Office MICROSOFT 97

Advanced Concepts
and Techniques

Office 97

MICROSOFT

Advanced Concepts and Techniques

Gary B. Shelly
Thomas J. Cashman
Misty E. Vermaat

Contributing Authors
Philip J. Pratt
James S. Quasney
Susan L. Sebok

**SHELLY
CASHMAN
SERIES**®

COURSE TECHNOLOGY
ONE MAIN STREET
CAMBRIDGE MA 02142

an International Thomson Publishing company **I**(**T**)**P**®

CAMBRIDGE   ALBANY   BONN   CINCINNATI   LONDON   MADRID   MELBOURNE

MEXICO CITY   NEW YORK   PARIS   SAN FRANCISCO   TOKYO   TORONTO   WASHINGTON

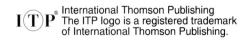

© **1998 Course Technology**
One Main Street
Cambridge, Massachusetts 02142

I(T)P® International Thomson Publishing
The ITP logo is a registered trademark
of International Thomson Publishing.

Printed in the United States of America

For more information, contact Course Technology:

Course Technology
One Main Street
Cambridge, Massachusetts 02142, USA

International Thomson Publishing Europe
Berkshire House
168-173 High Holborn
London, WC1V 7AA, United Kingdom

Thomas Nelson Australia
102 Dodds Street
South Melbourne
Victoria 3205 Australia

Nelson Canada
1120 Birchmont Road
Scarborough, Ontario
Canada M1K 5G4

International Thomson Editores
Campos Eliseos 385, Piso 7
Colonia Polanco
11560 Mexico D.F. Mexico

International Thomson Publishing GmbH
Konigswinterer Strasse 418
53227 Bonn, Germany

International Thomson Publishing Asia
Block 211, Henderson Road #08-03
Henderson Industrial Park
Singapore 0315

International Thomson Publishing Japan
Hirakawa-cho Kyowa Building, 3F
2-2-1 Hirakawa-cho, Chiyoda-ku
Tokyo 102, Japan

ISBN 0-7895-1335-8

PHOTO CREDITS: **Microsoft Word 97** *Project 4, pages WD 4.4-5* Map image © 1997 Photodisc, Inc. *Project 5, pages WD 5.2-3,* Boat, Courtesy of Corel Professional Photos CD-ROM Image usage; Thomas Jefferson, provided by North Wind Picture Archives; Hieroglyphics, provided by The British Museum. *Project 6, page WD 6.2, Women With Wheels* newsletter, Courtesy of The Quarterly Newsletter on Automobiles for Women; Landspeed Louise, Courtesy of Louise A. Noeth; *At-Home Dad* newsletter, Courtesy of Peter Baylies; *page WD 6.3, Newsletter Design* newsletter, Courtesy of The Newsletter Clearinghouse; Cat illustration provided by Rod Thomas; *Catnip* newsletter, Courtesy of Tufts University School of Veterinary Medicine; **Microsoft Excel 97** *Project 4, page E 4.4* Child, woman, logo, and spreadsheet, Courtesy of the Chicago Food Depository; *Project 5, pages E 5.2-3* Computer and keyboard and grass, Courtesy of Metatools, created by PhotoSpin; *Project 6, pages E 6.2-3* Copy machine and man, Courtesy of Corel Professional Photos CD-ROM Image usage; **Microsoft Access 97** *Project 3, pages A 3.2-3,* Dr. Thaddeus S. C. Lowe, provided by NorthWind Archives; Goodyear blimp photo, Courtesy of Goodyear Rubber and Tire Company; *Project 4, page A 4.4* Pelicans, Courtesy of Corel Professional Photos CD-ROM Image usage; *Project 5, pages A 5.2-3* Medieval man and Roman ruins, Courtesy of Corel Professional Photos CD-ROM Image usage; *Project 6, pages A 6.2-3* Indian, Indian painting, Brahman, and dragon, Courtesy of Corel Professional Photos CD-ROM Image usage; **Microsoft PowerPoint 97** *Project 3, pages PP 3.4-5,* Oil pump and charts, Courtesy of Corel Professional Photos CD-ROM Image usage; *Project 4, pages PP 4.2-3,* Magnifying glass, outline of body, overhead transparency, projector, gavel, judge, and globe, Courtesy of Corel Professional Photos CD-ROM Image usage.

6 7 8 9 10 BC 2 1 0 9

MICROSOFT Office 97

Advanced Concepts and Techniques

CONTENTS

▶ **PROJECT SIX**
CREATING A PROFESSIONAL NEWSLETTER

▶ **INTEGRATION FEATURE**
USING WORDART TO ADD SPECIAL
TEXT EFFECTS TO A WORD
DOCUMENT

Microsoft Excel 97   *E 4.1*

▶ **PROJECT FOUR**

CREATING TEMPLATES,
WORKBOOKS WITH
MULTIPLE WORKSHEETS,
AND WEB PAGES

▶ **PROJECT FIVE**

DATA TABLES, VISUAL BASIC FOR APPLICATIONS,
HYPERLINKS, AND SCENARIO MANAGER

Microsoft *Access* 97   **A 4.1**

▶ **PROJECT FOUR**
REPORTS, FORMS, AND
PUBLISHING REPORTS
TO THE WEB

▶ **PROJECT FIVE**
ENHANCING FORMS WITH OLE FIELDS,
HYPERLINKS, AND SUBFORMS

Microsoft PowerPoint 97 *PP 3.1*

Integration Case Studies   *I 1.1*

Preface

The Shelly Cashman Series® offers the finest textbooks in computer education. The Microsoft Office 97 books continue with the innovation, quality, and reliability that you have come to expect from this series. We are proud that both our Office 95 and Office 4.3 books are best-sellers, and we are confident that our Office 97 books will join their predecessors.

With Office 97, Microsoft has raised the stakes by adding a number of new features, especially the power of the Internet. The Shelly Cashman Series team has responded with Office 97 books that present the core application concepts required in any introductory application software course, as well as new features such as the Office 97 Internet tools.

In our Office 97 books, you will find an educationally sound and easy-to-follow pedagogy that combines a step-by-step approach with corresponding screens. Every project and exercise in the books are new and designed to take full advantage of the Office 97 features. The popular Other Ways and More About features have been amended to offer in-depth knowledge of Office 97. The all-new project openers provide a fascinating perspective on the subject covered in the project. The Shelly Cashman Series Office 97 books will make your computer applications class exciting and dynamic and one that your students will remember as one of their better educational experiences.

Objectives of This Textbook

Microsoft Office 97: Advanced Concepts and Techniques is intended for a one-quarter or one-semester advanced personal computer applications course. This book assumes that the student is familiar with the fundamentals of Microsoft Office 97, Microsoft Word 97, Microsoft Excel 97, Microsoft Access 97, and Microsoft PowerPoint 97. These introductory topics are covered in the companion textbook, *Microsoft Office 97: Introductory Concepts and Techniques*. The objectives of this book are as follows:

▶ To extend the student's basic knowledge of Microsoft Office and the four application tools: Word, Excel, Access, and PowerPoint.

▶ To help students demonstrate their proficiency in Microsoft Office applications. After completion of a two-course sequence with the companion textbook, *Microsoft Office 97: Introductory Concepts and Techniques*, this book prepares students to pass the Proficient level Microsoft Office User Specialist Exam for Microsoft Word 97 and Microsoft Excel 97 and the Expert level Microsoft Office User Specialist Exam for Microsoft Access 97 and Microsoft PowerPoint 97.

▶ To use practical problems to illustrate personal computer applications.

▶ To develop an exercise-oriented approach that allows students to learn by example.

▶ To encourage independent study and help those who are working on their own in a distance education environment.

When students complete the course using this textbook, they will have a firm knowledge of Microsoft Office and will be able to solve a variety of personal computer-related problems.

Approved by Microsoft as Courseware for the Microsoft Office User Specialist Program

Microsoft Office 97: Introductory Concepts and Techniques and *Microsoft Office 97: Advanced Concepts and Techniques* used in combination in a two-course sequence has been approved by Microsoft as courseware for the Microsoft Office User Specialist program. After completing the projects and exercises in these two companion textbooks, students will be prepared to take the Proficient level Microsoft Office User Specialist Exam for Microsoft Word 97 and Microsoft Excel 97 and the Expert level Microsoft Office User Specialist Exam for Microsoft Access 97 and Microsoft PowerPoint 97. By passing the certification exam for a Microsoft software program, students demonstrate their proficiency in that program to employers. These exams are offered at participating test centers, participating corporations, and participating employment agencies. For more information about certification, please visit Microsoft's World Wide Web site at http://microsoft.com/office/train_cert/.

The Shelly Cashman Approach

Features of the Shelly Cashman Series Office 97 books include:

▶ **Project Orientation:** Each project in the book uses the unique Shelly Cashman Series screen-by-screen, step-by-step approach.

▶ **Screen-by-Screen, Step-by-Step Instructions:** Each of the tasks required to complete a project is identified throughout the development of the project. Then, steps to accomplish the task are specified. The steps are accompanied by screens. Hence, students learn from this book the same as if they were using a computer.

▶ **Thoroughly Tested Projects:** The computer screens in the Shelly Cashman Series Office 97 books are captured from the author's computer. The screen is captured immediately after the author performs the step specified in the text. Therefore, every screen in the book is correct because it is produced only after performing a step, resulting in unprecedented quality in a computer textbook.

▶ **Multiple Ways to Use the Book:** This book can be used in a variety of ways, including: (a) Lecture and textbook approach — The instructor lectures on the material in the book. Students read and study the material and then apply the knowledge to an application on the computer; (b) Tutorial approach — Students perform each specified step on a computer. At the end of the project, students have solved the problem and are ready to solve comparable student assignments; (c) Other approaches — Many instructors lecture on the material and then require their students to perform each step in the project, reinforcing the material lectured. Students then complete one or more of the In the Lab exercises at the end of the project; and (d) Reference — Each task in a project is clearly identified. Therefore, the material serves as a complete reference.

▶ **Other Ways Boxes for Reference:** Microsoft Office 97 provides a wide variety of ways to carry out a given task. The Other Ways boxes included at the end of most of the step-by-step sequences specify the other ways to execute the task completed in the steps. Together, the steps and the Other Ways box make a comprehensive and convenient reference unit; you no longer have to reference tables at the end of a project or at the end of a book.

OtherWays

1. While in design mode select button, on Tools menu point to Macro, click Visual Basic Editor, click Properties Window button
2. While in design mode select button, press ALT+F11

More *About* **Run-Around**

The spacing around a graphic should be at least 1/8". Be sure the run-around is the same for all graphics in the newsletter. In Word, you can adjust the run-around of a selected frame by clicking the Format Picture button on the Picture toolbar, clicking the Wrapping tab, adjusting the Distance from text text boxes, and then clicking the OK button.

▶ More About Feature: The More About features in the margins provide background information that complements the topics covered, adding interest and depth to the learning process.

Organization of This Textbook

Microsoft Office 97: Advanced Concepts and Techniques consists of three projects and an integration feature on Microsoft Word 97, Microsoft Excel 97, and Microsoft Access 97; two projects and an integration feature on Microsoft PowerPoint 97; and three major case studies on integration. The projects in each of the first three applications of this textbook begin with Project 4 and the final application begins with Project 3, because they are a continuation of the projects found in the companion textbook *Microsoft Office 97: Introductory Concepts and Techniques.*

Advanced Word Processing Using Microsoft Word 97

This textbook begins by providing detailed instruction on how to use the advanced commands and techniques of Microsoft Word 97. The material is divided into three projects and the integration feature as follows:

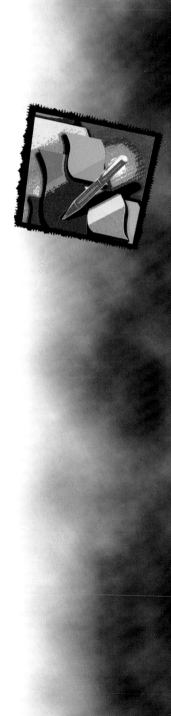

Project 4 – Creating a Document with a Title Page and Tables In Project 4, students work with tables in a document. Students learn how to add an outside border with color; add color to characters; download clip art from the Microsoft Clip Gallery Live page on the Web; change a floating picture to an inline picture; insert a section break; insert an existing document into an open document; save a document with a new file name; set and use tabs; create a table using the Draw Table feature; change the alignment of table cell text; change the direction of text in table cells; center a table; customize bullets in a list; and change the starting page number in a section.

Project 5 – Generating Form Letters, Mailing Labels, and Envelopes In Project 5, students learn how to generate form letters, mailing labels, and envelopes from a main document and a data source. Topics include creating and editing the three main documents and their associated data source; inserting the system date into a document; inserting merge fields into the main document; using an IF field; displaying and printing field codes; merging and printing the documents; selecting data records to merge and print; sorting data records to merge and print; viewing merged data in the main document; and inserting a bar code on the mailing labels and envelopes.

Project 6 – Creating a Professional Newsletter In Project 6, students learn how to use Word's desktop publishing features to create a newsletter. Topics include adding ruling lines; adding a bullet symbol; formatting a document into multiple columns; creating a dropped capital letter; framing and positioning graphics across columns; inserting a column break; adding a vertical rule between columns; creating a pull-quote; adding color to characters and lines; highlighting text; using the Format Painter button; creating and running a macro to automate a task; changing the color of a graphic; and adding text to a graphic.

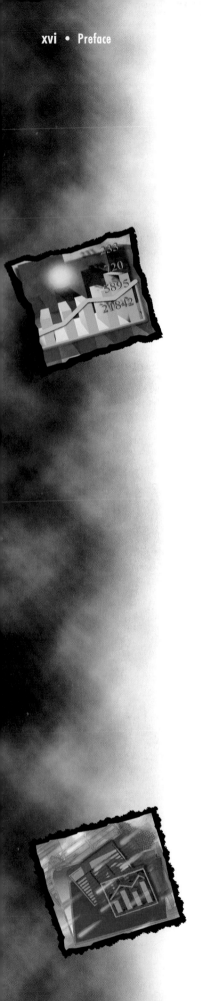

Integration Feature 2 – Using WordArt to Add Special Text Effects to a Word Document   In this section, students are introduced to WordArt, an application included with Word. Using the newsletter built in Project 6, students create a new headline in WordArt and then embed the new headline into the Word document. The following WordArt special effects are introduced: changing the shape of the text, stretching the text, bolding the text, and adding a shadow to the text.

Advanced Worksheets Using Microsoft Excel 97

Following the three advanced projects and integration feature on Microsoft Word 97, this textbook presents three advanced projects and an integration feature on Microsoft Excel 97. The topics presented are as follows:

Project 4 – Creating Templates, Workbooks with Multiple Worksheets, and Web Pages   In Project 4, students learn to create a template and consolidate data from multiple worksheets into one worksheet. Topics include: building and copying a template; adding worksheets to a workbook; manipulating data on multiple worksheets; 3-D cell references; drilling entries through worksheets; customized formats; comparison charts; adding comments to a cell; changing page setup characteristics; creating a Web page from a worksheet; and displaying Web pages using the Web toolbar.

Project 5 – Data Tables, Visual Basic for Applications, Hyperlinks, and Scenario Manager   In Project 5, students learn more about analyzing data in a worksheet and how to write macros using Visual Basic for Applications. Topics include: applying the PMT function to determine a monthly payment; using natural language formulas; analyzing data by (1) goal seeking, (2) creating a data table, and (3) creating a Scenario Summary Report worksheet; writing macros and recording macros that automate worksheet activities; creating a button and assigning a macro to it; adding a hyperlink to a worksheet; and protecting a worksheet.

Project 6 – Sorting and Filtering a Worksheet Database, Pivot Tables, and Creating a Data Map   In Project 6, students learn how to create, sort, and filter a database. Topics include: using a data form to create and maintain a database; creating subtotals; finding, extracting, and deleting records that pass a test; applying database and lookup functions; creating a data map; and creating a pivot table.

Integration Feature 2 – Embedding an Excel Worksheet in a Word Document Using Drag and Drop   In this section, students are introduced to embedding an Excel worksheet into a Word document. Topics include: tiling applications on the desktop; embedding using drag and drop; untiling applications on the desktop; and editing an embedded object.

Advanced Database Manipulation Using Microsoft Access 97

Following the advanced projects on Microsoft Excel 97, this textbook provides detailed instruction on advanced topics in Microsoft Access 97. The topics are divided into three projects and one integration feature as follows:

Project 4 – Reports, Forms, and Publishing Reports to the Web   In Project 4, students learn to create custom reports and forms. Topics include creating queries for reports; using Report Wizards; modifying a report design; saving a report; printing a report; creating a report with grouping and subtotals; removing totals from a report; and changing the characteristics of items on a report. They also learn how to publish the report they have created to the World Wide Web using the Publish to the Web Wizard. Other topics include creating an initial form using the FormWizard; modifying a form design; moving fields; and adding calculated fields and combo boxes. Students learn how to change a variety of field characteristics such as font styles, formats, and colors.

Project 5 – Enhancing Forms with OLE Fields, Hyperlinks, and Subforms   In Project 5, students learn to use date, memo, OLE, and hyperlink fields. Topics include incorporating these fields in the structure of a database; updating the data in these fields and changing the table properties; creating a form that uses a subform to incorporate a one-to-many relationship between tables; manipulating subforms on a main form; incorporating date, memo, OLE, and hyperlink fields in forms; and incorporating various visual effects in forms. Students also learn to use the hyperlink fields to access Web pages and to use date and memo fields in a query.

Project 6 – Creating an Application System Using Macros, VBA, and the Switchboard Manager   In Project 6, students learn how to create a switchboard system, a system that allows users to easily access tables, forms, and reports simply by clicking buttons. Topics include creating and running macros; adding command buttons to a form; adding a combo box for finding records to a form; modifying VBA code associated with an object on a form; and creating and using a switchboard system.

Integration Feature 2 – Linking Excel Worksheets to an Access Database   In this section, students learn how to link Excel Worksheets to an Access database. Topics include creating the Access database; linking the individual worksheets in a workbook to tables in the database; and using the linked worksheets.

Advanced Presentation Graphics Using Microsoft PowerPoint 97

The final Microsoft Office 97 software application covered in this textbook is Microsoft PowerPoint 97. The material is presented in two advanced projects and an integration feature as follows:

Project 3 – Using Embedded Visuals to Enhance a Slide Show   In Project 3, students create a presentation from a Microsoft Word outline and then enhance it with embedded visuals. Topics include creating a slide background using a picture; embedding a Microsoft Excel chart; creating and embedding an organization chart; embedding a picture; adding a border to a picture; scaling an object; ungrouping clip art; resizing objects; and applying slide transition and text preset animation effects.

Project 4 – Creating a Presentation Containing Interactive OLE Documents   In Project 4, students customize the presentation created in Project 3 by inserting a company logo, changing the Design Template, and then modifying the color scheme. Topics include drawing a company logo; creating a graphic image from text using Microsoft WordArt; grouping the logo and graphic image into a logo object; embedding an object on the Slide Master; changing organization chart formatting; using object linking and embedding to create a slide containing interactive documents; using guides to position and size objects; modifying PowerPoint options to end a presentation with a black slide; hiding a slide; animating an object; and running a slide show to display a hidden slide in an active interactive document.

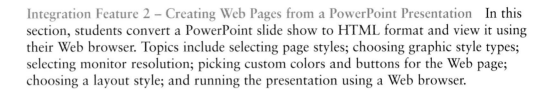

Integration Feature 2 – Creating Web Pages from a PowerPoint Presentation   In this section, students convert a PowerPoint slide show to HTML format and view it using their Web browser. Topics include selecting page styles; choosing graphic style types; selecting monitor resolution; picking custom colors and buttons for the Web page; choosing a layout style; and running the presentation using a Web browser.

Integration Case Studies

Following the four major Office applications are case studies on integration. In these case studies, students use the concepts and techniques presented in the projects and integration features in this book to integrate the Office 97 applications. The first case study requires students to embed an existing Excel worksheet into a Word document and then embed corresponding Excel charts into a PowerPoint presentation. The second case study requires students to use an existing Access database table as the data source in a Word form letter; students also are asked to use WordArt to create the letterhead for the form letter. The third case study requires the students to create an Access database table and then convert the table first to a Word document and then to an Excel worksheet.

End-of-Project Student Activities

A notable strength of the Shelly Cashman Series Office 97 books is the extensive student activities at the end of each project. Well-structured student activities can make the difference between students merely participating in a class and students retaining the information they learn. The activities in the Office 97 books include:

- ▶ **What You Should Know**   A listing of the tasks completed within a project together with the pages where the step-by-step, screen-by-screen explanations appear. This section provides a perfect study review for students.

- ▶ **Test Your Knowledge**   Four pencil-and-paper activities designed to determine students' understanding of the material in the project. Included are true/false questions, multiple-choice questions, and two short-answer activities.

- ▶ **Use Help**   Any user of Office 97 must know how to use Help, including the Office Assistant. Therefore, this book contains two Use Help exercises per project. These exercises alone distinguish the Shelly Cashman Series from any other set of Office 97 instructional materials.

- ▶ **Apply Your Knowledge**   This exercise requires students to open and manipulate a file on the Data Disk that accompanies the Office 97 books.

- ▶ **In the Lab**   Three in-depth assignments per project require students to apply the knowledge gained in the project to solve problems on a computer.

- ▶ **Cases and Places**   Seven unique case studies require students to apply their knowledge to real-world situations.

Instructor's Resource Kit

A comprehensive Instructor's Resource Kit (IRK) accompanies this textbook in the form of a CD-ROM. The CD-ROM includes an electronic Instructor's Manual (called *ElecMan*) and teaching and testing aids. The CD-ROM (ISBN 0-7895-1334-X) is available through your Course Technology representative or by calling one of the following telephone numbers: Colleges and Universities, 1-800-648-7450; High Schools, 1-800-824-5179; and Career Colleges, 1-800-477-3692. The contents of the CD-ROM are listed below.

▶ ElecMan (*Electronic Instructor's Manual*)   ElecMan is made up of Microsoft Word files. The files include lecture notes, solutions to laboratory assignments, and a large test bank. The files allow you to modify the lecture notes or generate quizzes and exams from the test bank using your own word processor. Where appropriate, solutions to laboratory assignments are embedded as icons in the files. When an icon appears, double-click it; the application will start and the solution will display on the screen. ElecMan includes the following for each project: project objectives; project overview; detailed lesson plans with page number references; teacher notes and activities; answers to the end-of-project exercises; test bank of 110 questions for every project (50 true/false, 25 multiple choice, and 35 fill-in-the-blank) with page number references; and transparency references. The transparencies are available through the Figures on CD-ROM described below.

▶ Figures on CD-ROM   Illustrations for every screen in the textbook are available. Use this ancillary to create a slide show from the illustrations for lecture or to print transparencies for use in lecture with an overhead projector.

▶ Course Test Manager   Course Test Manager is a powerful testing and assessment package that enables instructors to create and print tests from test banks designed specifically for Course Technology titles. In addition, instructors with access to a networked computer lab (LAN) can administer, grade, and track tests online. Students also can take online practice tests, which generate customized study guides that indicate where in the text students can find more information on each question.

▶ Lecture Success System   Lecture Success System files are designed for use with the application software package, a personal computer, and a projection device. The files allow you to explain and illustrate the step-by-step, screen-by-screen development of a project in the textbook without entering large amounts of data.

▶ Instructor's Lab Solutions   Solutions and required files for all the In the Lab assignments at the end of each project are available.

▶ Lab Tests/Test Outs   Tests that parallel the In the Lab assignments are supplied for the purpose of testing students in the laboratory on the material covered in the project or testing students out of the course.

▶ Student Files   All the files that are required by students to complete the Apply Your Knowledge and a few of the In the Lab exercises are included.

▶ Interactive Labs   Eighteen hands-on interactive labs that take students from ten to fifteen minutes each to step through help solidify and reinforce mouse and keyboard usage and computer concepts.

Shelly Cashman Online

Shelly Cashman Online is a World Wide Web service available to instructors and students of computer education. Visit Shelly Cashman Online at www.scseries.com. Shelly Cashman Online is divided into four areas:

▶ **Series Information**   Information on the Shelly Cashman Series products.

▶ **The Community**   Opportunities to discuss your course and your ideas with instructors in your field and with the Shelly Cashman Series team.

▶ **Teaching Resources**   Designed for instructors teaching from and using Shelly Cashman Series textbooks and software. This area includes password-protected instructor materials that can be downloaded, course outlines, teaching tips, and much more.

▶ **Student Center**   Dedicated to students learning about computers with Shelly Cashman Series textbooks and software. This area includes cool links, data from Data Disks that can be downloaded, and much more.

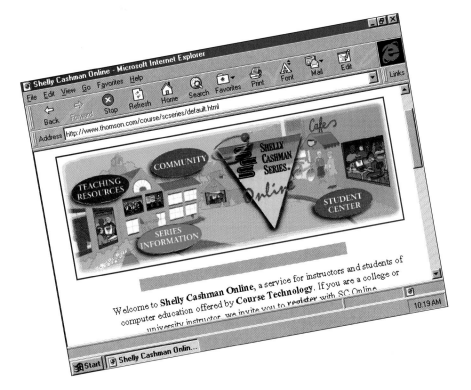

Acknowledgments

The Shelly Cashman Series would not be the leading computer education series without the contributions of outstanding publishing professionals. First, and foremost, among them is Becky Herrington, director of production and designer. She is the heart and soul of the Shelly Cashman Series, and it is only through her leadership, dedication, and tireless efforts that superior products are made possible. Becky created and produced the award-winning Windows 95 series of books.

Under Becky's direction, the following individuals made significant contributions to these books: Peter Schiller, production manager; Ginny Harvey, series specialist and developmental editor; Ken Russo, Mike Bodnar, Stephanie Nance, Greg Herrington, and Dave Bonnewitz, graphic artists; Jeanne Black, Quark expert; Patti Koosed, editorial assistant; Nancy Lamm, Lyn Markowicz, Marilyn Martin, Cherilyn King, and Steve Marconi, proofreaders; Cristina Haley, indexer; Sarah Evertson of Image Quest, photo researcher; and Peggy Wyman and Jerry Orton, Susan Sebok, and Nancy Lamm, contributing writers.

Special thanks go to Jim Quasney, our dedicated series editor; Lisa Strite, senior product manager; Lora Wade, associate product manager; Scott MacDonald and Tonia Grafakos, editorial assistants; and Sarah McLean, product marketing manager. Special mention must go to Suzanne Biron, Becky Herrington, and Michael Gregson for the outstanding book design; Becky Herrington for the cover design; and Ken Russo for the cover illustrations.

Gary B. Shelly
Thomas J. Cashman
Misty E. Vermaat

Visit Shelly Cashman Online at
www.scseries.com

Shelly Cashman Series – Traditionally Bound Textbooks

The Shelly Cashman Series presents the following computer subjects in a variety of traditionally bound textbooks. For more information, see your Course Technology representative or call one of the following telephone numbers: Colleges and Universities, 1-800-648-7450; High Schools, 1-800-824-5179; and Career Colleges, 1-800-477-3692.

COMPUTERS	
Computers	Discovering Computers: A Link to the Future, World Wide Web Enhanced
	Discovering Computers: A Link to the Future, World Wide Web Enhanced Brief Edition
	Using Computers: A Gateway to Information, World Wide Web Edition
	Using Computers: A Gateway to Information, World Wide Web Brief Edition
	Exploring Computers: A Record of Discovery 2e with CD-ROM
	A Record of Discovery for Exploring Computers 2e
	Study Guide for Discovering Computers: A Link to the Future, World Wide Web Enhanced
	Study Guide for Using Computers: A Gateway to Information, World Wide Web Edition
	Brief Introduction to Computers 2e (32-page)
WINDOWS APPLICATIONS	
Integrated Packages	Microsoft Office 97: Introductory Concepts and Techniques, Brief Edition (6 projects)
	Microsoft Office 97: Introductory Concepts and Techniques, Essentials Edition (10 projects)
	Microsoft Office 97: Introductory Concepts and Techniques (15 projects)
	Microsoft Office 97: Advanced Concepts and Techniques
	Microsoft Office 95: Introductory Concepts and Techniques (15 projects)
	Microsoft Office 95: Advanced Concepts and Techniques
	Microsoft Office 4.3 running under Windows 95: Introductory Concepts and Techniques
	Microsoft Office for Windows 3.1 Introductory Concepts and Techniques Enhanced Edition
	Microsoft Office: Advanced Concepts and Techniques
	Microsoft Works 4* • Microsoft Works 3.0*
Windows	Introduction to Microsoft Windows NT Workstation 4
	Microsoft Windows 95: Introductory Concepts and Techniques (96-page)
	Introduction to Microsoft Windows 95 (224-page)
	Microsoft Windows 95: Complete Concepts and Techniques
	Microsoft Windows 3.1 Introductory Concepts and Techniques
	Microsoft Windows 3.1 Complete Concepts and Techniques
Word Processing	Microsoft Word 97* • Microsoft Word 7* • Microsoft Word 6* • Microsoft Word 2.0
	Corel WordPerfect 8 • Corel WordPerfect 7 • WordPerfect 6.1* • WordPerfect 6* • WordPerfect 5.2
Spreadsheets	Microsoft Excel 97* • Microsoft Excel 7* • Microsoft Excel 5* • Microsoft Excel 4
	Lotus 1-2-3 97* • Lotus 1-2-3 Release 5* • Lotus 1-2-3 Release 4* • Quattro Pro 6
Database Management	Microsoft Access 97* • Microsoft Access 7* • Microsoft Access 2
	Paradox 5 • Paradox 4.5 • Paradox 1.0 • Visual dBASE 5/5.5
Presentation Graphics	Microsoft PowerPoint 97* • Microsoft PowerPoint 7* • Microsoft PowerPoint 4*
DOS APPLICATIONS	
Operating Systems	DOS 6 Introductory Concepts and Techniques
	DOS 6 and Microsoft Windows 3.1 Introductory Concepts and Techniques
Word Processing	WordPerfect 6.1 • WordPerfect 6.0 • WordPerfect 5.1
Spreadsheets	Lotus 1-2-3 Release 4 • Lotus 1-2-3 Release 2.4 • Lotus 1-2-3 Release 2.3
Database Management	dBASE 5 • dBASE IV Version 1.1 • dBASE III PLUS • Paradox 4.5
PROGRAMMING AND NETWORKING	
Programming	Microsoft Visual Basic 5
	Microsoft Visual Basic 4 for Windows 95* (available with Student version software)
	Microsoft Visual Basic 3.0 for Windows*
	QBasic • QBasic: An Introduction to Programming • Microsoft BASIC
	Structured COBOL Programming (Micro Focus COBOL also available)
Networking	Novell NetWare for Users
	Business Data Communications: Introductory Concepts and Techniques
Internet	The Internet: Introductory Concepts and Techniques (UNIX)
	Netscape Navigator 4: An Introduction
	Netscape Navigator 3: An Introduction • Netscape Navigator 2 running under Windows 3.1
	Netscape Navigator: An Introduction (Version 1.1)
	Netscape Composer
	Microsoft Internet Explorer 3: An Introduction
SYSTEMS ANALYSIS	
Systems Analysis	Systems Analysis and Design, Second Edition

*Also available as a Double Diamond Edition, which is a shortened version of the complete book

$\mathbf{S}$helly Cashman Series – **Custom Edition**® Program

If you do not find a Shelly Cashman Series traditionally bound textbook to fit your needs, the Shelly Cashman Series unique **Custom Edition** program allows you to choose from a number of options and create a textbook perfectly suited to your course. Features of the **Custom Edition** program are:

▶ Textbooks that match the content of your course

▶ Windows- and DOS-based materials for the latest versions of personal computer applications software

▶ Shelly Cashman Series quality, with the same full-color materials and Shelly Cashman Series pedagogy found in the traditionally bound books

▶ Affordable pricing so your students receive the **Custom Edition** at a cost similar to that of traditionally bound books

The table on the right summarizes the available materials.

For more information, see your Course Technology representative or call one of the following telephone numbers: Colleges and Universities, 1-800-648-7450; High Schools, 1-800-824-5179; and Career Colleges, 1-800-477-3692.

For Shelly Cashman Series information, visit Shelly Cashman Online at **www.scseries.com**

COMPUTERS	
Computers	Discovering Computers: A Link to the Future, World Wide Web Enhanced
	Discovering Computers: A Link to the Future, World Wide Web Enhanced Brief Edition
	Using Computers: A Gateway to Information, World Wide Web Edition
	Using Computers: A Gateway to Information, World Wide Web Brief Edition
	A Record of Discovery for Exploring Computers 2e (available with CD-ROM)
	Study Guide for Discovering Computers: A Link to the Future, World Wide Web Enhanced
	Study Guide for Using Computers: A Gateway to Information, World Wide Web Edition
	Introduction to Computers (32-page)

OPERATING SYSTEMS	
Windows	Microsoft Windows 95: Introductory Concepts and Techniques (96-page)
	Introduction to Microsoft Windows NT Workstation 4
	Introduction to Microsoft Windows 95 (224-page)
	Microsoft Windows 95: Complete Concepts and Techniques
	Microsoft Windows 3.1 Introductory Concepts and Techniques
	Microsoft Windows 3.1 Complete Concepts and Techniques
DOS	Introduction to DOS 6 (using DOS prompt)
	Introduction to DOS 5.0 or earlier (using DOS prompt)

WINDOWS APPLICATIONS	
Integrated Packages	Microsoft Works 4*
	Microsoft Works 3.0*
Microsoft Office	Using Microsoft Office 97 (16-page)
	Using Microsoft Office 95 (16-page)
	Microsoft Office 97:Introductory Concepts and Techniques, Brief Edition (396-page)
	Microsoft Office 97: Introductory Concepts and Techniques, Essentials Edition (672-page)
	Object Linking and Embedding (OLE) (32-page)
	Microsoft Outlook 97 • Microsoft Schedule+ 7
	Introduction to Integrating Office 97 Applications (48-page)
	Introduction to Integrating Office 95 Applications (80-page)
Word Processing	Microsoft Word 97* • Microsoft Word 7* • Microsoft Word 6* • Microsoft Word 2.0
	Corel WordPerfect 8 • Corel WordPerfect 7 • WordPerfect 6.1* • WordPerfect 6* • WordPerfect 5.2
Spreadsheets	Microsoft Excel 97* • Microsoft Excel 7* • Microsoft Excel 5* • Microsoft Excel 4
	Lotus 1-2-3 97* • Lotus 1-2-3 Release 5* • Lotus 1-2-3 Release 4* • Quattro Pro 6
Database Management	Microsoft Access 97* • Microsoft Access 7* • Microsoft Access 2*
	Paradox 5 • Paradox 4.5 • Paradox 1.0 • Visual dBASE 5/5.5
Presentation Graphics	Microsoft PowerPoint 97* • Microsoft PowerPoint 7* • Microsoft PowerPoint 4*

DOS APPLICATIONS	
Word Processing	WordPerfect 6.1 • WordPerfect 6.0 • WordPerfect 5.1
Spreadsheets	Lotus 1-2-3 Release 4 • Lotus 1-2-3 Release 2.4 • Lotus 1-2-3 Release 2.3
	Quattro Pro 3.0 • Quattro with 1-2-3 Menus
Database Management	dBASE 5 • dBASE IV Version 1.1 • dBASE III PLUS
	Paradox 4.5 • Paradox 3.5

PROGRAMMING AND NETWORKING	
Programming	Microsoft Visual Basic 5 • Microsoft Visual Basic 4 for Windows 95* (available with Student version software) • Microsoft Visual Basic 3.0 for Windows*
	Microsoft BASIC • QBasic
Networking	Novell NetWare for Users
Internet	The Internet: Introductory Concepts and Techniques (UNIX)
	Netscape Navigator 4: An Introduction
	Netscape Navigator 3: An Introduction
	Netscape Navigator 2 running under Windows 3.1
	Netscape Navigator: An Introduction (Version 1.1)
	Netscape Composer
	Microsoft Internet Explorer 3: An Introduction

*Also available as a mini-module

Microsoft *Word 97*

Project

Microsoft Word 97

Creating a Document with a Title Page and Tables

Objectives:

You will have mastered the material in this project when you can:

- ▶ Add color to characters
- ▶ Add an outside border with color to a paragraph
- ▶ Download clip art from the Microsoft Clip Gallery Live Web page
- ▶ Insert clip art into a document
- ▶ Change a floating picture to an inline picture
- ▶ Add a shadow to characters
- ▶ Insert a section break
- ▶ Return paragraph formatting to the Normal style
- ▶ Insert an existing document into an open document
- ▶ Save an active document with a new file name
- ▶ Set custom tabs
- ▶ Add an outside border to a table created with tabs
- ▶ Use the Draw Table feature to insert a table into a document
- ▶ Change alignment of data in table cells
- ▶ Change the direction of text in table cells
- ▶ Center a table between page margins
- ▶ Customize bullets in a list
- ▶ Create a header for a section
- ▶ Change the starting page number in a section

Charting a Course

Ancient Mapping,
Handwritten Computations,
and Contemporary Tables

Sea creatures — monstrous finned denizens of the ocean, lurking in the depths of the open seas, in readiness to pounce on and devour the unwary ships. The Seven Cities of Cibola — a tale that depicts an island far out into the Atlantic Ocean. Legend has it that, "there took ship seven Bishops, and went to Antilla, where each of them built a city; and lest their people should think to return to Spain, they set fire to their ships." Many who came to the island, never returned.

In the fourteenth and fifteenth centuries, these fanciful notions from the superstitious minds of medieval chartmakers embellished the first crude charts developed for seafaring explorers.

In a time when a sailor stood less than a fifty-fifty chance of returning home from a voyage, when ships were lost without a trace, few doubted that such charts told the truth. As more daring voyagers pushed beyond known limits, more accurate maps evolved with every journey. Soon, depth readings

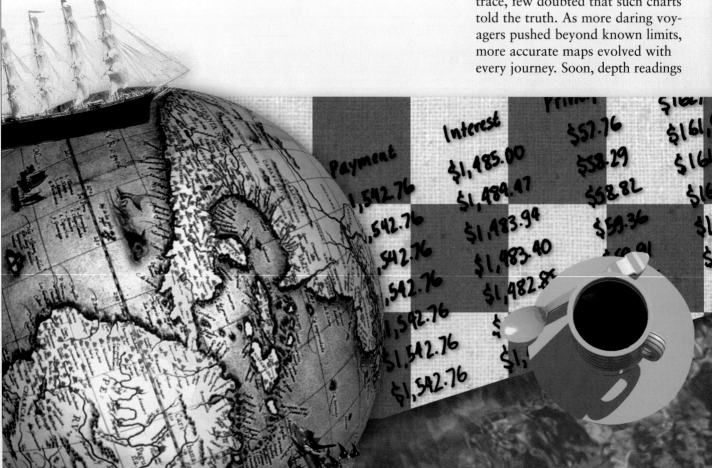

and ocean currents appeared on navigation maps. To this day, charting of the planet's land masses and oceans grows more sophisticated with modern technology to aid the effort.

Along with charts, various tables — especially tide tables that help ships avoid going aground — are important tools for the mariner, but another kind of table was just as important to early sailors as any scrap of paper. Looming mysteriously above Cape Town, South Africa is Table Mountain. With a top as flat as a football field, but vastly larger, its mystique is enhanced by frequent, sudden appearances of dense Antarctic fog on otherwise crystal-clear days, settling and spreading in a thin layer called the *Devil's tablecloth*. The mountain has served as beacon and inspiration to sailors, natives, and settlers for centuries. To the weary seafarer, Table Mountain meant a brief respite from the dangers of a daunting voyage, and ship captains gave lavish rewards to the first sailor to spy it.

From Latin *tabularis*, meaning board, the word, table, and its diminutive, tablet, have been used in varied contexts throughout human history. Medieval English accountants calculated sums on a checkered tablecloth, giving birth to the name Exchequer, Britain's royal treasury and the word cheque for bank drafts. Physicists consult the Periodic Table of Elements. Moses received the Ten Commandments on tablets of stone, while modern artists use digitized graphics tablets to enter drawings and sketches into a computer.

In the fast-paced '90s, you may not be required to chart the open seas. En route to a meeting via jet with laptop and mouse, however, the capability of creating tables and charts with ease and precision is a vital tool. Using Word 97 and the Draw Table feature in this project, you can create an attractive table, modify the structure, and enhance any document, proposal, or announcement you are asked to prepare. Apply borders and shading and add color for appeal.

The days of the drawing board are like ancient history. As we move into the twenty-first century, chart your course with the state-of-the-art business tools of Microsoft Word.

HOT AIR BALLOON RATES		
Passenger Types	Adult	Child
Peak Season — Sunrise	$120	$60
Peak Season — Sunset	$130	$65
Off Season — Sunrise	$90	$45
Off Season — Sunset	$100	$50

Microsoft
Word 97

Creating a Document with a Title Page and Tables

Case Perspective

The owners of Fiesta Balloon Tours have hired you, a Marketing major in your senior year at Canyon University, to design a sales proposal. In your first meeting with the owners, William and Anita Hampton, you try to learn as much about Fiesta Balloon Tours as possible. The Hamptons give you a business card that outlines the schedules of balloon outings, as well as company telephone numbers. They tell you that Fiesta Balloon Tours has been in business since 1979 and has a perfect passenger safety record. All pilots are certified and have more than 300 hours of flying experience. The balloons, which are inspected regularly, accommodate four to eight passengers.

In addition to the two-hour flight, passengers receive a Fiesta Balloon Tours T-shirt, personalized flight certificate, flight pin, and a feast of food and beverages upon landing. Mrs. Hampton provides you with a rate sheet for balloon outings. She mentions that Fiesta Balloon Tours also offers for purchase other products and services, and these items are on the rate sheet. At the conclusion of your meeting, you inform the Hamptons that you will complete the proposal for their review within a week.

Introduction

In all probability, sometime during your professional life, you will find yourself placed in a sales role. You might be selling to a customer or client a tangible product such as plastic or a service such as interior decorating. Within an organization, you might be selling an idea, such as a benefits package to company employees or a budget plan to upper management. To sell an item, whether tangible or intangible, you often will find yourself writing a proposal. Proposals vary in length, style, and formality, but all are designed to elicit acceptance from the reader.

A proposal may be one of three types: planning, research, or sales. A **planning proposal** offers solutions to a problem or improvement to a situation. A **research proposal** usually requests funding for a research project. A **sales proposal** offers a product or service to existing or potential customers.

Project Four – Sales Proposal

Project 4 uses Word to produce the sales proposal shown in Figures 4-1, 4-2 and 4-3 on the next three pages. The sales proposal is designed to persuade the public to select Fiesta Balloon Tours for a hot air balloon outing. The proposal has a colorful title page to grasp the reader's attention. The body of the sales proposal uses tables to summarize data.

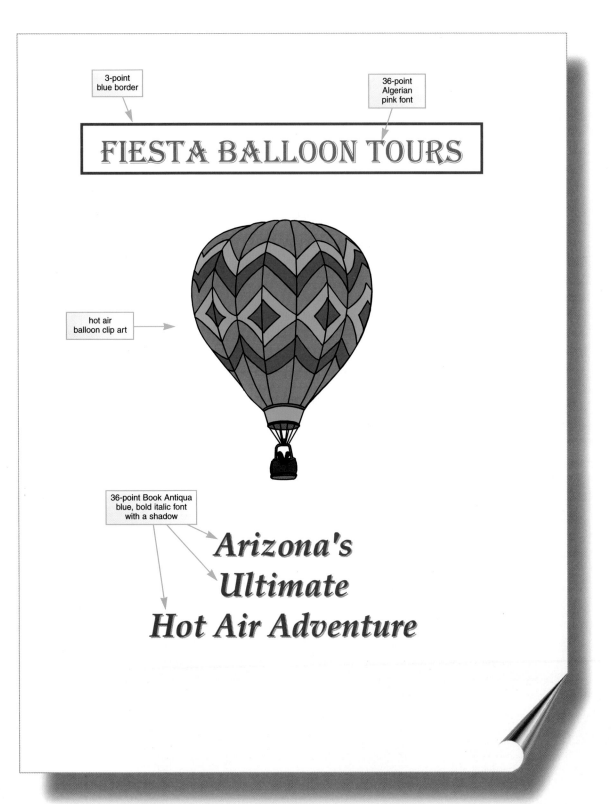

FIGURE 4-1

Fiesta Balloon Tours 1

Imagine gliding through the air, drifting with the clouds, and seeing a 360-degree view of the world below you. Fiesta Balloon Tours provides passengers with this breathtaking hot air adventure every day.

Fiesta Balloon Tours has been in business since 1979, and we are proud of our 100 percent passenger safety record. Each of our pilots is certified and has more than 300 hours of flying experience. Our balloons are of the highest quality and inspected regularly.

We offer two flights every day of the year, weather permitting. Our balloons accommodate four to eight passengers, in addition to the pilot. Because the temperature varies throughout the flight, wear comfortable clothing in layers.

HOT AIR BALLOON OUTINGS		
	Sunrise	Sunset
Start time	6:00 a.m.	7:00 p.m.
End time	10:00 a.m.	11:00 p.m.

box border surrounds table

table created using tabs

In addition to the two-hour flight, each passenger receives a Fiesta Balloon Tours T-shirt, personalized flight certificate, flight pin, and feast of gourmet food and beverages upon landing. The flight begins one hour after the start time, and the feast ends one hour after landing.

Rates vary depending on the season. Peak season runs from Memorial Day to Labor Day. Group and corporate rates are available, and we have senior citizen discounts. Reservations are required at least two weeks in advance of desired flight date and must be confirmed with a 50 percent down payment by check or credit card. If we must cancel a

FIGURE 4-2

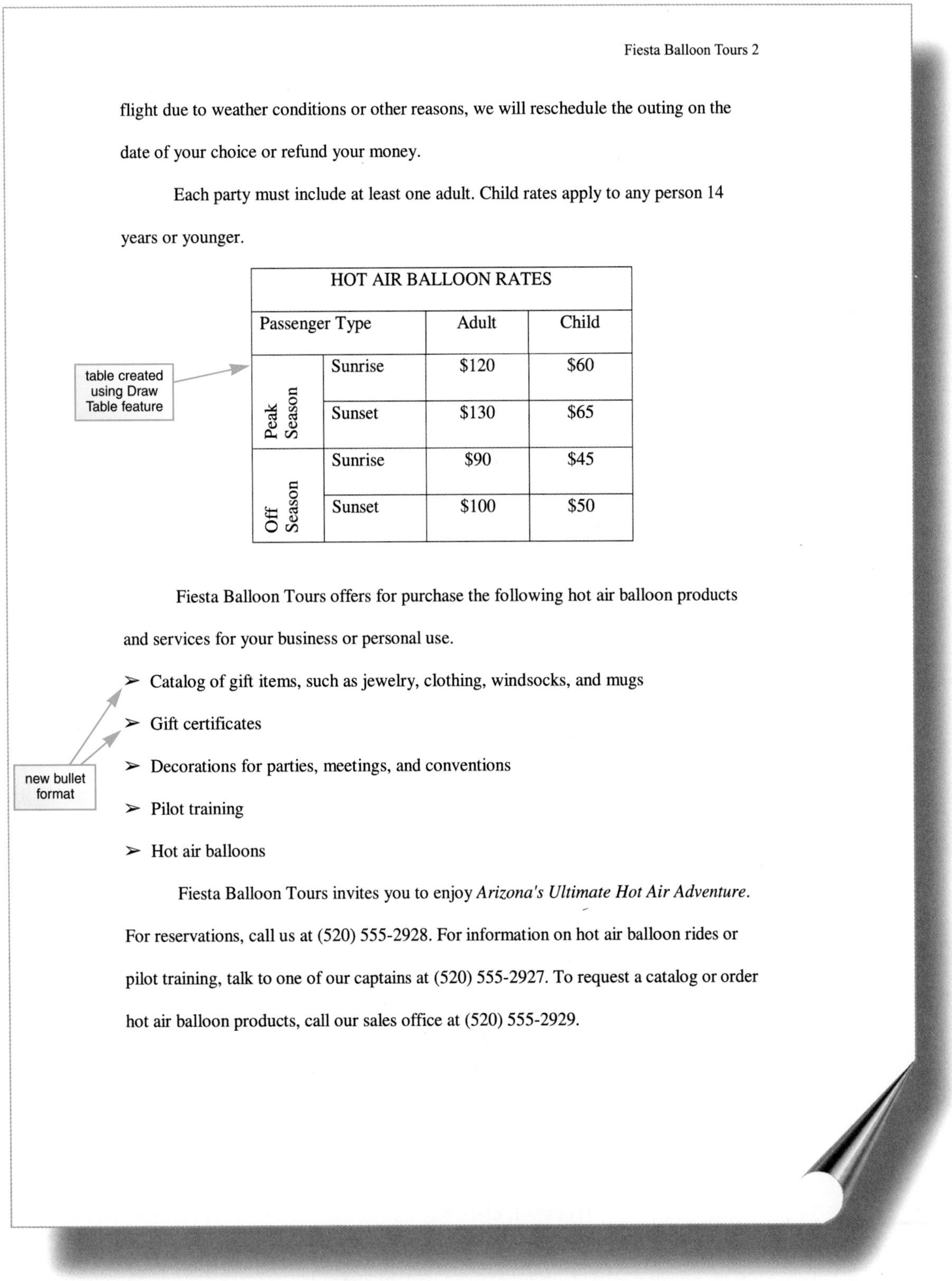

flight due to weather conditions or other reasons, we will reschedule the outing on the
date of your choice or refund your money.

Each party must include at least one adult. Child rates apply to any person 14
years or younger.

table created using Draw Table feature →

HOT AIR BALLOON RATES			
Passenger Type		Adult	Child
Peak Season	Sunrise	$120	$60
	Sunset	$130	$65
Off Season	Sunrise	$90	$45
	Sunset	$100	$50

Fiesta Balloon Tours offers for purchase the following hot air balloon products
and services for your business or personal use.

new bullet format →

➢ Catalog of gift items, such as jewelry, clothing, windsocks, and mugs

➢ Gift certificates

➢ Decorations for parties, meetings, and conventions

➢ Pilot training

➢ Hot air balloons

Fiesta Balloon Tours invites you to enjoy *Arizona's Ultimate Hot Air Adventure*.
For reservations, call us at (520) 555-2928. For information on hot air balloon rides or
pilot training, talk to one of our captains at (520) 555-2927. To request a catalog or order
hot air balloon products, call our sales office at (520) 555-2929.

FIGURE 4-3

Document Preparation Steps

Document preparation steps give you an overview of how the sales proposal in Figures 4-1, 4-2, and 4-3 on the previous pages will be developed. The following tasks will be completed in this project.

1. Create a title page using an outside border, color, shadows, and clip art.
2. Save the title page.
3. Insert an existing document below the title page in a new section.
4. Save the active document with a new file name.
5. Add a table to the document using custom tab stops.
6. Add a table to the document using the Draw Table feature.
7. Customize bullets in a list.
8. Add a header to the second section of the document.
9. Print the document.

The following pages contain a detailed explanation of each of these tasks.

Starting Word

Follow these steps to start Word or ask your instructor how to start Word for your system.

TO START WORD

1. Click the Start button on the taskbar.
2. Click New Office Document on the Start menu. If necessary, click the General tab when the New Office Document dialog box first opens.
3. Double-click the Blank Document icon on the General sheet.
4. If the Word screen is not maximized, double-click its title bar to maximize it.

Office starts Word. After a few moments, an empty document titled Document1 displays on the Word screen.

Displaying Nonprinting Characters

You may recall that it is helpful to display nonprinting characters that indicate where in the document you pressed the ENTER key, SPACEBAR, or TAB key. Follow this step to display nonprinting characters.

TO DISPLAY NONPRINTING CHARACTERS

1. If the Show/Hide ¶ button on the Standard toolbar is not already recessed, click it.

Word displays nonprinting characters in the document window, and the Show/Hide ¶ button on the Standard toolbar is recessed (Figure 4-4).

Creating a Title Page

A **title page** should be designed to catch the reader's attention. Therefore, the title page of the sales proposal in Project 4 (Figure 4-1 on page WD 4.7) contains color, an outside border, shadowed text, clip art, and a variety of fonts and point sizes. The steps on the following pages discuss how to create the title page in Project 4.

Changing the Top Margin

The first step in creating the title page for the sales proposal is to change the top margin to 1.5 inches. Because the default in Word is 1 inch, perform the following steps to change the top margin to 1.5 inches.

TO CHANGE THE TOP MARGIN

① Click File on the menu bar and then click Page Setup.

② If necessary, click the Margins tab when the Page Setup dialog box first opens.

③ Type 1.5 in the Top text box (Figure 4-4).

④ Click the OK button.

The top margin is set at 1.5 inches.

More *About*
Title Pages

Formal proposals often require a specific format for the title page. Beginning about 3-4" from the top margin, these components are each centered and on separate lines: title; the word, for; reader's name, position, organization, and address; the word, by; your name, position, and organization; and the date the proposal was written.

More *About*
Changing Margins

In page layout view, you can change the margins using the ruler. The current margins are shaded in gray, and the margin boundary is positioned where the gray meets the white. You drag the margin boundary to change the margin. Hold down the ALT key while dragging the margin boundary to display the margin settings.

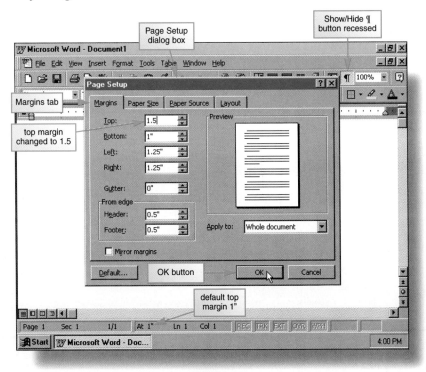

FIGURE 4-4

Adding Color to Characters

The next step in creating the title page is to enter the company name, centered using 36-point Algerian pink font. First, change the font, font size, and paragraph alignment. Then, use the Font Color button on the Formatting toolbar to add color to characters as shown on the next page.

TO FORMAT CHARACTERS

1 Click the Center button on the Formatting toolbar.

2 Click the Font box arrow on the Formatting toolbar and then click Algerian (or a similar font) from the list of available fonts.

3 Click the Font Size box arrow on the Formatting toolbar, scroll to and then click 36.

The font, font size, and paragraph alignment for the first line of the title are changed (Figure 4-5 below).

The next step is to change the color of the characters to pink.

Steps To Color Characters

1 **Point to the Font Color button arrow on the Formatting toolbar (Figure 4-5).**

The color that displays below the letter A on the Font Color button is the most recently used color for characters; thus, your color may differ from this figure.

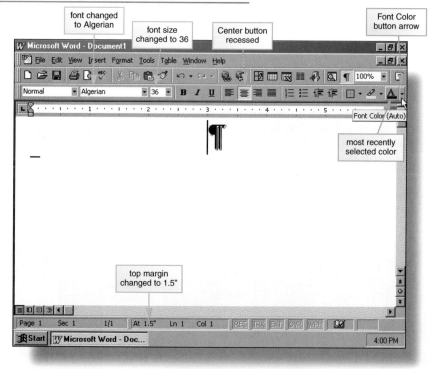

FIGURE 4-5

2 **Click the Font Color button arrow. When the color palette displays, point to the color Pink.**

Word displays a list of available colors for characters in the color palette (Figure 4-6). Automatic is the system default color, which usually is black.

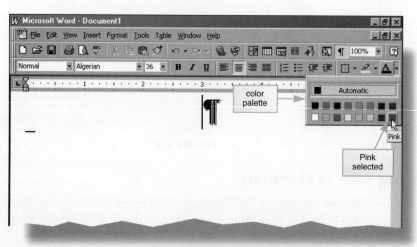

FIGURE 4-6

3 Click the color Pink. Type
FIESTA BALLOON TOURS **and
then press the ENTER key.**

*Word displays the first line
of the title page using the
36-point Algerian pink font
(Figure 4-7). Notice the
paragraph mark on line 2 also
is pink. To ensure that the next
characters you type are not pink,
you should change the color back
to automatic.*

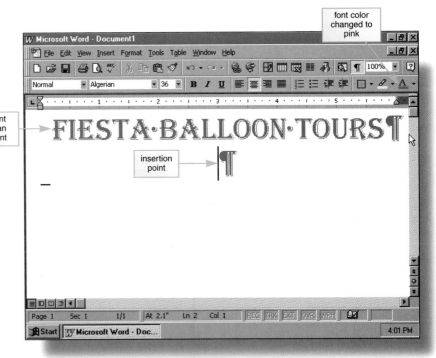

FIGURE 4-7

4 Click the Font Color button arrow
on the Formatting toolbar. When
the color palette displays, point
to Automatic (Figure 4-8).

5 Click Automatic.

*Word changes the font color to
automatic (Figure 4-9 on the next
page). The color of the paragraph
mark on line 2 changes to black
and so does the line on the Font
Color button.*

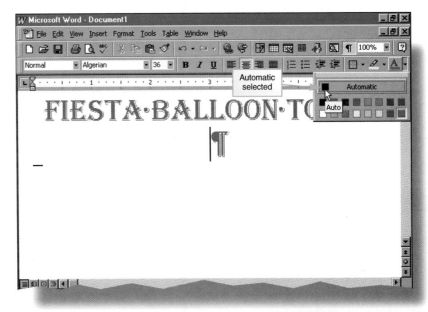

FIGURE 4-8

Adding a Shadow Box Border in Color with Shading

The next step is to surround the company name with a **border**. In Word, you
can add a border, also called a **rule**, to any edge of a paragraph. That is, borders
may be added above or below a paragraph, to the left or right of a paragraph, or
any combination of these sides. You can add borders by clicking the **Tables and
Borders button** on the Standard toolbar. When you click the Tables and Borders
button, the Tables and Borders toolbar displays on the screen and the Tables and
Borders button is recessed. Using the **Tables and Borders toolbar**, you also can add
color to a border.

Other Ways

1. Right-click paragraph mark
   or selected text, click Font
   on shortcut menu, click Font
   tab, click Color box arrow,
   click desired color, click
   OK button

2. On Format menu click Font,
   click Font tab, click Color
   box arrow, click desired
   color, click OK button

Perform the following steps to add a blue outside border around the company name.

Steps To Border a Paragraph

1 **Click somewhere in line 1 to position the insertion point in the company name. Point to the Tables and Borders button on the Standard toolbar (Figure 4-9).**

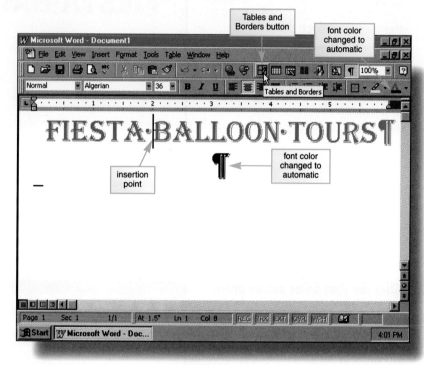

FIGURE 4-9

2 **Click the Tables and Borders button. If the Tables and Borders toolbar is floating on the Word screen, point to the title bar of the Tables and Borders toolbar.**

Word displays the Tables and Borders toolbar and switches to page layout view (Figure 4-10). Depending on the last position of this toolbar, it may be floating on the Word screen or it may be docked below the Formatting toolbar. You want it docked.

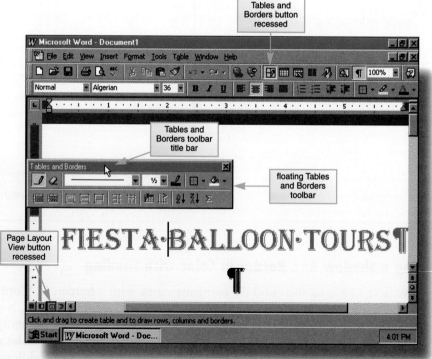

FIGURE 4-10

3 If the Tables and Borders toolbar is floating on the Word screen, double-click the title bar of the Tables and Borders toolbar.

Word docks the Tables and Borders toolbar below the Formatting toolbar.

FIGURE 4-11

4 Point to the Draw Table button on the Tables and Borders toolbar.

The Draw Table button is recessed when you first display the Tables and Borders toolbar (Figure 4-11). To border a paragraph, you do not want the Draw Table button recessed.

5 Click the Draw Table button. Click the Line Weight box arrow on the Tables and Borders toolbar and then point to 3 pt.

Word displays a list of available line weights (Figure 4-12). The Draw Table button is no longer recessed.

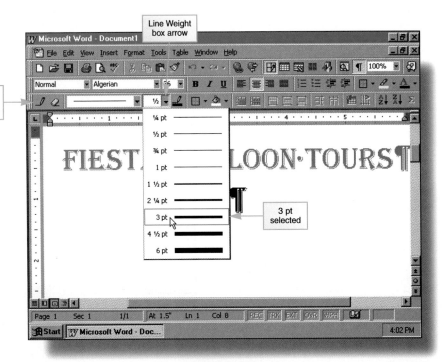

FIGURE 4-12

6 **Click 3 pt. If the Draw Table button is recessed, click it to deselect it.**

Word changes the line weight to 3 point.

7 **Click the Border Color button on the Tables and Borders toolbar. When the color palette displays, point to the color Blue.**

Word displays a color palette for border colors (Figure 4-13).

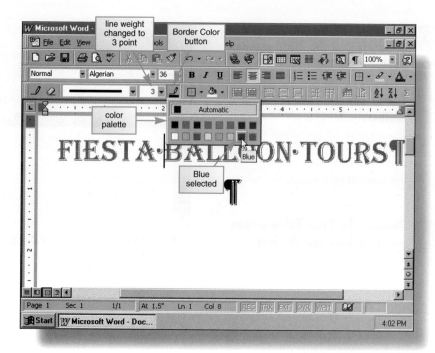

FIGURE 4-13

8 **Click the color Blue. If the Draw Table button is recessed, click it to deselect it.**

Word changes the color of the border lines to blue, as indicated in the Line Style box and the Border Color button.

9 **Click the Outside Border button on the Tables and Borders toolbar.**

*Word places an outside border around the company name on the title page (Figure 4-14). The **Outside Border button** on the Tables and Borders toolbar is recessed. Notice that the Outside Border button on the Formatting toolbar also is recessed. To ensure that the next border you draw is not 3-point blue, you should change the border line weight and color back to the default.*

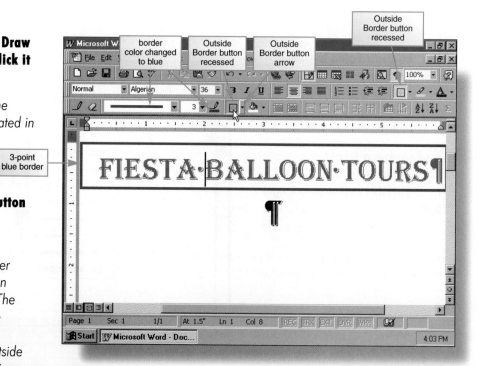

FIGURE 4-14

10 Click the Line Weight box arrow on the Tables and Borders toolbar and then click ½ pt. Click the Border Color button on the Tables and Borders toolbar and then click Automatic. Point to the Tables and Borders button on the Standard toolbar.

The line weight and border color are reset (Figure 4-15).

11 Click the Tables and Borders button.

The Tables and Borders toolbar no longer displays on the Word screen, and the Tables and Borders button is no longer recessed (Figure 4-16 on the next page).

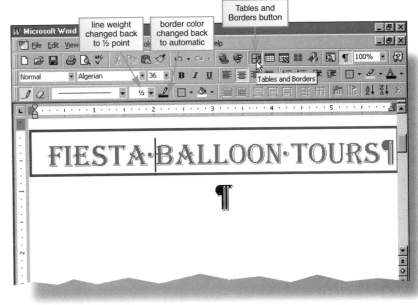

FIGURE 4-15

When you click the Outside Border button on the Tables and Borders toolbar, Word places a border around the entire paragraph. You can add a border to any edge of a paragraph from the **borders palette**. To display the borders palette, click the Outside Border button arrow (Figure 4-14). For example, to add a border to the left edge of a paragraph, position the insertion point somewhere in the paragraph, click the Outside Border button arrow, and then click **Left Border** on the borders palette. To remove a border from a paragraph, position the insertion point somewhere in the paragraph, click the Outside Border button arrow, and then click **No Border** on the borders palette.

Notice in Figure 4-14 that the Outside Border button on the Formatting toolbar also is recessed. Word actually provides two Outside Border buttons. If you want to place a border using the same color and size as the most recently defined border, then you simply click the Outside Border button on the Formatting toolbar. If you want to change the size or color of the border, however, you have to use the Tables and Borders toolbar or the Borders and Shading dialog box.

If you have a black-and-white printer, the colors other than black or white will print in shades of gray.

Importing and Resizing a Graphic

You may recall that Word 97 includes a series of predefined graphics called **clip art files** or **Windows metafiles**. These clip art files are located in the **Clip Gallery**, which contains its own Help system to assist you in locating an image suited to your application. If you cannot locate an appropriate clip art file in the Clip Gallery, Microsoft provides a special Web page with additional clips. If you have access to the Web, you can download clip art files from the Web page into the Clip Gallery. You insert, or import, these clip art files from the Clip Gallery into a Word document by clicking **Picture** on the Insert menu.

The next series of steps in this project are to download a hot air balloon clip art file from Microsoft's Clip Gallery Live Web page and then import the clip art file into the Word document.

> **Other Ways**
>
> 1. On Format menu click Borders and Shading, click Borders tab, click Box in Setting list, click desired style, color, and width, click OK button

> **More About Windows Metafiles**
>
> You can edit a Windows metafile by clicking the Drawing button on the Standard toolbar to display the Drawing toolbar. To separate the graphic into individual parts, select the graphic, click the Draw button on the Drawing toolbar, and then click Group. When you are finished making changes, click the Draw button again and click Regroup.

Note: The following steps assume you are using Microsoft Internet Explorer as your browser and that you have access to the Web. If you are not using Internet Explorer or you do not have access to the Web, you will need to perform a different set of steps. Your browser's handling of pictures on the Web will be discovered in Step 6. If necessary, you may be directed to follow the steps on page WD 4.21 to install the picture from the Data Disk that accompanies this book. If you do not have access to the Web, go directly to the steps on page WD 4.21.

Steps To Download Clip Art from Microsoft's Clip Gallery Live Web Page

1 **Click the paragraph mark below the company name to position the insertion point on line 2. Press the ENTER key to position the insertion point on line 3. Click Insert on the menu bar, point to Picture, and then point to Clip Art.**

The insertion point is on line 3 in the document (Figure 4-16). Because the submenu covers the insertion point, look on the status bar for the numeric location of the insertion point.

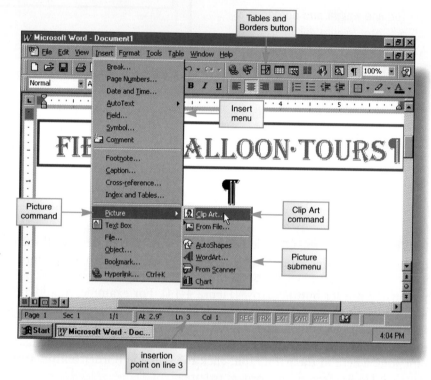

FIGURE 4-16

2 **Click Clip Art. If necessary, click the Clip Art tab when the Microsoft Clip Gallery dialog box first opens. Point to the Connect to Web for additional clips button.**

Word displays the Microsoft Clip Gallery dialog box (Figure 4-17). A list of clip art categories displays at the left of the dialog box. Clip art files associated with the selected category display to the right.

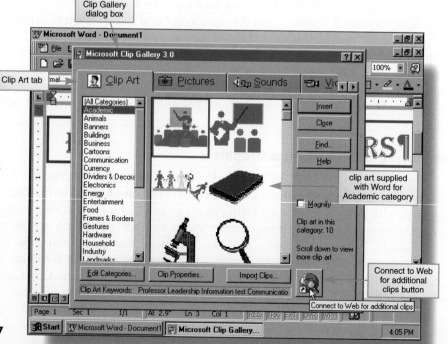

FIGURE 4-17

3 Click the Connect to Web for additional clips button. If a Connect to Web for More Clip Art, Photos, Sounds dialog box displays, click its OK button.

If you currently are not connected to the Web, Word connects you using your default browser. Microsoft Clip Gallery Live displays in a new window (Figure 4-18). The frame to the left of the window displays Microsoft's End-User License Agreement (EULA).

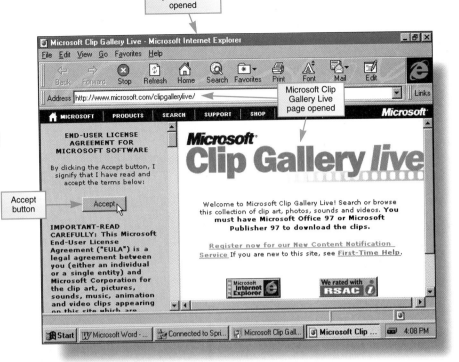

FIGURE 4-18

4 Read the EULA and then click the Accept button. When the Browse and Search buttons display in the left frame, be sure the ClipArt button is recessed, click the Search button and then type `balloon` in the Enter keywords text box.

Your browser replaces the EULA with buttons that enable you to locate clip art, pictures, sounds, and videos on the Web (Figure 4-19). The Browse button allows you to display categories similar to those in the Microsoft Clip Gallery dialog box. With the Search button, you type in a keyword and Microsoft searches through all the clips for matching images.

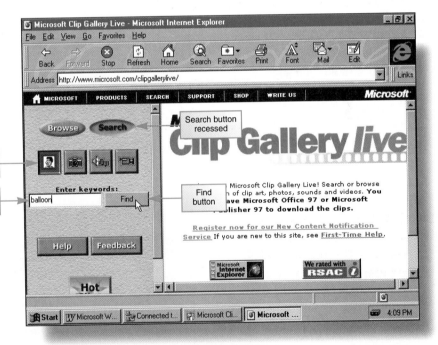

FIGURE 4-19

5 **Click the Find button.**

Your browser displays the clip art associated with keyword(s) you entered (Figure 4-20). The size of each clip art file displays below its name. To download a file into the Clip Gallery, you click the file name.

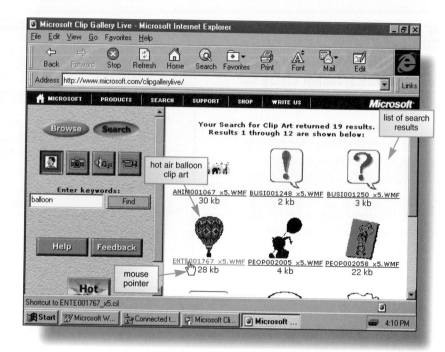

FIGURE 4-20

6 **Click the file name ENTE001767_x5.WMF. (If your browser displays a dialog box asking whether you want to open the file or save the file, click Open and then click the OK button. If your browser displays a dialog box and Open is not an option, close your browser window, click the Cancel button in the Microsoft Clip Gallery dialog box, then go to the steps on page WD 4.21.)**

Your browser downloads the file into your Microsoft Clip Gallery (Figure 4-21). If this is the first file downloaded, a new category called Downloaded Clips, is added to your category list.

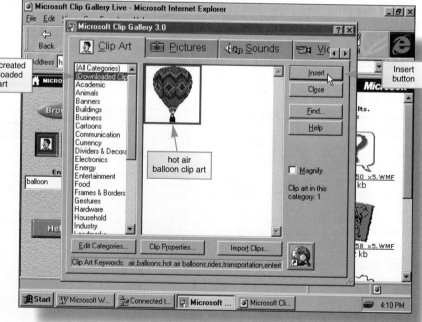

FIGURE 4-21

7 **If it is not already selected, click the hot air balloon clip art image and then point to the Insert button.**

8 Click the Insert button. If the Picture toolbar does not display, right-click the clip art image and then click Show Picture Toolbar on the shortcut menu.

Word inserts the hot air balloon clip art image into your document as a floating picture (Figure 4-22).

9 If necessary, close your Web browser window.

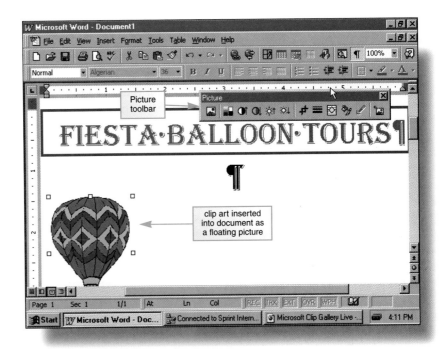

FIGURE 4-22

If you do not have access to the Web, you have to install the clip art file into the Microsoft Clip Gallery from the Data Disk that accompanies this book as described in the following steps.

TO INSTALL THE CLIP ART FROM THE DATA DISK

1 Click the paragraph mark below the company name to position the insertion point on line 2. Press the ENTER key to position the insertion point on line 3.

2 Click Insert on the menu bar, point to Picture on the Insert menu, and then point to Clip Art on the Picture submenu.

3 Click Clip Art. If necessary, click the Clip Art tab when the Microsoft Clip Gallery dialog box first opens.

4 Insert the Data Disk that accompanies this book into drive A.

5 Click the Start button on the taskbar, point to Programs on the Start menu, and then click Windows Explorer. When the Exploring window displays, scroll to the top of the All Folders side of the window and then click 3½ Floppy (A:) to select drive A. Double-click the Word folder in the Contents side of the window to display the contents of the Data Disk.

6 Double-click the file name ENTE001767_x5.CIL on the Data Disk. Close the Exploring window.

7 When the Microsoft Clip Gallery redisplays, click the balloon clip art and then click the Insert button.

Word inserts the hot air balloon clip art image into your document as a floating picture (see Figure 4-22 above).

Word imports a clip art file as a **floating picture**, which is a picture inserted in a layer over the text. An **inline picture**, on the other hand, is positioned directly in the text at the location of the insertion point. You change a floating picture to an inline picture using the **Format Picture dialog box**.

You may recall that you can resize a graphic by dragging its **sizing handles**. If you have a precise measurement for the graphic's dimensions, however, you can use the Format Picture dialog box to enter the exact width and height measurements.

Perform the following steps to change the clip art image from a floating picture to an inline picture and then resize it.

Steps **To Format a Picture**

1 If it is not already selected, click the balloon clip art image. (If the Picture toolbar does not display, right-click the clip art image and then click Show Picture Toolbar on the shortcut menu.) Point to the Format Picture button on the Picture toolbar.

Word displays the Picture toolbar when you select the clip art image (Figure 4-23). Recall that selected graphics display sizing handles at their corner and middle locations.

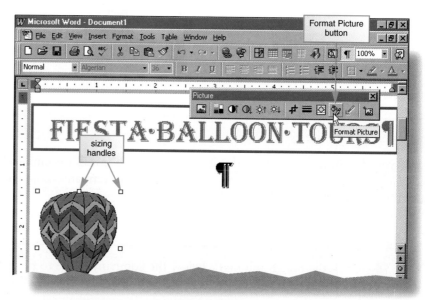

FIGURE 4-23

2 Click the Format Picture button. When the Format Picture dialog box displays, click the Position tab and then click Float over text to clear the check box.

Word displays the Format Picture dialog box (Figure 4-24). When the Float over text check box is selected, the image is a floating picture; when the check box is cleared, the image will be an inline picture.

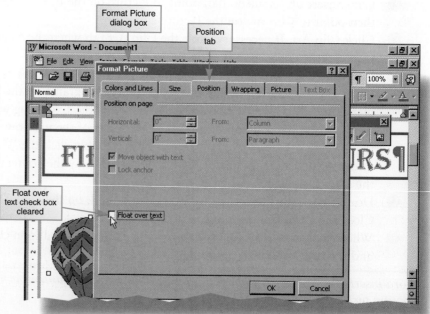

FIGURE 4-24

3 Click the Size tab. In the Size and rotate area, type 3 in the Height text box, type 3 in the Width text box, and then point to the OK button.

The numbers you enter in the Size and rotate area are in inches (Figure 4-25).

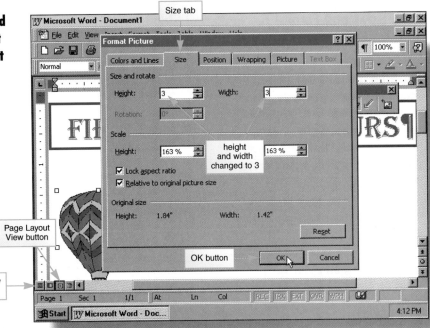

FIGURE 4-25

4 Click the OK button. Click outside the graphic to deselect it. Click the Normal View button at the bottom of the document window.

Word changes the graphic to an inline picture and resizes it to 3 inches by 3 inches (Figure 4-26). Notice the graphic is centered because the paragraph mark to which it is attached is centered. You switch to normal view to increase the work area in the Word window.

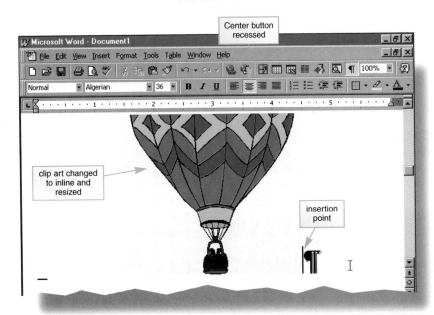

FIGURE 4-26

OtherWays

1. On Format menu click Picture, select desired settings, click OK button

Entering and Formatting the Company Slogan

The next step is to enter the company slogan below the graphic on the title page. The slogan is 36-point Book Antiqua blue, bold italic font. The characters also are formatted with a shadow. Because you need to display the Font dialog box to add a shadow to characters, you can change the font typeface, font style, and font size and color using the **Font dialog box** all at once, instead of using the Formatting toolbar. Perform the steps on the next page to enter the slogan and then format its characters using the Font dialog box.

Steps **To Enter and Format the Company Slogan**

1 **Position the insertion point at the end of the title page (after the balloon clip art). Press the ENTER key twice. Type** Arizona's **and then press the ENTER key. Type** Ultimate **and then press the ENTER key. Type** Hot Air Adventure **and then highlight the three paragraphs containing the company slogan. Right-click the selected slogan and then point to Font on the shortcut menu.**

All three lines of the company slogan are entered and selected (Figure 4-27). Notice when you type the slogan, it is formatted in all capital letters; this is because the Algerian font displays characters in uppercase.

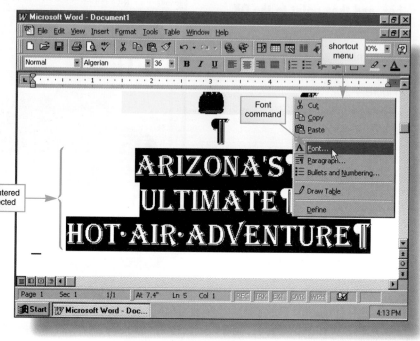

FIGURE 4-27

2 **Click Font. If necessary, click the Font tab when the Font dialog box first opens. Scroll through the list of fonts and then click Book Antiqua (or a similar font). Click Bold Italic in the Font style list box. If necessary, scroll through the list of font sizes and then click 36. Click the Color box arrow, scroll to and then click the color Blue. Click Shadow in the Effects area. Point to the OK button.**

The Preview area reflects the current selections (Figure 4-28).

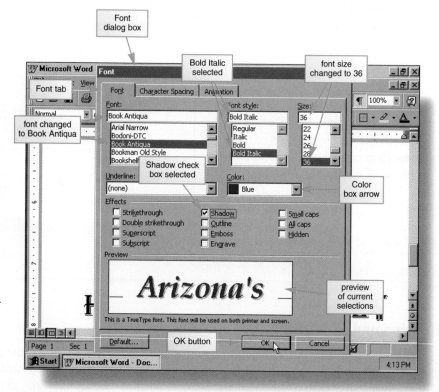

FIGURE 4-28

3 **Click the OK button. Click at the end of the slogan to remove the highlight.**

Word displays the company slogan formatted to 36-point Book Antiqua blue, bold italic font with a shadow (Figure 4-29).

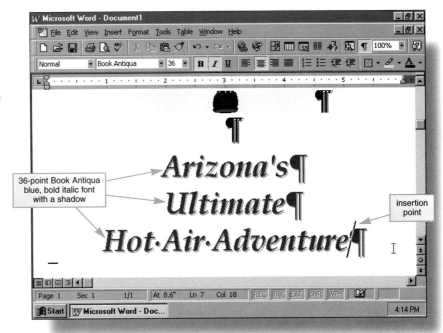

FIGURE 4-29

Saving the Title Page

Because you have finished the title page, you should save it by performing the following steps.

TO SAVE A DOCUMENT

1. Insert your floppy disk into drive A.
2. Click the Save button on the Standard toolbar.
3. Type `Fiesta Title Page` in the File name text box. Do not press the ENTER key after typing the file name.
4. Click the Save in box arrow and then click 3½ Floppy (A:).
5. Click the Save button in the Save As dialog box.

Word saves the document on a floppy disk in drive A with the file name Fiesta Title Page (Figure 4-30 on the next page).

The title page for the sales proposal is complete. The next step is to insert a draft of the proposal below the title page.

Inserting an Existing Document into an Open Document

Assume you already have prepared a draft of the body of the proposal and saved it with the file name Fiesta Balloon Tours Draft. You would like the draft to display on a separate page below the title page. Once the two documents display on the screen together as one document, you would like to save this active document with a new name so each of the original documents remains intact.

Other Ways

1. Click Font box arrow then select desired font, click Font Size box arrow then select desired font size, click Bold button, click Italic button, click Font Color button arrow then click color Blue, right-click selected text, click Font on shortcut menu, click Font tab, click Shadow, click OK button

2. On Format menu click Font, click Font tab, select desired font in Font list box, select desired style in Font style list box, select desired point size in Size list box, click Color box arrow then select desired color, click Shadow, click OK button

You want the inserted pages of the sales proposal to use the Times New Roman font and be left-aligned. That is, you want to return to the **Normal style**. Because the text to be entered at the insertion point currently is formatted for paragraphs to be centered using 36-point Book Antiqua blue, bold italic font, you should return to the Normal style as shown in the steps below.

Steps **To Return to the Normal Style**

1 **Be sure the insertion point is on the paragraph mark on line 7 and then press the ENTER key. Click the Style box arrow on the Formatting toolbar and then point to Normal.**

Word displays the list of available styles (Figure 4-30). Notice the paragraph mark on line 8 is formatted the same as the slogan because when you press the ENTER key, formatting is carried forward to the next paragraph.

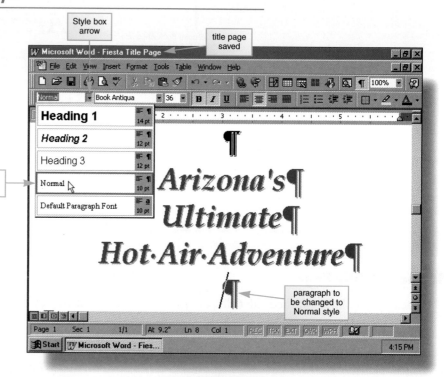

FIGURE 4-30

2 **Click Normal.**

Word returns the paragraph mark at the location of the insertion point to the Normal style (Figure 4-31). That is, the paragraph mark is left-aligned and the text to be entered is 10-point Times New Roman.

FIGURE 4-31

Inserting a Section Break

The draft of the sales proposal should appear on a separate page below the title page. The draft to be inserted requires different page formatting than the title page. Recall that you increased the top margin of the title page to 1.5 inches. The draft should have a top margin of 1 inch. To change margins for the draft of the proposal and retain the margins for the title page, you must create a new section in the document.

A Word document can be divided into any number of **sections**. All documents have at least one section. If during the course of creating a document, you would like to change the margins, paper size, page orientation, page number position, contents or position of headers, footers, or footnotes, you must create a new section. Each section may be formatted different from the others.

When you create a new section, a **section break** displays on the screen as a double dotted line separated by the words, Section Break. Section breaks do not print. When you create a section break, you specify whether or not the new section should begin on a new page. Perform the following steps to create a section break that begins on a new page.

More *About*
**Drafting a
Proposal**

All proposals should have an introduction, body, and conclusion. The introduction could contain the subject, purpose, statement of problem, need, background, or scope. The body may include available or required facilities, cost, feasibility, methods, timetable, materials, or equipment. The conclusion summarizes key points or requests some action.

 Steps To Create a Section Break

1 Be sure the insertion point is positioned on the paragraph mark on line 8. Click Insert on the menu bar and then click Break. When the Break dialog box displays, click Next page in the Section breaks area. Point to the OK button.

*Word displays the **Break dialog box** (Figure 4-32). The Next page option instructs Word to create a new page for the new section.*

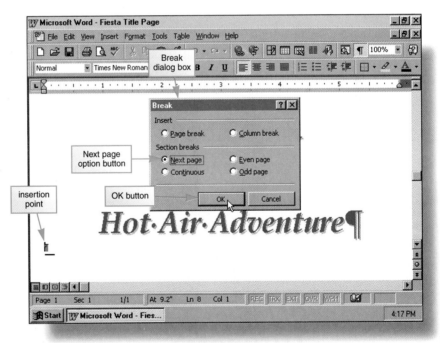

FIGURE 4-32

2 Click the OK button.

Word creates a section break in the document (Figure 4-33). The insertion point and paragraph mark are placed in the new section. Notice the status bar indicates the insertion point is on page 2 in section 2.

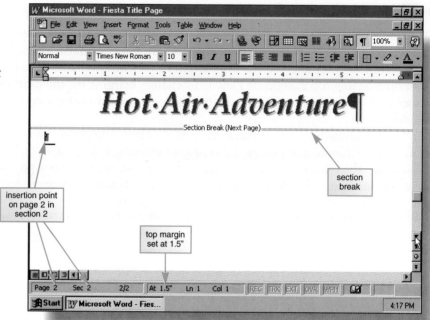

FIGURE 4-33

All section formatting is stored in the section break. You can delete a section break and all associated section formatting by selecting the section break, right-clicking the selection, and then clicking Cut on the shortcut menu. To select a section break, point to its left until the mouse pointer changes direction and then click. If you accidentally delete a section break, you can bring it back by clicking the Undo button on the Standard toolbar.

Notice in Figure 4-33 above that the top margin is set at 1.5 inches. Recall that the top margin of the new section containing the text of the draft of the sales proposal is to be set at 1 inch. Thus, follow these steps to change the top margin of section 2 to 1 inch.

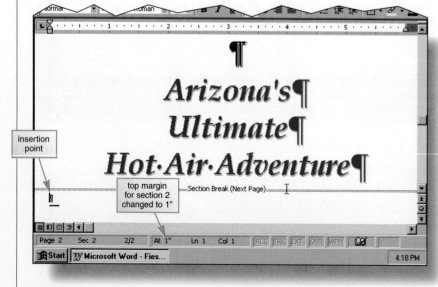

FIGURE 4-34

TO CHANGE THE TOP MARGIN

1. Be sure the insertion point is in section 2. Click File on the menu bar and then click Page Setup.
2. If necessary, click the Margins tab when the Page Setup dialog box first opens.
3. Type 1 in the Top text box.
4. Click the OK button.

The top margin is set at 1" (Figure 4-34).

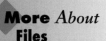

Inserting a Second Document into an Open Document

The next step is to insert the draft of the sales proposal below the section break. If you created the draft at an earlier time, you may have forgotten its name. Thus, you can display the contents of, or **preview**, any file before inserting it. Perform the following steps to insert the draft of the proposal into the open document.

More About Files

In the Insert and Open File dialog boxes, the Details button displays the name, size, type, and date modified of each file in the current folder. The Properties button displays items such as author name, last print date, creation and modification dates, number of pages, and other information for the selected file.

Steps To Insert a Second Document into an Open Document

1. **Insert the Data Disk that accompanies this book into drive A. Be sure the insertion point is positioned on the paragraph mark immediately below the section break. Click Insert on the menu bar and then point to File (Figure 4-35).**

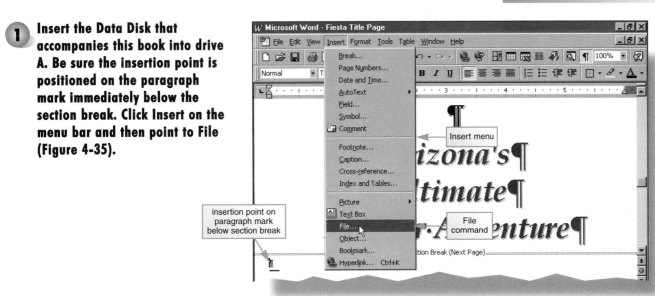

FIGURE 4-35

2. **Click File. When the Insert File dialog box displays, click the Look in box arrow and then click 3½ Floppy (A:). Double-click the Word folder. If it is not already recessed, click the Preview button. Click Fiesta Balloon Tours Draft and then point to the OK button.**

Word displays the Insert File dialog box (Figure 4-36). A list of available files in the Word folder on drive A displays. The contents of the selected file (Fiesta Balloon Tours Draft) display in the preview window.

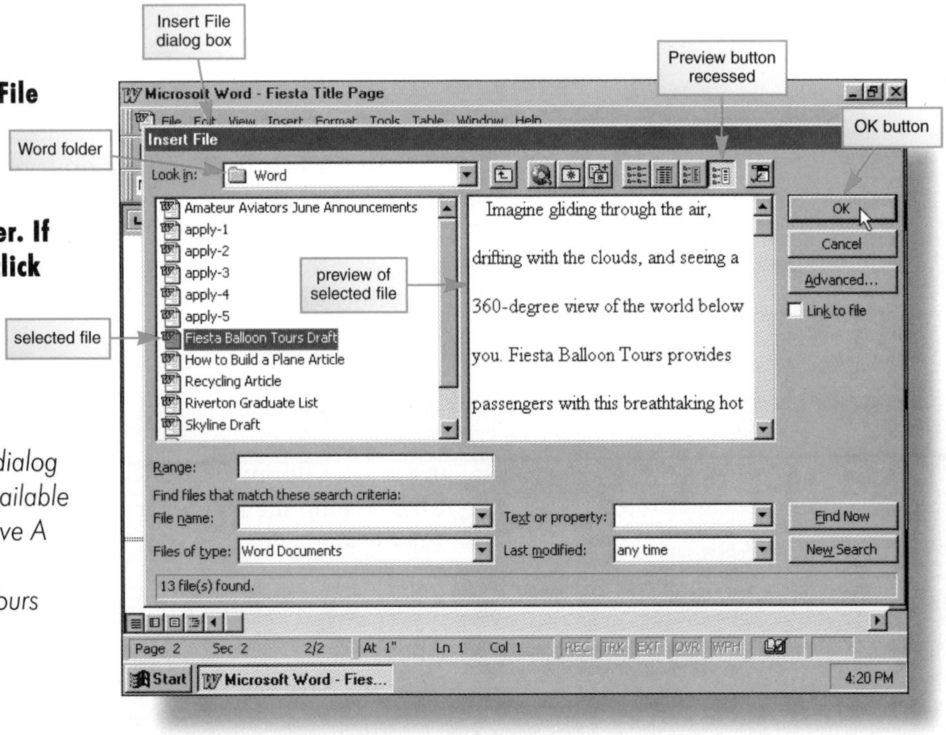

FIGURE 4-36

3 Click the OK button. When Word returns to the document window, press the SHIFT+F5 keys.

Word inserts the file, Fiesta Balloon Tours Draft, into the open document at the location of insertion point (Figure 4-37). The insertion point is positioned immediately below the section break, which was its location prior to inserting the new document. Pressing the SHIFT+F5 keys instructs Word to return the insertion point to your last editing location.

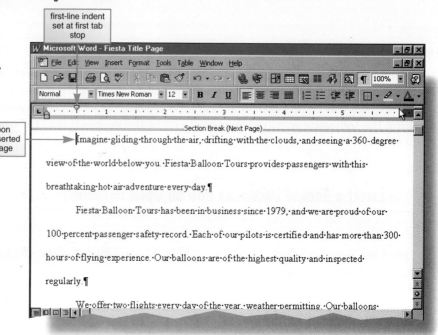

first-line indent
set at first tab
stop

Fiesta Balloon
Tours Draft inserted
below title page

FIGURE 4-37

◆**More** *About*
SHIFT+F5

Word remembers your last three editing or typing locations. Thus, you can press SHIFT+F5 up to three times to move the insertion point to prior editing locations in your document. This feature works even after you save and then re-open a document.

Word inserts the complete document immediately above the insertion point and positions the insertion point below the inserted document. Therefore, if the insertion point is positioned in the middle of the first document when you insert the second document, the first document continues after the end of the inserted document.

Previewing files before opening them is very useful if you have forgotten the name of a particular file. For this reason, you can preview files in both the Open and Insert File dialog boxes by clicking the **Preview button** in the respective dialog box.

Saving the Active Document with a New File Name

The current file name on the title bar is Fiesta Title Page, yet the active document contains both the title page and the draft of the sales proposal. Because you might want to keep the title page as a separate document called Fiesta Title Page, you should save the active document with a new file name. If you save the active document by clicking the Save button on the Standard toolbar, Word will assign it the current file name. Thus, use the following steps to save the active document with a new file name.

◆**More** *About*
File Save As

You can press F12 to display the Save As dialog box when you want to assign a new file name to an existing file.

TO SAVE AN ACTIVE DOCUMENT WITH A NEW FILE NAME

1. Insert your floppy disk into drive A.
2. Click File on the menu bar and then click Save As.
3. Type Fiesta Proposal in the File name text box. Do not press the ENTER key.
4. If necessary, click the Save in box arrow and then click 3½ Floppy (A:).
5. Click the Save button in the Save As dialog box.

Word saves the document on a floppy disk in drive A with the file name Fiesta Proposal (Figure 4-39 on page WD 4.32).

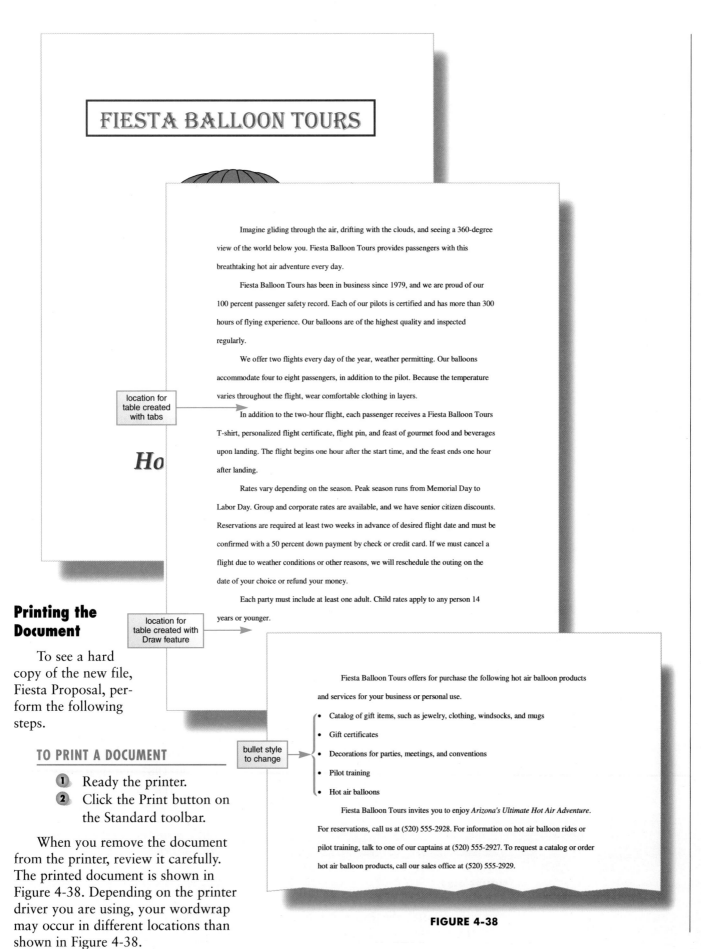

FIGURE 4-38

Printing the Document

To see a hard copy of the new file, Fiesta Proposal, perform the following steps.

TO PRINT A DOCUMENT

1. Ready the printer.
2. Click the Print button on the Standard toolbar.

When you remove the document from the printer, review it carefully. The printed document is shown in Figure 4-38. Depending on the printer driver you are using, your wordwrap may occur in different locations than shown in Figure 4-38.

More *About*
Proposal Wording

Be specific with descriptions in the sales proposal. Avoid vague, general, or abstract words, which could be misinterpreted by the reader. For example, the sentence, "the house is large" is too general. The sentence, "the house has 4,500 square feet with 5 bedrooms and 3 bathrooms" is more descriptive.

More *About*
Tab Stop Alignment

If you have a series of numbers that you want aligned on the decimal point, such as dollar amounts, use a decimal-aligned tab stop for the data. If you want text to be aligned with the right margin, such as a page number, place a right-aligned tab stop at the right margin, that is, where the gray meets the white on the ruler.

By adding two tables to the document and changing the bullet style, you can make the body of the proposal more pleasing to the eye. These enhancements to Project 4 are discussed in the following pages.

Setting and Using Tabs

Below the third paragraph of the sales proposal, you are to add a table that displays the starting and ending times of sunrise and sunset outings at Fiesta Balloon Tours. With Word, you can create tables by creating a Word table or by setting tab stops (as you would on a typewriter). In Project 3, you used the Insert Table button to create a Word table. For the first table in this project, you will set tab stops; for the second table that will be added later, you will draw a Word table.

Recall that Word, by default, places tab stops at every .5-inch mark on the ruler. You can use these default tab stops or set your own **custom tab stops**. When you set a custom tab stop, Word clears all default tab stops to the left of the custom tab stop. You also can specify how the text will align at a tab stop: left, centered, right, or decimal. Tab settings are stored in the paragraph mark at the end of each paragraph. Thus, each time you press the ENTER key, the custom tab stops are carried forward to the next paragraph.

The first step in creating this table is to center the title between the margins. If you simply click the Center button on the Formatting toolbar, the title will not be centered properly; instead, it will be one-half inch to the right of the center point because the first-line indent is set to the first tab stop (see Figure 4-37 on page WD 4.30). Thus, the first line of every paragraph is indented one-half inch. To properly center the title of the table, you must move the First Line Indent marker back to the left margin before clicking the Center button as described below.

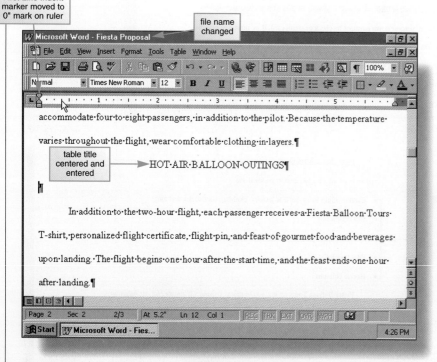

FIGURE 4-39

TO CENTER THE TITLE OF A TABLE

1. Position the insertion point at the end of the third paragraph (after the period following the word layers) and then press the ENTER key.
2. Drag the First Line Indent marker to the 0" mark on the ruler.
3. Click the Center button on the Formatting toolbar.
4. Type HOT AIR BALLOON OUTINGS and then press the ENTER key.
5. Press the CTRL+L keys.

The title displays centered properly (Figure 4-39).

The next step is to set custom tab stops for the data in the table. The text in the first tab stop should be left-aligned, the default; and the text in the last two tab stops should be right-aligned. Perform the following steps to set custom tab stops for the paragraph at the location of the insertion point.

 To Set Custom Tab Stops

1 **Be sure the insertion point is on the paragraph mark below the title of the table. Point to the 1.25" mark on the ruler (Figure 4-40).**

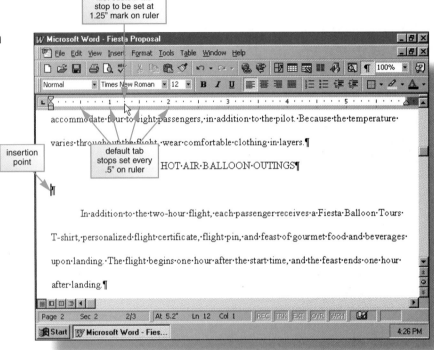

FIGURE 4-40

2 **Click the 1.25" mark on the ruler. Point to the Tab Alignment button at the left edge of the ruler.**

Word places a custom tab stop at the 1.25" mark on the ruler and removes the default tab stops at the .5" and 1" marks (Figure 4-41). A **tab marker** *displays on the ruler as a small dark capital L, the same symbol inside the* **Tab Alignment button***, which indicates the text entered at the tab stop will be left-aligned. You want the next custom tab stop to be right-aligned.*

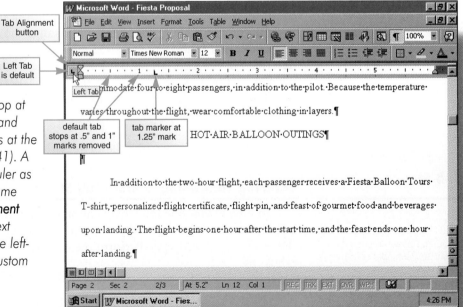

FIGURE 4-41

3 Click the Tab Alignment button twice.

The first time you click the Tab Alignment button, the symbol inside the Tab Alignment button changes to an upside down T, indicating a centered tab stop. The second click displays a mirror-image of a capital L, indicating the next custom tab stop set will be right-aligned (Figure 4-42).

FIGURE 4-42

4 Click the 3.25" mark on the ruler and then click the 4.5" mark on the ruler.

Word places custom tab stops at the 3.25" and 4.5" marks on the ruler and removes the default tab stops between the 1.25" and 3.25" marks and between the 3.25" and 4.5" marks. The tab markers display on the ruler as mirror-images of a capital L, indicating text typed at the tab stops will be right-aligned.

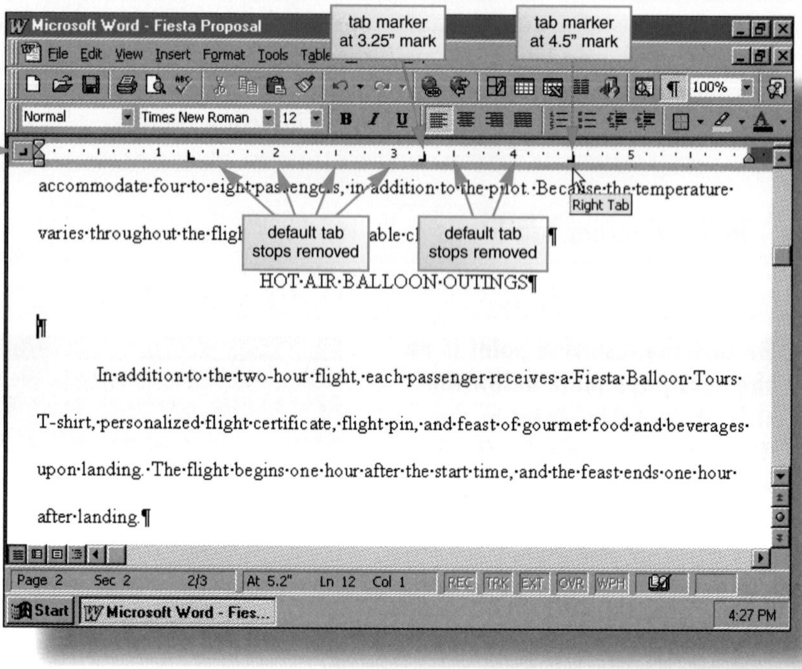

Other Ways

1. On Format menu click Tabs, enter tab stop position, click appropriate alignment, repeat if necessary, click OK button

More About Tab Stops

You can use the Tabs dialog box to change an existing tab stop's alignment or position on the ruler. You can also place leader characters in the empty space occupied by the tab. Leader characters, such as a series of dots, often are used in a table of contents to precede the page number. To display the Tabs dialog box, click Tabs on the Format menu.

If necessary, to move a custom tab stop drag the tab marker to the desired location on the ruler. If you wanted to change the alignment of a custom tab stop, you could first remove the existing tab stop and then insert a new one as described in the steps above. To remove a custom tab stop, point to the tab marker on the ruler and then drag the tab marker down and out of the ruler. You could also use the **Tabs dialog box** to change an existing tab stop's alignment or position. To display the Tabs dialog box, click Format on the menu bar and then click Tabs.

The next step in creating the table with tabs is to enter the text in the table.

Entering Text Using Custom Tab Stops

To move from one tab stop to another, you press the **TAB key**. A tab character displays in the empty space between tab stops and the insertion point moves to the next custom tab stop. Perform the following steps to enter text using custom tab stops.

TO ENTER TEXT USING CUSTOM TAB STOPS

1 Be sure the insertion point is positioned on the paragraph mark on line 12 in the sales proposal. Press the TAB key twice. Type Sunrise and then press the TAB key. Type Sunset and then press the ENTER key.

② Press the TAB key. Type
Start time and then
press the TAB key. Type
6:00 a.m. and then press
the TAB key. Type
7:00 p.m. and then press
the ENTER key.

③ Press the TAB key. Type
End time and then press
the TAB key. Type
10:00 a.m. and then
press the TAB key.
Type 11:00 p.m. and
then press the ENTER key.

*The first table in the sales
proposal displays as shown
in Figure 4-43.*

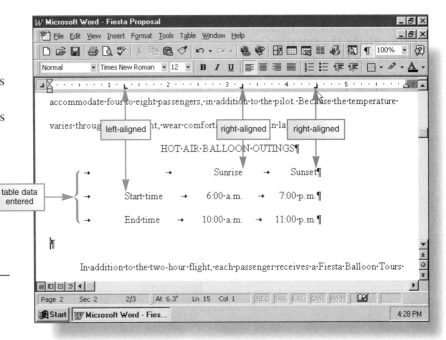

FIGURE 4-43

Adding a Border to a Table

To emphasize the table, you want
to add an outside border around it.
Recall that you place borders around a paragraph(s). Earlier in this project, you
used the Tables and Borders toolbar to add a 3-point blue border to a paragraph
on the title page and then changed the border back to its default size and color.
Because this border is to be the current border size and color, you can use the
Outside Border button on the Formatting toolbar. Because the table consists of
four separate paragraphs, including the title, you first select the paragraphs and
then add the border as shown in the following steps.

More *About*
Borders

If you don't want the border of
the current paragraph to extend
to the margins, drag the right or
left indent markers to the
desired location on the ruler.

 Steps **To Border a Table**

① **Select the four paragraphs in the
table and then point to the
Outside Border button on the
Formatting toolbar.**

*Word highlights the entire table
(Figure 4-44).*

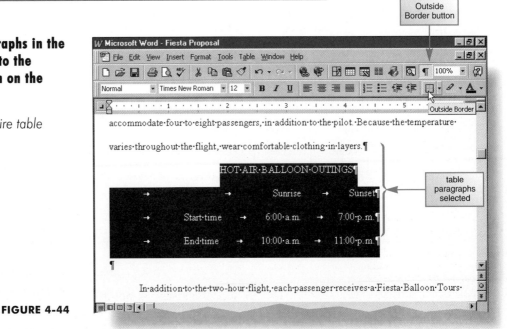

FIGURE 4-44

2 Click the Outside Border button. Click outside the selection to remove the highlight.

Word places a border around the selected paragraphs that extends from the left margin to the right margin of the document (Figure 4-45).

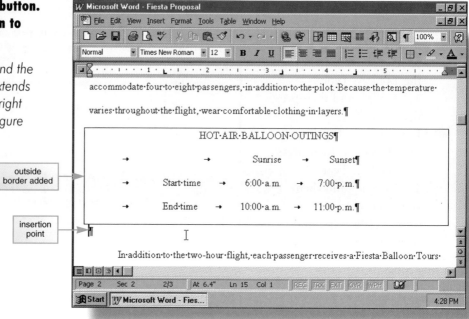

FIGURE 4-45

Creating a Table Using the Draw Table Feature

Below the sixth paragraph of the sales proposal draft (Figure 4-38 on page WD 4.31), you are to add another table. This table is more complicated than the previous one, so you are to create a Word table. In Project 3, you created a Word table using the Insert Table button on the Standard toolbar. When you have a simple table, one with the same number of rows and columns, use the Insert Table button to create a Word table. This table, however, is more complex (Figure 4-46). It contains a varying number of columns per row. To create a complex Word table, use the **Draw Table feature**.

You may recall that a Word table is a collection of rows and columns and that the intersection of a row and a column is called a **cell**. Cells are filled with data.

Within a table, you can easily rearrange rows and columns, change column widths, sort rows and columns, and sum the contents of rows and columns. You can use the Table AutoFormat dialog box to make the table display in a professional manner. You can also chart table data. For these reasons, many Word users create tables with the Insert Table button or the Draw Table feature, rather than using tabs as discussed in the previous section.

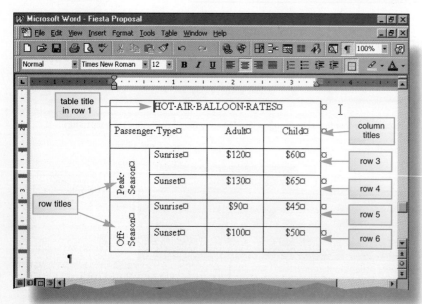

FIGURE 4-46

Drawing a Table

The first step is to draw an empty table in the document. To do this, you use the **Draw Table button** on the Tables and Borders toolbar. Perform the following steps to draw the table shown in Figure 4-46.

More *About* **Draw Table**

If you make a mistake while drawing a table, remember you can always click the Undo button to undo your most recent action.

Steps To Draw a Table

1 **Position the insertion point at the end of the sixth paragraph (after the period following the word younger) and then press the ENTER key. If necessary, click the Tables and Borders button on the Standard toolbar to display the Tables and Borders toolbar. If it is not already recessed, click the Draw Table button on the Tables and Borders toolbar. Move the mouse pointer into the document window to the location shown in Figure 4-47.**

Word displays the Tables and Borders toolbar and switches to page layout view (Figure 4-47). The mouse pointer shape changes to a pen when the Draw Table button is recessed. To draw the outside boundary of the table, you drag the pen pointer from one corner to the opposite diagonal corner of the desired table.

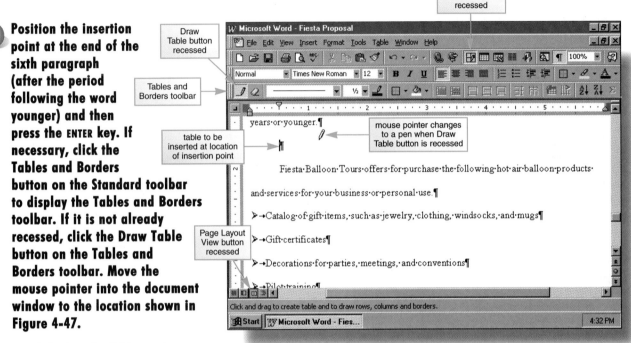

FIGURE 4-47

2 **Drag the pen pointer downward and to the right until the dotted rectangle is positioned similarly to the one shown in Figure 4-48.**

Word displays a dotted rectangle that shows the table's size (Figure 4-48).

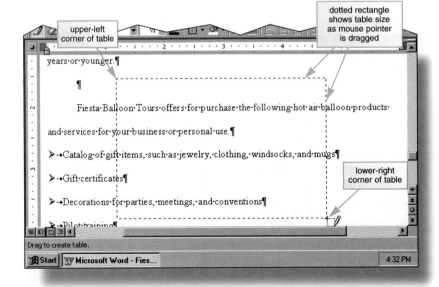

FIGURE 4-48

3 Release the mouse button. If necessary, scroll to display the entire table in the document window. (If the table is positioned in the wrong paragraph mark, click Table on the menu bar, click Select Table, and then drag the selected table to the correct paragraph mark.)

Word draws a table (Figure 4-49). If you wanted to redraw the table, you could click the Undo button on the Standard toolbar. If you wanted to resize the table, you would click the Draw Table button to turn off the Draw Table feature and then drag the table boundaries to their new locations. The next step is to begin drawing the rows and columns in the table.

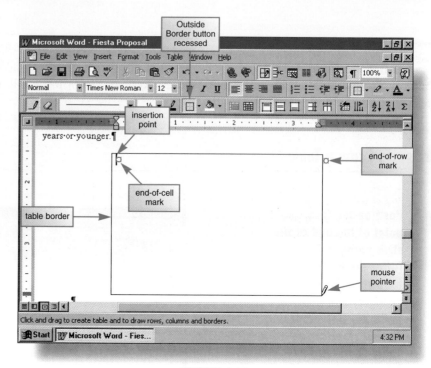

FIGURE 4-49

4 Be sure the Draw Table button is still recessed. Position the pen pointer as shown in Figure 4-50.

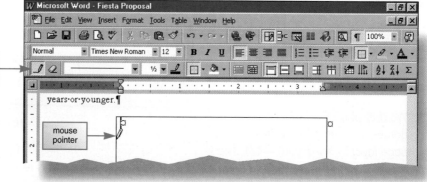

FIGURE 4-50

5 Drag the pen pointer to the right to draw a horizontal line.

*Word draws a horizontal line, which forms the bottom border of the first row in the table (Figure 4-51). If, while drawing rows and columns in the table, you want to remove and redraw a line, click the **Eraser button** on the Tables and Borders toolbar and then drag the eraser pointer through the line to erase. Click the Eraser button again to turn it off.*

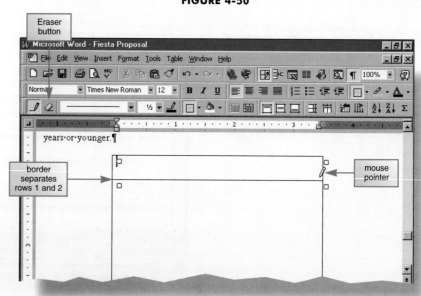

FIGURE 4-51

6 Be sure the Draw Table button is still recessed. Draw another horizontal line below the first as shown in Figure 4-52. Then, position the pen pointer as shown in Figure 4-52.

Word draws a second horizontal line to form the bottom border of the second row in the table (Figure 4-52). The pen pointer is positioned to draw the first column.

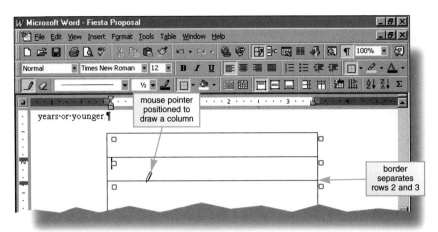

FIGURE 4-52

7 Draw three vertical lines to form the column borders as shown in Figure 4-53.

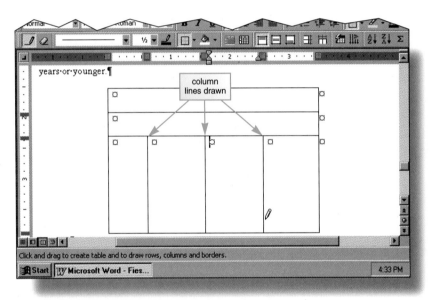

FIGURE 4-53

8 Draw four horizontal lines to form the row borders as shown in Figure 4-54.

The table displays as shown in Figure 4-54.

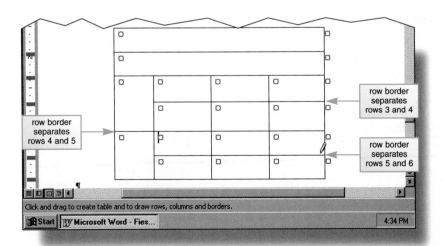

FIGURE 4-54

OtherWays

1. On Table menu click Draw Table, use pen pointer to draw table

More *About*
Table Columns

Column markers are located on the ruler and indicate the beginning and end of columns. A column boundary is the vertical gridline immediately to the right of a column in the table itself. To resize a column width, you drag the column boundary in the table or column marker on the ruler. Holding down the ALT key while dragging markers displays column width measurements.

All Word tables have a .5-point border. To change this border, you can use the Tables and Borders toolbar as described earlier in this project.

Recall that each row has an **end-of-row mark** (Figure 4-55 below), which is used to add columns to the right of a table, and each cell has an **end-of-cell mark,** which is used to select a cell. Notice the end-of-cell marks currently are **left-aligned** within each cell, which indicates the data will be left-aligned within the cells.

To format a table or data within a table, first you must select the cell(s) and then apply the appropriate formats. Because selecting table text is such a crucial function of Word tables, techniques to select these items are described in Table 4-1.

TABLE 4-1

ITEM TO SELECT	*ACTION*
Cell	Click the left edge of the cell.
Row	Click to the left of the row.
Column	Click the column's top gridline or border.
Contiguous cells, rows, or columns	Drag through the cells, rows, or columns.
Text in next cell	Press the TAB key.
Text in previous cell	Press the SHIFT+TAB keys.
Entire table	Click the table, click Table on the menu bar, then click Select Table.

If you look at the table drawn in Figure 4-54 on the previous page, the height of the rows varies and the width of the columns appears uneven. Perform the following steps to make the spacing between the columns and the rows even.

Steps **To Distribute Rows and Columns Evenly**

1 **If the Draw Table button on the Tables and Borders toolbar is recessed, click it to deselect it. Point to the left of the cell shown in Figure 4-55 until the mouse pointer changes direction.**

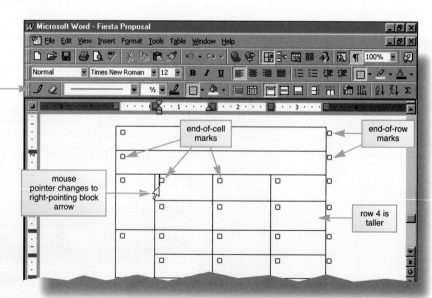

FIGURE 4-55

2 Drag through the cells to highlight the 12 cells shown in Figure 4-56.

The cells to be evenly distributed are selected (Figure 4-56).

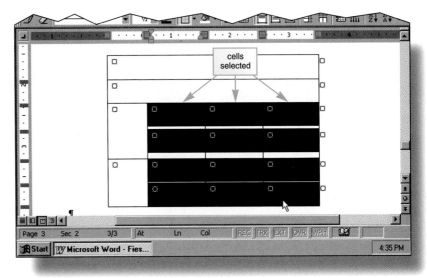

FIGURE 4-56

3 Click the Distribute Rows Evenly button on the Tables and Borders toolbar. Click the Distribute Columns Evenly button on the Tables and Borders toolbar. Click in the table to remove the highlight.

Word makes the height of the selected rows and the width of the selected columns uniform (Figure 4-57).

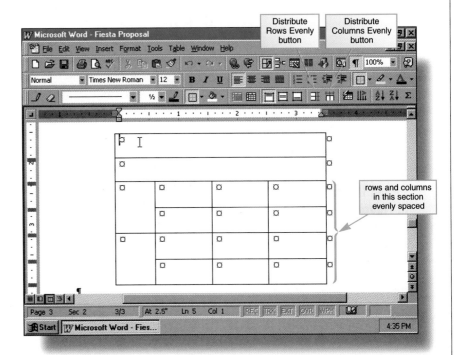

FIGURE 4-57

You notice you want to add two additional lines for column headings in the table. Perform the steps on the next page to continue drawing the table.

OtherWays

1. Select cells, on Table menu click Distribute Rows Evenly or Distribute Columns Evenly

2. Drag row or column boundaries (borders) on table

3. Drag row markers on vertical ruler or drag Move Table Column markers on horizontal ruler

4. On Table menu click Cell Height and Width, click appropriate tab, enter desired width or height, click OK button

Steps **To Draw More Table Lines**

1 Click the Draw Table button on the Tables and Borders toolbar. Position the mouse pointer as shown in Figure 4-58.

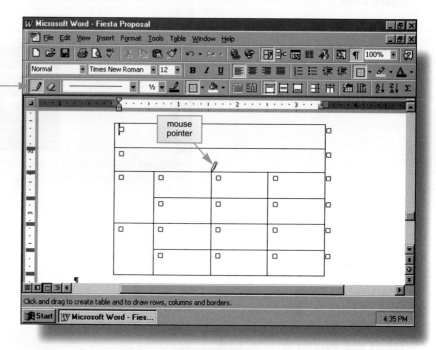

FIGURE 4-58

2 Draw a line upward extending the column border up. Draw a second line as shown in Figure 4-59. Click the Draw Table button on the Tables and Borders toolbar to deselect it.

The table is completely drawn (Figure 4-59).

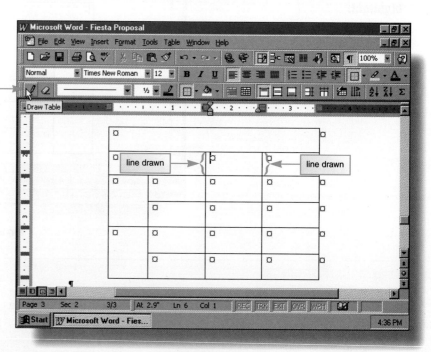

FIGURE 4-59

Entering the Data into the Table

The next step is to enter the data into the table. To advance from one column to the next, press the TAB key. To advance from one row to the next, also press the TAB key; do not press the ENTER key. The ENTER key is used to begin new paragraphs within a cell. Perform the following steps to enter the data into the table.

TO ENTER DATA INTO A TABLE

1 Click in the first cell of the table. Click the Center button on the Formatting toolbar. Type HOT AIR BALLOON RATES and then press the TAB key.

2 Type Passenger Type and then press the TAB key. Type Adult and then press the TAB key. Type Child and then press the TAB key.

3 Type Peak Season and then press the TAB key. Type Sunrise and then press the TAB key. Type $120 and then press the TAB key. Type $60 and then press the TAB key twice. Type Sunset and then press the TAB key. Type $130 and then press the TAB key. Type $65 and then press the TAB key.

4 Type Off Season and then press the TAB key. Type Sunrise and then press the TAB key. Type $90 and then press the TAB key. Type $45 and then press the TAB key twice. Type Sunset and then press the TAB key. Type $100 and then press the TAB key. Type $50 as the last entry.

The table data is entered (Figure 4-60).

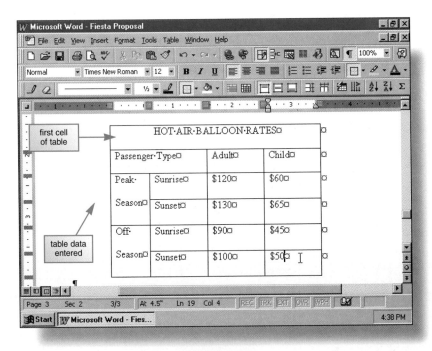

FIGURE 4-60

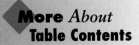

More *About*
Table Contents

You can sum a column or row of numbers in a table. First, click the cell where you want the sum to appear. Then, click Formula on the Table menu. If you agree with the formula Word proposes in the Formula dialog box, click the OK button; otherwise, delete the formula and then build your own formula through the Paste Function list box.

Just as with paragraphs, you can left-align, center, or right-align the end-of-cell marks in a table. The next step is to center the rates and respective column headings in the cells as shown on the next page.

Changing the Alignment of Data within Cells

The data you enter into the cells is by default left-aligned. You can change the alignment just as you would for a paragraph. Before changing the alignment, you must select the cell(s). Perform the following steps to center the end-of-cell marks for cells in the second and third columns below the title.

 Steps To Center Cell Contents

1 **Drag through the cells to center as shown in Figure 4-61. Point to the Center button on the Formatting toolbar.**

The cells to center are selected (Figure 4-61).

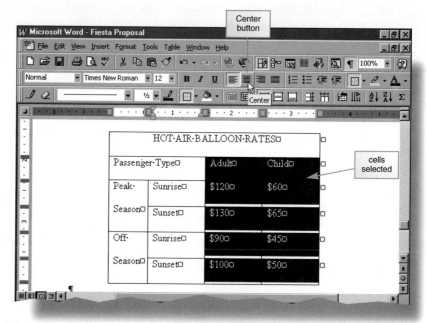

FIGURE 4-61

2 **Click the Center button. Click the selection to remove the highlight.**

Word centers the end-of-cell marks in the selected area (Figure 4-62). The Center button on the Formatting toolbar is recessed.

OtherWays

1. Select cells, click Paragraph on shortcut menu, click Indents and Spacing tab, click Alignment box arrow, click Centered, click OK button

2. Select cells, on Format menu click Paragraph, click Indents and Spacing tab, click Alignment box arrow, click Centered, click OK button

3. Select cells, press CTRL+E

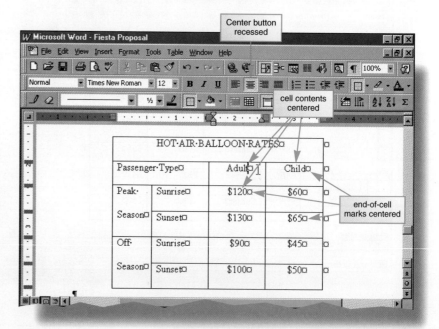

FIGURE 4-62

The next step is to **rotate** the row heading text, Peak Season and Off Season, so it displays vertically instead of horizontally.

Changing the Direction of Text in Cells

The data you enter in cells is, by default, displayed horizontally. You can change the text so it displays vertically. Changing the direction of text adds variety to your tables. Perform the following steps to display the row heading text vertically.

 Steps **To Vertically Display Text in a Cell**

More *About*
Shading

You can shade paragraphs or the cells in a table. To do this, click the cell(s) or paragraph(s) to shade, click the Shading Color button arrow on the Tables and Borders toolbar, then click the desired shade color on the shade palette. To remove shading, click None on the shade palette.

1 **Select the row heading text cells containing the words, Peak Season and Off Season. Point to the Change Text Direction button on the Tables and Borders toolbar.**

The cells to be formatted are selected (Figure 4-63).

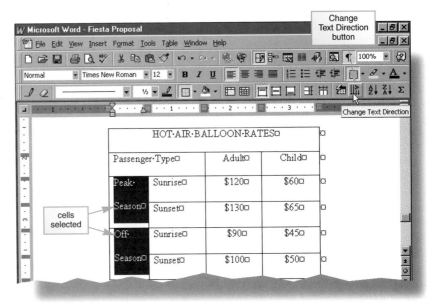

FIGURE 4-63

2 **Click the Change Text Direction button.**

The text displays vertically, top-to-bottom, in the selected cells (Figure 4-64). The first time you click the Change Text Direction button, the words display vertically so you read them from top to bottom.

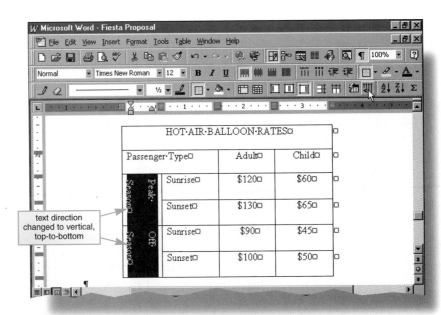

FIGURE 4-64

3 **With the cells still selected, click the Change Text Direction button again.**

The text displays vertically, bottom-to-top, in the selected cells (Figure 4-65). The second time you click the Change Text Direction button, the words display vertically so you read them from bottom to top. If you click the button a third time, the text would display horizontally again.

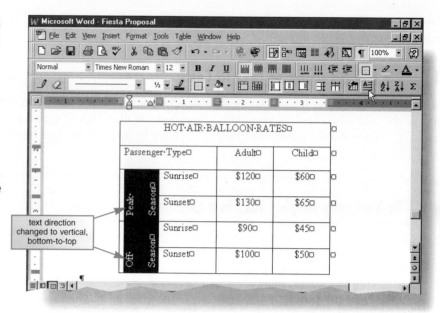

FIGURE 4-65

4 **Press the CTRL+1 keys. Click inside the selection to remove the highlight.**

Word formats the text in the selected cells to single-spacing (Figure 4-66). Recall that CTRL+1 is the keyboard shortcut for single-spacing paragraphs.

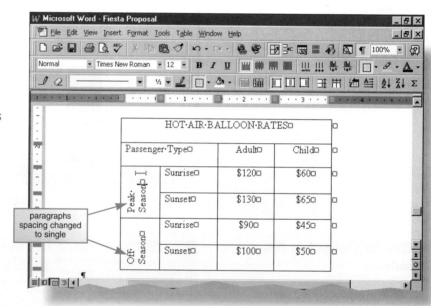

FIGURE 4-66

The next step is to center the table between the left and right margins of the document.

Centering a Table

The table currently is positioned on the screen where you drew it. Although it appears to be fairly close to the center point, you want it to be centered precisely between the left and right margins. To center the entire table, you first select the entire table and then click the Center button on the Formatting toolbar as shown in the following steps.

Steps To Center a Table

1 Make sure the insertion point is positioned somewhere inside the table. Click Table on the menu bar and then point to Select Table (Figure 4-67).

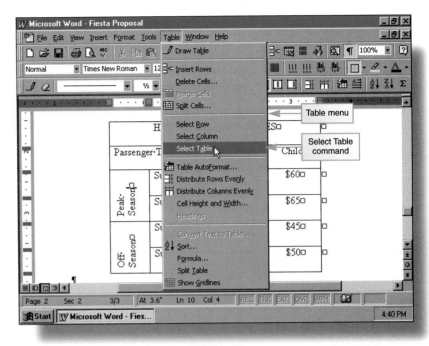

FIGURE 4-67

2 Click Select Table. Click the Center button on the Formatting toolbar. Click in the selection to remove the highlight. Click the Tables and Borders button on the Standard toolbar.

Word centers the table between the margins (Figure 4-68). Because the table is complete, you remove the Tables and Borders toolbar from the screen.

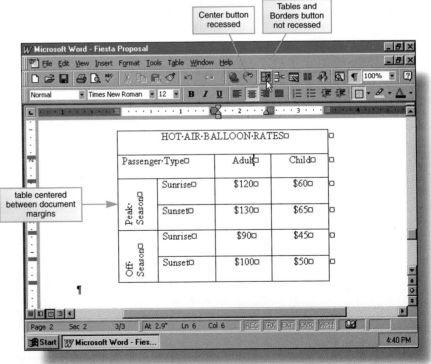

FIGURE 4-68

Other Ways

1. Select table, on Table menu click Cell Height and Width, click Row tab, click Center in Alignment area, click OK button

Working with Tables

At times you might want to add additional rows or columns to a table. To add a row to the end of a table, position the insertion point in the bottom right corner cell and then press the TAB key. Depending on the task you want to perform in a table, the function of the **Table button** on the Standard toolbar changes and the commands change on the Table menu and associated shortcut menu. To **add rows** in the middle of a table, select the row below where you want to insert a row and then click the **Insert Rows button** (the same button you clicked to insert a table) or click the **Insert Rows command** on the Table or shortcut menu. To **add a column** in the middle of a table, select the column to the right of where you want to insert a column and then click the **Insert Columns button** (the same button you clicked to insert a table) or click the **Insert Columns command** on the Table or shortcut menu. To add a column to the right of a table, select the end-of-row marks at the right edge of the table, then click the Insert Columns button or click the Insert Columns command on the Table or shortcut menu.

If you want to **delete row(s)** or **delete column(s)** from a table, select the row(s) or column(s) to delete and then click **Delete Rows** or **Delete Columns** on the Table or shortcut menu.

Adding Finishing Touches to the Document

The document requires two more enhancements: change the bullet type in the list of products and services for sale and add a header to the document.

Customizing Bullets in a List

You can add the default bullets, which are small circles, to a list by selecting the list and then clicking the **Bullets button** on the Formatting toolbar. In this project, you want the bullets to be arrow shaped. To change the bullet style, use the **Bullets and Numbering command** as shown in the following steps.

Steps **To Customize Bullets in a List**

1 **Scroll to and then select the paragraphs in the list. Right-click the selection. Point to Bullets and Numbering on the shortcut menu.**

A shortcut menu displays (Figure 4-69).

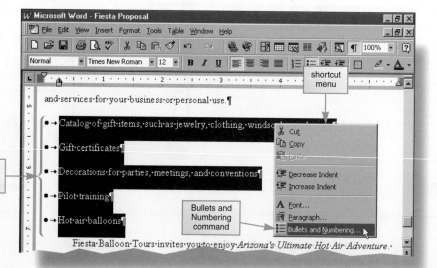

FIGURE 4-69

2 Click Bullets and Numbering. If necessary, click the Bulleted tab when the Bullets and Numbering dialog box first opens. Click the arrow shaped bullets and then point to the OK button.

Word displays the Bullets and Numbering dialog box (Figure 4-70). The arrow shaped bulleted list sample has a box around it, indicating it is selected.

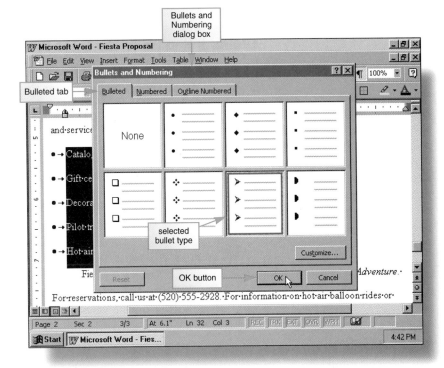

FIGURE 4-70

3 Click the OK button. Click outside the selection to remove the highlight.

Word places arrow shaped bullets to the left of each paragraph (Figure 4-71).

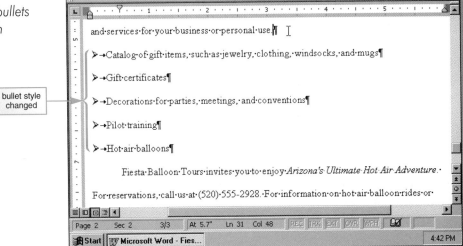

FIGURE 4-71

The next step is to add a header to the sales proposal.

Other**Ways**

1. Select the list, on Format menu click Bullets and Numbering, click Bullets tab, click desired bullet style, click OK button

Adding a Header to the Sales Proposal

You want the company name and page number to display on the sales proposal; you do not, however, want this header on the title page. Recall that the title page and the body of the sales proposal are in separate sections. You do not want a header in section 1, but you do want one in section 2. When you initially create a header, Word assumes you want it in all sections. Thus, when you create the header in section 2, you must instruct Word to not place it in section 1.

Currently, the insertion point is located in page 3 of the document. To illustrate creating the header, you will move the insertion point to the top of page 2. Follow these steps to display page 2 in the document window and then create the header for section 2.

TO DISPLAY THE PREVIOUS PAGE

1 Point to the double up arrow button above the Select Browse Object button on the vertical scroll bar. If the ScreenTip, Previous Page, displays below the double up arrow button, then click the button; otherwise, proceed with Step 2.

If you edited your document or table recently, the ScreenTip on the double up arrow button will not be Previous Page and the double up arrows will display in the color blue.

2 Click the Select Browse Object button on the vertical scroll bar. Point to the Browse by Page command (Figure 4-72).
3 Click the Browse by Page command. Click the Previous Page button.

Word displays page 2 at the top of the document window (Figure 4-73).

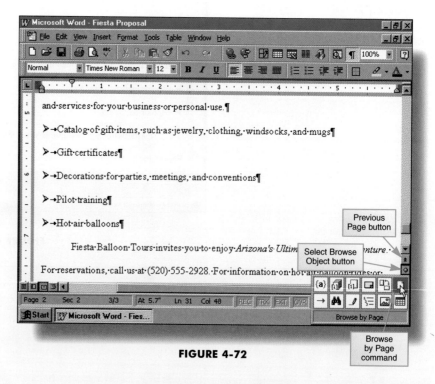

FIGURE 4-72

The next step is to create the header for section 2 of the document.

Steps To Add a Header to the Sales Proposal

1 **Click View on the menu bar and then click Header and Footer. Point to the Same as Previous button on the Header and Footer toolbar.**

*Word displays the Header and Footer toolbar (Figure 4-73). Notice the **Same as Previous button** is recessed, which instructs Word to place the header in the previous section also. Because you do not want this header in section 1, you do not want the Same as Previous button to be recessed.*

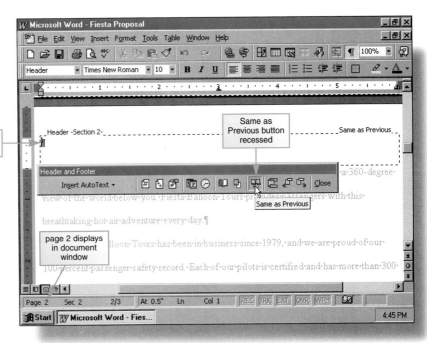

FIGURE 4-73

2 **Click the Same as Previous button. Click the Align Right button on the Formatting toolbar to right-align the header. Type** Fiesta Balloon Tours **and then press the SPACEBAR. Click the Insert Page Number button on the Header and Footer toolbar.**

Word displays the header for section 2 (Figure 4-74). The Same as Previous button no longer is recessed. Because Word begins numbering pages from the beginning of the document, the page number 2 displays in the header.

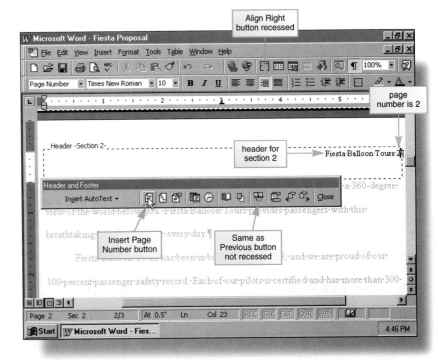

FIGURE 4-74

Notice in Figure 4-74 that the page number is a 2. You want to begin numbering the body of the sales proposal with a number 1. Thus, you need to instruct Word to begin numbering the pages in section 2 with a 1 as shown in the steps on the next page.

Steps **To Page Number Differently in a Section**

1 Click Insert on the menu bar and then point to Page Numbers (Figure 4-75).

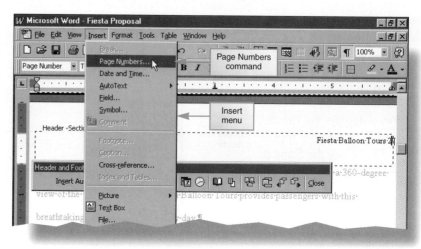

FIGURE 4-75

2 Click Page Numbers. When the Page Numbers dialog box displays, point to the Format button.

Word displays the Page Numbers dialog box (Figure 4-76).

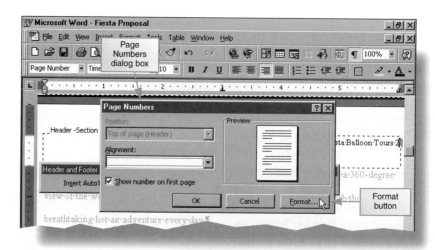

FIGURE 4-76

3 Click the Format button. When the Page Number Format dialog box displays, click Start at in the Page numbering area and then point to the OK button.

Word displays the Page Number Format dialog box (Figure 4-77). The number 1 displays in the Start at box, by default.

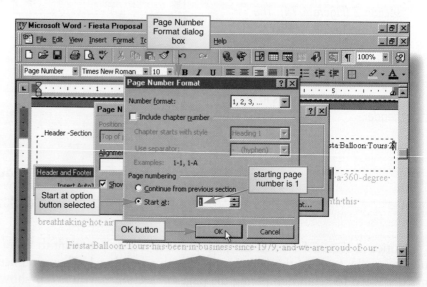

FIGURE 4-77

4 Click the OK button in the Page Number Format dialog box. When the Page Numbers dialog box redisplays, point to its Close button.

Word closes the Page Number Format dialog box and returns to the Page Numbers dialog box (Figure 4-78). This dialog box displays both an OK button and a Close button. Be sure to click the Close button, instead of the OK button, in the Page Numbers dialog box; otherwise, you will have another set of page numbers in the document.

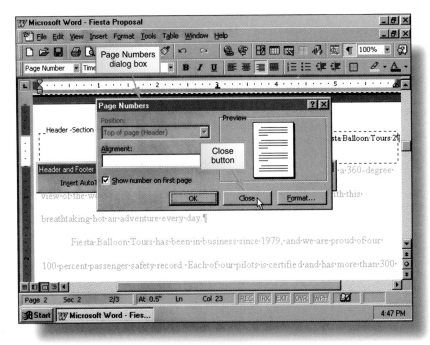

FIGURE 4-78

5 Click the Close button.

Word changes the starting page number for section 2 to the number 1 (Figure 4-79).

6 Click the Close Header and Footer button on the Header and Footer toolbar. If necessary, click the Normal View button at the bottom of the document window.

Word closes the Header and Footer toolbar and returns to normal view. Recall that headers and footers do not display on the screen in normal view.

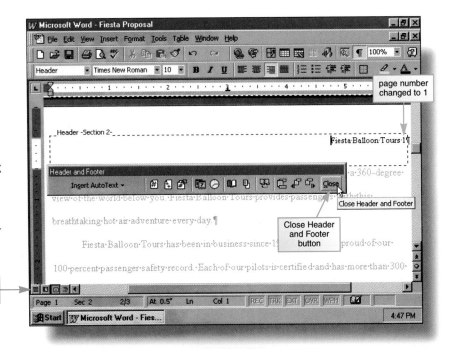

FIGURE 4-79

Check the spelling of the document by clicking the **Spelling and Grammar button** on the Standard toolbar. Save the document one final time by clicking the Save button on the Standard toolbar, and then print the sales proposal by clicking the Print button. The printed document displays as shown in Figure 4-80 on the next page.

Fiesta Balloon Tours 2

flight due to weather conditions or other reasons, we will reschedule the outing on the

date of your choice or refund your money.

Each party must include at least one adult. Child rates apply to any person 14

years or younger.

HOT AIR BALLOON RATES		
Passenger Type	Adult	Child
Sunrise	$120	$60

Peak Season

Off Season

Fiesta Balloon To

and services for your busi

➤ Catalog of gift items,

➤ Gift certificates

➤ Decorations for partie

➤ Pilot training

➤ Hot air balloons

Fiesta Balloon To

For reservations, call us a

pilot training, talk to one

hot air balloon products,

completed proposal

Fiesta Balloon Tours 1

Imagine gliding through the air, drifting with the clouds, and seeing a 360-degree

view of the world below you. Fiesta Balloon Tours provides passengers with this

breathtaking hot air adventure every day.

Fiesta Balloon Tours has been in business since 1979, and we are proud of our

100 percent passenger safety record. Each of our pilots is certified and has more than 300

hours of flying experience. Our balloons are of the highest quality and inspected

regularly.

We offer two

accommodate four to

varies throughout the

Sta

En

In addition to

T-shirt, personalized f

upon landing. The flig

after landing.

Rates vary dep

Labor Day. Group and

Reservations are requ

confirmed with a 50 p

FIESTA BALLOON TOURS

Arizona's
Ultimate
Hot Air Adventure

FIGURE 4-80

You have now finished Project 4. Follow this step to quit Word.

TO QUIT WORD

1   Click the Close button in the Word window.

The Word window closes.

Project Summary

Project 4 introduced you to creating a proposal with a title page and tables. First, you created a title page with a graphic, outside border, color, and characters in a variety of fonts and styles. You learned how to insert an existing document into the active document. Then, you saved the active document with a new file name. Next, you set custom tabs and used them to create a table. Then, you used the Draw Table feature to create a second table. Finally, you changed the bullet style in the list of items and created a header for the second section of the document.

What You Should Know

Having completed this project, you now should be able to perform the following tasks:

- Add a Header to the Sales Proposal *(WD 4.51)*
- Border a Paragraph *(WD 4.14)*
- Border a Table *(WD 4.35)*
- Center a Table *(WD 4.47)*
- Center Cell Contents *(WD 4.44)*
- Center the Title of a Table *(WD 4.32)*
- Change the Top Margin *(WD 4.11 and WD 4.28)*
- Color Characters *(WD 4.12)*
- Create a Section Break *(WD 4.27)*
- Customize Bullets in a List *(WD 4.48)*
- Display Nonprinting Characters *(WD 4.10)*
- Display the Previous Page *(WD 4.50)*
- Distribute Rows and Columns Evenly *(WD 4.40)*
- Download Clip Art from Microsoft's Clip Gallery Live Web Page *(WD 4.18)*
- Draw a Table *(WD 4.37)*
- Draw More Table Lines *(WD 4.42)*
- Enter and Format the Company Slogan *(WD 4.24)*
- Enter Data into a Table *(WD 4.43)*
- Enter Text Using Custom Tab Stops *(WD 4.34)*
- Format a Picture *(WD 4.22)*
- Format Characters *(WD 4.12)*
- Insert a Second Document into an Open Document *(WD 4.29)*
- Install Clip Art from the Data Disk *(WD 4.21)*
- Page Number Differently in a Section *(WD 4.52)*
- Print a Document *(WD 4.31)*
- Quit Word *(WD 4.55)*
- Return to the Normal Style *(WD 4.26)*
- Save a Document *(WD 4.25)*
- Save an Active Document with a New File Name *(WD 4.30)*
- Set Custom Tab Stops *(WD 4.33)*
- Start Word *(WD 4.10)*
- Vertically Display Text in a Cell *(WD 4.45)*

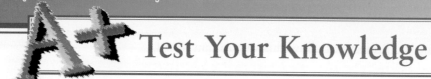

Test Your Knowledge

1 True/False

Instructions: Circle T if the statement is true or F if the statement is false.

T F 1. A research proposal offers a product or service to existing or potential customers.

T F 2. When Word displays the Tables and Borders toolbar, it switches to page layout view.

T F 3. One way to dock a floating toolbar is to click the title bar of the floating toolbar.

T F 4. If you have access to the Web, you can download clip art files from Microsoft's Clip Gallery Live Web page into the Clip Gallery.

T F 5. All documents have at least two sections.

T F 6. To save an active document with a new file name, click Save As on the File menu.

T F 7. To move a custom tab stop, drag the tab marker along the ruler.

T F 8. To create a complex table, use Word's Draw Table feature.

T F 9. By default, all Word tables have a 3-point border.

T F 10. To center a table, select the entire table and then click the Center button on the Formatting toolbar.

2 Multiple Choice

Instructions: Circle the correct response.

1. The Font Color button is located on the _____.
   a. menu bar
   b. Standard toolbar
   c. Formatting toolbar
   d. vertical scroll bar

2. In Word, you can add a border _____ a paragraph.
   a. above or below
   b. to the left or right of
   c. both a and b
   d. neither a nor b

3. To return the insertion point to your last editing location, press the _____ key(s).
   a. F5
   b. CTRL+F5
   c. SHIFT+F5
   d. ALT+F5

 Test Your Knowledge

4. Word, by default, places tab stops at every _____-inch mark on the ruler.
   a. .25
   b. .5
   c. 1
   d. none of the above

5. The Tab Alignment button is located on the _____.
   a. Standard toolbar
   b. Formatting toolbar
   c. vertical ruler
   d. horizontal ruler

6. The Outside Border button is located on the _____.
   a. Formatting toolbar
   b. Tables and Borders toolbar
   c. both a and b
   d. neither a nor b

7. When the Draw Table button is recessed, the mouse pointer shape changes to a(n) _____.
   a. pen
   b. eraser
   c. table
   d. letter D

8. To select noncontiguous cells, select the first cell, then press and hold down the _____ key while clicking the second cell.
   a. TAB
   b. CTRL
   c. ALT
   d. none of the above

9. The Change Text Direction button is located on the _____.
   a. Formatting toolbar
   b. Tables and Borders toolbar
   c. both a and b
   d. neither a nor b

10. To change the style of bullets on a list, _____.
    a. click the Bullets button on the Formatting toolbar
    b. click Bullets and Numbering on the Format menu
    c. press the CTRL+B keys
    d. both b and c

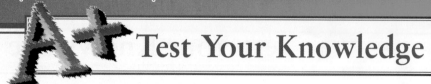

Test Your Knowledge

3 Understanding the Tables and Borders Toolbar

Instructions: In Figure 4-81, arrows point to several of the boxes and buttons on the Tables and Borders toolbar. In the spaces provided, briefly explain the purpose of each button or box.

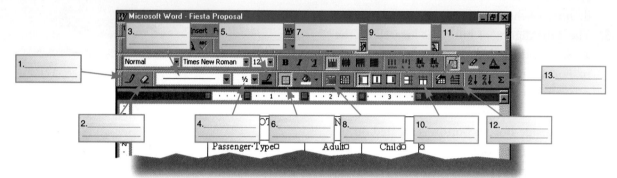

FIGURE 4-81

4 Understanding Custom Tab Stops

Instructions: Answer the questions below concerning Figure 4-82. The numbers in the figure correspond to question numbers below.

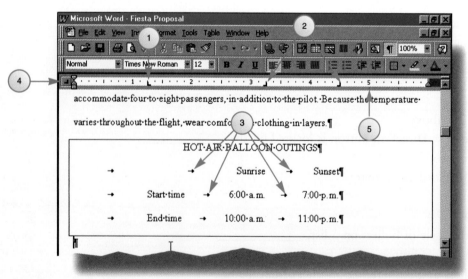

FIGURE 4-82

1. What is the alignment of the tab stop at the 1.25" mark?
2. What is the alignment of the tab stops at the 3.25" and 4.5" marks?
3. Why do the dark, right-pointing arrows display between the tab stops in the table?
4. What is the purpose of this button?
5. Why is a default tick mark at the 5" mark on the ruler?

Use Help

1 Reviewing Project Activities

Instructions: Perform the following tasks using a computer.

1. Start Word. If the Office Assistant is on your screen, click it to display its balloon. If the Office Assistant is not on your screen, click the Office Assistant button on the Standard toolbar.
2. Type `floating picture` in the What would you like to do? text box. Click the Search button. Click the Change a floating picture to an inline picture and vice-versa link. Read the information. Use the shortcut menu or Options button to print the information.
3. Click the Help Topics button to display the Help Topics: Microsoft Word dialog box. Click the Contents tab. Double-click the Changing the Appearance of Your Page book. Double-click the Inserting Page Breaks and Section Breaks book. Double-click the Types of section breaks topic. Read and print the information.
4. Click the Help Topics button. Click the Index tab. Type `colors` and then double-click the formatting topic. Read and print the information.
5. Click the Help Topics button. Click the Find tab. Type `complex tables` and then double-click the Create a complex table topic. Read and print the information.
6. Close any open Help window(s) by clicking its Close button. Close the Office Assistant.

2 Expanding on the Basics

Instructions: Use Word Help for a better understanding of the topics listed below. Answer the questions on your own paper or hand in the printed Help topic to your instructor.

1. In this project, you created a table using the Draw Table button on the Tables and Borders toolbar. Use the Office Assistant to answer the following questions about Word tables.
   a. What are the five new table features of Word 97?
   b. How do you sum a row or column of numbers in a table?
   c. How do you reference cells in a table in a formula?
   d. How do you split a single cell into multiple cells?
2. In this project, you added a border around a paragraph. Use the Contents tab in the Help Topics: Microsoft Word dialog box to answer the following questions about borders.
   a. How do you place a border around an entire page?
   b. How do you change a table's border?
   c. How do you add a box border around a single word?
3. In this project, you used tabs to create a table. Use the Index tab in the Help Topics: Microsoft Word dialog box to answer the following questions about tabs.
   a. How do you change the spacing between default tab stops?
   b. What are leader characters? How do you insert them in tab stops?
4. In this project, you created one table using tabs and another using the Draw Table feature. Word has three other types of tables: table of authorities, table of contents, and table of figures. For each of these three types of tables, (1) identify their purpose and (2) explain how to create them.

Apply Your Knowledge

1 Working with Tables

Instructions: Start Word. Open the document, apply-4, from the Word folder on the Data Disk that accompanies this book. The document is a table created with the Draw Table feature. You are to color the title lines, merge the cells of the column headings, change the direction of the row heading text, sum the columns, and format the data. The completed table is shown in Figure 4-83. You may need to refer to your Use Help 2 responses for assistance on tables.

Aquatics Unlimited									
Two-Year Comparison (in millions)									
		This Year				Last Year			
		1Q	2Q	3Q	4Q	1Q	2Q	3Q	4Q
Revenue	Sales	1650	1724	1850	1335	1425	1590	1765	1227
	Other	123	288	367	101	105	216	304	100
	Total	1773	2012	2217	1436	1530	1806	2069	1327
Expenses	Manufacturing	682	1150	1482	555	590	805	1298	413
	Research	157	265	339	112	135	207	313	98
	Administrative	222	314	356	141	214	300	316	133
	Total	1061	1729	2177	808	939	1312	1927	644

cell C8

cell C10

FIGURE 4-83

Apply Your Knowledge

Perform the following tasks.

1. Select the cell containing the title, Aquatics Unlimited. Center it and change its font size to 26. If necessary, click the Tables and Borders button on the Standard toolbar to display the Tables and Borders toolbar. Click the Shading Color button arrow on the Tables and Borders toolbar and then click the color Teal. Click the Font Color button arrow on the Formatting toolbar and then click the color White.

2. Select the cell containing the subtitle. Center it. Click the Font Color button arrow on the Formatting toolbar and then click the color Teal.

3. Select the cell containing the column heading, This Year, and the next three cells to its right. Click the Merge Cells button on the Tables and Borders toolbar to merge these four cells into one. Click the Center button to center the column heading over the four quarters. Repeat this procedure for the column heading Last Year.

4. Select the cells containing the 1Q, 2Q, 3Q, and 4Q headings. Center them.

5. Select the cells containing the row headings, Revenue and Expenses. Click the Change Text Direction button on the Tables and Borders toolbar twice. Drag the border line to the right of these cells until the width of the row headings' cells looks like Figure 4-83.

6. You cannot use the AutoSum button for the total revenue cells because this function sums all cells above the current cell; here, you want to sum the two revenue cells. AutoSum will include the 1Q, 2Q, 3Q, and so on, in the sums. Click the cell to contain the total revenue for the 1Q of this year. Click Table on the menu bar and then click Formula. Enter the following formula in the Formula text box: =SUM(C5:C6) and then click the OK button. Click the cell to contain the total revenue for the 2Q of this year. Click Table on the menu bar and then click Formula. Enter the following formula in the Formula text box: =SUM(D5:D6) and then click the OK button. Repeat this process for each total revenue cell – increasing the letter in the sum function by one each time you move one column to the right.

7. You cannot use AutoSum for the total expenses because this function sums all cells above the current cell; here, you want to sum only the three expense cells. Click the cell to contain the total expenses for the first quarter (1Q) of this year. Click Table on the menu bar and then click Formula. Enter the following formula in the Formula text box: =SUM(C8:C10) and then click the OK button. Click the cell to contain the total expenses for the second quarter (2Q) of this year. Click Table on the menu bar and then click Formula. Enter the following formula in the Formula text box: =SUM(D8:D10) and then click the OK button. Repeat this process for each total expense cell, increasing the letter in the sum function by one each time you move one column to the right.

8. Bold the cells containing This Year, Last Year, Revenue, Expenses, Total, and all total figures.

9. Select all the cells containing numbers and then click the Align Top button on the Formatting toolbar.

10. Click File on the menu bar and then click Save As. Use the file name Revised Aquatics Report to save the document on your Data Disk.

11. Print the revised document.

In the Lab

1 Creating a Proposal Using Tabs

Problem: The LakeView Sports Car Club is preparing for its Tenth Annual Car Show. As a member of the club and the resident computer expert, you have been asked to prepare the informal sales proposal announcing the event (Figures 4-84 and 4-85), which will be sent to all community residents.

Instructions:

1. Create the title page as shown in Figure 4-84. The sports car is located in the Transportation category of the Clip Gallery. Change the clip art to an inline picture and change its size to 75% of the original size (1.4" height by 5.4" width), if necessary.

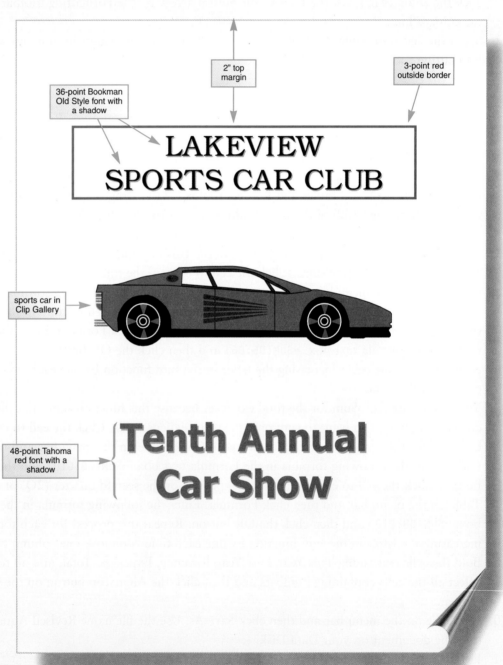

FIGURE 4-84

In the Lab

2. Insert a section break. Return to the normal style. Change the top margin to 1" for section 2. Adjust line spacing to double. Change the font size to 12 for the body of the proposal.

3. Enter the body of the proposal as shown in Figure 4-85. The body of the proposal has a list with square shaped bullets and a table created with tabs. The tabs are set at 1" (left-aligned), 3.5" and 4.5" (both centered).

4. Spell check the document. Save the document with LakeView Proposal as the file name.

5. View the document in print preview. Print the document from within print preview.

LakeView Sports Car Club invites you to join us for our *Tenth Annual Car Show*, the hottest auto event of the decade, on the weekend of October 10-11 in LakeView.

Bring the entire family! LakeView Sports Car Club has scheduled events for everyone. Admission is $2.00 per day for adults, and children under 12 are admitted free to all activities.

❑ More than 150 sports cars

❑ Parts Swap Meet

❑ Arts and crafts displays

❑ Carnival and children's games

❑ Live music, featuring the Nifty Fifties band

If you have a sports car that you would like to enter in the show or want to rent an arts and crafts booth, you still have time! Advance reservations must be made by Friday, October 2, by calling 555-4838.

VENDOR FEES		
	In Advance	At the Gate
Sports Car Vendor	$30	$35
Arts and Crafts Vendor	$20	$25

All participants are eligible for door prizes and commemorative T-shirts. Spectators at the car show will cast ballots for the *People's Choice Awards*. The Parts Swap Meet will have a *Name the Car Part* contest.

The car show and activities start at 9:00 a.m. and end at 7:00 p.m. each day. For more information, call 555-4838.

FIGURE 4-85

In the Lab

2 Creating a Proposal Using Downloaded Clip Art and the Draw Table Feature

Problem: You are manager of Spooky Treats, a Halloween store. To promote business, you decide to compose a sales proposal outlining your products. You develop the proposal shown in Figures 4-86 and 4-87.

Instructions:

1. Create the title page as shown in Figure 4-86. You are to download the clip art files from Microsoft's Clip Gallery Live Web page with the file names SPEC002182_x5, SPEC002183_x5, and SPEC002184_x5. To reach these files, type Halloween celebration in the Search text box. If you do not have access to the Web, you can install these files from the Data Disk that accompanies this book. Change the clip art images to inline pictures and change their sizes as indicated in Figure 4-86.

FIGURE 4-86

In the Lab

2. Insert a section break. Return to the normal style. Change the top margin to 1" for section 2. Adjust line spacing to double.

3. Create the body of the proposal as shown in Figure 4-87. The body of the proposal has a table created with the Draw Table button. Use the AutoSum button for the Clown Totals. The formulas for the Pirate Totals of adult, teen, and child outfits are as follows: =SUM(C6:C7), =SUM(D6:D7), and =SUM(E6:E7), respectively. Center the table between the page margins.

4. Spell check the document. Save the document with Spooky Treats Proposal as the file name.

5. View the document in print preview. Print the document from within print preview.

Spooky Treats is a full-service Halloween store offering a huge selection of Halloween merchandise. We stock a complete line of high-quality costumes, masks, makeup, and accessories for adults, teens, and children at very reasonable prices.

Sample Price List		Adult	Teen	Child
Clown	Costume	28.99	15.99	13.99
	Accessories	16.99	14.99	7.99
	Total	45.98	30.98	21.98
Pirate	Costume	21.99	14.99	13.99
	Accessories	14.99	12.99	8.99
	Total	36.98	27.98	22.98

Costumes and accessories are sold separately. For example, the clown costume consists of a one-piece, multicolored suit with matching collar and hat. The accessories include a rainbow wig, red nose, white gloves, striped socks, and makeup.

Our salespeople are professional and courteous and are trained in makeup application techniques to answer any questions you have or provide you with any instruction you may require.

Spooky Treats has supplied the best in Halloween attire and accessories from our same location for the past 10 years at 104 Southwestern Avenue, Chicago, Illinois. Let us outfit you this Halloween. Come by and see us or place your order by telephone and request a catalog at 312-555-0826.

FIGURE 4-87

In the Lab

3 Enhancing a Draft of a Proposal

Problem: You are the owner of Skyline Office Rentals. One of your employees has drafted an informal sales proposal to be sent to prospective clients around the country (Figure 4-89). You decide to add pizzazz to the proposal by creating a title page (Figure 4-88). You also add a couple of tables to the body of the proposal.

Instructions:

1. Create the title page as shown in Figure 4-88. The office buildings clip art is located in the Buildings category of the Clip Gallery. Change the clip art to an inline picture.

FIGURE 4-88

In the Lab

2. Insert the draft of the body of the proposal below the title page using the File command on the Insert menu. The draft is called Skyline Draft in the Word folder on the Data Disk that accompanies this book. The draft of the body of the proposal is shown in Figure 4-89. Be sure to change the top margin to 1" for section 2.

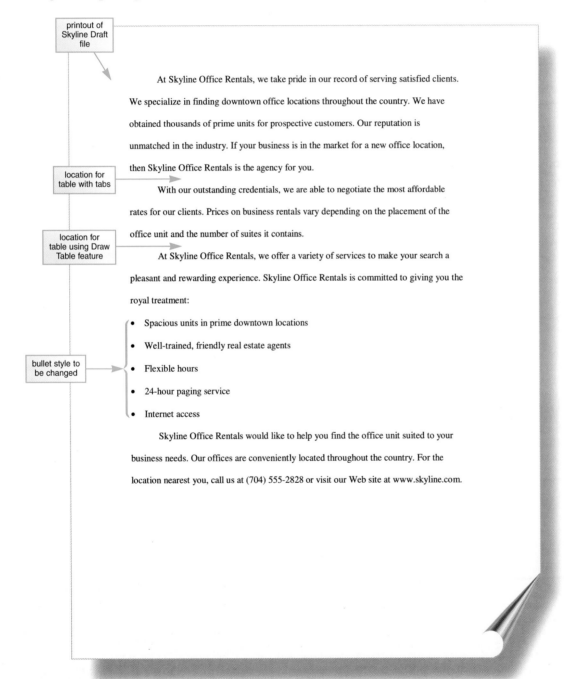

FIGURE 4-89

(continued)

In the Lab

Enhancing a Draft of a Proposal *(continued)*

3. Add the following table, created with tabs, below the first paragraph in the proposal. Double-space the table and set custom tab stops at 1", 3", and 4.5". Draw an outside border around the table. Above the table, center and bold the title, Skyline Track Record.

	# OF CLIENTS	# OF UNITS RENTED
This Year	5692	5109
Last Year	4998	4514

4. Use the Draw Table button to create the following table below the second paragraph in the proposal. Double-space the table. Center the table between the page margins. Above the table, center and bold the title, Average Monthly Rental Prices.

Average Monthly Rental Prices				
		2-ROOM	3-ROOM	4-ROOM
Lower Floors	Window Unit	1025	1245	1475
	Inside Unit	895	1035	1275
Upper Floors	Window Unit	1445	1665	1895
	Inside Unit	1265	1465	1675

5. Change the style of the bullet characters in the list.
6. Add a header to section 2 of the proposal.
7. Save the active document with the file name Skyline Proposal using the Save As command on the File menu.
8. View the document in print preview. Print the document from within print preview.

Cases and Places

The difficulty of these case studies varies: ❯ are the least difficult; ❯❯ are more difficult; and ❯❯❯ are the most difficult.

1 ❯ Your school probably has one or more facilities open to both students and the general public; e.g., a day-care center, a fitness center, a cafeteria, or the library. Select one of these facilities that interests you. Obtain information about the facility using one or more of these fact-gathering techniques: visit the facility and use its resources; collect brochures and other literature about the facility; interview an employee of the facility; interview a visitor to the facility. Then, draft a sales proposal for the facility to send to the general public as a marketing tool. Be sure the proposal includes at least one table and has a creative cover page with appropriate color and graphics.

2 ❯ Hobbies can be exciting and interesting, ranging from snow skiing to photography to making crafts. Pick a hobby of your own, a family member, or friend and then acquire as much information about it as possible. Assume you are the chairperson of a club that meets monthly to discuss this hobby; the club also sponsors a variety of social events. You want to recruit new members to the club. Draft a sales proposal for the club to send to the general public as a marketing tool. Be sure the proposal includes at least one table and has a creative cover page with appropriate color and graphics.

3 ❯❯ Assume you are president of the Student Government Organization at your school and that you have concerns about an issue on campus, such as security, computer availability, facilities for the disabled, or student advising/registration. Select an item from this list, or one of your own, that you feel needs improvement at your school. Investigate how other schools locally and nationally handle the same issue. Visit the library or *surf* the Internet for guidelines on preparing a planning proposal. Draft a planning proposal for the Student Government Organization to submit to your school's Board of Directors that recommends some action the school should take to improve the situation you investigated. Be sure the proposal includes at least one table and has an appropriate cover page.

4 ❯❯ As a concerned resident, you have a suggestion(s) for improving the quality of life in your neighborhood. Such suggestions might include initiating a recycling program, creating a bike lane or path on main roads, or placing speed bumps or a stop sign at an area populated with young children. Select an item from this list, or one of your own, that you feel would benefit your neighborhood. Investigate how other communities have implemented the same type of program successfully. Visit the library or *surf* the Internet for guidelines on preparing a planning proposal. Draft a planning proposal that recommends some action to be taken to improve the situation you investigated. Be sure the proposal includes at least one table and has an appropriate cover page.

Cases and Places

5 ▶▶ Assume you have graduated recently from your school with a degree in your field of study. The department head of your major has contacted you for suggestions on improving the abilities and skills of students in your major. She wants your recommendation(s) on changing the curriculum. Obtain evidence to support your recommendation(s) such as interviewing local businesses that hire your school's graduates, using the Internet to discover how other school's curricula are organized, or surveying recent alumni of your program. Visit the library or *surf* the Internet for guidelines on preparing a planning proposal. Draft a planning proposal that recommends your suggestions to the department head. Be sure the proposal includes at least one table and has an appropriate cover page.

6 ▶▶▶ As chair of the Resources and Planning Committee for your school, you have been assigned the task of writing a proposal to acquire new hardware and/or software for your school. The proposal must contain figures on the current hardware and/or software configurations on campus, as well as the proposed configurations. A minimum of two proposed cost quotations must be provided, with sources of the quotations cited. Obtain evidence to support your proposal such as current industry trends in the computer field. Visit the library or *surf* the Internet for guidelines on preparing a research proposal. Draft a research proposal that presents your findings, suggests two alternatives, and then recommends your suggested configuration to your school's decision-making body. Be sure the proposal includes at least one table and has an appropriate cover page.

7 ▶▶▶ As director of the outside sales force at a local company, you are responsible for providing each salesperson with a company car. Each year you must submit a proposal to the president for approval. Your recommended vehicle must meet current safety regulations. You also must provide figures on leasing, renting, and purchasing each of three different makes of vehicles. The quotations must list the dealer from which the figures were obtained or the Internet address, if obtained via the Internet. Visit the library or *surf* the Internet for guidelines on preparing a research proposal. Draft a research proposal that presents your safety findings; suggests purchase, lease, and rent alternatives for three different makes; and then recommends your suggestion. Be sure the proposal includes at least one table and has an appropriate cover page.

Microsoft Word 97

Generating Form Letters, Mailing Labels, and Envelopes

Objectives:

You will have mastered the material in this project when you can:

▶ Explain the merge process
▶ Create a letterhead
▶ Explain the terms, data field and data record
▶ Create a data source
▶ Switch from a data source to the main document
▶ Insert merge fields into the main document
▶ Use an IF field in the main document
▶ Merge and print form letters
▶ Selectively merge and print form letters
▶ Sort a data source
▶ Address and print mailing labels
▶ Address and print envelopes

Pharaoh's Favorite

A Man of Letters

As the sun sets in the west to begin its nightly journey into day, a barge crosses the mythic Nile, bearing an ornate stone coffin. On the western bank, the burial chamber is transferred to an ox-drawn sledge. Priests clad in leopard skins, chanting ritual prayers and wafting incense, lead a solemn procession of mourners. Finally, they reach a splendid mortuary tabernacle next to the royal temples of ancient Thebes and inter the mummy of a man who lived to be eighty.

The last rites of a powerful Pharaoh or some regal personage?

No. It is the funeral of a commoner, a scribe, who rose to become vizier to Pharaoh Amenhotep III, who reigned during Egypt's New Kingdom. Next to the Pharaoh himself, scribes were the most important officials in ancient Egypt. As people of letters, they supervised virtually all public activity, from tallying harvests to levying taxes.

Since the first cuneiform alphabet enabled mankind to preserve thoughts on clay tablets, the world has respected, even revered, its writers. History owes much to those who recorded their wisdom in letters. One of the more prolific letter writers of all time was Thomas Jefferson. Fortunately for historians, he was also a dedicated scientist and used a patented duplicating machine — called a polygraph — to make a copy of each letter he wrote. As he moved a quill pen attached to the machine, a complex system of gears and pulleys moved a second quill in unison with his movements, even dipping the second pen in an inkwell when he dipped his. Not exactly *form* letters, but "formed letters," for sure.

Early popular novelists used collections of letters to tell their stories. In the modern novel, *The Color Purple*, Alice Walker continues this tradition, using "Dear God" letters to tell a poignant story. Walker and other writers sometimes are called *belletrists*, practitioners of the fine art of *belles-lettres*, a literary style so highly regarded for its aesthetic value, that content becomes secondary.

Today, letters are the principal feature of modern enterprise, with form letters ranking foremost in the order of business. Most of us receive dozens of them every year. Though usually considered "junk mail," they serve a vital function, helping businesses reach potential customers.

You are a correspondent of sorts when you are required to demonstrate your creative writing skills. You may be asked to organize a school bazaar and recruit your fellow classmates to assist during the event. A family reunion might require your expertise in the form of an announcement to all your relatives, or at some time soon, you may seek an employment position in your field of study. All these tasks can be simplified using the many Word features presented in this project to create form letters. With Word 97, you can design custom letterheads, create a data source, and generate mailing labels or envelopes. Then, pull it all together using the Mail Merge feature, and you are off to the post office.

As a man or woman of letters, take your aspirations to the limits. Apply your creative talents and succeed.

Microsoft
Word 97

Generating Form Letters, Mailing Labels, and Envelopes

Case Perspective

Connie L. Peterson, president of Arrow Electronics, has asked Henry Thomas in the Information Center to send a letter to all customers informing them of the upcoming year-end clearance sale. The letter should arrive in the customers' hands around December 8 because the sale is to run for the last two weeks of the year. Instead of typing a separate letter to each customer, which could be very time consuming, Henry uses a form letter. The form letter contains the identical information that is to be in all the letters. He also creates a separate file containing the names and addresses of each customer; this file is called a data source. Then, he merges the data source with the form letter so an individual letter prints for each customer. Henry also creates and prints mailing labels and envelopes for each customer in the data source.

This year, Connie has indicated she wants to have two separate discount rates: one for VIP Club members and another, lower discount, for regular customers. That is, VIP Club members are to receive a 25 percent discount and all other customers are to receive a 10 percent discount.

Introduction

Form letters are used regularly in both business and personal correspondence. The basic content of a group of form letters is similar; however, items such as name, address, city, state, and zip code change from one letter to the next. Thus, form letters are personalized to the addressee. An individual is more likely to open and read a personalized letter than a standard Dear Sir or Dear Madam letter. Form letters usually are sent to a group of people. **Business form letters** include announcements of sales to customers or explanation of company benefits to employees. **Personal form letters** include letters of application for a job or invitations to participate in a sweepstakes giveaway. Once form letters are generated, envelopes must be addressed or mailing labels printed for the envelopes.

Project Five – Form Letters, Mailing Labels, and Envelopes

Project 5 illustrates the generation of a business form letter and corresponding mailing labels and envelopes. The form letter is sent to all current customers, informing them of the year-end clearance sale. The discount percentage rate varies, depending on whether or not the customer is a member of the VIP Club. The process of generating form letters involves creating a main document for the form letter and a data source, and then merging, or *blending*, the two together into a series of individual letters as shown in Figure 5-1.

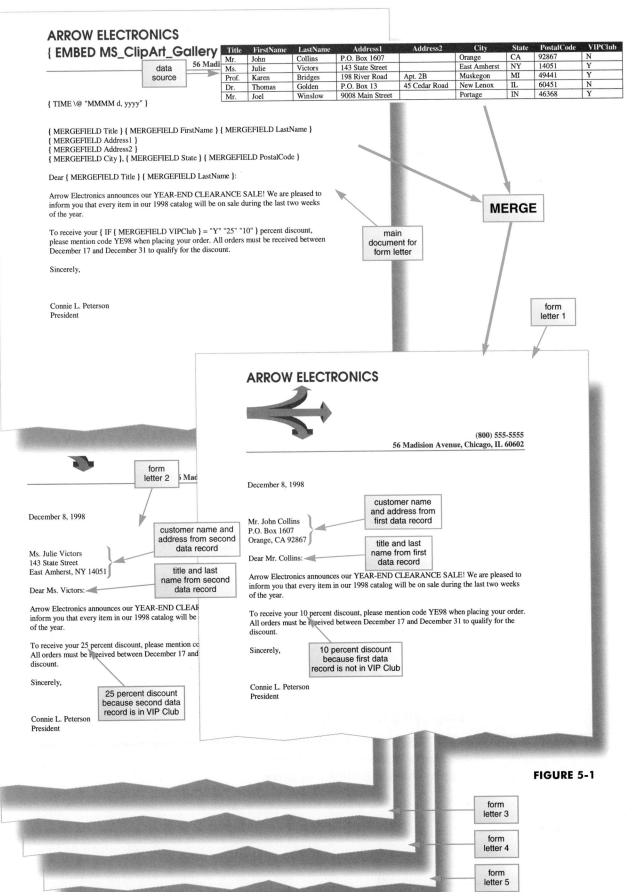

FIGURE 5-1

Merging

Merging is the process of combining the contents of a data source with a main document. The **main document** contains the constant, or unchanging, text, punctuation, spaces, and graphics. In Figure 5-1 on the previous page, the main document represents the portion of the form letters that is identical from one merged letter to the next. Conversely, the **data source** contains the variable, or changing, values in each letter. In Figure 5-1, the data source contains five different customers. One form letter is generated for each customer listed in the data source.

Document Preparation Steps

Document preparation steps give you an overview of how the main document, data source, and form letters in Figure 5-1 and corresponding mailing labels and envelopes will be developed. The following tasks will be completed in this project.

1. Create a letterhead for Arrow Electronics correspondence.
2. Identify the main document as a form letter.
3. Create a data source.
4. Create the main document for the form letter.
5. Merge and print the form letters.
6. Create and print mailing labels.
7. Create and print envelopes.

The following pages contain a detailed explanation of each of these tasks.

Starting Word

Follow these steps to start Word or ask your instructor how to start Word for your system.

TO START WORD

① Click the Start button on the taskbar.
② Click New Office Document on the Start menu. If necessary, click the General tab when the New Office Document dialog box first opens.
③ Double-click the Blank Document icon in the General sheet.
④ If the Word screen is not maximized, double-click its title bar to maximize it.

Office starts Word. After a few moments, an empty document titled Document1 displays.

Displaying Nonprinting Characters

It is helpful to display nonprinting characters that indicate where in the document you pressed the ENTER key, SPACEBAR, or TAB key. Follow this step to display the nonprinting characters.

TO DISPLAY NONPRINTING CHARACTERS

1 If the Show/Hide ¶ button on the Standard toolbar is not recessed, click it.

Word displays nonprinting characters in the document window, and the Show/Hide ¶ button on the Standard toolbar is recessed (Figure 5-2 on the next page).

Creating Company Letterhead

In many businesses, letterhead is preprinted on stationery that is used by everyone throughout the corporation. In some organizations, however, preprinted letterhead may not be purchased because of its expense. An alternative for these companies is to create their own letterhead and save it in a file. Then, company employees can open the letterhead file when they begin a document, create their document on the letterhead file, and then save their document with a new name – to preserve the original letterhead file.

In Project 5, the letterhead at the top of the main document is created with a header as described in the steps below.

TO CREATE COMPANY LETTERHEAD

1 Click View on the menu bar and then click Header and Footer. Click the Font box arrow on the Formatting toolbar and then click Albertus Extra Bold (or a similar font). Click the Font Size box arrow on the Formatting toolbar and then click 20. Click the Bold button on the Formatting toolbar. Click the Font Color button arrow and then click Dark Blue. Type ARROW ELECTRONICS and then press the ENTER key.

2 Click Insert on the menu bar, point to Picture, and then click Clip Art. If necessary, click the Clip Art tab when the Microsoft Clip Gallery dialog box first opens. Scroll through the list of categories and then click Shapes. Scroll through the shapes and then click the three-way arrow with the keywords, Alternative Options Disagreement Change. Click the Insert button to insert the floating picture into the header.

3 If the Picture toolbar does not display, right-click the clip art image and then click Show Picture Toolbar on the shortcut menu. Click the Format Picture button on the Picture toolbar. When the Format Picture dialog box displays, click the Position tab and then click Float over text to clear the check box. Click the Size tab. In the Scale area, type 25 in the Height and Width text boxes and then click the OK button. Click the paragraph mark to the right of the clip art image.

4 Press the TAB key twice. Click the Font box arrow on the Formatting toolbar and then click Times New Roman. Click the Font Size box arrow on the Formatting toolbar and then click 12. Type (800) 555-5555 and then press the ENTER key. Press the TAB key twice. Type 56 Madison Avenue, Chicago, IL 60602 and then press the ENTER key three times. Click the Font Color button arrow and then click Automatic.

The letterhead displays in the header area (Figure 5-2 on the next page).

More *About* **Letterhead Design**

Letterhead designs vary. Some are centered at the top of the page, while others have text or graphics aligned with the left and right margins. Another style places the company's name and logo at the top of the page with the address and other information at the bottom. Well-designed letterheads add professionalism to correspondence.

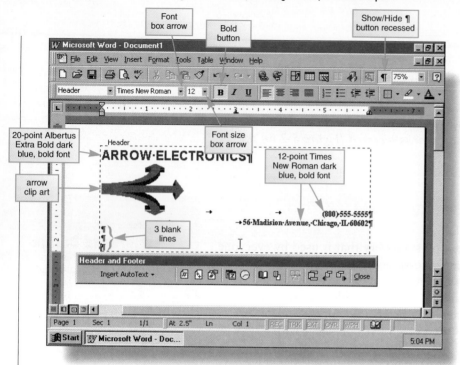

FIGURE 5-2

Adding a Bottom Border to a Paragraph

To add more professionalism to the letterhead, you would like to draw a horizontal line from the left margin to the right margin immediately below the address line. Recall that in Word, you can draw a solid line, called a **border**, to any edge of a paragraph. That is, borders may be added above or below a paragraph, to the left or right of a paragraph, or any combination of these sides. In Project 4, you added an outside border to the company name on the title page of the sales proposal. Here, you will add a bottom border to a paragraph. Perform the following steps to add a 1½-point red bottom border to a paragraph.

Steps **To Bottom Border a Paragraph**

1 **Position the insertion point in the address line of the header. If necessary, click the Tables and Borders button on the Standard toolbar to display the Tables and Borders toolbar. Click the Line Weight box arrow on the Tables and Borders toolbar and then click 1 ½ pt. Click the Border Color button on the Tables and Borders toolbar and then click the color Red on the color palette. Click the Outside Border button arrow on the Tables and Borders toolbar, then point to the Bottom Border button on the border palette.**

Word displays the border palette (Figure 5-3). Using the border palette, you can add a border to any edge(s) of a paragraph(s).

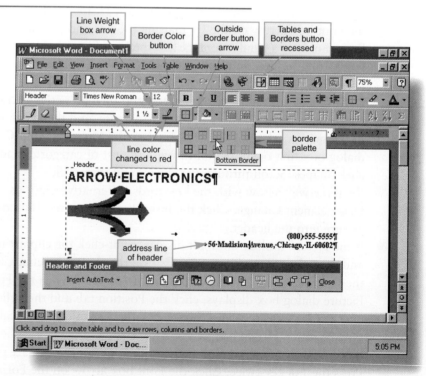

FIGURE 5-3

2 **Click the Bottom Border button on the border palette.**

Word places a 1½-point red bottom border below the paragraph containing the insertion point (Figure 5-4).

3 **Click the Tables and Borders button on the Standard toolbar to remove the Tables and Borders toolbar from the Word window. Click the Close Header and Footer button on the Header and Footer toolbar.**

Word returns to the document window (Figure 5-5 on the next page). Recall that a header does not display on the screen in normal view.

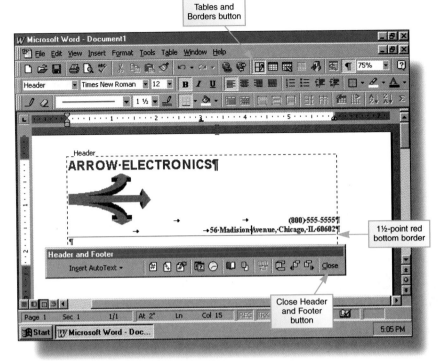

FIGURE 5-4

Now that you have created the company letterhead, the next step is to save it in a file.

TO SAVE THE COMPANY LETTERHEAD IN A FILE

1 Insert your floppy disk into drive A.
2 Click the Save button on the Standard toolbar.
3 Type the file name `Arrow Letterhead` in the File name text box. Do not press the ENTER key after typing the file name.
4 If necessary, click the Save in box arrow and then click 3½ Floppy (A:).
5 Click the Save button in the Save As dialog box.

Word saves the document on a floppy disk on drive A with the file name, Arrow Letterhead (Figure 5-5 on the next page).

More *About*
Letterhead Contents

All letterheads should contain the following items: complete legal name of company, group, or individual; full street address including any building, room, or suite number, and post office box; city, state, and zip code. Other items often found on letterhead include a logo, department name, telephone number, fax number, and e-mail address.

Identifying the Main Document and Creating the Data Source

Creating form letters requires merging a main document with a data source. To create form letters using Word's mail merge, first, you identify the main document and then create or specify the data source; next, create the main document; and finally, merge the data source with the main document to generate and print the form letters.

Identifying the Main Document

The first step in the mail merge process it to open the document you will use as the main document. If it is a new document, click the New button on the Standard toolbar. Because the main document in this project is to contain Arrow Electronics' letterhead, you should leave the file Arrow Letterhead open in the document window. Once the main document file is open, you must identify it as such to Word's mail merge as shown in these steps.

Steps To Identify the Main Document

1 **Click Tools on the menu bar and then point to Mail Merge (Figure 5-5).**

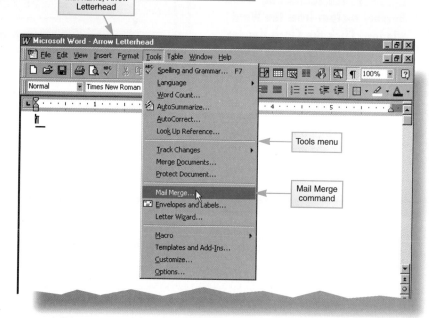

letterhead saved with name, Arrow Letterhead

Tools menu

Mail Merge command

FIGURE 5-5

2 **Click Mail Merge. When the Mail Merge Helper dialog box displays, point to the Create button.**

Word displays the Mail Merge Helper dialog box (Figure 5-6). Using this dialog box, you can identify the main document and create the data source. Notice the instructions at the top of this dialog box.

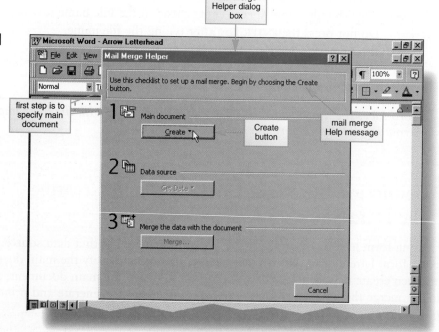

Mail Merge Helper dialog box

first step is to specify main document

Create button

mail merge Help message

FIGURE 5-6

3 Click the Create button. Point to Form Letters.

Word displays a list of main document types (Figure 5-7).

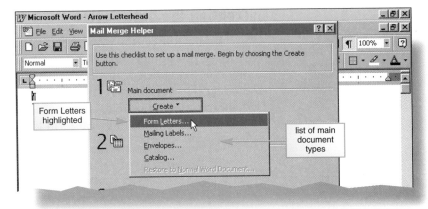

FIGURE 5-7

4 Click Form Letters.

Word displays a Microsoft Word dialog box asking if you want to use the active document window for the form letters (Figure 5-8). The current active document window is Arrow Letterhead. The Active Window button uses Arrow Letterhead as the main document, whereas the New Main Document button creates a new document window for the main document – a procedure similar to clicking the New button on the Standard toolbar.

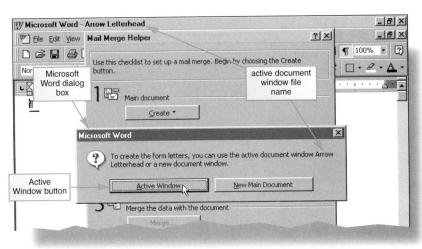

FIGURE 5-8

5 Click the Active Window button.

Word returns to the Mail Merge Helper dialog box (Figure 5-9). The merge type is identified as Form Letters and the main document is A:\Arrow Letterhead.doc, the letterhead for Arrow Electronics. An Edit button now displays in the Mail Merge Helper dialog box so you can modify the contents of the main document.

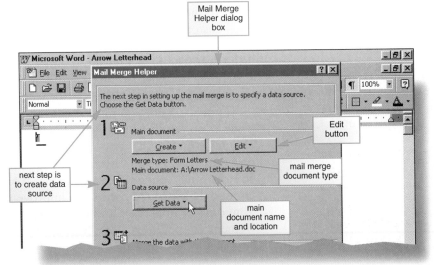

FIGURE 5-9

At this point, you do not create the main document; you simply identify it. As indicated in the Mail Merge Helper dialog box, the next step is to create the data source. After you create the data source, you will enter the main document text.

Creating the Data Source

A data source is a Word table (Figure 5-10). Recall that a **Word table** is a series of rows and columns. The first row of the data source is called the **header row**. Each row below the header row is called a **data record**. Data records contain the text that varies from one merged document to the next. The data source for this project contains five data records. In this project, each data record identifies a different customer. Thus, five form letters will be generated from this data source.

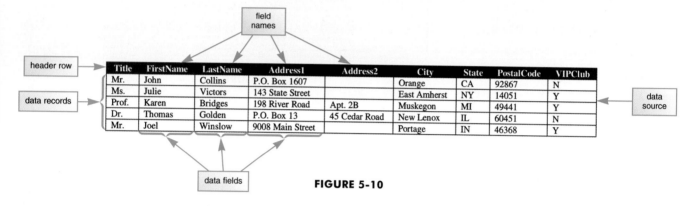

field names

header row

data records

Title	FirstName	LastName	Address1	Address2	City	State	PostalCode	VIPClub
Mr.	John	Collins	P.O. Box 1607		Orange	CA	92867	N
Ms.	Julie	Victors	143 State Street		East Amherst	NY	14051	Y
Prof.	Karen	Bridges	198 River Road	Apt. 2B	Muskegon	MI	49441	Y
Dr.	Thomas	Golden	P.O. Box 13	45 Cedar Road	New Lenox	IL	60451	N
Mr.	Joel	Winslow	9008 Main Street		Portage	IN	46368	Y

data source

data fields

FIGURE 5-10

More *About*
Data Sources

A data source does not have to be a Word table. Instead, it could be an Outlook address book, an Access database table, or an Excel spreadsheet. If the necessary records already exist in one of these Office applications, you can instruct Word to use the existing file as the data source for the mail merge.

More *About*
Terminology

The terms, field and record, come from the computer programming field of study. Don't be intimidated by these terms. A field is simply a column in a table, and a record is a row. Instead of the term field, some programmers use the terms variable or attribute to identify a column of data.

Each column in the data source is called a **data field**. A data field represents a group of similar data. In this project, the data source contains nine data fields: Title, FirstName, LastName, Address1, Address2, City, State, PostalCode, and VIPClub.

In a data source, each data field must be uniquely identified with a name, called a **field name**. For example, the name FirstName represents the field (column) containing the first names of the customers. Field names are placed in the header row of the data source to identify the name of each column.

The first step in creating a data source is to decide which fields it will contain. That is, you must identify the information that will vary from one merged document to the next. In Project 5, each record contains up to nine different fields for each customer: a courtesy title (e.g., Mrs.), first name, last name, first line of street address, second line of street address (optional), city, state, zip code, and VIP Club. The field VIPClub is either the value, Y, for Yes or the value, N, for No depending on whether the customer is a member of the VIP Club. The discount percent is determined based on the value of the VIPClub field.

For each field, you must decide on a field name. Field names must be unique. That is, no two field names may be the same. Field names may be up to 40 characters in length, can contain only letters, numbers, and the underscore (_), and must begin with a letter. Field names cannot contain spaces. Because data sources often contain the same fields, Word provides you with a list of thirteen commonly used field names. To improve the readability of field names, Word uses a mixture of uppercase and lowercase letters to separate words within the field (remember spaces are not allowed). You will use eight of the thirteen field names supplied by Word: Title, FirstName, LastName, Address1, Address2, City, State, and PostalCode. You will delete the other five field names from the list supplied by Word. That is, you will delete JobTitle, Company, Country, HomePhone, and WorkPhone. In this project, the only field that Word does not supply is the VIPClub field. Thus, you will add a field name called VIPClub.

Fields and related field names may be listed in any order in the data source. The order of fields has no effect on the order they will print in the main document.

Perform the following steps to create a new data source.

 Steps **To Create a Data Source in Word**

1 **In the Mail Merge Helper dialog box, click the Get Data button and then point to Create Data Source.**

Word displays a list of data source options (Figure 5-11). You can create your own data source in Word, use a data source already created in Word, or use files from Access or Excel as a data source.

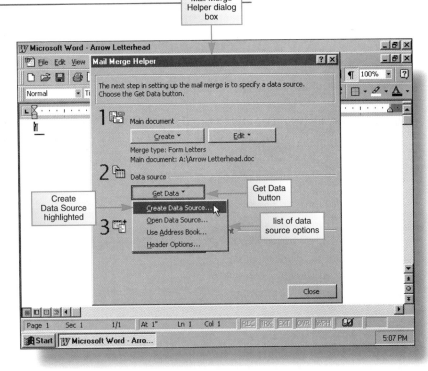

FIGURE 5-11

2 **Click Create Data Source. When the Create Data Source dialog box displays, click JobTitle in the Field names in header row list box.**

Word displays the Create Data Source dialog box (Figure 5-12). In the Field names in header row list box, Word displays a list of commonly used field names. You can remove a field name from this list if you do not want it to be in the header row of your data source. JobTitle is highlighted for removal.

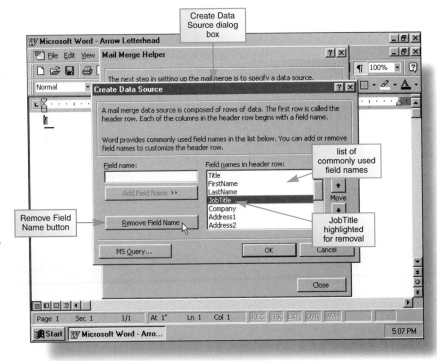

FIGURE 5-12

3 **Click the Remove Field Name button. With the Company field highlighted, click the Remove Field Name button. Scroll to the bottom of the Field names in header row list box. Click Country in the Field names in header row list box. Click the Remove Field Name button. With HomePhone highlighted, click the Remove Field Name button. With WorkPhone highlighted, click the Remove Field Name button.**

Word removes five field names from the Field names in header row list (Figure 5-13). The remaining fields in the Field names in header row list box are to be included in the data source. The last field name removed, WorkPhone, displays in the Field name text box.

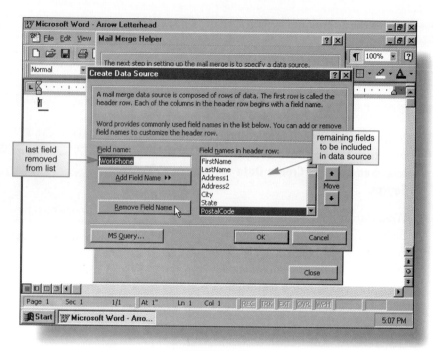

FIGURE 5-13

4 **Type VIPClub in the Field name text box and then point to the Add Field Name button (Figure 5-14).**

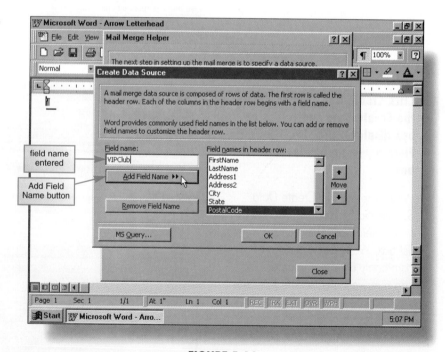

FIGURE 5-14

5 Click the Add Field Name button. Point to the OK button.

Word adds the VIPClub field name to the bottom of the Field names in header row list box (Figure 5-15).

FIGURE 5-15

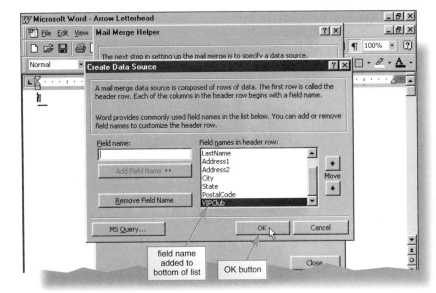

field name added to bottom of list

OK button

---

6 Click the OK button.

Word displays the Save As dialog box. You assign a file name to the data source in this dialog box.

7 **Type** Arrow Customer List **and, if necessary, change the drive to 3½ Floppy (A:). Point to the Save button in the Save As dialog box.**

Word displays the file name, Arrow Customer List, in the File name text box (Figure 5-16). The data source for Project 5 will be saved with the file name, Arrow Customer List.

Save As dialog box

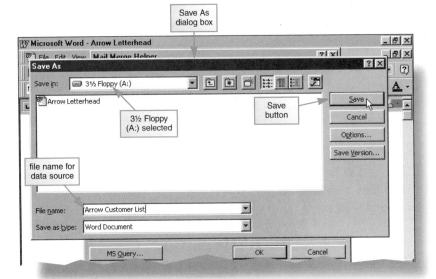

3½ Floppy (A:) selected

Save button

file name for data source

FIGURE 5-16

---

8 Click the Save button.

Word displays a Microsoft Word dialog box asking if you would like to edit the data source or edit the main document at this point (Figure 5-17). Because you want to add data records to the data source, you will edit the data source now.

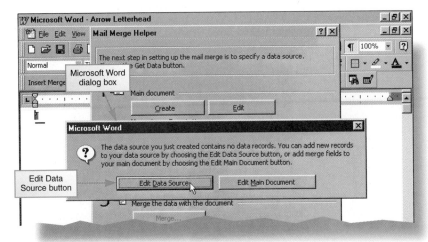

Microsoft Word dialog box

Edit Data Source button

FIGURE 5-17

9 Click the Edit Data Source button.

Word displays a *Data Form dialog box* (Figure 5-18). You can use this dialog box to enter the data records into the data source. Notice the field names from the header row are displayed along the left edge of the dialog box with an empty text box to the right of each field name. The insertion point is in the first text box.

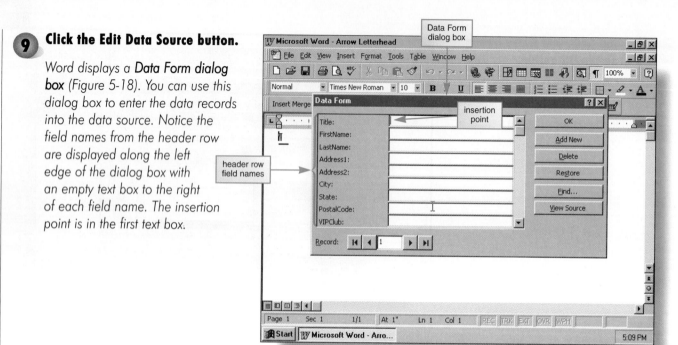

FIGURE 5-18

10 Type Mr. and then press the TAB key. Type John and then press the TAB key. Type Collins and then press the TAB key. Type P.O. Box 1607 and then press the TAB key twice. Type Orange and then press the TAB key. Type CA and then press the TAB key. Type 92867 and then press the TAB key. Type N and then point to the Add New button.

The first data record values are entered in the Data Form dialog box (Figure 5-19). Notice you press the TAB key to advance from one text box to the next. If you notice an error in a text box, click the text box and then correct the error as you would in the document window. Clicking the Add New button displays another blank form, which you can use to add another data record.

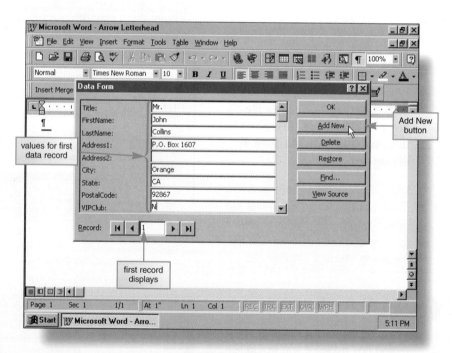

FIGURE 5-19

11 **Click the Add New button. Type**
Ms. **and then press the TAB key.**
Type Julie **and then press the**
TAB key. Type Victors **and then**
press the TAB key. Type 143
State Street **and then press**
the TAB key twice. Type East
Amherst **and then press the TAB**
key. Type NY **and then press the**
TAB key. Type 14051 **and then**
press the TAB key. Type Y **and**
then point to the Add New
button.

The second data record is entered
(Figure 5-20).

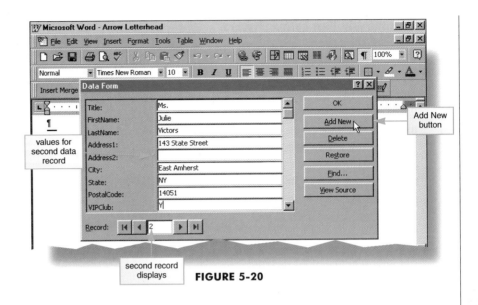

FIGURE 5-20

12 **Click the Add New button. Type**
Prof. **and then press the TAB**
key. Type Karen **and then press**
the TAB key. Type Bridges **and**
then press the TAB key. Type 198
River Road **and then press the**
TAB key. Type Apt. 2B **and then**
press the TAB key. Type
Muskegon **and then press the TAB**
key. Type MI **and then press the**
TAB key. Type 49441 **and then**
press the TAB key. Type Y **and**
then point to the Add New
button.

The third data record is entered
(Figure 5-21).

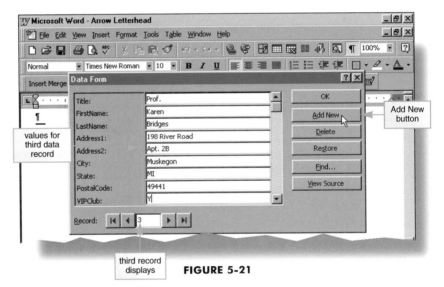

FIGURE 5-21

13 **Click the Add New button. Type**
Dr. **and then press the TAB key.**
Type Thomas **and then press the**
TAB key. Type Golden **and then**
press the TAB key. Type P.O.
Box 13 **and then press the TAB**
key. Type 45 Cedar Road **and**
then press the TAB key. Type New
Lenox **and then press the TAB**
key. Type IL **and then press the**
TAB key. Type 60451 **and then**
press the TAB key. Type N **and**
then point to the Add New
button.

The fourth data record is entered
(Figure 5-22).

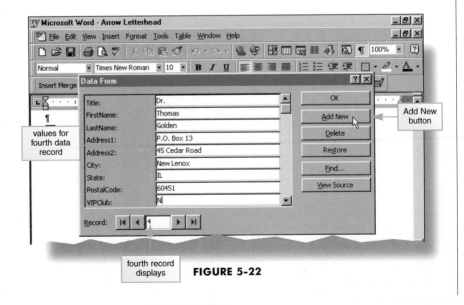

FIGURE 5-22

14 Click the Add New button. Type Mr. and then press the TAB key. Type Joel and then press the TAB key. Type Winslow and then press the TAB key. Type 9008 Main Street and then press the TAB key twice. Type Portage and then press the TAB key. Type IN and then press the TAB key. Type 46368 and then press the TAB key. Type Y and then point to the View Source button.

The fifth, and last, data record is entered (Figure 5-23). All of the data records have been entered into the data source, but Word has not saved the records in the file, Arrow Customer List.

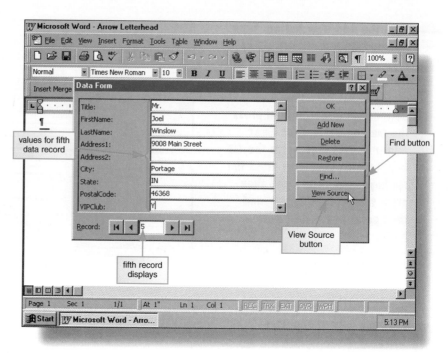

FIGURE 5-23

15 Click the View Source button. Click the Save button on the Standard toolbar. If gridlines do not display in your table, click Table on the menu bar and then click Show Gridlines.

*Word displays the data records in table form (Figure 5-24). Because the data records are not saved in the data source file when you fill in the Data Form dialog box, you must save them here. The **Database toolbar** displays below the Formatting toolbar.*

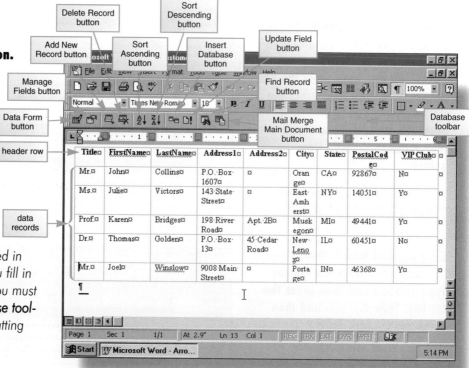

FIGURE 5-24

More *About*
Data Sources

The data source is a table. Thus, you can format it using the Table AutoFormat dialog box. If the printed data source is too wide for the paper, change to landscape orientation by clicking Page Setup on the File menu, clicking the Paper Size tab, clicking Landscape, then clicking the OK button.

All of the data records have been entered into the data source and saved with the file name, Arrow Customer List. If, when you are entering your data records into the Data Form dialog box, you accidentally click the OK button instead of the Add New button, Word will return to the main document. To return to the

Data Form dialog box and continue adding data records, click the Edit Data Source button on the Mail Merge toolbar shown in Figure 5-26 on page WD 5.20.

Editing Records in the Data Source

In the **Data Form dialog box**, you can add, change, or delete data records. To **add a new record**, click the Add New button as shown in the previous steps. To **change an existing record**, display it in the Data Form dialog box by clicking the appropriate Record button(s) or using the Find button to locate a particular data item (see Figure 5-23). For example, to find Karen Bridges, you could click the Find button, enter her title, Prof., in the Find What text box and then click the OK button. Once you have changed an existing record's data, click the OK button in the Data Form dialog box. To **delete a record**, display it in the Data Form dialog box, and then click the Delete button. If you accidentally delete a data record, click the Restore button to bring it back.

You also can add, change, and delete data records when you are viewing the source in table form as shown in Figure 5-24. Click the Add New Record button on the Database toolbar to **add a blank row** to the bottom of the table and then fill in the field values. To **delete a row**, click somewhere in the row and then click the Delete Record button on the Database toolbar. Because the data source is a Word table, you also can add and delete records the same way you add and delete rows in a Word table, which was discussed in Project 4.

The data source is complete. If you wish, you can print the data source by clicking the Print button on the Standard toolbar. The next step is to switch from the data source to the main document so you can enter the contents of the form letter into the main document.

Steps **To Switch from the Data Source to the Main Document**

1 **Point to the Mail Merge Main Document button on the Database toolbar (Figure 5-25).**

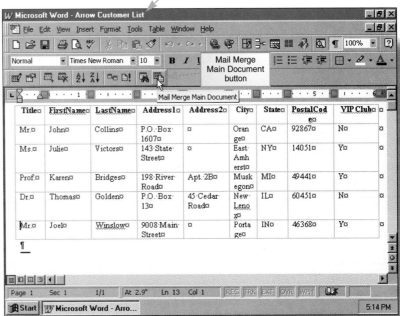

FIGURE 5-25

More *About*
Organizing Data

Organize the information in a data source so it is reusable. For example, you may want to print a person's title, first, middle, and last name (e.g., Ms. Jane L. Verlow) in the inside address but only the title and last name in the salutation (Dear Ms. Verlow). Thus, you should break the name into separate fields: title, first name, middle initial, and last name.

2 **Click the Mail Merge Main Document button.**

*Word opens the main document (Figure 5-26). The **Mail Merge toolbar** displays below the Formatting toolbar in place of the Database toolbar. When you are viewing the data source, the Database toolbar displays; and when you are viewing the main document, the Mail Merge toolbar displays. The title bar displays the file name Arrow Letterhead because Arrow Electronics' letterhead currently is the main document.*

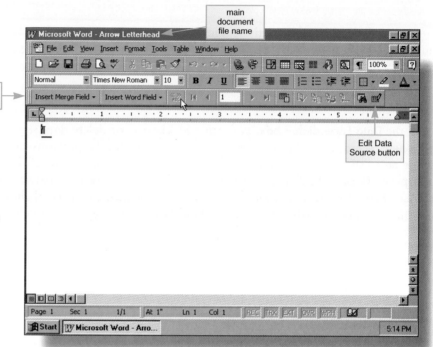

FIGURE 5-26

Creating the Main Document for the Form Letter

The next step is to create the **main document**, which is the form letter (see Figure 5-1 on page WD 5.5). The form letter is based on a **block style** letter. That is, all paragraphs are left-aligned. The current date displays in the left corner of the form letter below the letterhead. Keep in mind that you created the letterhead earlier as a header and saved it in a file called Arrow Letterhead.

You may recall that all business letters have common elements such as a date line, inside address, message, complimentary close, and signature block. The form letter in this project is a business letter that follows these guidelines:

▶ Inside address is three blank lines below the date line
▶ Salutation is one blank line below the inside address
▶ Letter message is one blank line below the salutation
▶ Paragraphs within the message are separated by one blank line
▶ Complimentary close is one blank line below the message
▶ Signature block is three blank lines below the complimentary close

The steps on the following pages illustrate how to create the main document for the form letter.

Saving the Main Document with a New File Name

The main document currently has the name Arrow Letterhead, the name of the letterhead for Arrow Electronics. Because you want the letterhead to remain unchanged, you should save the main document with a new file name as described in these steps.

More *About*
Business Letters

All business letters must contain the following items from top to bottom: date line, inside address, body or message, and signature block. Many business letters contain additional items such as a special mailing notation, attention line, salutation, subject line, complimentary close, reference initials, and enclosure notation.

TO SAVE THE MAIN DOCUMENT WITH A NEW FILE NAME

1. If necessary, insert your floppy disk into drive A.
2. Click File on the menu bar and then click Save As.
3. Type `Arrow Form Letter` in the File name text box. Do not press the ENTER key.
4. If necessary, click the Save in box arrow and then click 3½ Floppy (A:).
5. Click the Save button in the Save As dialog box.

Word saves the main document on a floppy disk in drive A with the file name, Arrow Form Letter (Figure 5-27 below).

Redefining the Normal Style

When you enter a document, its text and paragraphs are based on the Normal style. The **Normal style** is defined as single-spaced, left-aligned paragraphs containing characters in 10-point Times New Roman font. In this project, you want all of the characters to be in 12 point. You can change the font size of all characters you type from 10 to 12 by clicking the Font Size box arrow and then clicking 12 in the list. If you use this procedure, however, the current date and the discount percent will be in 10 point because they are Word fields, and Word fields are inserted based on the Normal style. Thus, you have to redefine the Normal style to 12 point.

Perform the following steps to redefine the Normal style to 12 point for this document.

Steps To Redefine the Normal Style

1 Click Format on the menu bar and then point to Style (Figure 5-27).

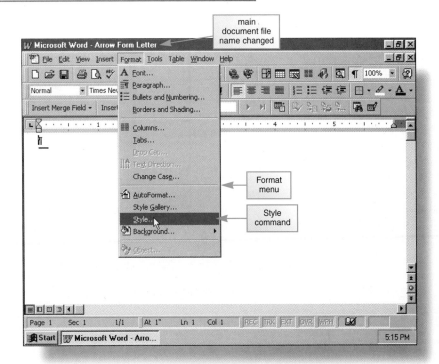

FIGURE 5-27

<table><tr><td>

More *About*
Styles

Some organizations redefine the Normal style to 12 point for all documents. That is, when they start Word, the Formatting toolbar indicates the default font size is 12 point. If your school has redefined the Normal style, then nothing will happen when you follow the steps to redefine it because it has already been redefined.
</td></tr></table>

2 **Click Style. When the Style dialog box displays, point to the Modify button.**

Word displays the Style dialog box (Figure 5-28). You can modify any of the styles listed in the Styles list box.

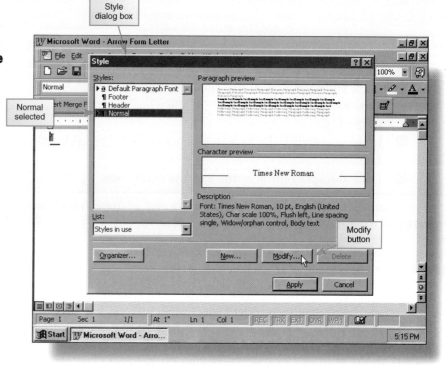

FIGURE 5-28

3 **Be sure Normal is selected in the Styles list box and then click the Modify button. When the Modify Style dialog box displays, click the Format button and then point to Font.**

Word displays the Modify Style dialog box (Figure 5-29). Using this dialog box, you can change characteristics about a style's characters (font), paragraphs, tabs, borders, language, frames, and numbering.

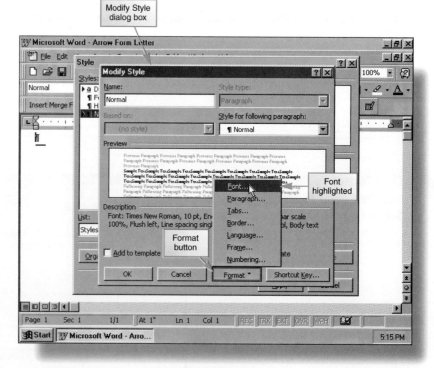

FIGURE 5-29

4 **Click Font. When the Font dialog box displays, click 12 in the Size list box and the point to the OK button.**

Word displays the Font dialog box (Figure 5-30). Using this dialog box, you can change characteristics of a style's font.

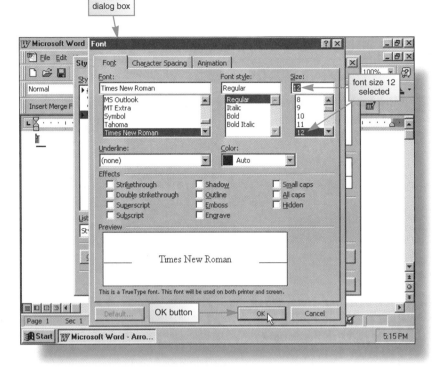

FIGURE 5-30

5 **Click the OK button in the Font dialog box. When the Modify Style dialog box redisplays, click the OK button. When the Style dialog box redisplays, click the Apply button.**

Word redefines the Normal style to 12 point (Figure 5-31).

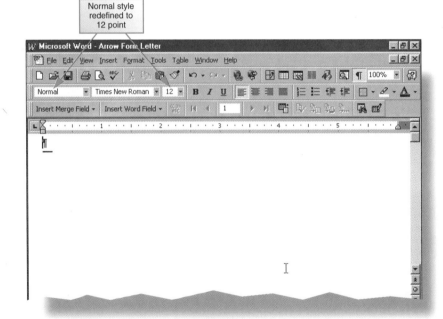

FIGURE 5-31

Inserting the Current Date in the Form Letter

When sending letters to the customers, you want the current date to print below the letterhead. Word provides a method of inserting the computer's system date into a document. In this way, if you type the letter today and print it at a later date, it will print the current date. Follow the steps on the next page to insert the current date in the main document.

More *About* **Dates**

If you do not want the date to change to the current date each time you print a document, do not make it a field. That is, do not click the Update automatically check box in the Date and Time dialog box when you insert the current date.

Steps To Insert the Current Date into a Document

1 Click Insert on the menu bar and then point to Date and Time (Figure 5-32).

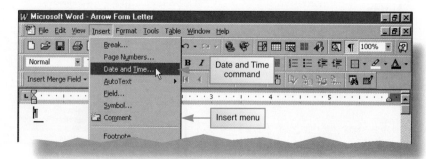

FIGURE 5-32

2 Click Date and Time. When the Date and Time dialog box displays, click the format December 8, 1998 (the current date on your screen). If it is not selected, click Update automatically.

*Word displays the **Date and Time dialog box** (Figure 5-33). A list of available formats for showing the current date and time displays. Your screen will not show December 8, 1998; instead, it will display the current system date stored in your computer. The current date will display in the main document according to the highlighted format.*

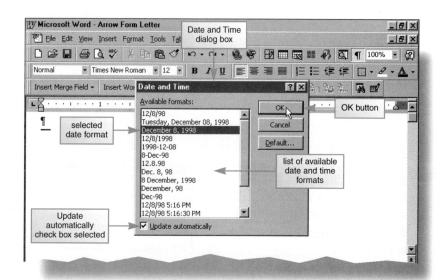

FIGURE 5-33

3 Click the OK button. Press the ENTER key four times. If your date is shaded, click Tools on the menu bar, click Options, click the View tab, click the Field shading box arrow, click When selected, then click the OK button.

Word displays the current date in the main document (Figure 5-34). The insertion point is on line 5 with three blank lines above it.

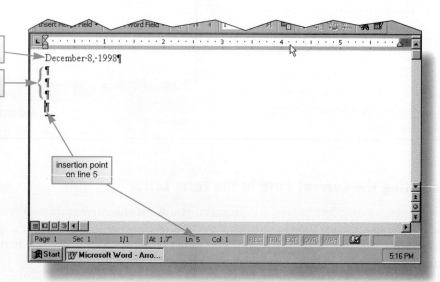

FIGURE 5-34

The current date is actually a field that Word updates when it prints the document. If you open the document at a later date, Word will not update the date on the screen until you print the document. If you would like to update the field on the screen prior to printing, click the date and then press the F9 key. If, for some reason, you want to delete the date field from the main document, double-click it, right-click the selection, and then click Cut on the shortcut menu.

The next step is to enter the inside address on the letter. The contents of the inside address are located in the data source. Thus, you insert fields from the data source into the main document.

Inserting Merge Fields into the Main Document

Earlier in this project, you created the data source for the form letter. The first record in the data source, the header row, contains the field names of each field in the data source. To link the data source to the main document, you must insert these field names into the main document. In the main document, these field names are called **merge fields** because they merge, or combine, the main document with the contents of the data source. When a field is inserted into the main document from the data source, Word surrounds the field name with **chevrons**. These chevrons mark the beginning and ending of a merge field. Chevrons are not on the keyboard; therefore, you cannot type them directly into the document. They display as a result of inserting a merge field with the **Insert Merge Field button** on the Mail Merge toolbar.

Perform the following steps to create the inside address and salutation using fields from the data source.

◆ **More** *About* **Fields**

When you position the insertion point in a field, the entire field is shaded gray. The shading displays on the screen only to help you identify fields; the shading does not print on a hard copy. Thus, the date and merge fields appear shaded when you click them. To select an entire field, you must double-click it.

 Steps **To Insert Merge Fields into the Main Document**

1 **Be sure the insertion point is on line 5 in the main document. Click the Insert Merge Field button on the Mail Merge toolbar. In the list of fields, point to Title.**

Word displays a list of fields from the data source (Figure 5-35). The field you select will be entered at the location of the insertion point in the main document.

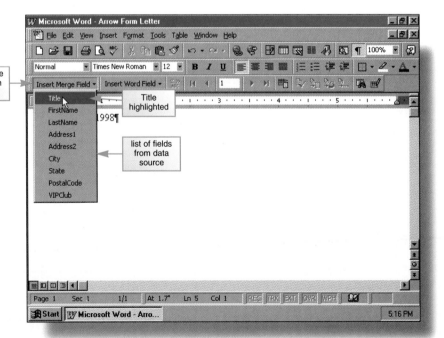

FIGURE 5-35

2 **Click Title. When the list of fields disappears from the screen, press the SPACEBAR.**

Word displays the field name, Title, surrounded with chevrons in the main document (Figure 5-36). When you merge the data source with the main document, the customer's title (e.g., Mr. or Ms.) will print at the location of the merge field Title. One space follows the ending chevron after the Title merge field.

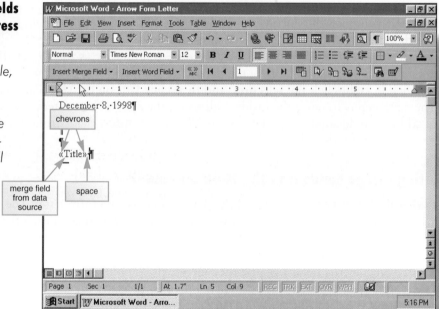

FIGURE 5-36

3 **Click the Insert Merge Field button on the Mail Merge toolbar and then click FirstName. Press the SPACEBAR. Click the Insert Merge Field button and then click LastName. Press the ENTER key. Click the Insert Merge Field button and then click Address1. Press the ENTER key. Click the Insert Merge Field button and then click Address2. Press the ENTER key. Click the Insert Merge Field button and then click City. Type , (a comma) and then press the SPACEBAR. Click the Insert Merge Field button and then click State. Press the SPACEBAR. Click the Insert Merge Field button and then click PostalCode.**

The inside address is complete (Figure 5-37).

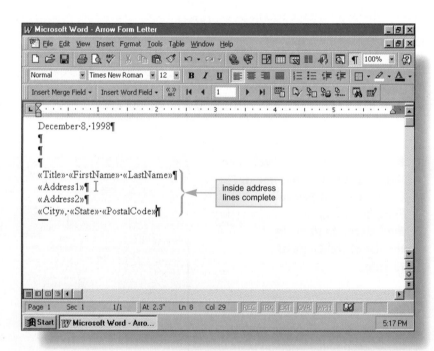

FIGURE 5-37

Entering the Salutation and Body of the Form Letter

The next step is to enter the salutation and then the first paragraph in the body of the form letter. The first paragraph contains *constant*, or unchanging, text to be printed in each form letter. Perform the following steps to enter the salutation and the first paragraph in the body of the form letter.

TO ENTER THE SALUTATION AND FIRST PARAGRAPH IN THE FORM LETTER

1 Press the ENTER key twice. Type Dear and then press the SPACEBAR. Click the Insert Merge Field button and then click Title. Press the SPACEBAR. Click the Insert Merge Field button and then click LastName. Type : (a colon).

2 Press the ENTER key twice. If the Office Assistant displays, click its Cancel button. Type Arrow Electronics announces our YEAR-END CLEARANCE SALE!

3 Press the SPACEBAR. Type We are pleased to inform you that every item in our 1998 catalog will be on sale during the last two weeks of the year.

The salutation and body of the form letter display as shown in Figure 5-38. Depending on your printer driver, your wordwrap may occur in different locations.

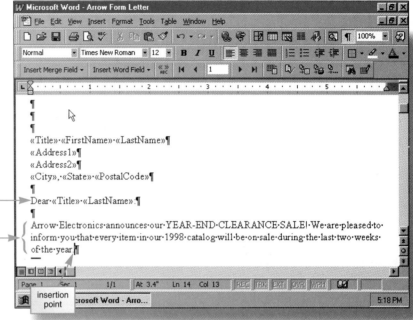

FIGURE 5-38

Using an IF Field to Conditionally Print Text in a Form Letter

In addition to merge fields, you can insert other types of fields in your main document. One type of field is called an **IF field**. One form of the IF field is: If a condition is true, then perform an action. For example, If Mary is a student, then inform her of the good student discount program for car insurance. This type of IF field is called **If...Then**. Another form of the IF field is: If a condition is true, then perform an action; else perform a different action. For example, If the weather is sunny, we will go to the beach; else we will go the movies. This type of IF field is called **If...Then...Else**.

In Project 5, the form letter checks whether the customer is a member of the VIP Club. If the customer is a member, then the discount is 25 percent. If the customer is not a member of the VIP Club, then the discount is 10 percent. For Word to determine which discount percent to use, you must enter an If...Then...Else: If VIP Club is equal to Y (for Yes), then print 25 percent as the discount, else print 10 percent as the discount.

The phrase that appears after the word If is called a **condition**. A condition is comprised of an expression, followed by a comparison operator, followed by a final expression.

EXPRESSIONS The **expression** in a condition can be a merge field, a number, a string of characters, or a mathematical formula. Word surrounds a string of characters with quotation marks ("). Place two quotation marks together ("") to indicate an empty, or **null**, expression.

More *About* **Field Codes**

If, when you insert fields into a document, the field displays surrounded by braces instead of chevrons and extra instructions appear between the braces, then field codes have been turned on. To turn off field codes and display the field results, press ALT+F9, which toggles between field codes and field results.

More *About* **Word Fields**

In addition to the IF field, Word provides other fields that may be used in form letters. For example, the ASK and FILLIN fields prompt the user to enter data for each record in the data source. The SKIP RECORD IF field instructs the mail merge to not generate a form letter for a data record if a specific condition is met.

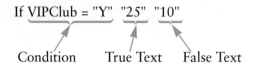

More *About*
IF Fields

The term, IF field, comes from computer programming. Don't be intimidated by the terminology. An IF field simply specifies a decision. Some programmers refer to it as an IF statement. An IF field can be quite simple or complex. Complex IF fields include nested IF fields, which is a second IF field inside true or false text of the first IF field.

COMPARISON OPERATORS The **comparison operator** in a condition must be one of six characters: = (equal to or matches the text), <> (not equal to or does not match text), < (less than), <= (less than or equal to), > (greater than), >= (greater than or equal to).

If the result of a condition is true, then the **true text** is evaluated; otherwise, if the result of the condition is false, the **false text** is evaluated. In Project 5, the first expression in the condition is a merge field (VIPClub); the comparison operator is an equal sign (=); and the second expression is the text "Y". The true text is "25" and the false text is "10". That is, the complete IF field is as follows:

$$\text{If VIPClub} = \text{"Y"} \quad \text{"25"} \quad \text{"10"}$$

Condition   True Text   False Text

Perform the following steps to insert the IF field into the form letter.

Steps **To Insert an IF Field into the Main Document**

1 **Press the ENTER key twice. Type** To receive your **and then press the SPACEBAR. Click the Insert Word Field button on the Mail Merge toolbar. When the list of Word fields displays, point to If...Then...Else.**

A list of Word fields that may be inserted into the main document displays (Figure 5-39).

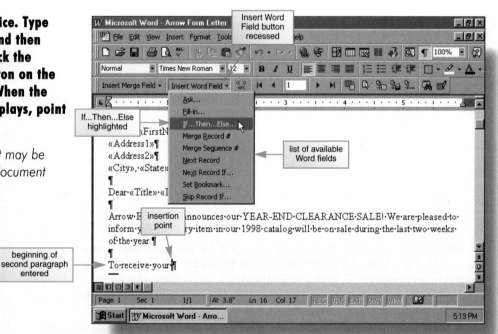

FIGURE 5-39

2 Click If...Then...Else. When the Insert Word Field: IF dialog box displays, point to the Field name box arrow.

Word displays the Insert Word Field: IF dialog box (Figure 5-40). You can specify the condition in the IF area of this dialog box.

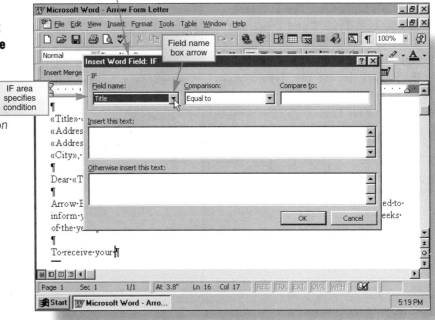

FIGURE 5-40

3 Click the Field name box arrow. Scroll through the list of fields and then point to VIPClub.

Word displays a list of fields from the data source (Figure 5-41).

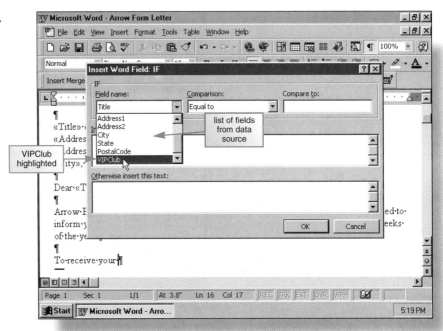

FIGURE 5-41

4 **Click VIPClub. Click the Compare to text box. Type** Y **and then press the TAB key. In the Insert this text text box, type** 25 **and then press the TAB key. Type** 10 **in the Otherwise insert this text text box.**

The entries in the Insert Word Field: IF dialog box are complete (Figure 5-42).

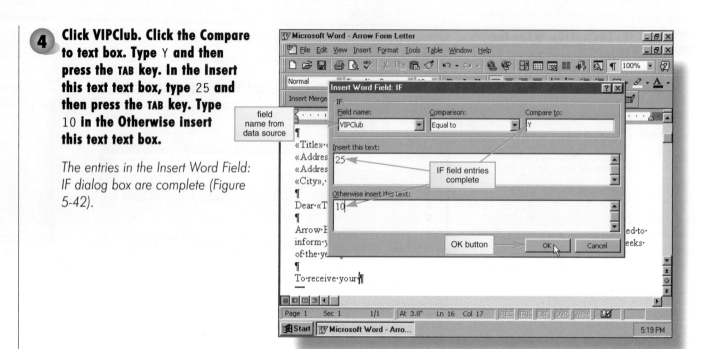

FIGURE 5-42

5 **Click the OK button.**

Word returns to the document. The discount percent, 10, displays at the location of the insertion point because the first record in the data source is not a member of the VIP Club.

6 **Press the SPACEBAR. Type** percent discount, please mention code YE98 when placing your order. **Press the SPACEBAR. Type** All orders must be received between December 17 and December 31 to qualify for the discount. **Press the ENTER key twice. Type** Sincerely, **and then press the ENTER key four times. Type** Connie L. Peterson **and then press the ENTER key. Type** President **in the signature block.**

The form letter is complete (Figure 5-43).

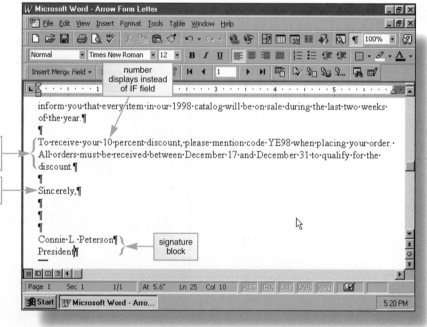

FIGURE 5-43

The main document for the form letter is complete. You should save it again by clicking the Save button on the Standard toolbar.

Displaying Field Codes

Notice that the IF field does not display in the document window; instead, the value of the IF field, called the **field results,** displays. That is, the number 10 displays because the first data record contains a customer that is not a member of the VIP Club.

The IF field is referred to as a **field code,** and the default mode for Word is field codes off. Thus, field codes will not print or display unless you turn them on. You use one procedure to display field codes on the screen and a different procedure to print them on a hard copy. Whether field codes are on or off on your screen has no effect on the print merge process. The following steps illustrate how to turn on field codes so you may see them on the screen. Most Word users turn on field codes only to verify their accuracy. Because field codes tend to clutter the screen, you may want to turn them off after checking their accuracy.

 Steps To Turn Field Codes On or Off for Display

1 **Press the ALT+F9 keys. Scroll up the document to view the field codes.**

Word displays the main document with field codes on (Figure 5-44). With field codes on, the term, MERGEFIELD, appears before each field from the data source. The IF field also displays. With field codes on, braces surround the fields instead of chevrons.

2 **Press the ALT+F9 keys again.**

Word turns field codes off in the main document.

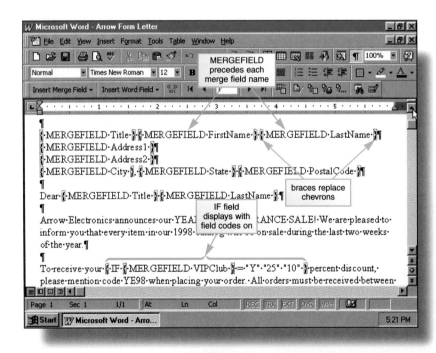

FIGURE 5-44

More *About* **Fields**

If you wanted to lock a field so that its field results cannot be changed, click the field and then press CTRL+F11. To subsequently unlock a field so that it may be updated, click the field and then press CTRL+SHIFT+F11.

Other Ways

1. On Tools menu click Options, click View tab, click Field Codes, click OK button

Printing Field Codes

You also may want to print the field codes version of the form letter so you have a hard copy of the fields for future reference (see Figure 5-47). Field codes can be printed using the Print dialog box. When you print field codes, you must remember to turn off the field codes option so future documents print field results rather than field codes. For example, with field codes on, merged form letters will display field codes instead of data. Perform the following steps to print the field codes in the main document and then turn off the field codes print option for future printing.

 To Print Field Codes in the Main Document

1 **Click File on the menu bar and then click Print. When the Print dialog box displays, point to the Options button.**

Word displays the Print dialog box (Figure 5-45).

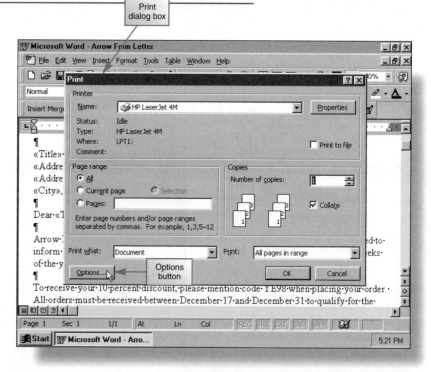

FIGURE 5-45

2 **Click the Options button. When the next Print dialog box displays, click Field codes in the Include with document area.**

Word displays another Print dialog box (Figure 5-46). The Field codes check box is selected.

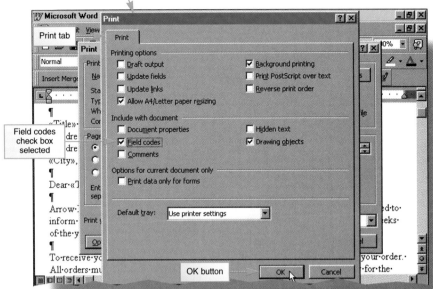

FIGURE 5-46

3 **Click the OK button in the active Print dialog box. When Word returns to the first Print dialog box, click the OK button.**

Word sends the main document with field codes to the printer (Figure 5-47). Notice the date field and IF field display on the printout.

4 **Click File on the menu bar and then click Print. Click the Options button. Turn off field codes by clicking Field codes. Click the OK button in the active Print dialog box and then click the Close button in the Print dialog box.**

The field codes have been turned off. No future documents will print field codes. If you accidentally click the Print button, instead of the Close button, in the Print dialog box, you will print the main document again – without field codes.

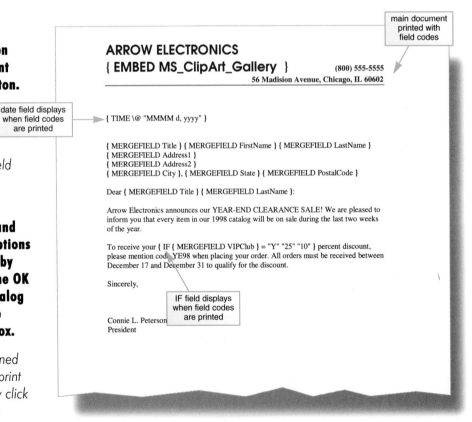

FIGURE 5-47

OtherWays

1. Press CTRL+P, click Options button, click Field codes, click OK button in Print dialog box, click OK button

2. On Tools menu click Options, click Print tab, click Field codes, click OK button, click Print button on Standard toolbar

Merging the Documents and Printing the Letters

The data source and main document for the form letter are complete. The next step is to merge them together to generate the individual form letters as shown in the following steps.

Steps To Merge the Documents and Print the Form Letters

1 Press the CTRL+HOME keys to move the insertion point to the beginning of the document. Point to the Merge to Printer button on the Mail Merge toolbar (Figure 5-48).

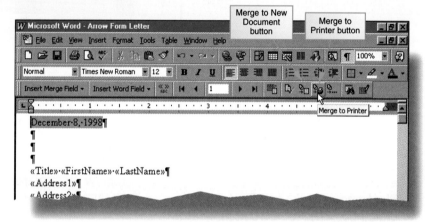

FIGURE 5-48

2 Click the Merge to Printer button. When the Print dialog box displays, click the OK button.

Word displays the Print dialog box and then sends the form letters to the printer. Form letters for five customers print (Figure 5-49).

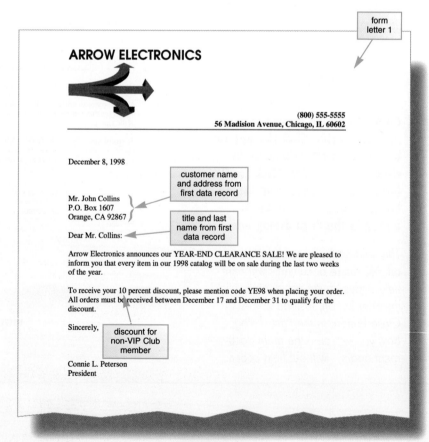

FIGURE 5-49

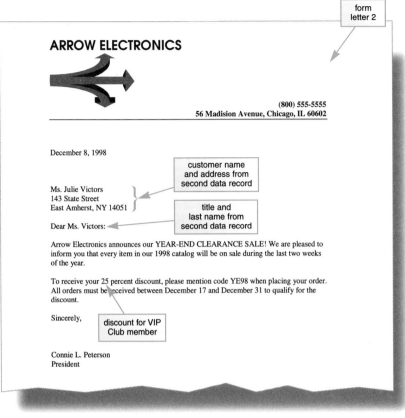

FIGURE 5-49 (continued)

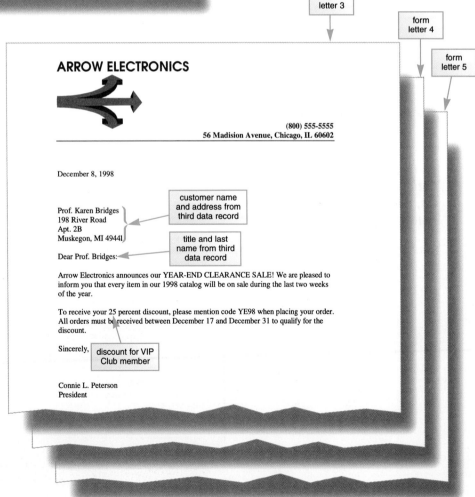

OtherWays

1. Click Mail Merge button on Mail Merge toolbar, click Merge to box arrow, click Printer in list box, click Merge button

2. Click Mail Merge Helper button on Mail Merge toolbar, click Merge button, click Merge to box arrow, click Printer in list box, click Merge button in Merge dialog box, click Close button

More *About*
Opening Form Letters

When you open the main document, the associated data source also automatically opens in a separate document window. If, however, you open the data source, only the data source opens. Thus, to generate form letters at a later date, simply open the main document and then click the Merge to Printer button.

The contents of the data source merge with the merge fields in the main document to generate the form letters. One form letter for each customer is generated because each customer is a separate record in the data source. Notice that the address lines *suppress* blanks. That is, customers without a second address line begin the city on the line immediately below the first address line. Also notice that the discount percent changes from one letter to the next based on whether or not the customer is a member of the VIP Club.

If you notice errors in your form letters, you can edit the main document the same way you edit any other document. Then, you can save your changes and merge again.

Instead of printing the form letters, you could send them into a new document window by clicking the **Merge to New Document button** on the Mail Merge toolbar (Figure 5-48 on page WD 5.34). With this button, you view the merged form letters to verify their accuracy before sending them to the printer. When you are finished viewing the merged form letters, close the document window by clicking the Close button at the right edge of the menu bar and then click the No button to not save the document. In addition, you could save the merged form letters into a file and then print the file containing the letters at a later time using the Print button on the Standard toolbar.

Selecting Data Records to Merge and Print

Instead of merging and printing all of the records in the data source, you can choose which records will merge, based on a condition you specify. For example, to merge and print only those customers who are not a member of the VIP Club, perform the following steps.

Steps ▶ **To Selectively Merge and Print Records**

① **Click the Mail Merge button on the Mail Merge toolbar. When Word displays the Merge dialog box, point to the Query Options button.**

Word displays the Merge dialog box (Figure 5-50).

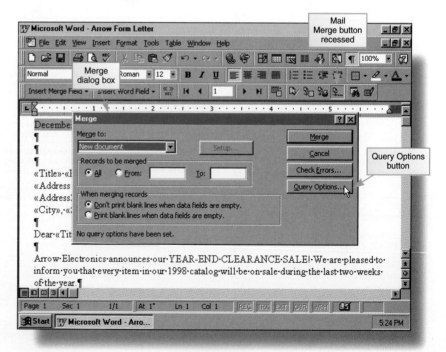

FIGURE 5-50

2 Click the Query Options button. If necessary, click the Filter Records tab when the Query Options dialog box first opens. Click the Field box arrow to display a list of fields from the data source. Scroll to the bottom of the list and then click VIPClub. In the Compare to text box, type N and then point to the OK button.

Word displays the Query Options *dialog box (Figure 5-51). VIPClub displays in the Field box, Equal to displays in the Comparison box, and N displays in the Compare to text box.*

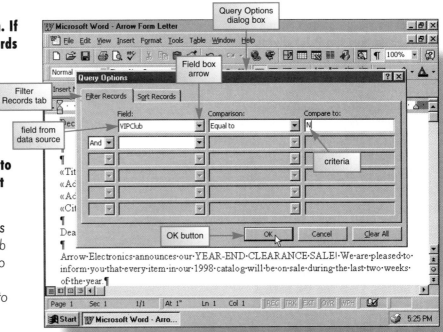

FIGURE 5-51

3 Click the OK button. When the Merge dialog box redisplays, click the Merge to box arrow and then click Printer. Point to the Merge button in the Merge dialog box.

Word returns to the Merge dialog box (Figure 5-52). You can merge to the printer or to a new document window using this dialog box.

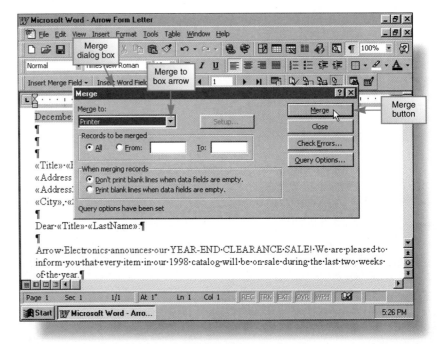

FIGURE 5-52

4 **Click the Merge button. When Word displays the Print dialog box, click the OK button.**

Word prints the form letters that match the specified condition: VIPClub is Equal to N (Figure 5-53). Two form letters print because two customers are not members of the VIP Club.

5 **Click the Mail Merge button on the Mail Merge toolbar. Click the Query Options button in the Merge dialog box. Click the Clear All button. Click the OK button. Click the Close button in the Merge dialog box.**

Word removes the specified condition so that future merges will not be restricted to VIPClub is Equal to N.

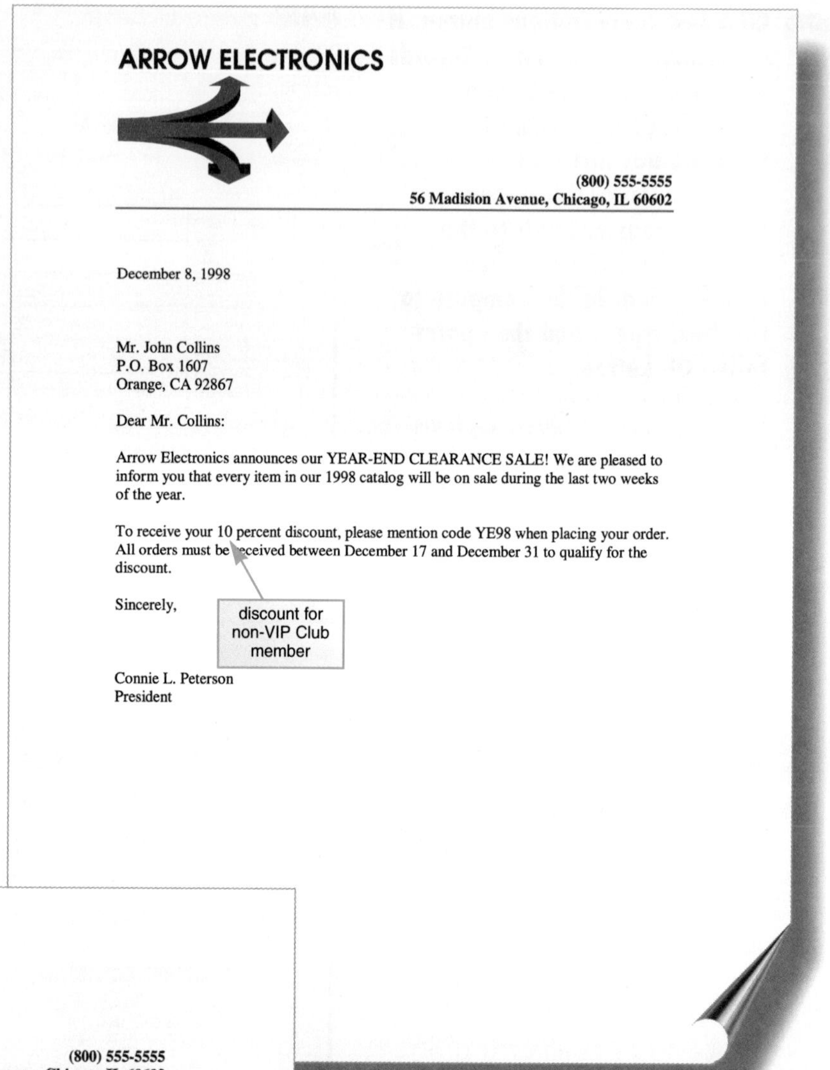

ARROW ELECTRONICS

(800) 555-5555
56 Madision Avenue, Chicago, IL 60602

December 8, 1998

Mr. John Collins
P.O. Box 1607
Orange, CA 92867

Dear Mr. Collins:

Arrow Electronics announces our YEAR-END CLEARANCE SALE! We are pleased to inform you that every item in our 1998 catalog will be on sale during the last two weeks of the year.

To receive your 10 percent discount, please mention code YE98 when placing your order. All orders must be received between December 17 and December 31 to qualify for the discount.

Sincerely,

> discount for
> non-VIP Club
> member

Connie L. Peterson
President

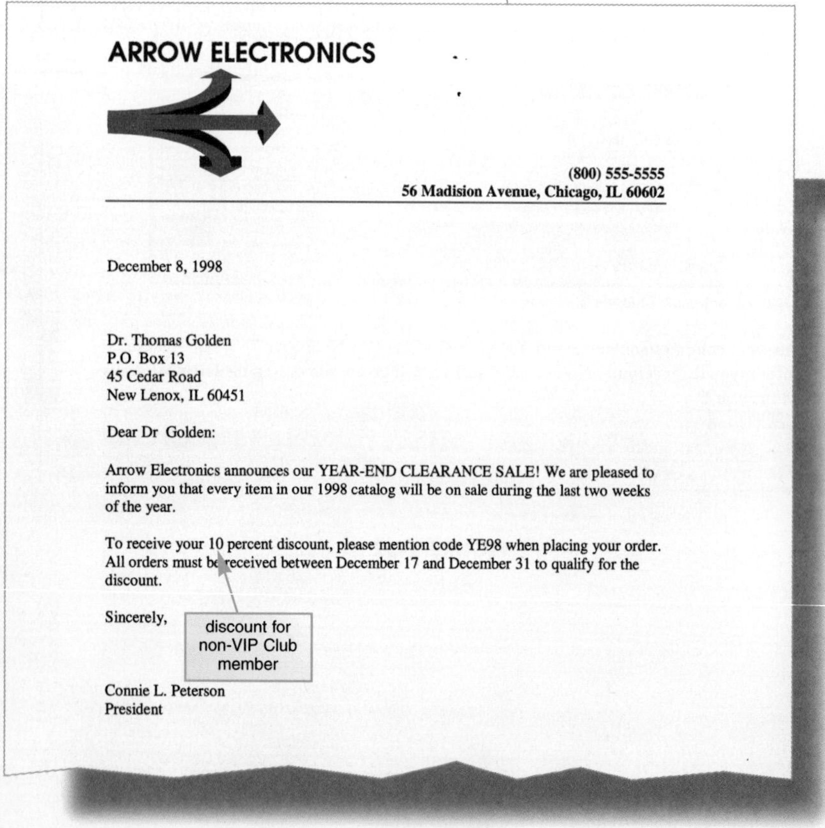

ARROW ELECTRONICS

(800) 555-5555
56 Madision Avenue, Chicago, IL 60602

December 8, 1998

Dr. Thomas Golden
P.O. Box 13
45 Cedar Road
New Lenox, IL 60451

Dear Dr Golden:

Arrow Electronics announces our YEAR-END CLEARANCE SALE! We are pleased to inform you that every item in our 1998 catalog will be on sale during the last two weeks of the year.

To receive your 10 percent discount, please mention code YE98 when placing your order. All orders must be received between December 17 and December 31 to qualify for the discount.

Sincerely,

> discount for
> non-VIP Club
> member

Connie L. Peterson
President

FIGURE 5-53

OtherWays

1. Click Mail Merge Helper button on Mail Merge toolbar, click Merge button, click Query Options button, enter condition, click OK button, click Merge to box arrow, click Printer in list box, click Merge button in Merge dialog box, click Close button

Sorting Data Records to Merge and Print

If you mail your form letters using the U.S. Postal Service's bulk rate mailing service, the post office requires you to sort and group the form letters by zip code. Thus, follow these steps to sort the data records by zip code.

Steps **To Sort the Data Records**

---

1 Click the Mail Merge button on the Mail Merge toolbar. When Word displays the Merge dialog box, click the Query Options button. If necessary, click the Sort Records tab when the Query Options dialog box first opens. Point to the Sort by box arrow.

Word displays the Query Options dialog box (Figure 5-54). You can order the data source records by any of its fields. For example, you could alphabetize by LastName or order by PostalCode.

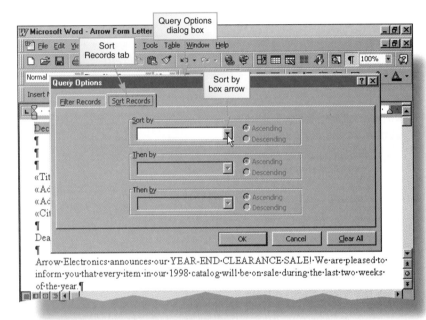

FIGURE 5-54

2 Click the Sort by box arrow to display a list of fields from the data source. Scroll to the bottom of the list and then click PostalCode.

Word displays PostalCode in the Sort by box (Figure 5-55). The Ascending option button is selected. Thus, the smallest zip code (those beginning with zero) will be at the top of the data source and the largest will be at the bottom.

3 Click the OK button. When the Merge dialog box redisplays, click the Close button.

The data records are sorted by zip code.

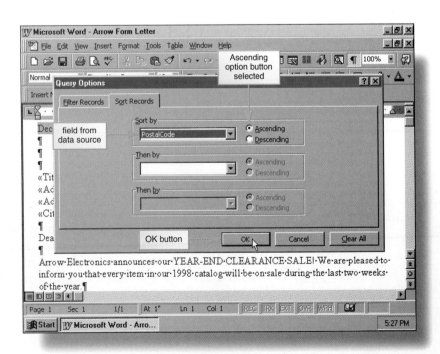

FIGURE 5-55

If you chose to merge the form letters again at this point, Word would print them in order of zip code; that is, the letter to Julie Victors would print first and the letter to John Collins would print last.

Because you want the mailing labels and envelopes to print in order of zip code, leave the sort condition set in the Query Options dialog box.

Viewing Merged Data

You can verify the order of the data records without printing them by using the **View Merged Data button** on the Mail Merge toolbar as shown below.

Steps To View Merged Data in the Main Document

1 **Click the View Merged Data button on the Mail Merge toolbar.**

Word displays the contents of the first data record in the main document, instead of the merge fields (Figure 5-56). The View Merged Data button is recessed.

2 **Click the View Merged Data button on the Mail Merge toolbar again.**

Word displays the merge fields in the main document, instead of the field values.

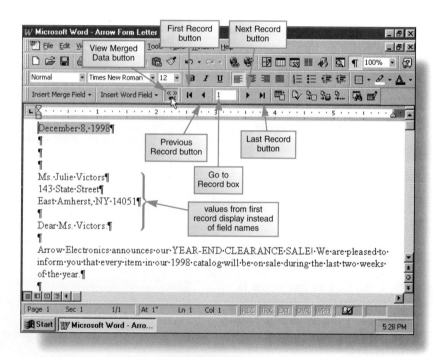

FIGURE 5-56

When you are viewing merged data in the main document (the View Merged Data button is recessed), you can click the **Last Record button** on the Mail Merge toolbar to display the values in the last record in the data source, the **Next Record button** to display the values in the next consecutive record number, the **Previous Record button** to display the values in the previous record number, or the **First Record button** to display the values in record one. You also can click in the **Go to Record box**, type the record number you want to display in the main document, and then press the ENTER key.

Addressing and Printing Mailing Labels

Now that you have printed the form letters, the next step is to address **mailing labels** for the envelopes of the form letters. The mailing labels will use the same data source as the form letter, Arrow Customer List. The format and content of the mailing labels will be exactly the same as the inside address in the main document for the form letter. That is, the first line will contain the customer's title, followed by the first name, followed by the last name. The second line will contain the customer's street address, and so on.

If your printer can print graphics, you can add a **POSTNET delivery-point bar code**, usually referred to as simply a **bar code,** above the address on each mailing label. Using a bar code speeds up the delivery service by the U.S. Postal Service. A bar code represents the addressee's zip code and first street address.

Follow the same basic steps as you did to create the main document for the form letters when you create the main document for the mailing labels. The major difference is that the data source already exists because you created it earlier in this project. The following pages illustrate how to address and print mailing labels from an existing data source.

Steps To Address and Print Mailing Labels from an Existing Data Source

1 **Point to the New button on the Standard toolbar (Figure 5-57).**

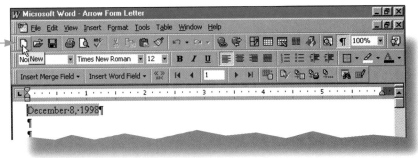

FIGURE 5-57

2 **Click the New button. Click File on the menu bar and then click Save As. Type** Arrow Mailing Labels **in the File name text box. If necessary, click the Save in box arrow and then click 3½ Floppy (A:). Click the Save button in the Save As dialog box. Click Tools on the menu bar and then click Mail Merge. When the Mail Merge Helper dialog box displays, click the Create button. Point to Mailing Labels.**

Word displays a new document window for the mailing labels (Figure 5-58). The file name of the new document is Arrow Mailing Labels.

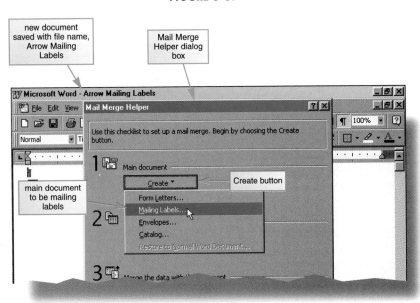

FIGURE 5-58

3 **Click Mailing Labels.**

A Microsoft Word dialog box displays asking if you want to use the active window for the mailing labels (Figure 5-59). The active window is Arrow Mailing Labels, which is the one you want.

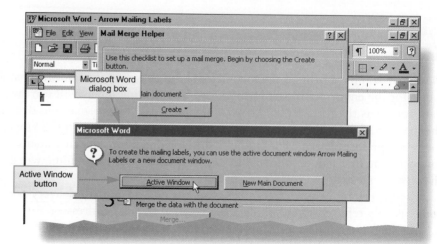

FIGURE 5-59

4 **Click the Active Window button. When the Mail Merge Helper dialog box displays, click the Get Data button and then point to Open Data Source.**

Word returns to the Mail Merge Helper dialog box (Figure 5-60). The merge type is identified as mailing labels for the main document. Because you will use the same data source as you did for the form letters, you will open a data source instead of creating one.

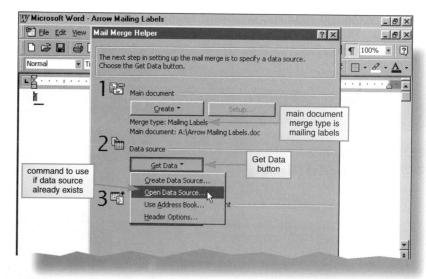

FIGURE 5-60

5 **Click Open Data Source. When Word displays the Open Data Source dialog box, click the Look in box arrow and then, if necessary, click 3½ Floppy (A:). Click the file name, Arrow Customer List, and then point to the Open button in the Open Data Source dialog box.**

Word displays the Open Data Source dialog box (Figure 5-61). You use the existing data source, Arrow Customer List, to generate the mailing labels.

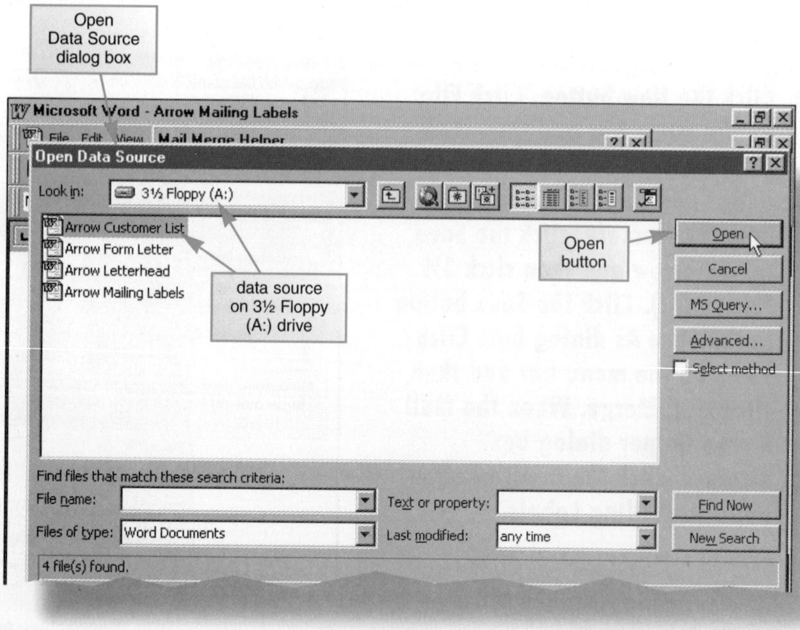

FIGURE 5-61

6 **Click the Open button.**

A Microsoft Word dialog box displays asking if you want to set up the main document, which is a mailing label layout in this case (Figure 5-62).

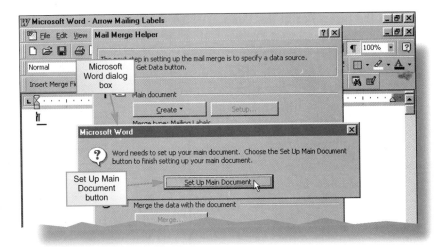

FIGURE 5-62

7 **Click the Set Up Main Document button. When the Label Options dialog box displays, click the desired Avery product number.**

*Word displays the **Label Options dialog box** (Figure 5-63). If you have a dot matrix printer, your printer information will differ from this figure. The Product number list box displays the product numbers for all possible Avery mailing label sheets compatible with your printer. The Label information area displays details about the selected Avery product number.*

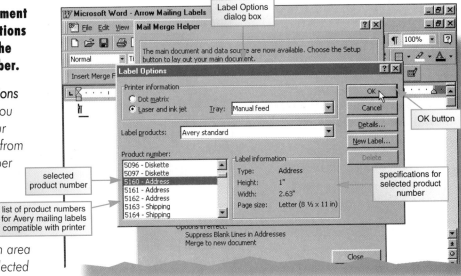

FIGURE 5-63

8 **Click the OK button.**

*Word displays the **Create Labels dialog box.** You can insert merge fields into the Sample label area of this dialog box the same way you inserted merge fields into the main document for the form letter.*

9 **Follow Steps 1 through 3 on pages WD 5.25 and WD 5.26 to address the mailing label. Point to the Insert Postal Bar Code button.**

The mailing label layout is complete (Figure 5-64).

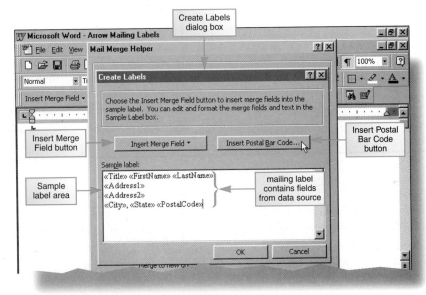

FIGURE 5-64

10 Click the Insert Postal Bar Code button. When the Insert Postal Bar Code dialog box displays, click the Merge field with ZIP code box arrow and then click PostalCode in the list. Click the Merge field with street address box arrow and then click Address1 in the list.

Word displays the Insert Postal Bar Code dialog box (Figure 5-65). A bar code contains the zip code and the first address line. Thus, PostalCode displays in the Merge field with ZIP code box and Address1 displays in the Merge field with street address box.

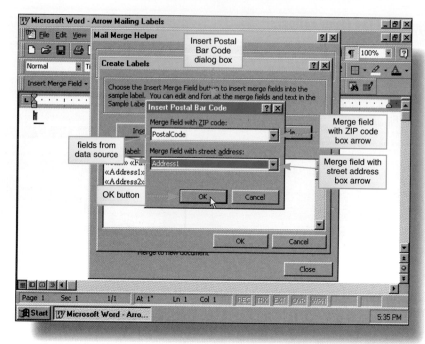

FIGURE 5-65

11 Click the OK button in the Insert Postal Bar Code dialog box.

Word returns to the Create Labels dialog box, which indicates where the bar code will print on each mailing label (Figure 5-66).

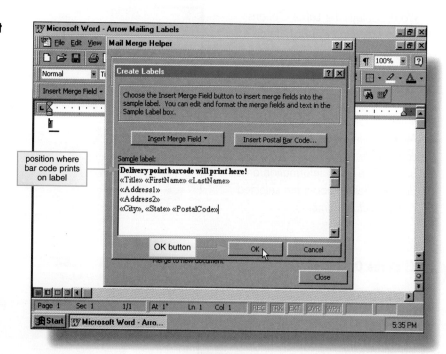

FIGURE 5-66

12 Click the OK button. Click the Close button in the Mail Merge Helper dialog box. When the main document displays in the document window, click the Merge to Printer button on the Mail Merge toolbar. When the Print dialog box displays, click the OK button.

Word returns to the document window with the mailing label layout as the main document (Figure 5-67). If your mailing labels display an error message indicating the zip code portion of the bar code is not valid, ignore the message because the bar codes will print correctly.

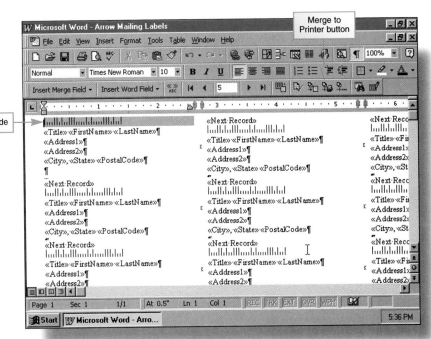

FIGURE 5-67

13 Retrieve the mailing labels from the printer.

The mailing labels print as shown in Figure 5-68. The mailing labels print in zip code order because earlier in this project you sorted the data source by zip code.

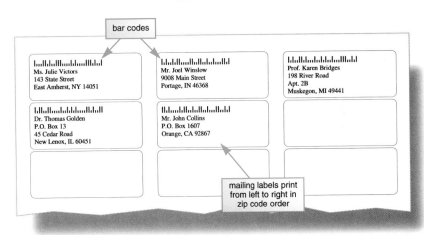

FIGURE 5-68

Saving the Mailing Labels

You should save the mailing labels again because you have made several changes since the initial save.

TO SAVE A DOCUMENT A SECOND TIME

1 Click the Save button on the Standard toolbar.

Word saves the main document for the mailing labels on a floppy disk in drive A with the same file name, Arrow Mailing Labels.

Addressing and Printing Envelopes

Instead of generating mailing labels to affix to envelopes, your printer may have the capability of printing directly onto the envelopes. To print the label information directly on the envelopes, you will follow the same basic steps as you did to generate the mailing labels. Perform the following steps to address and print the envelopes.

Steps **To Address and Print Envelopes from an Existing Data Source**

1 **Click the New button on the Standard toolbar. Click File on the menu bar and then click Save As. Type** Arrow Envelopes **in the File name text box. If necessary, click the Save in box arrow and then click 3½ Floppy (A:). Click the Save button in the Save As dialog box. Click Tools on the menu bar and then click Mail Merge. When the Mail Merge Helper dialog box displays, click the Create button and then point to Envelopes.**

Word displays a new document window for the main document for the envelopes (Figure 5-69). The file name of the new document is Arrow Envelopes.

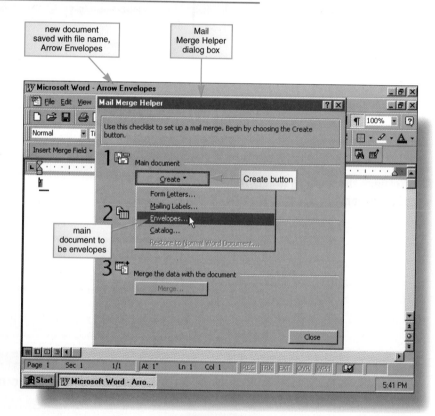

FIGURE 5-69

More *About*
Envelopes

Instead of addressing envelopes from a data source, you can print an envelope(s) for a single address. Click Envelopes and Labels on the Tools menu, click the Envelopes tab, type the name, delivery address, and return address in the appropriate text boxes, then click the Print button in the Envelopes and Labels dialog box.

2 Click Envelopes. In the Microsoft Word dialog box, click the Active Window button. When the Mail Merge Helper dialog box displays, click the Get Data button and then click Open Data Source. When Word displays the Open Data Source dialog box, click the Look in box arrow and then, if necessary, click 3½ Floppy (A:). Click the file name, Arrow Customer List, and then click the Open button in the Open Data Source dialog box. In the Microsoft Word dialog box, click the Set Up Main Document button. If necessary, click the Envelope Options tab when the Envelope Options dialog box first opens.

Word displays the *Envelope Options dialog box* (Figure 5-70). The *Envelope Options sheet* is used to specify size of the envelopes. Depending on your printer, your Envelope Options sheet may differ from this figure.

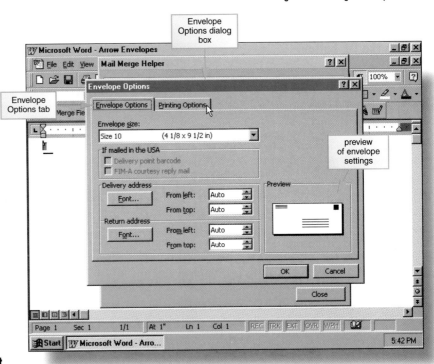

FIGURE 5-70

3 Click the Printing Options tab.

Word displays the *Printing Options sheet* in the Envelope Options dialog box (Figure 5-71). In the Feed method area, you can indicate how the envelopes are positioned in the printer. Depending on your printer, your Printing Options sheet may differ from this figure.

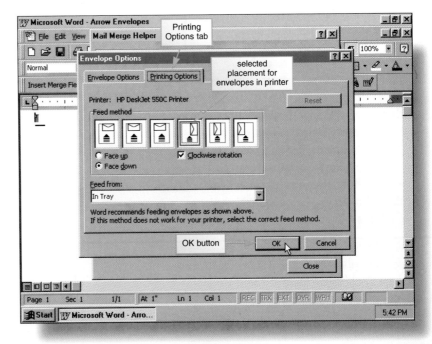

FIGURE 5-71

4 **Click the OK button.**

*Word displays the **Envelope address dialog box.** You insert merge fields into the Sample envelope address area of the this dialog box the same way you inserted merge fields into the main document for the mailing labels and the main document for the form letter.*

5 **Follow Steps 9 through 11 on pages WD 5.43 and WD 5.44 to address the envelopes with a bar code.**

Word displays the completed envelope layout (Figure 5-72).

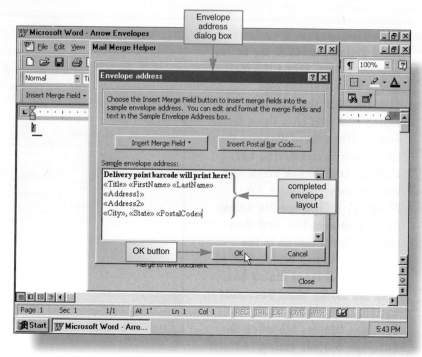

FIGURE 5-72

6 **Click the OK button in the Envelope address dialog box. When the Mail Merge Helper dialog box displays, click the Close button. When the main document displays in the document window, click the return address and type** Arrow Electronics **and then press the ENTER key. Type** 56 Madison Avenue **and then press the ENTER key. Type** Chicago, IL 60602 **and then click the Save button on the Standard toolbar. If necessary, insert envelopes in the printer. Click the Merge to Printer button on the Mail Merge toolbar. When the Print dialog box displays, click the OK button.**

Word returns to the document window with the envelope layout as the main document (Figure 5-73). If your envelope displays an error message indicating the zip code portion of the bar code is not valid, ignore the message because the bar code will print correctly.

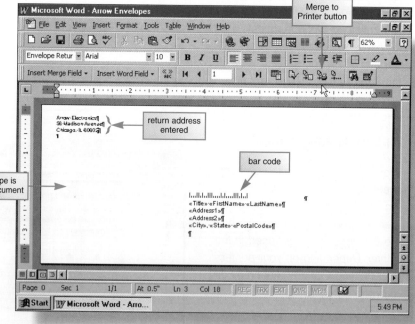

FIGURE 5-73

7 **Retrieve the envelopes from the printer.**

The envelopes print as shown in Figure 5-74. The envelopes print in zip code order because earlier in this project you sorted the data source by zip code.

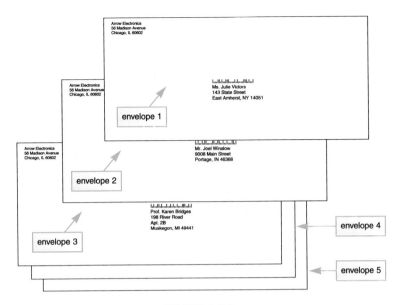

FIGURE 5-74

Closing All Open Files and Quitting Word

You currently have four files open: Arrow Customer List, Arrow Form Letter, Arrow Mailing Labels, and Arrow Envelopes. Rather than closing each one individually, you can close all open files at once as described in these steps.

TO CLOSE ALL OPEN DOCUMENTS

1 Press and hold the SHIFT key. While holding the SHIFT key, click File on the menu bar. Release the SHIFT key.

2 Click Close All.

3 If the Microsoft Word dialog box displays, click the Yes button to save any changes made to the individual documents. If you do not want the data records to be saved in sorted order (by zip code), you would click the No button when Word asks if you want to save changes to Arrow Customer List.

Word closes all open documents and displays a blank document window.

Project 5 is complete. Follow this step to quit Word.

TO QUIT WORD

1 Click the Close button in the Word window.

The Word window closes.

More *About*
Closing Form Letters

Word always asks if you want to save changes when you close a main document, even if you just saved the document. If you are sure that no additional changes were made to the document, click the No button; otherwise, click the Yes button – just to be safe.

Project Summary

Project 5 introduced you to generating form letters and their corresponding mailing labels and envelopes. First, you created the Arrow Electronics letterhead, then identified the main document and created a data source. Next, you created the main document for the form letter. The form letter included merge fields and an IF field. In this project, you learned how to merge and print all the form letters, as well as only certain records in the data source. You also learned how to sort the data source records. Finally, you addressed and printed mailing labels and envelopes to accompany the form letters.

What You Should Know

Having completed this project, you now should be able to perform the following tasks:

- Address and Print Envelopes from an Existing Data Source *(WD 5.46)*
- Address and Print Mailing Labels from an Existing Data Source *(WD 5.41)*
- Bottom Border a Paragraph *(WD 5.8)*
- Close All Open Documents *(WD 5.49)*
- Create a Data Source in Word *(WD 5.13)*
- Create Company Letterhead *(WD 5.7)*
- Display Nonprinting Characters *(WD 5.7)*
- Enter the Salutation and the First Paragraph in the Form Letter *(WD 5.27)*
- Identify the Main Document *(WD 5.10)*
- Insert an IF Field into the Main Document *(WD 5.28)*
- Insert Merge Fields into the Main Document *(WD 5.25)*
- Insert the Current Date into a Document *(WD 5.24)*
- Merge the Documents and Print the Form Letters *(WD 5.34)*
- Print Field Codes in the Main Document *(WD 5.32)*
- Quit Word *(WD 5.49)*
- Redefine the Normal Style *(WD 5.21)*
- Save a Document a Second Time *(WD 5.45)*
- Save the Company Letterhead in a File *(WD 5.9)*
- Save the Main Document with a New File Name *(WD 5.21)*
- Selectively Merge and Print Records *(WD 5.36)*
- Sort the Data Records *(WD 5.39)*
- Start Word *(WD 5.6)*
- Switch from the Data Source to the Main Document *(WD 5.13)*
- Turn Field Codes On or Off for Display *(WD 5.31)*
- View Merged Data in the Main Document *(WD 5.40)*

 Test Your Knowledge

1 True/False

Instructions: Circle T if the statement is true or F if the statement is false.

T F   1. Sorting is the process of blending a data source into a main document.
T F   2. A data source contains the variable, or changing, text in a form letter.
T F   3. A data source is always a Word table.
T F   4. When a data source is the current document, the buttons on the Standard toolbar change.
T F   5. To redefine the Normal style, click the Normal Style button on the Standard toolbar to display the Redefine Style dialog box.
T F   6. To insert a merge field into the main document, type the beginning chevron, followed by the field name, followed by the ending chevron.
T F   7. A condition is composed of an expression, a comparison operator, and a final expression.
T F   8. Use one procedure to display field codes on the screen and another procedure to print them.
T F   9. When field codes are off, the word, MERGEFIELD, displays in front of every merge field in the main document.
T F   10. When merging a data source to a main document, Word by default suppresses empty fields from the data source.

2 Multiple Choice

Instructions: Circle the correct response.

1. To display the border palette, click the _____ button.
   a. Border Palette   b. Rule   c. Palette   d. none of the above
2. Each row in a data source is called a _____.
   a. character   b. field   c. record   d. file
3. The first row in a data source is called the _____.
   a. header row   b. data row   c. initial row   d. start row
4. To update a field, such as the current date, in the document window, press the _____ key.
   a. F6   b. F7   c. F8   d. F9
5. Which of the following is an invalid field name?
   a. FirstNameofCustomer   b. Title   c. Local_Resident   d. 1st_Name
6. In the main document, the Mail Merge toolbar is located between the _____ and the _____.
   a. title bar, menu bar   c. Formatting toolbar, ruler
   b. menu bar, Standard toolbar   d. Standard toolbar, Formatting toolbar
7. In an IF field, a null string is represented as _____.
   a. " " " "   b. "NULL"   c. "0"   d. " "
8. Which of the following mathematical operators stands for not equal to or does not match?
   a. !=!   b. <=   c. >=   d. none of the above

(continued)

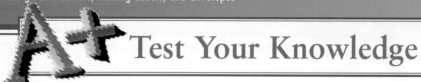

Test Your Knowledge

Multiple Choice *(continued)*

9. Text expressions in an IF field must be surrounded by _____.
   a. equal signs (=)   b. apostrophes (')   c. quotation marks (")   d. hyphens (-)
10. When field codes are off, merge fields in the main document are surrounded by _____.
    a. quotation marks   b. chevrons   c. parenthesEs   d. none of the above

3 Understanding the Database Toolbar

Instructions: In Figure 5-75, arrows point to various buttons on the Database toolbar when a data source is the active document. In the spaces provided, identify each button.

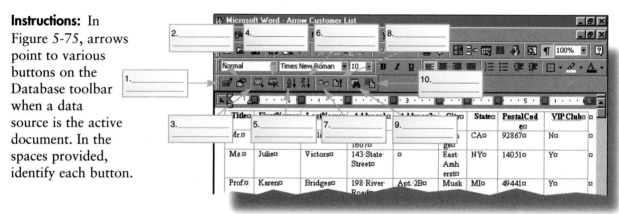

FIGURE 5-75

4 Understanding the Mail Merge Toolbar

Instructions: In Figure 5-76, arrows point to various buttons on the Mail Merge toolbar. In the spaces provided, identify each button.

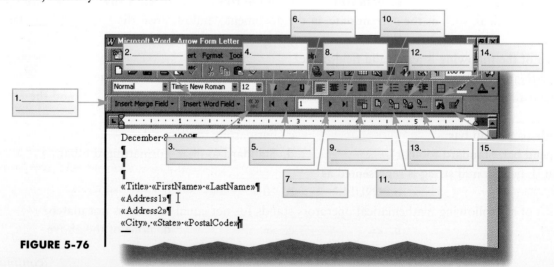

FIGURE 5-76

Use Help

1 Reviewing Project Activities

Instructions: Perform the following tasks using a computer.

1. Start Word. If the Office Assistant is on your screen, click it to display its balloon. If the Office Assistant is not on your screen, click the Office Assistant button on the Standard toolbar.
2. Type create a data source in the What would you like to do? text box. Click the Search button. Click the Create a new mail-merge data source in Word topic. Read and print the information.
3. Click the Help Topics button to display the Help Topics: Microsoft Word dialog box. Click the Contents tab. Double-click the Assembling Documents with Mail Merge book. Double-click the Customizing Mail Merge with Word Fields book. Double-click the Merge fields topic. Read and print the information.
4. Click the Help Topics button. Click the Index tab. Type styles in the top text box labeled 1 and then double-click the changing topic in the list box labeled 2. Read and print the information.
5. Click the Help Topics button. Click the Find tab. Type fields and then double-click the About fields topic. Read and print the information. Close any open Help window and the Office Assistant.

2 Expanding on the Basics

Instructions: Use Word Help to better understand the topics listed below. Answer the questions on your own paper or hand in the printed Help topic to your instructor.

1. In this project, you merged a main document to a data source. Sometimes when using mail merge, error messages display or you need to change existing settings. Use the Office Assistant to determine how to remedy these situations.
   a. You get a message saying your data file is a mail merge main document. How do you remove the main document designation from the data source?
   b. How do you change the mailing label or envelope size in an existing main document?
2. In this project, you created a data source as a Word table. Use the Contents tab in the Help Topics: Microsoft Word dialog box to answer the following questions about external data sources.
   a. What types of files, other than a Word table, can be used as a data source?
   b. What is a header source? When should you use one?
   c. What Office programs can you use to make a list of names and addresses for mail merge?
3. In this project, you addressed envelopes using the existing data source. Use the Index tab in the Help Topics: Microsoft Word dialog box to determine how to address a single envelope.
4. In this project, you created a condition in the mail merge main document. Use the Find tab in the Help Topics: Microsoft Word dialog box to give an example of a multiple selection rule (condition) using the And; also give an example using the Or. Then, explain each of the examples.

Apply Your Knowledge

1 Working with a Form Letter

Instructions: Start Word. Open the document, apply-5, from the Word folder on the Data Disk that accompanies this book. The document is a main document for Riverton College. You are to print field codes in the main document (Figure 5-77), edit and print a data source, and then merge the form letters to a file and the printer.

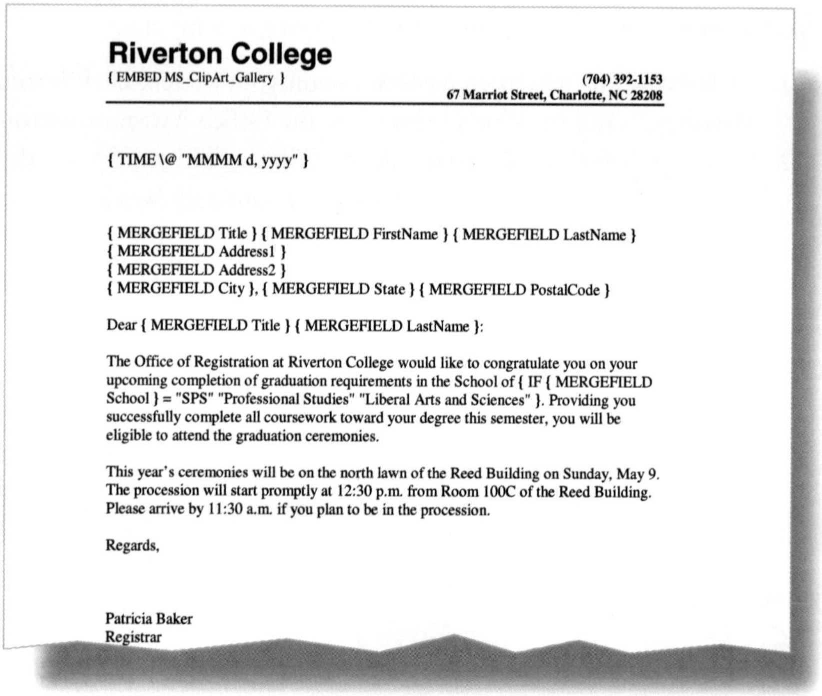

Perform the following tasks.

1. Click the Print button on the Standard toolbar.

2. Click File on the menu bar and then click Print. Click the Options button in the Print dialog box. Click Field codes to select the check box and then click the OK button. When the Print dialog box redisplays, click the OK button.

Riverton College
{ EMBED MS_ClipArt_Gallery }
                   (704) 392-1153
67 Marriot Street, Charlotte, NC 28208

{ TIME \@ "MMMM d, yyyy" }

{ MERGEFIELD Title } { MERGEFIELD FirstName } { MERGEFIELD LastName }
{ MERGEFIELD Address1 }
{ MERGEFIELD Address2 }
{ MERGEFIELD City }, { MERGEFIELD State } { MERGEFIELD PostalCode }

Dear { MERGEFIELD Title } { MERGEFIELD LastName }:

The Office of Registration at Riverton College would like to congratulate you on your upcoming completion of graduation requirements in the School of { IF { MERGEFIELD School } = "SPS" "Professional Studies" "Liberal Arts and Sciences" }. Providing you successfully complete all coursework toward your degree this semester, you will be eligible to attend the graduation ceremonies.

This year's ceremonies will be on the north lawn of the Reed Building on Sunday, May 9. The procession will start promptly at 12:30 p.m. from Room 100C of the Reed Building. Please arrive by 11:30 a.m. if you plan to be in the procession.

Regards,

Patricia Baker
Registrar

FIGURE 5-77

3. Click File on the menu bar and then click Print. Click the Options button in the Print dialog box. Click Field codes to turn off the check box and then click the OK button. When the Print dialog box redisplays, click the Close button.

4. Click the Edit Data Source button on the Mail Merge toolbar and then click the View Source button to display the data source, Riverton Graduate List, as a Word table.

5. Click the Add New Record button on the Database toolbar. Add a record containing your personal information; use SPS as the School.

6. Click Table on the menu bar and then click Table AutoFormat. When the Table AutoFormat dialog box displays, scroll through the list of formats, and then click Grid 8. Click the OK button.

7. Click in the LastName column of the data source. Click the Sort Ascending button on the Database toolbar.

8. Click File on the menu bar and then click Save As. Use the file name Revised Riverton Graduate List.

9. Click the Print button on the Standard toolbar.

10. Click the Mail Merge Main Document button on the Database toolbar.

11. Click the Merge to New Document button on the Mail Merge toolbar. Click the Print button on the Standard toolbar. Click File on the menu bar and then click the Close button. Click the No button in the Microsoft Word dialog box.

12. Click the Merge to Printer button on the Mail Merge toolbar. Click the OK button.

13. Press and hold the SHIFT key and then click File on the menu bar. Release the SHIFT key. Click Close All.

1 Creating a Data Source, Form Letter, and Mailing Labels

Problem: Janice Rivers, the owner of Rose Card and Gift Shop, has asked you to notify all customers of the shop's new holiday hours. You decide to send a form letter (Figure 5-78) to all customers.

Instructions:

1. Create the letterhead shown at the top of Figure 5-78 using a header. Save the letterhead with the file name Rose Letterhead.

2. Begin the mail merge process by clicking Tools on the menu bar and then clicking Mail Merge. Specify the current document window as the main document.

3. Create the data source shown in Figure 5-79.

4. In the Data Form dialog box, click the View Data Source button to view the data source in table form. Save the data source with the name Rose Customer List.

5. Print the data source.

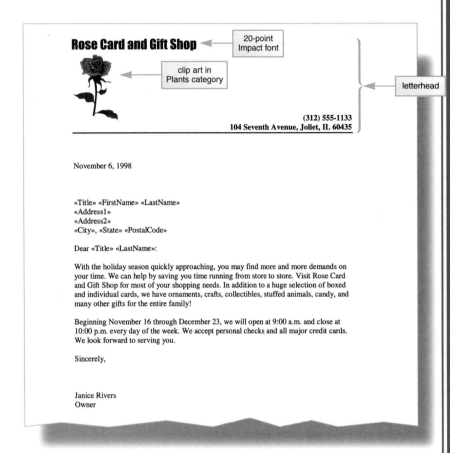

FIGURE 5-78

6. Switch to the main document. Save the main document with a new file name, Rose Form Letter. Change the Normal style to a font size of 12 for the main document. Create the main document for the form letter shown in Figure 5-78. The current date should print at the top of the form letter.

7. Save the main document for the form letter again.

8. Print the main document.

Title	FirstName	LastName	Address1	Address2	City	State	PostalCode
Mr.	Ian	Peters	P.O. Box 19		Orland Park	IL	60462
Ms.	Charlotte	Winters	44 River Road		Joliet	IL	60435
Mrs.	Karen	Bissel	105 Lake Street	Apt. 3D	New Lenox	IL	60451
Dr.	John	Groves	P.O. Box 67		Mokena	IL	60448
Mr.	Samuel	Easton	123 Michigan Avenue	Apt. 5A	Joliet	IL	60435

FIGURE 5-79

(continued)

In the Lab

Creating a Data Source, Form Letter, and Mailing Labels *(continued)*

9. Merge and print the form letters.
10. Click the New button on the Standard toolbar and then address mailing labels using the same data source you used for the form letters. Put bar codes on the mailing labels.
11. Save the mailing labels with the name Rose Mailing Labels.
12. Print the mailing labels.
13. If your printer allows, address envelopes using the same data source you used for the form letters. Put bar codes on the envelopes. Save the envelopes with the name Rose Envelopes. Print the envelopes.

2 Creating a Data Source and a Form Letter with an IF Field

Problem: You are the owner of Magic Time! You have decided to use a form letter to offer a discount to all current customers (Figure 5-80). For those customers who recently ordered a full magic act, you offer a 20% discount; for those who ordered a mini performance, you offer a 10% discount. You decide to use an IF field for this task.

Instructions:

1. Create the letterhead shown at the top of Figure 5-80 using a header. Save the letterhead with the file name, Magic Time Letterhead.

2. Begin the mail merge process by clicking Tools on the menu bar and then clicking Mail Merge. Specify the current document window as the main document.

3. Create the data source shown in Figure 5-81.

4. In the Data Form dialog box, click the View Data Source button to view the data source in table form. Save the data source with the name Magic Time Customer List.

5. Print the data source.

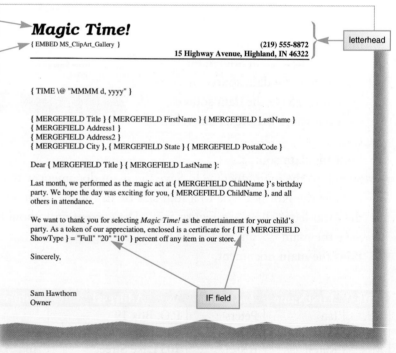

FIGURE 5-80

In the Lab

Title	FirstName	LastName	Address1	Address2	City	State	PostalCode	ChildName	ShowType
Mrs.	Juanita	Evans	175 Gordon Drive		Highland	IN	46322	Bobby	Full
Mr.	Frank	Zimmer	P.O. Box 15		Munster	IN	46321	Jackie	Mini
Ms.	Louise	Roseman	198 Hohman Avenue	Apt. 3A	Hammond	IN	46322	Julie	Mini
Mr.	Conrad	Jones	81 Duluth Street		Highland	IN	46322	Johnny	Full
Mrs.	Brenda	Duley	145 Calumet Avenue	Apt. 17	Hammond	IN	46323	Amanda	Mini

FIGURE 5-81

6. Switch to the main document. Save the main document with a new file name, Magic Time Form Letter. Change the Normal style to a font size of 12 for the main document. Create the main document for the form letter shown in Figure 5-80. The current date should print at the top of the form letter. The IF field tests if ShowType is equal to Full; if it is, then the discount is 20%; otherwise the discount is 10%.

7. Save the main document for the form letter again.

8. Print the main document with field codes on. Do not forget to turn the field codes off.

9. Merge and print the form letters.

3 Creating a Form Letter Using an Access Database as the Data Source

Problem: On Target Travel would like to thank its customers for their business (Figure 5-82). The customer list is stored in an Access database table. If you are using the *Complete Concepts and Techniques* book, the database file is on the Data Disk that accompanies this book; otherwise, see your instructor for the location of the database file. You are to use the Access database table as the data source in the form letters.

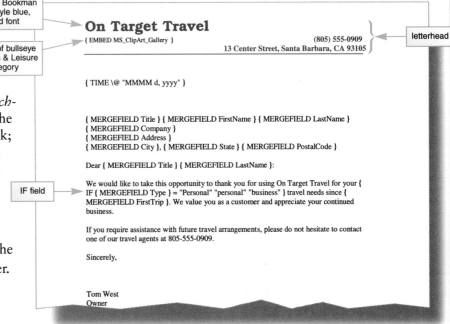

FIGURE 5-82

Instructions:

1. Create the letterhead shown at the top of Figure 5-82 using a header. Save the letterhead with the file name On Target Letterhead.

2. Begin the mail merge process by clicking Tools on the menu bar and then clicking Mail Merge. Specify the current document window as the main document.

(continued)

In the Lab

Creating a Form Letter Using an Access Database as the Data Source *(continued)*

3. In the Open Data Source dialog box, click the Files of type box arrow and then click MS Access Databases. Click On Target Client List and then click the Open button. Click Customers in the Microsoft Access dialog box and then click the OK button.

4. Click the Edit the Main Document button. Save the main document with a new file name, On Target Form Letters. Change the Normal style to a font size of 12 for the main document. Create the main document for the form letter shown in Figure 5-82 on the previous page. The current date should print at the top of the form letter. The IF field tests the Type field value: if Type is Personal, then print the word personal; otherwise print the word business.

5. Save the main document for the form letter again.

6. Print the main document with field codes. Do not forget to turn off the field codes after printing them.

7. Merge and print the form letters.

8. Click the New button on the Standard toolbar and address mailing labels using the same data source you used for the form letters. Put bar codes on the mailing labels.

9. Save the mailing labels with the name On Target Mailing Labels.

10. Print the mailing labels.

11. If your printer allows, address envelopes using the same data source you used for the form letters. Put bar codes on the envelopes. Save the envelopes with the name On Target Envelopes. Print the envelopes.

Cases and Places

The difficulty of these case studies varies: ◗ are the least difficult; ◗◗ are more difficult; and ◗◗◗ are the most difficult.

1 ◗ Your school is organizing a bazaar for the weekend of May 16 and May 17. The bazaar will have food booths, arts and crafts, door prizes, games, and contests. As event coordinator, you are responsible for recruiting your fellow classmates to assist during the bazaar. A variety of positions are required: food preparation, food sales, arts and crafts sales, booth setup, announcers, game directors, ticket collectors, cashiers, and more. Create a form letter persuading your classmates to assist during the bazaar. Be sure the form letter has an attractive letterhead containing the school name, address, and an appropriate clip art file. Obtain the names and addresses of five of your classmates and use them as records in the data source. Then, address and print accompanying labels or envelopes for the form letters.

2 ◗ You are coordinating the tenth-annual family reunion for your relatives. The reunion will be held at Grover Park in Wilmington on Saturday, August 8. You have reserved the pavilion at the park from 11:00 a.m. to 6:00 p.m. Each family is to bring a dish for eight to share. You will be providing burgers and brats for the grill, as well as all condiments and paper products. Family members should also bring mitts, bats, volleyballs, horseshoes, and other outdoor game equipment. Create a form letter announcing the family reunion to your relatives. Be sure the form letter has an attractive letterhead with your family name and an appropriate clip art file. Obtain the names and addresses of five of your family members and use them as records in the data source. Then, address and print accompanying labels or envelopes for the form letters.

3 ◗◗ You are currently seeking an employment position in your field of study. You already have prepared a resume and would like to send it to a group of potential employers. You decide to design a cover letter to send with the resume. Obtain a recent newspaper and cut out five classified advertisements pertaining to your field of study. Create the cover letter for your resume as a form letter. Be sure the cover letter has an attractive letterhead containing your name, address, and telephone number, as well as an appropriate clip art file. Use the information in the classified ads for the data source. The data source should contain potential employers' names, addresses, and position type. Use an IF field in your cover letter that prints the words, full-time or part-time, where appropriate, which will depend on whether or not it is a full-time position. Be sure to add a field to your data source for the comparison. Then, address and print accompanying labels or envelopes for the cover letters. Turn in the want ads with your printouts.

Cases and Places

200 MHz

4 ▶▶ Everyone has strong opinions about one or more of many subjects related to government issues (e.g., taxation, welfare, the justice system, etc.). Pick a subject of interest to you and then draft a letter persuading our congressmen to take some action regarding your position. Create your letter as a form letter. Be sure the letter has an attractive letterhead containing your name, address and telephone number, as well as an appropriate clip art file. Surf the Internet for five current senators or representatives. Use their names, addresses, party affiliation, and position as records in your data source. Use two IF fields in your form letter: one to print the party affiliation (Republican or Democrat), where appropriate, and the other to print their position (senator or representative), where appropriate. Be sure to add fields to your data source for these comparisons. Then, address and print accompanying labels or envelopes for the cover letters.

5 ▶▶ You are director of a local charity organization, which receives donations for many causes. This month's theme is health. Pick a health issue of concern to you (e.g., cancer, diabetes, AIDS, etc.) and then draft a letter persuading local businesses to donate to your charity so you can forward the contribution to the appropriate facility. Obtain the names of two facilities in your area, such as hospitals or hospices. Research your health issue either at the library or on the Internet to obtain impressive statistics and other information and then create a form letter containing your research findings. Be sure the letter has an attractive letterhead with an appropriate clip art file. Obtain the actual names and addresses of five major industries in your area. Use these businesses as records in your data source. Use an IF field in your form letter to print the name of the facility closest (e.g., hospital or hospice) to the business from which you seek a donation. Then, address and print accompanying labels or envelopes for the cover letters.

6 ▶▶▶ If Microsoft Access is installed on your system, you can use it to create a table and then use that table as the data source in a mail merge document. Start Access and then create the table in Project 5 on page WD 5.12 as an Access database table. You may need to use Help in Access to assist you in the procedure for creating and saving a database that contains a table. Quit Access. Start Word. Begin the mail merge process as discussed in Project 5. When specifying the data source, click Open Data Source. In the Open Data Source dialog box, change the file type to MS Access Databases and then click the database name of the file you created in Access. Create the form letter in Project 5 so it uses the fields in the Access database table. Then, address and print accompanying labels or envelopes for the cover letters.

7 ▶▶▶ If Microsoft Access is installed on your system, you can use it to create a table and then use that table as the data source in a mail merge document. Start Access and then create the table for the In the Lab 2 exercise as an Access table (Figure 5-81 on page WD 5.57). You may need to use Help in Access to assist you in the procedure for creating and saving a database that contains a table. Quit Access. Start Word. Begin the mail merge process as discussed in Project 5. When specifying the data source, click Open Data Source. In the Open Data Source dialog box, change the file type to MS Access Databases and then click the database name of the file you created in Access. Create the form letter in Figure 5-80 on page WD 5.56 so it uses the fields in the Access database table. Then, address and print accompanying labels or envelopes for the cover letters.

Microsoft *Word 97*

Creating a Professional Newsletter

Objectives:

You will have mastered the material in this project when you can:

▌ Define desktop publishing terminology
▌ Add ruling lines above and below paragraphs
▌ Insert special symbols in a document
▌ Format a document into multiple columns
▌ Format a dropped capital letter in a paragraph
▌ Position a graphic between columns
▌ Insert a column break
▌ Place a vertical rule between columns
▌ Create a pull-quote
▌ Use the Format Painter button
▌ Create a macro to automate a task
▌ Run a macro
▌ Delete a macro
▌ Change the color(s) in a graphic
▌ Add a text box to a graphic
▌ Place a border on a page

Project 6

From **A**cademic to **Z**estful

A Newsletter for Every Interest

Women With Wheels. At- Home Dad. Penn State Sports Medicine Newsletter. From the church bulletin to the condominium association activity log, a newsletter exits to suit basically every interest. Each year an estimated 200,000 newsletters are published regularly in the United States, and more than 20,000 appear on the Internet. These numbers are growing as computer users discover desktop publishing software and the dynamic formatting features of word processing programs such as Microsoft Word 97.

Internet neophytes can surf to *NewbieNewz,*™ a free Net newsletter that offers helpful cyberspace advice and instruction. The two million American fathers who stay home with their preschoolers can cure their isolation and find helpful child-care and home business tips with *At-Home Dad*, which was started and is produced by a father who lost his job. The stress and special health problems affecting workers who work when the majority of people sleep are explored in *Shiftworker News*.

Other specialty newsletters have been created, such as *Catnip* for feline

---

Volume VII, No. 2

Women With Wheels ™

The Quarterly Newsletter on [...]

Automobile Rallying is Great Fun
by: Susan Frissell, Ph.D.

Now that Summer is here it is rally time! In the past couple of years, I've had the pleasure of being involved in several auto "rallies." Rallies with sport clubs, media associations, and specialty groups (convertibles, sport/GT cars). And, it's been far too much fun! In fact, the people, the enthusiasm, and the comraderie are almost palpable.

There are rallies that are strictly for fun, and there are rallies for the serious driver. Time-and-Distance rallies are the type of rally you're more likely to find in connection with the avid sports-car club member. For instance, Corvette owners, Porsche owners, and the like, may participate in a Time-and-Distance rally where specific methods of timing, penalties and scoring are adhered to. Time-and-Distance rally scoring is based on the ability of contestants to maintain certain predetermined average speeds over a measured course. Time is an essential ingredient, although distance may also be used as a tie-breaker or as an additional [...]

Just What is a Rally?

There are a wide variety of auto events that are classified as "rallies." A group of sports-car enthusiasts might get together and plan a picnic, following a specific route. Sponsored by the Club, this cruise may also be referred to as a "tour" or "caravan." As a member of The Midwest Automotive Media Association (M.A.M.A.), I participate in a test-drive of several new model vehicles, provided by the manufacturers. We refer to our twice-a-year events as "rallies", and as members, we drive a specific route, switching cars and drivers at various checkpoints along the [...]

Registration for most, if not all, rallies requires an entrance fee. This can range anywhere from $16 to a couple of thousand dollars (The Great North American Race). Generally, the fees are very reasonable, and will sometimes include snacks (cold drinks, cookies, etc.) at the checkpoints or rest stops, as well as mo- [...] events, such as T-shirts, key chains, etc. [...] included in your packet, [...] route instructions. Thus [...] to go, and what average speeds to [...] along the route. In short, they [...] get where you're [...] the exact [...]

Why rally, [...]
And it's easy to do [...]
the family van, sta[...]
Winning—or serious[...]

LANDSPEED LOUISE

SUMMER

AT-HOME DAD NETWORK

AT-HOME DAD NETWORK ™

DAD-TO-DAD

With summer just around the corner, many DAD-to-DAD chapters will be taking their activities outside! A few events planned for the Atlanta chapter include: weekend camping and canoe trip, field trip to a horse ranch, and picnics in the park. So, put on the shorts and T-shirts and hit the outdoors! Speaking of T-shirts, DAD-to-DAD will have T-shirts available to purchase very soon for both children and adults. Look for further info in the next At-Home Dad newsletter. Also, please call me at (770) 643-5964, or dadtodad@aol.com if you need help either getting started or deciding on what activities are best.

Curtis Cooper - Founder, DAD-to-DAD

CHARLOTTESVILLE

March has been an active month for the Charlottesville-Albemarle Dad-to-Dad group. Three more fathers have expressed an interest in the group as a result of some television coverage, an ad in the C-Ville Weekly and a friendly invitation at Jungle Max. We've even had one very brave mother come to one of the play sessions. Also, Michael Duggan has worked hard to create a Home Page for our group on the Comet.Net Web Site. Use the address http://www.comet.net/clubs/dad-to-dad and check us out! Oprah presented the Parent of the Week Award to [...] Cooper. The segment on Curtis [...] proud, and it proved to be an [...] follow-up to the story about our [...] Later that week, our group size [...] three! One father and his daught[...] like to join us if we ever do a [...] playgroup. He's also intereste[...] Dads' Night-Out Dinners. Anot[...] and his child plan to join us on[...] We'll try to schedule tw[...] playgroups for this month.
- Dan Dunsmore, Charlottesv[...]

If you would like to send a [...] update for publication about yo[...] to-DAD chapter or any pl[...] experiences, please send it to our [...] will share it with the readers.

NETWORK BUZZ

Keith Dilley, the at-home dad of sextuplets (profiled in issue 3), has gone to "work" as an airline reservationist. (Ah, the easy life!) His kids are now 3 years old. To keep them in the playroom they use 3 metal baby gates on top of each other, slimed with vaseline.

Brian Basset, the cartoonist who draws Adam, the at-home dad comic strip, now has E-mail. Cyberdads can drop him a line at adamathome@aol.com. See page 7 for info on his new book.

ALL RIGHT! I HAVE E-MAIL!

If you get this early enough and have cable, check out CNBC's feature on this newsletter, Tues, May 28th at 7pm EST, on their show called *The Money Club.* [...]Home Dad readers Casey Spencer [...] appeared on the [...]

NETWOR[...]
Please ad[...]
Network [...]
Brightwood [...]
or e-mail to [...]

Name [...]

Penn State Sports Medicine Newsletter - Volum... - Microsoft Internet Explorer

File   Edit   View   Go   Favorites   Help

Back   Forward   Stop   Refresh   Home   Search   Favorites   Print   Font   Mail   Edit

Address http://cac.psu.edu/~hgk2/may97.html

Links Best of the Web   Today's Links   Web Gallery   Product News   Micros[...]

PENN STATE

SPORTS MEDICINE NEWSLETTER
The Newsletter of Athletic Performance

Volume 5, Number 9. May '97

Table of Contents

☐ Supraventricular Tachycardis: Your Cheatin' Heart

lovers, published by Tufts University School of Veterinary Medicine, the *Frugal Bugle* for penny-pinchers, *Childfree Network* for individuals without children who desire equity in the corporate world, *Women with Wheels* for consumers wanting to learn about maintaining and purchasing cars, and *Naturally Well* for health-conscious individuals interested in homeopathic remedies. Other newsletter titles need no explanation: *Thrifty Traveler*, *Spirit of Route 66*, *FluteSounds*, *Growth Stock Outlook*, and *Dreaded Broccoli*.

Baby boomers' interests account for an upswing in specialized publications. For example, *Homeground*, a quarterly newsletter started by a former gardening columnist, and *Virtual Garden*, a newsletter on the Internet being read more than 35,000 times a week, are among the newsletters filling the gardening niche. Also, more than 30 health and nutrition newsletters have sprung up in the past decade with such titles as *Health After 50*, *Nutrition Advocate*, *What Doctors Don't Tell You*, *Health Wisdom for Women*, and *Yale Children's Health Letter*.

Internet users can find a plethora of electronic newsletters, some which also are available in printed versions. Investors might surf to the *Prime Time Investor Mutual Fund Family Newsletters*, which offers more than 100 newsletters discussing thousands of mutual funds and *The Right Investments*, giving daily performance results. Sports lovers can find *Sports Talk NFL News*, the *Trout Talk Fantasy Football Newsletter*, and the *Penn State Sports Medicine Newsletter*. Scientists can discover such diverse sites as the *NATO Science Forum*, the *Electronic Zoo*, and the *History of Australian Science Newsletter*.

A newsletter to evaluate other newsletters even exists. Each month the reviewers for *Newsletter Design* critique publications submitted by organizations. Calling itself a publication for "the desktop generation," *Newsletter Design* examines the overall layout, design, nameplate, shading, ruling lines, and graphics and then offers suggestions for improvement.

Americans are reading print and electronic newsletters in record numbers to satisfy their needs for education and entertainment. And with knowledge of basic design and the formatting features in word processing software, writers can satisfy this thirst for knowledge by using newsletters to express themselves.

Project 6

Microsoft Word 97

Creating a Professional Newsletter

Case Perspective

Tom Watson is president of Amateur Aviators, a club for the hobby pilot. Each month Tom prepares the club's newsletter. Because he has built two biplanes, he decides that this month's feature article will cover the basics of building a plane. He types the article in a Word document, covering items such as buying a kit, workspace, and hangar and concludes with a frequently asked questions and answers section. When finished, Tom realizes the article is quite long – about 650 words. Although the monthly newsletter usually is one page, he decides to make it two pages so the entire article will be in this newsletter. He also types the June announcements into a Word file containing about 150 words; the announcements remind members of the annual dues deadline, the July fly-in, and the Aviator's Catalog.

Now Tom's task is to design the newsletter so the How to Build a Plane article spans the first two columns of page 1 and then continues on page 2; the announcements always are located in the third column of the first page of the *Amateur Aviators* newsletter.

Introduction

Professional looking documents, such as newsletters and brochures, often are created using desktop publishing software. With **desktop publishing software**, you can divide a document into multiple columns, insert pictures and wrap text around them, change fonts and font sizes, add color and lines, and so on to make the document original and attractive. A traditionally held opinion of desktop publishing software, such as PageMaker or Ventura, is that it enables you to load an existing word processing document and enhance it through formatting not provided in your word processor. Word, however, provides you with many of the formatting features that you would find in a desktop publishing package. Thus, you can create professional newsletters and brochures directly within Word.

Project Six – Newsletter

Project 6 uses Word to produce the monthly newsletter shown in Figures 6-1 and 6-2 on the next two pages. The newsletter is a monthly publication for members of Amateur Aviators. Notice that it incorporates the desktop publishing features of Word. The newsletter is divided into three columns; includes a graphic of an airplane and a pull-quote, both with text wrapped around them; has both horizontal and vertical lines to separate distinct areas; has page borders; and uses different fonts, font sizes, and color for various characters and the graphic.

nameplate

ruling lines

AMATEUR AVIATORS

vertical rule

issue information line

Monthly Newsletter

subhead

Vol. VI •June 1998

drop cap

G ET READY

Many preliminary decisions need to be made before you invest in the materials to build your plane. One major factor is cost. Home-built aircraft prices range from $10,000 to $100,000, depending on the make and model. Other major decisions include plan type, shop space, and hangar. This month's feature article addresses these items, as well as frequently asked questions with their answers.

PURCHASING PLAN

Plans and complete kits both are available. A kit has the plans as well as the materials for the plane, which helps to make construction much faster and easier. If you buy your own materials from the purchased plans, however, you can save a considerable amount of money.

If you purchase just the plans, you should have some prior experience with planes and construction. Usually, but not always, the plans come with a materials list. Then, you can

purchase all of the materials at fly markets, from catalogs, or at aircraft supply houses. If you are not familiar with building planes, you will want to buy a

HOW TO BUILD A PLANE

kit, which comes with the plans and all accompanying major materials.

BUYING A KIT

Certain kits require more expertise than others. You can put all the components together yourself, or you can order them pre-assembled. For example, if you are not familiar with welding techniques, then you may be able to order a pre-welded frame. If you have never molded fiberglass parts, you may be able to order pre-made fiberglass parts. The same holds true for sheet metal parts. Wing fabric can be shipped as raw material or already sewn to fit. These pre-assembled kits are especially helpful for the first-time aircraft builder.

Article continues on Page 2...

ANNUAL DUES

It's that time of year again. Annual dues must be received by August 15, 1998. We need your continued support. If you have not yet paid your dues, please send a check or money order for $45 to Howard Peterson at P.O. Box 17, Belmont, California 94002.

MONTHLY FLY-IN

Our July fly-in is scheduled for the morning of Saturday, July 11, at the Hargrove Airport in Oshkosh, Wisconsin. Starting at 6:30 a.m., we are serving a breakfast buffet of pancakes, eggs, bacon, sausage, ham, potatoes, grits, and beverage for $4.50 per person. Please plan to join us. In case of rain, we will fly-in and meet on Sunday, July 12. If you have any questions or would like to help cook food for the breakfast, call Pamela Williams at (754) 555-0980.

AVIATOR'S CATALOG

To order a catalog of plans, kits, and other materials, call (312) 555-1212.

FIGURE 6-1

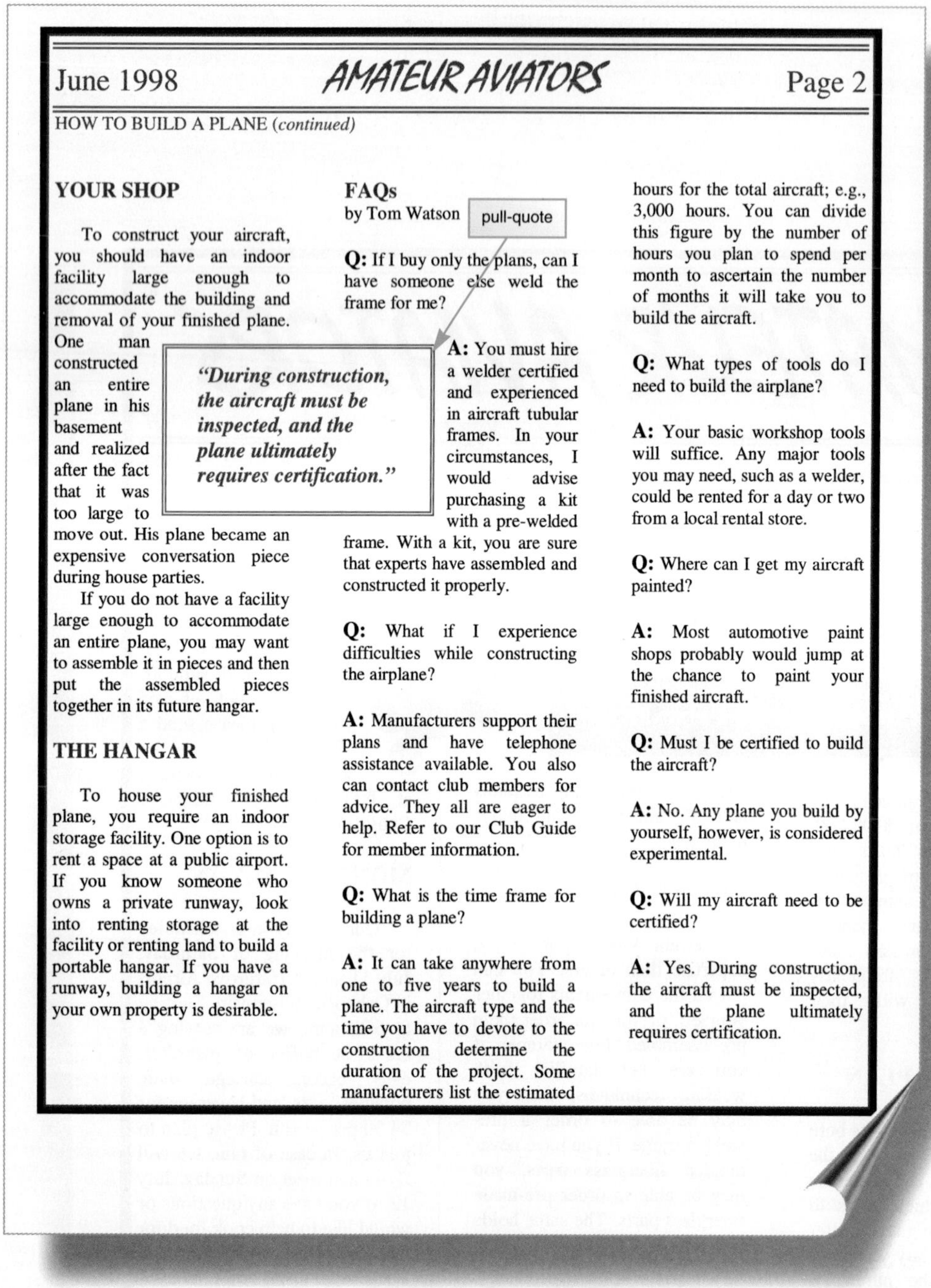

June 1998   *AMATEUR AVIATORS*   Page 2

HOW TO BUILD A PLANE (*continued*)

YOUR SHOP

To construct your aircraft, you should have an indoor facility large enough to accommodate the building and removal of your finished plane. One man constructed an entire plane in his basement and realized after the fact that it was too large to move out. His plane became an expensive conversation piece during house parties.

If you do not have a facility large enough to accommodate an entire plane, you may want to assemble it in pieces and then put the assembled pieces together in its future hangar.

THE HANGAR

To house your finished plane, you require an indoor storage facility. One option is to rent a space at a public airport. If you know someone who owns a private runway, look into renting storage at the facility or renting land to build a portable hangar. If you have a runway, building a hangar on your own property is desirable.

FAQs
by Tom Watson

pull-quote

Q: If I buy only the plans, can I have someone else weld the frame for me?

> *"During construction, the aircraft must be inspected, and the plane ultimately requires certification."*

A: You must hire a welder certified and experienced in aircraft tubular frames. In your circumstances, I would advise purchasing a kit with a pre-welded frame. With a kit, you are sure that experts have assembled and constructed it properly.

Q: What if I experience difficulties while constructing the airplane?

A: Manufacturers support their plans and have telephone assistance available. You also can contact club members for advice. They all are eager to help. Refer to our Club Guide for member information.

Q: What is the time frame for building a plane?

A: It can take anywhere from one to five years to build a plane. The aircraft type and the time you have to devote to the construction determine the duration of the project. Some manufacturers list the estimated

hours for the total aircraft; e.g., 3,000 hours. You can divide this figure by the number of hours you plan to spend per month to ascertain the number of months it will take you to build the aircraft.

Q: What types of tools do I need to build the airplane?

A: Your basic workshop tools will suffice. Any major tools you may need, such as a welder, could be rented for a day or two from a local rental store.

Q: Where can I get my aircraft painted?

A: Most automotive paint shops probably would jump at the chance to paint your finished aircraft.

Q: Must I be certified to build the aircraft?

A: No. Any plane you build by yourself, however, is considered experimental.

Q: Will my aircraft need to be certified?

A: Yes. During construction, the aircraft must be inspected, and the plane ultimately requires certification.

FIGURE 6-2

Desktop Publishing Terminology

As you create professional looking newsletters and brochures, you should be aware of several desktop publishing terms. In Project 6 (Figures 6-1 on the previous page and 6-2), the **nameplate**, or **banner**, is the top portion of the newsletter above the three columns. It contains the title of the newsletter and the **issue information line**. The horizontal lines in the nameplate are called **rules**, or **ruling lines**.

Within the body of the newsletter, a heading, such as GET READY, is called a **subhead**. The vertical line dividing the second and third columns on page 1 is a **vertical rule**. The text that wraps around the airplane graphic is referred to as **wrap-around text**, and the space between the graphic and the words is called the **run-around**.

Document Preparation Steps

Document preparation steps give you an overview of how the newsletter in Figures 6-1 and 6-2 will be developed. The following tasks will be completed in this project:

1. Create the nameplate.
2. Format the first page of the body of the newsletter.
3. Format the second page of the newsletter.
4. Enhance the newsletter with color using the Format Painter button and a macro.
5. Edit the graphic in the newsletter.

The following pages contain a detailed explanation of each of these tasks.

Because this project involves several steps requiring you to drag the mouse, you may want to cancel an action if you drag to the wrong location. Remember that you can always click the Undo button on the Standard toolbar to cancel your most recent action.

Starting Word

Follow these steps to start Word or ask your instructor how to start Word for your system.

TO START WORD

1. Click the Start button on the taskbar.
2. Click New Office Document on the Start menu. If necessary, click the General tab when the New Office Document dialog box first opens.
3. Double-click the Blank Document icon in the General sheet.
4. If the Word screen is not maximized, double-click its title bar to maximize it.

Office starts Word. After a few moments, an empty document titled Document1 displays on the Word screen.

Displaying Nonprinting Characters

It is helpful to display nonprinting characters that indicate where in the document you pressed the ENTER key, SPACEBAR, or TAB key. Thus, you should display the nonprinting characters as described below.

TO DISPLAY NONPRINTING CHARACTERS

1. If the Show/Hide ¶ button on the Standard toolbar is not already recessed, click it.

Word displays nonprinting characters in the document window, and the Show/Hide ¶ button on the Standard toolbar is recessed (Figure 6-3 on the next page).

Redefining the Normal Style

Recall from Project 5 that your desired document settings may differ from Word's default settings. In these cases, it is good practice to define your document settings and save these settings in the Normal style to ensure that the entire document follows the same style. Much of the text in the newsletter in Project 6 has a font size of 12. Use the steps on the next page to redefine the Normal style to a font size of 12, if your default is a font size other than 12. For a detailed example of the procedure summarized on the next page, refer to pages WD 5.21 through 5.23 in Project 5.

More *About*
Newsletters

Most newsletters are sent automatically to a defined population on a regular basis; e.g., weekly, monthly, semi-annually, etc. The recipients may be paying subscribers or non-paying subscribers, such as community or church members. A newsletter should contain interesting articles and announcements, especially if the recipient has paid to receive it.

More *About* **Font Size**

Many word processors have a default font size of 10 point. In some fonts, 10 point is small and difficult to read for many people. Because many people wear reading glasses, desktop publishers recommend a font size of 12 point for newsletters so that it can be easily read by people of all ages.

TO REDEFINE THE NORMAL STYLE

1 Click Format on the menu bar and then click Style.

2 When the Style dialog box displays, be sure Normal is selected in the Styles list box and then click the Modify button.

3 When the Modify Style dialog box displays, click the Format button and then click Font.

4 When the Font dialog box displays, click 12 in the Size list box and then click the OK button in the Font dialog box.

5 Click the OK button in the Modify Style dialog box, then click the Apply button in the Style dialog box.

Word redefines the Normal style to 12 point.

Changing All Margin Settings

As you may recall, Word is preset to use standard 8.5-by-11-inch paper, with 1.25-inch left and right margins and 1-inch top and bottom margins. For the newsletter in this project, you want the left, right, and top margins to be .5 inch and the bottom margin to be 1 inch. Thus, you want to change the left, right, and top margin settings as described in the following steps.

TO CHANGE ALL MARGIN SETTINGS

1 Click File on the menu bar and then click Page Setup.

2 When the Page Setup dialog box displays, type .5 in the Top text box and then press the TAB key twice; type .5 in the Left text box and then press the TAB key; type .5 in the Right text box and then point to the OK button (Figure 6-3).

3 Click the OK button to change the margin settings for this document.

Once you have completed Step 2, the Page Setup dialog box displays as shown in Figure 6-3. Depending on the printer you are using, you may need to set the margins differently for this project.

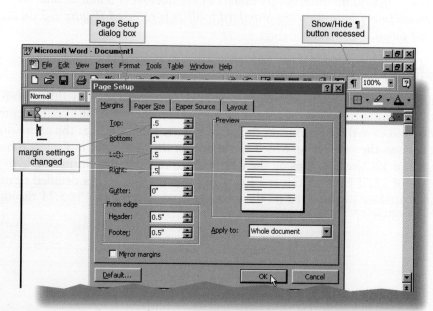

FIGURE 6-3

Creating the Nameplate

The nameplate in Project 6 consists of all the text above the multiple columns (see Figure 6-1 on page WD 6.5). The nameplate is composed of the newsletter title, AMATEUR AVIATORS, and the issue information line. The steps on the following pages illustrate how to create the nameplate for the first page of the newsletter in Project 6.

Entering the Newsletter Title

In Project 6, the newsletter title is formatted to 72-point Mistral teal, bold italic font. Follow these steps to format and enter the newsletter title.

TO FORMAT AND ENTER TEXT

1. Click the Font box arrow on the Formatting toolbar. Scroll to and then click Mistral (or a similar font) in the list.
2. Click the Font Size box arrow on the Formatting toolbar. Scroll to and then click 72 in the list.
3. Click the Bold button on the Formatting toolbar. Click the Italic button on the Formatting toolbar.
4. Click the Center button on the Formatting toolbar.
5. Click the Font Color button arrow on the Formatting toolbar and then click the color Teal.
6. Type AMATEUR AVIATORS and then press the ENTER key.
7. Click the Align Left button on the Formatting toolbar.

Word displays the newsletter title in 72-point Mistral teal, bold italic font (Figure 6-4).

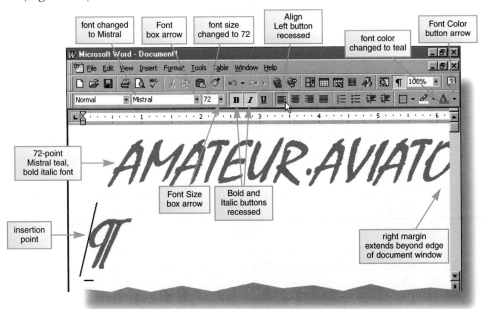

FIGURE 6-4

More *About* **Nameplates**

The nameplate should contain, at a minimum, the title and date of the newsletter. The title should be displayed in as large a font size as possible. You may also include a logo in the nameplate. Many nameplates include a headline outlining the function of the newsletter. Some nameplates also include a short table of contents.

When you changed the margin settings earlier in this project, the right margin moved beyond the right edge of the document window. Thus, part of the newsletter title does not display in the document window.

Zooming page width brings both the left and right margins of a document into view in the document window. If the left and right margins do not both display in the document window, follow these steps to zoom page width.

TO ZOOM PAGE WIDTH

1. Click the Zoom box arrow on the Standard toolbar.
2. Click Page Width in the list.

Word brings both the left and right margins into view in the document window (Figure 6-5).

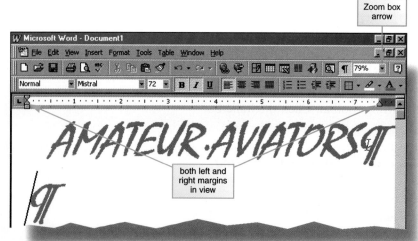

Zoom box arrow

both left and right margins in view

FIGURE 6-5

The next step is to add rules, or ruling lines, above and below the newsletter title.

Adding Ruling Lines to Divide Text

In Word, you use borders to create **ruling lines**. Borders can be placed on any edge of a paragraph(s), that is, the top, bottom, left, or right edges. Ruling lines generally display both above and below a paragraph. Perform the following steps to place ruling lines above and below the newsletter title.

TO ADD RULING LINES

1. Click somewhere in the newsletter title.
2. If necessary, click the Tables and Borders button on the Standard toolbar to display the Tables and Borders toolbar.
3. Click the Line Style box arrow on the Tables and Borders toolbar and then click the first set of double lines in the list.
4. Click the Line Weight box arrow on the Tables and Borders toolbar and then click 1 ½ pt.
5. Click the Border Color button on the Tables and Borders toolbar and then click the color Red.
6. Click the Outside Border button arrow on the Tables and Borders toolbar and then click Top Border. Click the Border button arrow again and then point to Bottom Border (Figure 6-6).
7. Click Bottom Border.
8. Click the Tables and Borders button on the Standard toolbar to remove the Tables and Borders toolbar. Click the Normal View button at the bottom of the Word screen.

Once you have completed Step 6, the newsletter title and Tables and Borders toolbar display as shown in Figure 6-6.

Recall that borders are part of paragraph formatting. If you press the ENTER key in a bordered paragraph, the border will carry forward to the next paragraph. To avoid this, move the insertion point outside of the bordered paragraph before pressing the ENTER key.

The next step is to enter the issue information line in the nameplate.

Inserting Symbols into a Document

The issue information line in this project contains the volume number and date of the newsletter. It also displays a large round dot between the volume number and the date of the newsletter. This special symbol, called a **bullet**, is not on the keyboard. You insert bullets and other special symbols, such as letters in the Greek alphabet and mathematical characters, using the Symbol dialog box. Perform the following steps to add a bullet symbol in the issue information line.

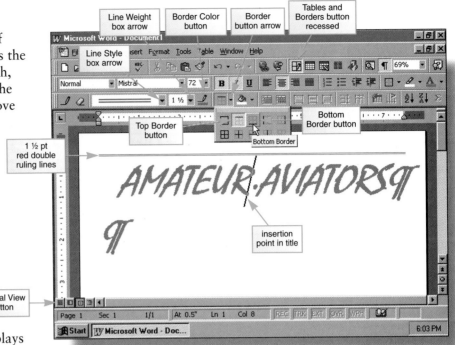

FIGURE 6-6

Steps **To Insert a Symbol into Text**

1 **Click the paragraph mark on line 2. Change the font to Times New Roman. Change the font size to 12 point. Be sure the Bold button is recessed. Click the Italic button to deactivate it. Type** Monthly Newsletter **and then click the Tab Alignment button on the ruler twice. Click the 7.375" mark on the ruler.**

The first part of the issue information line is entered (Figure 6-7). The volume and date information should be right-aligned; however, the words, Monthly Newsletter, should be at the left margin. Thus, you want one part of the paragraph to be left-aligned and the other to be right-aligned. Because you can specify only one type of alignment for a single paragraph, you must use a right-aligned custom tab stop for the volume and date information. You cannot click a tab directly at the right margin, which explains why you click the 7.375" mark and then drag the tab marker to the right margin.

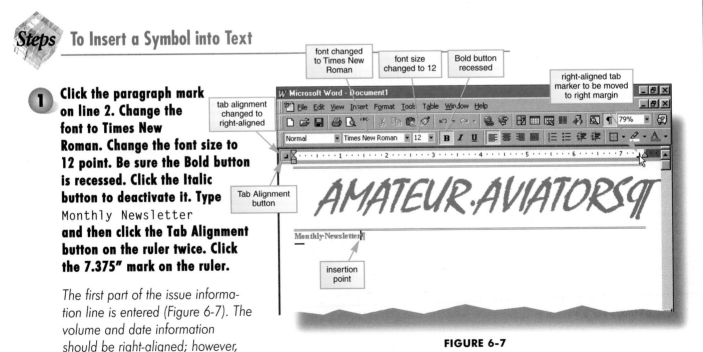

FIGURE 6-7

2 Drag the right-aligned tab marker from the 7.375" mark on the ruler to the 7.5" mark on the ruler (where the gray meets the white). Press the TAB key. Type Vol. VI and then press the SPACEBAR. Click Insert on the menu bar and then point to Symbol.

The volume information displays at the right margin of the document (Figure 6-8). Notice the right-aligned tab marker is positioned directly on top of the right margin on the ruler.

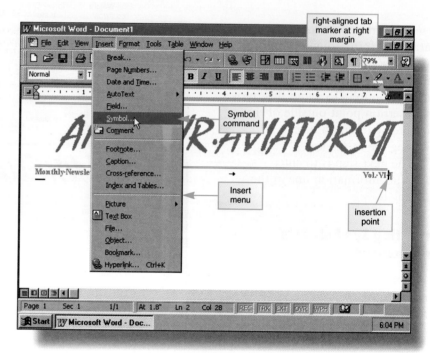

FIGURE 6-8

3 Click Symbol. If necessary, click the Symbols tab when the Symbol dialog box first opens. If necessary, click the Font box arrow in the Symbol dialog box and then click Symbol. If it is not already selected, click the bullet symbol. Click the Insert button.

Word displays the *Symbol dialog box* (Figure 6-9). When you click a symbol in the list, it becomes enlarged so that you can see it more clearly. A selected symbol is highlighted. Because you clicked the Insert button, the bullet symbol appears in the document to the left of the insertion point. At this point, you can insert additional symbols or close the Symbol dialog box.

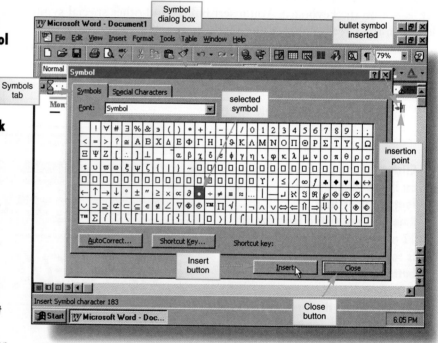

FIGURE 6-9

4 Click the Close button in the Symbol dialog box. Press the SPACEBAR. **Type** June 1998 **and then press the** ENTER **key. Click in the issue information line. If necessary, click the Tables and Borders button on the Standard toolbar to display the Tables and Borders toolbar. Click the Border button arrow on the Tables and Borders toolbar and then click Bottom Border. Click the Tables and Borders button on the Standard toolbar. Click the Normal View button at the bottom of the Word screen. Click the paragraph mark on line 3. Click the Bold button on the Formatting toolbar to deactivate it. Click the Font Color button arrow on the Formatting toolbar and then click Automatic. Scroll up to display the entire nameplate.**

The issue information line is complete (Figure 6-10).

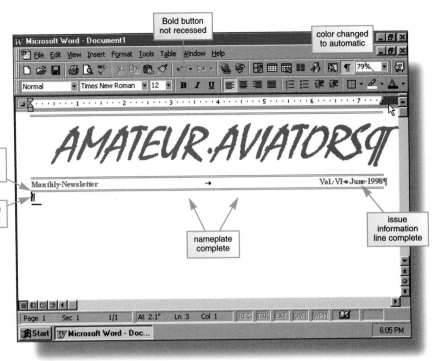

FIGURE 6-10

Other Ways
1. Type ALT+0 (zero) followed by ANSI character code for symbol using numeric keypad

You also can insert ANSI characters into a document by entering the ANSI code directly into the document. The **ANSI characters** are a predefined set of characters, including both characters on the keyboard and special characters, such as the bullet symbol. To enter the ANSI code, make sure the NUM LOCK key is on. Press and hold the ALT key and then type the number zero followed by the ANSI code for the character. You *must* use the numeric keypad when entering the ANSI code. For a complete list of ANSI codes, see your Microsoft Windows documentation.

The nameplate is now complete. The next step is to enter and format the body of the newsletter.

Formatting the First Page of the Body of the Newsletter

The body of the newsletter in this project is divided into three columns (see Figure 6-1 on page WD 6.5). The airplane graphic displays across the first, second, and third columns on page 1. A vertical rule separates the second and third columns on page 1. The steps on the following pages illustrate how to format the first page of the body of the newsletter using these desktop publishing features.

More *About*
Newspaper
Columns

Narrow columns are generally
easier to read than wide ones;
however, because columns can
be too narrow, try to have
between five and fifteen words
per line. To do this, you may
need to adjust the column width,
the font size, or the leading.
Leading is the line spacing,
which can be adjusted through
the Paragraph dialog box in
Word.

Formatting a Document into Multiple Columns

With Word, you can create two types of columns: parallel columns and snaking columns. **Parallel columns,** or table columns, are created with the Insert Table button. You created parallel columns in Project 4. The text in **snaking columns,** or newspaper columns, flows from the bottom of one column to the top of the next. The body of the newsletter in Project 6 uses snaking columns.

When you begin a document in Word, it has one column. You can divide a portion of a document or the entire document into multiple columns. Within each column, you can type, modify, or format text.

To divide a portion of a document into multiple columns, you first must insert a section break. In this project, the nameplate is one column and the body of the newsletter is three columns. Thus, you must insert a continuous section break below the nameplate. *Continuous* means you want the new section on the same page as the previous section. Perform the following steps to divide the body of the newsletter into three columns.

Steps To Insert a Continuous Section Break

1 **With the insertion point on line 3, press the ENTER key twice. Click Insert on the menu bar and then click Break. Click Continuous in the Section breaks area of the Break dialog box. Point to the OK button.**

Word displays the Break dialog box (Figure 6-11). Continuous means you want the new section on the same page as the previous section.

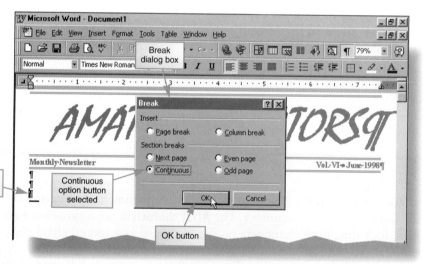

FIGURE 6-11

2 **Click the OK button.**

Word inserts a section break above the insertion point (Figure 6-12). The insertion point now is located in section 2.

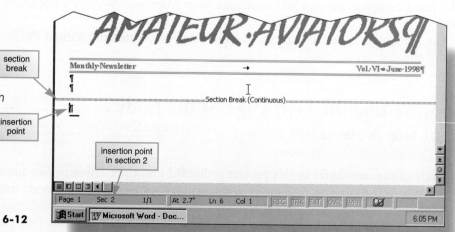

FIGURE 6-12

The next step is to format the second section to three columns.

 **To Format Columns**

1 **Be sure the insertion point is in section 2. Click the Columns button on the Standard toolbar.**

Word displays the columns list graphic below the Columns button (Figure 6-13).

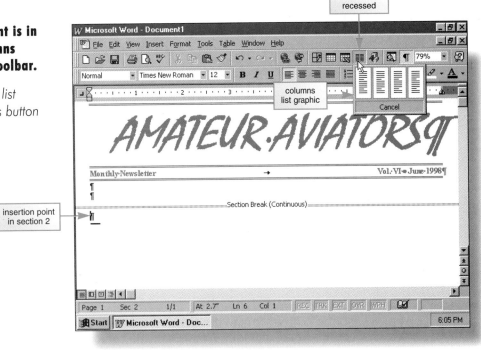

FIGURE 6-13

2 **Point to the third column in the columns list graphic (Figure 6-14).**

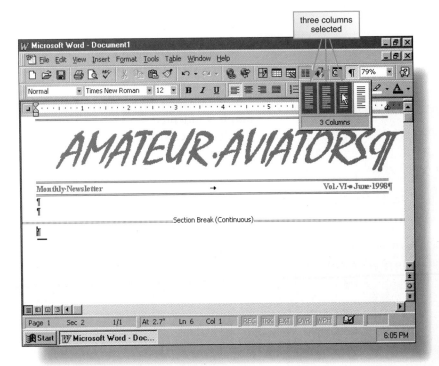

FIGURE 6-14

3 **Click the third column. If necessary, click the Zoom box arrow and then click Page Width.**

Word divides the section containing the insertion point into three evenly sized and spaced columns (Figure 6-15). Notice that the ruler indicates the size of the three columns. Word switches to page layout view because columns do not display properly in normal view.

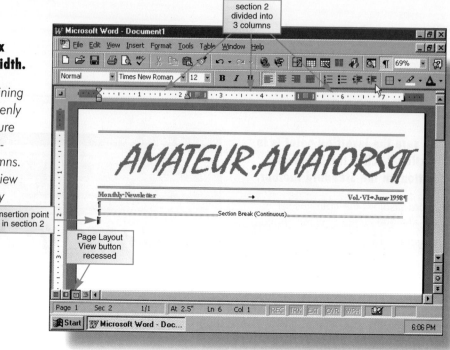

FIGURE 6-15

When you use the Columns button to create columns, Word creates columns of equal width. You can create columns of unequal width by clicking Columns on the Format menu.

Entering a Subhead and Associated Text

Subheads are headings placed throughout the body of the newsletter, such as GET READY. In this project, the subheads are bold and have a font size of 14. The text below the subheads is **justified**, which means that the left and right margins are aligned, like the edges of newspaper columns. The first line of each paragraph is indented .25 inch. Perform the following steps to enter the first subhead and its associated text.

Steps To Enter Subheads and Associated Text

1 Change the font size to 14. Click the Bold button. Type GET READY and then click the Bold button. Change the font size back to 12 and then press the ENTER key twice. Drag the First Line Indent marker on the ruler to the .25" mark.

The first subhead is entered and the insertion point is indented .25 inch (Figure 6-16).

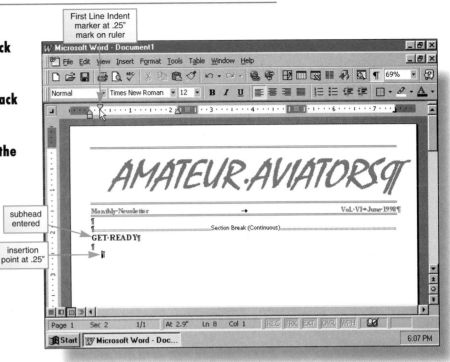

FIGURE 6-16

2 Click the Justify button on the Formatting toolbar. Type the paragraph below the GET READY subhead. The paragraph is shown in Figure 6-18 on the next page.

Word aligns both the left and right edges of the paragraph automatically (Figure 6-17). Notice that extra space is placed between some words when you justify text.

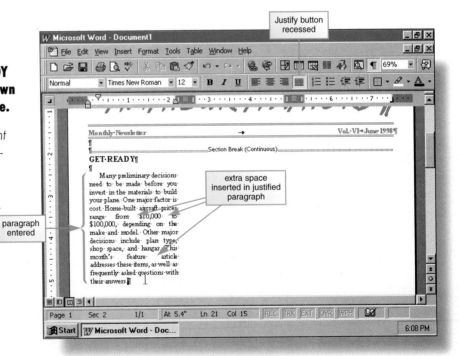

FIGURE 6-17

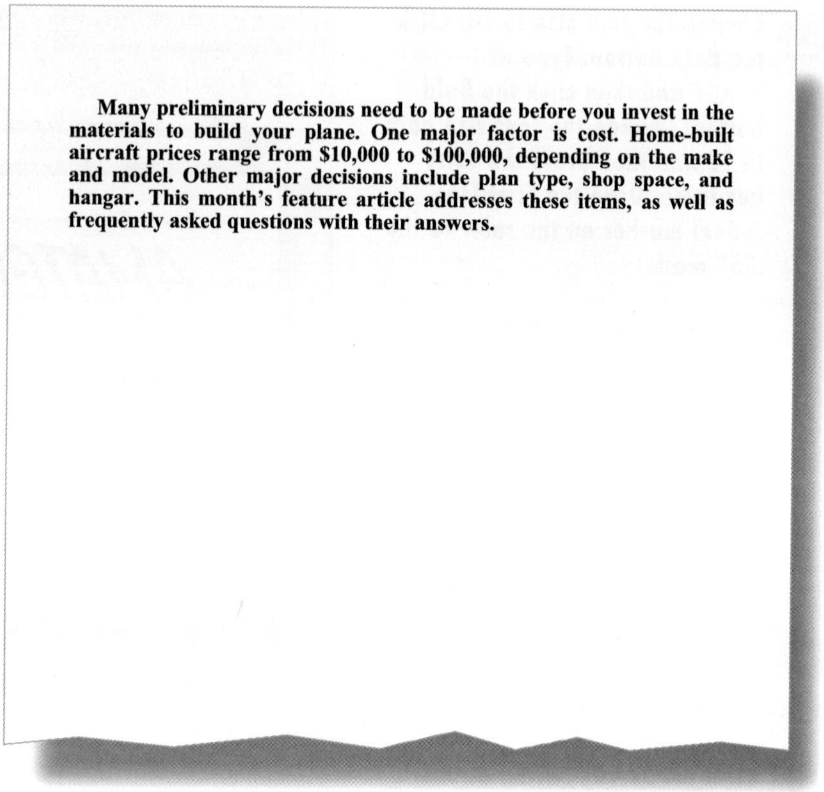

Many preliminary decisions need to be made before you invest in the materials to build your plane. One major factor is cost. Home-built aircraft prices range from $10,000 to $100,000, depending on the make and model. Other major decisions include plan type, shop space, and hangar. This month's feature article addresses these items, as well as frequently asked questions with their answers.

FIGURE 6-18

Saving the Newsletter

Because you have performed several steps, you should save the newsletter as described in the steps.

TO SAVE THE NEWSLETTER IN A FILE

1. Insert your floppy disk into drive A.
2. Click the Save button on the Standard toolbar.
3. Type Amateur Aviators Newsletter in the File name text box. Do not press the ENTER key.
4. Click the Save in box arrow and then click 3½ Floppy (A:).
5. Click the Save button in the Save As dialog box.

Word saves the document on a floppy disk in drive A with the file name, Amateur Aviators Newsletter (Figure 6-19).

Inserting the Remainder of the Newsletter Feature Article

Instead of entering the rest of this article into the newsletter for this project, you can insert the file named, How to Build a Plane Article, which is located on the Data Disk that accompanies this book, into the newsletter. This file contains the remainder of the newsletter article. Perform the following steps to insert the How to Build a Plane Article into the newsletter.

Steps **To Insert a File into the Newsletter**

1 **Press the ENTER key. Drag the first-line indent marker back to the 0″ mark on the ruler. Press the ENTER key again. Insert the Data Disk that accompanies this book into drive A. Click Insert on the menu bar and then click File. If necessary, click the Look in box arrow and then click 3½ Floppy (A:). Double-click the Word folder. If it is not already recessed, click the Preview button. Click How to Build a Plane Article.**

Word displays the Insert File dialog box (Figure 6-19). The contents of the selected file (How to Build a Plane Article) display when the Preview button is recessed. The file will be inserted at the location of the insertion point in the document.

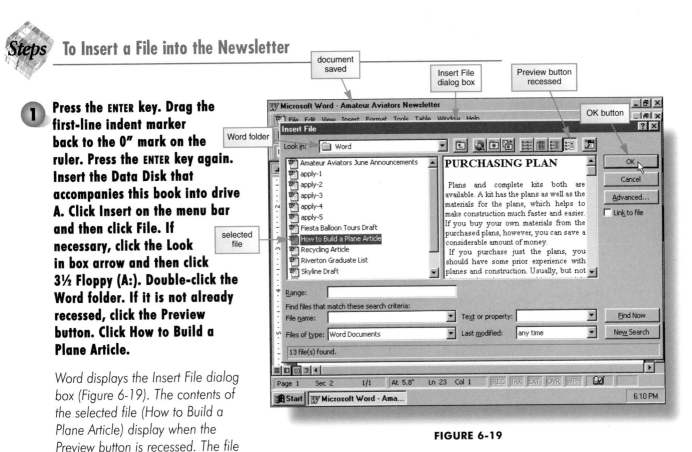

FIGURE 6-19

2 **Click the OK button. Replace the Data Disk with your floppy disk.**

Word inserts the file, How to Build a Plane Article, into the file Amateur Aviators Newsletter at the location of the insertion point (Figure 6-20).

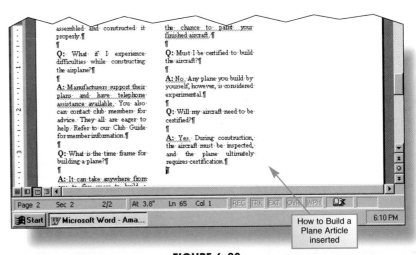

FIGURE 6-20

Creating a Dropped Capital Letter

You can format the first character or word in a paragraph to be dropped. A **dropped capital letter**, or **drop cap**, appears larger than the rest of the characters in the paragraph. The text in the paragraph wraps around the dropped capital letter. Perform the steps on the next page to create a dropped capital letter for the GET READY subhead in the newsletter.

More *About*
Drop Caps

A drop cap often is used to mark the beginning of an article. An alternative is a stick-up cap, which extends into the left margin, rather than sinking into the first few lines of the text. To insert a stick-up cap, click In Margin in the Drop Cap dialog box.

Steps **To Create a Dropped Capital Letter**

1 Press the CTRL+HOME keys to scroll to the top of the document window. Click anywhere in the GET READY paragraph. Click Format on the menu bar and then point to Drop Cap.

The insertion point is in the GET READY paragraph (Figure 6-21).

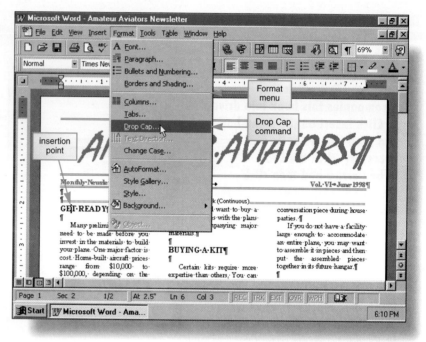

FIGURE 6-21

2 Click Drop Cap. Click Dropped in the Position area of the Drop Cap dialog box.

Word displays the Drop Cap dialog box (Figure 6-22).

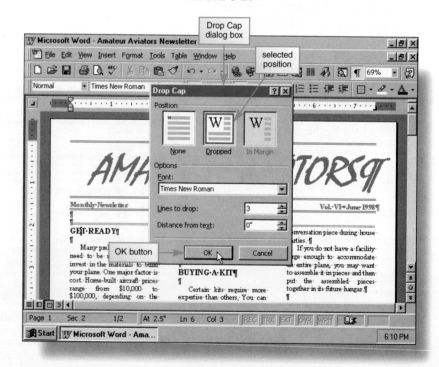

FIGURE 6-22

3 **Click the OK button.**

*Word drops the letter G in
the GET READY paragraph,
and wraps subsequent text
around the dropped capital G
(Figure 6-23).*

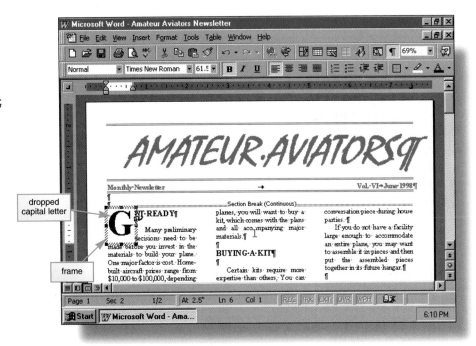

FIGURE 6-23

When you drop cap a letter, Word places a **frame** around it. A framed object is one that you can position anywhere on the page.

The next step is to insert the airplane graphic and position it across the first, second, and third columns.

Positioning Graphics on the Page

Recall that you insert a graphic into a document using the Picture command on the Insert menu. You can import graphics from the Microsoft Clip Gallery that accompanies Word, or you can import them from the Microsoft Clip Gallery Live page on the Web. In Project 4, after you imported the graphic, you turned off the Float over text check box in the Format Picture dialog box so the picture became part of a paragraph. In this project, you want to position the graphic across multiple columns; thus, you will not turn off the Float over text check box.

Perform the steps on the next page to download an airplane graphic from Microsoft's Clip Gallery Live Web page, import the clip art file into the document, and then position the graphic across the first, second, and third columns of page 1 in the newsletter.

NOTE: The steps on the next page assume you are using Microsoft Internet Explorer as your browser and that you have access to the Web. If you are not using Internet Explorer or you do not have access to the Web, you will need to perform a different set of steps. Your browser's handling of pictures on the Web will be discovered in Step 2. If necessary, you may be directed to follow the steps on page WD 6.23 to install the picture from the Data Disk that accompanies this book. If you do not have access to the Web, go directly to the steps on page WD 6.23.

More *About*
Graphics

The use of real photographs in a newsletter adds professionalism to the document. You can insert them yourself if you have a scanner; otherwise, you can work with a print shop. When using photos, you may need to crop, or trim out, the edges. If you have a scanner, you can crop the images on your own computer.

Steps To Download Clip Art from Microsoft's Clip Gallery Live Web Page

1 Scroll through the document and position the insertion point on the paragraph mark above the subhead PURCHASING PLAN in the first column. Click Insert on the menu bar, point to Picture, and then click Clip Art. If necessary, click the Clip Art tab when the Microsoft Clip Gallery dialog box first opens. Click the Connect to Web for additional clips button. If a Connect to Web for More Clip Art, Photos, Sounds dialog box displays, click its OK button. When the Clip Gallery Live window opens, click the Accept button in the left frame. Be sure the ClipArt button is recessed, click the Search button, type planes in the Enter keywords text box, then click the Find button.

Microsoft Clip Gallery Live displays in a new window (Figure 6-24). Recall that to download a file into the Microsoft Clip Gallery, you click the file name that displays below the clip art graphic.

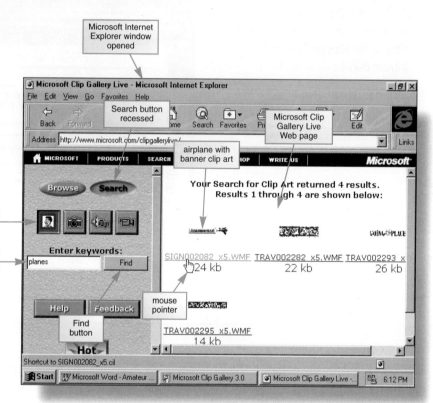

FIGURE 6-24

2 **Click the file name SIGN002082_x5.WMF. (If your browser displays a dialog box asking whether you want to open the file or save the file, click Open and then click the OK button. If your browser displays a dialog box and Open is not an option, close your browser window, click the Close button in the Microsoft Clip Gallery dialog box, then go to the steps below).**

Your browser downloads the file into your Microsoft Clip Gallery in the Downloaded Clips category (Figure 6-25).

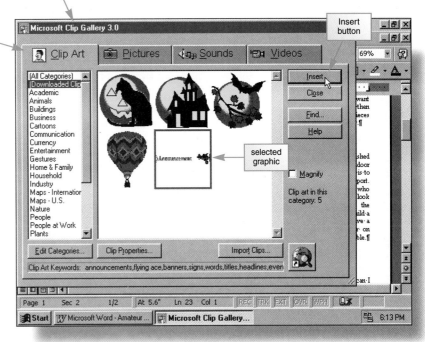

FIGURE 6-25

3 **If it is not already selected, click the airplane graphic and then click the Insert button. Close your browser window.**

Word inserts the airplane graphic into your document as a floating picture (Figure 6-26 on the next page).

If you do not have access to the Web, you have to install the clip art file into the Microsoft Clip Gallery from the Data Disk that accompanies this book as described in the following steps.

TO INSTALL THE CLIP ART FILE FROM THE DATA DISK

1 Position the insertion point on the paragraph mark above the subhead PURCHASING PLAN in first column.

2 Click Insert on the menu bar, point to Picture on the Insert menu, and then point to Clip Art on the Picture submenu.

3 Click Clip Art. If necessary, click the Clip Art tab when the Microsoft Clip Gallery dialog box first opens.

4 Insert the Data Disk that accompanies this book into drive A.

5 Click the Start button on the taskbar, point to Programs on the Start menu, and then click Windows Explorer. When the Exploring window displays, scroll to the top of the All Folders side of the window and then click 3½ Floppy (A:) to select drive A. Double-click the Word folder in the Contents side of the window to display the contents of the Data Disk.

6. Double-click the file name SIGN002082_x5.cil on the Data Disk. Close the Exploring window.

7. When the Microsoft Clip Gallery redisplays, click the airplane clip art and then click the Insert button. Replace the Data Disk with your floppy disk.

Word inserts the airplane clip art graphic into your document as a floating picture (Figure 6-26 below).

The next step is to specify how the text is to wrap around the graphic and then position the graphic across the first, second, and third columns of page 1 in the newsletter.

Steps **To Position a Graphic Anywhere on a Page**

1. **If necessary, click the airplane graphic to select it. If the Picture toolbar does not display, right-click the clip art graphic and then click Show Picture Toolbar on the shortcut menu. Point to the Format Picture button on the Picture toolbar.**

Word selects the airplane graphic (Figure 6-26). Recall that selected graphics display surrounded by sizing handles at each corner and middle location.

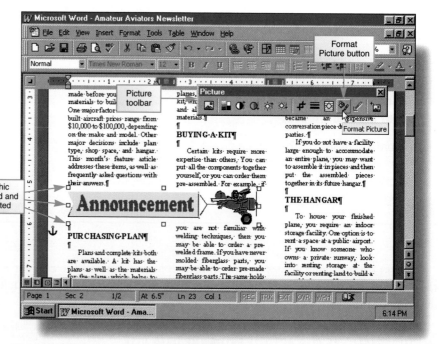

FIGURE 6-26

2 **Click the Format Picture button. When the Format Picture dialog box displays, click the Wrapping tab and then click Square in the Wrapping style area.**

*Word displays the Format Picture dialog box (Figure 6-27). The **wrapping styles** specify how the text in the document displays with the graphic.*

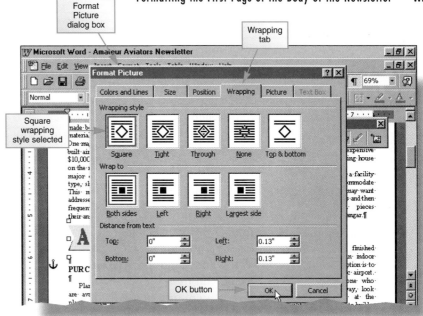

FIGURE 6-27

3 **Click the OK button. Point to the edge of the graphic so the mouse has a four-headed arrow attached to it.**

Word changes the wrapping style to square so the text boxes around the graphic (Figure 6-28). When the mouse has a four-headed arrow attached to it, you can drag the graphic to any location in the document.

FIGURE 6-28

4 **Drag the graphic to the desired location. (Try to position the graphic as close as possible to Figure 6-29. You may have to drag the airplane graphic a couple of times to position it properly.) Click outside the graphic to remove the selection.**

As the graphic moves, a dotted border indicates its new location. When you release the mouse button, the graphic is positioned at the new location (Figure 6-29). Depending on the printer you are using, your wordwrap may occur in different locations.

FIGURE 6-29

Notice in Figure 6-29 on the previous page that the text in columns one and three wraps around the airplane graphic. Thus, it is called **wrap-around text**. The wrap around forms a square because of the wrapping style set in Step 2. The space between the airplane graphic and the wrap-around text is called the **run-around**.

The next step is to place the monthly announcements in column three of the newsletter.

Inserting a Column Break

Notice in Figure 6-1 on page WD 6.5 that the third column is not a continuation of the article. The third column contains several announcements. The How to Build a Plane article actually is continued on the second page of the newsletter. You want the monthly announcements to be separated into the third column. Thus, you must force a **column break** at the bottom of the second column. Word inserts a column break at the location of the insertion point.

The first step is to force the article to continue on the next page with a **next page section break** and then insert a column break at the bottom of the second column so the announcements always display in the third column.

Steps **To Insert a Next Page Section Break**

1 **Scroll through the document to display the bottom of the second column of the first page in the document window. Click before the Y in the subhead YOUR SHOP. Click Insert on the menu bar and then click Break. Click Next page in the Section breaks area of the Break dialog box.**

The insertion point is at the beginning of the subhead YOUR SHOP (Figure 6-30).

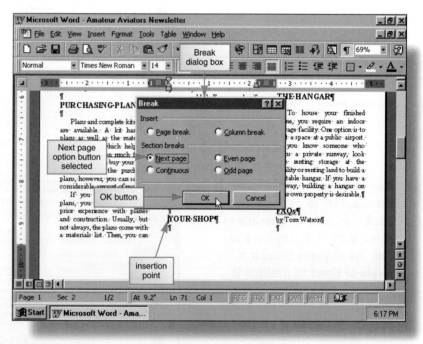

FIGURE 6-30

2 **Click the OK button.**

Word inserts a section break at the location of the insertion point (Figure 6-31). The rest of the article displays on page 2 of the document because the section break included a page break. On page 1, the bottom of the second column and the entire third column are empty.

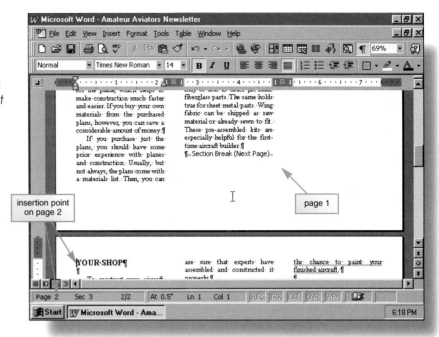

FIGURE 6-31

Because you want the monthly announcements to begin at the top of the third column, the next step is to enter a column break at the end of the text in the second column as shown in these steps.

 Steps **To Insert a Column Break**

1 **Position the insertion point at the end the second column on the first page of the newsletter. Press the ENTER key two times. Drag the First Line Indent marker to the 0" mark on the ruler in column 2. Click the Italic button on the Formatting toolbar. Type** Article continues on Page 2... **and then click the Italic button again. Press the ENTER key. Click Insert on the menu bar and then click Break. Click Column break in the Break dialog box.**

The insertion point is immediately below the message, Article continues on Page 2 (Figure 6-32).

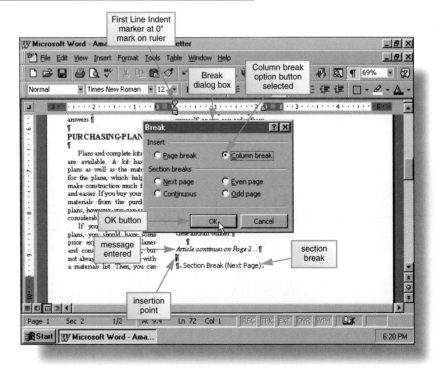

FIGURE 6-32

2 **Click the OK button.**

Word inserts a column break at the bottom of the second column and advances the insertion point to the top of the third column (Figure 6-33).

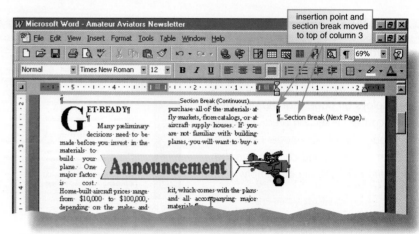

FIGURE 6-33

OtherWays

1. Press CTRL+SHIFT+ENTER

More *About* **Jump Lines**

An article that spans multiple pages should contain a jump or jump line, which informs the reader where to look for the rest of the article or story. The message on the first page is called a jump-to line, and a jump-from line marks the beginning of the continuation. The alignment of the jump-to and jump-from lines should be the same.

To eliminate having to enter the entire column of announcements into the newsletter, you can insert the file, Amateur Aviators June Announcements, which is located on the Data Disk that accompanies this book, into the third column of the newsletter. The file contains all of the announcements for this June issue.

TO INSERT A FILE INTO A COLUMN OF THE NEWSLETTER

1 Insert the Data Disk that accompanies this book into drive A.

2 With the insertion point at the top of the third column, click Insert on the menu bar and then click File.

3 When the Insert File dialog box displays, if necessary, click the Look in box arrow and then click 3½ Floppy (A:). If necessary, double-click the Word folder. If it is not already recessed, click the Preview button. If necessary, click Amateur Aviators June Announcements.

4 Click the OK button. Replace with the Data Disk with your floppy disk.

Word inserts the file, Amateur Aviators June Announcements, into the third column of the newsletter (Figure 6-34).

The next step is to place a vertical rule between the second and third columns in the newsletter.

Adding a Vertical Rule Between Columns

In newsletters, you often see a vertical rule separating columns. With Word, you can place a vertical rule between *all* columns by clicking the Columns command on the Format menu and then clicking the Line between check box.

FIGURE 6-34

In this project, you want a vertical rule between *only* the second and third columns. To do this, you add a left border placed several points from the text. Recall that a point is approximately 1/72 of an inch. Perform the following steps to add a vertical rule between the second and third column in the newsletter.

Steps **To Add a Vertical Rule Between Columns**

① **Drag the mouse from the top of the third column down to the bottom of the third column. Click Format on the menu bar and then point to Borders and Shading.**

Word highlights the entire third column of page 1 in the newsletter (Figure 6-35).

FIGURE 6-35

② **Click Borders and Shading. If necessary, click the Borders tab when the Borders and Shading dialog box first opens. Point to the left side of the diagram in the Preview area.**

Word displays the Borders and Shading dialog box (Figure 6-36). By clicking sides of the diagram in the Preview area, you can apply borders to the selected paragraph(s).

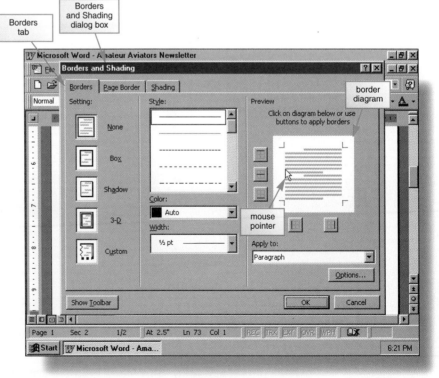

FIGURE 6-36

3 **Click the left side of the diagram in the Preview area. Point to the Options button.**

Word draws a border on the left edge of the diagram (Figure 6-37).

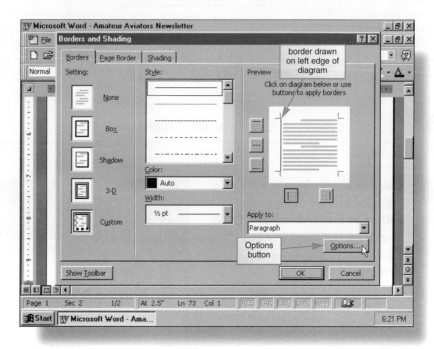

FIGURE 6-37

4 **Click the Options button. When the Border and Shading Options dialog box displays, change the Left text box to 15 pt.**

The Preview shows the border positioned 15 points from the left edge of the paragraph (Figure 6-38).

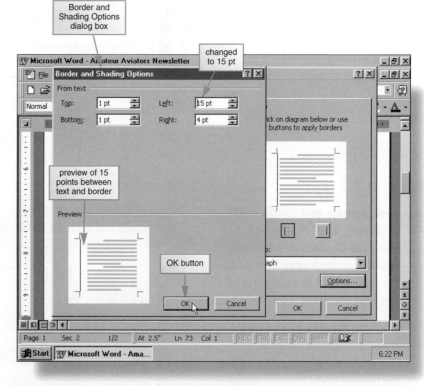

FIGURE 6-38

5 Click the OK button in the Borders and Shading Options dialog box. When the Borders and Shading dialog box redisplays, click its OK button. Click in the selection to remove the highlight.

Word draws a border positioned 15 points from the left edge of the text (Figure 6-39). A vertical rule displays between the second and third columns of the newsletter.

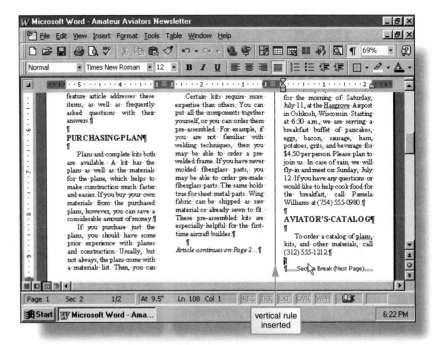

FIGURE 6-39

The first page of the newsletter is formatted completely.

Formatting the Second Page of the Newsletter

The second page of the newsletter continues the article that began in the first two columns of page 1 (see Figure 6-2 on page WD 6.6). The nameplate on the second page is more concise than the one on the first page of the newsletter. In addition to the text in the article, page two contains a pull-quote. The following pages illustrate how to format the second page of the newsletter in this project.

Creating the Nameplate on the Second Page

Because the document currently is formatted into three columns and the nameplate is a single column, the next step is to change the number of columns to one at the top of the second page. Recall that each time you change the number of columns in a document, you must insert a new section. You will then format the section to one column and enter the nameplate into the section as described in the steps on the next page.

More *About*
Vertical Rules

A vertical rule is used to guide the reader through the newsletter. If a multi-column newsletter contains a single article, then place a vertical rule between every column. If, however, different columns present different articles, then place a vertical rule between each article instead of each column.

Steps To Format the Second Page Nameplate

1 Scroll through the document and position the mouse pointer at the top left corner of the second page of the newsletter. Click Insert on the menu bar and then click Break. When the Break dialog box displays, click Continuous in the Section breaks area. Point to the OK button.

Word displays the Break dialog box (Figure 6-40). This section break will place the nameplate on the same physical page as the three columns of the continued article.

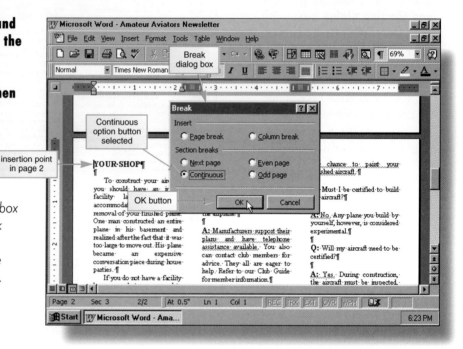

FIGURE 6-40

2 Click the OK button.

Word inserts a section break above the insertion point.

3 Press the UP ARROW key to position the insertion point in section 3 on the section break. Click the Columns button on the Standard toolbar. Point to the first column in the columns list graphic.

Word highlights the left column in the columns list graphic and displays 1 Column below the graphic (Figure 6-41). The current section, for the nameplate, will be formatted to one column.

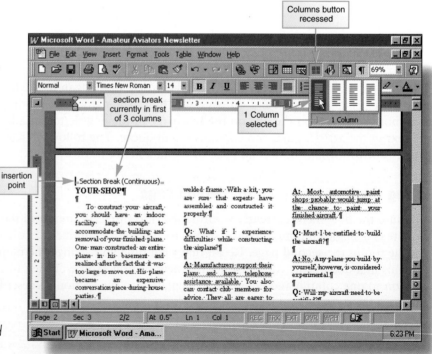

FIGURE 6-41

4 **Click the first column in the columns list graphic.**

Word formats the current section to one column (Figure 6-42).

section 3 is one column

section 4 is three columns

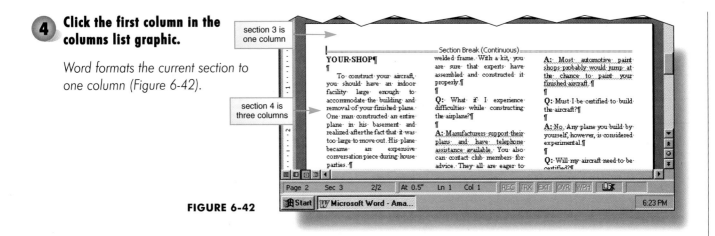

FIGURE 6-42

The next step is to enter the nameplate and a continued message at the top of the first column in the second page of the newsletter.

TO ENTER THE NAMEPLATE AND CONTINUED MESSAGE ON THE SECOND PAGE

1 Change the font size to 12. Click the Bold button on the Formatting toolbar. Press the ENTER key twice. Press the UP ARROW key. Change the font size to 20 point. Click the Font Color button arrow on the Formatting toolbar and then click the color Teal. Type June 1998 as the date.

2 Click the Tab Alignment button on the ruler as many times as necessary to change the alignment to centered. Click the 3.75" mark on the ruler to place a centered tab stop at that location. Change the font size to 28. Click the Bold and Italic buttons on the Formatting toolbar. Press the TAB key. Change the font to Mistral. Type AMATEUR AVIATORS and then click the Bold and Italic buttons. Change the font size back to 20. Change the font back to Times New Roman.

3 Click the Tab Alignment button on the ruler to change the alignment to right-aligned. Click the 7.375" mark on the ruler to place a right-aligned tab stop at that location. Drag the right-aligned tab marker to the 7.5" mark (the right margin). Press the TAB key. Type Page 2 and then press the ENTER key.

4 Click the line typed in Steps 1 through 3. Click the Tables and Borders button on the Standard toolbar. Click the Line Style box arrow and then click the first set of double lines in the list. Click the Border button arrow on the Tables and Borders toolbar and then click Top Border. Click the Border button arrow on the Tables and Borders toolbar and then click Bottom Border. Click the Tables and Borders button on the Standard toolbar.

5 Click the paragraph mark in line 2. Change the font size to 12. Type HOW TO BUILD A PLANE and then press the SPACEBAR. Click the Italic button on the Formatting toolbar. Type (continued) and then click the Italic button. Change the color back to Automatic. Press the ENTER key.

More *About* **Inner Page Nameplates**

The top of the inner pages of the newsletter may or may not have a nameplate. If you choose to create one for your inner pages, it should not be the same as, or compete with, the one on the first page. Inner page nameplates usually contain only a portion of the nameplate from the first page of a newsletter.

The nameplate and article continued message for page two are complete (Figure 6-43 on the next page).

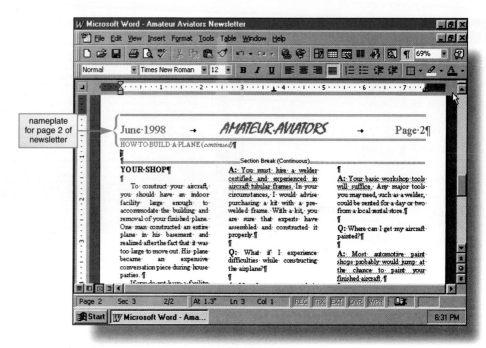

FIGURE 6-43

Because you want to be sure the FAQs section of the newsletter begins at the top of the second column on page 2, you insert a column break at the bottom of the first column as described in these steps.

TO INSERT A COLUMN BREAK

1. Scroll to the bottom of the first column on page 2 and then position the insertion point to the left of the subhead, FAQs.
2. Click Insert on the menu bar and then click Break.
3. Click Column break in the Break dialog box and then click the OK button.

Word inserts a column break in the first column and positions the FAQs text at the top of the second column (Figure 6-44).

The next step is to insert a pull-quote between the first and second columns on page two of the newsletter.

Inserting a Pull-Quote

A **pull-quote** is a quotation pulled, or copied, from the text of the document and given graphic emphasis so it stands apart and grasps the attention of the reader. The newsletter in this project has a pull-quote on the second page between the first and second columns (see Figure 6-2 on page WD 6.6).

To create a pull-quote, you must copy the text in the existing document to the Clipboard and then paste it into a column of the newsletter. To position it between columns, you place a **text box** around it and then move it to the desired location. Perform the following steps to create the pull-quote.

◆ More *About*
Pull-Quotes

Because of their bold emphasis, pull-quotes should be used sparingly in a newsletter. Pull-quotes are especially useful for breaking the monotony of long columns of text. Quotation marks are not required around a pull-quote; but if you use them, use curly (or smart) quotes instead of straight quotes.

Steps **To Create a Pull-Quote**

1 **Scroll to the bottom of the third column of the newsletter and highlight the entire last sentence of the article (do not select the paragraph mark).**

The text for the pull-quote is highlighted (Figure 6-44).

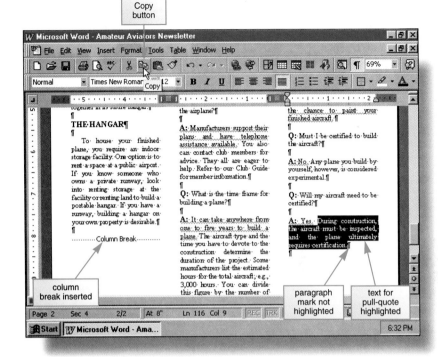

FIGURE 6-44

2 **Click the Copy button on the Standard toolbar. Scroll up the document and then click immediately below the THE HANGAR subhead in column 1 on page 2. Click the Paste button on the Standard toolbar. Type a quotation mark (") at the end of the pull-quote, and then type a quotation mark (") at the beginning of the pull-quote.**

The pull-quote displays below the THE HANGAR subhead (Figure 6-45).

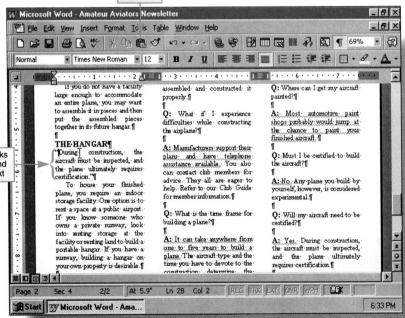

FIGURE 6-45

3 Select the entire pull-quote (do not select the paragraph mark). Click Insert on the menu bar and then point to Text Box (Figure 6-46).

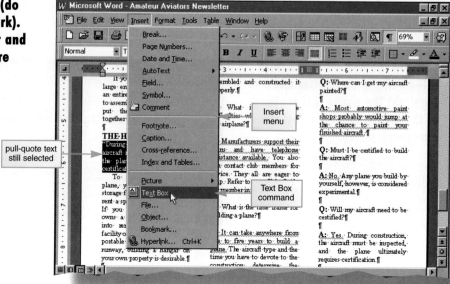

FIGURE 6-46

4 Click Text Box.

Word places a frame around the pull-quote, so that it may be positioned anywhere on the page and formatted.

5 Click the pull-quote. Click Format on the menu bar and then click Paragraph. If necessary, click the Indents and Spacing tab when the Paragraph dialog box first opens. In the Indentation area, change Left to 0.2″ and Right to 0.2″ to increase the amount of space between the left and right edges of the pull-quote and frame. In the Spacing area, change Before to 6 pt and After to 6 pt to increase the amount of space above and below the pull-quote.

*Word displays the **Paragraph dialog box** (Figure 6-47). The pull-quote will have a 0.2-inch space on the left and right edges and 6 points - approximately one blank line - above and below it.*

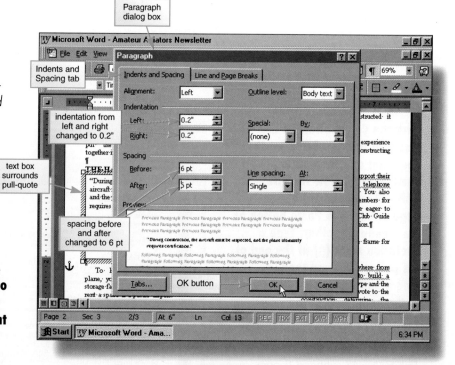

FIGURE 6-47

6 Click the OK button. Drag through the pull-quote text. Click the Font Size box arrow and then click 14. Click the Bold and Italic buttons on the Formatting toolbar. Click inside the pull-quote to remove the highlight.

Word displays the pull-quote left-aligned with a 0.2-inch space between the border and the frame on the left and right sides. Approximately one blank line displays between the border and frame on the top and bottom sides (Figure 6-48). Notice that Word places a border around the pull-quote. When you add a text box, Word automatically places a border around it and the Text Box toolbar displays. You want to change the border around the pull-quote.

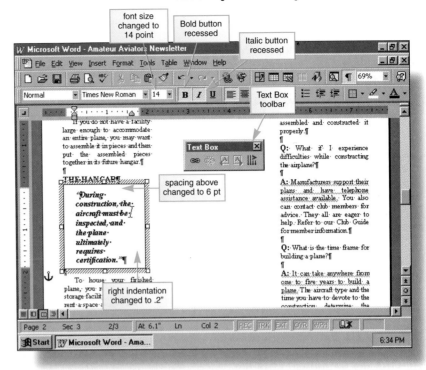

FIGURE 6-48

7 Click Format on the menu bar and then point to Text Box (Figure 6-49).

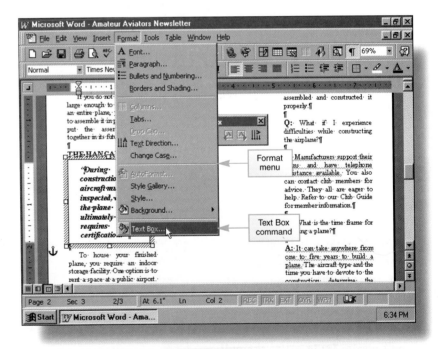

FIGURE 6-49

8 Click Text Box. If necessary, click the Colors and Lines tab when the Format Text Box dialog box first opens. Click the Line Color box arrow and then click the color Red. Click the Line Style box arrow and then click the 3 pt double lines graphic in the list.

Word displays the Format Text Box dialog box (Figure 6-50).

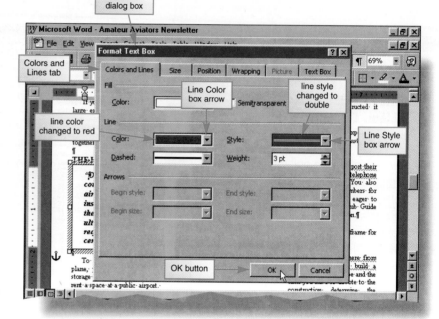

FIGURE 6-50

9 Click the OK button. Click the frame to select it and then point to the right-middle sizing handle on the frame.

Word changes the border around the text box (Figure 6-51).

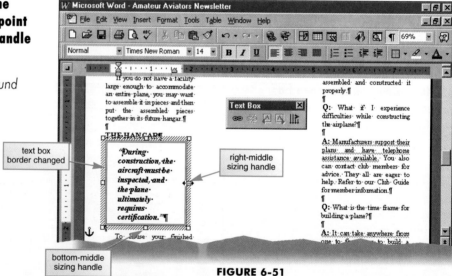

FIGURE 6-51

10 Drag the right-middle sizing handle to make the pull-quote a bit wider so the pull-quote text looks more balanced. Then, drag the bottom-middle sizing handle up to reduce the height of the pull-quote. Try to resize the pull-quote as close to Figure 6-52 as possible. Position the mouse pointer on the frame so it has a four-headed arrow attached to it.

The text in the pull-quote wraps more evenly (Figure 6-52).

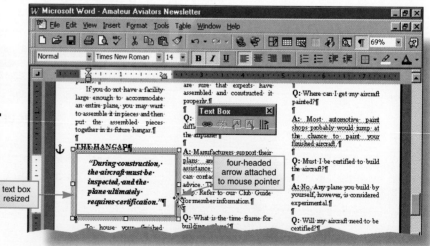

FIGURE 6-52

11 Drag the frame to its new position (Figure 6-53). You may need to drag it a couple of times to position it similarly to this figure. Try to position it as close to Figure 6-53 as possible. Depending on your printer, your wordwrap may occur in different locations. Click outside the frame to remove the selection.

The pull-quote is complete (Figure 6-53).

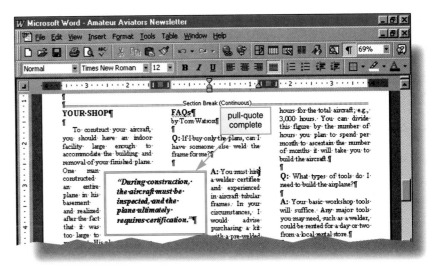

FIGURE 6-53

The second page of the newsletter is complete. Save this project again by clicking the Save button on the Standard toolbar.

The next step is to enhance the newsletter with colors and borders.

Enhancing the Newsletter with Color and a Page Border

You already have added color to many of the characters and lines in the newsletter in Project 6. You also want to color all of the subheads, edit the airplane graphic, and add a border around each page of the newsletter. The following pages illustrate these tasks.

The first step is to color the dropped capital letter.

TO COLOR THE DROP CAP

1. Scroll to the top of the newsletter and then select the dropped capital letter by clicking to its left.
2. Click the Font Color button arrow on the Formatting toolbar and then click the color Violet.

Word changes the color of the dropped capital letter to violet (Figure 6-54 on the next page).

Using the Format Painter Button

All of the subheads are to be colored violet. Instead of selecting each subhead one at a time and then changing its color with the Font Color button, you can change the color of the first subhead and then copy its formatting (which includes the color) to another location. To do this, use the **Format Painter button** on the Standard toolbar as shown on the next page.

More *About* **Printing Color**

Some printers do not have enough memory to print a wide variety of images and color. In these cases, the printer prints up to a certain point on a page and then chokes – resulting in only the top portion of the document printing. Check with your instructor whether your printer has enough memory to work with colors.

More *About* **Highlighting**

To add color to an e-mail communication or online document, you highlight the text instead of changing the font's color. Highlighting this text alerts the reader to the text's importance, much like a highlight marker does in a textbook. To highlight text, select it, click the Highlight button arrow, and then click the desired color.

Steps **To Use the Format Painter Button**

1 **Drag through the remaining characters in the subhead, ET READY. (It may be easier to drag from right to left because of the frame around the dropped capital letter.) Click the Font Color button on the Formatting toolbar. Click somewhere in the subhead GET READY, other than the drop cap. Click the Format Painter button on the Standard toolbar. Move the mouse pointer into the document window.**

*The mouse pointer changes to an I-beam with a small paint brush to its left when the **Format Painter button** is recessed (Figure 6-54). The insertion point is in the 14-point Times New Roman violet, bold font of the subhead GET READY. The format painter has copied this font.*

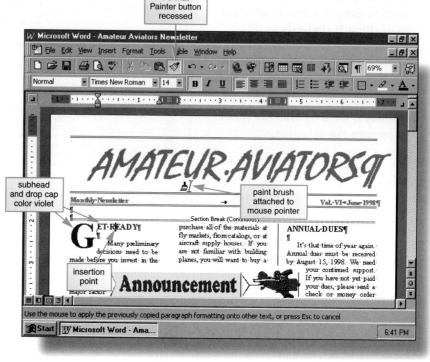

FIGURE 6-54

2 **Scroll through the newsletter to the next subhead, PURCHASING PLAN. Select the subhead by clicking to its left. Click outside the selection to remove the highlight.**

Word copies the 14-point Times New Roman violet, bold font to the PURCHASING PLAN subhead (Figure 6-55). The Format Painter button on the Standard toolbar is no longer recessed.

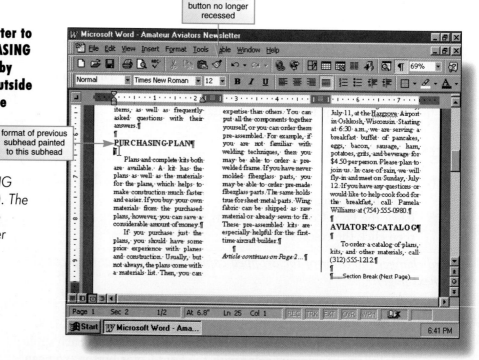

FIGURE 6-55

If you want to copy character formatting to multiple locations in a document, double-click the Format Painter button, which will remain recessed until you click it again. Highlight each location to which you want the format copied. When you are finished copying the character formatting, click the Format Painter button again to restore the normal I-beam pointer.

In this newsletter, you want each subhead to be the color violet. You could use the Format Painter button to color each subhead. Because several subheads remain, an easier technique is to create a macro for the character formatting as discussed in the next section.

Using a Macro to Automate a Task

A **macro** is composed of a series of Word commands or instructions that are grouped together as a single command. This single command is a convenient way to automate a difficult or lengthy task. Macros often are used by Word users for formatting or editing activities, to combine multiple commands into a single command, or to display a dialog box with a single keystroke.

To create a macro, you begin the **Word macro recorder** and then record a series of actions. The recorder is similar to a movie camera, in that it records all actions you perform on a document over a period of time. Once the macro is recorded, you can run it any time you want to perform that same set of actions.

When Word records a macro, it stores a series of instructions using Visual Basic, its **macro language**. **Visual Basic** is a powerful programming language available with Word. If you are familiar with programming techniques, you can write your own macros or edit one recorded earlier.

The macro for this project will format characters to the 14-point Times New Roman violet, bold font when you press the ALT+V keys. Perform the following steps to record this macro.

Steps To Record a Macro

① **Position the insertion point in the BUYING A KIT subhead. Point to the REC indicator on the status bar.**

Because the BUYING A KIT subhead already is formatted to 14-point Times New Roman bold, the formatting required for the macro will require only the addition of the color violet (Figure 6-56). Thus, the positioning of the insertion point in this step is for convenience only; it is not required.

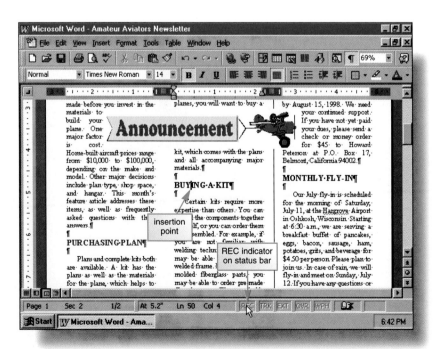

FIGURE 6-56

More *About* **Macros**

If you are familiar with computer programming techniques, you can edit an existing macro. To do this, click Macro on the Tools menu, click Macros on the Macro submenu, click the name of the macro in the Macros dialog box, and then click the Edit button to display the macro contents in the Visual Basic Editor window. When finished, save the macro and then click Close on the File menu.

2 Double-click the REC indicator on the status bar. When the Record Macro dialog box displays, type `FormatSubheads` in the Macro name text box. Point to the Keyboard button.

*Word displays the **Record Macro** dialog box (Figure 6-57). Macro names must begin with a letter, can contain only letters and numbers with no spaces, and can be a maximum length of 80 characters. You can assign a macro to a button on a toolbar, a command in a menu, or a shortcut key. For this macro, you want to press the ALT+V keys to make selected characters the 14-point Times New Roman violet, bold font.*

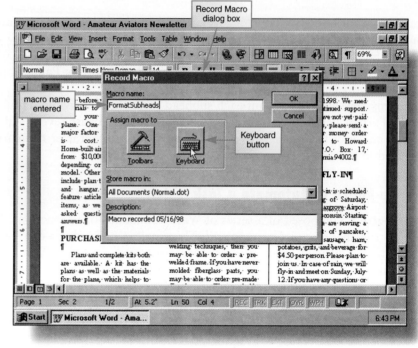

FIGURE 6-57

3 Click the Keyboard button. When the Customize Keyboard dialog box displays, press the ALT+V keys and then point to the Assign button.

*Word displays the **Customize Keyboard dialog box** (Figure 6-58). The shortcut keys you pressed display in the Press new shortcut key text box. If the shortcut key already has a function in Word, it displays in the Currently assigned to area. In this case, ALT+V is unassigned.*

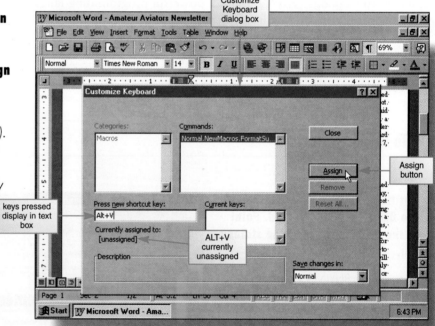

FIGURE 6-58

4 Click the Assign button and then point to the Close button in the Customize Keyboard dialog box.

Word assigns the shortcut key to the macro named FormatSubheads (Figure 6-59).

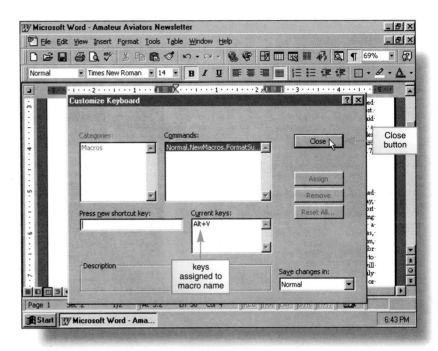

FIGURE 6-59

5 Click the Close button.

Word displays a Stop Recording toolbar in the document window (Figure 6-60).

FIGURE 6-60

6 Click Format on the menu bar and then point to Font (Figure 6-61).

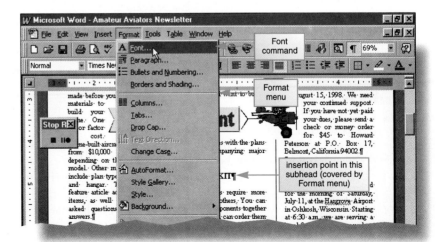

FIGURE 6-61

7 **Click Font. If necessary, click the Font tab when the Font dialog box first opens. Click the Color box arrow; scroll to and then click Violet in the list. Be sure the font is Times New Roman, the font style is Bold, and the font size is 14. Point to the OK button.**

Word displays the Font dialog box (Figure 6-62). The formatting for the subheads, 14-point Times New Roman violet, bold font, is selected.

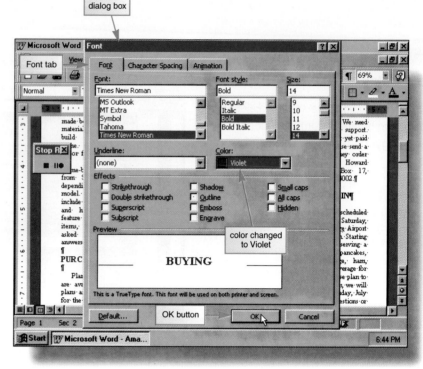

FIGURE 6-62

8 **Click the OK button. Point to the Stop Recording button on the Stop Recording toolbar.**

Word stores the settings in the Font dialog box in the FormatSubheads macro (Figure 6-63). A portion of the subhead is formatted with the color violet.

9 **Click the Stop Recording button.**

Word closes the Stop Recording toolbar and dims the REC indicator on the status bar (see Figure 6-64).

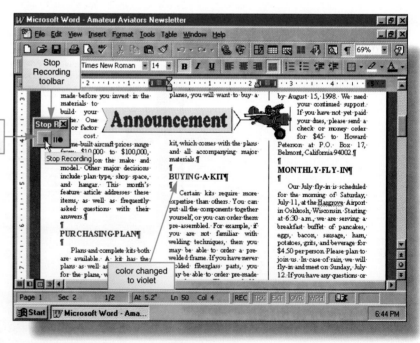

FIGURE 6-63

If, while recording a macro, you want to perform some actions that should not be part of the macro, click the **Pause Recording button** on the Stop Recording toolbar to suspend the recording (Figure 6-60 on the previous page). When you want to continue recording, click the Pause Recording button again.

The next step is to run the macro using the shortcut keys ALT+V as shown in the following steps.

Steps **To Run a Macro**

① **Select the BUYING A KIT subhead (Figure 6-64).**

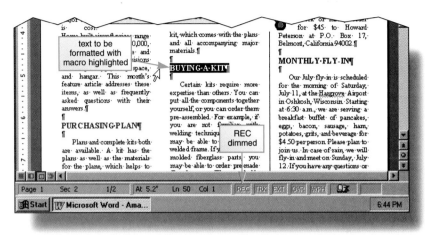

FIGURE 6-64

② **Press the ALT+V keys. Click outside the highlight to remove the selection.**

Word locates the instructions stored for the macro ALT+V and then performs its instructions (Figure 6-65). The characters in the subhead are the 14-point Times New Roman violet, bold font.

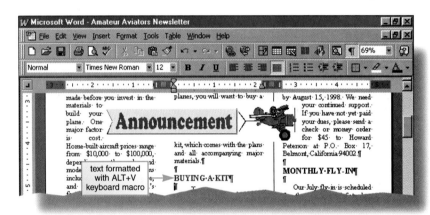

FIGURE 6-65

OtherWays

1. On Tools menu point to Macro, click Macros, click macro name in Macro name list box, click Run button

The remaining subheads and the pull-quote in the newsletter must be colored as described in the steps below.

TO COLOR THE REMAINING TEXT IN THE NEWSLETTER

① Select the ANNUAL DUES subhead and then press the ALT+V keys.
② Repeat the procedure in Step 1 for each of these subheads: MONTHLY FLY-IN, AVIATOR'S CATALOG, YOUR SHOP, THE HANGAR, and FAQs.
③ Select the pull-quote by dragging from the left quotation mark through the right quotation mark. Click the Font Color button arrow on the Formatting toolbar and then click the color Teal. Click outside the selection to remove the highlight.

The characters in the newsletter are colored (Figure 6-66 on the next page).

Word stores macros in the Normal template; thus, they are available to every Word document on your system. For this reason, you should delete the macro just created by following the steps on the next page.

More *About* **Color**

Because they are difficult to read, avoid using light colors, like yellow, orange, or light green for text. Graphics also should use bright, bold colors so that they stand out. If you do not have a color printer, still change the colors because the colors will print in shades of black and gray, which adds variety to your newsletter.

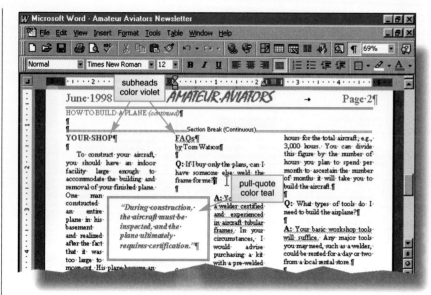

FIGURE 6-66

TO DELETE A MACRO

1 Click Tools on the menu bar, point to Macro, and then click Macros.

2 Click the macro name FormatSubheads in the Macro name list.

3 Click the Delete button.

4 Click the Yes button in the Microsoft Word dialog box. Click the Close button in the Macros dialog box.

Word deletes the FormatSubheads macro; thus, ALT+V is no longer assigned to any Word instructions.

The next step is to change the color of the airplane graphic and change the slogan in the banner object of the graphic.

Editing a Graphic

The banner object of the airplane graphic in the newsletter is yellow. To change its color and add text to it, you use the **Drawing toolbar**. Through the drawing toolbar, you can create **drawing objects** such as rectangles, squares, polygons, ellipses, and lines. Perform the following steps to edit the airplane graphic.

 To Edit a Graphic

1 Scroll through the document and then click the airplane graphic to select it. Click the Drawing button on the Standard toolbar.

*The airplane graphic is selected (Figure 6-67). The **Drawing button** on the Standard toolbar is recessed, and the Drawing toolbar displays at the bottom of the Word screen.*

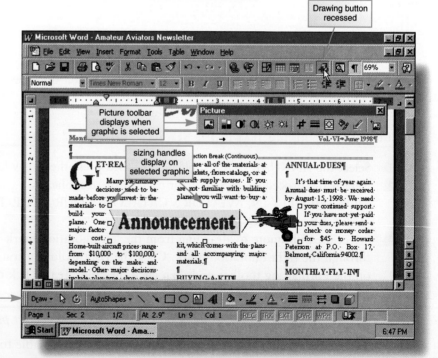

FIGURE 6-67

2 Click the Draw button on the Drawing toolbar and then point to Ungroup on the Draw menu (Figure 6-68).

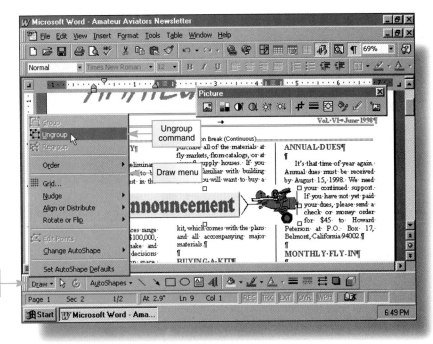

FIGURE 6-68

3 Click Ungroup.

The airplane graphic is separated into its individual objects (Figure 6-69). You can edit each individual object.

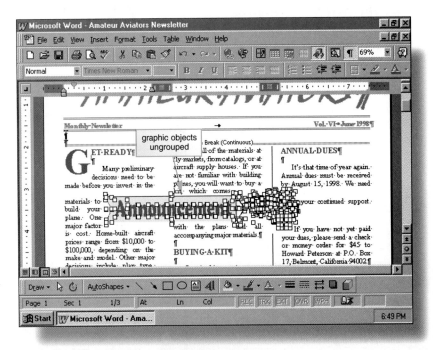

FIGURE 6-69

4 Click outside the graphic to deselect the objects. Click the letter A in the word, Announcement. While holding down the SHIFT key, click each remaining letter in the word, Announcement. If you accidentally click any other object, click outside the graphic and begin this step again.

Word selects each letter in the word, Announcement (Figure 6-70). Be careful not to select any other object in the graphic.

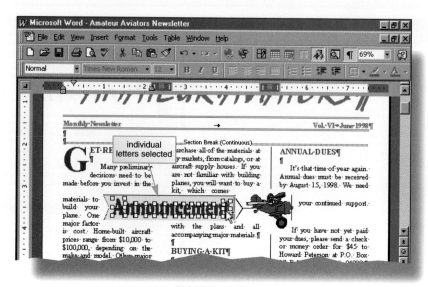

FIGURE 6-70

5 Click the Cut button on the Standard toolbar. Click the banner object to select it. Click the Fill Color button arrow on the Drawing toolbar and then point to the color Teal.

Word removes the word, Announcement, from the banner (Figure 6-71). The banner object has sizing handles, indicating it is selected.

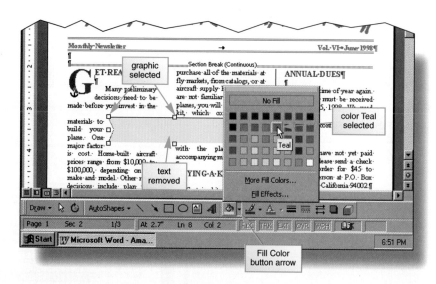

FIGURE 6-71

6 Click the color Teal. Click the Text Box button on the Drawing toolbar. Point in the banner object about .25 inch from its top and left edges.

*Word colors the inside of the banner teal (Figure 6-72). The mouse pointer changes to a plus sign when the Text Box button is recessed. You drag the mouse pointer to outline a **text box**, in which you then can type.*

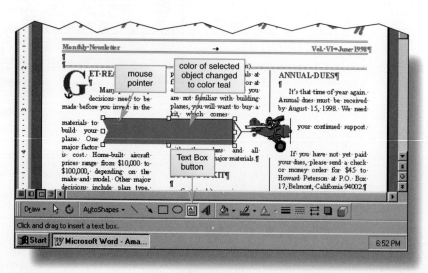

FIGURE 6-72

7 Drag so a text box approximately 2 inches wide and .25 inch high displays in the banner object. Point to the Fill Color button on the Drawing toolbar.

Word creates a text box inside the banner object (Figure 6-73). The Fill Color button displays the color teal because it is the most recently selected color.

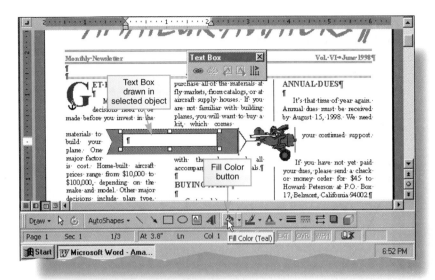

FIGURE 6-73

8 Click the Fill Color button on the the Drawing toolbar. Click the Font Color button arrow and then point to the color White.

Word displays the list of available font colors (Figure 6-74).

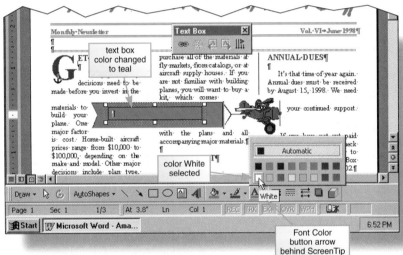

FIGURE 6-74

9 Click the color White and then click the Bold button on the Formatting toolbar. Type HOW TO BUILD A PLANE in the text box.

Word displays the slogan in a text box in the banner object (Figure 6-75). Notice the text box has a border around it.

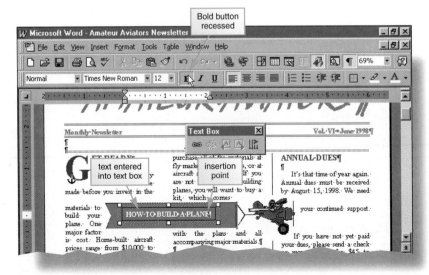

FIGURE 6-75

10 Click Format on the menu bar and then click Text Box. If necessary, click the Colors and Lines tab when the Format Text Box dialog box first opens. Click the Line Color box arrow and then click No Line.

Word displays the *Format Text Box dialog box* (Figure 6-76).

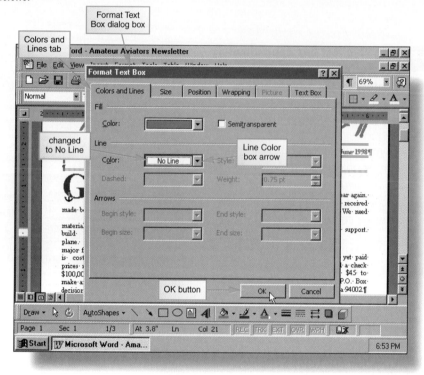

FIGURE 6-76

11 Click the OK button. Click the Draw button on the Drawing toolbar and then point to Regroup.

Word removes the border from around the text box (Figure 6-77). Because you are finished editing the airplane, you want to regroup the individual objects into one large object.

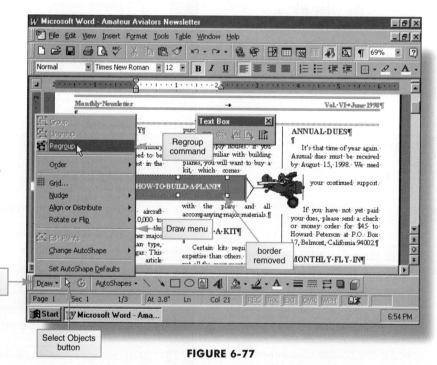

FIGURE 6-77

12 Click Regroup. (If the Regroup command is dimmed, click the Select Objects button on the Drawing toolbar, drag the dotted rectangle around the entire graphic, click the Draw button on the Drawing toolbar, and then click Group to regroup the objects into a single object.) Click the Drawing button on the Standard toolbar to remove the Drawing toolbar. Click outside the graphic to remove the selection.

Word regroups the individual objects into a single object (Figure 6-78). The Drawing toolbar no longer displays at the bottom of the screen.

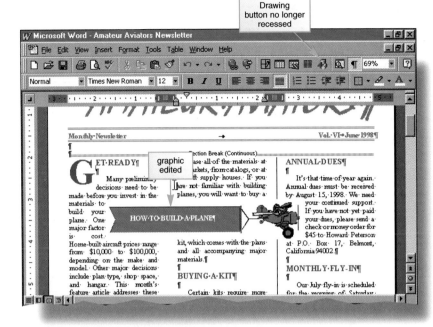

FIGURE 6-78

The final step in enhancing the newsletter is to add a border around each page.

Adding a Page Border

You have added borders to the edges of a paragraph(s). In Word, you can also add a border around the perimeter of an entire page. These page borders add professionalism to your documents. Perform the following steps to add a teal page border to the pages of the newsletter.

More *About* **Graphics**

Some images in the Microsoft Clip Gallery are Windows metafiles, and you may edit any of the metafiles. Other graphics supplied with Office, also in the Clip Gallery, are called bitmap images. You cannot edit bitmap images. To determine the file type, click the Clip Properties button in the Clip Gallery dialog box.

Steps **To Add a Page Border**

1 Click Format on the menu bar and then click Borders and Shading. If necessary, click the Page Border tab when the Borders and Shading dialog box first opens. Click the Box option in the Setting area; scroll to the bottom of the Style list box and then click the last style in the list; click the Color box arrow and then click Teal; point to the Options button.

Word displays the Borders and Shading dialog box (Figure 6-79). The page border is set to a 3-point Teal box.

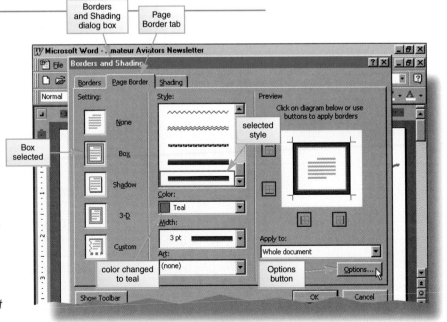

FIGURE 6-79

2 Click the Options button. When the Border and Shading Options dialog box displays, click the Measure from box arrow and then click Text. Change the Top setting to 4 pt and the bottom setting to 0 pt.

Word displays the Border and Shading Options dialog box (Figure 6-80).

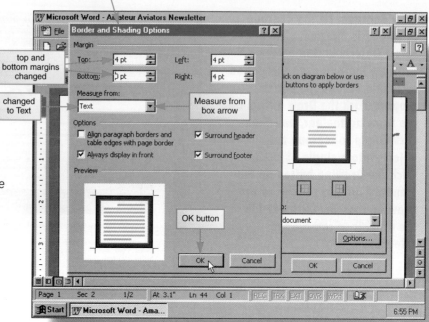

FIGURE 6-80

3 Click the OK button in the Border and Shading Options dialog box. When the Borders and Shading dialog box redisplays, click its OK button.

Word places a page border on each page of the newsletter (Figure 6-81).

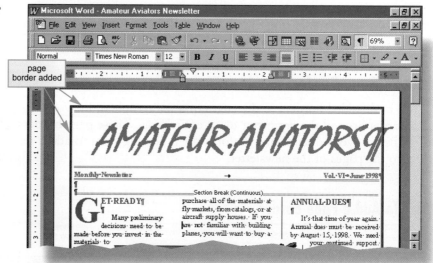

FIGURE 6-81

The newsletter is complete. You should save the document again, print it, and then quit Word.

TO SAVE AND PRINT THE DOCUMENT

1 Click the Save button on the Standard toolbar.

2 Click the Print button on the Standard toolbar.

The printed newsletter is shown in Figures 6-1 and 6-2 on pages WD 6.5 and WD 6.6.

TO QUIT WORD

① Click the Close button in the Word window.

The Word window closes.

Project Summary

Project 6 introduced you to creating a professional looking newsletter using desktop publishing features. You created a nameplate with ruling lines. You formatted the body of the newsletter into three columns and added a vertical rule between the second and third columns. You learned how to move graphics and a pull-quote between columns. You used the Format Painter button and learned how to create a macro. Finally, you edited a graphic and added a page border to the newsletter.

What You Should Know

Having completed this project, you should now be able to perform the following tasks:

▶ Add a Page Border *(WD 6.51)*

▶ Add a Vertical Rule Between Columns *(WD 6.29)*

▶ Add Ruling Lines *(WD 6.10)*

▶ Change All Margin Settings *(WD 6.8)*

▶ Color the Drop Cap *(WD 6.39)*

▶ Color the Remaining Text in the Newsletter *(WD 6.45)*

▶ Create a Dropped Capital Letter *(WD 6.20)*

▶ Create a Pull-Quote *(WD 6.35)*

▶ Delete a Macro *(WD 6.46)*

▶ Display Nonprinting Characters *(WD 6.7)*

▶ Download Clip Art from Microsoft's Clip Gallery Live Web Page *(WD 6.22)*

▶ Edit a Graphic *(WD 6.46)*

▶ Enter Subheads and Associated Text *(WD 6.17)*

▶ Enter the Nameplate and Continued Message on the Second Page *(WD 6.33)*

▶ Format and Enter Text *(WD 6.9)*

▶ Format Columns *(WD 6.15)*

▶ Format the Second Page Nameplate *(WD 6.32)*

▶ Insert a Column Break (WD 6.27 and WD 6.34)

▶ Insert a Continuous Section Break *(WD 6.14)*

▶ Insert a File into a Column of the Newsletter *(WD 6.28)*

▶ Insert a File into the Newsletter *(WD 6.19)*

▶ Insert a Next Page Section Break *(WD 6.26)*

▶ Insert a Symbol into Text *(WD 6.11)*

▶ Install the Clip Art File from the Data Disk *(WD 6.23)*

▶ Position a Graphic Anywhere on a Page *(WD 6.24)*

▶ Quit Word *(WD 6.53)*

▶ Record a Macro *(WD 6.41)*

▶ Redefine the Normal Style *(WD 6.8)*

▶ Run a Macro *(WD 6.45)*

▶ Save and Print the Document *(WD 6.52)*

▶ Save the Newsletter in a File *(WD 6.18)*

▶ Start Word *(WD 6.7)*

▶ Use the Format Painter Button *(WD 6.40)*

▶ Zoom Page Width *(WD 6.10)*

Test Your Knowledge

1 True/False

Instructions: Circle T if the statement is true or F if the statement is false.

T F 1. Word 97 provides many of the desktop publishing features you would find in a specialized package.

T F 2. The space between an object and the text that wraps around the object is called run-around.

T F 3. To format the first character of a paragraph as a dropped capital letter, click the Drop Cap button on the Formatting toolbar.

T F 4. Snaking columns are created with the Columns button on the Standard toolbar.

T F 5. The default number of columns in a document is one.

T F 6. To move a graphic between or across columns, the Float over text check box must be deselected.

T F 7. When you insert a text box, Word places a border around it.

T F 8. A pull-quote is a quotation mark displayed in a font size larger than 40 points.

T F 9. The Drawing toolbar displays below the Formatting toolbar.

T F 10. A paragraph border displays around the perimeter of a page.

2 Multiple Choice

Instructions: Circle the correct response.

1. In the desktop publishing field, the _____ is located at the top of a newsletter.
   a. box border
   b. nameplate
   c. wrap-around text
   d. pull-quote

2. To insert special characters and symbols into a document, _____.
   a. click Symbol on the Insert menu
   b. press and hold the ALT key and then type a zero followed by the ANSI character code
   c. either a or b
   d. neither a nor b

3. Each section in a document can have its own _____.
   a. number of columns
   b. margins settings
   c. headers
   d. all of the above

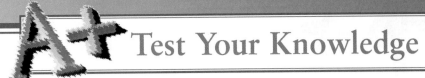

4. To add a vertical rule between columns, select the column and then _____.
   a. on the Tools menu, click Vertical Rule
   b. on the Format menu, click Borders and Shading
   c. click the Rule button on the Standard toolbar
   d. click the Rule button on the Drawing toolbar

5. Which of the following is a valid macro name?
   a. Print Hard Copy
   b. Print2HardCopies
   c. Print&SaveDocument
   d. both b and c are valid macro names

6. When Word records a macro, it stores a series of instructions using _____.
   a. Visual Basic
   b. Excel
   c. Access
   d. PowerPoint

7. To copy the formatting of text, click the text, click the _____ on the Standard toolbar, then select the text where you want to copy the formatting.
   a. Copy button
   b. Paste button
   c. Format Painter button
   d. Copy button and then the Paste button

8. When the first letter in a paragraph is larger than the rest of the characters in the paragraph, the letter is called a _____.
   a. large cap
   b. big cap
   c. drop cap
   d. enlarged cap

9. The REC indicator is located on the _____.
   a. vertical scroll bar
   b. horizontal scroll bar
   c. status bar
   d. taskbar

10. To add a page border, _____.
    a. on the Format menu, click Borders and Shading
    b. on the Format menu, click Page Border
    c. right-click the page and then click Border on the shortcut menu
    d. click the Page Border button on the Standard toolbar

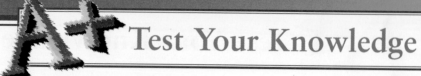

3 Understanding the Drawing Toolbar

Instructions: In Figure 6-82, arrows point to several of the buttons on the Drawing toolbar. In the spaces provided, briefly explain the purpose of each button.

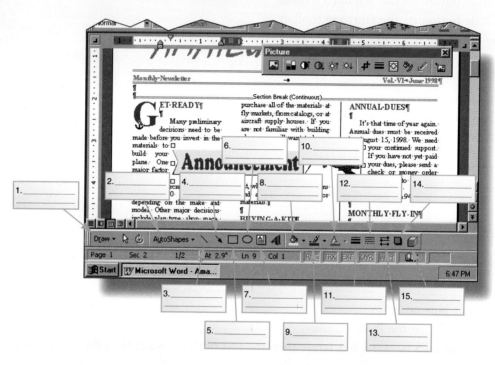

FIGURE 6-82

4 Understanding Desktop Publishing Terminology

Instructions: In the spaces provided, briefly define each of the desktop publishing terms listed.

TERM

1. nameplate
2. ruling line
3. vertical rule
4. issue information line
5. subhead
6. wrap-around text
7. run-around
8. pull-quote
9. banner
10. drop cap

DEFINITION

? Use Help

1 Reviewing Project Activities

Instructions: Perform the following tasks using a computer.

1. Start Word.
2. If the Office Assistant is on your screen, click it to display its balloon. If the Office Assistant is not on your screen, click the Office Assistant button on the Standard toolbar.
3. Type macros in the What would you like to do? text box. Click the Search button. Click the Using macros to automate tasks link. Read the information. Use the shortcut menu or the Options button to print the information.
4. Click the Help Topics button to display the Help Topics: Microsoft Word dialog box. Click the Contents tab. Double-click the Changing the Appearance of Your Page book. Double-click the Positioning Text Using Newspaper Columns book. Double-click the Newspaper columns topic. Click each of the links and read their Help information. Right-click each link's help information and then click Print Topic on the shortcut menu.
5. Click the Help Topics button. Click the Index tab. Type page borders and then double-click the page borders, adding topic. Click the Add a border to a page in a document link. Read and print the information.
6. Click the Help Topics button. Click the Find tab. Type format painter and then double-click the Copy character and paragraph formats topic. Read and print the information.
7. Close any open Help window(s) by clicking its Close button. Close the Office Assistant.

2 Expanding on the Basics

Instructions: Use Word Help to better understand the topics listed below. Answer the questions on your own paper or hand in the printed Help topic to your instructor.

1. In this project, you created a page border to enhance the newsletter. Use the Office Assistant to determine the definition of a watermark and then determine how to add one to a Word document.
2. In this project, you created newspaper, or snaking, columns in the newsletters. Use the Contents tab in the Help Topics: Microsoft Word dialog box to answer the following questions about newspaper columns.
    a. How do you change the number of newspaper columns in a section?
    b. How can you change the width of a newspaper column in a section?
    c. How do you remove newspaper columns from a section?
3. In this project, you used a macro. Use the Index tab in the Help Topics: Microsoft Word dialog box to answer the following questions about macros.
    a. What if, when you record a macro, you accidentally perform an action you do not want to record?
    b. Can a macro be renamed? If so, how?
4. In this project, you inserted the bullet symbol into the newsletter. Use the Find tab in the Help Topics: Microsoft Word dialog box to answer these questions about symbols.
    a. How do you enter the following international symbols into a document? ò, ó, Ö, ø, ¿, ß
    b. How do you assign a symbol to a shortcut key?

Apply Your Knowledge

1 Editing an Embedded Object

Instructions: Start Word. Performing the steps below, you are to edit a Windows metafile. The edited graphic is shown in Figure 6-83.

Perform the following tasks.

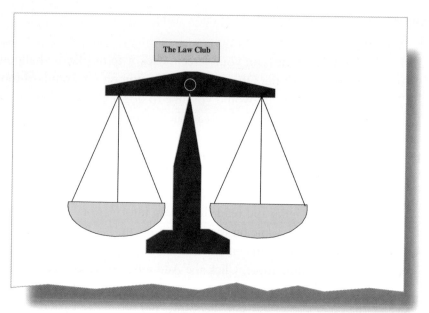

FIGURE 6-83

1. Click Insert on the menu bar, point to Picture, and then click Clip Art. If necessary, click the Clip Art tab when the Microsoft Clip Gallery dialog box first opens. Click the Signs category and then click the scales graphic. Click the Insert button to insert the scales graphic into the document window.

2. Click the Drawing button on the Standard toolbar to display the Drawing toolbar.

3. Click the Draw button on the Drawing toolbar and then click Ungroup.

4. Click the left scale in the graphic to select it. Click the Fill Color button arrow on the Drawing toolbar and then click the color Gold to change the scale's color to gold. Click the Line Color button arrow on the Drawing toolbar and then click the color Dark Red to change the line color to dark red.

5. Repeat Step 4 for the right scale.

6. Click the stand in the graphic to select it. Click the Fill Color button arrow on the Drawing toolbar and then click the color Violet. Click the Line Color button arrow on the Drawing toolbar and then click the color Gold.

7. Click the Text Box button on the Drawing toolbar and then drag a text box above the graphic about .25 inch high by 1.50 inches long to create a text box.

8. Change the font size to 12. Click the Bold button and the Center button on the Formatting toolbar. Click the text box and then type The Law Club as the club name. Resize the text box, if necessary. With the text box still selected, click the Font Color button arrow on the Drawing toolbar and then click the color Violet.

9. Click the Fill Color button arrow on the Drawing toolbar and then click the color Gold. Click the Line Color button arrow on the Drawing toolbar and then click the color Violet.

10. Save the edited graphic with The Law Club Graphic as the file name.

11. Print the edited graphic.

In the Lab

1 Creating a Newsletter from an Article and Announcements on File

Problem: You are an associate editor of the *Village News* newsletter for the Village of New Treppor. The 32nd edition is due out next Monday. The Village's new recycling program is to be the feature article (Figure 6-84). The recycling article and the announcements have been prepared and are on the Data Disk that accompanies this book.

Instructions:

1. Change the top, left, and right margins to .5 inch; change the bottom margin to .75 inch. Depending on your printer, you may need different margin settings.

2. Redefine the Normal style to a font size of 12.

3. Create the nameplate using the formats identified in Figure 6-84. Create a continuous section break below the nameplate. Format section 2 to three columns.

4. Insert the recycling article into section 2 below the nameplate. The article is in a file called Recycling Article in the Word folder on the Data Disk that accompanies this book. If necessary, switch to Page Layout View.

5. Insert a column break at the end of the recycling article. Insert the announcements into column 3 of section 2. The article is in a file called Village News Announcements in the Word folder on the Data Disk that accompanies this book.

Callouts in figure:

3-point dark red page border

72-point Algerian dark red, bold font

14-point Times New Roman dark red font

Times New Roman dark red, bold italic font for pull-quote

14-point Times New Roman teal, bold font for subheads

3-point green ruling lines

VILLAGE NEWS

Weekly Newsletter   No. 32 • July 20, 1998

RECYCLING

Beginning this Monday, the Village will initiate a curbside recycling program. To participate, simply pick up a green recycling bin at the Village Hall. The hours are Monday to Friday from 8:00 a.m. to 4:30 p.m. and Saturday from 8:00 a.m. to 1:00 p.m. The first recycling bin is free to each Village resident. Additional bins may be obtained for a fee of $3.50. The following sections of this newsletter outline the types of material that may be recycled.

"The first recycling bin is free to each Village resident."

BOTTLES & CANS

Both clear and colored food and drink glass bottles and aluminum cans may be recycled. Labels do not need to be removed; nor do the containers need to be washed. Broken bottles are not accepted.

PAPER

Most paper can be recycled. We require that you separate paper into the three individual groups: newspapers, magazines and catalogs, and mixed paper.

Inserts and advertisements may be left in the newspapers. Mixed paper includes white and colored paper, cardboard, cereal boxes, junk mail, and brown paper bags. Plastic window envelopes are recyclable.

Contaminated paper products may not be recycled and include paper coated with food, covered with wax, soaked in oil, or laminated.

PLASTIC

Types 1 and 2 plastic jugs and bottles are accepted. Milk jugs and soda bottles generally are recyclable in our program; motor oil and anti-freeze containers are not. Check the bottom of the jug or bottle for the code number. Because caps are not recyclable, remove all bottle caps from jugs and bottles.

OTHER NOTES

Johnny's Grocery in the Village Square will accept plastic grocery and produce sacks for recycling. The store is open 24-hours a day for your convenience.

HELP WANTED

Our fifth annual Summerfest is scheduled for the weekend of August 8 and 9. Activities include arts and crafts booths, volleyball games, antique car show, food and drink stands, live entertainment, children's contests, and bingo. We need volunteers to collect tickets, staff booths, and coordinate events. If you are interested, please call Jean at 555-2312.

WAFFLE BREAKFAST

The Village is sponsoring a Waffle Breakfast at the VFW on Center Street on Saturday, August 16, from 6:30 to 10:00 in the morning. Meal includes a waffle, 2 eggs, bacon or sausage, and juice. Cost is $3.99 per adult and $1.99 per child. The food is being donated by The Country Kitchen. All proceeds from this event will be donated to the Charity House. Please plan to attend.

DID YOU KNOW?

You can pay your water bills at the Village Bank or at Johnny's Grocery. If you have any questions, please come in and ask.

FIGURE 6-84

(continued)

In the Lab

Creating a Newsletter from an Article and Announcements on File *(continued)*

6. Format the newsletter according to Figure 6-84 on the previous page. Place a vertical rule between the second and third columns. Use the Format Painter button and a macro to automate some of your formatting tasks.
7. Save the document with Village News Newsletter as the file name.
8. Print the newsletter.

2 Creating a Newsletter from an Article on File

Problem: You are secretary for the National Campers Society and responsible for the monthly preparation of *Campers Society*, a newsletter for the club. The September edition, due out in two weeks, is to rate Trail Blaze Park in the feature article (Figure 6-85). The Trail Blaze Park review article has been prepared and is on the Data Disk that accompanies this book. You need to type the announcements.

Instructions:

1. Change the top, left, and right margins to .5 inch; change the bottom margin to .75 inch. Depending on your printer, you may need different margin settings.
2. Redefine the Normal style to a font size of 12.
3. Create the nameplate using the formats identified in Figure 6-85. Create a continuous section break below the nameplate. Format section 2 to three columns.
4. Insert the Trail Blaze Article file into section 2 below the nameplate. The article is in a file called Trail Blaze Article in the Word folder on the Data Disk that accompanies this book. If necessary, switch to Page Layout View.
5. Insert a column break at the end of Trail Blaze Article. Enter the announcements into column 3 of section 2. The first line of each paragraph is indented .25 inch.
6. Format the newsletter according to Figure 6-85. The clip art is in the Screen Beans category of the Microsoft Clip Gallery; resize the clip art to 45%. Place a vertical rule between the second and third columns. Use the Format Painter button and a macro to automate some of your formatting tasks.
7. Save the document with Campers Society Newsletter as the file name.
8. Print the newsletter.

3 Creating a Newsletter from Scratch

Problem: You are the editor of *Surfing Today*, a new monthly newsletter for the subscribers to the Internet. The first edition is due out in November. An introduction to the Internet is to be the feature article (Figure 6-86 on page WD 6.62). You need to enter the feature article, as well as announcements.

In the Lab

3-point green page border

48-point Arial Black blue, bold font

14-point Times New Roman blue font

½-point red triple ruling lines

CAMPERS SOCIETY

Monthly Newsletter   Issue 66 • September 1998

clip art fill color light blue, line color blue-gray

14-point Times New Roman green, bold font for subheads

FOUR STARS!

Trail Blaze Park in Round Lake, Illinois, receives a four-star rating from the National Campers Society. Located on more than 7,500 acres of beautiful rolling hills with thousands of oak trees and roomy campsites, the park has two lakes stocked with game fish and another lake for swimming and boating. The park provides comfortable, clean camping facilities with both outdoor and indoor activities for all ages. This article highlights the features of Trail Blaze Park.

RECREATION

One major attraction of this park is that all activities are free to all overnight guests. For the camper that enjoys the outdoors, Trail Blaze Park provides swimming in a clear water lake or an Olympic-sized heated pool, tennis, basketball, horseshoes, hiking, nature walks, canoeing, ping-pong, golf, shuffleboard, rowboating, fishing, and horseback riding. For children, the fun includes hayrides, video games, four playgrounds, and wagon rides.

Evening activities include bingo, movies, concerts, and square dances. An enclosed recreation room has frequent nighttime children's programs, such as games, sing-a-longs, scavenger hunts, and cartoons.

FACILITIES

The park has 550 hook-up sites. Of these, 200 are full hook-ups that include water, sewer, and 30-amp electric for $18 per day. The remaining 350 are water and 20-amp electric for $15 per day. A total of 75 primitive, or tent, sites are available for $10 per day.

The park provides modern restrooms, hot showers, laundry facilities, and public telephones. A camp store is located at the park's entrance that supplies snacks, groceries, firewood, camping supplies, and fishing supplies. No fishing license is required!

For reservations, directions, or more information, call Karen at (847) 555-8867.

MEMBER DISCOUNTS

As a National Campers Society member, you are entitled to many benefits. Discounts include a 10 percent reduction on campsites at over 3,000 parks nationwide; members-only RV and auto insurance protection at low rates; 15 percent discount on parts and supplies at participating facilities; and an annual coupon book. To receive your free National Campers Society card and a complete benefits guide, call Mike at (312) 555-0088.

FREE CATALOG

Campers Discount Supply has air conditioners, awnings, jacks, heaters, refrigerators, fans and vents, kitchen accessories, generators, trailer parts, covers, and many more hard-to-find camping supplies. For a free color catalog, call toll-free at (800) 555-4400.

REMINDER

Annual dues of $40 must be paid by September 30. Please send check to National Campers Society, P.O. Box 776, Chicago, IL 60601.

FIGURE 6-85

Instructions:

1. Change the top, left, and right margins to .5 inch; change the bottom margin to .75 inch. Depending on your printer, you may need different margin settings.
2. Redefine the Normal style to a font size of 12.
3. Create the nameplate using the formats identified in Figure 6-86 on the next page. Create a continuous section break below the nameplate. Format section 2 to three columns.

(continued)

In the Lab

Creating a Newsletter from Scratch *(continued)*

4. If necessary, switch to Page Layout View. Enter the Internet article into section 2 below the nameplate.

5. Insert a continuous section break at the end of the Internet article. Format section 3 to two columns. Type the announcements into section 3 at the bottom of the page.

6. Format the newsletter according to Figure 6-86. Place a vertical rule between all columns in section 2; place a vertical rule between the columns in section 3. Use the Line between check box in the Columns dialog box (Format menu) to do this. Use the Format Painter button and a macro to automate some of your formatting tasks.

7. Save the document with Surfing Today Newsletter as the file name.

8. Print the newsletter.

3-point dark blue page border

72-point Arial Narrow green, bold font

14-point Times New Roman green font

clip art in Maps – International category of Microsoft Clip Gallery

14-point Times New Roman dark blue, bold font for subheads

2¼-point bright green ruling line

½-point pink double ruling lines

SURFING TODAY

Monthly Newsletter

Vol. I • No. 1 • November 1998

WELCOME

For this first monthly issue of Surfing Today, we plan to introduce you to the basics of the Internet. With each subsequent issue, you will be exposed to another exciting feature of the Internet. For example, how to do research; view stock prices; shop for services and merchandise; display weather maps; obtain pictures, movies, audio clips, and information stored on computers around the world; and converse with people worldwide.

THE INTERNET

The Internet is a collection of networks, each of which is composed of a collection of smaller networks; for example,

on a college campus, the network in the student lab can be connected to the faculty computer network, which is connected to the administration network, and they all can connect to the Internet.

Networks are connected with high-, medium-, and low-speed data lines that allow data to move from one computer to another. The separate networks connect to the Internet through computers.

WORLD WIDE WEB

Modern computer systems have the capability to deliver information in a variety of ways, such as graphics, sound, video clips, animation, and, of course, regular text. On the Internet, this multimedia capability is available in the form of hypermedia, which is any variety of computer media.

Hypermedia is accessed through the use of a hypertext link, or simply link, which is a special software pointer that points to the location of the computer on which the hypermedia is stored and to the hypermedia itself. A link can point to hypermedia on any computer hooked into the Internet that is running the proper software. Thus, a hypertext link on a computer in New York can point to a picture on a computer in Los Angeles.

The collection of hypertext links throughout the Internet creates an interconnected network of links called the World Wide Web, which also is referred to as the Web, or WWW. Each computer within the Web containing hypermedia that can be referenced by hypertext links is called a Web site. Thousands of Web sites around the world can be accessed through the Internet.

FAQs

Frequently Asked Questions, or FAQs, are a common type of informal publishing on the Internet. A FAQ file answers questions of interest to a particular group of people. For example, one FAQ file addresses questions on Internet documentation styles for research papers.

NEXT MONTH

Next month's issue will discuss how to use Netscape Navigator, an Internet browser. Netscape Navigator provides graphical display of plain and formatted text, hypertext, online access to graphs, images, audio and video clips, and multimedia and hypermedia documents.

FIGURE 6-86

Cases and Places

The difficulty of these case studies varies: ❶ are the least difficult; ❶❶ are more difficult; and ❶❶❶ are the most difficult.

1 ❶ Your school has decided to publish a one-page monthly newsletter to be sent to the community. You have been assigned the task of designing the newsletter and writing the first issue. The newsletter should contain an informative article about the school. Select a topic about your school that would interest the community; e.g., a curricula, the fitness center, the day care center, the bookstore, the Student Government Organization, registration, the student body, a club, a sports team, and so on. Obtain information for your article by interviewing a campus employee or a student, visiting the school library, or reading brochures published by your school. The article should span the first two columns of the newsletter, and the third column should contain announcements for the school. Enhance the newsletter with color, ruling lines, and a page border. Use an appropriate clip art graphic or a pull-quote in the newsletter.

2 ❶ You are a member of the Pen Pal Club, which unites people across the world. The club publishes a monthly newsletter for its members. Each newsletter features one member and lists announcements. You are the feature member this month; thus, you have been assigned the task of designing and writing the newsletter. The newsletter should contain an interesting article about you; e.g., interests, hobbies, employment, major, family, friends, and so on. The article should span the first two columns of the newsletter, and the third column should contain announcements for the club. Enhance the newsletter with color, ruling lines, and a page border. Use an appropriate clip art graphic or a pull-quote in the newsletter.

3 ❶❶ You are an associate editor of *Village News*, a one-page newsletter for the Village of New Treppor. Last week's edition is shown in Figure 6-84 on page WD 6.59. The 33rd edition is due out in three weeks. Your assignment is to decide on a feature article for the *Village News* newsletter and develop some announcements. Use your home community as the basis for your feature article and announcements. Your article could address an item such as one of these: an issue facing the community, a major upcoming event, a celebration, a new program, an election or campaign, and so on. Visit the Chamber of Commerce or other government agency in your community to obtain background information for your article. The newsletter should contain both the feature article and community announcements. Enhance the newsletter with color, ruling lines, and a page border using colors different from those used in Figure 6-84. Use an appropriate clip art graphic or a pull-quote in the newsletter.

Cases and Places

4 ▶▶ You are secretary for the National Campers Society and responsible for the monthly preparation of *Campers Society*, a one-page newsletter for the club. Last month's edition is shown in Figure 6-85 on page WD 6.61. The October edition is due out in two weeks. Your assignment is to decide on a feature article for *Campers Society* and develop some announcements. The feature article cannot rate a campground; instead, develop a feature article of interest to campers. For example, your feature article could discuss types of recreational vehicles, items to pack for a camping trip, how to care for your camper, or any other item of interest to you. Visit a campground, the library, or a local dealership for information for your article. The newsletter should contain both the feature article and announcements, which you need to develop. Enhance the newsletter with color, ruling lines, and a page border using colors different from those used in Figure 6-85. Use an appropriate clip art graphic or a pull-quote in the newsletter.

5 ▶▶ You are the editor of *Surfing Today*, a one-page monthly newsletter for the subscribers to the Internet. Last month's edition is shown in Figure 6-86 on page WD 6.62. The next edition is due out in two weeks. Your assignment is to decide on a feature article for *Surfing Today* and develop some announcements. The feature article should provide information about some aspect of the Internet. Your article could address an item such as one of these: a Web browser, how to develop a home page, an interesting Internet site, HTML, an Internet provider, and so on. Surf the Internet for information in your article. The newsletter should contain both the feature article and announcements, which you need to develop. Enhance the newsletter with color, ruling lines, and a page border using colors different from those in Figure 6-86. Use an appropriate clip art graphic or a pull-quote in the newsletter.

6 ▶▶▶ You are a member of the local chapter of a computer user group. The group has decided to publish a two-page monthly newsletter. You must decide on a title for the newsletter. Your assignment is to design the newsletter and develop the first issue. The newsletter should have a feature article and some announcements for the user group. Your feature article should address a computer-related item such as a new hardware platform, an interesting software application, an exciting Internet site, price comparisons, a local computer center, and so on. Use the Internet, textbooks, teachers, user manuals, user guides, and magazines for information in your article. The newsletter should contain both the feature article that spans both pages of the newsletter and user group announcements on the first page of the newsletter. Enhance the newsletter with color, ruling lines, and a page border. Use an appropriate clip art graphic and a pull-quote in the newsletter.

7 ▶▶▶ You are a member of a package vacation club. Because you have a background in desktop publishing, you prepare the monthly two-page newsletter for club members. Your assignment is to design the newsletter and develop the next issue. The newsletter should have a feature article and some announcements for club members. Your feature article should discuss some exciting vacation site, which can be anywhere in the world. Use the Internet, a local travel agency, literature or brochures, or a public library for information on your travel spot. The newsletter should contain the feature article that spans both pages of the newsletter and user group announcements on the first page of the newsletter. Enhance the newsletter with color, ruling lines, and a page border. Use an appropriate clip art graphic and a pull-quote in the newsletter.

Using WordArt to Add Special Text Effects to a Word Document

Case Perspective

Recall that in Project 6, you were asked to design the June newsletter for the Amateur Aviators. Thus, you created the newsletter shown in Figures 6-1 and 6-2 on pages WD 6.5 and WD 6.6 and submitted it to the club president, Tom Watson, for his approval. He was very impressed with the design you created. Now, he has asked you to enhance the title somehow. He wants it to have a bit more pizzazz. You decide to look into the capabilities of WordArt, a supplementary Office application that allows you to create interesting text effects.

You will need the newsletter created in Project 6 so you can modify the title. (If you did not create the newsletter, see your instructor for a copy of it.) You will use WordArt to add special text effects to the title. WordArt is an application included with Microsoft Office. Depending on how Office was installed on your system, you may not have WordArt. If Office was installed using the Typical setup option, then you will need to run the Setup program again to install WordArt.

Introduction

Microsoft Office includes supplemental applications (WordArt, Equation, Organization Chart, and Graph) that allow you to create a visual object and then insert the object into an Office document. With WordArt, you create text with special effects; Equation allows you to create mathematical equations; you create company organization charts with Organization Chart; and Graph enables you to create charts. Thus, a **visual object** can be a graphic, equation, or chart. The application used initially to create the object is referred to as the **source application**.

When you insert, or **embed**, an object into an Office document, the object becomes part of the Office document. Because the Office document contains the embedded object, the Office document is referred to as the **container file**. In some cases, when you double-click an object embedded into an Office document, the object's source application opens inside the Office application, allowing you to edit the object directly from within Office. Any changes you make to the object are reflected immediately in the Office document.

This Integration Feature illustrates the procedure to use WordArt to add special text effects to the title of the *Amateur Aviators* newsletter. The revised newsletter is shown in Figure 1 on the next page. Notice the title waves and has a gradient color scheme.

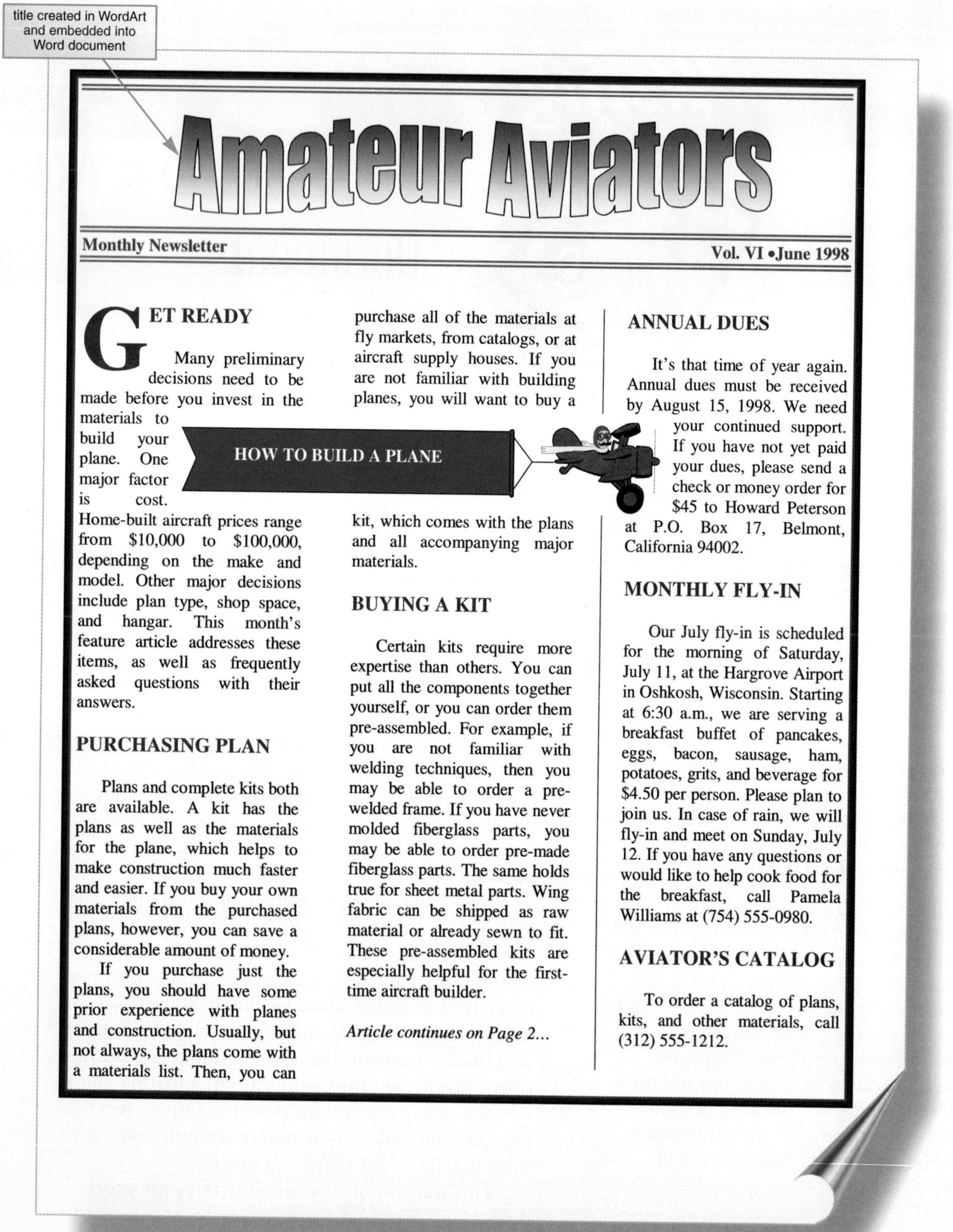

title created in WordArt and embedded into Word document

Amateur Aviators

Monthly Newsletter   **Vol. VI •June 1998**

GET READY

Many preliminary decisions need to be made before you invest in the materials to build your plane. One major factor is cost. Home-built aircraft prices range from $10,000 to $100,000, depending on the make and model. Other major decisions include plan type, shop space, and hangar. This month's feature article addresses these items, as well as frequently asked questions with their answers.

PURCHASING PLAN

Plans and complete kits both are available. A kit has the plans as well as the materials for the plane, which helps to make construction much faster and easier. If you buy your own materials from the purchased plans, however, you can save a considerable amount of money.

If you purchase just the plans, you should have some prior experience with planes and construction. Usually, but not always, the plans come with a materials list. Then, you can purchase all of the materials at fly markets, from catalogs, or at aircraft supply houses. If you are not familiar with building planes, you will want to buy a

HOW TO BUILD A PLANE

kit, which comes with the plans and all accompanying major materials.

BUYING A KIT

Certain kits require more expertise than others. You can put all the components together yourself, or you can order them pre-assembled. For example, if you are not familiar with welding techniques, then you may be able to order a pre-welded frame. If you have never molded fiberglass parts, you may be able to order pre-made fiberglass parts. The same holds true for sheet metal parts. Wing fabric can be shipped as raw material or already sewn to fit. These pre-assembled kits are especially helpful for the first-time aircraft builder.

Article continues on Page 2...

ANNUAL DUES

It's that time of year again. Annual dues must be received by August 15, 1998. We need your continued support. If you have not yet paid your dues, please send a check or money order for $45 to Howard Peterson at P.O. Box 17, Belmont, California 94002.

MONTHLY FLY-IN

Our July fly-in is scheduled for the morning of Saturday, July 11, at the Hargrove Airport in Oshkosh, Wisconsin. Starting at 6:30 a.m., we are serving a breakfast buffet of pancakes, eggs, bacon, sausage, ham, potatoes, grits, and beverage for $4.50 per person. Please plan to join us. In case of rain, we will fly-in and meet on Sunday, July 12. If you have any questions or would like to help cook food for the breakfast, call Pamela Williams at (754) 555-0980.

AVIATOR'S CATALOG

To order a catalog of plans, kits, and other materials, call (312) 555-1212.

FIGURE 1

Removing the Current Title

To create the WordArt object, the first step is to open the Amateur Aviators Newsletter file and then remove the current title as described in the following steps.

TO REMOVE THE CURRENT TITLE

1️⃣ Start Word and then open the Amateur Aviators Newsletter file created in Project 6. (If you did not create the newsletter in Project 6, see your instructor for a copy of it.)

2️⃣ If it is not already recessed, click the Show/Hide ¶ button on the Standard toolbar.

3️⃣ Drag through the title to select it. Be careful NOT to select the paragraph mark following the title. Right-click the selection (Figure 2).

4️⃣ Click Cut on the shortcut menu.

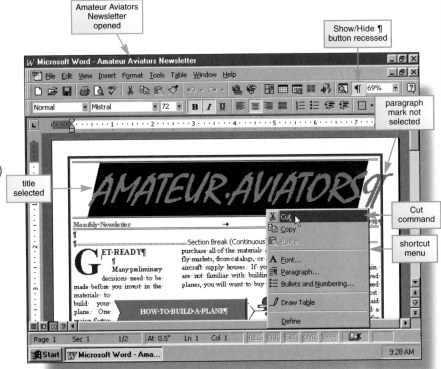

FIGURE 2

Word removes the title from the newsletter (Figure 3 on the next page). The insertion point is positioned where the title originally was located. It is important to leave the original paragraph mark to ensure enough room (72-point, in this case) is available for the WordArt object.

Creating a WordArt Object

As discussed earlier, **WordArt** is an application that enables you to add special text effects to a document. In this Integration Feature, you will use WordArt to create a new title for the *Amateur Aviators* newsletter. WordArt is the source application because that is where the title will be created. The Word document is the container file because it will contain the **WordArt object,** the title. The following pages explain how to insert a WordArt object into a Word document and then use WordArt to add special effects to the text itself.

The first step in creating a WordArt object is to **insert,** or **embed,** the object into a Word document. WordArt inserts at the location of the insertion point. Follow the steps on the next page to insert a WordArt object into a Word document.

▶ **More** *About*
WordArt Objects

Keep in mind that WordArt objects are drawing objects and are not treated as Word text. Thus, if you misspell the contents of a WordArt object and then spell check the document, Word will not catch the misspelled word(s) in the WordArt text. Also, WordArt objects display only in page layout view.

Steps **To Insert a WordArt Object into a Word Document**

1 **Click Insert on the menu bar, point to Picture, and then point to WordArt.**

Notice the insertion point is positioned on the paragraph mark on line 1 of the newsletter (Figure 3).

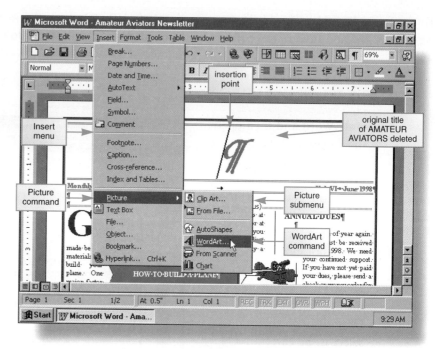

FIGURE 3

2 **Click WordArt. When the WordArt Gallery dialog box displays, if necessary, click the style in the upper-left corner.**

The WordArt Gallery dialog box displays (Figure 4). Because you will add your own special text effects, the style in the upper-left corner is selected.

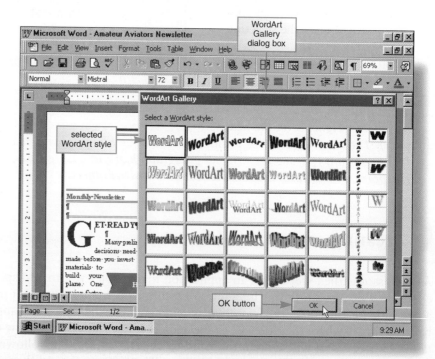

FIGURE 4

3 **Click the OK button. When the Edit WordArt Text dialog box displays, type** Amateur Aviators **and then click the Font box arrow. Scroll to and then click Impact. Click the Size box arrow, scroll to and then click 60.**

The Edit WordArt Text dialog box displays (Figure 5). In this dialog box, you can enter the WordArt text, and change its font and font size.

4 **Click the OK button.**

The WordArt text (object) displays in the document window (Figure 6 on the next page).

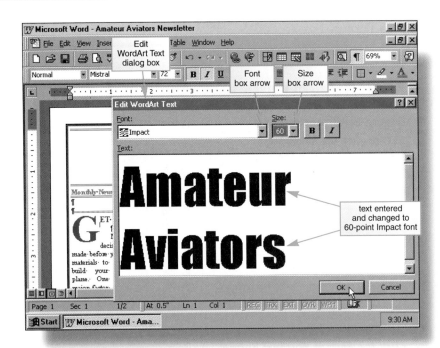

FIGURE 5

Notice in Figure 6 on the next page that when the WordArt object is selected, the **WordArt toolbar** displays. Recall that selected objects display with **sizing handles** at their middle and corner locations. If, for some reason, you wanted to change the WordArt text, its font, or its font size, you would click the **Edit Text button** on the WordArt toolbar to display the Edit WordArt text dialog box.

To change the size (width and height) of WordArt text, you drag the sizing handles on the selected WordArt object to the appropriate locations – just as you resize any other graphic.

If, for some reason, you wanted to delete WordArt text, you would right-click the WordArt object and then click the Cut button on the shortcut menu.

Adding Special Effects to WordArt Text

The next step is to enhance the WordArt text. Enhancing includes changing its color, shape, and location. The steps on the following pages outline these enhancements.

Formatting the WordArt Text

In Figure 6, the WordArt text (the title) is formatted so the text in the newsletter wraps around it; you do not want the newsletter text to wrap around the WordArt text. In addition, you want to add color to the WordArt text. Perform the steps on the next page to format the WordArt text.

Other Ways

1. Click Insert WordArt button on Drawing toolbar, select WordArt style, enter WordArt text, click OK button

More About Special Effects

If you want WordArt to format your text, click the desired WordArt style in the WordArt Gallery dialog box (Figure 4). If you want to rotate your text, click the Free Rotate button on the WordArt toolbar, drag a corner of the WordArt object in the direction you want it rotated, and then click the Free Rotate button again to deselect it.

Steps   **To Format the WordArt Text**

1 Point to the Format WordArt button on the WordArt toolbar (Figure 6). If your screen does not display the WordArt toolbar, right-click the WordArt object and then click Show WordArt Toolbar.

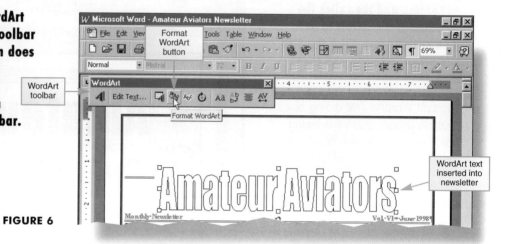

FIGURE 6

2 Click the Format WordArt button. If necessary, click the Wrapping tab when the Format WordArt dialog box first opens. Click None in the Wrapping style area.

The Format WordArt dialog box displays (Figure 7). In the Wrapping sheet, you can specify how the words in the document will wrap around the WordArt object.

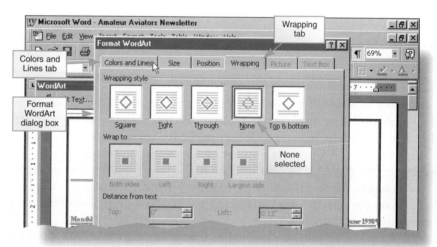

FIGURE 7

3 Click the Colors and Lines tab. Click the Fill Color box arrow and then point to Fill Effects.

The options in the Colors and Lines sheet display (Figure 8). In this sheet, you can change the color of the WordArt text.

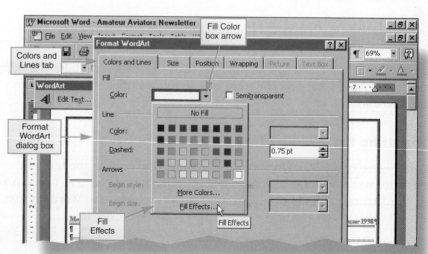

FIGURE 8

4 Click Fill Effects. When the Fill Effects dialog box displays, if necessary, click the Gradient tab, and then click Two colors. Click the Color 1 box arrow and then click Teal. Click the Color 2 box arrow and then click White.

The Fill Effects dialog box displays (Figure 9). In this dialog box, you can change the color scheme for the WordArt text.

5 Click the OK button in the Fill Effects dialog box and then click the OK button in the Format WordArt dialog box.

The WordArt text displays formatted with a teal-to-white gradient color scheme (Figure 10 below).

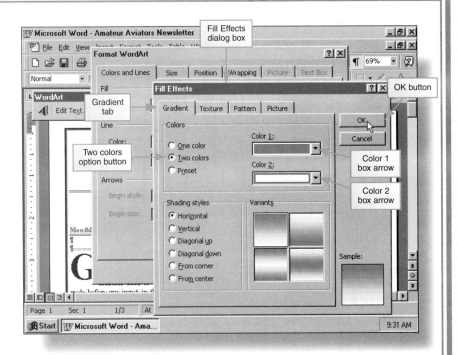

FIGURE 9

Moving WordArt Text

Notice in Figure 10 that the WordArt text is positioned on top of the newsletter text; this is because you changed wrapping to none in the previous steps. Now, you can move the WordArt text as you would any other drawing object. That is, drag the WordArt object to the desired location as shown in the steps below.

 Steps To Move a WordArt Object

1 If the WordArt object is not selected, click it to select it. Point in the WordArt object so the mouse pointer displays a four-headed arrow.

*The mouse pointer changes to include a **four-headed arrow** when positioned in a WordArt object (Figure 10).*

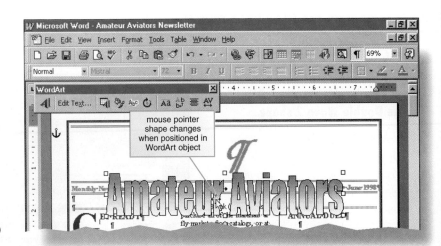

FIGURE 10

2 **Drag the WordArt object to the desired location.**

As you drag, a dotted outline moves to show where the dropped WordArt object will display if the mouse button is released at that location (Figure 11).

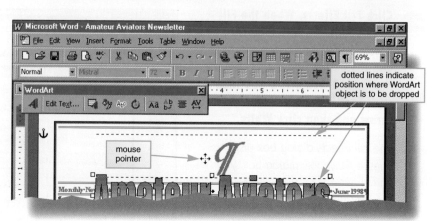

FIGURE 11

3 **Release the mouse button.**

The WordArt object is moved to the desired location (Figure 12).

FIGURE 12

Changing the WordArt Shape

WordArt provides a variety of shapes to make your WordArt text more interesting. Perform the following steps to change the WordArt text to a wavy shape.

Steps **To Change the WordArt Shape**

1 **Click the WordArt Shape button on the WordArt toolbar. Point to the Double Wave 2 shape.**

WordArt displays a graphic list of available shapes (Figure 13). The WordArt text forms itself into the selected shape when you click a shape.

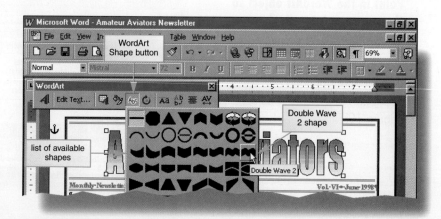

FIGURE 13

2 Click Double Wave 2. Click below the WordArt text as shown in the figure to remove the selection and remove the WordArt toolbar. Click the Show/Hide ¶ button on the Standard toolbar to remove nonprinting characters from the screen.

The title displays in the double wave 2 shape (Figure 14). The WordArt text is complete.

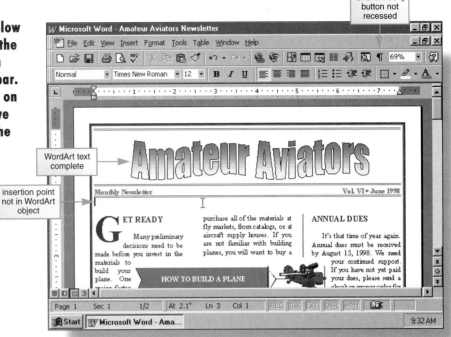

FIGURE 14

Saving and Printing the Newsletter and Quitting Word

The revision of the newsletter is now complete. You should save it with a new file name, print it, and then quit Word.

Summary

This Integration Feature introduced you to the concept of embedding an object created in WordArt into a Word document. You learned how to insert a WordArt object, add WordArt special features to the WordArt text, and move the WordArt object.

What You Should Know

Having completed this Integration Feature, you now should be able to perform the following tasks:

- Change the WordArt Shape *(WDI 2.8)*
- Format the WordArt Text *(WDI 2.6)*
- Insert a WordArt Object into a Word Document *(WDI 2.4)*
- Move a WordArt Object *(WDI 2.7)*
- Remove the Current Title *(WDI 2.3)*

 In the Lab

1 Using Help

Instructions: Start Word. If the Office Assistant is on your screen, click it to display its balloon. If the Office Assistant is not on your screen, click the Office Assistant button on the Standard toolbar. Type share information in the What would you like to do? text box. Click the Search button. Click the Use linked and embedded objects to share information between Office programs topic. Read and print the information. Click the Help Topics button to display the Help Topics: Microsoft Word dialog box. Click the Find tab. Type WordArt and then double-click the Arrange text and graphics on a page topic. Read and print the information. Close any open Help window or dialog box by clicking its Close button. Close the Office Assistant.

2 Embedding a WordArt Object into a Newsletter

Problem: You created the *Village News* newsletter shown in Figure 6-84 on page WD 6.59 in Project 6. You decide to redo the title, VILLAGE NEWS, using WordArt.

Instructions: Open the file Village News Newsletter from your floppy disk. (If you did not create the newsletter, see your instructor for a copy of it.) Delete the current title from the document. Be sure not to delete the paragraph mark following the title. Insert a WordArt object at the location of the title using the Insert command on the Picture menu. Enter the title VILLAGE NEWS, use the font Courier New, the font size 66, and bold it. Format the WordArt object to no wrapping and gradient colors of Dark Red to White. Change the shape of the WordArt text to Deflate Bottom. Quit WordArt. Save the file using the Save As command on the File menu with Village News Newsletter Revised as the file name. Print the revised file.

3 Embedding a WordArt Object into a Newsletter

Problem: You created the *Surfing Today* newsletter shown in Figure 6-86 on page WD 6.62 in Project 6. You decide to redo the title, SURFING TODAY, using WordArt.

Instructions: Open the file Surfing Today Newsletter from your floppy disk. (If you did not create the newsletter, see your instructor for a copy of it.) Delete the current title from the document. Be sure not to delete the paragraph mark following the title. Insert a WordArt object at the location of the title using the Insert command on the Picture menu. Enter the title SURFING TODAY, use the font Comic Sans MS, and the font size 60. Format the WordArt object to no wrapping and gradient colors of Sky Blue to Sea Green. Change the shape of the WordArt text to Wave 1. Quit WordArt. Save the file using the Save As command on the File menu with Surfing Today Newsletter Revised as the file name. Print the revised file.

Index

NOTE TO READER: This index contains references for Projects 1 through 6 and the Integration Features of the book, *Microsoft Word 97: Complete Concepts and Techniques*. The same references can be used for Word Projects 1 through 3 and Integration Feature 1 in the book, *Microsoft Office 97: Introductory Concepts and Techniques*, and Word Projects 4 through 6 and Integration Feature 2 in the book, *Microsoft Office 97: Advanced Concepts and Techniques*.

Microsoft **Word 97**

Microsoft Excel 97

Creating Templates, Workbooks with Multiple Worksheets, and Web Pages

Objectives:

You will have mastered the material in this project when you can:

▶ Create and use a template
▶ Copy data between worksheets in a workbook
▶ Drill an entry through worksheets
▶ Format ranges across multiple worksheets in a workbook
▶ Utilize custom format codes
▶ Add a worksheet to the workbook
▶ Create formulas that use 3-D references to cells in different sheets in a workbook
▶ Summarize data using consolidation
▶ Draw a 3-D Pyramid chart
▶ Add comments to cells
▶ Add a header or footer to a workbook
▶ Change the page margins
▶ Create a Web page from worksheet data

Food for Thought

Worksheets Help Serve the Needy

At least one in every 10 Americans relies on food pantries and soup kitchens to avoid going hungry. Sixty percent of these people have graduated from high school and have attended college.

They are helped in part by the efforts of Second Harvest, the nation's largest hunger-relief charity network of food banks. Corporate donors, local businesses, and individuals provide surplus food to the food banks, which, in turn, distribute the food to 40,000 local agencies. The 2,500 employees and 30,000 volunteers, including sorority and fraternity members, feed 15 million adults and 11 million children annually.

The Greater Chicago Food Depository, one of Second Harvest's more than 180 food banks, collects donated or surplus food from wholesale food manufacturers, produce distributors, food store chains, and restaurants. The food is gathered by Food Depository drivers, delivered at warehouses, and collected at food drives.

GREATER CHICAGO FOOD DEPOSITORY

The products are distributed later to charitable food pantries, soup kitchens, and shelters throughout Chicago.

The Food Depository distributes more than 25 million pounds of food each year. In the past, employees kept track of these products using manual methods. More recently, they have developed Microsoft Excel worksheets, similar to the ones you will create in this project, that organize, tabulate, and summarize the hundreds of pallets and thousands of pounds of food shipped each week to its two warehouses. These worksheets are useful particularly now because restaurants and food packagers receive food deliveries just when they need it. This means less surplus food is available for donations. In addition, improved quality control at processing plants results in fewer mislabeled and slightly damaged cans and boxes being supplied.

Now when drivers deliver the products at the warehouses, employees keep track of inventory and also project storage needs by using the Excel worksheets. One of their worksheets contains a template to enter the quantity of salvage goods, and a second worksheet has another template to record items that need to be repacked. For example, employees use a template to record receipt of 100 cases of tomato juice, each of which contains one dozen, 24-ounce cans.

Workers then generate reports from each Excel worksheet. The Salvage Report summarizes the quantity of food that was delivered, such as number of cans of juice or pounds of fresh lettuce, how much was usable, and how much was spoiled due to dents or expired dates. A second report, the Repack Listing, specifies the items that were divided to bring to various food pantries.

Each night, the employees study the worksheets to see the amounts of dry, refrigerated, and frozen products in stock and the amounts expected to arrive the following day. At that point, they survey the 91,000-square-foot main warehouse to ensure sufficient room exists for these products. For example, if a large delivery of frozen food is on the schedule, sufficient freezer space must be available to accommodate these goods when they arrive.

The Excel worksheets certainly are food for thought for helping feed more than 300,000 Chicagoans annually through the efforts of the Greater Chicago Food Depository.

Project 4

Microsoft
Excel 97

Creating Templates, Workbooks with Multiple Worksheets, and Web Pages

Case Perspective

In the past three years, Awesome Sound Bites (ASB) has grown from obscurity into eminence, becoming one of the premier small companies in the United States. The company, which sells five categories of speakers, has opened stores in Los Angeles, Chicago, and New York, all of which are thriving. Even more exciting is that a major competitor recently approached ASB's president Arnold Ladd about buying the company. The competitor has requested that Arnold supply a report that shows the total gross profit potential of the company based on the year-end inventory of speakers. The gross profit potential for a single speaker is determined by applying a 65% margin to its average unit cost.

Now that each of the three stores has submitted their end-of-year inventory reports to the main office, Arnold has asked you to consolidate the inventory data on one worksheet and to create a chart that compares the gross profit potentials of the speaker categories. He also wants you to create a Web page from the worksheet to be posted for viewing on the company's intranet.

Introduction

Many business-type applications, such as the one described in the Case Perspective, require worksheet data from several worksheets in a workbook to be summarized on one worksheet. As you will learn in this project, Excel makes the process of consolidation easy. Suppose your firm maintains data for four different units within the company on four separate worksheets in a workbook. You can click the tabs at the bottom of the Excel window to move from worksheet to worksheet. If you want to summarize the data on a totals worksheet, you can enter formulas that reference cells found on the other worksheets, which allows you to summarize worksheet data. The process of summarizing worksheet data found on multiple worksheets on one worksheet is called **consolidation**.

Another important concept is the use of a template. A **template** is a special workbook or worksheet you can create and then use as a pattern to create new, similar workbooks or worksheets. A template usually consists of a **general format** (worksheet title, column and row titles, and numeric format) and formulas that are common to all the worksheets. For example, in the Awesome Sound Bites report, the worksheets for each of the three stores and the company worksheet would be identical, except for the numbers. For such an application, it is to your advantage to create a template, save it, and then copy it as many times as necessary to a workbook.

Finally, this project introduces you to creating a Web page from worksheet data by saving it as an HTML file. Once the worksheet data is saved as HTML, you can view the worksheet data as a Web page using a World Wide Web browser.

Project Four – Awesome Sound Bites Profit Potential

From your meetings with Arnold Ladd, you have accumulated the following workbook specifications:

Needs: The workbook Arnold has in mind will require five worksheets — one for each of the three stores, a summary worksheet for the company, and a chart on a separate sheet that compares the profit potential based on the sales of the different speakers categories (Figure 4-1).

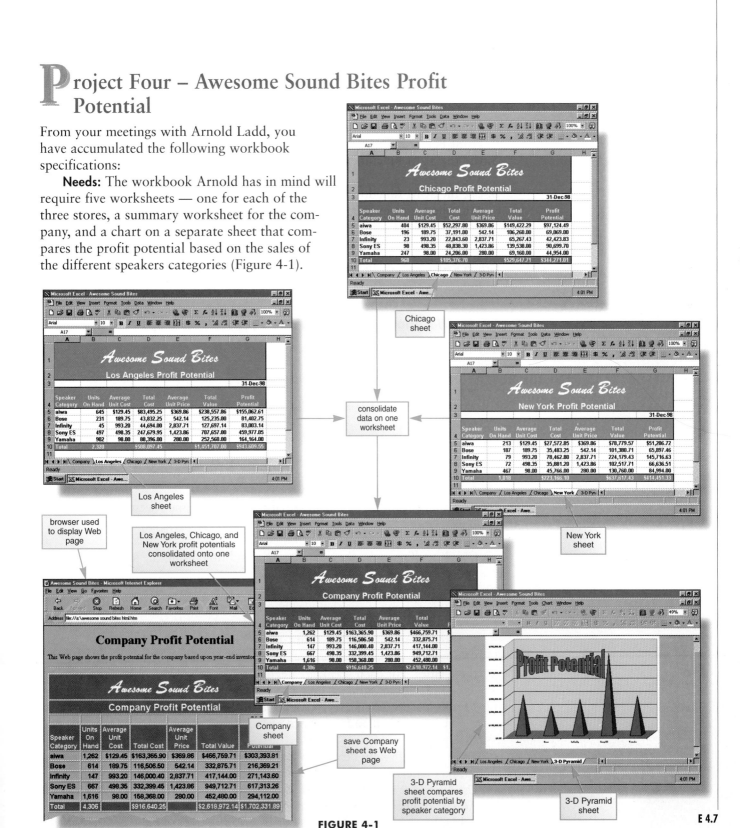

FIGURE 4-1

Arnold also wants the company worksheet to be available on the intranet as a Web page for internal company use.

Because the three stores sell the same five categories of speakers, the inventory worksheets are identical, except for the units on hand. You thus can create a template (Figure 4-2) and then copy it three times into the workbook.

Source of Data: The units on hand for each category of speaker will be collected from the business managers of the respective stores. The average unit cost of each speaker category is available from the main office.

Calculations: The following calculations are required for the template (Figure 4-2):

1. Total Cost in column D = Units On Hand * Average Unit Cost
2. Average Unit Price in column E = Average Unit Cost * $(1 / (1 - .65))$
3. Total Value in column F = Units On Hand * Average Unit Price
4. Profit Potential in column G = Total Value - Total Cost
5. Use the SUM function in columns B, D, F, and G to total the sums in row 10.
6. Use the SUM function to determine the Units On Hand totals on the Company sheet. For example, assigning the SUM function to cell B5 on the Company sheet sums the values in cell B5 on the Los Angeles sheet, Chicago sheet, and New York sheet (Figure 4-1 on the previous page).

Graph Requirements: Include a 3-D Pyramid chart on a separate chart sheet that compares the profit potential for each speaker category.

Template, Workbook, and Web Page Preparation Steps

The following preparation steps summarize how the template shown in Figure 4-2 and the workbook shown in Figure 4-1 will be developed in Project 4.

1. Start Excel.
2. Assign the Bold style to all cells in the worksheet and increase column widths.
3. Enter the worksheet titles, row titles, column titles, and system date.
4. Use the fill handle to enter dummy data for the Units On Hand in column B and Average Unit Cost in column C.
5. Enter the required formulas.
6. Save the workbook as a template using the file name Awesome Sound Bites Template.
7. Format the template.
8. Check spelling, save the template a second time using the same file name, and then close it.
9. Add a new sheet to the workbook. Copy Sheet1 to the three blank sheets in the workbook. Save the workbook as Awesome Sound Bites.
10. On all four sheets, replace the Average Unit Cost dummy data in column C with the actual Average Unit Cost data.
11. Change the worksheet titles and sheet names to represent each of the three cities. For each speaker category, replace the Units On Hand dummy data with the actual data submitted by the three stores.
12. Modify the worksheet title and sheet name of the Company sheet. Enter the SUM function and copy it to consolidate the data on the three store sheets on the Company sheet.
13. Draw a 3-D Pyramid chart that compares the profit potential of the five speaker categories. Place the chart on a separate chart sheet.
14. Use WordArt to create a chart title.
15. Add a comment to cell A13 on the Company sheet.
16. Add a header to and change the margins of the five sheets.

More *About*
Consolidation

Besides consolidating data within a single workbook, you can consolidate data across different workbooks using the Consolidate command on the Data menu. For more information, click Contents and Index on the Help menu, click the Index tab, and obtain information on the topic consolidating data.

17. Save, preview, and print the workbook.
18. Create a Web page from the Company sheet.
19. Quit Excel.
20. View the Company Web page using a Web browser.

The following pages contain a detailed explanation of these tasks.

Starting Excel

To start Excel, follow the steps you used at the beginning of Project 1. These steps are summarized below:

TO START EXCEL

Step 1: Click the Start button. Click New Office Document on the Start menu. If necessary, click the General tab in the New dialog box.

Step 2: Double-click the Blank Workbook icon.

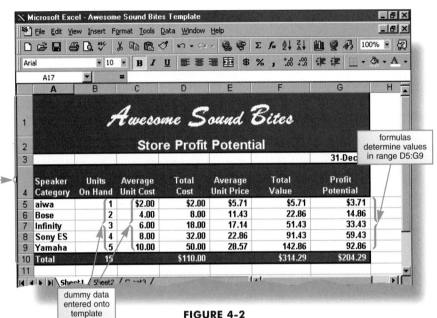

FIGURE 4-2

Creating the Template

Learning how to use templates is important, especially if you plan to use a similar worksheet design or layout for several worksheets or workbooks. In Project 4, for instance, the four worksheets in the inventory workbook (Figure 4-1) are nearly identical. Thus, the first step in building the Awesome Sound Bites workbook is to create and save a template that contains the labels, formulas, and formats used in each of the sheets. Once the template is saved to disk, you can use it every time you begin developing a similar workbook. Because templates help speed and simplify their work, many Excel users create a template for each application on which they work. Templates can be simple — possibly using a special font or worksheet title — or more complex — perhaps utilizing specific formulas and page setup characteristics, like the template for Project 4.

To create and modify a template, you simply follow the same basic steps used to create and modify a workbook. The only difference between developing a workbook and a template is the way you save the file.

> **More** *About*
> **Templates**
>
> Templates can be a powerful tool for developing consistency among worksheets. Templates can contain: (1) text and graphics, such as a company name and logo; (2) formats and page layouts, such as styles and custom headers and footers; and (3) formulas or macros.

Bolding the Font and Changing Column Widths of the Template

The first step in this project is to change the font style of the entire template to bold so that all entries are emphasized. You also must change the column widths as follows: columns A, B, C, and E = 9.00; column D = 11.00; and columns F and G = 13.00.

TO BOLD THE FONT AND CHANGE THE COLUMN WIDTHS IN THE TEMPLATE

Step 1: Click the Select All button immediately above row heading 1 and to the left of column heading A.

Step 2: Click the Bold button on the Standard toolbar. Click cell A1.

Step 3: Drag through column headings A, B, and C. While holding down the CTRL key, click column heading E. Drag the right boundary of column heading E until the ScreenTip, Width: 9.00, displays.

Step 4: Drag the right boundary of column heading D until the ScreenTip, Width: 11.00, displays.

Step 5: Drag through column headings F and G. Drag the right boundary of column heading G until the ScreenTip, Width: 13.00, displays.

The Bold style is assigned to all cells in the worksheet. Columns A, B, and C have a width of 9.00. Column D has a width of 11.00. Columns F and G have a width of 13.00.

Entering the Template Title and Row Titles

The following steps enter the worksheet titles in cells A1 and A2 and the row titles in column A.

TO ENTER THE TEMPLATE TITLE AND ROW TITLES

Step 1: Click cell A1. Type Awesome Sound Bites and then press the DOWN ARROW key. Type Store Profit Potential and then press the DOWN ARROW key twice to make cell A4 active.

Step 2: Type Speaker and then press ALT+ENTER. Type Category and then press the DOWN ARROW key.

Step 3: With cell A5 active, enter the remaining row titles in column A as shown in Figure 4-3.

The template title and row titles display in column A as shown in Figure 4-3. Because the entry in cell A4 requires two lines, Excel automatically increases the height of row 4.

Entering Column Titles and the System Date

The next step is to enter the column titles in row 4 and the system date in cell G3.

TO ENTER COLUMN TITLES AND THE SYSTEM DATE IN THE TEMPLATE

Step 1: Click cell B4. Type Units and then press ALT+ENTER. Type On Hand and then press the RIGHT ARROW key.

Step 2: Type Average and then press ALT+ENTER. Type Unit Cost and then press the RIGHT ARROW key.

Step 3: With cell D4 active, enter the remaining column titles in row 4 as shown in Figure 4-3.

Step 4: Select the column titles (range A4:G4). Click the Center button on the Formatting toolbar.

Step 5: Click cell G3. Type =now() and then press the ENTER key.

More *About*
Formatting

You can apply formats to an entire workbook by clicking the Select All button (or pressing CTRL+A) and then choosing the Select All Sheets command on the shortcut menu that displays when you right-click a sheet tab.

Step 6: Right-click cell G3. Click Format Cells on the shortcut menu. When the Format Cells dialog box displays, click the Number tab, and then click Date in the Category list box. Click 04-Mar-97 in the Type list box. Click the OK button.

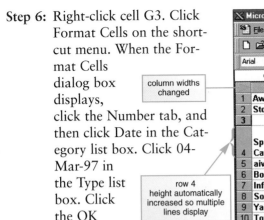
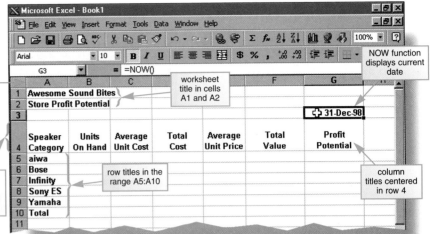

FIGURE 4-3

The column titles and system date display as shown in Figure 4-3.

Entering Dummy Data in the Template

When you are creating a template, you should use **dummy data** in place of actual data to verify the formulas in the template. Selecting simple numbers like 1, 2, and 3 allows you to check quickly to see if the formulas are generating the proper results. While creating the Awesome Sound Bites Template in Project 4, dummy data is used for the Units On Hand in the range B5:B9 and the Average Unit Costs in the range C5:C9.

The dummy data is entered by using the fill handle to create a series of numbers in columns B and C. The series in column B begins with 1 and increments by 1; the series in column C begins with 2 and increments by 2. Recall from Project 3 that to create a series you enter the first two numbers so Excel can determine the increment amount. If the cell to the right of the start value is empty, however, you can create a series by entering only one number. Perform the following to create the two series of numbers.

 Steps **To Enter Dummy Data in the Template Using the Fill Handle**

1 **Type** 1 **in cell B5 and press the ENTER key. Select the range B5:C5. Drag the fill handle through cells B9 and C9 and hold down the left mouse button.**

Excel surrounds the range B5:C9 with a gray border (Figure 4-4). A ScreenTip displays showing the final value in the series that will be assigned to cell B9.

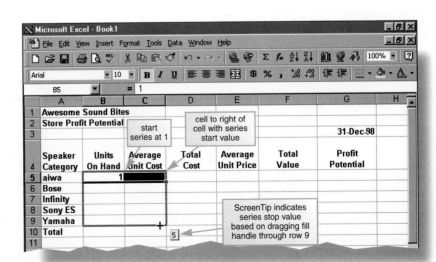

FIGURE 4-4

2 Release the left mouse button.

Excel creates the series 1 through 5 in increments of 1 in the range B5:B9 (Figure 4-5).

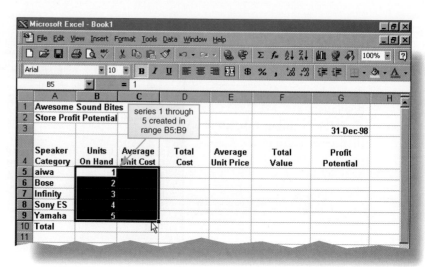

FIGURE 4-5

3 Click cell C5. Type 2 and then press the DOWN ARROW key. Type 4 and then press the ENTER key. Select the range C5:C6. Drag the fill handle through cell C9.

Excel creates the series 2 through 10 in increments of 2 in the range C5:C9 (Figure 4-6).

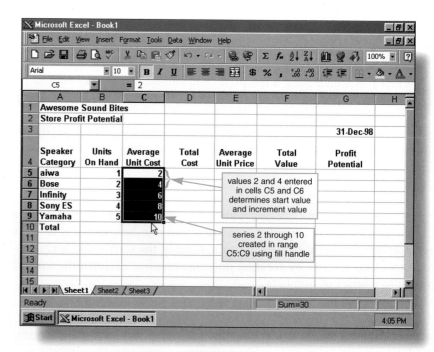

FIGURE 4-6

It is important to remember that, if you create a linear series by selecting the cell to the right of the start value, that cell must be empty.

The most common types of series used in Excel are: a **date/time series** (Jan, Feb, Mar, ...), an **AutoFill series** (1, 1, 1, ...), and a **linear series** (1, 2, 3...). A fourth type of series is a growth series. A **growth series** multiplies values by a constant factor. You can create a growth series by pointing to Fill on the Edit menu and then clicking Series. When the Series dialog box displays, click the Growth option button and then click the OK button. For example, if you enter 2 in cell D5 and 4 in cell D6, select the range D5:D15, and then follow the above steps, Excel will create the series 2, 4, 8, 16, 32, 64, 128, 256, 512, 1024, 2048 in the range D5:D15.

Entering the Formulas in the Template

The next step is to enter the four formulas for the first speaker category (aiwa) in the range D5:G5. The four formulas to enter are shown in Table 4-1.

CELL	DESCRIPTION	FORMULA	ENTRY
Table 4-1			
D5	Total Cost	Units On Hand x Average Unit Cost	=B5*C5
E5	Average Unit Price	Average Unit Cost x (1 / (1-.65))	=C5*(1 / (1 - .65))
F5	Total Value	Units On Hand x Average Unit Price	=B5 * E5
G5	Profit Potential	Total Value – Total Cost	=F5 – D5

The most difficult formula to understand in Table 4-1 is the one that determines the average unit price, which also is called the average selling price. To make a net profit, companies must sell their merchandise for more than the unit cost of the merchandise plus the company's operating expenses (taxes, store rent, upkeep, and so forth). To determine what selling price to set for an item, companies often first establish a desired gross profit margin.

The **margin** is the sum of the operating expenses and net profit. Most companies look for a margin of from 60% to 75%. Awesome Sound Bites, for example, tries to make a margin of 65% on their products. The formula for the average unit price in Table 4-1 helps them determine the price at which to sell an item so that the company ends up with 65% of the selling price as their gross profit. For example, if an item costs Awesome Sound Bites $1.00, they must sell it for $2.86 ($1.00 x (1/(1-.65))) to make a 65% margin. Of this $2.86, $1.00 goes to pay the cost of the item; the other $1.86 is the gross profit potential (65% x $2.86).

The following steps use Point mode to enter the four formulas in Table 4-1 in the range D5:G5. After the formulas are entered for the aiwa speaker in row 5, the formulas will be copied for the remaining speaker categories.

 Steps **To Enter the Formulas Using Point Mode and Determine Totals in the Template**

1 **Click cell D5. Type = to start the formula. Click cell B5. Type * and then click cell C5. Click the Enter box in the formula bar or press the ENTER key.**

*The formula =B5*C5 displays in the formula bar and the value 2 (1 x 2) displays as the total cost in cell D5 (Figure 4-7).*

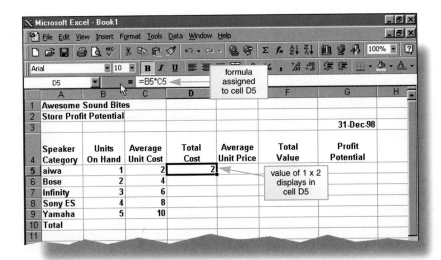

FIGURE 4-7

2 **Click cell E5. Type = to start the formula. Click cell C5. Type * and then type** (1/(1-.65)) **as the remainder of the formula. Click the Enter box in the formula bar or press the ENTER key.**

The value 5.7142857 displays as the average unit price in cell E5 and the formula =C5(1/(1-0.65)) displays in the formula bar (Figure 4-8). Excel automatically adds the zero (0) prior to the decimal point in the formula.*

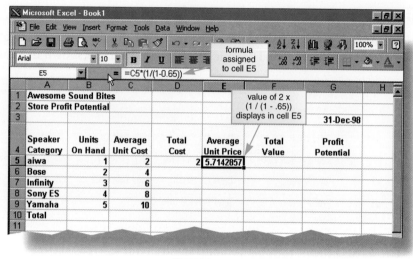

FIGURE 4-8

3 **Click cell F5. Type = to start the formula. Click cell B5. Type * and then click cell E5. Click the Enter box in the formula bar or press the ENTER key.**

*The value 5.714285714 (1 x 5.714285714) displays as the total value in cell F5 and the formula =B5*E5 displays in the formula bar (Figure 4-9). Even though the formulas in cell E5 and F5 generate the same result, cell E5 displays the value 5.714285714 as 5.7142857, because of the width of column E.*

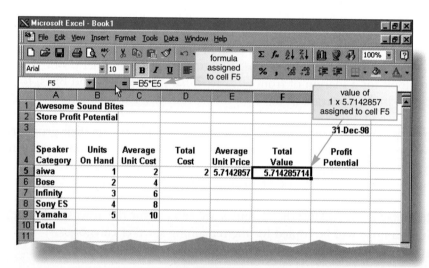

FIGURE 4-9

4 **Click cell G5. Type = to start the formula. Click cell F5. Type - and then click cell D5. Click the Enter box in the formula bar or press the ENTER key.**

The value 3.714285714 (5.714285714 – 2) displays as the profit potential in cell G5 and the formula =F5 – D5 displays in the formula bar (Figure 4-10).

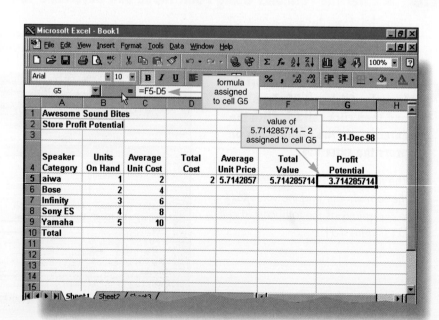

FIGURE 4-10

5 **Select the range D5:G5 and then point to the fill handle.**

The range D5:G5 is highlighted and the mouse pointer changes to a crosshair (Figure 4-11).

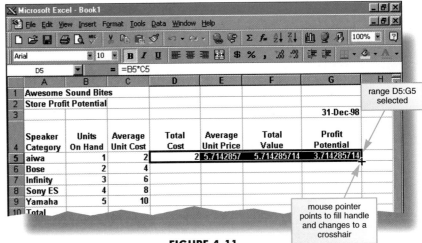

FIGURE 4-11

6 **Drag down through the range D6:G9.**

Excel copies the formulas in the range D5:G5 to the range D6:G9. Excel automatically adjusts the cell references so each formula references the data in the row to which it is copied (Figure 4-12).

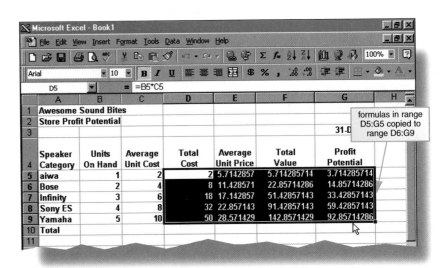

FIGURE 4-12

7 **Click cell B10. Click the AutoSum button on the Standard toolbar twice. Click cell D10. Click the AutoSum button twice. Select the range F10:G10. Click the AutoSum button.**

The totals for columns B, D, F, and G display in row 10 (Figure 4-13).

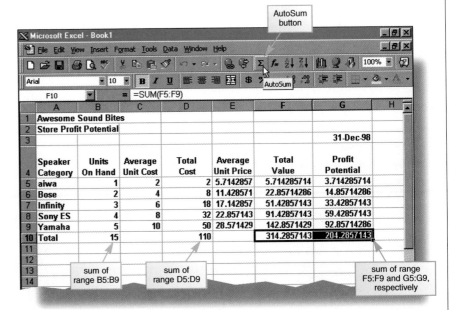

FIGURE 4-13

ore *About*
File Extensions

If the MS-DOS extension .xlt shows in your title bar following the file name, it means that the option not to show the MS-DOS extension is not selected on the View sheet in the Options dialog box in Explorer.

The values Excel generates from the formulas are based on the dummy data entered in columns B and C. After you save and format the template, you will use it to create the Awesome Sound Bites workbook. You then will enter the actual data for the different speaker categories.

Saving the Template

Saving a template is just like saving a workbook, except that you select Template in the Save as type box in the Save As dialog box. The following steps save the template on a floppy disk using the file name Awesome Sound Bites Template.

Steps **To Save a Template**

① **Click the Save button on the Standard toolbar. When the Save As dialog box displays, type** Awesome Sound Bites Template **in the File name box. Click the Save as type box arrow and then click Template.**

② **Click the Save in box arrow and then click 3½ Floppy (A:). Point to the Save button in the Save As dialog box.**

The Save As dialog box displays as shown in Figure 4-14.

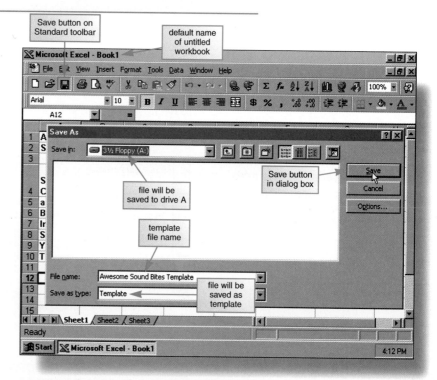

FIGURE 4-14

③ **Click the Save button.**

Excel saves the template Awesome Sound Bites on the floppy disk in drive A. The file name Awesome Sound Bites Template displays in the title bar as shown in Figure 4-15.

OtherWays

1. On File menu click Save As, type file name, select Template in Save as type box, select drive or folder, click OK button
2. Press CTRL+S, type file name, select Template in Save as type box, select drive or folder, click OK button

Formatting the Template

The next step is to format the template so it displays as shown in Figure 4-15. As you format the template, keep in mind that each of the sheets for which the template is used will use the same formats. The following list summarizes the steps required to format the template.

1. Change the font size of the template title in cells A1 and A2. Center cells A1 and A2 across columns A through G.
2. Change the background color, change the font color, and add a heavy outline border to the nonadjacent ranges A1:G2, A4:G4, and A10:G10.
3. Assign the Currency style format with a floating dollar sign to the nonadjacent ranges C5:G5 and D10:G10.
4. Assign a Custom style format to the range C6:G9.
5. Assign a Comma style format to the ranges B5:B10.

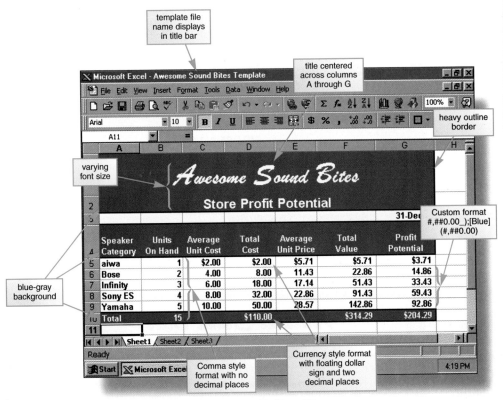

FIGURE 4-15

Formatting the Template Title

The steps used to format the template title include: changing cell A1 to 26-point Brush Script MT font (or a similar font); increasing the point size of the first character in each word in cell A1 to 36-point font; changing cell A2 to 16-point Arial font; and centering both titles over columns A through G. Perform the steps on the next page to format the template title.

Steps To Format the Template Title

1 Click cell A1. Click the Font box arrow on the Formatting toolbar and then click Brush Script MT (or a similar font) in the Font list box. Click the Font Size box arrow on the Formatting toolbar and then click 26. Double-click cell A1 to activate in-cell editing. Drag across the letter A in the word Awesome. Click the Font Size box arrow on the Formatting toolbar and then click 36. With in-cell editing active, drag across the letters S in Sound and B in Bites one at a time and then change the font size to 36.

The title displays as shown in Figure 4-16.

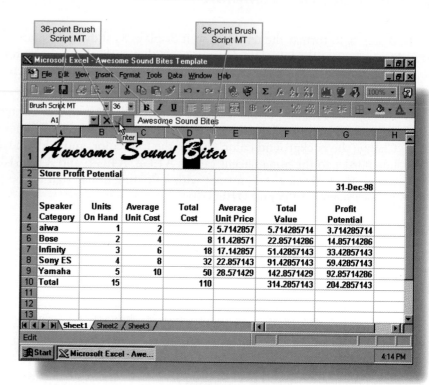

FIGURE 4-16

2 Click the Enter box in the formula bar or press the ENTER key.

3 Select the range A1:G1. Click the Merge and Center button on the Formatting toolbar.

Excel centers the title over columns A through G and merges the range A1:G1 into one cell.

4 Click cell A2. Click the Font box arrow on the Formatting toolbar and then click Arial (or a similar font) in the Font list box. Click the Font Size box arrow on the Formatting toolbar and then click 16. Select the range A2:G2. Click the Merge and Center button on the Formatting toolbar.

Excel centers the title over columns A through G and merges the range A2:G2 into one cell. The template displays as shown in Figure 4-17.

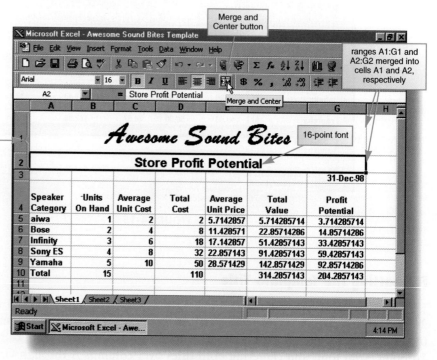

FIGURE 4-17

When you increase the font size, Excel automatically increases the heights of rows 1 and 2 so the tallest letter will display properly in the cells.

Changing the Background Color, Font Colors, and Adding Outlines

To further emphasize the titles, you can change the background and font color, and add a heavy outline border to the ranges A1:G2, A4:G4, and A10:G10. You can format the ranges one at a time. Because the same format will be applied to all three ranges, however, you can use the CTRL key to select the nonadjacent ranges and then format them at the same time. The following steps show how to format all three nonadjacent ranges at one time.

Steps To Change the Background and Font Colors and Add Outline Borders

1 Select the range A1:A2. While holding down the CTRL key, select the nonadjacent ranges A4:G4 and A10:G10. Click the Fill Color button arrow on the Formatting toolbar and then point to the color blue-gray (column 7, row 2) on the Fill Color palette.

The Fill Color palette displays, showing available background colors (Figure 4-18).

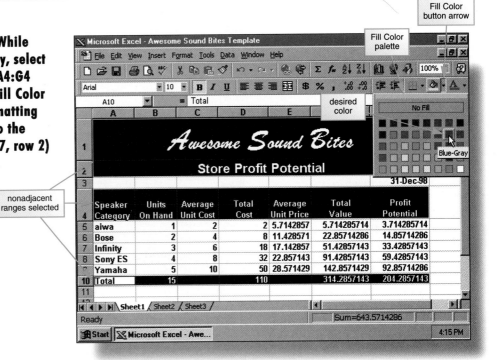

FIGURE 4-18

More *About*
Merging Cells

If you merge cells, then only the leftmost one can be activated. For example, in Figure 4-17, if you use the Name Box or Go To command to activate any of the merged cells A1 through G1, Excel will activate cell A1.

2 **Click blue-gray.**

Excel changes the background color of the selected ranges to blue-gray.

3 **Click the Font Color button arrow and then point to the color white (column 8, row 8) on the Font Color palette.**

The Font Color palette displays (Figure 4-19). The nonadjacent ranges A1:A2, A4:G4, and A10:G10 remain selected.

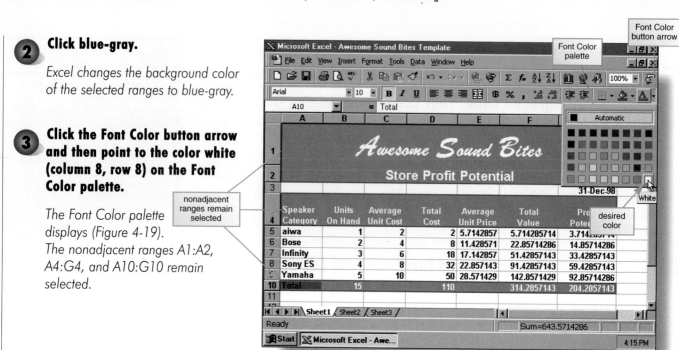

FIGURE 4-19

4 **Click white.**

Excel changes the font color of the selected ranges to white.

5 **Click the Borders button arrow and then point to the heavy outline border (column 4, row 3) on the Borders palette.**

The Borders palette displays (Figure 4-20). The nonadjacent ranges remain selected.

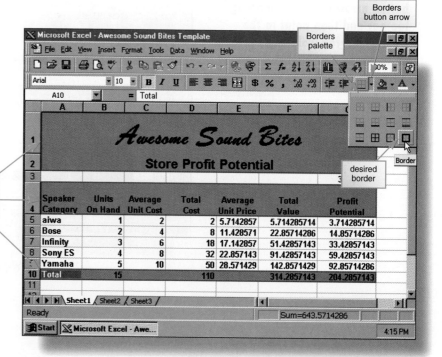

FIGURE 4-20

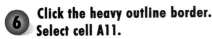

6 **Click the heavy outline border.**
Select cell A11.

The template displays as shown in
Figure 4-21.

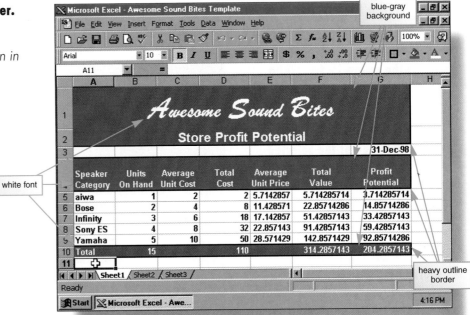

FIGURE 4-21

Applying Number Formats Using the Format Dialog Box

As shown in Figure 4-15 on page E 4.17, the template for this project follows the standard accounting format for a table of numbers; that is, it displays floating dollar signs in the first row of numbers (row 5) and the totals row (row 10). Recall that while a *fixed* dollar sign always displays in the same position in a cell (regardless of the number of significant digits), a *floating* dollar sign always displays immediately to the left of the first significant digit. To assign a fixed dollar sign to rows 5 and 10, you simply select the range and click the Currency button on the Formatting toolbar. Assigning a floating dollar sign, by contrast, requires you to select the desired format from the Format Cells dialog box.

The steps on the next page use the Format Cells dialog box to assign a Currency style with a floating dollar sign and two decimal places to the range C5:G5 and B10:G10.

Other Ways

1. On Format menu click Cells, click Patterns tab to change background, click Font tab to change font, click Border tab to change border
2. Right-click range, click Format Cells on shortcut menu, click Patterns tab to change background, click Font tab to change font, click Border tab to change border

**More *About*
Formatting**

Excel has formats for Zip Codes, telephone numbers, and social security numbers. Click Special in the Category list box in the Format Cells dialog box. The formats will display in the Type list box. These formats automatically will add dashes in the appropriate positions. All you have to do is enter the digits.

Steps To Assign a Currency Style Using the Format Dialog Box

1 **Select the range C5:G5. While holding down the CTRL key, select the nonadjacent range D10:G10.**

2 **Right-click one of the selected ranges.**

Excel displays the shortcut menu (Figure 4-22).

3 **Click Format Cells on the shortcut menu.**

4 **When the Format Cells dialog box displays, click the Number tab. Click Currency in the Category list box. Click the third item ($1,234.10) in the Negative numbers list box and then point to the OK button.**

The Format Cells dialog box displays as shown in Figure 4-23. The selected format will apply a Currency style with a floating dollar sign and two decimal places to the selected ranges.

5 **Click the OK button.**

Excel assigns the Currency style with a floating dollar sign and two decimal places to the selected ranges (Figure 4-15 on page E 4.17).

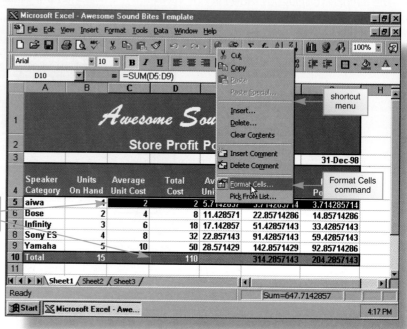

FIGURE 4-22

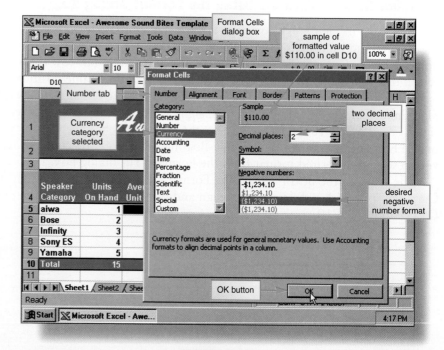

FIGURE 4-23

OtherWays

1. On Format menu click Cells, click Number tab, select format, click OK button
2. Press CTRL+1, click Number tab, select format, click OK button

Creating a Customized Format Code

Every format style listed in the Category list box in Figure 4-23 has a format code assigned to it. A **format code** is a series of format symbols (Table 4-2) that define how a format displays. To view the entire list of format codes that come with Excel, select Custom in the Category list box. You even can create your own format codes or modify the customized ones that come with Excel. Before you begin to create your own format codes or modify a customized format code, you should understand their makeup.

As shown below, a format code can have up to four sections: positive numbers, negative numbers, zeros, and text. Each section is divided by a semicolon.

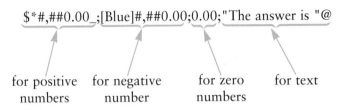

$$\$*\#,\#\#0.00\_;[\text{Blue}]\#,\#\#0.00;0.00;"\text{The answer is }"@$$

for positive numbers for negative number for zero numbers for text

A format code need not have all four sections. For most applications, a format code will have only a positive section and possibly a negative section.

More *About* **Creating Customized Formats**

Each format symbol within the format code has special meaning. Table 4-2 summarizes the more often used format symbols and their meanings. For additional information on creating format codes, click Contents and Index on the Help menu, click the Find tab, type format codes in the top text box labeled 1, click the word codes in the middle list box labeled 2, and then double-click Create a Custom number format in the lower list box labeled 3.

Table 4-2		
FORMAT SYMBOL	**EXAMPLE OF SYMBOL**	**DESCRIPTION**
# (number sign)	###.##	Serves as digit placeholder. If there are more digits to the right of the decimal point than there are number signs, Excel rounds the number. Extra digits to the left of the decimal point are displayed.
0 (zero)	0.00	Functions like number sign (#), except that if the number is less than one, Excel displays a zero in the ones place.
. (period)	#0.00	Ensures a decimal point will display in the number. The placement of symbols determines how many digits display to left and right of the decimal point.
% (percent sign)	0.00%	Displays numbers as percentages of 100. Excel multiplies the value of the cell by 100 and displays a percent sign after the number.
, (comma)	#,##0.00	Displays comma as a thousands separator.
( )	#0.00;(#0.00)	Displays negative numbers surrounded by parentheses.
$ or + or -	$#,##0.00;($#,##0.00)	Displays a floating sign ($, +, or -).
* (asterisk)	$* ##0.00	Displays a fixed sign ($, +, or -) to the left in the cell followed by spaces until the first significant digit.
[color]	#.##;[Red]#.##	Displays the characters in the cell in the designated color. In the example, positive numbers display in the default color and negative numbers display in red.
" " (quotation marks)	$0.00 "Surplus";$-0.00 "Shortage"	Displays text along with numbers entered in cell
_	#,##0.00_)	Skips the width of the character that follows the underline.

The next step is to assign a customized Comma style to the range C6:G9. If you wanted to assign the standard Comma style, you would select the Currency category and the Comma style using the Format Cells dialog box. To assign a customized Comma style, you select the Custom category, select a format code close to the desired one, and then modify or customize it. Perform the steps on the next page to assign a customized format code. The last step uses buttons on the Formatting toolbar to assign a Comma style with no decimal places to column B.

Steps   To Create a Custom Format Code

1 Select the range C6:G9. Right-click the range. Click Format Cells on the shortcut menu. When the Format Cells dialog box displays, click Custom in the Category list box.

2 Scroll down and click #,##0.00_);[Red](#,##0.00) in the Type list box. In the Type text box, change the word Red to Blue.

The Format Cells dialog box displays as shown in Figure 4-24. The Custom format has been modified to display negative numbers in blue. Excel displays a sample of the first number in the selected range in the Sample area.

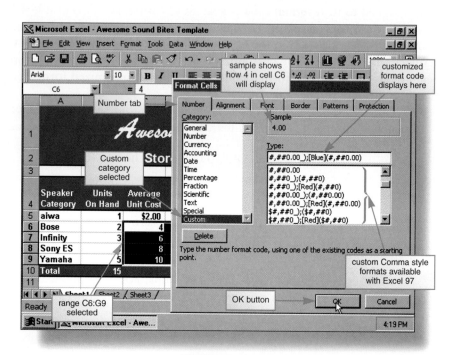

FIGURE 4-24

3 Click the OK button.

4 Select the range B5:B10. Click the Comma Style button on the Formatting toolbar. Click the Decrease Decimal button on the Formatting toolbar twice. Select cell A11.

The numbers in the template display as shown in Figure 4-25. When numbers with more than three whole number digits are entered in the range B5:B10, the Comma style format will show in the range.

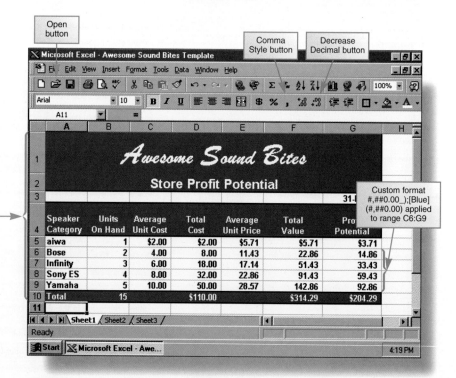

FIGURE 4-25

OtherWays

1. On Format menu click Cells, click Number tab, select format, click OK button

2. Press CTRL+1, click Number tab, select format, click OK button

When you create a new custom format code, Excel adds it to the bottom of the Custom category Type list to make it available for future use.

Spell Checking and Saving the Template

With the template complete, the next step is to spell check the template and then save it.

TO SPELL CHECK AND SAVE THE TEMPLATE

Step 1: Click cell A1. Click the Spelling button on the Standard toolbar. Change any misspelled words.

Step 2: Click the Save button on the Standard toolbar. Click Close on the File menu.

Excel saves the template to a floppy disk using the file name Awesome Sound Bites Template. Excel closes the template.

The basic worksheet portion of the template is complete. The next step is to use the template to create a workbook that uses multiple worksheets.

Alternative Uses of Templates

Before continuing on and using the template to create the Awesome Sound Bites workbook, you should be aware of some additional uses of templates. As you have seen when you begin a new Office document, Excel includes a default Workbook template, which you double-click to open a new workbook.

You can create a template — specifying desired fonts, formatting, column widths, or any other defaults — and then save it to the **Xlstart folder**. Templates stored in the Xlstart folder are called **autotemplates**. Once a template is saved in the Xlstart folder, you can select it by clicking the New command on the File menu. For example, if you save the Awesome Sound Bites Template file to the Xlstart folder, you then can open it by clicking the New command on the File menu. If you store a formatted template in the Xlstart folder using the file name Book, Excel uses it as the default Workbook template every time you begin or insert a blank workbook.

Creating a Workbook From a Template

Once you have saved the template to disk, you can begin the second phase of this project: using the template to create the Awesome Sound Bites workbook shown in Figure 4-1 on page E 4.7. As shown by the three tabs at the bottom of Figure 4-25, Excel's default Blank Workbook template includes three worksheets. The Awesome Sound Bites workbook, however, requires four sheets — one for each of the three stores and one for the company totals. A worksheet thus must be added to the workbook. Perform the steps on the next page to add a worksheet to the workbook.

Steps To Add a Worksheet to a Workbook

1 **Click the Open button on the Standard toolbar. When the Open dialog box displays, click the Files of type box arrow and click Templates. Click the Look in box arrow and click 3½ Floppy (A:). Double-click Awesome Sound Bites Template.**

Excel opens the file, Awesome Sound Bites Template, as shown earlier in Figure 4-25 on page 4.24.

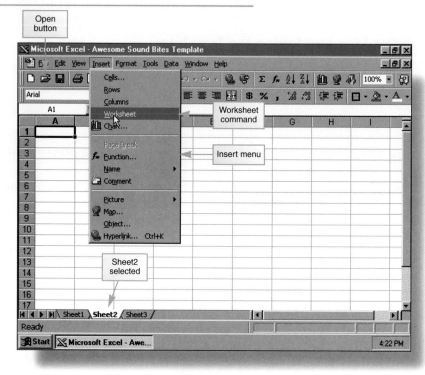

FIGURE 4-26

2 **Click the Sheet2 tab at the bottom of the screen. Click Insert on the menu bar and point to Worksheet.**

The Insert menu displays with the Worksheet command highlighted (Figure 4-26).

3 **Click Worksheet.**

Excel adds a fourth worksheet between Sheet1 and Sheet2. Recall that Sheet1 contains the template. As shown on the sheet tab, Sheet4 is the name of the new worksheet (Figure 4-27).

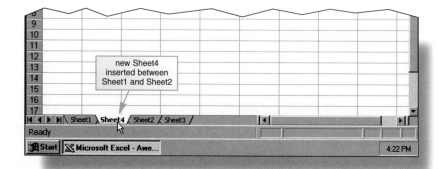

FIGURE 4-27

OtherWays

1. Right-click sheet tab, click Insert, double-click Worksheet icon

2. Right-click sheet tab, click Move or Copy, click Create a copy check box, click OK button

You can continue adding worksheets until the workbook contains 255 work-sheets. An alternative to adding worksheets to a workbook once it is open is to change the default number of worksheets before you open a new workbook. To change the default number of worksheets in a blank workbook, click Option on the Tools menu, click the General tab, and change the number in the Sheets in new workbook box.

With four worksheets in the workbook, you now can copy the template on the Sheet1 worksheet to the three blank worksheets in the workbook.

Steps **To Create a Workbook From a Template**

1 Click the Sheet1 tab to display the template. Click the Select All button and then click the Copy button on the Standard toolbar.

The template is selected as shown in Figure 4-28. The template, including all data and formats, is copied to the Clipboard.

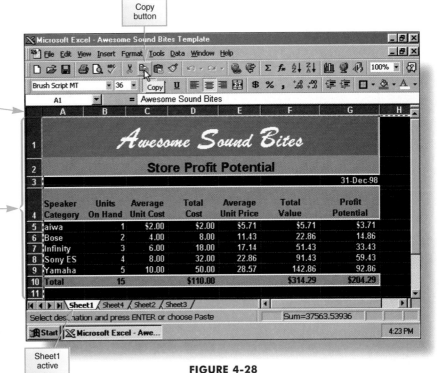

FIGURE 4-28

2 Click the Sheet4 tab. While holding down the SHIFT key, click the Sheet3 tab so all three blank worksheets are selected. Click the Paste button on the Standard toolbar.

The template is copied to Sheet4, Sheet2, and Sheet3. Because multiple sheets are selected, the term [Group] follows the template name in the title bar (Figure 4-29).

3 Click the Sheet1 tab. Click Save As on the File menu. Type
Awesome Sound Bites **in the File name text box. Click Microsoft Excel Workbook in the Save as type list box. If necessary, click 3½ Floppy (A:) in the Save in list box. Click the Save button.**

Excel saves the workbook on the floppy disk in drive A using the file name Awesome Sound Bites. Sheet1 is the active worksheet.

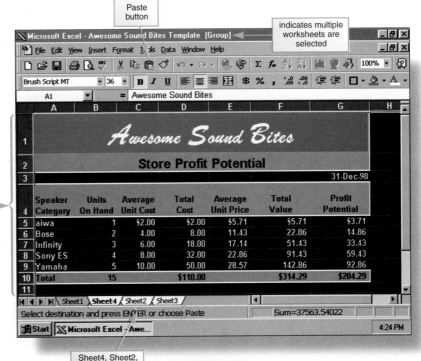

FIGURE 4-29

Table 4-3	
SPEAKER CATEGORY	**AVERAGE UNIT COST**
aiwa	129.45
Bose	189.75
Infinity	993.20
Sony ES	498.35
Yamaha	98.00

Drilling an Entry Down Through Worksheets

The next step is to enter the average unit cost for each speaker category (Table 4-3) in the range C5:C9. The average unit costs for each category are identical on all four sheets. For example, the average unit cost for the aiwa speaker category in cell C5 will be $129.45 on all four sheets. To speed data entry, Excel allows you to enter a number once and drill it through worksheets so it displays in the same cell on all the selected worksheets. This technique is referred to as **drilling an entry**. The following steps drill the five average unit cost entries through all four worksheets.

 Steps To Drill an Entry Through Worksheets

1 **With Sheet1 active, hold down the SHIFT key and then click the Sheet3 tab.**

All four tabs at the bottom of the screen are selected. The word Sheet1 on the first tab is bold, indicating it is the active sheet (Figure 4-30).

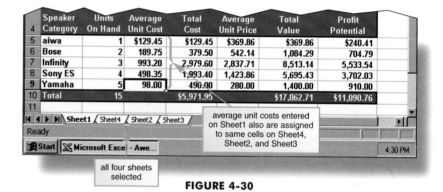

4	Speaker Category	Units On Hand	Average Unit Cost	Total Cost	Average Unit Price	Total Value	Profit Potential
5	aiwa	1	$129.45	$129.45	$369.86	$369.86	$240.41
6	Bose	2	189.75	379.50	542.14	1,084.29	704.79
7	Infinity	3	993.20	2,979.60	2,837.71	8,513.14	5,533.54
8	Sony ES	4	498.35	1,993.40	1,423.86	5,695.43	3,702.03
9	Yamaha	5	98.00	490.00	280.00	1,400.00	910.00
10	Total	15		$5,971.95		$17,062.71	$11,090.76
11							

Sheet1 / Sheet4 / Sheet2 / Sheet3

average unit costs entered on Sheet1 also are assigned to same cells on Sheet4, Sheet2, and Sheet3

all four sheets selected

FIGURE 4-30

2 **Click cell C5. Type** 129.45 **and then press the DOWN ARROW key. Enter the four remaining average unit costs in Table 4-3 in the range C6:C9.**

The average unit cost entries display as shown in Figure 4-30.

average unit costs display on all four sheets

template copied to four sheets, one for each store location and one for the company

Sheet1

Sheet4

Sheet2

	Awesome Sound Bites						
	Store Profit Potential						
							31-Dec-98
4	Speaker Category	Units On Hand	Average Unit Cost	Total Cost	Average Unit Price	Total Value	Profit Potential
5	aiwa	1	$129.45	$129.45	$369.86	$369.86	$240.41
6	Bose	2	189.75	379.50	542.14	1,084.29	704.79
7	Infinity	3	993.20	2,979.60	2,837.71	8,513.14	5,533.54
8	Sony ES	4	498.35	1,993.40	1,423.86	5,695.43	3,702.03
9	Yamaha	5	98.00	490.00	280.00	1,400.00	910.00
10	Total	15		$5,971.95		$17,062.71	$11,090.76

Sheet3

FIGURE 4-31

3 **One at a time, click the Sheet1 tab, the Sheet4 tab, the Sheet2 tab, and the Sheet3 tab.**

The four sheets are identical (Figure 4-31). Each is made up of the data and formats assigned earlier to the template.

In the previous set of steps, you entered five new numbers on one worksheet. As shown in Figure 4-31, by drilling the entries through the four other worksheets, twenty new numbers now display, five on each of the four worksheets. This ability to drill data through worksheets is an efficient way to enter data that is common among worksheets. For example, you could have used this technique to create the entire Awesome Sound Bites workbook without the use of a template.

Modifying the Los Angeles Sheet

With the skeleton of the Awesome Sound Bites workbook created, the next step is to modify the individual sheets. The following steps modify the Los Angeles sheet by changing the sheet name and worksheet title, changing the color of the title and total rows, and entering the units on hand in column B.

TO MODIFY THE LOS ANGELES SHEET

Step 1: Double-click the Sheet4 tab and then type Los Angeles as the sheet name.

Step 2: Double-click cell A2, drag through the word Store, and type Los Angeles to change the worksheet title.

Step 3: Select the range A1:A2. While holding down the CTRL key, select the nonadjacent ranges A4:G4 and A10:G10. Click the Fill Color button arrow on the Formatting toolbar. Click the color green (column 4, row 2) on the Fill Color palette.

Step 4: Enter the data listed in Table 4-4 in the range B5:B9.

Step 5: Click the Save button on the Standard toolbar.

The Los Angeles sheet displays as shown in Figure 4-32.

Table 4-4

CELL	UNITS ON HAND
B5	645
B6	231
B7	45
B8	497
B9	902

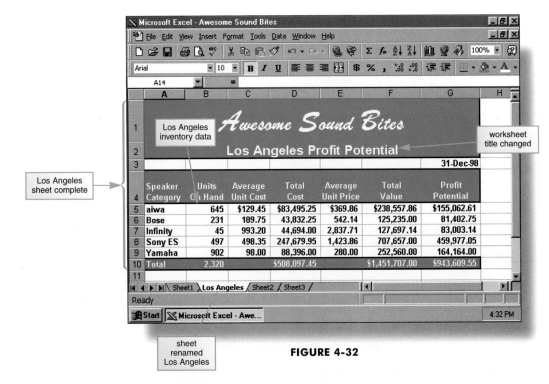

FIGURE 4-32

As you enter the new data, Excel immediately recalculates all the formulas.

Modifying the Chicago Sheet

The following steps modify the the Chicago sheet.

TO MODIFY THE CHICAGO SHEET

Step 1: Double-click the Sheet2 tab and then type `Chicago` as the sheet name.

Step 2: Double-click cell A2, drag through the word Store, and type `Chicago` as the worksheet title.

Step 3: Select the range A1:A2. While holding down the CTRL key, select the nonadjacent ranges A4:G4 and A10:G10. Click the Fill Color button arrow on the Formatting toolbar. Click the color red (column 1, row 3) on the Fill Color palette.

Step 4: Enter the data in Table 4-5 in the range B5:B9.

Step 5: Click the Save button on the Standard toolbar.

The Chicago sheet displays as shown in Figure 4-33.

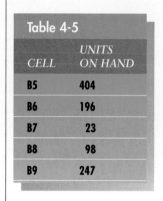

Table 4-5	
CELL	UNITS ON HAND
B5	404
B6	196
B7	23
B8	98
B9	247

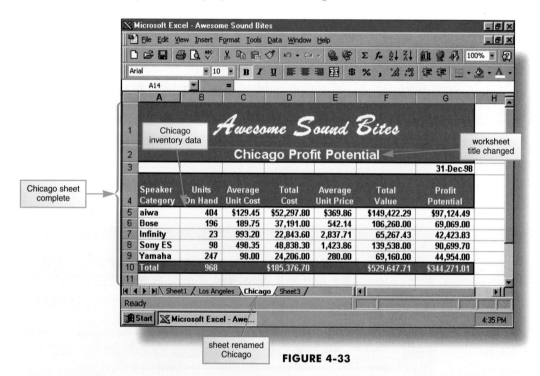

FIGURE 4-33

Modifying the New York Sheet

Like the Los Angeles and Chicago sheets, the sheet name, worksheet title, data, and background colors must be changed on the New York sheet. The following steps modify the New York sheet.

TO MODIFY THE NEW YORK SHEET

Step 1: Double click the Sheet3 tab and then type New York as the sheet name.

Step 2: Double click cell A2, drag through the word Store and type New York to change the worksheet title.

Step 3: Select the range A1:A2. While holding down the CTRL key, select the nonadjacent ranges A4:G4 and A10:G10. Click the Fill Color button arrow on the Formatting toolbar. Click the color orange (column 2, row 2) on the Fill Color palette.

Step 4: Enter the data in Table 4-6 in the range B5:B9.

Step 5: Click the Save button on the Standard toolbar.

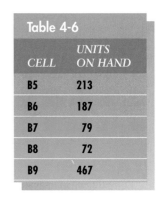

Table 4-6	
CELL	**UNITS ON HAND**
B5	213
B6	187
B7	79
B8	72
B9	467

The New York sheet displays as shown in Figure 4-34.

FIGURE 4-34

With the three store sheets complete, the next step is to modify Sheet1, which will serve as the consolidation worksheet containing totals of the data on the Los Angeles, Chicago, and New York sheets. Because this sheet contains totals of the data, you need to understand how to reference cells in other sheets in a workbook before modifying Sheet1.

Referencing Cells in Other Sheets in a Workbook

To reference cells in other sheets in a workbook, you use the sheet name, which serves as the **sheet reference**, and the cell reference. For example, you refer to cell B5 on the Los Angeles sheet as shown on the next page.

More *About*
Entering Data

You can automate entering the data in Table 4-6 by selecting the range to enter data into prior to entering the data. Excel will move down to the next cell when you press the ENTER key and then over to the next column within the range when you reach the bottom of the range.

=Los Angeles!B5

sheet reference   exclamation   cell
or sheet name   point   reference

Using this method, you could sum cell B5 on the three store sheets by selecting cell B5 on the Sheet1 sheet and then entering:

=Los Angeles!B5 + Chicago!B5 + New York!B5

A much quicker way to total this is to use the SUM function as follows:

=SUM(Los Angeles:New York!B5)

The SUM argument (Los Angeles:New York!B5) instructs Excel to sum cell B5 on each of the three sheets (Los Angeles, Chicago, and New York). The colon (:) between the first sheet and the last sheet means to include these sheets and all sheets in between, just as it does with a range of cells on a sheet. A range that spans two or more sheets in a workbook, such as Los Angeles:New York!B5, is called a **3-D range**. The reference to this range is a **3-D reference**.

A sheet reference, such as Los Angeles!, is always absolute. Thus, the sheet reference remains constant when you copy formulas.

Entering a Sheet Reference

You can enter a sheet reference in a cell by typing it or by clicking the appropriate sheet tab while in Point mode. When you click the sheet tab, Excel activates the sheet and automatically adds the sheet name and an exclamation point after the insertion point in the formula bar. Next, click or drag through the cells you want to reference on the sheet.

If the range of cells to be referenced is located on several worksheets (as when selecting a 3-D range), click the first sheet tab and then drag through the cell or range of cells. Next, while holding down the SHIFT key, click the sheet tab of the last sheet you want to reference. Excel will include the cell(s) on the end sheets and all the sheets in between.

Modifying the Company Sheet

The next step is to modify the Company sheet by changing sheet names and titles and entering the SUM function in each cell in the range B5:B9. The SUM functions will determine the total units on hand by speaker category for the three stores. Cell B5, for instance, will equal the sum of the aiwa speaker category units on hand in cells Los Angeles!B5, Chicago!B5, and New York!B5. Before determining the totals, perform the following steps to change the sheet name from Sheet1 to Company and the worksheet title to Company Profit Potential.

TO RENAME A SHEET

Step 1: Double-click the Sheet1 sheet tab.
Step 2: Type Company and then click cell B5.
Step 3: Double-click cell A2, drag through the word Store, and type Company as the worksheet title.

Excel changes the name of Sheet1 to Company and the worksheet title to Company Profit Potential.

More *About*
3-D References

If you are adding numbers on noncontiguous sheets, hold down the CTRL key rather than the SHIFT key when selecting the sheets.

The following steps enter the 3-D references used to determine the total units on hand for each of the five speaker categories.

 Steps **To Enter and Copy 3-D References**

1 **With cell B5 selected on the Company sheet, click the AutoSum button on the Standard toolbar.**

The SUM function displays without a selected range (Figure 4-35).

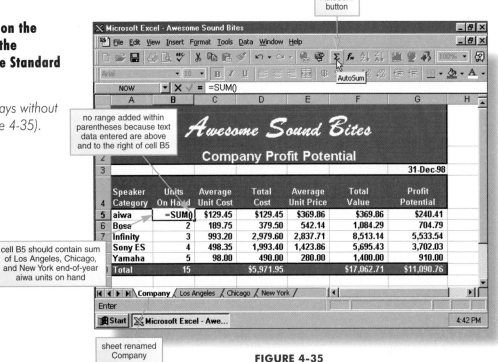

FIGURE 4-35

2 **Click the Los Angeles tab and then click cell B5. While holding down the SHIFT key, click the New York tab.**

A moving border or marquee surrounds cell Los Angeles!B5 (Figure 4-36). All four sheet tabs are highlighted; the Los Angeles tab displays in bold because it is the active sheet. The SUM function displays in the formula bar.

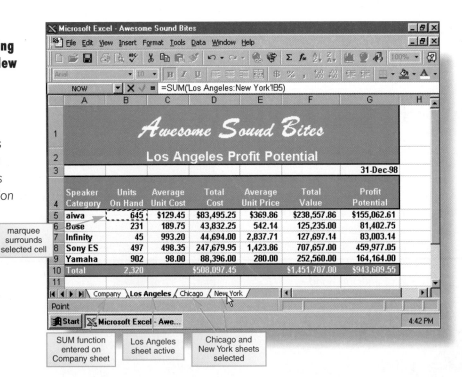

FIGURE 4-36

3 **Click the Enter box in the formula bar or press the ENTER key.**

The SUM function is entered and the Company sheet becomes the active sheet. The sum of the cells Los Angeles!B5, Chicago!B5, and New York!B5 displays in cell B5 of the Company sheet. The SUM function assigned to cell B5 displays in the formula bar (Figure 4-37).

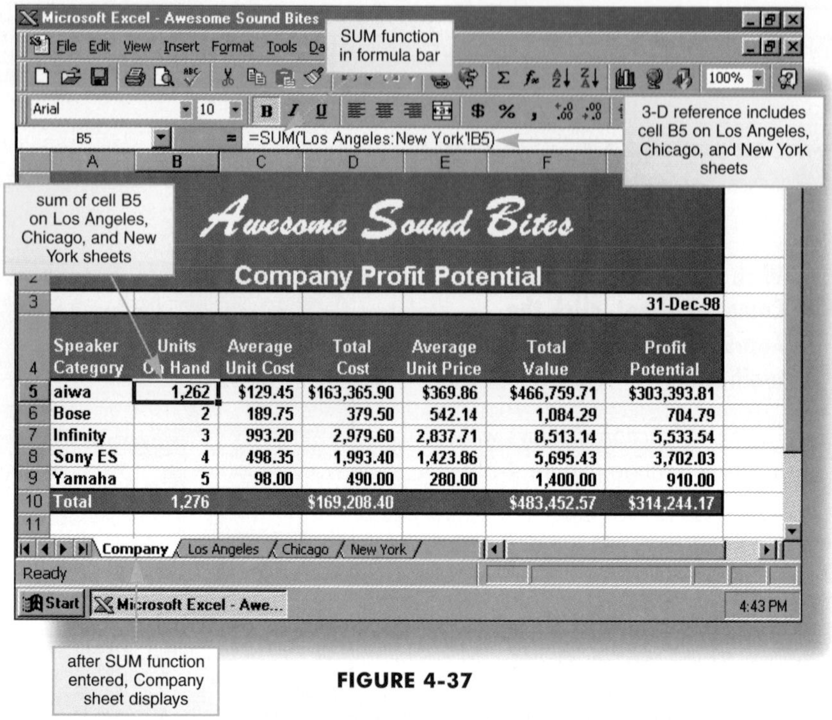

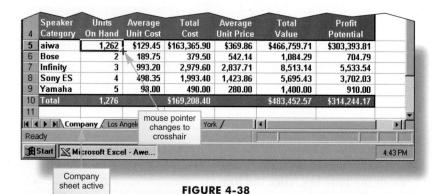

FIGURE 4-37

4 **With cell B5 active, point to the fill handle.**

The mouse pointer changes to a crosshair (Figure 4-38).

FIGURE 4-38

5 **Drag the fill handle through cell B9.**

Excel copies the SUM function in cell B5 to the range B6:B9 (Figure 4-39). Excel automatically adjusts the cell references in the SUM function to reference the corresponding cells on the other three sheets in the workbook. The total units on hand for each speaker category displays.

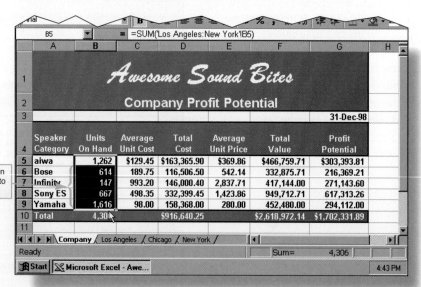

FIGURE 4-39

6 **Click cell A14 and then scroll to the top of the Company sheet.**

All the formulas in cell A10 of the Company sheet are recalculated based on the total units on hand for each speaker category. The Company sheet is complete (Figure 4-40).

7 **Click the Save button on the Standard toolbar to save the Awesome Sound Bites workbook.**

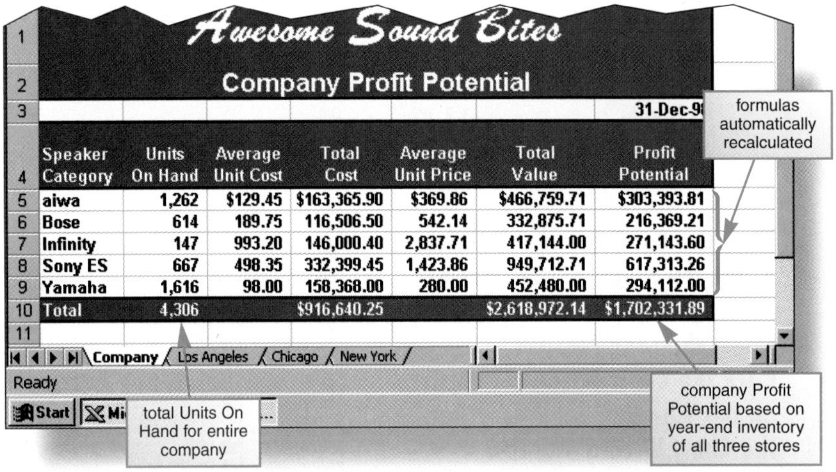

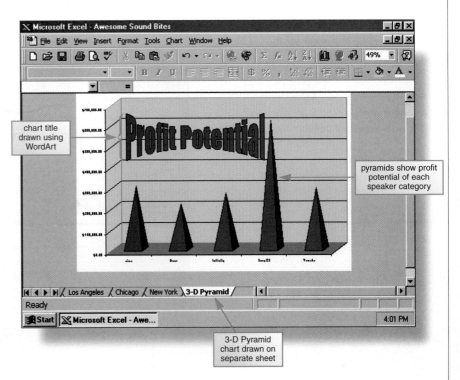

Speaker Category	Units On Hand	Average Unit Cost	Total Cost	Average Unit Price	Total Value	Profit Potential
aiwa	1,262	$129.45	$163,365.90	$369.86	$466,759.71	$303,393.81
Bose	614	189.75	116,506.50	542.14	332,875.71	216,369.21
Infinity	147	993.20	146,000.40	2,837.71	417,144.00	271,143.60
Sony ES	667	498.35	332,399.45	1,423.86	949,712.71	617,313.26
Yamaha	1,616	98.00	158,368.00	280.00	452,480.00	294,112.00
Total	4,306		$916,640.25		$2,618,972.14	$1,702,331.89

FIGURE 4-40

OtherWays

1. Click Paste Function button, click Math & Trig in Function Category list box, click SUM in Function name list box, click OK button, enter parameters, click OK button
2. On Insert menu click Function, click Math & Trig in Function Category list box, click SUM in Function name list box, click OK button, enter parameters, click OK button
3. Click Edit Formula box in formula bar, click SUM in Function list box, enter parameters, click OK button

As shown in cell G10 in Figure 4-40, Awesome Sound Bites has a year-end profit potential of $1,702,331.89, based on the inventory data submitted by the three stores. If a store calls in a correction to the units on hand for any speaker category, Arnold Ladd, CEO of Awesome Sound Bites, simply has to select the sheet that represents the store and enter the correction. All formulas, including those on the Company sheet, will be recalculated immediately, and Arnold quickly can see the most up-to-date total for profit potential.

With the four worksheets in the Awesome Sound Bites workbook complete, the next step is to draw a 3-D Pyramid chart.

Drawing a 3-D Pyramid Chart

The 3-D Pyramid chart is similar to a 3-D Bar chart in that it can be used to show trends or illustrate comparisons among items. The 3-D Pyramid chart on the Company sheet in Figure 4-41, for example, compares the profit potential of each of the five speaker categories.

FIGURE 4-41

The following steps create the 3-D Pyramid chart.

Steps To Draw a 3-D Pyramid Chart

1 With the Company sheet active, select the range A5:A9. While holding down the CTRL key, select the range G5:G9. Click the Chart Wizard button on the Standard toolbar. When the Chart Wizard – Step 1 of 4 – Chart Type dialog box displays, click Pyramid in the Chart type list box.

The Chart Wizard – Step 1 of 4 – Chart Type dialog box displays as shown in Figure 4-42. The nonadjacent range selection displays behind the dialog box.

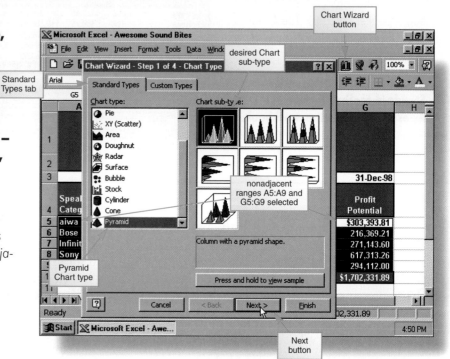

FIGURE 4-42

2 Click the Next button.

The Chart Wizard – Step 2 of 4 – Chart Source Data dialog box displays with a sample of the 3-D Pyramid chart and the nonadjacent data range selection (Figure 4-43). Because nonadjacent ranges are selected down the sheet, Excel automatically determines series are in columns.

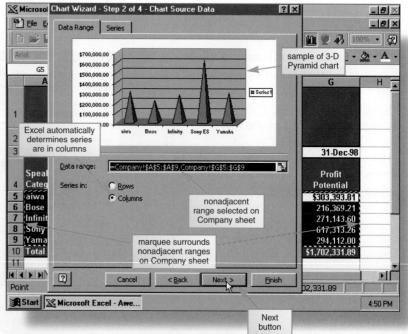

FIGURE 4-43

3 Click the Next button. When the Chart Wizard – Step 3 of 4 – Chart Options dialog box displays, click the Legend tab. Click the Show Legend check box so the legend does not display with the chart.

The Chart Wizard – Step 3 of 4 – Chart Options dialog box displays as shown in Figure 4-44.

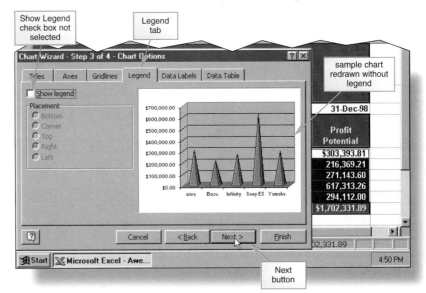

FIGURE 4-44

4 Click the Next button. When the Chart Wizard – Step 4 of 4 – Chart Location dialog box displays, click the As new sheet option button.

The Chart Wizard – Step 4 of 4 – Chart Location dialog box displays as shown in Figure 4-45. Because the As new sheet option button is selected, the chart will be drawn on a separate chart sheet.

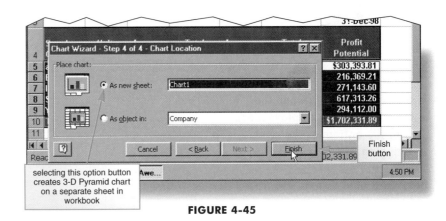

FIGURE 4-45

5 Click the Finish button.

Excel draws the 3-D Pyramid chart. The chart sheet, which is named Chart1, is inserted as the first sheet in the workbook (Figure 4-46).

6 Double-click the Chart1 tab and then type 3-D Pyramid as the sheet name. Press the ENTER key. Drag the 3-D Pyramid to the right of the New York sheet. Click the wall of the chart. Click the Fill Color arrow on the Formatting toolbar and click Light Green. Click one of the pyramids. Click the Fill Color arrow on the Formatting toolbar and click Blue-Gray.

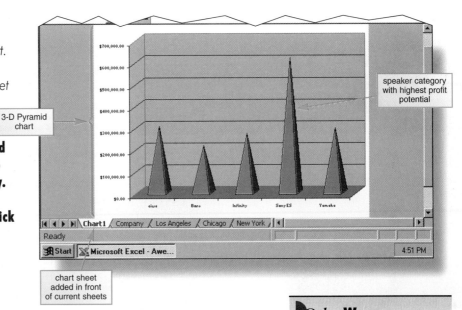

OtherWays

1. Select chart range, press F11

The 3-D Pyramid chart in Figure 4-46 on the previous page compares the profit potential of the five speaker categories. You can see from the chart that the Sony ES speaker category has the greatest profit potential and that the Bose speaker category has the least profit potential.

Adding a Chart Title Using the WordArt Tool

In earlier projects, you added a chart title by using the Chart Wizard and then formatted it using the Formatting toolbar. This section shows you how to add a chart title and create special text formatting effects using the WordArt tool. The **WordArt tool** allows you to create shadowed, skewed, rotated, and stretched text on a chart sheet or worksheet. You start the WordArt tool by clicking the WordArt button on the Drawing toolbar.

Steps To Add a Chart Title Using the WordArt Tool

1 **With the chart sheet active, click the Drawing button on the Standard toolbar. When the Drawing toolbar displays, dock it at the bottom of the screen by dragging it.**

The Drawing toolbar displays at the bottom of the screen (Figure 4-47).

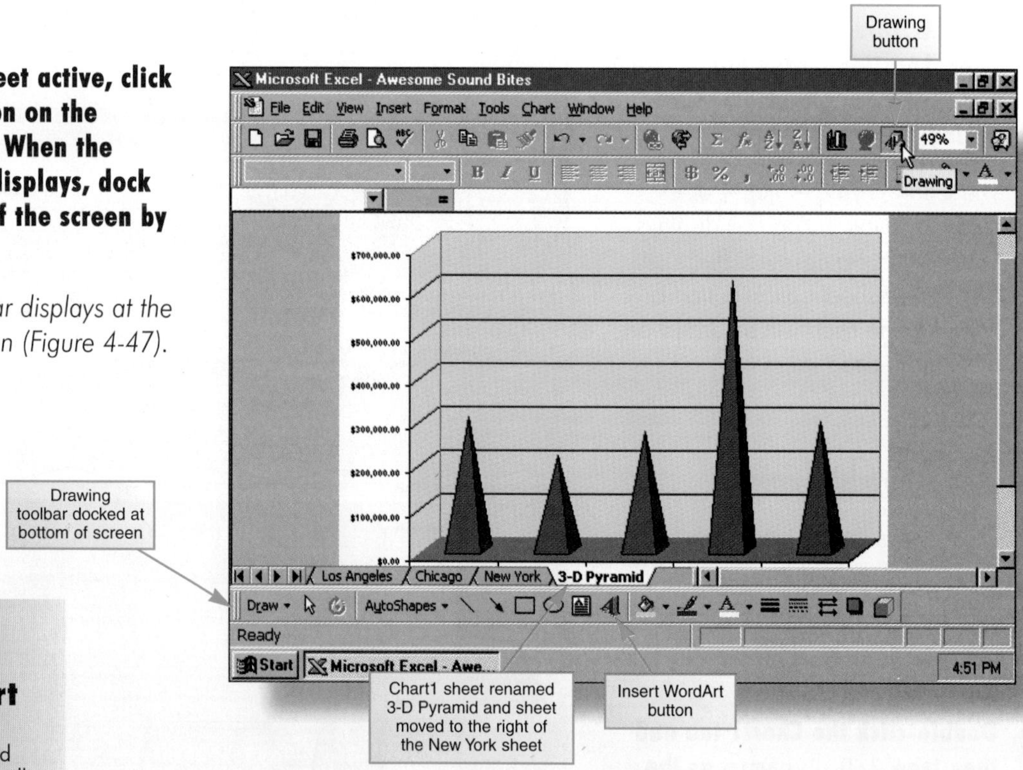

Drawing button

Drawing toolbar docked at bottom of screen

Chart1 sheet renamed 3-D Pyramid and sheet moved to the right of the New York sheet

Insert WordArt button

FIGURE 4-47

2 Click the Insert WordArt button on the Drawing toolbar. When the WordArt Gallery dialog box displays, click the design in column 4, row 1 of the Select a WordArt style area.

The WordArt Gallery dialog box displays as shown in Figure 4-48.

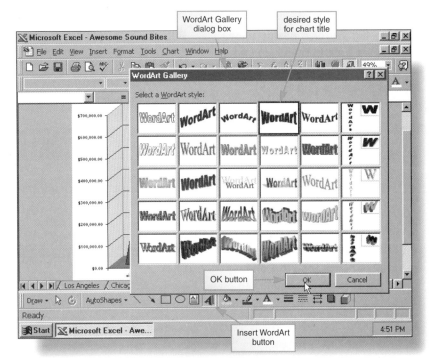

FIGURE 4-48

3 Click the OK button. When the Edit WordArt Text dialog box displays, type Profit Potential as the title of the 3-D Pyramid chart.

The Edit WordArt Text dialog box displays as shown in Figure 4-49. Profit Potential will be the chart title.

FIGURE 4-49

4 Click the OK button.

The WordArt displays in the middle of the chart sheet (Figure 4-50). The WordArt toolbar displays.

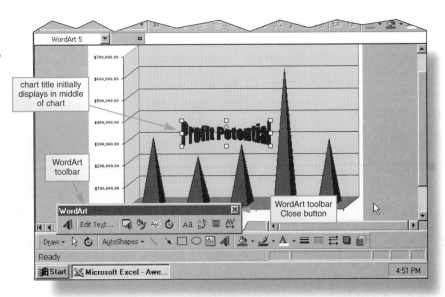

FIGURE 4-50

5 Drag the WordArt design above the pyramids in the chart and drag the sizing handles to resize it as shown in Figure 4-51.

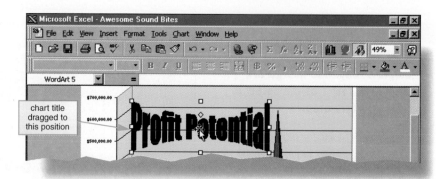

FIGURE 4-51

6 With the WordArt design selected, click the Fill Color button arrow and change the color of the design to blue-gray (row 7, column 2) on the Fill Color palette.

The color of the WordArt design changes to blue-gray (Figure 4-52). Even though the title appears to be made up of text, the chart title is a design. You thus use the Fill Color button, rather than the Font Color button, to change the color.

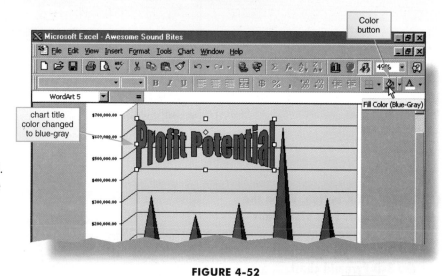

FIGURE 4-52

7 Click outside the chart area. Click the Close button on the WordArt toolbar. Click the Drawing button on the Standard toolbar.

Excel hides the WordArt and Drawing toolbars. The 3-D Pyramid chart now is complete (Figure 4-53).

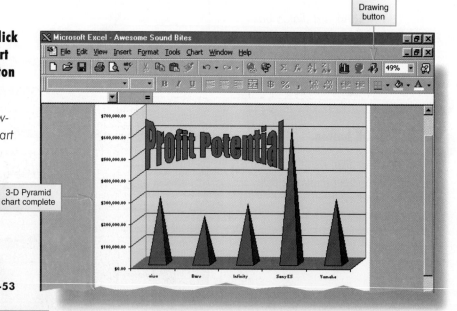

FIGURE 4-53

Other Ways

1. On Insert menu point to Picture, click WordArt on Picture submenu
2. Right-click toolbar, click WordArt, click Insert WordArt button

Once you add a WordArt design to your workbook, you can use the WordArt toolbar to edit it. The buttons on the WordArt toolbar and their functions are described in Table 4-7. Like the other Excel toolbars, you can display or hide the WordArt toolbar by right-clicking any toolbar and then clicking WordArt on the shortcut menu.

Adding Comments to a Workbook

Comments or **notes** in a workbook are used to describe the function of a cell, a range of cells, a sheet, or the entire workbook. Comments are used to identify workbooks and clarify entries that might otherwise be difficult to understand.

In Excel you can assign comments to any cell in the worksheet by using the Comment command on the Insert menu. Once a comment is assigned, you can read the comment by pointing to the cell. Excel will display the comment in a comment box. In general, overall workbook comments should include the following:

1. Worksheet title
2. Author's name
3. Date created
4. Date last modified (use N/A if it has not been modified)
5. Template(s) used, if any
6. A short description of the purpose of the worksheet

Table 4-7

BUTTON	NAME	FUNCTION
	Insert WordArt	Start WordArt tool
Edit Text...	Edit Text	Edit text in design
	WordArt Gallery	Display WordArt Gallery dialog box
	Format WordArt	Format design
	WordArt Shape	Change shape of design
	Free Rotate	Rotate design
Aa	WordArt Same Letter Heights	Switch between same and different letter height in design
	WordArt Vertical Text	Change design from horizontal to vertical
	WordArt Alignment	Change alignment of design
	WordArt Character Spacing	Change character spacing in design

The following steps assign a workbook comment to cell A13 on the Company sheet.

Steps To Assign a Comment to a Cell

1 **Click the Company tab to display the Company sheet. Right-click cell A13. Point to the Insert Comment command on the shortcut menu.**

The shortcut menu displays (Figure 4-54).

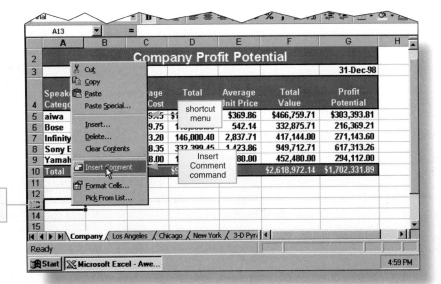

FIGURE 4-54

2 **Click Insert Comment. When the comment box displays, drag the lower-right handle to resize the comment box as shown in Figure 4-55.**

Excel adds a small red triangle, called a **comment indicator,** *to cell A13. A small black arrow attached to the comment box points to the comment indicator (Figure 4-55).*

3 **Enter the comment shown in Figure 4-55 in the comment box.**

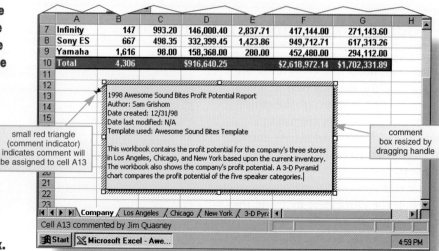

FIGURE 4-55

4 **Click cell A20 and then point to cell A13.**

The comment box displays (Figure 4-56).

5 **Click the Save button on the Standard toolbar to save the workbook.**

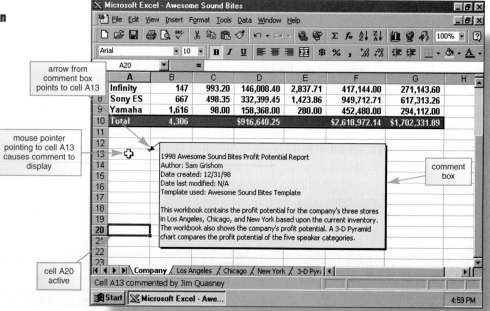

FIGURE 4-56

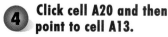
The comment indicator in the upper-right corner of the cell indicates the cell has a comment associated with it (cell A13 in Figure 4-56). To read the comment, point to the cell and the note will display on the worksheet. To edit the comment, right-click the cell and then click Edit Comment, or click the cell and press SHIFT+F2. To delete the comment, right-click the cell and then click Delete Comment.

More *About* **Comments**

You can print comments by clicking the Comments arrow on the Sheet sheet in the Page Setup dialog box.

Adding a Header and Changing the Margins

A **header** is printed at the top of a every page in a printout. A **footer** is printed at the bottom of every page in a printout. By default, both the header and footer are blank. You can change either so that information, such as the workbook author, date, page number, or tab name, prints at the top or bottom of each page.

Sometimes you will want to change the margins to increase or decrease the white space surrounding the printed worksheet or chart. The default **margins** in Excel are set to the following: Top = 1"; Bottom = 1"; Left = .75"; Right = .75". You also can center a printout horizontally and vertically.

Changing the header and footer and changing the margins are all part of the **page setup**, which defines the appearance and format of a page. To change page setup characteristics, select the desired sheet(s) and click the Page Setup command on the File menu. Remember to select all the sheets you want to modify before you change the headers, footers, or margins, because the page setup characteristics will change only on selected sheets.

As you modify the page setup, remember that Excel does not copy page setup characteristics when one sheet is copied to another. Thus, even if you assigned page setup characteristics to the template before copying it to the Awesome Sound Bites workbook, the page setup characteristics would not copy to the new sheet. The following steps use the Page Setup dialog box to change the headers and margins and center the printout horizontally.

More *About* Templates

Applying page setup characteristics to a template will not work because they are not part of the pasted worksheets. Thus, the page setup characteristics assigned to a template only will apply to the first sheet in a workbook created by copying the template to multiple worksheets in the workbook.

More *About* Headers and Footers

You can turn off headers and footers for a printout by selecting (none) in the Header list box and in the Footer list box on the Header/Footer sheet in the Page Setup dialog box. This is useful when printing charts for slides.

 Steps To Change the Header and Margins and Center the Printout Horizontally

1 **If necessary, click the Company sheet tab to make it active. While holding down the SHIFT key, click the 3-D Pyramid sheet tab. Click File on the menu bar and then point to Page Setup.**

Excel displays the File menu (Figure 4-57). The five sheet tabs at the bottom of the window are selected.

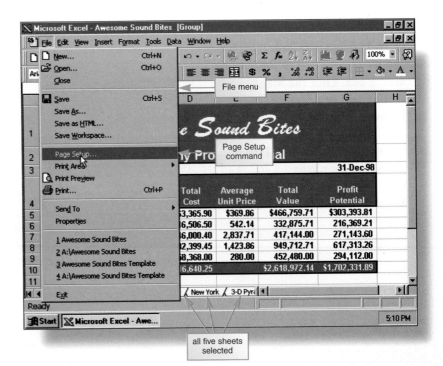

FIGURE 4-57

2 **Click Page Setup. When the Page Setup dialog box displays, click the Header/Footer tab. Point to the Custom Header button.**

Samples of the default header and footer display (Figure 4-58). The entry (none) indicates that the headers and footers are blank.

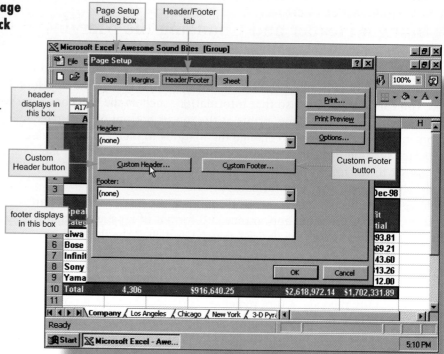

FIGURE 4-58

3 **Click the Custom Header button. When the Header dialog box displays, click the Left section text box. Type** Sam Grishom **and then press the ENTER key to go to the next line. Type** Profit Potential **and then click the Center section text box. Click the Sheet Name button in the Header dialog box. Click the Right section text box. Type** Page **followed by a space and then click the Page Number button in the Header dialog box. Type a space and then type** of **followed by a space. Click the Total Pages button. Point to the OK button.**

The Header dialog box appears with the new header as shown in Figure 4-59.

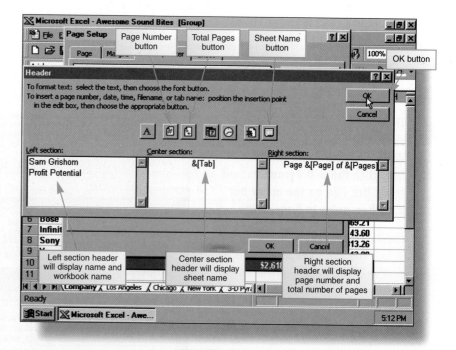

FIGURE 4-59

4 **Click the OK button in the Header dialog box.**

The Header/Footer sheet in the Page Setup dialog box displays as shown in Figure 4-60.

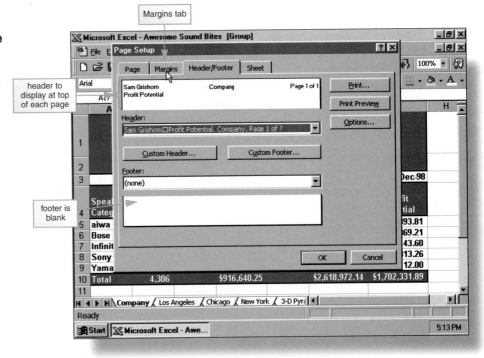

FIGURE 4-60

5 **Click the Margins tab in the Page Setup dialog box. Click the Horizontally check box to center the worksheet on the page. Click the Top box and type** 1.5 **to change the top margin to 1.5″.**

The Margins sheet in the Page Setup dialog box displays as shown in Figure 4-61.

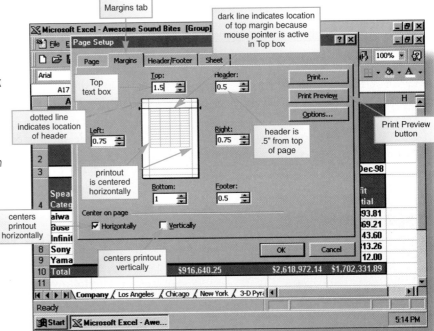

FIGURE 4-61

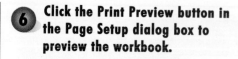 **Click the Print Preview button in the Page Setup dialog box to preview the workbook.**

The Company sheet displays as shown in Figure 4-62. Although difficult to read, the header displays at the top of the page. You can click the Zoom button to get a better view of the page.

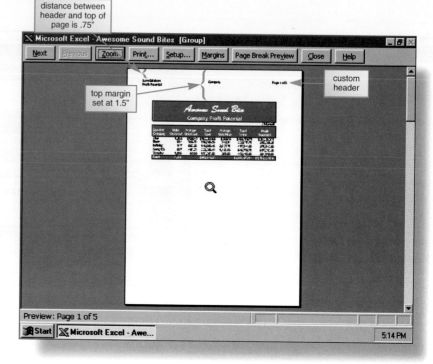 **When you are finished previewing the printout, click the Close button. Click the Save button on the Standard toolbar to save the workbook with the new page setup characteristics.**

FIGURE 4-62

Table 4-8		
BUTTON	**CODE**	**FUNCTION**
A		Displays the Font dialog box
	&[Page]	Inserts a page number
	&[Pages]	Inserts the total number of pages
	&[Date]	Inserts the system date
	&[Time]	Inserts the system time
	&[File]	Inserts the file name of the workbook
	&[Tab]	Inserts the tab name

When you click a button in the Header dialog box (Figure 4-59 on page E 4.44), Excel enters a code (similar to a format code) into the active header section. A code such as &[Page] instructs Excel to insert the page number. Table 4-8 summarizes the buttons, their codes, and their functions in the Header or Footer dialog box.

Printing the Workbook

The following steps print the workbook.

TO PRINT THE WORKBOOK

Step 1: Ready the printer.
Step 2: If the five sheets in the workbook are not selected, click the Company tab and then, while holding down the SHIFT key, click the 3-D Pyramid tab.
Step 3: Click the Print button on the Standard toolbar.

The workbook prints as shown in Figures 4-63a and 4-63b.

(a)

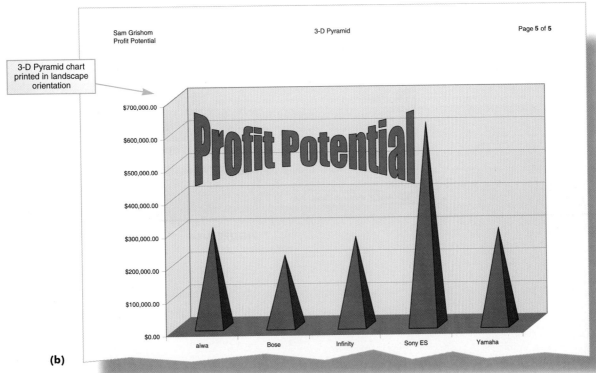

(b)

FIGURE 4-63

Creating a Web Page From an Excel Worksheet

Companies such as Awesome Sound Bites often publish Web pages for internal use on their intranet. An **intranet** is a closed network that can be used to store Web pages like the Internet; an intranet is closed in the sense that only employees and other authorized individuals are allowed to view the Web pages. Arnold Ladd has asked you to create a Web page from the Company sheet. This Web page will be posted to the company's intranet and viewed by management using a **browser**, such as Microsoft Internet Explorer or Netscape Navigator.

Like the documents on the Internet, documents on an intranet are saved in HTML format. **HTML** stands for Hypertext Markup Language, which allows you to mark or tag a document so it can be viewed by a browser. With Excel, you can convert workbook data, such as a worksheet or chart, to HTML by using the **Save as HTML command** on the File menu. You do not have to add HTML tags (special codes) to the worksheet data, because the Save as HTML command instructs Excel to add the tags for you automatically.

The following steps save the range A1:G10 on the Company sheet of the Awesome Sound Bites workbook as HTML.

Steps To Create a Web Page from an Excel Worksheet

1 Insert a floppy disk in drive A. While holding down the SHIFT key, click the Company tab. Select the range A1:G10. On the File menu, point to Save as HTML.

The File menu displays as shown in Figure 4-64.

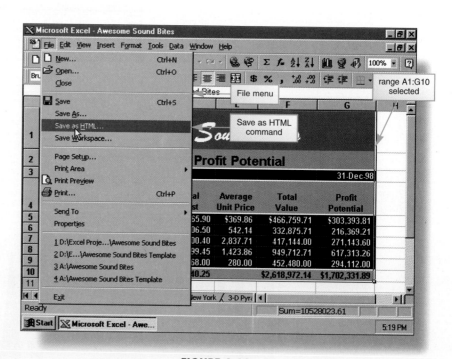

FIGURE 4-64

2 Click Save as HTML. When the Internet Assistant Wizard – Step 1 of 4 dialog box displays, click Chart "3-D Pyramid" in the Ranges and charts to convert list box and then click the Remove button.

The Internet Assistant Wizard – Step 1 of 4 dialog box displays (Figure 4-65). Excel automatically selects any range or chart within the selected range. Because this project does not require that the chart be converted to HTML, it is removed.

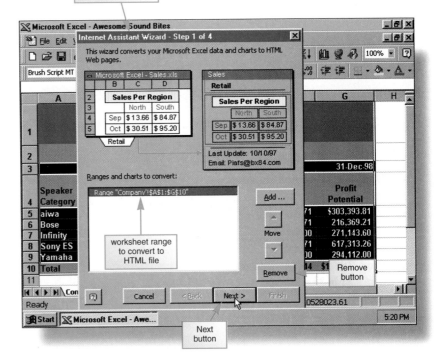

FIGURE 4-65

3 Click the Next button.

The Internet Assistant Wizard – Step 2 of 4 dialog box displays with the Create an independent, ready-to-view HTML document... option button selected (Figure 4-66).

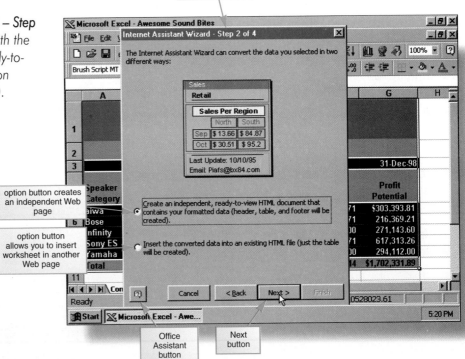

FIGURE 4-66

4 Click the Next button. Type Awesome Sound Bites Profit Potential **in the Header text box. Type** This Web page shows the profit potential for the company based on year-end inventory. **in the Description below header text box. Click the two check boxes to insert horizontal lines before and after the worksheet data. Type** 12/31/98 **in the Last Update on text box. Type** Sam Grishom **(or your name) in the By text box. Type** grishoms@msn.com **(or your Email address) in the Email text box.**

The Internet Assistant Wizard – Step 3 of 4 dialog box displays as shown in Figure 4-67.

5 Click the Next button. When the Internet Assistant – Step 4 of 4 dialog box displays, type a:\Awesome Sound Bites.htm **in the File path text box.**

The Internet Assistant Wizard – Step 4 of 4 dialog box displays as shown in Figure 4-68.

6 Click the Finish button. Close the workbook.

Excel saves the range A1:G10 of the Company sheet in the Awesome Sound Bites workbook on the floppy disk in drive A as an HTML file.

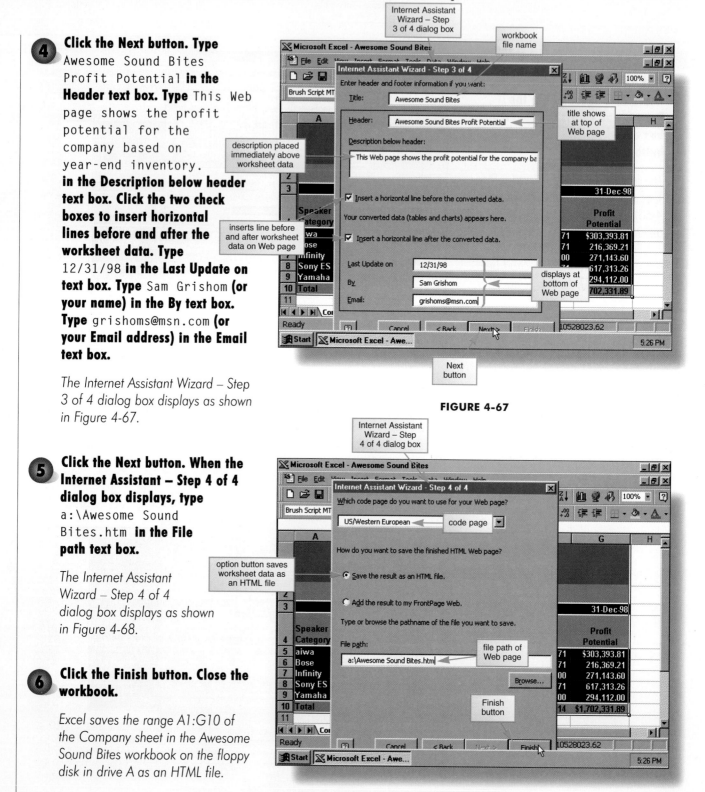

FIGURE 4-67

FIGURE 4-68

All of the text entered in response to the Internet Assistant Wizard – Step 3 of 4 dialog box is optional. You should, however, keep the reader in mind and add text and lines to make the Web page easier to interpret and more professional in appearance.

In Step 5, the file path was entered in response to the Internet Assistant Wizard – Step 4 of 4 dialog box. The **file path** indicates where you want to store the HTML file. To specify a file path, you first enter the drive letter, followed by a colon (:) and a backslash (\). If the file will be stored in one or more folders, type the name of the folders that contain the file, placing a backslash before each folder name. After the last folder name, type the file name. The file name should be preceded by a backslash. Following the file name, type a period (.) and then the three character **extension**. In the case of the HTML file, the extension is htm. The extension is important and must be included for your browser to locate the HTML file. The path name used in this project is shown below:

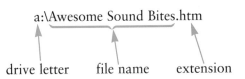

a:\Awesome Sound Bites.htm

drive letter   file name   extension

Viewing a Web Page Using the Web Toolbar

Once the worksheet data is saved as a Web page, you can use your browser or the Web toolbar in Excel to display it. The following steps show how to launch your browser using Excel's Web toolbar. Before you perform these steps, make sure that the Awesome Sound Bites workbook is closed and that an empty workbook displays on the screen.

 Steps **To View a Web Page Using the Web Toolbar**

1 **Click the New button on the Standard toolbar. Insert the floppy disk with the HTML file into drive A. Click the Web Toolbar button on the Standard toolbar. When the Web toolbar displays, type the file path** a:\awesome sound bites.htm **in the Address box.**

The Web toolbar displays (Figure 4-69). The file path displays in the Address box.

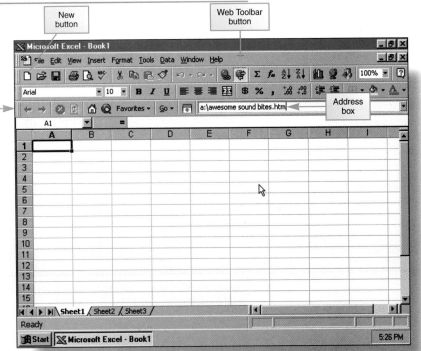

FIGURE 4-69

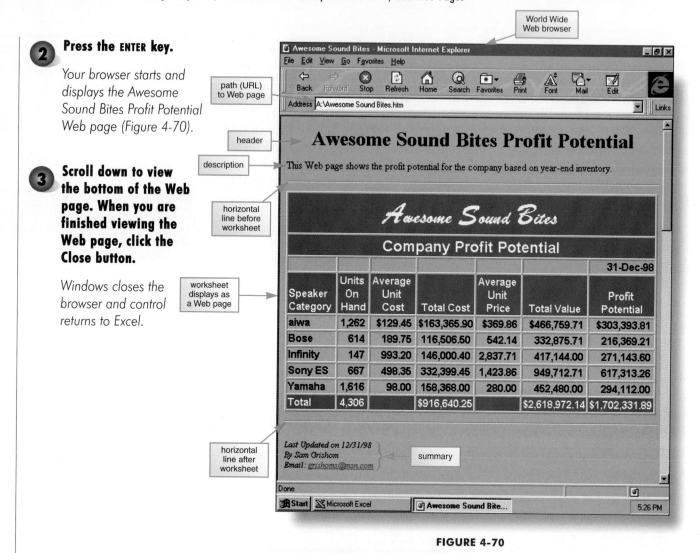

2 **Press the ENTER key.**

Your browser starts and displays the Awesome Sound Bites Profit Potential Web page (Figure 4-70).

3 **Scroll down to view the bottom of the Web page. When you are finished viewing the Web page, click the Close button.**

Windows closes the browser and control returns to Excel.

FIGURE 4-70

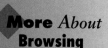

More *About* Browsing

An alternative to clicking the Close button to quit your browser is to click the Back button (Figure 4-70). When you click the Back button, the system returns control to Excel because the Excel Web toolbar was used to start your browser.

As you can see from Figure 4-70, Excel creates a professional-looking Web page that resembles a worksheet. It maintains consistency with the worksheet by drawing outlines of the cells.

If you study Figures 4-67 on page E 4.50 and 4-70, you can see how the text entries made in response to the Internet Assistant Wizard – Step 3 of 4 dialog box impact the Web page. For example, the header in Figure 4-67 displays in a large bold font in Figure 4-70. The description below the header results in the introductory sentence. The check boxes selected in Figure 4-67 improve the appearance of the Web page by drawing horizontal lines before and after the worksheet data. The date, name, and Email address appear at the bottom of the Web page.

If you click on the Email address at the bottom of the Web page, your Email program will start and the Email message automatically will be addressed to grishoms@msn.com.

Quitting Excel

To quit Excel, complete the following steps.

TO QUIT EXCEL

Step 1: Click the Close button on the right side of the title bar.
Step 1: If the Microsoft Excel dialog box displays, click the No button.

Project Summary

Arnold Ladd, president and CEO of Awesome Sound Bites, is sure to be pleased with many aspects of the workbook developed in this project. The use of multiple sheets, for example, allows for better organization of the data, while the 3-D Pyramid chart makes it easy to pinpoint the speaker category with the greatest profit potential. Further, the Web page showing the company's profit potential can be published on the company's intranet so all the managers can view it using a browser. Perhaps the best aspect of the way the workbook is used, however, is the use of the template: even if the buyout doesn't work out, Arnold can use the template in the future to add additional stores to the existing workbook or create new, similar workbooks.

This project introduced you to creating and using a template, customizing formats, changing chart types, and drawing and enhancing a 3-D Pyramid chart using WordArt. You also learned how to reference cells in other sheets and add comments to a cell. To enhance a printout, you learned how to add a header and footer and to change margins. Finally, you learned how to create a Web page from your worksheet data.

What You Should Know

Having completed this project, you now should be able to perform the following tasks:

- Add a Chart Title Using the WordArt Tool (E 4.38)
- Add a Worksheet to a Workbook (E 4.26)
- Assign a Comment to a Cell (E 4.41)
- Assign a Currency Style Using the Format Dialog Box (E 4.22)
- Bold the Font and Change the Column Widths in the Template (E 4.10)
- Change the Background and Font Colors and Add Outline Borders (E 4.19)
- Change the Header and Margins and Center the Printout Horizontally (E 4.43)
- Create a Custom Format Code (E 4.24)
- Create a Web Page from an Excel Worksheet (E 4.48)
- Create a Workbook from a Template (E 4.27)
- Draw a 3-D Pyramid Chart (E 4.36)
- Drill an Entry Through Worksheets (E 4.28)
- Enter and Copy 3-D References (E 4.33)
- Enter Dummy Data in the Template Using the Fill Handle (E 4.11)
- Enter the Formulas Using Point Mode and Determine Totals in the Template (E 4.13)
- Enter Column Titles and the System Date in the Template (E 4.10)
- Enter the Template Title and Row Titles (E 4.10)
- Format the Template Title (E 4.18)
- Modify the Chicago Sheet (E 4.30)
- Modify the Los Angeles Sheet (E 4.29)
- Modify the New York Sheet (E 4.31)
- Print the Workbook (E 4.46)
- Quit Excel (E 4.53)
- Rename a Sheet (E 4.32)
- Save a Template (E 4.16)
- Spell Check and Save the Template (E 4.25)
- Start Excel (E 4.9)
- View a Web Page Using the Web Toolbar (E 4.51)

 Test Your Knowledge

1 True/False

Instructions: Circle T if the statement is true or F is the statement is false.

T F 1. A small red triangle, called a comment indicator, displays in the upper-right corner of a cell that has a comment assigned to it.

T F 2. HTML stands for Hypertext Markup Language.

T F 3. A path name is made up of a drive letter, file name, and extension.

T F 4. A sheet reference in a three-dimensional range always is relative.

T F 5. You can create a workbook from a template by copying the template to the Clipboard and then pasting it to one or more sheets in a workbook.

T F 6. Summarizing data that appears on multiple worksheets on one worksheet is called consolidation.

T F 7. Page setup characteristics will apply to all sheets that are copied from a template.

T F 8. To save a template, you use the same command on the File menu that you use to save a workbook.

T F 9. When multiple sheets are selected, changes you make to cells on the displayed sheet will affect the same cells on all of the selected sheets.

T F 10. The WordArt tool is accessible through a button on the Formatting toolbar.

2 Multiple Choice

Instructions: Circle the correct response.

1. The digit placeholder in a format code is represented by the _____ symbol.
   a. #   b. *   c. !   d. @

2. A header contains _____ section(s).
   a. 1   b. 2   c. 3   d. 4

3. To create a Web page from an Excel worksheet, click the _____ command on the File menu.
   a. Save   b. New   c. Save as HTML   d. Save as Hyperlink

4. The Page Setup dialog box allows you to _____.
   a. view format codes   c. turn off the gridlines on a worksheet
   b. turn off headers and footers   d. all of these

5. A format code is a series of format symbols that define the formats for _____.
   a. text   b. currency   c. dates   d. all of these

6. Autotemplates are stored in the _____ folder.
   a. Startup   b. Xlstart   c. Template   d. Format

7. To save a workbook as a template, select Template in the _____ list box.
   a. Save in   b. File name   c. Save as type   d. Options

8. _____ numbers are entered into a worksheet to test formulas and functions.
   a. Dummy   b. Variance   c. Test   d. none of these

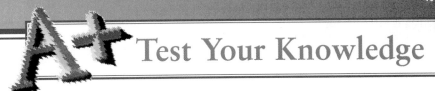

Test Your Knowledge

9. You can add a comment to a cell on a worksheet by clicking the _____ command on the Insert menu.
   a. Comment
   b. Name
   c. Note
   d. Object

10. If you store a template in the Xlstart folder using the file name _____, then Excel uses the formats assigned to the template every time you start Excel.
    a. Template
    b. Book
    c. Start
    d. Default

3 Understanding 3-D References

Instructions: The workbook in Figure 4-71 is made up of four sheets labeled Order 1, Order 2, Order 3, and Inventory. Assume cell A4 is active on the Inventory sheet. Write the formula or function that accomplishes each of the tasks below. All of the four tasks below are independent of one another.

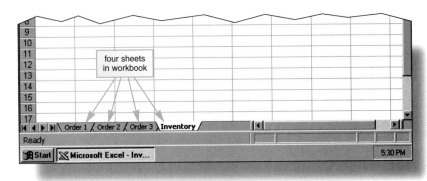

FIGURE 4-71

   a. Assign cell Inventory!A4 the product of cell I5 on the Order 1 sheet times cell A17 on the Order 2 sheet.

      Formula: _____

   b. Assign cell Inventory!A4 the sum of cell A15 on each of the three Order sheets.

      Formula: _____

   c. Assign cell Inventory!A4 the product of cell D5 on the Inventory sheet times the quantity of cell H7 on the Order 3 sheet plus cell A3 on the Order 2 sheet.

      Formula: _____

   d. Assign cell Inventory!A4 the value in cell F15 on the Order 3 sheet.

      Formula: _____

   e. Assign cell Inventory!A4 the expression A * (B / 4 + 1) - (D * F / 2 + A) where the value of A is cell E5 on the Inventory sheet, B is cell G3 on the Order 1 sheet, D is cell A12 on the Order 3 sheet, and F is cell E3 on the Order 2 sheet.

      Formula: _____

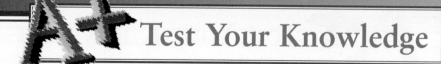 Test Your Knowledge

4 Understanding Customized Formats

Instructions: Using Table 4-2 on page E 4.23, determine the results that will display in the Results In and Color columns of Table 4-9. Assume that the width of the Results In column is 10.00, meaning it will display 10 characters (including special characters). If the Results In column is not wide enough to display the entire resulting value, enter a series of 10 asterisks in the Results In column. Use the letter b to indicate positions containing blank characters.

To determine the answers, you may want to open a new blank Excel worksheet, format the column widths to 10.00, and enter the numbers shown in Table 4.9. As examples, the first two problems in the table are complete. If the number displays in a color other than black, indicate the color in the Color column; otherwise, enter N/A.

Table 4-9

PROBLEM	CELL CONTENTS	FORMAT ASSIGNED	RESULTS IN	COLOR
1	-214	$#,###0_);[Red]($#,###0)	bbbb($214)	Red
2	88.5	#,###.00	bbbbb88.50	N/A
3	0	#,###.00_);[Red](#,###.00)	_____	____
4	0.092548	###.#####	_____	____
5	6	+##0.##	_____	____
6	-0.458255	0.000%	_____	____
7	96	#,##0	_____	____
8	56.326	$#,###,###	_____	____
9	225896.532	$#,###,##0.00	_____	____
10	0.8	#,##0.00	_____	____
11	14875466	#,###.00_);[Blue](#,###.00)	_____	____
12	0.21	$#,##0_);[Red]($#,###0)	_____	____
13	6	-#0.00	_____	____
14	0.4	$* ##0.00	_____	____
15	-35982.115	#,###.00_);[Blue](#,###.00)	_____	____

Use Help

1 Reviewing Project Activities

Instructions: Perform the following tasks using a computer.

1. Start Excel.
2. Click the Contents and Index command on the Help menu. Click the Contents tab. Double-click the Formatting Worksheets book and then double-click the Formatting Numbers, Dates, and Times book. One at a time, double-click the links under the book title. Read and then right-click each topic to print. Click the Help Topics button to return to the Help Topics: Microsoft Excel dialog box. Hand the printouts in to your instructor.
3. If the Help Topics: Microsoft Excel dialog box is not on the screen, click the Contents and Index command on the Help menu. Click the Find tab. Type 3-D references in the top text box labeled 1. Double-click Data consolidation by using 3-D references in the lower list box labeled 3. Click the two links. Read and then right-click each topic to print. Click the Help Topics button to return to the Help Topics: Microsoft Excel dialog box. Hand the printouts in to your instructor.
4. If the Help Topics: Microsoft Excel dialog box is not on the screen, click the Contents and Index command on the Help menu. Click the Index tab. Type web in the top text box labeled 1, then double-click toolbar under Web in the lower list box labeled 2. Double-click the topic, About Microsoft Excel and the Internet. Click the four links. Read and then right-click each topic to print. Click the Help Topics button to return to the Help Topics: Microsoft Excel dialog box. Hand the printouts in to your instructor.
5. If the Help Topics: Microsoft Excel dialog box is not on the screen, click the Contents and Index command on the Help menu. Click the Index tab. Type publish on the Web in the top text box labeled 1, then double-click the topic, publishing data on the Internet, in the lower list box labeled 2. Read and print the information. Click each link. Read and print the information. Close the Microsoft Excel Help window. Hand the printouts in to your instructor.

2 Expanding on the Basics

Instructions: Perform the following tasks using a computer.

1. Start Excel.
2. Click the Contents and Index command on the Help menu. Click the Index tab. Type templates in the top text box labeled 1. Double-click templates in the lower list box labeled 2. When the Topics Found dialog box displays, double-click Guidelines for storing templates. Read and then right-click to print. Click the Help Topics button to return to the Help Topics: Microsoft Excel dialog box. Hand the printout in to your instructor.
3. If the Help Topics: Microsoft Excel dialog box is not on the screen, click the Contents and Index command on the Help menu. Click the Index tab and then type combination chart in the top text box labeled 1. Double-click the topic, combination charts, in the lower list box labeled 2. Click each link to read and then right-click to print. Close the Microsoft Excel Help window. Hand the printouts in to your instructor.

Apply Your Knowledge

1 Using 3-D References in a Workbook

Instructions: Follow the steps below to consolidate the four weekly sheets on the Monthly Totals sheet in the workbook Monthly Sales. The Monthly Totals sheet should appear as shown in the lower screen in Figure 4-72.

1. Open the workbook Monthly Sales from the Excel folder on the Data Disk that accompanies this book.

2. One-by-one, click the first four tabs and review the weekly totals. Click on the Monthly Totals tab.

3. Determine the monthly totals by using the SUM function and 3-D references to sum the quantity and cost for each inventory item.

4. Save the workbook using the file name Monthly Totals 1.

5. Add a header that includes your name and course number in the Left section, the computer laboratory exercise number (Apply 4-1) in the Center section, and the system date and your instructor's name in the Right section.

6. Select all five sheets and then print them. Select the Monthly Totals sheet. Save the workbook with the new page setup using the same file name.

Week 1 Wholesale Totals

Inventory	Cost	Quantity	Total Cost
0115	25.01	20	500.20
0126	9.45	15	141.75
0322	28.99	8	231.92
0201	17.64	50	882.00
Total	**81.09**	**93**	**$1,755.87**

Week 2 Wholesale Totals

Inventory	Cost	Quantity	Total Cost
0115	25.01	10	250.10
0126	9.45	21	198.45
0322	28.99	15	434.85
0201	17.64	35	617.40
Total	**81.09**	**81**	**$1,500.80**

Week 3 Wholesale Totals

Inventory	Cost	Quantity	Total Cost
0115	25.01	30	750.30
0126	9.45	10	94.50
0322	28.99	0	-
0201	17.64	30	529.20
Total	**81.09**	**70**	**$1,374.00**

Week 4 Wholesale Totals

Inventory	Cost	Quantity	Total Cost
0115	25.01	20	500.20
0126	9.45	25	236.25
0322	28.99	5	144.95
0201	17.64	40	705.60
Total	**81.09**	**90**	**$1,587.00**

Monthly Wholesale Totals

Inventory	Cost	Quantity	Total Cost
0115	25.01	80	2000.8
0126	9.45	71	670.95
0322	28.99	28	811.72
0201	17.64	155	2734.2
Total	**81.09**	**334**	**$6,217.67**

Ready

Start | Microsoft Excel - Mon... | 5:31 PM

FIGURE 4-72

1 Designing a Business Template

Problem: For the first month of your work-study program, you have been serving up special sandwiches at the on-campus deli. The deli manager knows your real specialty is designing workbooks and wants to utilize your Excel skills. She has asked you to create a template for all of the deli employees to use when they create new Excel workbooks (Figure 4-73).

Instructions: Perform the following steps to create a template.

1. Change the font of all cells to 12-point Times New Roman. Increase all row heights to 18. Assign the Comma style to all cells. (*Hint:* Click the Select All button to make these changes.)

2. Add a comment to cell G1 to identify the template and its purpose, as shown in Figure 4-73. Include your name as the author.

3. Enter the titles in cells A1 and A2, as shown in Figure 4-73. In cell A1, change the font of cell A1 to a 24-point violet script font of your choice. In cell A2, change the font to 14-point Times New Roman. Use the Format Cells dialog box to assign an indigo bottom border (column 2, row 2 in the Line Style area) to the range A2:H2.

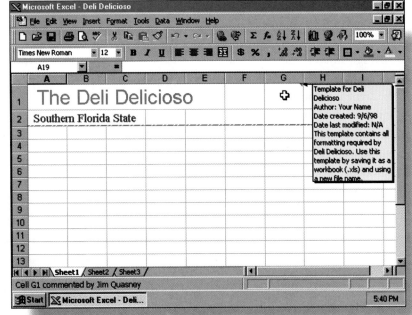

FIGURE 4-73

4. Enter your name, course, computer laboratory assignment (Lab 4-1), date, and instructor name in the range A8:A12.

5. Save the template using the file name Deli Delicioso Template. Use the Save As command to save the template, selecting Template in the Save File as type list box.

6. Print the template and comment. To print the comment, click the Sheet tab in the Page Setup dialog box. Click the Comments box arrow and then click At end of sheet. The comment will print on a separate sheet. After the comment prints, deselect printing the comment by clicking the Comment box arrow on the Sheet tab in the Page Setup dialog box and then clicking (None).

7. Close the template and then reopen it. Save the template as a regular workbook using the file name Deli Delicioso. Close the workbook.

In the Lab

2 Creating a Multiple-Sheet Sales Breakdown Workbook Using a Template

Problem: Sky Pony Gifts specializes in Southwestern and Native American crafts. The company has stores in three Idaho cities — Twin Falls, Sandpoint, and Coeur d' Alene — and a corporate office in Santa Fe, New Mexico. All of the store franchises sell their products through in-store purchases and by phone, mail, and Email. Every year, the corporate officers in Santa Fe use a template to create a year-end retail sales breakdown workbook. The workbook contains four sheets, one for each of the three stores and one for the franchise totals. The Franchise Totals sheet displays as shown in Figure 4-74.

The template is stored in the Excel folder on the Data Disk that accompanies this textbook. Mr. Allison, a corporate officer, has asked you to use the template to create the year-end retail sales breakdown workbook.

Instructions: Perform the following tasks.

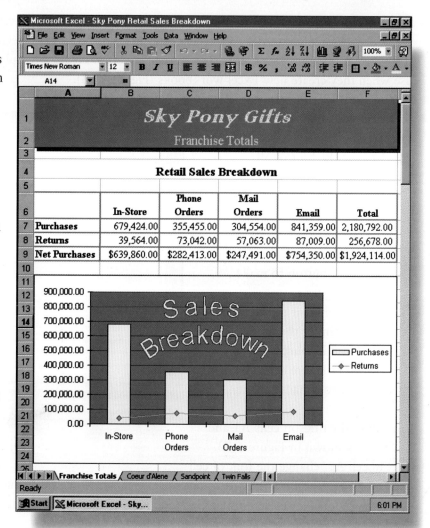

FIGURE 4-74

1. Open the template, Sky Pony Template, from the Excel folder on the Data Disk. Add a worksheet to the workbook and then paste the template to Sheet2, Sheet3, and Sheet4. Save the workbook using the file name Sky Pony Retail Sales Breakdown. Make sure Microsoft Excel Workbook is selected in the Save as type list box.

2. Rename the sheet tabs to Coeur d'Alene, Sandpoint, Twin Falls, and Franchise Totals. Enter the data in Table 4-10 onto the three city sheets. On each sheet, change the title in cell A2 to reflect the city. Choose a different background color for each sheet.

3. On the Franchise Totals sheet, use the SUM function, 3-D references, and the fill handle to total the corresponding cells on the three city sheets. The Franchise Totals sheet should resemble the top of Figure 4-74. Save the workbook by clicking the Save button on the Standard toolbar.

In the Lab

4. Create an embedded Line-Column chart in the range A11:F24 on the Franchise Totals sheet. Chart the range A6:E8 on the Franchise Totals sheet. Create the chart as shown in Figure 4-74 by clicking the Custom Types tab and then clicking the Built-in option button, if necessary. Select the first Line - Column option in the Chart type list box. Refer to Expanding on the Basics, number 2 on page E 4.57 for further explanation of the combination chart. Format the chart colors, as shown in Figure 4-74. Click the Save button on the Standard toolbar to save the workbook.

Table 4-10		COEUR d'ALENE	SANDPOINT	TWIN FALLS
In-Store	Sales	253,147	325,689	100,588
	Returns	12,743	15,760	11,061
Phone	Sales	128,564	161,220	65,671
	Returns	24,782	22,589	25,671
Mail	Sales	92,501	139,212	72,841
	Returns	18,230	19,179	19,654
Email	Sales	319,874	422,631	98,854
	Returns	26,632	38,577	21,800

5. Click the WordArt button on the Drawing toolbar and select the style in column 3, row 1 and then click the OK button. When the Edit WordArt Text dialog box displays, type Sales and then press the ENTER key. Type Breakdown to complete the title. Highlight the text, select 32-point Arrus font (or a similar font), and deselect the Bold style, if necessary. Click the OK button. Use the WordArt Shape button on the WordArt toolbar to select the Arch Up (Curve) option, and then click the Format WordArt button to format the WordArt similar to Figure 4-74. Click the WordArt Character Spacing Button and then click the Loose option.

6. Select all four sheets. Change the header to include your name, course, computer laboratory exercise (Lab 4-2), date, and instructor's name. Change the footer to include the page number and total pages. Print the entire workbook. Save the workbook with the new page setup characteristics.

3 Creating and Using a Consolidated Profit Forecast Template

Problem: Hawaiian Grove Pineapple Growers is seeking additional representatives to distribute their pineapples globally. The owners have decided to create a Web page with a link to their worksheet to show their annual profits. You have been asked to create the workbook and the Web page. The workbook is to include three worksheets, each with a 3-D Pie chart. Two of the worksheets pertain to the Honolulu and Los Angeles outlets. The third worksheet is used to consolidate the data found on the Honolulu and Los Angeles worksheets.

Instructions Part 1: Perform the following steps to create the template shown in Figure 4-75 on the next page.

1. Change the font in all cells to 11-point Arial bold. Change the active column widths to the following: A = 19.00, B through E = 12.00, and F = 13.00. Increase the height of row 1 to 77.25 and row 2 to 21.00.

(continued)

In the Lab

Creating and Using a Consolidated Profit Forecast Template *(continued)*

2. Enter the subtitle `Pineapple Growers` in cell A2 and then change its font to 16-point Bookman Old Style (or a similar font). Center the subtitle over the columns A through F. Enter the column titles in row 3 and the row titles in column A. Italicize the column titles and the row title in cell A6. Format cell A8 to 14-point italic underlined font. Assign cell A2 and the range A8:F12 a light yellow font and a green background.

3. Click the Insert WordArt button on the Drawing toolbar and then select the WordArt style in row 4, column 3 of the WordArt Gallery dialog box. Type `Hawaiian Grove` as the WordArt text and change its font to 28-point Bookman Old Style bold (or a similar font). Resize and center the design to fit in the range A1:F1 as shown in Figure 4-75. Save the template as Hawaiian Grove Template.

4. Enter the dummy data shown in Figure 4-75 into the range B9:E12 in the Assumptions table. Enter all percentages with a trailing percent sign. Format cell B9 to a Currency style with a floating dollar sign and two decimal places. Format the range B10:E12 to a Percentage style with two decimal places. Format the table and add the colors shown in Figure 4-75.

5. The values that display in rows 4 through 6 are based on the assumptions in rows 9 through 12. A surcharge is added to the expenses whenever the Qtr Growth rate is negative. Enter the following formulas into the worksheet:
   a. Sales in cell B4: =B9
   b. Sales in cell C4: =B4 * (1 + C10)

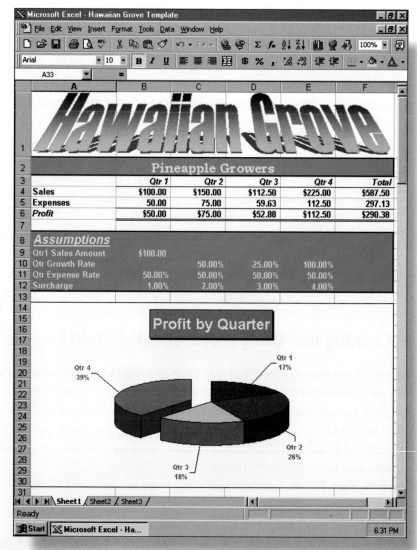

FIGURE 4-75

In the Lab

c. Copy cell C4 to the range D4:E4.

d. Expenses in cell B5: =IF(B10 < 0, B4 * (B11 + B12), B4 * B11)

e. Profit in cell B6: =B4 - B5

f. Copy the range B5:B6 to C5:E6.

g. Use the SUM function to determine totals in column F.

6. Create a 3-D Pie chart that shows the contribution of each quarter to the total profit, as shown in Figure 4-75. Use the chart range B3:E3 and B6:E6. Format the 3-D Pie chart as shown in Figure 4-75.

7. Save the template using the file name Hawaiian Grove Template. Make sure Template is selected in the Save as type box when you save the template. Close the template.

8. Open the template and copy it to the other two sheets. Rename the sheets Los Angeles, Honolulu, and Company.

9. Change the assumptions for Honolulu to the following: Qtr1 Sales Amount (cell B9) = $355,500; Qtr2 Growth Rate (cell C10) = 2.50%; Qtr3 Growth Rate (cell D10) = -1.75%; Qtr4 Growth Rate (cell E10) = 2.25%; Qtr Expense Rate (cells B11 through E11) = 53.00%, 55.00%, 42.75%, and 52.00%; Surcharge (cells B12 through E12) = 1.50%, 2.25%, 4.25%, and 3.75%. Change the assumptions for Los Angeles to the following: Qrt1 Sales Amount (cell B9) = 465,750; Qtr2 Growth Rate (cell C10) = -2.00%; Qtr3 Growth Rate (cell D10) = 3.00%; Qtr4 Growth Rate (cell E10) = 4.25%; Qtr Expense Rate (cells B11 through E11) = 52.00%, 48.00%, 53.00%, and 59.00%; Surcharge (cells B12 through E12) = 2.00%, 2.50%, 1.25%, and 3.00%.

10. Delete the Assumptions table from the Company sheet. Use 3-D references and the fill handle to determine totals on the Company sheet. You should end up with the following totals in column F on the Company sheet: Sales = $3,326,385.72; Expenses = $1,758,469.01; and Profit = $1,567,916.71. If necessary, change the format in row 5 to the Comma style after copying the formulas.

11. Change the chart range so that each pie chart refers to the data on the same sheet. (*Hint:* One at a time, activate the charts on the Honolulu and Los Angeles sheets. Click the Chart Wizard button and change the range in the Chart Wizard dialog box so the range reflects the active sheet.) Save the workbook using the file name Hawaiian Grove.

12. Select all three sheets. Change the header to include your name, course, computer laboratory exercise (Lab 4-3), date, and instructor's name. Change the footer to include the page number and total pages. Print and then save the workbook.

Instructions Part 2: Decrease each of the quarter expense rates (B11:E11) for both cities by 2.5%. You should end up with a company total profit of $1,651,076.35 in cell F6 of the Company sheet. Close the workbook without saving the changes.

(continued)

In the Lab

Creating and Using a Consolidated Profit Forecast Template *(continued)*

Instructions Part 3: Perform the following steps to create a Web page.

1. Open the workbook Hawaiian Grove. Select the range A2:F6 on the Company sheet and click the Save as HTML command on the File menu. When the Internet Assistant Wizard – Step 1 of 4 dialog box displays, remove all the ranges except for the range A2:F6.

2. In the Internet Assistant Wizard – Step 2 of 4 dialog box, click the option button to create the Web page as an independent file.

3. When the Internet Assistant Wizard – Step 3 of 4 dialog box displays, type Hawaiian Grove Pineapple Growers in the Header box. In the Description box, type Annual sales for 1997 after being in business only two years. Distributorships are available in your city now! as the entry. Add a horizontal line before and after the converted data. Type today's date, your name, and Email address for the footer.

4. Save the HTML file to drive A. Enter the path name a:\Excel\Hawaiian Grove.htm.

5. Use the Web toolbar in Excel to enter the path name of the Hawaiian Grove Web page (a:\Excel\Hawaiian Grove.htm). When the Web page displays, print it. Close the browser and then close Excel.

Cases and Places

The difficulty of these case studies varies: ▶ are the least difficult; ▶▶ are more difficult; and ▶▶▶ are the most difficult.

1 ▶ Multimedia Mega Store has four departments, which are categorized by profit margin: computers (42%), electronics (36%), small appliances (13%), and large appliances (10%). Use the annual sales in Figure 4-76 to develop a template for determining next year's marketing needs. Include sales, profit margins, profits (sales * profit margin), total sales, and total profits. Also include functions to determine the most and least profitable categories. Use the template to create a worksheet for each year and a consolidated worksheet for the store. Add an embedded chart that reflects the store's profits each year by category.

2 ▶ Deb's Delights is a small deli renowned for its lunch menu. Deb keeps track of spoilage and loss on paper (Figure 4-77), but wants to find a better way to track her costs. Create a template that Deb can use to track her losses more effectively. Include the following for each item: Profit Potential = Amount Purchased * (Retail Cost – Wholesale Cost); Loss = # Past Pull Date * Wholesale Cost; and, Net Profit = Profit Potential – Loss.

Cases and Places

Multimedia Mega Store		
DEPARTMENTS	LAST YEAR'S SALES	THIS YEAR'S SALES
Computers	$552,000	$625,000
Electronics	420,000	486,000
Small Appliances	312,000	310,000
Large Appliances	275,000	202,000

FIGURE 4-76

Item	Amount Purchased	# Past Pull Date	Wholesale Cost	Retail Cost
Milk (gallons)	10	2	1.66	7.20
Sour Cream (pints)	4	0	0.68	1.50
Sliced Bread (loaves)	48	4	0.99	4.00
Rolls (bags)	36	2	1.20	3.00
Salami (lbs.)	15	3	0.84	1.19
Chicken (lbs.)	40	4	0.94	1.33

FIGURE 4-77

3 ▶▶ Elegant Weddings, Inc. has been a successful full-service wedding planning company for 12 years in Seattle, Washington. After launching their Web site three years ago, they have attracted so many clients from Europe that the owners opened a shop in London. The Seattle and London shops' assets last year, respectively, were: cash $317,325 and $132,650, accounts receivable $107,125 and $74,975, marketable securities $196,425 and $76,250, inventory $350,395 and $175,750, and equipment $25,000 and $17,500. The liabilities for each store were: notes payable $28,300 and $26,000, accounts payable $78,450 and $80,125, and income tax payable $62,000 and $20,000. The stockholders' equity was: common stock $731,170 and $268,375 and retained earnings $96,350 and $82,625. Design a template as a balance sheet to reflect the figures above. Include totals for total assets, total liabilities, total stockholders' equity, and liabilities and stockholders' equity. Use the template to create a balance sheet for each store and a consolidated balance sheet for the corporation.

4 ▶▶ World of Flowers has noticed a sharp increase in business since they started a Web site that allows people to order flowers over the Internet. They also have started a free flower information service on the Web that has contributed to an additional increase in sales. The owner of World of Flowers needs a worksheet representation of the business increases based on the data in Figure 4-78 on the next page. Create one worksheet for each year and one for the totals, adding a column for quarter totals and a row for item totals. Include the percentage of annual growth (1999 – 1998) / 1998. Add an embedded 3-D Area chart comparing the annual growth of each item.

Cases and Places

World of Flowers				
	QTR	BOUQUETS	SPECIAL	OUT OF STATE
1998	1	21,547.23	2,201.88	0
	2	26,568.31	3,525.01	0
	3	31,697.11	2,436.65	0
	4	42,435.35	3,567.21	0
1999	1	24,568.31	3,825.98	2
	2	31,717.11	4,856.47	23
	3	32,114.15	4,569.22	54
	4	48,291.45	6,212.73	72

FIGURE 4-78

5 ▶▶▶ When a printing company receives a job from a customer, there are usually multiple tasks involved (four color printing, making plates or film, cutting, folding, etc.) that may involve measurements, such as ink weight. Visit a local printer, find out how each job is estimated, and how ink is measured to obtain a desired color. Create a template from a hypothetical printing job, including any formulas or functions needed. The template should show how a printing job is estimated based on 10,000 copies, two-sided, three colors, and folded in thirds.

6 ▶▶▶ Using the Internet, access the National Weather Service at http://www.nws.noaa.gov/ and create a template summarizing the weekly weather conditions for a city near you. Consider factors such as high and low temperatures, median temperature, humidity, and precipitation. Use at least five factors for each day of the week, using functions to find weekly averages, highs, and lows. Include a chart to illustrate one weather factor. Use the template to record and chart the weather for two weeks and create a consolidated worksheet based on the entire two-week period.

7 ▶▶▶ Travel agencies book vacations around the world, getting clients to their destinations using a variety of modes of transportation. Visit a travel agency and find out the six most popular travel destinations and the three most popular ways to get there. Create a template that can track travel destinations and transportation mode for a one-week period. Include the prices for each mode of transportation. Use the template to create worksheets that span the period of a month. Create a consolidated worksheet that illustrates the most popular travel destination and the mode of transportation. Add an embedded chart to display this data.

Microsoft Excel 97

Data Tables, Visual Basic for Applications, Hyperlinks, and Scenario Manager

Objectives:

You will have mastered the material in this project when you can:

- ▶ Use natural language formulas
- ▶ Determine the monthly payment of a loan using the financial function PMT
- ▶ State the purpose of the FV and PV functions
- ▶ Build a data table to analyze data in a worksheet
- ▶ Write a macro in Visual Basic to automate data entry into a worksheet
- ▶ Use the Macro Recorder to create a macro
- ▶ Execute macros
- ▶ Analyze worksheet data by changing values and goal seeking
- ▶ Add hyperlinks to a workbook
- ▶ Use Excel's Scenario Manager to record and save different sets of what-if assumptions and the corresponding results of formulas
- ▶ Protect and unprotect cells

Project 5

Click the Tires

Hit the Road with

Vehicle Worksheets

The days of plaid-jacketed, tire-kicking car salesmen may be dwindling as consumers turn to computer technology to buy their dream cars. Using the Internet, buyers can research, locate, and finance anything from a sports car to an all-terrain vehicle.

The number of automotive-related Internet sites grows steadily. Every domestic and foreign vehicle manufacturer had its own Web site by July 1995; and all dealers are expected to be online in a few years. You can surf to these sites to compare models and price options, and when you are ready to buy, you can find the nearest dealer selling your ideal car. If necessary, the next step may be arranging financing through an online creditor.

For example, if you dream about cruising down the highway in a Ford Mustang GT, you can research the vehicle at the Ford Motor Company's site. After viewing pictures of the car's

research

locate

finance

interior and exterior, watching a video, and reading performance data, you select the model, options, and equipment packages. A worksheet computes a window sticker with the manufacturer's suggested retail price (MSRP), taking into account discounts and destination and delivery charges.

If that final figure exceeds the amount in your savings account, you can click the link to the Ford Credit site for help. A powerful feature of this site is that you can change values to analyze the worksheet data. Using Microsoft Excel's financial functions, you will be performing similar operations to analyze data in the Excel worksheet you will complete in this project.

For starters, at the Ford Credit Financial Planner page, you enter your monthly take-home pay and the amounts you spend on housing, groceries, gas, clothing, entertainment, and other expenses. Using calculations in a worksheet, the planner determines the amount that is available. Financial experts recommend using no more than 20 percent of this figure for the vehicle loan. If your car payment exceeds this amount, you will be forced to tighten your budget in other areas such as entertainment.

The next step is to explore whether leasing or financing is the best option. Another worksheet, the Lease vs. Finance Calculator, references the MSRP you determined previously and then prompts you for additional information, including the amount of your down payment or trade-in allowance. Again, experts suggest the 20 percent number as a minimum down-payment amount so that you will not owe more on the vehicle than it is worth during the term of the loan. When you enter these numbers and click the Calculate button, a macro executes using the payment financial function to determine the monthly payment for both the lease and finance options. You can change the length of the loan to 24, 36, 48, and 60 months to see variations in the monthly payment amounts.

After a house, a vehicle generally is a consumer's second major purchase in a lifetime; manufacturers know it is an acquisition people make after researching and comparing models. The Ford Credit site receives about 12 million hits per month, so buyers are realizing that clicking the tires is an attractive way to get rolling.

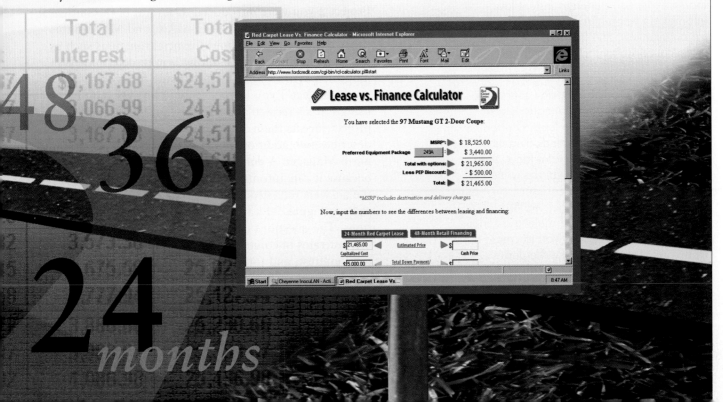

Microsoft
Excel 97

Data Tables, Visual Basic for Applications, Hyperlinks, and Scenario Manager

Case Perspective

Susan Dexter recently was named manager of the loan department for SavU Bank. Susan started at SavU Bank as a teller and quickly rose through the ranks because she is innovative, reliable, and has excellent communication skills. Her major goal during her first few months as manager is to computerize the loan department so that loan officers can generate instant loan information when a customer comes in for an interview. She has hired you as her technical consultant to help her achieve this goal.

Susan recently took a one-day course on Microsoft Excel at the local community college, during which she learned about Excel's many capabilities, including its financial functions and what-if tools. She also learned that macros can be written to ensure that occasional Excel users, such as the loan officers, can be guided through a task without the chance of making a serious mistake. Susan has asked you to create a workbook that will generate the desired loan information at the click of a button, while ensuring that the loan officers will not render the worksheet useless by entering data into the wrong cells. She also has requested that you include a hyperlink to the bank's 1998 Statement of Condition.

Introduction

Two of the most powerful aspects of Excel are its wide array of functions and its capability to automate worksheet data analysis and answer what-if questions. In Project 2 you were introduced to several of the statistical functions, such as AVERAGE, MAX, and MIN. In this project you will learn about financial functions such as the PMT function, which allows you to determine a monthly payment for a loan (left side of Figure 5-1a).

In Project 3 you learned how to analyze data by using Excel's recalculation feature and goal seeking. This project revisits these two methods of analyzing data and describes two additional ones — data tables and Scenario Manager. A **data table** is a powerful what-if tool because it can automate your data analyses and organize the answers returned by Excel. The data table on the right in Figure 5-1a answers 11 different what-if questions. The questions pertain to the effect the 11 different interest rates in column D have on the monthly payment, total interest, and total cost of a loan.

A **macro**, such as the one shown in Figure 5-1b, is a series of Visual Basic statements. **Visual Basic statements** tell Excel how to carry out an operation, such as selecting a range or clearing a selection. This particular macro accepts loan data so Excel can calculate the monthly payment in the data table; clicking the New Loan button

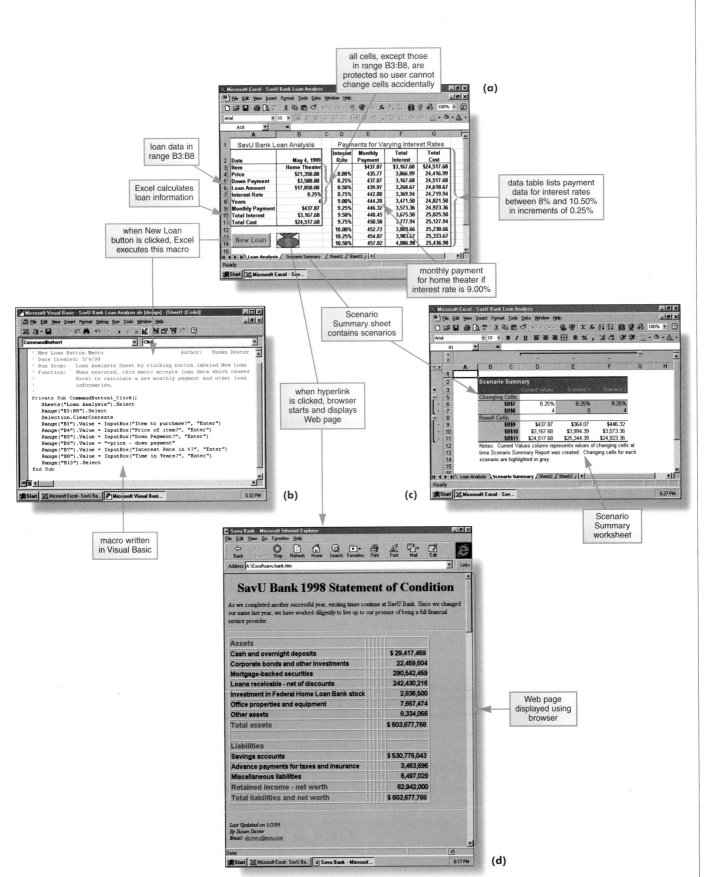

all cells, except those in range B3:B8, are protected so user cannot change cells accidentally **(a)**

loan data in range B3:B8

Excel calculates loan information

when New Loan button is clicked, Excel executes this macro

data table lists payment data for interest rates between 8% and 10.50% in increments of 0.25%

monthly payment for home theater if interest rate is 9.00%

Scenario Summary sheet contains scenarios

when hyperlink is clicked, browser starts and displays Web page

macro written in Visual Basic **(b)**

(c)

Scenario Summary worksheet

Web page displayed using browser

(d)

FIGURE 5-1

More *About*
Solution Templates

There is a set of templates available with Excel that provides solutions to common business problems. To view the templates, click New on the File menu, and then click the Spreadsheet Solutions tab. Many more templates that solve a wide range of problems are available at the Microsoft Excel Free Stuff site. To visit the site, start Excel, point to Microsoft on the Web on the Help menu, and then click the Free Stuff command. One template, called Loan Manager, offers a partial solution to the problem being solved in this project.

(left side of Figure 5-1a on page E 5.5) executes the macro. Creating a macro is a form of **programming**. The programming language you use with Excel 97 is called **Visual Basic for Applications** or **VBA**.

Like using data tables, Excel's Scenario Manager is an Excel feature that allows you to analyze data. Scenario Manager is a what-if tool that allows you to record and save different sets of what-if assumptions used to forecast the outcome of a worksheet model (Figure 5-1c on page E 5.5).

Another key feature of Excel is its capability to add hyperlinks to a worksheet. Hyperlinks are built-in links (URLs or file path names) to other Office documents or HTML files (also called Web pages). A hyperlink can be assigned to text in a cell or to an object, such as the moneybag clip art in Figure 5-1a. When you click the moneybag in Figure 5-1a, Excel starts your browser and displays a Web page (Figure 5-1d on page E 5.5). The Web page, which contains SavU Bank's 1998 Statement of Condition, can be stored as a local file, a page on an intranet, or a page on the World Wide Web.

Finally, this project introduces you to cell protection. Cell protection ensures that you do not inadvertently change values that are critical to the worksheet.

Project Five – SavU Bank Loan Analysis

From your meeting with Susan Dexter you have determined the following needs, source of data, calculations, and special requirements.

Needs: An easy-to-read worksheet (Figure 5-1a) that determines the monthly payment, total interest, and total cost for a loan; a button on the worksheet that executes a macro (Figure 5-1b on page E 5.5) that requests the loan officer to enter the new loan data; a macro that prints the worksheet in landscape orientation; a Scenario Summary worksheet (Figure 5-1c) that summarizes what-if questions; and, a hyperlink assigned to an object so that when the object is clicked the SavU Bank's 1998 Statement of Condition Web page displays (Figure 5-1d).

Source of Data: The data (item, price of item, down payment, interest rate, and term of the loan in years) is determined by the loan officer and customer when they initially meet for the loan.

Calculations: The following calculations must be made for each loan (see column B in Figure 5-1a):

1. Loan Amount = Price – Down Payment
2. Monthly Payment, determined using the PMT function
3. Total Interest = 12 x Years x Monthly Payment – Loan Amount
4. Total Cost = 12 x Years x Monthly Payment + Down Payment

The data table, which involves calculations, will be created using the Table command on the Data menu.

Special Requirements: Protect the worksheet in such a way that the loan officers cannot enter data mistakenly into wrong cells. Include a macro that automatically prints the loan information in landscape orientation and then resets the print orientation to portrait.

More *About*
Visual Basic for Applications

All of the applications in Office 97 (Word, Excel, Access, and PowerPoint) use Visual Basic for Applications (Figure 5-1b). Thus, what you learn in this project applies to the other applications as well. Today, Visual Basic is the most widely used Windows programming language.

Preparation Steps

The following preparation steps summarize how the workbook will be developed in Project 5.

1. Start Excel.
2. Enter the worksheet section title, row titles, and system date for the loan analysis section.
3. Save the workbook.
4. Enter the loan data.
5. Determine the monthly payment, total interest, and total cost.
6. Create the data table using the Table command.
7. Create the New Loan button and assign a macro to it.
8. Use the Macro Recorder to create a macro to print the worksheet.
9. Print the worksheet using the recorded macro.
10. Create a hyperlink to a Web page.
11. Use the Scenarios command to create a Scenario Summary worksheet.
12. Protect the worksheet.
13. Save the workbook and quit Excel.

Starting Excel

To start Excel, Windows 95 must be running. Perform the following steps to start Excel.

TO START EXCEL

Step 1: Click the Start button on the taskbar.
Step 2: Click New Office Document. If necessary, click the General tab in the New dialog box.
Step 3: Double-click the Blank Workbook icon.

Excel starts and a blank workbook titled Book1 displays.

Changing the Font of the Entire Worksheet

The first step in this project is to change the font of the entire worksheet to bold to ensure that the characters in the worksheet stand out.

TO CHANGE THE FONT OF THE ENTIRE WORKSHEET

Step 1: Click the Select All button immediately above row heading 1 and to the left of column heading A.
Step 2: Click the Bold button on the Formatting toolbar.

As you enter text and numbers onto the worksheet, they will display in bold.

Entering the Section Title, Row Titles, and System Date

The next step is to enter the loan analysis section title, row titles, and system date. To make the worksheet easier to read, the width of columns A and B and the height of rows 1 and 2 will be increased. The worksheet title also will be changed from 10-point to 12-point font.

More *About*
Starting Excel at Startup

To start Excel when you start Windows, copy the Excel application icon to the Startup folder. Any program in the Startup folder automatically starts when Windows starts.

More *About*
Formatting Across Worksheets

To assign formats to all the cells in all the worksheets in a workbook, click the Select All button, then right-click a tab and click Select All Sheets. Next, assign the formats. To deselect the sheets, hold down the SHIFT key and click the Sheet1 tab. You also can select a cell or a range of cells and then select all sheets to assign formats to a cell or a range of cells on all the sheets in a workbook.

TO ENTER THE SECTION TITLE, ROW TITLES, AND SYSTEM DATE

Step 1: Click cell A1. Type SavU Bank Loan Analysis as the section title and then click the Enter box or press the ENTER key. Select cells A1 and B1. Click the Merge and Center button on the Formatting toolbar.

Step 2: With cell A1 active, click the Font Size box arrow on the Formatting toolbar and then click 12. Click the Font Color button arrow on the Formatting toolbar and then click the color red (column 1, row 3) on the Font Color palette.

Step 3: Position the mouse pointer on the bottom boundary of row heading 1 and then drag down until the ScreenTip, Height: 21.00, displays.

Step 4: Click cell A2 and type Date as the row title. Click the Enter box or press the ENTER key.

Step 5: Position the mouse pointer on the bottom boundary of row heading 2 and then drag down until the ScreenTip, Height: 27.00, displays.

Step 6: Enter the following row titles:

CELL	ENTRY	CELL	ENTRY	CELL	ENTRY
A3	Item	A6	Loan Amount	A9	Monthly Payment
A4	Price	A7	Interest Rate	A10	Total Interest
A5	Down Payment	A8	Years	A11	Total Cost

Step 7: Select columns A and B. Position the mouse pointer on the right boundary of column heading B and then drag until the ScreenTip, Width: 16.00, displays.

Step 8: Click cell B2. Type =now() and then click the Enter box or press the ENTER key.

Step 9: Right-click cell B2 and then click Format Cells on the shortcut menu. When the Format Cells dialog box displays, click the Number tab, click Date in the Category list box, click March 4, 1997 in the Type list box, and click the OK button. If necessary, increase the width of column B to 18.00 points to display the entire date.

Step 10: Click the Save button on the Standard toolbar. Save the workbook using the file name SavU Bank Loan Analysis.

The loan analysis section title, row titles, and system date display as shown in Figure 5-2.

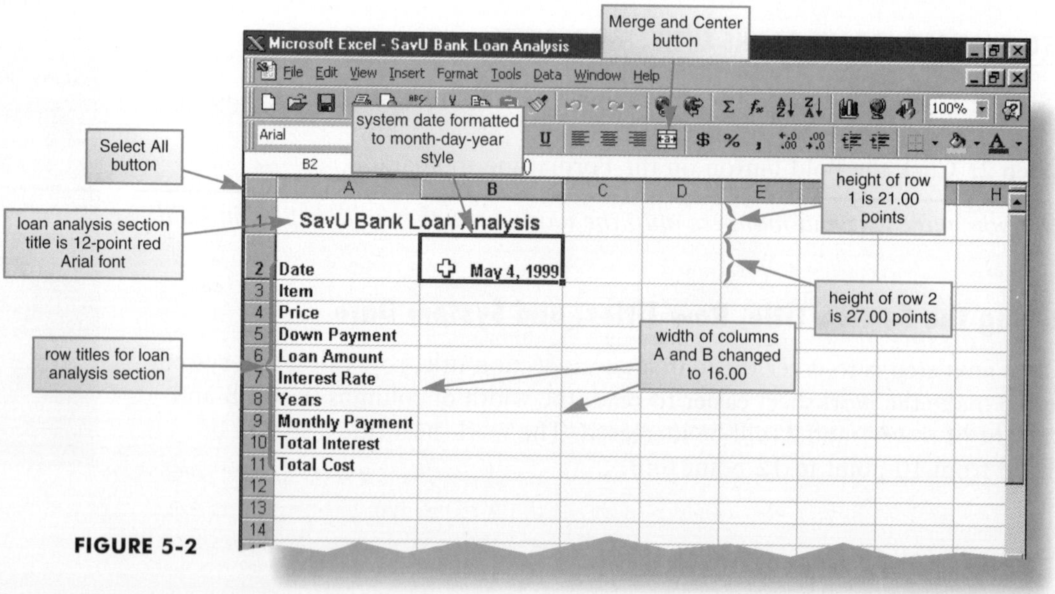

More *About* Displaying Shortcut Menus

Excel requires that you point to the object (cell, range, toolbar) on the screen when you right-click to display the corresponding shortcut menu. For example, if you select the range A1:D5, and right-click with the mouse pointer on cell F10, then the shortcut menu pertains to cell F10, and not the range A1:D5.

FIGURE 5-2

Outlining and Adding Borders to the Loan Analysis Section of the Worksheet

The following steps add an outline to separate the loan analysis section in the range A1:B11 from the data table in the range D1:G14. To further subdivide the row titles and numbers in the loan analysis section, light borders also are added within the outline as shown in Figure 5-1a on page E 5.5.

TO ADD AN OUTLINE AND BORDERS

Step 1: Select the range A2:B11. Right-click the selected range.

Step 2: Click Format Cells. When the Format Cells dialog box displays, click the Border tab. Click the Color box arrow. Click the color red (column 1, row 3) on the palette. Click the heavy border in the Style area (column 2, row 6). Click the Outline box in the Presets area. Click the OK button.

Step 3: Select the range A2:B2. Click the Borders button arrow on the Formatting toolbar. Click the bottom border (column 2, row 1) on the Borders palette. Select the range A2:A11. Click the Borders button arrow on the Formatting toolbar. Click the right border (column 4, row 1) on the Borders palette. Click cell A13 to deselect the range A2:A11.

The loan analysis section is outlined in red. The section has a heavy black border dividing the date in row 2 from the rest of the rows and a light black border dividing the two columns (Figure 5-3).

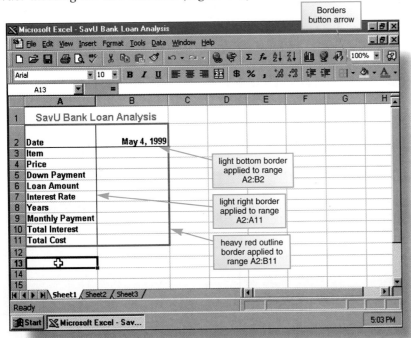

FIGURE 5-3

Formatting Cells Before Entering Values

While you usually format cells after you enter the values, Excel also allows you to format cells before the values are entered. The following steps, for example, assign the Currency style format with a floating dollar sign to the ranges B4:B6 and B9:B11 before the values are entered.

TO FORMAT CELLS BEFORE ENTERING VALUES

Step 1: Select the range B4:B6. While holding down the CTRL key, select the nonadjacent range B9:B11. Right-click one of the selected ranges.
Step 2: Click Format Cells. When the Format Cells dialog box displays, click the Number tab.
Step 3: Click Currency in the Category list box and then click the fourth format, ($1234.10), in the Negative numbers list box.
Step 4: Click the OK button.

The ranges B4:B6 and B9:B11 are assigned the Currency style format with a floating dollar sign. As you enter numbers into these cells, the numbers will display in this format.

Entering the Loan Data

As shown in Figure 5-1a on page E 5.5, five items make up the loan data in the worksheet: the item to be purchased, the price of the item, the down payment, the interest rate, and the number of years until the loan is paid back (also called the term of the loan). These items are entered into cells B3 through B5 and cells B7 and B8. The following steps describe how to enter the following loan data: Item – Home Theater; Price – $21,350.00; Down Payment – $3,500.00; Interest Rate – 8.25%; and Years – 4.

TO ENTER THE LOAN DATA

Step 1: Click cell B3. Enter Home Theater and then, with cell B3 still active, click the Align Right button on the Formatting toolbar. Click cell B4 and enter 21350 for the price of the home theater. Click cell B5 and enter 3500 for the down payment.
Step 2: Click cell B7. Enter 8.25% for the interest rate. Click cell B8 and enter 4 for the number of years.

The loan data displays in the worksheet as shown in Figure 5-4.

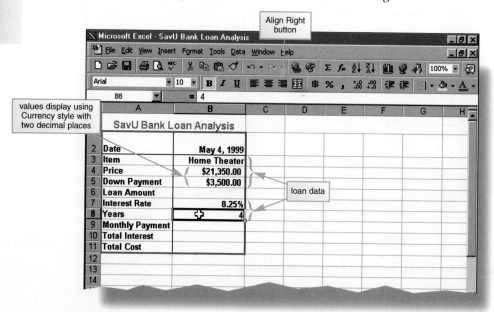

FIGURE 5-4

The values in cells B4 and B5 display using the Currency style with two decimal places, because this format was assigned to the cells prior to entering the values. Excel also automatically formats the interest rate to the Percent style with two decimal places, because the percent sign (%) was appended to 8.25 when it was entered into cell B7.

Calculating the four remaining entries in the Loan Analysis section of the worksheet — loan amount (cell B6), monthly payment (cell B9), total interest (cell B10), and total cost (cell B11) — requires you to enter formulas that reference cells B4, B5, B7, and B8. The formulas will be entered using natural language.

Entering the Loan Amount Formula Using Natural Language

The first formula entered will determine the loan amount in cell B6 by subtracting the down payment in cell B5 from the price in cell B4. You could do this by entering the formula = B4 – B5 in cell B6. Excel also allows you to enter formulas using names — not cell references — to identify the cells. Row titles or column titles, for example, can be used as names to reference cells. Thus, instead of entering the formula = B4 – B5, you can enter the formula = Price – Down Payment (Price is the row title of cell B4 and Down Payment is the row title of cell B5). A formula entered using row titles or column titles is called a **natural language formula**. As shown in the following steps, when you enter a natural language formula, you do not have to worry about capitalizing letters.

Steps To Enter the Loan Amount Formula Using Natural Language

More *About*
Natural Language Formulas

You can write natural language formulas, which use their own column and row headings rather than cell references, making it easier to create and understand calculations. If a formula references cells that are not in the same column or row as the formula you are creating, then you still can use names, rather than cell references, by using the Name Box in the formula bar to name the cells you want to reference.

1. **Click cell B6. Type** =price - down payment. **Point to the Enter box.**

   The natural language formula displays in cell B6 and in the formula bar (Figure 5-5).

   row titles used in formula reference cells in same row

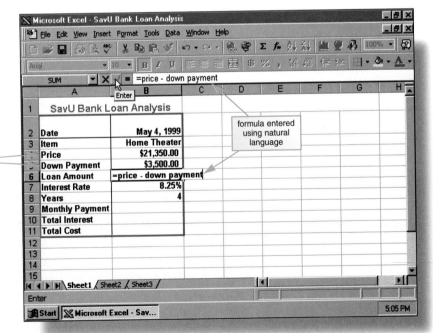

FIGURE 5-5

Click the Enter box.

Excel assigns the formula =Price – Down Payment to cell B6. The result of the formula ($17,850.00) displays in cell B6 (Figure 5-6).

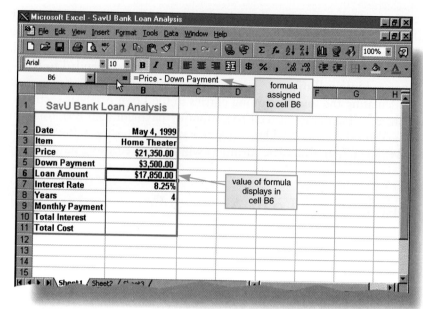

FIGURE 5-6

When using natural language formulas in a column, remember that Excel uses the values in the row that corresponds to the row titles used in the formula. For example, if you entered the formula =price – down payment in cell C6, Excel will reference cell C4 for Price and cell C5 for Down Payment. Since both cells are empty, the result in cell C6 will be zero (0).

An alternative to using natural language formulas is to use the Name Box on the formula bar or the **Name command** on the **Insert menu** to assign names to cells B4 and B5. Then, you can enter formulas anywhere on the worksheet using the defined names; the references always will refer to cells B4 and B5.

Determining the Monthly Payment

The next step is to determine the monthly payment for the loan. You can use Excel's PMT function to determine the monthly payment (cell B9) on the basis of the loan amount (cell B6), the interest rate (cell B7), and the number of years for payments, or term, of the loan (cell B8). The **PMT function** has three arguments — rate, payments, and loan amount — and its general form is

=PMT(rate, payments, loan amount)

where rate is the interest rate per payment period, payments is the number of payments, and loan amount is the amount of the loan.

In the worksheet in Figure 5-6, cell B7 displays the *annual* interest rate. Because the interest on a loan is their gross profit, however, loan institutions calculate interest on a monthly basis. The rate value in the PMT function is thus Interest Rate / 12 (cell B7 divided by 12), rather than just Interest Rate (cell B7). The number of payments (or periods) in the PMT function is 12 * Years (12 times cell B8) because there are 12 months, or 12 payments, per year.

Excel considers the value returned by the PMT function to be a debit and therefore, returns a negative number as the monthly payment. To display the monthly payment as a positive number, you can enter a negative sign before the loan amount. Thus, the loan amount is equal to –Loan Amount. The PMT function for cell B9 is

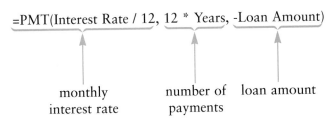

=PMT(Interest Rate / 12, 12 * Years, -Loan Amount)

monthly interest rate   number of payments   loan amount

More *About* **the PMT Fuction**

An alternative to requiring the user to enter an interest rate in percent form, such as 8.25%, is to allow the user to enter the interest rate as a number without an appended percent sign (8.25) and then divide the interest rate by 1200, rather than 12.

The following steps use the PMT function to determine the monthly payment in cell B9.

TO ENTER THE PMT FUNCTION

Step 1: Click cell B9. Type `=pmt(interest rate / 12, 12 * years, -loan amount)` as the function.

Step 2: Click the Enter box or press the ENTER key.

With cell B9 active, the PMT function displays in the formula bar (Figure 5-7). Excel displays the monthly payment $437.87 in cell B9, based on a loan amount of $17,850.00 (cell B6) with an annual interest rate of 8.25% (cell B7) for 4 years (cell B8).

You could have entered the PMT function by clicking the Paste Function button on the Standard toolbar. When the Paste Function dialog box displays, click Financial in the Function category list box and then click PMT in the Function name list box. In addition to the PMT function, Excel provides over 50 additional **financial functions** to help you solve the most complex finance problems. These functions save you from entering long, complicated formulas to obtain needed results. Table 5-1 summarizes three of the more often used financial functions.

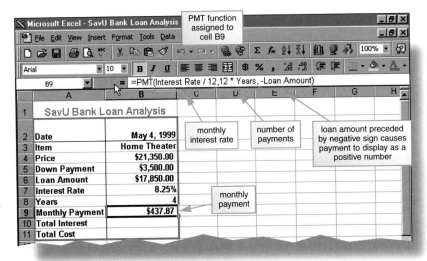

FIGURE 5-7

Table 5-1	
FUNCTION	DESCRIPTION
FV(rate, periods, payment)	Returns the future value of an investment based on periodic, constant payments and a constant interest rate.
PMT(rate, periods, loan amount)	Returns the payments for a loan based on periodic, constant payments and a constant interest rate.
PV(rate, periods, payment)	Returns the present value of an investment; that is, the total amount that a series of payments is worth now.

More *About* Auditing a Worksheet

You can use the Audit command on the Tools menu or the Auditing toolbar to locate the cells that provide data to a formula. The Trace Precedent command on the Audit submenu draws arrows from the cells referenced in a formula to the formula in the active cell. The Trace Dependent command draws arrows from the active cell to any cells containing formulas that reference it.

Determining the Total Interest and Total Cost

The next step is to determine the total interest (SavU Bank's gross profit) and the borrower's total cost of the item being purchased. The total interest (cell B10) is equal to:

$$=12 * \text{Years} * \text{Monthly Payment} - \text{Loan Amount}$$

The total cost of the item to be purchased (cell B11) is equal to:

$$=12 * \text{Years} * \text{Monthly Payment} + \text{Down Payment}$$

To enter the total interest and total cost formulas, perform the following steps.

TO DETERMINE THE TOTAL INTEREST AND TOTAL COST

Step 1: Click cell B10. Enter the formula =12 * years * monthly payment - loan amount to determine the total interest.

Step 2: Click cell B11. Enter the formula =12 * years * monthly payment + down payment to determine the total cost.

Step 3: Click cell A13. Click the Save button on the Standard toolbar to save the workbook using the file name SavU Bank Loan Analysis.

Excel displays a total interest of $3,167.68 in cell B10 and a total cost of $24,517.68 in cell B11 for the home theater (Figure 5-8).

With the loan analysis section of the worksheet complete, you can determine the monthly payment, total interest, and total cost for any reasonable loan data. After entering the data table in the next section, alternative loan data will be entered to illustrate Excel's recalculation feature.

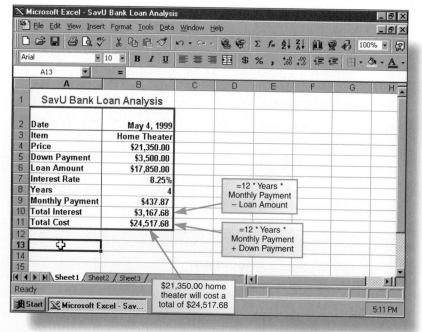

FIGURE 5-8

Using a Data Table to Analyze Worksheet Data

You already have seen that, if a value in a cell changes in a worksheet, Excel immediately recalculates and stores the results of any formulas that reference the cell. But what if you want to compare the results of the formula for several different values? Writing down or trying to remember all the answers to the what-if questions would be unwieldy. If you use a data table, however, Excel will organize the answers in the worksheet for you automatically.

A **data table** is a range of cells that shows the answers generated by formulas in which different values have been substituted. This data table shown on the right side of Figure 5-9, for example, displays the resulting monthly payment, total interest, and total cost values based on different interest rates in column D.

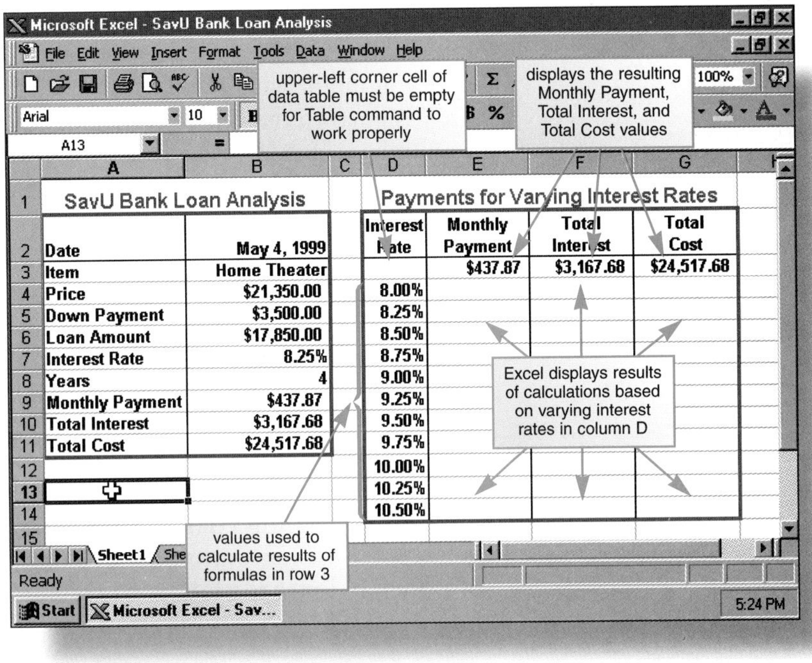

Data tables are built in an unused area of the worksheet (in this case, the range D1:G14). Within the table, you can vary one or two values and Excel will display the results of the specified formulas in table form. The right side of Figure 5-9 illustrates the makeup of a one-input data table. With a **one-input data table**, you vary the value in one cell (in this project, cell B7, the interest rate). Excel then calculates the results of one or more formulas (in this project monthly payment, total interest, and total cost) and fills the table with the results. A **two-input data table** allows you to vary the values in two cells, but you only can apply it to one formula. (See In the Lab 2 on page E 5.55 for an example of a two-input data table.)

The interest rates that will be used to analyze the loan formulas in this project range from 8.00% to 10.50%, increasing in increments of 0.25%. The data table in Figure 5-10 illustrates the impact of varying the interest rate on three formulas: the monthly payment (cell B9), total interest paid (cell B10), and the total cost of the item to be purchased (cell B11).

To construct the data table in Figure 5-10, you will complete the following steps: (1) adjust the widths of columns C through G; (2) enter the data table section title and column titles in the range D1:G2; (3) use the fill handle to enter the series of varying interest rates in column D; (4) enter the formulas in the range E3:G3 for which you want the data table to determine answers; (5) use the **Table command** on the **Data menu** to define the range D3:G14 as a data table and then identify the interest rate in cell B7 as the **input cell**, the one you want to vary; and (6) outline the data table to highlight it.

FIGURE 5-9

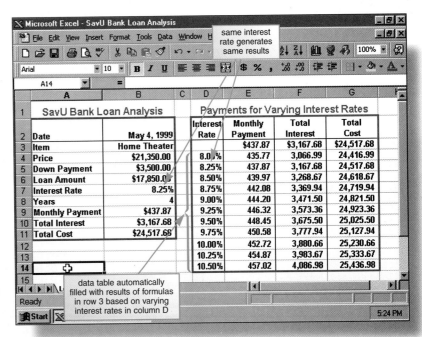

FIGURE 5-10

In the steps that follow, the columns are set to specific widths so the data table will fit in the same window with the loan analysis section. Keep in mind that you might have to adjust the widths of columns after the numbers and text are assigned to the cells, because numbers too large to fit across a cell will display as number signs (#). As you design a worksheet, make the best possible estimate of column widths and then change them later as required.

TO ENTER THE DATA TABLE TITLE AND COLUMN TITLES

Step 1: Change the widths of columns C through G as follows: C = 3.00; D = 6. 71; and E, F, and G = 11. 29.

Step 2: Click cell D1 and enter `Payments for Varying Interest Rates` as the data table section title.

Step 3: Click the Font Size arrow on the Formatting toolbar and then click 12. Click the Font Color button on the Formatting toolbar to change the font color to red. Select the range D1:G1 and click the Merge and Center button on the Formatting toolbar.

Step 4: Enter the following column titles in range D2:G2, as shown in Figure 5-11. Press ALT+ENTER as needed to enter the titles on two lines.

CELL	ENTRY
D2	Interest Rate
E2	Monthly Payment
F2	Total Interest
G2	Total Cost

Step 5: Select the range D2:G2 and then click the Center button on the Formatting toolbar.

The data table title and column headings display as shown in Figure 5-11.

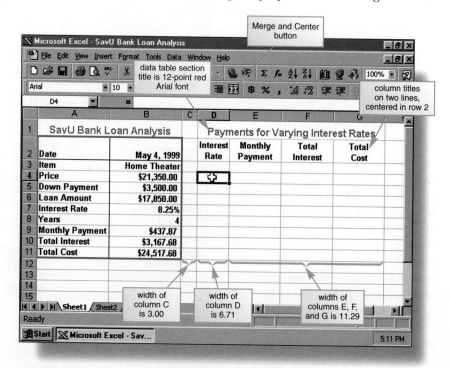

FIGURE 5-11

Creating a Percent Series Using the Fill Handle

The next step is to create the percent series in column D using the fill handle.

 Steps **To Create a Percent Series Using the Fill Handle**

1 Click cell D4 and enter 8.00% as the first number in the series. Select cell D5 and enter 8.25% as the second number of the series.

2 Select the range D4:D5 and point to the fill handle. Drag the fill handle through cell D14 and hold.

Excel shades the border of the copy and paste area (Figure 5-12). The ScreenTip, 10.50%, displays below the fill handle, indicating the last value in the series. This value will display in cell D14.

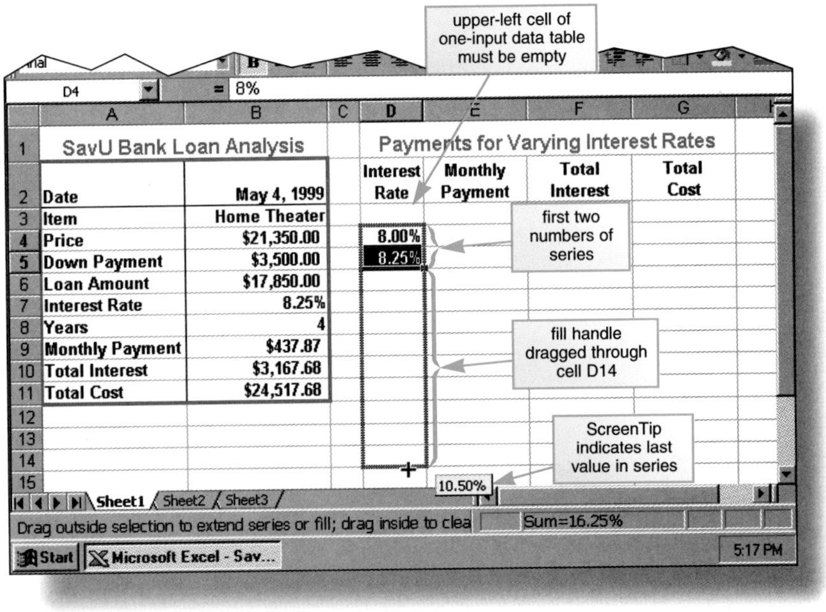

FIGURE 5-12

3 Release the mouse button. Click cell E3.

Excel generates the series of numbers from 8.00% to 10.50% in the range D4:D14 (Figure 5-13). The series increases in increments of 0.25%.

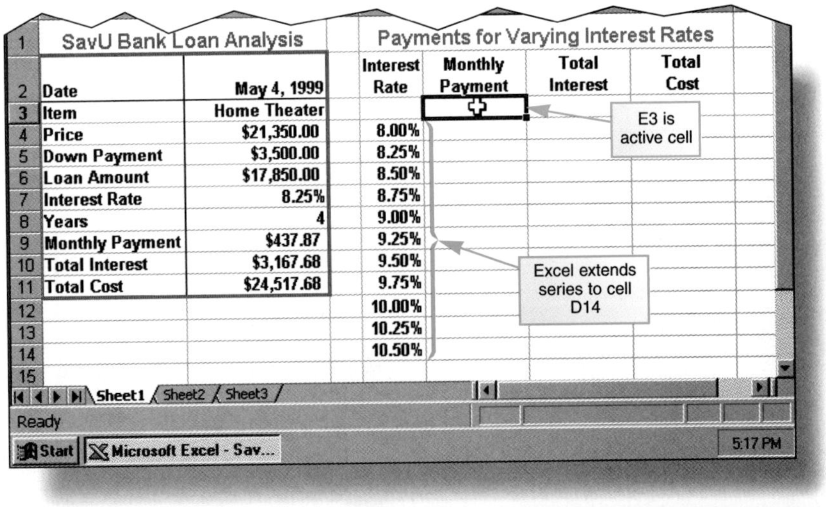

FIGURE 5-13

The percents in column D are the values Excel will use to calculate the formulas entered at the top of the data table in row 3. Notice that the series was started in cell D4, not cell D3, because the cell immediately above the series and to the left of the formulas in the data table must be empty for a one-input data table.

OtherWays

1. Enter initial values, select initial values and range to fill, on Edit menu point to Fill, click Series, click Columns, click Linear, click OK button

2. Enter initial values, select initial values, right-drag fill handle through range to fill, click Fill Series on shortcut menu

More *About* Formulas in Data Tables

Any experienced Excel user will tell you that to enter the formulas at the top of the data table, you should enter the cell reference or name of the cell preceded by an equal sign. This ensures that if you change the original formula in the worksheet, Excel automatically will change the corresponding formula in the data table.

Entering the Formulas in the Data Table

The next step in creating the data table is to enter the three formulas in row 3 in cells E3, F3, and G3. The three formulas are the same as the monthly payment formula in cell B9, the total interest formula in cell B10, and the total cost formula in cell B11.

Excel provides three ways to enter these formulas in the data table: (1) retype the formulas in cells E3, F3, and G3; (2) copy cells B9, B10, and B11 to cells E3, F3, and G3, respectively; or (3) enter the formulas =b9 in cell E3, =b10 in cell F3, and enter =b11 in cell G3.

Using the cell references preceded by an equal sign to define the formulas in the data table is the better alternative because: (1) it is more efficient; and (2) if you change any of the formulas in the range B9:B11, the formulas at the top of the data table are updated automatically.

TO ENTER THE FORMULAS IN THE DATA TABLE

Step 1: With cell E3 active, type =b9 and then press the RIGHT ARROW key.
Step 2: Type =b10 in cell F3 and then press the RIGHT ARROW key.
Step 3: Type =b11 in cell G3 and then click the Enter box or press the ENTER key.
Step 4: Drag across the range E3:G3. Click the Borders button arrow on the Formatting toolbar. Click the no border option (column1, row 1) on the Borders palette. Click cell D3.

The results of the formulas display in the range E3:G3 (Figure 5-14). Excel automatically assigns the Currency style format to cells E3 through G3 based on the formats assigned to cells B9 through B11.

More *About* Applying Formats

When you assign a formula to a cell, Excel formats the cell the same as the first cell reference. Thus, in Figure 5-14, the =b9 assigned to cell E3 instructs Excel to apply the format in cell B9 to cell E3.

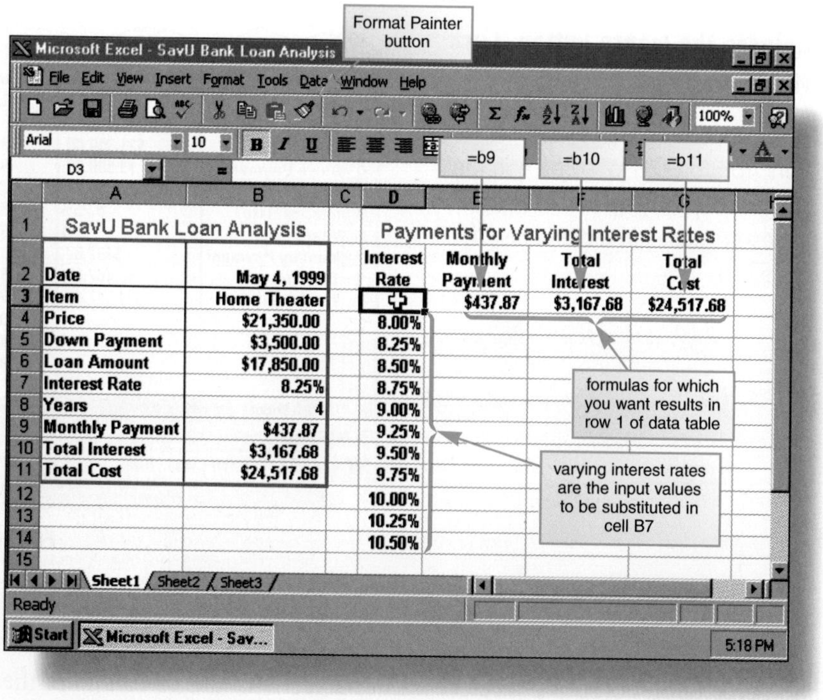

FIGURE 5-14

Defining the Data Table

After creating the percent interest rates series in column D and entering and formatting the formulas in row 3, the next step is to define the range D3:G14 as a data table.

Steps **To Define a Range as a Data Table**

1 **Select the range D3:G14. Point to Table on the Data menu.**

*Excel displays the **Data menu** (Figure 5-15). The range to be defined as the data table begins with the formulas in row 3. The section title and column headings in the range D1:G2 are not part of the data table, even though they identify the section and columns in the table.*

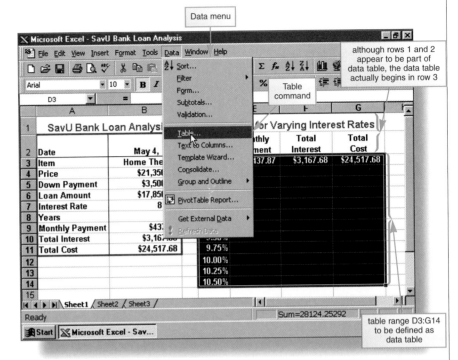

FIGURE 5-15

2 **Click the Table command. When the Table dialog box displays, click the Column input cell text box. Click cell B7 or type** B7 **as the input cell.**

*A marquee surrounds the selected cell B7, indicating it will be the input cell in which values from the data table are substituted. Excel assigns cell B7 to the **Column input cell text box** in the **Table dialog box** (Figure 5-16).*

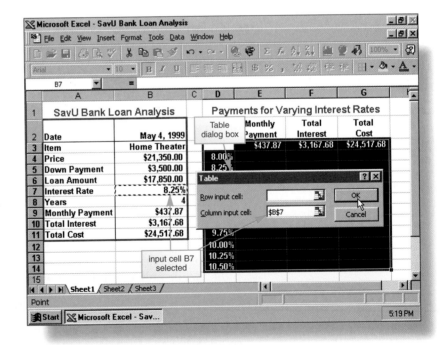

FIGURE 5-16

3 Click the OK button.

Excel calculates the results of the three formulas in row 3 for each interest rate in column D and immediately fills columns E, F, and G of the data table (Figure 5-17). The resulting values for each interest rate are displayed in the corresponding row.

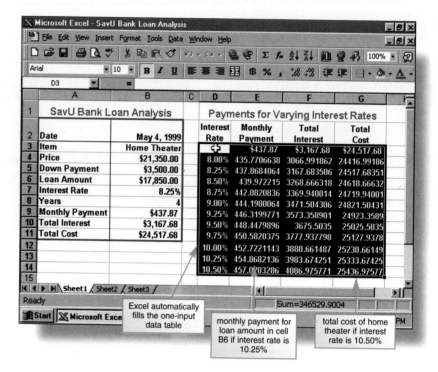

FIGURE 5-17

In Figure 5-17, the data table displays the monthly payment, total interest, and total cost for the interest rates in column D. For example, if the interest rate is 8.25% (cell B7), the monthly payment is $434.87 (cell B9). If, however, the interest rate is 10.25% (cell D13), the monthly payment is $454.87 rounded to the nearest cent (cell E13). If the interest rate is 10.50% (cell D14), then the total cost of the home theater is $25,436.98 (cell G14) rounded to the nearest cent, rather than $24,517.68 (cell B11). Thus, a 2.25% increase in the interest rate results in a $919.30 increase in the total cost of the home theater.

The following list details important points you should know about data tables:

1. The formula(s) you are analyzing must have a cell reference to the input cell.
2. You can have as many active data tables in a worksheet as you want.
3. For a data table with one varying value, the cell in the upper-left corner of the table (cell D3 in Figure 5-17) must be empty.
4. While only one value can vary in a one-input data table, the data table can analyze as many formulas as you want.
5. To add additional formulas to a one-input data table, enter them in adjacent cells in the same row as the current formulas (row 3 in Figure 5-17) and then define the entire new range as a data table by using the Table command on the Data menu.
6. You delete a data table as you would delete any other item on a worksheet. That is, select the data table and press the DELETE key.

Formatting the Data Table

The next step is to format the data table to improve its readability.

TO OUTLINE AND FORMAT THE DATA TABLE

Step 1: Select the range E4:G14. Click the Comma Style button on the Formatting toolbar.

Step 2: Select the range D2:G14. Right-click the selected range.

Step 3: Click Format Cells on the shortcut menu. When the Format Cells dialog box displays, click the Border tab.

Step 4: Click the Color box arrow. Select red (column 1, row 3) on the palette. Click the heavy border in the Style area (column 2, row 6). Click the Outline button in the Presets area. Click the OK button.

Step 5: Select the range D2:G2. Click the Borders button arrow on the Formatting toolbar. Click the light bottom border (column 2, row 1) on the Borders palette.

Step 6: Select the range D2:D14. Click the Borders button arrow on the Formatting toolbar. Click the light right border (column 4, row 1) on the Borders palette. Repeat this step for the ranges E2:E14 and F2:F14. Click cell A14.

Step 7: Double click the Sheet1 tab. Type Loan Analysis as the sheet name and then press the ENTER key.

Step 8: Click the Save button on the Standard toolbar to save the workbook using the file name SavU Bank Loan Analysis.

The worksheet displays as shown in Figure 5-18.

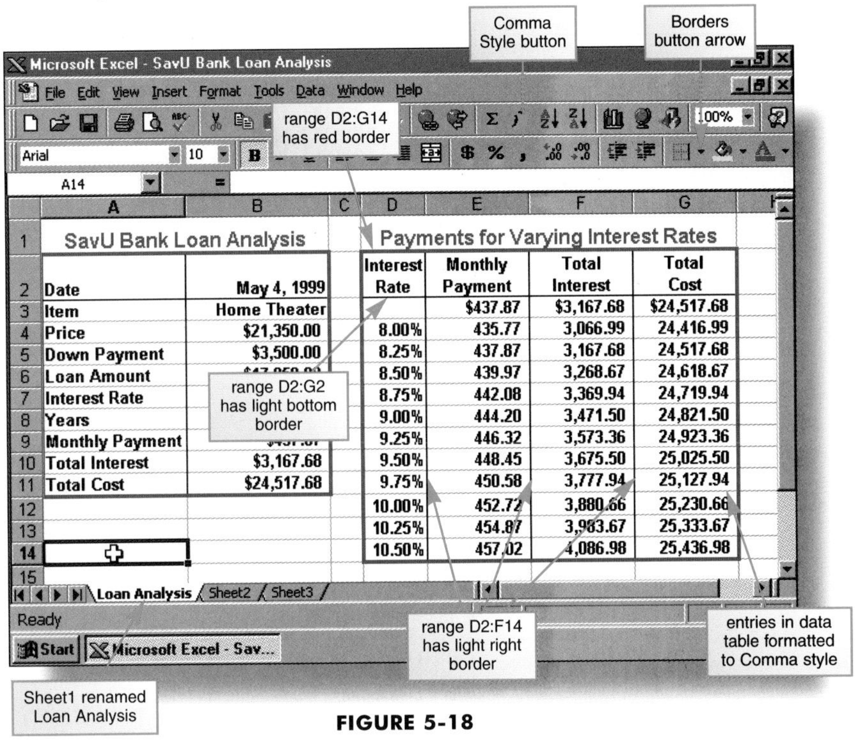

FIGURE 5-18

More *About* Undoing Formats

If you started to assign formats to a range and then realize you made a mistake and want to start over, select the range, click Style on the Format menu, click Normal in the Style Name list box, and click the OK button.

Entering New Loan Data

Once the loan analysis and data table sections of the worksheet are complete, you can use them to generate new loan information. For example, assume you want to purchase a home for $296,350.00. You estimate you have $65,000.00 from the sale of your current home to use for a down payment and you want the loan for a term of 15 years. SavU Bank currently is charging 8.25% interest for a 15-year loan. The steps on the next page show how to enter the new loan data.

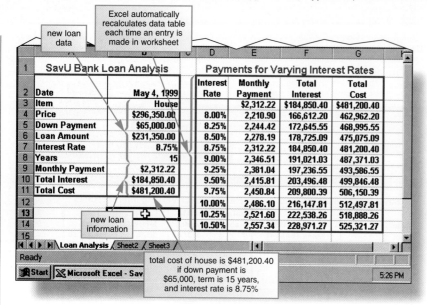

new loan
data

Excel automatically
recalculates data table
each time an entry is
made in worksheet

	SavU Bank Loan Analysis		Payments for Varying Interest Rates			
			Interest Rate	Monthly Payment	Total Interest	Total Cost
2	Date	May 4, 1999		$2,312.22	$184,850.40	$481,200.40
3	Item	House	8.00%	2,210.90	166,612.20	462,962.20
4	Price	$296,350.00	8.25%	2,244.42	172,645.55	468,995.55
5	Down Payment	$65,000.00	8.50%	2,278.19	178,725.09	475,075.09
6	Loan Amount	$231,350.00	8.75%	2,312.22	184,850.40	481,200.40
7	Interest Rate	8.75%	9.00%	2,346.51	191,021.03	487,371.03
8	Years	15	9.25%	2,381.04	197,236.55	493,586.55
9	Monthly Payment	$2,312.22	9.50%	2,415.81	203,496.48	499,846.48
10	Total Interest	$184,850.40	9.75%	2,450.84	209,800.39	506,150.39
11	Total Cost	$481,200.40	10.00%	2,486.10	216,147.81	512,497.81
12			10.25%	2,521.60	222,538.26	518,888.26
13			10.50%	2,557.34	228,971.27	525,321.27

new loan
information

Loan Analysis / Sheet2 / Sheet3

Ready

Start | Microsoft Excel - Sav...   5:26 PM

total cost of house is $481,200.40
if down payment is
$65,000, term is 15 years,
and interest rate is 8.75%

FIGURE 5-19

TO ENTER NEW LOAN DATA

Step 1: Click cell B3. Type House and press the DOWN ARROW key.

Step 2: In cell B4, type 296350 and press the DOWN ARROW key.

Step 3: In cell B5, type 65000 and press the DOWN ARROW key twice.

Step 4: In cell B7, type 8.75% and press the DOWN ARROW key.

Step 5: In cell B8, type 15 and then click cell B13.

Excel automatically recalculates the loan information in cells B6, B9, B10, B11, and the data table (Figure 5-19).

As you can see from Figure 5-19, the monthly payment for the house is $2,312.22. The total interest (SavU Bank's gross profit) is $184,850.40. By paying for the house over a 15-year period, you actually pay a total cost of $481,200.40 for a $296,350.00 house. As shown in the example, you can use the Loan Analysis worksheet to calculate the loan information for any reasonable loan data.

Creating a Macro to Automate Loan Data Entry

As noted, a macro is made up of a series of Visual Basic statements that tell Excel how to complete a task. Macros such as the one in Figure 5-20 can be used to automate routine workbook tasks, such as entering new data into a worksheet.

If you are developing a worksheet for users who know little or nothing about computers and worksheets, you should use macros to automate as much as possible. In the previous section, for example, you entered the data for a 15-year house loan to calculate new loan information. A novice user, however, might not know what cells to select or how much loan data is required to obtain the desired results. To facilitate entering the loan data, a worksheet and macro can be set up so the user simply clicks a button to execute the macro. The instructions that make up the macro (Figure 5-20) then guide the user through entering the required loan data in the range B3:B8.

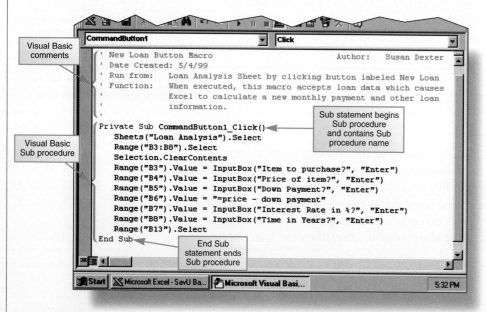

Visual Basic
comments

Visual Basic
Sub procedure

CommandButton1   Click

```
'  New Loan Button Macro                    Author:    Susan Dexter
'  Date Created: 5/4/99
'  Run from:     Loan Analysis Sheet by clicking button labeled New Loan
'  Function:     When executed, this macro accepts loan data which causes
'                Excel to calculate a new monthly payment and other loan
'                information.
'
Private Sub CommandButton1_Click()
    Sheets("Loan Analysis").Select
    Range("B3:B8").Select
    Selection.ClearContents
    Range("B3").Value = InputBox("Item to purchase?", "Enter")
    Range("B4").Value = InputBox("Price of item?", "Enter")
    Range("B5").Value = InputBox("Down Payment?", "Enter")
    Range("B6").Value = "=price - down payment"
    Range("B7").Value = InputBox("Interest Rate in %?", "Enter")
    Range("B8").Value = InputBox("Time in Years?", "Enter")
    Range("B13").Select
End Sub
```

Sub statement begins
Sub procedure
and contains Sub
procedure name

End Sub
statement ends
Sub procedure

Start | Microsoft Excel - SavU Ba... | Microsoft Visual Basi...   5:32 PM

FIGURE 5-20

Before the macro can be entered, the button that executes the macro must be added to the worksheet.

Adding a Button to the Worksheet to Execute a Macro

The most common way to execute a macro in Excel is to create a button with an assigned macro on the worksheet. Clicking the button executes the macro. To create the button, click the **Command Button button** on the **Control Toolbox toolbar**. You size and locate the button in the same way you size and locate an embedded chart. You then assign properties and the macro to the button while Excel is in **design mode**. When you first create a button, Excel automatically switches to design mode. The following steps add the button to the worksheet.

 Steps To Add a Button to the Worksheet

1 **Right-click one of the toolbars at the top of the screen. When the shortcut menu displays, click Control Toolbox.**

The Control Toolbox toolbar displays.

2 **Click the Command Button button on the Control Toolbox toolbar. If the Exit Design Mode toolbar displays, click its Close button. Move the mouse pointer (a cross hair) to the upper-left corner of cell A13. Drag the mouse pointer so the rectangle defining the button area appears as shown in Figure 5-21 and hold.**

When you click the Command Button button, Excel automatically switches to design mode. You know Excel is in design mode when the Design Mode button on the Control Toolbox toolbar is recessed. A light border surrounds the proposed button area in the worksheet (Figure 5-21).

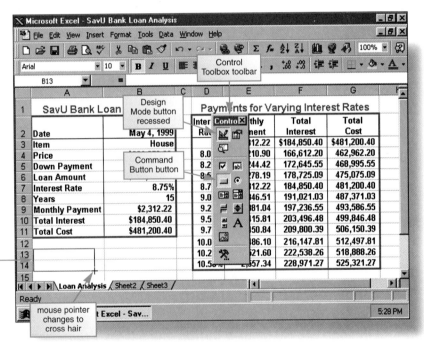

FIGURE 5-21

3 Release the left mouse button.

Excel displays the button with the default title CommandButton1 (Figure 5-22). Because Excel is in design mode and the button is selected, the button is surrounded by a shaded border and has sizing handles. While in design mode, you can resize the button, change the title of the button, set button properties, and assign the button a macro.

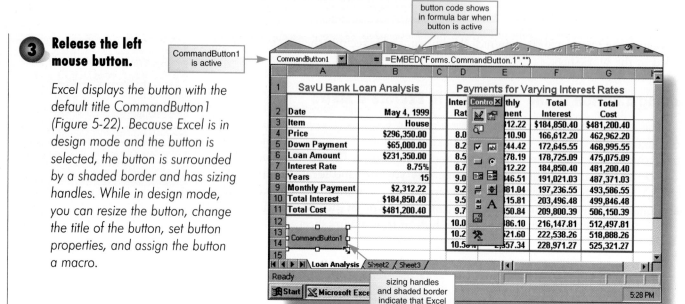

FIGURE 5-22

With the button created, the next step is to change the name on the button from CommandButton1 to New Loan and then adjust or set several of the button's properties.

Editing the Button Name and Setting Button Properties

To change the name of the button, Excel must be in design mode. You then right-click the button to display its shortcut menu. The Edit command on the CommandButton Object submenu allows you to change the button's name.

In addition to its name, a button has other default properties, several of which will be changed in the steps that follow. The button title font, for example, will be changed. In addition, the **PrintObject property** will be set to False so the button does not print when the worksheet is printed.

To Change the Name of a Button and Set Its Properties

1 While in design mode, right-click the button, point to CommandButton Object on the shortcut menu and point to Edit.

When you point to the button while in design mode, the mouse pointer changes to an arrow and a plus sign with four arrowheads. Right-clicking the button displays a shortcut menu. The Edit command is selected on the CommandButton Object submenu (Figure 5-23).

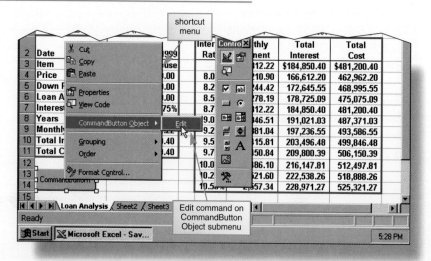

FIGURE 5-23

2 **Click Edit. Drag across the button title CommandButton1. Type** New Loan **as the button title and then click cell B13.**

The button displays as shown in Figure 5-24.

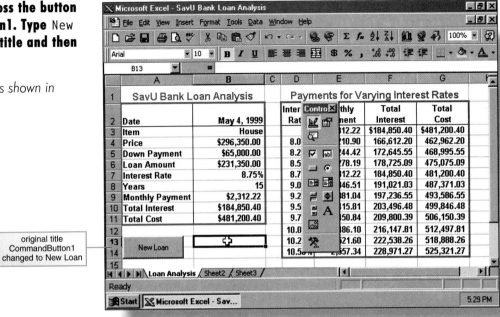

original title CommandButton1 changed to New Loan

FIGURE 5-24

3 **Right-click the button and point to Properties on the shortcut menu.**

The shortcut menu displays (Figure 5-25).

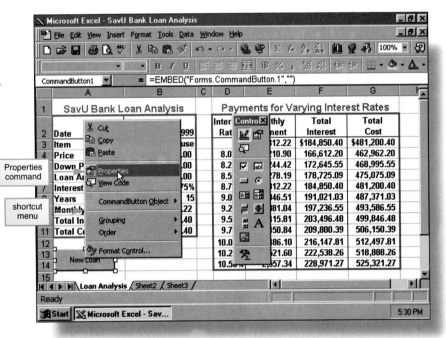

Properties command

shortcut menu

FIGURE 5-25

4 Click Properties. When the Properties window displays, click the Alphabetic tab. Click Font and then click the Font button that appears in the right column of the Font row. When the Font dialog box displays, click Bold in the Font style box and click 12 in the Size box. Click the OK button.

5 Click ForeColor in the Properties window. In the right column, click the ForeColor down arrow, click the Palette tab, and click the color red (column 2, row 3) on the palette. Click PrintObject in the Properties window. In the right column, double-click the word True to change it to False.

The Properties window displays as shown in Figure 5-26. Changing the PrintObject property from True to False instructs Excel not to print the button when the worksheet is printed.

6 Click the Close button on the Properties window.

The command button displays with the new properties (Figure 5-27).

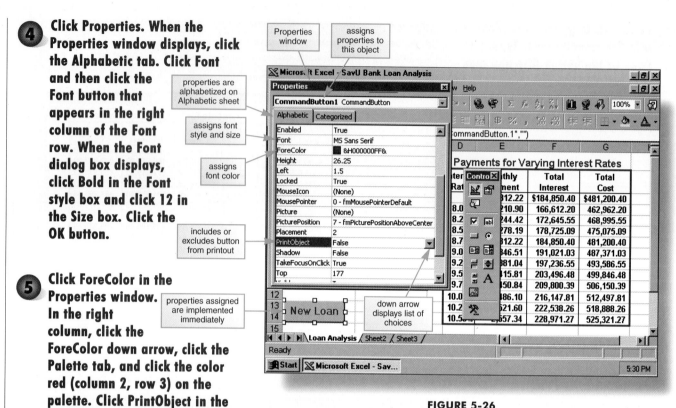

FIGURE 5-26

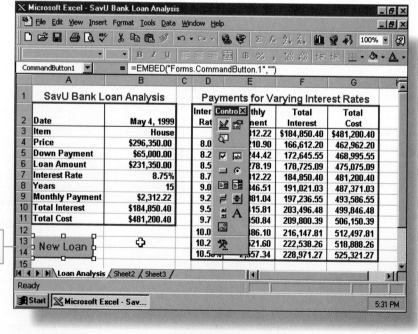

FIGURE 5-27

OtherWays

1. While in design mode select button, on Tools menu point to Macro, click Visual Basic Editor, click Properties Window button

2. While in design mode select button, press ALT+F11

Over 25 button properties display in the Properties window. Depending on the application, you can modify any one of these properties, much like you changed the Font and PrintObject properties in the previous steps. One property that could have been changed, for example, was the shape of the mouse pointer when it is positioned over the button. Excel provides over 14 different mouse pointer shapes from which to choose.

The next step is to enter the macro that will execute when you click the New Loan button. Macros are made up of Visual Basic statements. Thus, before entering the macro, you should understand the fundamentals of Visual Basic statements.

Visual Basic Statements

As noted, Visual Basic for Applications (VBA) is a powerful programming language that you can use to automate most of the workbook activities described thus far in this book. Visual Basic statements (or **Visual Basic code**) are instructions that tell Excel to execute a specific task. In the case of Project 5, all the statements are entered into a single **Sub procedure**. A Sub procedure begins with a **Sub statement** and ends with an **End Sub statement** (see Figure 5-20 on page E 5.22).

The Sub statement includes the name of the Sub procedure, which Excel determines from the original name of the button (CommandButton1) and the event that causes the macro to execute (Click). Thus, the name of the Sub procedure is CommandButton1_Click.

Remark (or comment) statements begin with the word **Rem** or an apostrophe ('). In Figure 5-20, there are seven comment lines prior to the Sub statement. These comments contain overall procedure documentation and are placed above the Sub statement. Rem statements have no effect on the execution of a macro; they simply provide information about the macro, such as name, creation date, and function.

In this project you will use seven Visual Basic statements and one Visual Basic function, as listed in Table 5-2. InputBox is a **function** rather than a statement because it returns a value to the Sub procedure.

Table 5-2	
VISUAL BASIC STATEMENTS	*DESCRIPTION*
Rem or '	Initiates a comment
Sub name ()	Begins a Sub procedure
Sheets("sheet name").Select	Selects the worksheet to affect
Range("range").Select	Selects a range
Selection.ClearContents	Clears the selected range
Range("cell").Value	Assigns the value following the equal sign to the cell
InputBox("Message", "Title of Dialog Box")	Displays *Message* in a dialog box with the title *Title of Dialog Box*
End Sub	Ends a Sub procedure

Planning a Macro

When you execute a macro, Excel steps through the Visual Basic statements one at a time, beginning at the top of the Sub procedure. Thus, when you plan a macro, remember that the order in which you place the statements in the procedure determines the sequence of execution. Excel bypasses any statements that begin with Remark, Rem, or an apostrophe (').

Once you know what you want the macro to do, write it out on paper. Then, before entering the macro into the computer, test it by putting yourself in the position of Excel and stepping through the instructions one at a time. As you do so, think about how it affects the worksheet. Testing a macro before entering it is called **desk checking** and is an important part of the development process. Adding comments before each procedure as you enter the macro will help you remember the purpose of the macro at a later date.

Entering a Macro for a Button

To enter the button's macro, double-click the button while Excel is in design mode. Excel activates the Visual Basic Editor and displays the Microsoft Visual Basic window. The **Visual Basic Editor** is a full-screen editor, which allows you to enter a macro by typing the lines of Visual Basic code (statements) as if you were using word processing software. At the end of a line, you press the ENTER key or use the DOWN ARROW key to move to the next line. If you make a mistake in a statement, you can use the arrow keys and the DELETE or BACKSPACE keys to correct it. You also can move the insertion point to previous lines to make corrections.

The following steps activate the Visual Basic Editor and enter and assign the button's macro.

Steps To Enter and Assign a Macro to a Button

1 **With Excel in design mode, double-click the New Loan button. If necessary, click the Close button on the Project Explorer window on the left and then click the Maximize button to maximize the Code window on the right.**

Excel starts the Visual Basic Editor and displays the Microsoft Visual Basic window shown in Figure 5-28. Because the Visual Basic Editor was started by double-clicking the button, the Visual Basic Editor automatically inserts the Sub and End Sub statements.

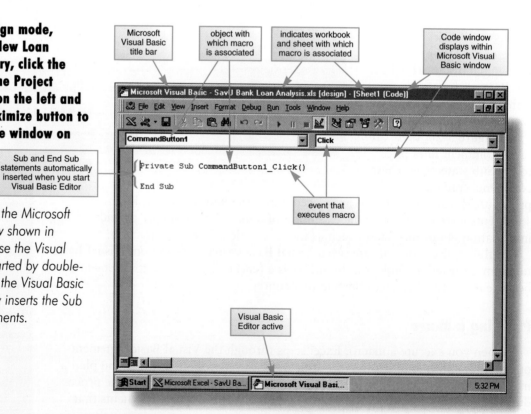

FIGURE 5-28

2 Click to the left of the letter P in the word Private and press the ENTER key to add a blank line before the Sub statement. Move the insertion point to the blank line and type the seven comment statements as shown in Figure 5-29. Remember to enter an apostrophe at the beginning of each comment line.

Excel automatically displays the comment lines in green.

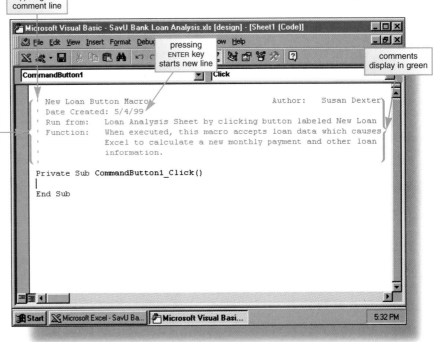

FIGURE 5-29

3 Move the insertion point to the blank line between the Sub and End Sub statements. Type the Sub procedure as shown in Figure 5-30. Indent all lines between the Sub statement and End Sub statement by three spaces for clarity.

The macro displays as shown in Figure 5-30.

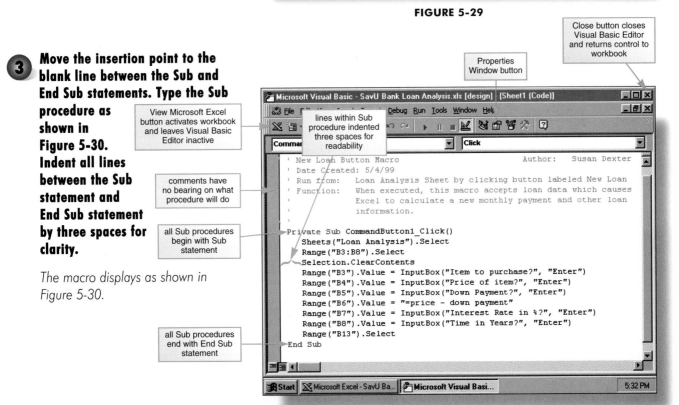

FIGURE 5-30

4 Click the Close button on the right side of the Microsoft Visual Basic title bar to return to the worksheet.

The Visual Basic Editor closes and the Loan Analysis sheet displays (Figure 5-31).

5 If necessary, right-click any toolbar and then click Control Toolbox to display the Control Toolbox toolbar. Click the Exit Design Mode button on the Control Toolbox toolbar. Click the Close button on the right side of the Control Toolbox toolbar title bar to hide it. Click the Save button on the Standard toolbar.

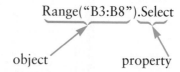

FIGURE 5-31

OtherWays

1. While in design mode select button, on Tools menu point to Macro, click Visual Basic Editor, on Insert menu click Module
2. Press ALT+F11, on Insert menu click Module

More About
Buttons on a Toolbar

Each button on a toolbar has a macro assigned to it. For example, when you click the Save button on the Standard toolbar, the macro assigned to the button executes and steps you through saving the workbook. You can add a new button to a toolbar and assign it a macro.

More About Macros and Visual Basic Statements

Visual Basic for Applications uses many more statements than those presented here. Even this simple macro, however, should help you understand the basic makeup of a Visual Basic statement. For example, each of the statements within the Sub procedure includes a period. The entry on the left side of the period tells Excel which object on the worksheet you want to affect. An **object** can be a cell, a range, a chart, a button, the worksheet, or the workbook. The entry on the right side of the period tells Excel what you want to do to the object. The right side of the period is called the **property**. For example, in the statement

$$Range(\text{``B3:B8''}).Select$$

object   property

the range B3:B8 is the range and select is the property. When the macro is executed, the statement Range("B3:B8").Select instructs Excel to select the range B3:B8 as if you used the mouse to select the range B3:B8 by dragging. Several of the statements in Figure 5-30 on the previous page also include equal signs. An equal sign instructs Excel to make an assignment to a cell. For example, when executed as part of the macro,

$$Range(\text{``B3''}).Value = InputBox(\text{``Item to purchase?''}, \text{``Enter''})$$

instructs Excel to display an Enter dialog box with the prompt message, Item to purchase?, and then assigns cell B3 the value entered by the user in response to the dialog box.

Because the second and third statement in the Sub procedure clears the range B3:B8, the formula in cell B6 has to be reentered. When executed, the seventh statement in the Sub procedure

Range("B6").Value = "=price – down payment"

reenters or assigns the formula =price – down payment to cell B6.

The next to the last statement in the Sub procedure selects cell B13, just as if you clicked cell B13 in the worksheet. Finally, the last statement in the Sub procedure, End Sub, ends the Sub procedure and control returns to the worksheet from which the Sub procedure was executed.

Creating and using a button and its macro is a five-step process: (1) create the button; (2) edit the button; (3) assign properties to the button; (4) enter the macro for the button; and (5) execute the macro by clicking the button. The next section discusses the final step – executing the macro.

Executing the Macro

The next step is to use the New Loan button to enter loan data. Remember that, when the macro executes, the second and third statements clear the range. Thus, any cell with a formula that includes a division operation might display the diagnostic message **#DIV/0!**, because clearing the range deletes the divisor value.

Follow the steps below to enter the loan data for a Jeep priced at $23,500.00. Assume the customer plans to make a down payment of $7,500.00 and wants the loan for 5 years. SavU Bank is charging 9.75% interest.

> ### More *About*
> ### Executing Macros
>
> Never execute a macro without first saving the workbook. If a save operation is part of the macro, then save the workbook under another name. A runaway macro can ruin a workbook.

 Steps **To Execute the Macro and Enter New Loan Data**

1 **Click the New Loan button. When Excel displays the first Enter dialog box with the prompt message, Item to purchase?, type** Jeep **as the item.**

Excel selects the Loan Analysis sheet. It then selects the range B3:B8 and clears the range. Next, it displays the Enter dialog box shown in Figure 5-32. Jeep is entered as the item to purchase.

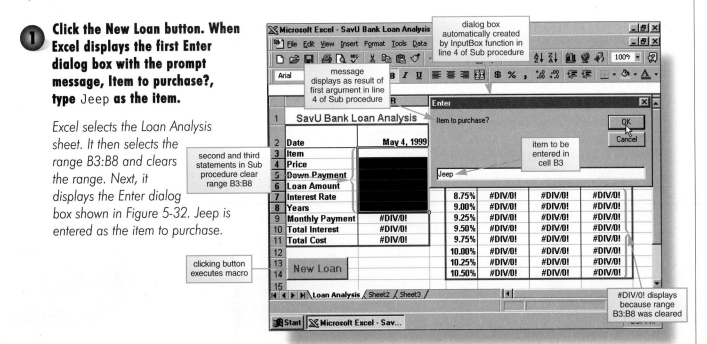

FIGURE 5-32

2 Click the OK button in the Enter dialog box or press the ENTER key. When Excel displays the next Enter dialog box with the prompt message, Price of item?, type 23500 **as the price.**

Excel assigns the text Jeep to cell B3 and displays the second Enter dialog box (Figure 5-33).

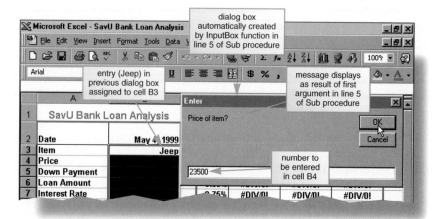

FIGURE 5-33

3 Click the OK button in the Enter dialog box. When Excel displays the next Enter dialog box with the prompt message, Down Payment?, type 7500 **as the down payment.**

Excel assigns the number 23500 to cell B4 and displays the third Enter dialog box (Figure 5-34).

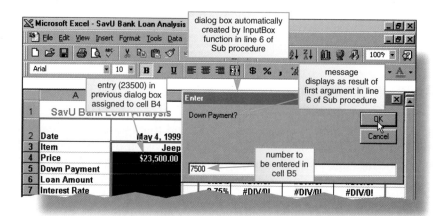

FIGURE 5-34

4 Click the OK button in the Enter dialog box. When Excel displays the next Enter dialog box with the prompt message, Interest Rate in %?, type 9.75% **as the interest rate. (Remember to type the percent (%) sign.)**

Excel assigns the number 7500 to cell B5. It then assigns the formula =price – down payment to cell B6. Next, it displays the fourth Enter dialog box (Figure 5-35).

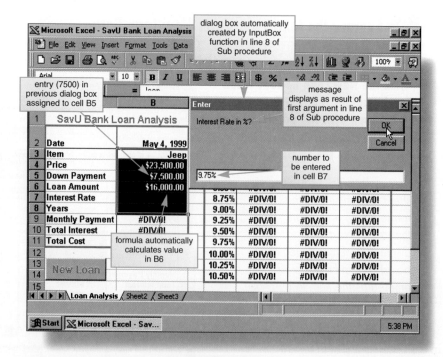

FIGURE 5-35

5 Click the OK button in the Enter dialog box. When Excel displays the next Enter dialog box with the prompt message, Time in Years?, type 5 as the number of years.

Excel assigns 9.75% to cell B7 and then displays the fifth Enter dialog box (Figure 5-36).

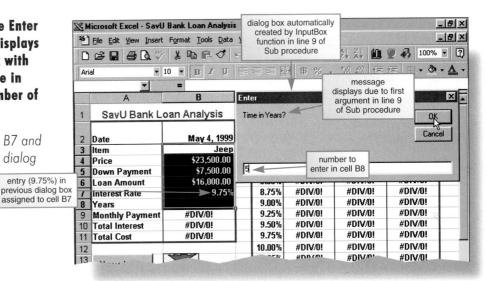

FIGURE 5-36

6 Click the OK button in the Enter dialog box.

Excel assigns 5 to cell B8 and then recalculates the loan information for the new loan data. Cell B13 is the active cell (Figure 5-37).

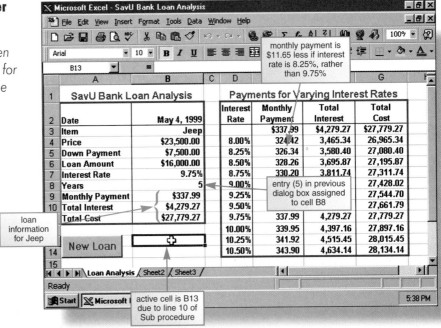

FIGURE 5-37

Figure 5-37 shows that the monthly payment for the Jeep is $337.99 (cell B9), the total interest is $4,279.27 (cell B10), and the total cost is $27,779.27 (cell B11). Furthermore, Excel automatically recalculates new results in the data table (range D3:G14) for the new loan data.

Based on this example, you can see the significance of using a macro to automate the worksheet tasks, especially if the users know little about computers. In this worksheet, each time the New Loan button is clicked, the macro guides the SavU Bank loan officers through entering the loan data and placing it in the correct cells.

More *About*
the Macro
Recorder

Record short procedures you
can call and use from a main
procedure. This makes your
code easier to manage, reuse,
and debug.

Recording a Macro

Excel has a **macro recorder** that creates a macro automatically, based on a series of actions you perform while it is recording. Like a tape recorder, the macro recorder records everything you do to a workbook over a period of time. The macro recorder can be turned on, during which time it records your activities, and then turned off to stop the recording. Once the macro is recorded, it can be **played back** (executed) as often as you want. To play back a recorded macro, you can do one of the following:

1. Assign the macro to a button on the worksheet and then click the button (as shown in this project).
2. Assign the macro to a custom button on a toolbar and then click the toolbar button.
3. Point to **Macro** on the Tools menu and then click the **Macros command** on the Macro submenu.
4. Click the **Run Macro button** on the Visual Basic toolbar.
5. Add a command to the Tools menu that plays back the macro and then choose the command.
6. Assign the macro to a graphic, such as a chart or clip art, and then click the graphic.
7. Assign a shortcut key to the macro and then press the shortcut key.

The following series of steps show you how to record a macro to print the Loan Analysis worksheet in landscape orientation and then return the orientation to portrait. Before you invoke the Macro Recorder, save the workbook using the same file name to ensure that no data is lost.

TO RECORD A MACRO TO PRINT THE LOAN ANALYSIS WORKSHEET IN LANDSCAPE ORIENTATION

Step 1: Click the Save button on the Standard toolbar to save the workbook using the file name SavU Bank Loan Analysis.

Step 2: Point to Macro on the Tools menu and then click Record New Macro on the Macro submenu.

Step 3: When the Record Macro dialog box displays, type the macro name PrintLandscape in the Macro name text box. Click the Shortcut key text box. While holding down the SHIFT key, press the letter L to set CTRL+SHIFT+L as the shortcut key.

Step 4: Click the OK button.

*Excel displays the **Stop Recording button** on the Stop Recording toolbar and displays the message, Recording, on the status bar at the bottom of the screen. The Macro Recorder is on, meaning that any actions you perform will be recorded.*

Step 5: Complete the following actions:
   a. Click Page Setup on the File menu.
   b. When the Page Setup dialog box displays, click the Page tab.
   c. Click the Landscape option button and then click the Print button.
   d. When the Print Dialog box displays, click the OK button.
   e. Click Page Setup on the File menu.
   f. Click the Portrait option button and then click the OK button.

Step 6: Click the Stop Recording button.

More *About*
Recording Macros

The macro recorder is a neat
tool for discovering Visual Basic
programming methods. But there
are limitations to recording
macros. You cannot record the
following: (1) conditional
branches; (2) looping structures;
(3) calculated selections and references; (4) certain built-in functions and dialog boxes; and, (5)
custom dialog boxes. Once
recorded, however, you can
modify and enhance your
recorded macros by using the
Microsoft Visual Basic Editor.

As you step through the actions, you can see the steps the macro will execute once it is recorded. If you recorded the wrong actions, point to Macro on the Tools menu and then click Macros on the Macro submenu. When the **Macro dialog box** displays, click the name of the macro (PrintLandscape) and then click the Delete button. Finally, rerecord the macro.

Playing Back a Recorded Macro

The following steps show you how to play back the recorded macro Print-Landscape by using the shortcut key CTRL+SHIFT+L. Recall that the shortcut key was established in Step 3 of the previous set of steps.

TO PLAY BACK A RECORDED MACRO

Step 1: Press CTRL+SHIFT+L.

The Excel window blinks as the macro is executed. The report prints as shown in Figure 5-38.

Step 2: Click the Save button on the Standard toolbar to save the workbook with the recorded macro.

More *About*
Viewing a
Recorded Macro

You can view the macro that the Macro Recorder created by pointing to Macro on the Tools menu and clicking Macros. When the Macro dialog box displays, select the macro PrintLandscape and click the Edit button. As you can see, the PrintLandscape macro is 70 Visual Basic statements long.

SavU Bank Loan Analysis	
Date	May 4, 1999
Item	Jeep
Price	$23,500.00
Down Payment	$7,500.00
Loan Amount	$16,000.00
Interest Rate	9.75%
Years	5
Monthly Payment	$337.99
Total Interest	$4,279.27
Total Cost	$27,779.27

Payments for Varying Interest Rates

Interest Rate	Monthly Payment	Total Interest	Total Cost
	$337.99	$4,279.27	$27,779.27
8.00%	324.42	3,465.34	26,965.34
8.25%	326.34	3,580.40	27,080.40
8.50%	328.26	3,695.87	27,195.87
8.75%	330.20	3,811.74	27,311.74
9.00%	332.13	3,928.02	27,428.02
9.25%	334.08	4,044.70	27,544.70
9.50%	336.03	4,161.79	27,661.79
9.75%	337.99	4,279.27	27,779.27
10.00%	339.95	4,397.16	27,897.16
10.25%	341.92	4,515.45	28,015.45
10.50%	343.90	4,634.14	28,134.14

FIGURE 5-38

As an alternative to pressing CRTL+SHIFT+L to play back the macro, point to Macro on the Tools menu and click Macros on the Macro submenu. When the Macro dialog box displays, double-click PrintLandscape in the middle box. You also can display the Macro dialog box by clicking ALT+F8.

Goal Seeking to Determine the Down Payment for a Specific Monthly Payment

If you know the result you want a formula to generate, you can use goal seeking to determine what value is needed in a particular cell to produce that result. The example on the next page uses the Goal Seek command to determine what down payment is required to make the monthly payment for the Jeep exactly $275.00.

Steps To Determine the Down Payment for a Specific Monthly Payment Using Goal Seek

1 **Click cell B9, the cell with the monthly payment amount. Click Goal Seek on the Tools menu. When the Goal Seek dialog box displays, type 275 in the To value text box. Click the By changing cell text box. In the worksheet, click cell B5.**

The Goal Seek dialog box displays as shown in Figure 5-39. In the dialog box, the first text box indicates the cell for which you want to seek a goal (cell B9), the second text box indicates the specific value you are seeking ($275.00), and the third text box indicates the cell to vary to reach that goal (cell B5).

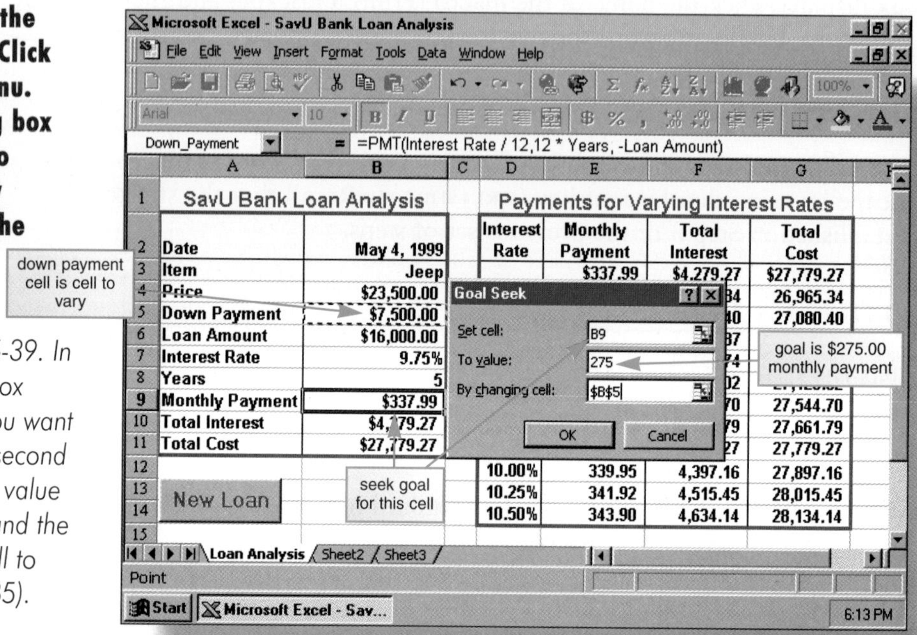

FIGURE 5-39

2 **Click the OK button.**

Excel displays the Goal Seek Status dialog box, indicating it has found an answer. Excel also changes the monthly payment in cell B9 to the goal ($275.00) and changes the down payment in cell B5 to $10,481.78 (Figure 5-40).

3 **Click the Cancel button in the Goal Seek Status dialog box to undo the changes to the worksheet.**

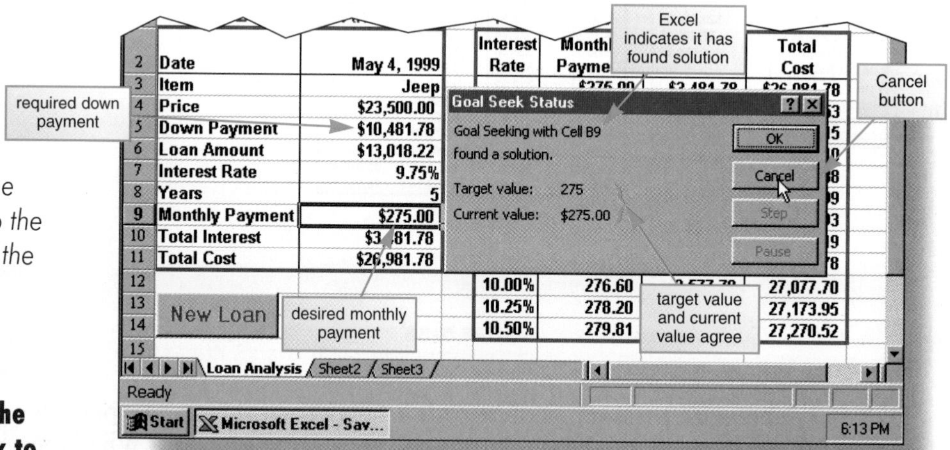

FIGURE 5-40

As shown in Figure 5-40, if you want to pay exactly $275.00 a month and the Jeep costs $23,500.00, the interest rate is 9.75%, and the term is 5 years, then you must pay a down payment of $10,481.78.

In this goal seeking example, you do not have to directly reference the cell to vary in the formula or function. For example, the monthly payment formula in cell B9 is =PMT(Interest Rate / 12, 12 * Years, -Loan Amount). This formula does not include a direct reference to the down payment. Because the loan amount, which is referenced in the PMT function, is based on the down payment, however, Excel is able to goal seek on the monthly payment by varying the down payment.

If you had clicked the OK button instead of the Cancel button in Step 3, then Excel would have stored the changes to the worksheet based on the goal seek activity. If you do click the OK button, you can reset the worksheet to the values displayed prior to goal seeking by clicking the Undo button on the Standard toolbar.

dding a Hyperlink to the Worksheet

A **hyperlink** is a pointer that points to the location of a computer on which a destination file is stored and the destination file itself. With Excel, you easily can create hyperlinks to other files on your personal computer, your network, or the World Wide Web. The destination file (or hyperlinked file) can be any Office document or an HTML file (Web page). There are two primary worksheet elements to which you can assign a hyperlink:

1. text — enter text in a cell and make the text a hyperlink; text hyperlinks display blue and underlined; and
2. embedded graphic — draw or insert a graphic, such as clip art, and then make the graphic a hyperlink.

In both cases, the **Insert Hyperlink button** on the Standard toolbar is used to assign the hyperlink to the worksheet element.

Assigning a Hyperlink to an Embedded Graphic

The following steps show how to assign a hyperlink to a graphic. The destination file is a Web page that contains the SavU Bank 1998 Statement of Condition. The destination file, savu bank.htm, is located in the Excel folder on the Data Disk that accompanies this book.

 To Assign a Hyperlink to an Embedded Graphic

① **Point to Picture on the Insert menu and then point to Clip Art on the Picture submenu.**

The Insert menu and Picture submenu display as shown in Figure 5-41.

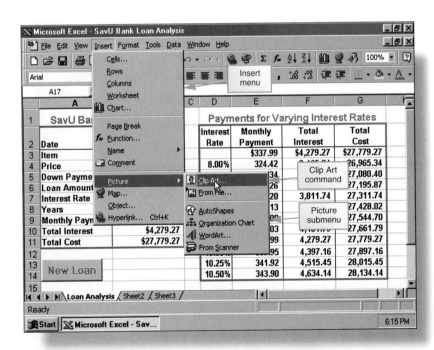

FIGURE 5-41

> **More** *About*
> **Hyperlinks**
>
> You can embed hyperlinks into an Excel worksheet that easily connect to important information on your local disk, on your company's intranet, or on the World Wide Web. The information can be a Web page or another Microsoft Office document, such as an Excel workbook.

2 Click Clip Art. When the Microsoft Clip Gallery 3.0 dialog box displays, click the Clip Art tab, and then select Currency in the Category list box on the left. Click the moneybag graphic and point to the Insert button. If the moneybag graphic is not available, choose another graphic.

The Microsoft Clip Gallery 3.0 dialog box displays as shown in Figure 5-42.

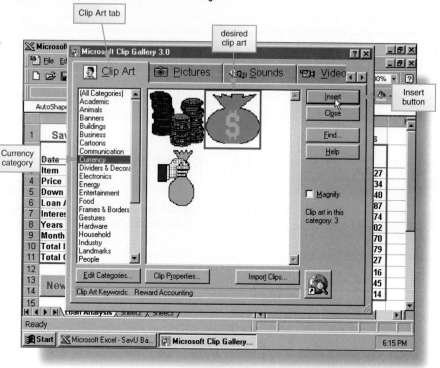

FIGURE 5-42

3 Click the Insert button. If the Picture toolbar displays, click its Close button to hide it. Use the sizing handles to size and move the moneybag graphic so it displays as shown in Figure 5-43. With the graphic selected, point to the Insert Hyperlink button on the Standard toolbar.

Excel embeds the graphic in the worksheet. The graphic is resized and placed next to the right of the New Loan button.

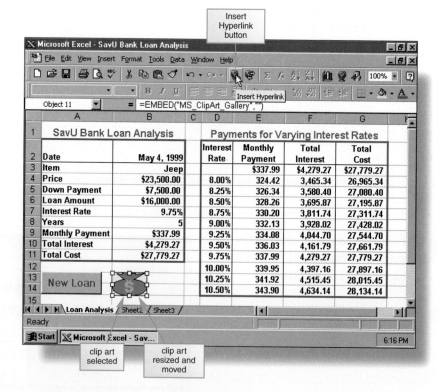

FIGURE 5-43

4 Click the Insert Hyperlink button. When the Insert Hyperlink dialog box displays, type `a:\excel\savu bank.htm` **in the Link to file or URL text box. Point to the OK button.**

The Insert Hyperlink dialog box displays as shown in Figure 5-44. If prompted, save the workbook by clicking the Save button on the Standard toolbar.

5 Click the OK button. Click cell A6 to deselect the graphic. Click the Save button on the Standard toolbar.

Excel assigns the hyperlink, a:\excel\savu bank.htm, to the moneybag graphic. The workbook is saved using the file name SavU Bank Loan Analysis.

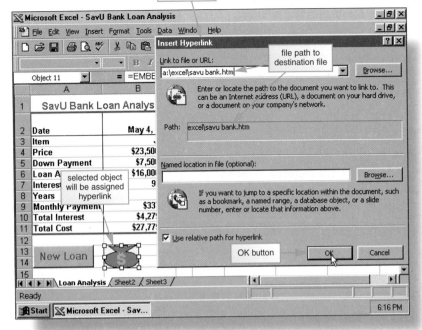

FIGURE 5-44

To edit the hyperlink, right-click the moneybag graphic to select it and then click the Insert Hyperlink button on the Standard toolbar.

Displaying a Hyperlinked File

The next step is to display the hyperlinked file by clicking the moneybag graphic on the worksheet. Once you assign a hyperlink to an element in your worksheet, you can position the mouse pointer over the element to display the hyperlink as a ScreenTip. Clicking the element will display the hyperlinked file, as shown in the following steps.

More *About* **Hyperlinks**

You can jump to a specific location in the HTML file, such as a bookmark, by entering the information in the second text box in the Insert Hyperlink dialog box (Figure 5-44).

 Steps **To Display a Hyperlinked File**

1 Insert the Data Disk that accompanies this book into drive A. Point to the moneybag graphic.

The hyperlink displays as a ScreenTip (Figure 5-45).

FIGURE 5-45

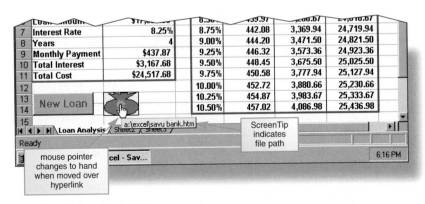

2 **Click the moneybag graphic.**

Excel starts your browser and displays the HTML file (Figure 5-46). The HTML file contains the SavU Bank 1998 Statement of Condition.

3 **When you are finished viewing the HTML file, click the Back button to return to Excel.**

The browser closes and the Loan Analysis worksheet displays in the active window.

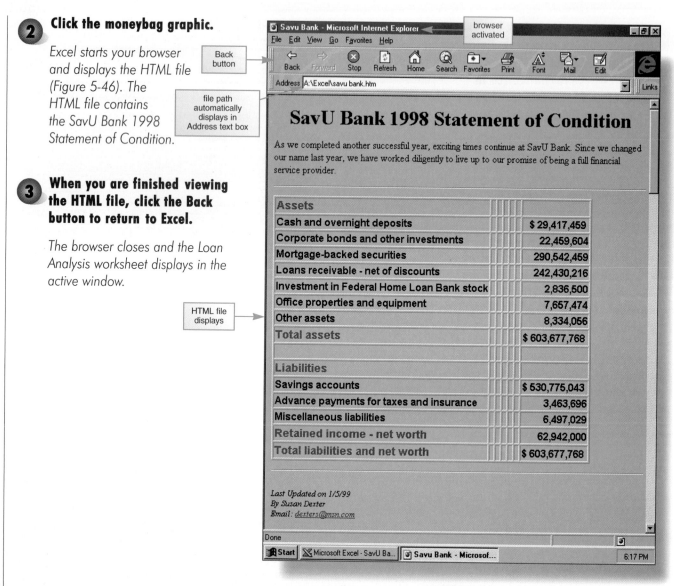

FIGURE 5-46

If the hyperlink does not connect you to the destination file, make sure you typed the correct hyperlink in the Link to file or URL text box on the Insert Hyperlink dialog box. If you entered the hyperlink correctly and it still does not work, check to be sure the file exists in the Excel folder on the Data Disk.

Using Scenario Manager to Analyze Data

An alternative to using a data table to analyze worksheet data is to use Excel's Scenario Manager. The Scenario Manager allows you to record and save different sets of what-if assumptions (data values) called **scenarios**. For example, earlier in this project (Figure 5-18 on page E 5.21), a monthly payment of $437.87 was determined for a home theater loan based on the following loan data: Item – Home Theater; Price – $21,350.00; Down Payment – $3,500.00; Interest Rate – 8.25%; and Years – 4. One scenario for the home theater loan might be: " What is the monthly payment, total interest, and total cost if the interest rate remains the same (8.25%) but the number of years changes from 4 to 5?". Another scenario might be: " What is the monthly payment, total interest, and total cost if the interest rate is increased by 1% to 9.25% and the number of years remains at 4?". Each set of values in these examples represents a what-if assumption. The primary uses of Scenario Manager are to:

1. create different scenarios with multiple sets of changing cells;
2. build a summary worksheet that contains the different scenarios; and
3. view the results of each scenario on your worksheet.

The following sections show how to use the Scenario Manager for each of the three uses listed above. Once you create the scenarios, you can instruct Excel to build the summary worksheet. The summary worksheet that the Scenario Manager generates is actually an outlined worksheet (Figure 5-47) that you can print and manipulate like any other worksheet. An **outlined worksheet** is one that contains symbols (buttons) above and to the left, which allows you to collapse and expand row and columns.

More *About*
Scenario Manager

Worksheets are used primarily for what-if analysis. You enter values into cells and instantaneously the results change in the dependent cells. As you continue to change values in the key cells, you lose the previous results. If you want to go back, you have to reenter the data. Scenario manager allows you to store the different sets of values (called scenarios) so you can redisplay them easily with a few clicks of the mouse button. Each scenario can have up to 32 sets of changing cells for each scenario.

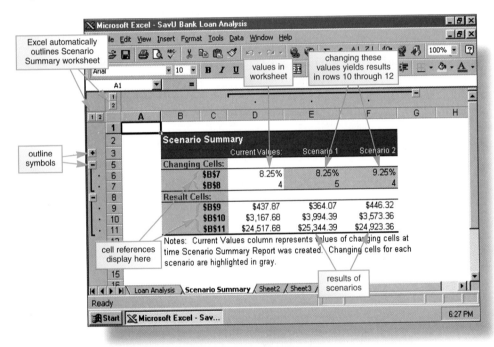

FIGURE 5-47

Before illustrating the Scenario Manager, enter the home theater loan data as shown in the following steps.

TO REENTER LOAN DATA

Step 1: Click the New Loan button.
Step 2: Enter the following data as requested: Item – Home Theater; Price – 21350; Down Payment – 3500; Interest Rate – 8.25%; and Years – 4.

The steps on the next page create the two scenarios and the Scenario Summary worksheet shown in Figure 5-47 by using the **Scenarios command** on the Tools menu. The Scenario Summary worksheet displays the monthly payment, total interest, and total cost for the current values in the SavU Bank Loan Analysis worksheet and for the two additional scenarios. The current interest rate value is 8.25% and the current time in years is 4. The first scenario sets the interest rate to 8.25% and the number of years to 5. The second scenario sets the interest rate to 9.25% and the number of years to 4.

Steps To Create Scenarios and a Scenario Summary Worksheet

1 Point to Scenarios on the Tools menu (Figure 5-48).

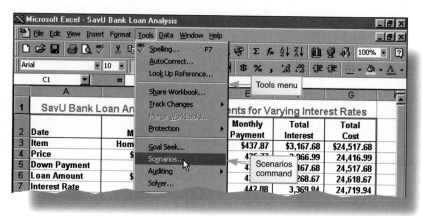

FIGURE 5-48

2 Click Scenarios.

The *Scenario Manager dialog box* displays, informing you that no scenarios are defined (Figure 5-49). It also instructs you to choose Add to add scenarios.

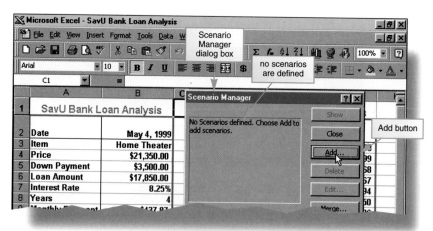

FIGURE 5-49

3 Click the Add button to add a scenario. When the Add Scenario dialog box displays, type Scenario 1 in the Scenario name text box. Click the Changing cells text box and then drag through the range B7:B8 on the worksheet.

The *Add Scenario dialog box* changes to the *Edit Scenario dialog box.* A marquee displays around the cells to change Interest Rate in cell B7 and Years in cell B8. Excel assigns the range $B$7:$B$8 to the *Changing cells text box* (Figure 5-50).

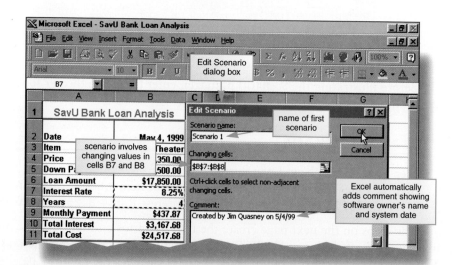

FIGURE 5-50

4 **Click the OK button. When the Scenario Values dialog box displays, click the $B$8 text box and type** 5 **as the value.**

The Scenario Values dialog box displays as shown in Figure 5-51. Changing the value in the $B$8 box to 5 instructs Excel that this scenario uses a term of five years.

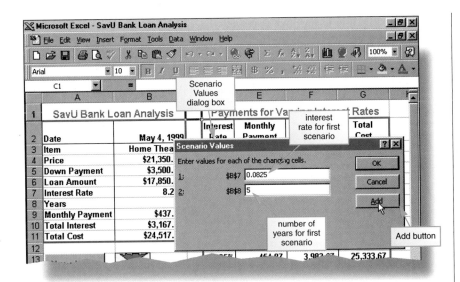

FIGURE 5-51

5 **Click the Add button to add the scenario. When the Add Scenario dialog box displays, type** Scenario 2 **in the Scenario name text box.**

The Add Scenario dialog box displays as shown in Figure 5-52. Excel automatically assigns the range B7:B8 to the Changing Cells text box because this range was used in the previous scenario.

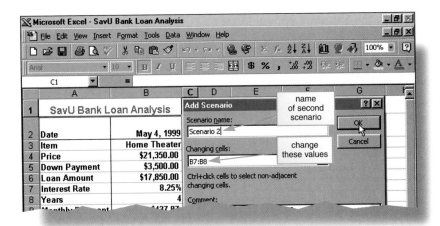

FIGURE 5-52

6 **Click the OK button. When the Scenario Values dialog box displays, type** 0.0925 **in the $B$7 text box. If necessary, type** 4 **in the $B$8 text box.**

The Scenario Values dialog box displays as shown in Figure 5-53. Changing the value in the $B$7 text box to 0.0925 instructs Excel that this scenario uses an interest rate of 9.25%.

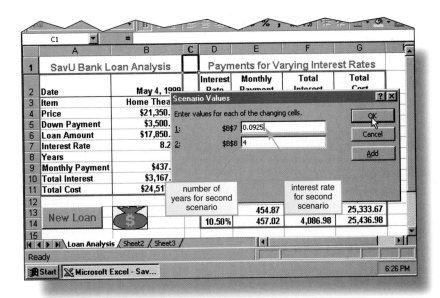

FIGURE 5-53

7 **Because this is the last scenario to add, click the OK button.**

The Scenario Manager dialog box displays with the two named scenarios in the Scenarios list (Figure 5-54).

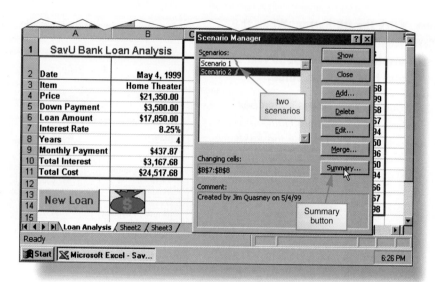

FIGURE 5-54

8 **Click the Summary button. When the Scenario Summary dialog box displays, drag through the range B9:B11 to select the cells for which you want results.**

The Scenario Summary dialog box displays as shown in Figure 5-55. Cells B9, B10, and B11 are selected as the results cells. A marquee displays around these cells and the range $B$9:$B$11 displays in the Results cells text box.

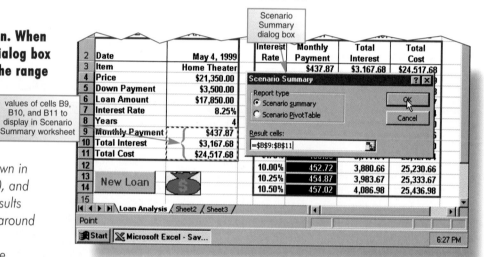

FIGURE 5-55

9 **Click the OK button in the Scenario Summary dialog box.**

The Scenario Summary worksheet displays as shown in Figure 5-56.

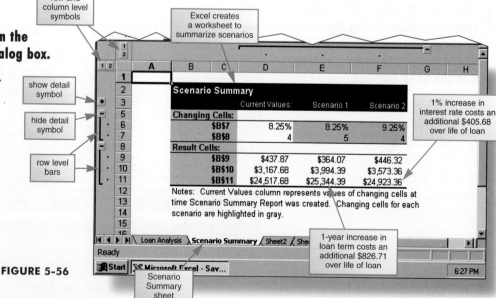

FIGURE 5-56

Column D in the Scenario Summary worksheet in Figure 5-56 shows the results of the current values in the Loan Analysis worksheet; columns E and F show the results of the two scenarios. The Scenario Summary worksheet makes it easier to compare the results of the scenarios. For example, in Scenario 1 (column E), the interest rate is the same as in the Current Values (column D), but the term of the loan is 5 years rather than 4 years. Because the loan is paid over a greater length of time, the monthly payment is $73.80 less per month. The total cost of the loan, however, increases by $826.71 to $25,344.39.

In Scenario 2, the number of years is the same as the Current Values, but the interest rate is 1% greater. The 1% change increases the monthly payment by $8.45 per month and raises the total cost of the home theater to $24,923.36 — $405.68 more than the Current Values loan data.

Working with an Outlined Worksheet

Excel automatically outlines the Scenario Summary worksheet. The **outline symbols** display above and to the left of the worksheet (Figure 5-56). You click the outline symbols to expand or collapse the worksheet. For example, if you click the **show detail symbol**, Excel displays additional rows or columns that are summarized on the displayed row or column. If you click a **hide detail symbol**, Excel hides any detail rows that extend through the length of the corresponding **row level bar** or **column level bar**. You also can expand or collapse a worksheet by clicking the **row level** or **column level** symbols above and to the left of row title 1.

An outline is especially useful when working with large worksheets. To remove an outline, point to **Group and Outline** on the Data Menu and then click **Clear Outline** on the Group and Outline submenu.

◆ **More** *About*
Outlined
Worksheets

You can outline any worksheet by clicking Auto Outline on the Group and Outline submenu. You display the Group and Outline submenu by pointing to Group and Outline on the Data menu.

Applying Scenarios Directly to a Worksheet

When you work with scenarios, you do not have to create the Scenario Summary Report worksheet shown in Figure 5-56. Instead, you can create the scenarios following the first seven steps of the previous example and then use the Show button in the Scenario Manager dialog box to apply the scenarios directly to the worksheet for which they were created. The following steps show how to apply the two scenarios created earlier directly to a worksheet.

 Steps To Apply Scenarios Directly to a Worksheet

 Click the Loan Analysis tab. Click Scenarios on the Tools menu.

The Scenario Manager dialog box displays (Figure 5-57).

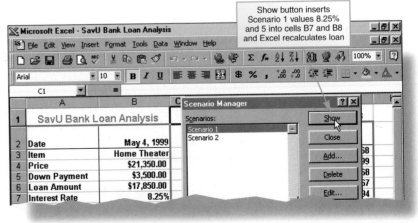

FIGURE 5-57

2 **With Scenario 1 selected in the Scenarios list box, click the Show button.**

Excel inserts the values from Scenario 1 into the worksheet and then automatically recalculates all formulas (Figure 5-58). The entries in the range B7:B11 change so they agree with the Scenario 1 results in column E of the Scenario Summary Report worksheet shown in Figure 5-56.

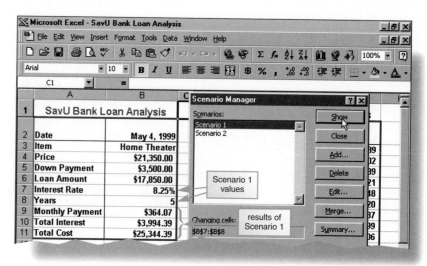

FIGURE 5-58

3 **Click Scenario 2 in the Scenarios list box in the Scenario Manager dialog box. Click the Show button.**

Excel inserts the values from Scenario 2 into the worksheet and then automatically recalculates all formulas (Figure 5-59). Again, the results in the worksheet agree with the Scenario 2 results in column F of the Scenario Summary Report worksheet shown in Figure 5-56 on page E 5.44.

4 **Click the Close button in the Scenario Manager dialog box. Click the Undo button on the Standard toolbar twice to return the worksheet to the one shown in Figure 5-55 on page E 5.44.**

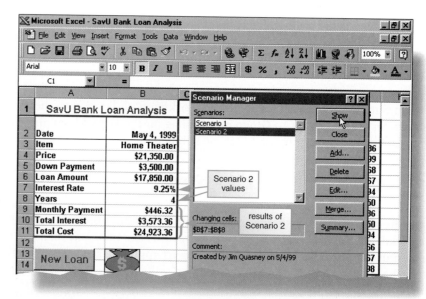

FIGURE 5-59

You can undo the scenario results by clicking the Undo button on the Standard toolbar. If you want, you then can click the Redo button on the Standard toolbar to again display the scenario results.

Scenario Manager is an important what-if tool for organizing your assumptions. Using Scenario Manager, you can define different scenarios with up to 32 changing cells per scenario. Once you have entered the scenarios, you can show them one by one as illustrated in the previous example, or you can create the Scenario Summary worksheet.

Protecting the Worksheet

When building a worksheet for novice users, you should protect the cells in the worksheet that you don't want changed, such as cells that contain text and formulas.

When you create a new worksheet, all the cells are unprotected. **Unprotected cells,** or **unlocked cells,** are cells whose values you can change at any time. **Protected cells,** or **locked cells,** are cells that you cannot change. If a cell is protected and the user attempts to change its value, Excel displays a dialog box with a message indicating the cells are protected.

You should protect cells only after the worksheet has been fully tested and displays the correct results. Protecting a worksheet is a two-step process:

1. Select the cells you want to leave unprotected and change their cell protection settings to unprotected.
2. Protect the entire worksheet.

At first glance, these steps may appear to be backwards. Once you protect the entire worksheet, however, you cannot change anything, including the protection of individual cells. Thus, you first set the cells you want to leave unprotected and then protect the entire worksheet.

In the loan analysis worksheet (Figure 5-60), the user should make changes to only five cells: the item in cell B3; the price in cell B4; the down payment in cell B5; the interest rate in cell B7; and the years in cell B8. These cells thus must remain unprotected. Also, because of the way the New Loan button macro works, cell B6 should be unprotected. The remaining cells in the worksheet should be protected so they cannot be changed by the user.

The following steps show how to protect the loan analysis worksheet.

 Steps **To Protect a Worksheet**

① Select the range B3:B8, the range to unprotect. Right-click the selected range. Click Format Cells on the shortcut menu. When the Format Cells dialog box displays, click the Protection tab. Click the Locked check box.

*The Protection sheet in the Format Cells dialog box displays with the check mark removed from the **Locked** check box (Figure 5-60).*

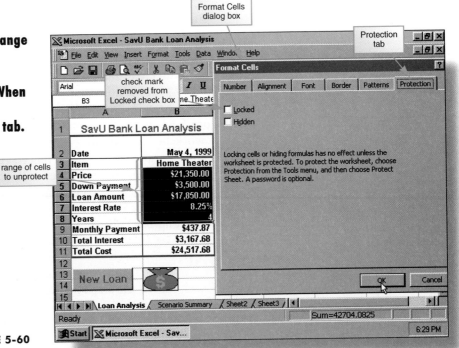

FIGURE 5-60

2 **Click the OK button. Point to Protection on the Tools menu and then point to Protect Sheet on the Protection submenu.**

Excel displays the Tools menu and Protection submenu (Figure 5-61).

FIGURE 5-61

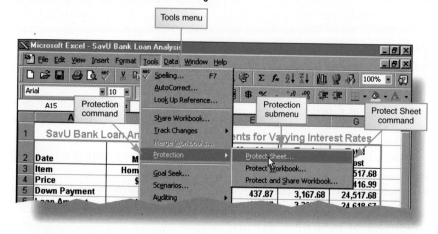

3 **Click Protect Sheet on the Protection submenu.**

The Protect Sheet dialog box displays (Figure 5-62). All three check boxes are selected, thus protecting the worksheet from changes to contents, objects, and scenarios.

4 **Click the OK button. Click the Save button on the Standard toolbar to save the protected workbook.**

All the cells in the worksheet are protected, except for the range B3:B8.

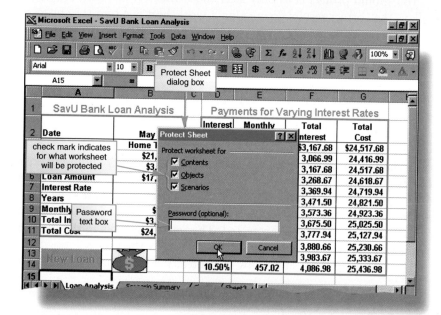

FIGURE 5-62

The Protect Sheet dialog box in Figure 5-62 lets you enter a password. You should create a **password** when you want to keep others from changing the worksheet from protected to unprotected.

If you want to protect more than one sheet, select them before you begin the protection process or click **Protect Workbook** on the Protection submenu that displays (Figure 5-61) when you point to Protection on the Tools menu.

With the worksheet protected, you still can click the New Loan button to execute the macro because the cells referenced (B3:B8) by the macro are unprotected. If you try to change any protected cell, however, Excel displays a dialog box with a diagnostic message. To change any cells in the worksheet such as titles or formulas, unprotect the document by pointing to Protection on the Tools menu and then clicking **Unprotect Sheet.**

Quitting Excel

To quit Excel, follow the steps below.

TO QUIT EXCEL

Step 1: Click the Close button on the right side of the title bar.
Step 2: If the Microsoft Excel dialog box displays, click the No button.

More *About*
Closing Files

If you have multiple workbooks opened, you can close them all at the same time by holding down the SHIFT key when you click the File menu. The Close command changes to Close All. Click Close All and Excel will close all open workbooks.

Project Summary

The workbook you developed in this project will handle all of Susan Dexter's requirements for the loan department at SavU Bank. The loan information, including the data table and Scenario Summary worksheet, is easy to read, which will help with customer relations. The macro created to accept loan data and the protection features of Excel ensures that the loan officers will not enter or change values in the wrong cells. The hyperlink associated with the moneybag clip art gives the loan officer quick access to the SavU Bank 1998 Statement of Condition to answer customer questions. Finally, the macro created to print the worksheet will simplify getting a copy to the customer.

In this project you learned how to apply the PMT function to determine the monthly payment of a loan and then learned how to enter natural language formulas. You also learned how to analyze data by creating a data table and working with the Scenario Manager. This project also explained how macros are used to automate worksheet tasks, after which you learned how to add a button and assign a macro to it. The button was used to execute the macro. You learned how to add a hyperlink to a worksheet. You also learned how to record a macro and play it back. Finally, you learned how to protect a document so a user can change only the contents of unprotected cells.

What You Should Know

Having completed this project, you now should be able to perform the following tasks:

▶ Add a Button to the Worksheet *(E 5.23)*

▶ Add an Outline and Borders *(E 5.9)*

▶ Apply Scenarios Directly to the Worksheet *(E 5.45)*

▶ Assign a Hyperlink to an Embedded Graphic *(E 5.37)*

▶ Change the Font of the Entire Worksheet *(E 5.7)*

▶ Change the Name of a Button and Set Its Properties *(E 5.24)*

▶ Create a Percent Series Using the Fill Handle *(E 5.17)*

▶ Create Scenarios and a Scenario Summary Worksheet *(E 5.42)*

▶ Define a Range as a Data Table *(E 5.19)*

▶ Determine the Down Payment for a Specific Monthly Payment Using Goal Seek *(E 5.36)*

▶ Determine the Total Interest and Total Cost *(E 5.14)*

▶ Display a Hyperlinked File *(E 5.39)*

▶ Enter and Assign a Macro to a Button *(E 5.28)*

▶ Enter the Formulas in the Data Table *(E 5.18)*

▶ Enter New Loan Data *(E 5.22)*

▶ Enter the Data Table Title and Column Titles *(E 5.16)*

▶ Enter the Loan Amount Formula Using Natural Language *(E 5.11)*

▶ Enter the Loan Data *(E 5.10)*

▶ Enter the PMT Function *(E 5.13)*

▶ Enter the Section Title, Row Titles, and System Date *(E 5.8)*

▶ Execute the Macro and Enter New Loan Data *(E 5.31)*

▶ Format Cells Before Entering Values *(E 5.10)*

▶ Outline and Format the Data Table *(E 5.21)*

▶ Play Back a Recorded Macro *(E 5.35)*

▶ Protect a Worksheet *(E 5.47)*

▶ Quit Excel *(E 5.48)*

▶ Record a Macro to Print the Loan Analysis Worksheet in Landscape Orientation *(E 5.34)*

▶ Reenter Loan Data *(E 5.41)*

▶ Start Excel *(E 5.7)*

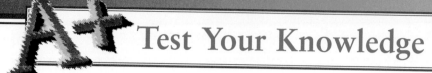 Test Your Knowledge

1 True/False

Instructions: Circle T if the statement is true or F if the statement is false.

T F 1. The Command Button button is found on the Drawing toolbar.
T F 2. To keep cells unprotected, highlight them before you click the Protect Sheet command.
T F 3. A hyperlink points to a file.
T F 4 To assign properties to a button, double-click the button while in design mode.
T F 5. The Scenario Manager allows you to record and save different sets of what-if assumptions.
T F 6. The upper-left cell in a one-input data table must be empty.
T F 7. =Balance – Payment is an example of a natural language formula.
T F 8. Use Goal Seek when you do not know the result you want a formula to produce.
T F 9. An apostrophe at the beginning of a Visual Basic statement indicates a comment.
T F 10. A data table is a function.

2 Multiple Choice

Instructions: Circle the correct response.

1. The input cell in a one-input data table is the _____.
   a. cell you want to vary
   b. upper-left cell of the data table
   c. cell you want to remain constant
   d. none of the above

2. To assign a macro to a command button, _____ while Excel is in design mode.
   a. click the Macro command on the Tools menu
   b. click the Button Macro command on the Insert menu
   c. double-click the button
   d. right-click the button and then click the Edit command

3. Click the _____ button on the Standard toolbar to assign a hyperlink to a worksheet element.
   a. Insert Hyperlink   b. Insert Object   c. Web Toolbar   d. Command Toolbox

4. A data table is created _____.
   a. on a data sheet   b. on a chart sheet   c. on a macro sheet   d. on a worksheet

5. The interest rate is _____ in the argument for the PMT function when the payments are calculated monthly.
   a. multiplied by 12   b. divided by 12   c. multiplied by 6   d. divided by 6

6. When using natural language formulas in a column, Excel uses the values in the _____ as the formula that corresponds to the row titles.
   a. same column   b. adjacent column   c. same row   d. adjacent row

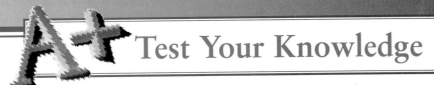

Test Your Knowledge

7. Use the _____ function to determine the future value of an investment.

   a SLN   b. PMT   c. PV   d. FV

8. You can record the actions you perform on a worksheet by pointing to _____ on the Tools menu and then clicking the Macros command.

   a. Visual Basic Editor   b. Macro   c. Customize   d. Record New Macro

9. Use the _____ command to summarize what-if questions.

   a. Goal Seek   b. Table   c. Protect Sheet   d. Visual Basic

10. To set the properties for a button, right-click the button and then click _____ on the button's shortcut menu.

    a. Design Mode   b. Properties   c. Command Button   d. Edit

3 Understanding Macro Functions

Instructions: In the spaces provided, write the Visual Basic statement that completes the specified task.

1. Select the range A1:D3 on the worksheet: _____

2. Clear the selected range: _____

3. Accept a value from the user and assign it to cell A1 on the worksheet: _____

4. Assign the formula =J5 * J6 to cell A2 on the worksheet: _____

5. End the Sub procedure: _____

6. Select cell B16: _____

7. Add the comment *Created by JSQ*: _____

4 Understanding Functions, Data Analysis, and Worksheet Protection

Instructions: Answer the following questions.

1. Write a function to determine the monthly payment (PMT function) on a loan of $225,000 over a period of 30 years, at an annual interest rate of 10.75%. Make sure the function returns the monthly payment as a positive number.

2. Write a function to determine the future value (FV function) of a $575 a month investment for 20 years if the interest rate is fixed at 6.75% and compounded monthly.

3. Explain the difference between a protected cell and an unprotected cell. How do you change the contents of a cell that is protected?

Use Help

1 Reviewing Project Activities

Instructions: Perform the following tasks using a computer.

1. Start Excel. Click the Contents and Index command on the Help menu to display the Help Topics: Microsoft Excel dialog box. Click the Contents tab. Double-click the Creating Formulas and Auditing Workbooks book. Double-click the Working with Labels and Names book. Double-click the topic, About labels and names in formulas. Read and print the information. Click each link (words in green) and read the information. Click the Help Topics button. Double-click the topic, Create a name to represent a formula and constant value link. Read and print the information. Click the Help Topics button and then double-click the topic, Name cells in a workbook. Read and print the information. Hand the printouts in to your instructor. Close the Help window.

2. If the Help Topics: Microsoft Excel dialog box is not on the screen, click the Contents and Index command on the Help menu. Click the Find tab. Type financial in the top text box labled 1 and then double-click Financial functions in the lower list box labled 3. Read and print the information. Click the Help Topics button. Hand the printout in to your instructor.

3. If the Help Topics: Microsoft Excel dialog box is not on the screen, click the Contents and Index command on the Help menu. Click the Index tab. Type Visual in the top text box labeled 1. Under the topic, Visual Basic Editor in the lower list box labeled 3, double-click these topics one at a time: (1) recording macros and (2) running macros. After you double-click the second topic, running macros, double-click each topic in the Topics Found dialog box. Read and print the information. Click any links and read the information. Hand the printout in to your instructor.

4. Close the Help Topics: Microsoft Excel dialog box and then click the Office Assistant button on the Standard toolbar. Obtain information on the How do I create a Scenario Summary report? topic. Read and print the information. Hand the printout in to your instructor.

2 Expanding on the Basics

Instructions: Perform the following tasks using a computer.

1. Start Excel. Click the Contents and Index command on the Help menu to display the Help Topics: Microsoft Excel dialog box. Click the Contents tab. Double-click the Creating Formulas and Auditing Workbooks book. Double-click the topic, Troubleshoot formulas and error values. Read and print the information. Click each link (button) and read the information on the various error messages. Hand the printouts in to your instructor.

2. If the Help Topics: Microsoft Excel dialog box is not on the screen, click the Contents and Index command on the Help menu. Use the Index tab to collect information on the following topics: goal seeking, creating one-input and two-input data tables, and using the Visual Basic Editor to retrieve external data. Hand in one printout on each topic to your instructor. Quit Help.

3. Press ALT+F11 to start the Visual Basic Editor and display the Microsoft Visual Basic window. Click the Contents and Index command on the Help menu. Use the Find tab to collect information on writing Visual Basic statements. Display information on this and related topics. Read and print the information. Hand in three printouts to your instructor.

1 Assigning a Command Macro to a Button and Protecting a Worksheet

Instructions: Start Excel and perform the following tasks.

1. Open the workbook LED Fabrications (Figure 5-63) from the Excel folder on the Data Disk that accompanies this book.

2. Display the Control Toolbox toolbar. Add the button shown in Figure 5-63 to the lower-right corner of the worksheet. Change the button title to Inventory. Set the button properties so the background color, foreground color, and text appear as shown in Figure 5-63. Assign the macro shown in Figure 5-64 to the button. Print the macro. Briefly explain the function of each of the five Visual Basic statements between Sub and End Sub procedures. Close the Microsoft Visual Basic Editor. Click the Exit Design Mode button on the Control Toolbox toolbar. Hide the Control Toolbox toolbar.

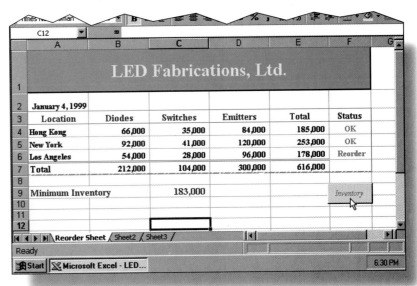

FIGURE 5-63

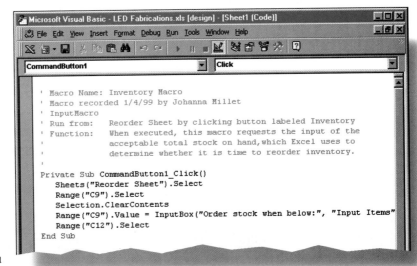

FIGURE 5-64

3. Use the Format Cells command on the shortcut menu to unprotect cell C9. Use the Protection command on the Tools menu to protect the worksheet. Try to enter a value in any cell other than C9. What happens? Write your answer at the bottom of the macro printout.

4. Click the Inventory button and type 200,000 as the entry. The words in the Status column (column F) change based on the value entered. Print the worksheet. Press CTRL+` and print the formulas version of the worksheet. Press CTRL+` to display the values version. Use the button to enter 178,000 and then print the worksheet.

5. Save the worksheet as LED Fabrications 2.

In the Lab

1 Determining the Monthly Mortgage Payment

Problem: You are a work study student for a local bank and have been asked to build a worksheet (Figure 5-65) that determines the monthly payment on a loan. The worksheet must include a one-input data table that shows the monthly payment, total interest, and total cost for a loan for varying years. Because loan officers who are not familiar with Microsoft Excel will use the worksheet, you have decided to create a button and assign it a macro (Figure 5-66) that will guide the loan officers through entering the loan data.

Determining a Monthly Loan Payment		Payments for Varying Interest Rates			
Item	98 Ford Explorer	**Interest**	**Monthly Payment**	**Total Cost**	**Total Interest**
Price	$29,500.00		$531.18	$36,370.57	$6,870.57
Down Payment	$4,500.00	8.50%	512.91	35,274.80	5,774.80
Interest Rate	10.00%	9.00%	518.96	35,637.53	6,137.53
Years	5	9.50%	525.05	36,002.79	6,502.79
		10.00%	531.18	36,370.57	6,870.57
Loan Amount	$25,000.00	10.50%	537.35	36,740.85	7,240.85
Monthly Payment	$531.18	11.00%	543.56	37,113.63	7,613.63
		11.50%	549.82	37,488.91	7,988.91
	New Loan				

Monthly Payment / Sheet2 / Sheet3

Ready

Start Microsoft Excel - 19f...   6:45 PM

FIGURE 5-65

Instructions: With a blank worksheet on the screen, perform the following tasks.

1. Change the font of the worksheet to bold Times New Roman. Change the column widths to the following: A = 13.86; B = 13.00; C = 2.57; D = 7.00; and E, F, and G = 14.43.

2. Enter the Determining a Monthly Loan Payment section of the worksheet in columns A and B. Change the title of the worksheet in cell A1 to 14-point font and center it across columns A and B.

3. Enter the following loan data: Item = 98 Ford Explorer; Price = $29,500; Down Payment = $4,500; Interest Rate = 10.00%; and Years = 5. Format the range B4:B10 as shown in Figure 5-65.

4. Assign cell B9 the following formula using natural language: =Price – Down Payment

5. Assign cell B10 the following PMT function using natural language: =PMT(Interest Rate / 12, 12 * Years, -Loan Amount)

6. Enter the Payments for the Varying Interest Rates section of the worksheet. Assign cell E4 the formula =B10, cell F4 the formula =12 * B7 * B10 + B5, and cell G4 the formula =F4 – B4. Use the fill handle to create the series in the range D5:D11. Create a data table in the range D4:G11 using the Table command on the Data menu. Use cell B6 as the input cell.

7. Save the worksheet using the file name Monthly Loan Payment.

8. Change the text Down Payment in cell A5 to Down Pymt and then click cell B9. Notice that the name also changes in the Formula. Change the text Down Pymt in cell A5 back to Down Payment.

9. Rename the sheet Monthly Payment. Add your name, course, computer laboratory assignment number (Lab 5-1), date, and instructor name in column A beginning in cell A15. Print the worksheet. Press CTRL+` and print the formulas version. Press CTRL+` to display the values version. Click the Save button on the Standard toolbar to save the workbook.

10. Display the Control Toolbox toolbar. If necessary, click the Design Mode button on the Control Toolbox toolbar to place Excel in design mode. Create a button in column B below the Determining a Monthly Loan Payment section, as shown in Figure 5-65. Right-click the button and use the

appropriate commands on the shortcut menu to change the name of the button and format it as shown. Set the PrintObject property to False.

11. Double-click the button and assign it the macro shown in Figure 5-66. Print the macro. Close the Microsoft Visual Basic Editor, click the Exit Design Mode button on the Control Toolbox toolbar, and then hide the Control Toolbox toolbar. Unprotect the range B3:B7. Protect the worksheet. Click the Save button on the Standard toolbar to save the workbook.

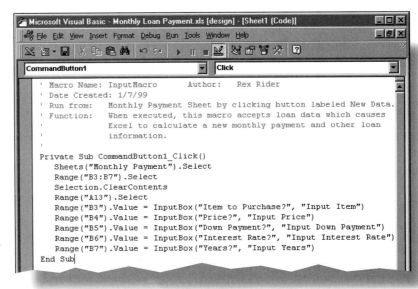

FIGURE 5-66

12. Use the newly created button to determine the monthly payment for the following loan data and print the worksheet for each data set: (a) Item = Office Building; Price = $300,000; Down Payment = $75,000; Interest Rate = 9.50%; and Years = 30; (b) Item = House; Price = $155,500; Down Payment = $30,000; Interest Rate = 10.75%; and Years = 20. The Monthly Payment for (a) is $1,891.92 and for (b) is $1,274.11.

13. Click cell B10 and use the Trace Precedents command and Trace Dependents command on the Audit submenu (Tools menu) to find cells referenced by the formula and cells dependent on the formula.

2 Determining the Future Value of an Investment

Problem: The investment company for which you work is in need of a Future Value worksheet (Figure 5-67 on the next page) that its sales force can use on their computers as they work with customers in the field. Being able to calculate a future value allows the sales force to tell the customer what a constant monthly payment in a fixed interest account will be worth after a certain period of time.

Instructions: With a blank workbook on the screen, perform the following tasks.

1. Bold the entire worksheet. Change the column widths of the entire worksheet to 16.14.
2. Enter the Future Value Computations section of the worksheet (A1:E4), as shown in Figure 5-67. Assign cell B2 the NOW function so it displays the system date and then format the system date so it appears as shown in Figure 5-67. Enter the following data in cells B3, B4, and E2: Monthly Payment (B3) = $200.00; Interest Rate (B4) = 4.75%; and Years (E2) = 15.
3. Assign cell E3 the following formula: =FV(B4 / 12, 12 * E2, -B3)
4. Assign cell E4 the following formula: =12 * E2 * B3

(continued)

In the Lab

Determining the Future Value of an Investment *(continued)*

5. Enter the Varying Interest Rate and Monthly Payment data table. Assign cell A7 the entry =E3. Assign cells B7, C7, D7, and E7 the following monthly payments: $100.00, $150.00, $250.00, and $300.00, respectively. Use the fill handle to create the series 5.00% to 6.75% in the range A8:A15, increasing the values in increments of 0.25%. Create a data table in the range A7:E15 using the Table command from the Data menu. Use cell B3 as the row input cell and cell B4 as the column input cell. Rename the sheet Future Values.

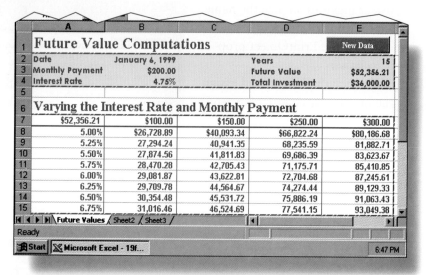

FIGURE 5-67

6. Add your name, course, computer laboratory assignment number (Lab 5-2), date, and instructor name in column A beginning in cell A19. Save the workbook using the file name Future Value. Print the worksheet with the future value data shown

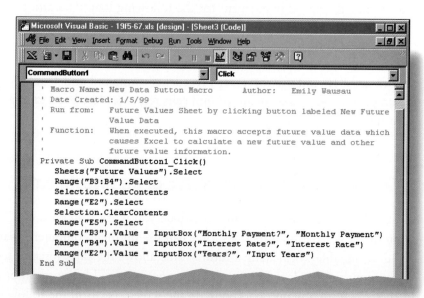

FIGURE 5-68

in Figure 5-67. Press CTRL+` and print the formulas version of the worksheet. Press CTRL+` to display the values version.

7. Display the Control Toolbox toolbar. Create a button in cell E1, as shown in Figure 5-67.

8. If necessary, click the Design Mode button on the Control Toolbox toolbar to place Excel in design mode. Change the name of the button to New Data. Bold the font in the button name. Set the foreground and background colors of the button as shown in Figure 5-67. Set PrintObject to False. Double-click the New Data button. Create the macro shown in Figure 5-68. Click the Exit Design Mode button on the Control Toolbox toolbar. Hide the Control Toolbox toolbar.

In the Lab

9. Unprotect cells B3, B4, and E2, and the range B7:E7. Protect the worksheet. Click the Save button on the Standard toolbar to save the workbook.

10. Use the New Data button in cell E1 (Figure 5-67) to determine the future value for the following data and print the worksheet for each data set: (a) Monthly Payment = $300.00; Interest Rate = 8.00%; Years = 20. Also make the following changes: cell B7 = $400; cell C7 = $500; cell D7 = $600; cell E7 = $700; and (b) Monthly Payment = $25.00; Interest Rate = 7.25%; Years = 10. Also make the following changes: cell B7 = $50; cell C7 = $75; cell D7 = $100; cell E7 = $125. The future value in cell E3 for (a) is $176,706.12 and for (b) is $4,387.17.

3 Building an Amortization Table and Analyzing Data

Problem: Each student in your Office Automation course is assigned a real-world project, which involves working with a local company. For your project, you are working with the TrustUs Loan Company, a subsidiary of SavU Bank. The manager of TrustUs has asked you to create the loan information worksheet in Figure 5-69 and the Scenario Summary worksheet in Figure 5-70 on the next page. He also wants a hyperlink added to the worksheet that displays the SavU Bank 1998 Statement of Condition. Finally, he wants you to demonstrate the goal seeking capabilities of Excel.

Instructions: With a blank worksheet on the screen, perform the following tasks to create the two worksheets.

1. Bold the entire worksheet. Enter the worksheet title in cell A1 and increase its font size to 16. Enter the text in the ranges A2:A4 and D2:D4. Enter $323,000.00 (price) in cell B2, $41,000.00 (down payment) in cell B3, 9.75% (interest rate) in cell E2, and 30 (years) in cell E3 (Figure 5-69). Determine the loan amount in cell B4 by using the formula =B2 – B3. Determine the monthly payment in cell E4 by entering the PMT function =PMT(E2 / 12, 12 * E3, -B4)

2. Increase the widths of columns A through E to 15.00. Center the worksheet title over the range A1:E1. Color the background of the range A2:E4 and add a heavy outline to the range.

(continued)

FIGURE 5-69

TrustUs Loan Company

	A	B	C	D	E
1			**TrustUs Loan Company**		
2	Price	$323,000.00		Rate	9.75%
3	Down Pymt	$41,000.00		Years	30
4	Loan Amount	$282,000.00		Monthly Pymt	$2,422.82
5		Year	Beginning Balance	Ending Balance	Paid On Principal	Interest Paid
6	1	$282,000.00	$280,348.72	$1,651.28	$27,422.50
7	2	280,348.72	278,529.04	1,819.68	$27,254.11
8	3	278,529.04	276,523.80	2,005.24	$27,068.54
9	4	276,523.80	274,314.07	2,209.73	$26,864.05
10	5	...14.07		...25.07	...6 638.74
32	27	95,980.87	75,359.87	20,621.00	$8,452.79
33	28	75,359.87	52,636.00	22,723.87	$6,349.92
34	29	52,636.00	27,594.82	25,041.19	$4,032.60
35	30	27,594.82	-	27,594.82	$1,478.97
36			Subtotal	$282,000.00	$590,213.56
37			Down Pymt		$41,000.00
38			Total Cost		$913,213.56

In the Lab

Building an Amortization Table and Analyzing Data *(continued)*

3. Enter the column titles for the amortization schedule in the range A5:E13. An **amortization schedule** is a tabular report that shows the gradual extinguishment of a loan. Use the fill handle to generate the series of years in the range A6:A35.

4. Assign the formulas and functions to the cells indicated in Table 5-3.

5. Copy cell B7 to the range B8:B35. Copy the range C6:E6 to the range C7:E35. Draw the borders shown in Figure 5-69. Rename the tab Loan Information.

6. Save the workbook using the file name TrustUs Loan Company. Print the worksheet with the loan data and loan information in Figure 5-68. Press CTRL+` and print the formulas version of the worksheet using the Fit to option.

7. Insert the clip art shown in the range C2:C4. The clip art comes from the People category in the Clip Art library. Assign the hyperlink a:\excel\savu bank.htm to the clip art. Display and print the Web page. You must have the Data Disk that accompanies this book in drive A to display the Web page.

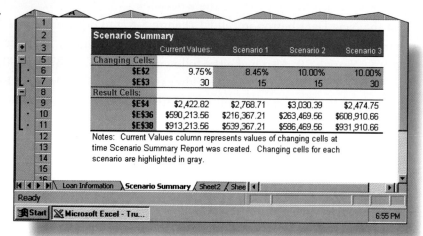

FIGURE 5-70

Table 5-3	
CELL	FORMULA OR FUNCTION
B6	=B4
C6	=IF(A6 <= $E$3, PV($E$2 / 12, 12 * ($E$3 - A6), -$E$4),0)
D6	=B6 - C6
E6	=IF(B6 > 0, 12 * $E$4 - D6, 0)
B7	=C6
D36	=SUM(D6:D35)
E36	=SUM(E6:E35)
E37	=B3
E38	=D36 + E36 + E37

8. Unprotect the ranges B2:B4 and E2:E3. Protect the worksheet. Save the worksheet.

9. Use Excel's goal seeking capabilities to determine the down payment required for the loan data in Figure 5-69 if the monthly payment is set to $2,000.00. The down payment that results for a monthly payment of $2,000.00 is $90,212.97. Print the worksheet with the new monthly payment of $2,000.00. Change the down payment in cell B3 back to $41,000.00.

10. Use Scenario Manager to create a Scenario Summary worksheet (Figure 5-70) for the following scenarios: (1) Interest Rate = 8.45% and Years = 15; (2) Interest rate = 10.00% and Years = 15; and (3) Interest Rate = 10.00% and Years = 30. After the Scenario Summary worksheet displays, move the Scenario Summary tab to the immediate right of the Loan Information. Print the Scenario Summary worksheet. Activate the Loan Information worksheet and save the workbook.

Cases and Places

The difficulty of these case studies varies: ▶ are the least difficult; ▶▶ are more difficult; and ▶▶▶ are the most difficult.

1 ▶ After much research, Jennifer Nelson has decided which computer she wants to buy. She will pay for the computer by making monthly payments over a period of three years. Before she buys the computer, Jennifer wants to know how much she actually will pay for the computer with all the interest. Create a worksheet based on the information provided by Jennifer. The cost of the computer is $2,500; the interest is 11% for 3 years; and her payment is $81.85 a month.

2 ▶ The value of an asset frequently declines over time. When the value falls at a steady rate, the loss is called a **straight-line depreciation (SLN)**. Depreciation is considered a business expense. Straight-line depreciation is based on an asset's initial cost, how long it can be used (called useful life), and the price at which it eventually can be sold (called average value). John Perez, president of San Diego Trucking, recently purchased a new truck. John wants a worksheet that uses a financial function to show the truck's straight-line depreciation (SLN) and a formula to determine the annual rate of depreciation. John has supplied the following information: Cost – $42,395; Salvage – $11,000; Life – 6 years; and Rate of depreciation – SLN / Cost.

John is not sure for how much he will be able to sell the truck. Create a data table that shows straight-line depreciation and rate of depreciation for salvage costs from $7,000 to $16,000, in $1,000 increments.

3 ▶▶ As a graduation present, your parents have decided to help you buy a car. The only stipulation they made was that the payments are no more than $175.00 per month. Develop a two-input data table with varying interest rates (from 8.5% to 12.5% by increments of 0.5%) and costs (from $7,500 to $10,000 by increments of $500). You hope to be able to get a car for about $9,000 with a 10% interest rate on a 6-year loan. Use the cost of the car as the row input cell, the interest rate as the column input cell, and reference the cell with the payment function in the upper-left cell of the data table. Calculate the payment using the Payment (PMT) function. Divide the interest rate by 12 and multiply the years by 12. See In the Lab 2 on page E 5.55 and Microsoft Excel Help for more information on the layout of a two-input data table.

4 ▶▶ You have just landed the job of your dreams and you know that in six months you will be able to qualify for a home loan. You have your eye on a house with a price of $185,000. You have $40,000 for a down payment. The bank is charging 8.75% for a 15-year loan. Determine the monthly payment.

You need to get an idea of what the payment will be based on different interest rates, down payments, and home prices. Create a worksheet and data table to vary the interest rate from 8.5% to 11% in increments of 0.5% and show the resulting monthly payments. Because you also want to be able to use this for other items you intend to purchase, create a button that will prompt you for the item, cost, down payment, interest rate, and the number of years. Use Goal Seek to adjust the down payment to fit your payment ceiling of $725.00.

Cases and Places

5 ▶▶▶ Your parents are disappointed that they were unable to contribute more to your education. Because they don't want the same thing to happen to your little sister, they want to create a future value worksheet based on investing $200 a month at 6% for 10 years. Use the FV function to determine the future value of the investment. Create a two-input data table to determine the future values for investments of $300, $400, $500, and $600 at the following interest rates: 6%, 7.5%, 9%, and 10.5%.

6 ▶▶▶ Some things "hold their value;" that is, they are worth almost as much after five years have passed as they were when brand new. How well does computer equipment hold its value? Using old magazines, find the original selling price of at least one personal computer and two or more peripheral devices (printers, hard disks, video cards, RAM, and so on). Visit a vendor that deals with used computer equipment and find out how much would be paid for each item today.

Develop a worksheet that uses the original price, current value, and number of years that have passed to calculate the straight-line depreciation (SLN) for each item. Add a button that finds the straight-line depreciation of any item based on the item's initial cost, salvage value (value today), and useful life to date. Try to discover what type of computer equipment holds its value best and see if you can guess why.

7 ▶▶▶ For most people, buying a car not only means finding one they like, it also entails finding one they can afford. Many dealerships offer financing plans to prospective buyers. Visit an automobile dealership and pick out your favorite car. Talk to a salesperson about the cost, down payment, amount that must be borrowed, annual loan interest rate, and length of time for which the loan runs. With this information, develop a worksheet to calculate your monthly payment (PMT), total cost, and total interest. Consider a number of cars before making a decision and then assign a button to the worksheet that ascertains the monthly payment for any car based on the car's cost, required down payment, interest rate, and payment periods.

Sorting and Filtering a Worksheet Database, Pivot Tables, and Creating a Data Map

Objectives:

You will have mastered the material in this project when you can:

▶ Create a worksheet database
▶ Use a data form to display records, add records, delete records, and change field values in a worksheet database
▶ Sort a worksheet database on one field or multiple fields
▶ Display automatic subtotals
▶ Use a data form to find records that meet comparison criteria
▶ Filter data to display records that meet comparison criteria
▶ Use the advanced filtering features to display records that meet comparison criteria
▶ Apply database functions to generate information about a worksheet database
▶ Use the VLOOKUP function to look up a value in a table
▶ Create and format a data map
▶ Analyze a worksheet database using a pivot table

Project 6

Cloning Allowed Here

Photocopiers Push Your Buttons

"Can I make a copy of your notes?" you ask a classmate after you have missed class. You trudge to the library and drop coins in the photocopy machine to reproduce the materials. Throughout the world, billions of photocopies are made each day, and businesses spend nearly 10 percent of their revenues on document production.

In 1938, Chester Carlson, a patent attorney and part-time inventor, developed the first photocopy machine. He called the process electrophotography. He spent years trying to sell his invention, without success. Business executives and entrepreneurs did not believe a market existed for a copier when carbon paper worked just fine.

In 1944, Carlson changed the name to xerography, a term derived from the Greek words for "dry" and "writing." He sold his rights to a company that coined the word, Xerox, as the trademark for the new invention. The copier and the words, xerography (to describe the process) and Xerox (to identify the products), were introduced simultaneously in 1948.

Now, 50 years later, when you set your original sheet of paper on the glass, a system of lamps, mirrors, and lenses expose the image on a belt that has a positive electrical charge of static electricity. Wherever the image is projected on the belt, that area remains charged. All other areas are exposed to light and discharge the static electricity. Then magnetic rollers brush the belt with dry ink having a negative charge. Because opposite charges are attracted to each other, the dry ink adheres to the positive image on the belt. Then a sheet of paper moves onto the belt, receives a positive charge, and pulls the dry ink off the roller. Finally, the paper moves between two rollers that apply heat and then fuse the ink into the paper.

Many companies use the xerography process today, and they need various types of belts, rollers, drums, and other parts. The service industry needs an inventory of parts to repair broken copiers or perform preventive maintenance. Tracking these repairs and maintaining an adequate inventory are simplified by keeping records in worksheet databases, which are similar to the Microsoft Excel worksheet database you will create and use in this project.

Danka Business Systems markets, supplies, and services copiers and other office equipment worldwide. When Danka customers call to report a problem, a dispatcher locates the customer records in the database and schedules appointments for office visits.

Technicians are assigned and stock their vehicles with an inventory of parts. They assess the situation and call the dispatcher if they need a part not stocked in their vehicles. The dispatcher records the part request in the customer's database record and prints reports listing these parts. Warehouse staff receive the reports and retrieve the parts from the shelves.

At month end, the worksheet program sorts the records to generate reports detailing how many parts each technician used and how much inventory remains. Supervisors use these reports to monitor the repairs and forecast parts.

By tracking the customers' repairs in a database, Danka hopes to push their buttons and keep the machines reproducing clearly.

Customer Records

	A	B	C	D	E	F	G	H
3	Company	Contact name	address	phone	model	purchase date		
4	ABC Link	John Flint	130 Fern D	714-555-2339	Canon	4/20/95		
5	Chuck's Painting	Amy Johnson	23 Dale Grove	714-555-5544	Minolta	3/12/94		
6	Data Corp.	Jack Tucker	311 Birchwood	714-555-8001	Canon	12/2/96		
7	Data Ltd.	Jim Fears	617 College	714-565-5632	Richo	7/10/95		
8	Data Track	Michelle Nancy	41 Lafayette	714-562-5561	Xerox	7/23/95		
9	Express Form	Kim Lute	476 Fulton	310-312-5689	Canon	8/24/96		
10	Foster & Son	Gene Grace	247 Fuller	310-903-5574	Minolta	1/15/97		
11	Handers	Nancy Fox	201 Plymouth	818-965-1023	Minolta	3/18/97		
12	Lee & Wright	Lyn Christy	912 Devonshire	818-965-4853	Richo	10/30/95		
13	Nex Com	Roy Evans	346 Vernon	909-590-2301	Richo	8/26/96		
14	One Step	Betty Gonzales	216 Four Mile	909-590-4430	Minolta	7/3/94		
15	Service Step	Marilyn Foreman	223 N. Jackson	909-532-7730	Minolta	6/23/96		
16	Sound Co.	Henry Green	3294 E. Devon	818-964-0365	Canon	4/12/94		
17	Trucking 4 U	Jim Hiker	1632 W. Clark	818-964-8236	Xerox	3/26/95		
18	Voice Track	Bill Vaughn	787 N. Monroe	818-965-8530	Xerox	2/20/97		

Photocopier machine parts

	A	B	C	D	E	F	G	H	I	J
3	Part	Vender	Part #	shipping code	stock					
4	Drum roll	can	125-332	44900563	yes					
5	20-Bin Sorter	min	124-356	44900532	yes					
6	40-Bin Sorter	xer	523-965	44905624	yes					
7	fuse rack	ric	510-326	46565502	yes					
8	Data Controller	can	521-263	13235646	yes					
9	Intelligent Commander	min	124-256	54616546	yes					
10	Interface kit	min	124-632	54216545	yes					
11	Memory card	min	124-562	46545165	yes					
12	Plug-In counter	xer	124-560	54313451	yes					
13	Fusing system	ric	510-653	45421543	yes					
14	Lamp	ric	534-063	57545785	yes					
15	Belt	xer	532-056	33263156	yes					
16	Roller	can	562-451	32154321	yes					
17	Drum	can	125-632	32453245	yes					
18	Feeder	can	125-623	35134650	yes					
19	Hold tray	can	125-650	54351504	yes					
20	Sort kit	xer	125-063	54561215	yes					
21	Fuse kit	xer	540-356	57435150	yes					
22	Circuit set	xer	758-250	43215407	yes					
23	Heater	ric	465-023	53432123	yes					

Project 6

Microsoft
Excel 97

Sorting and Filtering a Worksheet Database, Pivot Tables, and Creating a Data Map

Case Perspective

Apothecary is a pharmaceutical company that specializes in vitamin and mineral supplements. Kelsy Young, who is the national sales manager for Apothecary, oversees one dozen sales representatives spread equally between four states: Florida, Texas, Pennsylvania, and Arizona. Kelsy recently purchased a laptop computer and Microsoft Office, which she plans to use to analyze the sales force as she travels between offices.

Kelsy plans to use Excel to create, maintain, and query a worksheet database containing data about the Apothecary sales force. She has learned through Help that a pivot table can be used to obtain different summary views of the data in the database. She also wants to create a data map of the United States that shows the states covered by the sales force and state-by-state quota comparisons between this year's sales quota and last year's sales quota. Kelsy has assigned you the challenge of creating the database, pivot table, and data map. She also wants you to demonstrate how to query the database using Excel's database capabilities and how to use the VLOOKUP function.

Introduction

A **worksheet database**, also called a **database** or **list**, is an organized collection of data. For example, telephone books, grade books, and lists of company employees are databases. In these cases, the data related to a person is called a **record**, and the data items that make up a record are called **fields**. In a database of company employees, each employee would have a separate record; some of the fields in the records might be name, hire date, age, and gender.

A worksheet's row and column structure can be used easily to organize and store a database (Figure 6-1). Each row of a worksheet can be used to store a record and each column to store a field. Additionally, a row of column titles at the top of the worksheet can be used as **field names** that identify each field.

Once you enter a database into a worksheet, you can use Excel to:

1. add and delete records;
2. change the values of fields in records;
3. sort the records so that they appear in a different order;
4. determine subtotals for numeric fields;
5. display records that meet comparison criteria;
6. analyze data using database functions; and
7. summarize information about the database using a pivot table.

This project illustrates all seven of these database capabilities as well as how to create a data map.

Project Six – Apothecary Sales Representative Database

FIGURE 6-1

From your meeting with Kelsy Young, you have determined the following needs, source of data, and graph specifications.

Needs: Create a sales representative database (Figure 6-1). The field names, columns, types of data, and column widths are described in Table 6-1. Because Kelsy will use the database online as she travels between offices, it is important that it be readable and that the database is visible on the screen. Therefore, some of the column widths listed in Table 6-1 are determined from the field names and not the maximum length of the data.

Once the database is entered into the worksheet, it will be sorted and manipulated to illustrate how quickly information can be generated from a database. One way to generate information is to create a pivot table (Figure 6-2 on the next page). A **pivot table** gives you the ability to summarize data in the database and then rotate the table's row and column titles to show different views of the summarized data.

COLUMN TITLES (FIELD NAMES)	COLUMN	TYPE OF DATA	COLUMN WIDTH
Lname	A	Text	8.14
Fname	B	Text	6.71
Hire Date	C	Date	9.00
Age	D	Numeric	5.00
Gender	E	Text	7.00
Educ	F	Text	5.00
Sales Area	G	Text	12.00
St	H	Text	2.71
99 $ Quota	I	Numeric	11.00
98 $ Quota	J	Numeric	11.00

Table 6-1

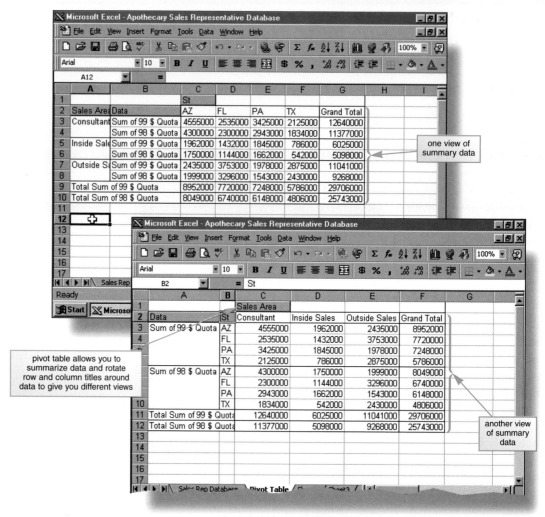

FIGURE 6-2

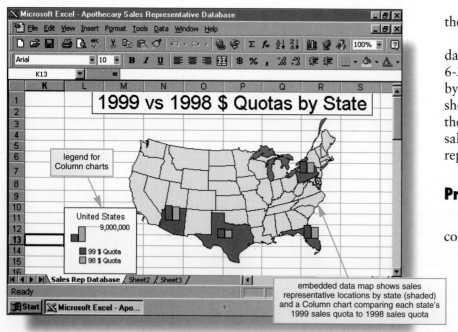

FIGURE 6-3

Source of Data: Kelsy will supply the data required for the database.

Graph Specifications: Create a data map of the United States (Figure 6-3) that shows the states covered by the sales force. The data map also should show comparisons between the 1999 sales quotas and the 1998 sales quotas for each sales representative.

Project Steps

The following tasks will be completed in this project.

1. Start the Excel program.
2. Enter and format the worksheet database title and column titles.
3. Assign the name Database to row 8 and row 9. Save the workbook.

4. Enter the data into the database using a data form.
5. Display sales representative records using a data form.
6. Sort the records in the database.
7. Determine quota subtotals.
8. Use a data form to display records that meet comparison criteria one at a time.
9. Filter the database using the AutoFilter command.
10. Filter the database using the Advanced Filter command.
11. Extract employee records that meet comparison criteria from the database.
12. Apply database functions to the database to generate information.
13. Create and format a data map.
14. Create and manipulate a pivot table.
15. Save and print the workbook.
16. Quit Excel.

The following pages contain a detailed explanation of each of these steps.

Starting Excel

To start Excel, follow the steps below.

TO START EXCEL

Step 1: Click the Start button. Click New Office Document on the Start menu.
Step 2: Double-click the Blank Workbook icon in the New Office Document dialog box.

Creating a Database

There are three steps to creating a database in Excel:

1. set up the database;
2. assign the range containing the database a name; and
3. enter the data into the database.

These steps are similar to what you would do with a more traditional database package, such as Access, Approach, FoxPro, or Paradox. The following pages illustrate these three steps for creating the Apothecary Sales Representative database.

Setting Up a Database

Setting up the database involves entering field names in a row in the worksheet and changing the column widths so the data will fit in the columns. Follow these steps to change the column widths to those specified in Table 6-1 on page E 6.5, change the height of row 7 to 18 points and row 8 to 15 points, and enter and format the database title and column titles (field names).

Although Excel does not require a database title to be entered in cell A7, it is a good practice to include one on the worksheet to show where the database begins. The steps on the next page also changes the name of Sheet1 to Sales Rep Database and saves the workbook using the file name Apothecary Sales Representative Database.

◆ **More** *About* **Databases**

Although Excel is not a true database management system, such as Access, FoxPro, or Paradox, it does give you many of the same capabilities as these dedicated systems. For example, in Excel you can create a database; add, change, and delete data in the database; sort data in the database; query the database; and create forms and reports.

TO SET UP A DATABASE

Step 1: Use the mouse to change the column widths as follows: A = 8.14, B = 6.71, C = 9.00, D = 5.00, E = 7.00, F = 5.00, G = 12.00, H = 2.71, I = 11.00, and J = 11.00.

Step 2: Click cell A7 and enter Apothecary Sales Representative Database as the worksheet database title.

Step 3: With cell A7 active, click the Font Size button on the Formatting toolbar and then click 14 in the Font list. Position the mouse pointer on the lower boundary of row heading 7. When the mouse pointer changes to a split double arrow, drag down until the ScreenTip, Height: 18.00, displays.

Step 4: Enter the column titles in row 8 as shown in Figure 6-4. Change the height of row 8 to 15.00. Select the range A7:J8. Click the Bold button on the Formatting toolbar. Click the Font Color button on the Formatting toolbar and then click red (column 1, row 3) on the Font Color palette.

Step 5: Select the range A8:J8. Right-click the selected range and click Format Cells on the shortcut menu. Click the Border tab. Click the Color arrow in the Line area and then click red (column 1, row 3). Click the heavy border in the Style box (column 2, row 6). Click the Underline button on the left side of the Border area. Click the OK button.

Step 6: Click column heading E to select the entire column. Click the Center button on the Formatting toolbar so that all entries in column E will be centered. Click column heading I and then drag through column heading J to select both columns. Click the Comma Style button on the Formatting toolbar. Click the Decrease Decimal button on the Formatting toolbar twice so that all entries in columns I and J will display using the Comma style with zero decimal places. Click cell A10.

Step 7: Double-click the Sheet1 tab at the bottom of the screen. Type Sales Rep Database as the sheet name. Press the ENTER key.

Step 8: Click the Save button on the Standard toolbar. When the Save As dialog box displays, type Apothecary Sales Representative Database in the File name box. Select 3½ Floppy (A:) in the Save in box and then click the Save button.

The worksheet displays as shown in Figure 6-4.

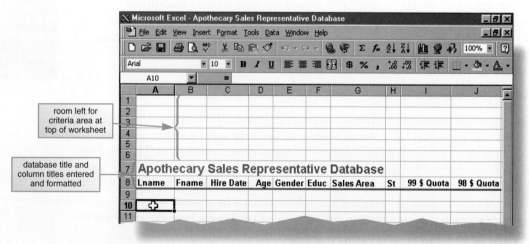

FIGURE 6-4

Naming a Database

Although Excel usually can identify a **database range** when you invoke a database-type command, assigning the name Database to the range eliminates any confusion when commands are entered to manipulate the database. Thus, as you create the Apothecary Sales Representative database shown in Figure 6-1 on page E 6.5, you first assign to the range A8:J9 the name Database by selecting the range and typing Database in the Name Box in the formula bar. The range assigned the name Database includes the column titles (row 8) and one blank row (row 9) below the column titles. The blank row is for expansion of the database. As records are added using a data form, Excel automatically expands the named range Database to include the last record.

TO NAME THE DATABASE

Step 1: Select the range A8:J9. Click the Name Box in the formula bar and type Database as the name for the selected range.
Step 2: Press the ENTER key.

The worksheet displays as shown in Figure 6-5.

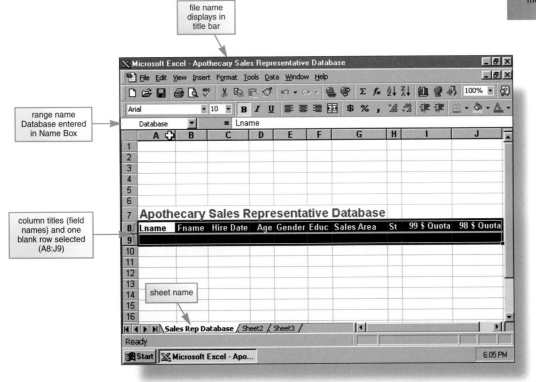

FIGURE 6-5

Using the Name Box in the formula bar to name a range is a useful tool for many spreadsheet operations. For example, if you name a cell or range of cells that you often select, you then can select the cell or range of cells by clicking the name in the Name Box list.

Entering Records into the Database Using a Data Form

After assigning the name Database to rows 8 and 9, a data form is used to enter the sales representative records. A **data form** is an Excel dialog box that lists the field names in the database and provides corresponding boxes in which you enter the field values. The following steps add the sales representative records to the database as shown in Figure 6-1 on page E 6.5.

Steps | To Enter Records into a Database Using a Data Form

1 Click cell A9 to deselect the range A8:J9. Point to Form on the Data menu.

The Data menu displays as shown in Figure 6-6.

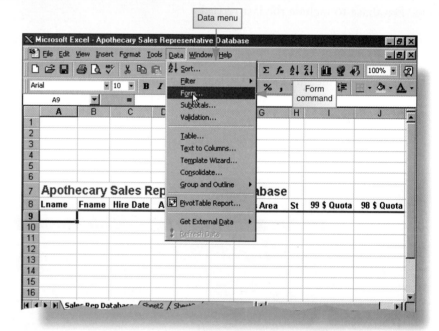

FIGURE 6-6

2 Click Form.

Excel displays the data form (Figure 6-7) with the sheet name Sales Rep Database in the title bar. The data form automatically includes the field names and corresponding boxes for entering the field values. Excel selects the field names in the range A8:J8 because they are at the top of the range named Database.

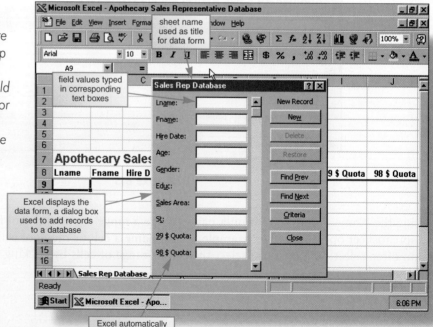

FIGURE 6-7

3 Enter the first sales representative record into the data form as shown in Figure 6-8. Use the mouse or the TAB key to move the insertion point down to the next box . If you make a mistake, use the mouse or SHIFT+TAB keys to move the insertion point to the previous box in the data form to edit the entry.

FIGURE 6-8

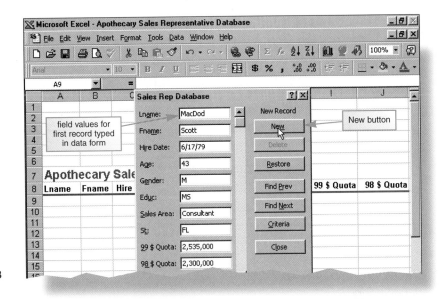

4 Click the New button in the data form. Type the second sales representative record into the data form as shown in Figure 6-9.

Excel adds the first sales representative record to row 9 in the database range on the worksheet. The second record displays on the data form (Figure 6-9).

FIGURE 6-9

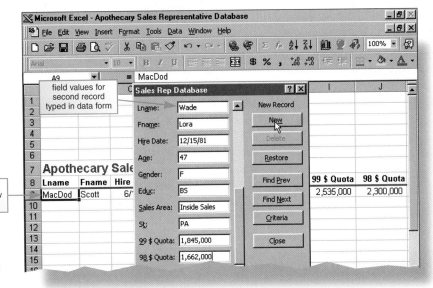

5 Click the New button on the data form to enter the second sales representative record. Use the data form to enter the next nine sales representative records in rows 11 through 19, as shown in Figure 6-1 on page E 6.5. Type the last sales representative record into the data form (row 20 of Figure 6-1).

Excel enters the sales representative records into the database range as shown in Figure 6-10. The last record displays on the data form.

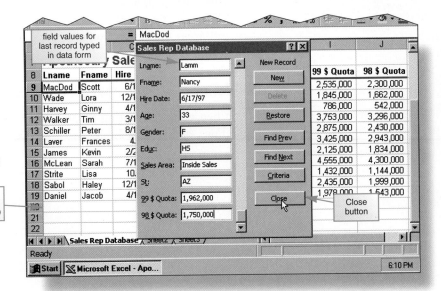

FIGURE 6-10

6 With the last record typed in the data form, click the Close button to complete the record entry. Click the Save button on the Standard toolbar to save the workbook using the file name **Apothecary Sales Representative Database.**

The data form closes and Excel enters the last sales representative record in row 20 of the database. The Apothecary Sales Representative Database displays as shown in Figure 6-11.

all records entered in Apothecary Sales Representative Database

	A	B	C	D	E	F	G	H	I	J
7	**Apothecary Sales Representative Database**									
8	**Lname**	**Fname**	**Hire Date**	**Age**	**Gender**	**Educ**	**Sales Area**	**St**	**99 $ Quota**	**98 $ Quota**
9	MacDod	Scott	6/17/79	43	M	MS	Consultant	FL	2,535,000	2,300,000
10	Wade	Lora	12/15/81	47	F	BS	Inside Sales	PA	1,845,000	1,662,000
11	Harvey	Ginny	4/15/82	38	F	AAS	Inside Sales	TX	786,000	542,000
12	Walker	Tim	3/19/83	39	M	BS	Outside Sales	FL	3,753,000	3,296,000
13	Schiller	Peter	8/12/84	37	M	AAS	Outside Sales	TX	2,875,000	2,430,000
14	Laver	Frances	4/9/85	47	F	BS	Consultant	PA	3,425,000	2,943,000
15	James	Kevin	2/20/87	57	M	MS	Consultant	TX	2,125,000	1,834,000
16	McLean	Sarah	7/15/91	55	F	HS	Consultant	AZ	4,555,000	4,300,000
17	Strite	Lisa	10/2/94	29	F	AAS	Inside Sales	FL	1,432,000	1,144,000
18	Sabol	Haley	12/15/96	39	F	MS	Outside Sales	AZ	2,435,000	1,999,000
19	Daniel	Jacob	4/15/97	32	M	BS	Outside Sales	PA	1,978,000	1,543,000
20	Lamm	Nancy	6/17/97	33	F	HS	Inside Sales	AZ	1,962,000	1,750,000
21										
22										

FIGURE 6-11

You also could create the database by entering the records in columns and rows as you would enter data into any worksheet and then assigning the name Database to the range (A8:J20). The data form was illustrated here because it is considered to be a more accurate and reliable method of data entry, which automatically extends the range of the name Database to include any new records.

Moving From Field to Field on a Data Form

As described in Step 3, you can move from field to field on a data form using the TAB key, or you can hold down the ALT key and press the key that corresponds to the underlined letter in the name of the field to which you want to move. An underlined letter in a field name is called an **access key**. Thus, to select the field titled Fna̲me in Figure 6-10 on the previous page, you would hold down the ALT key and press the M key (ALT+M), because M is the access key for the field name Fna̲me.

Guidelines to Follow When Creating a Database

When you are creating a database in Excel, you should follow some basic guidelines, as listed in Table 6-2.

Using a Data Form to View Records and Change Data

At any time while the worksheet is active, you can use the Form command on the Data menu to display records, add new records, delete records, and change the data in records. When a data form is opened initially, Excel displays the first record in the database. To display the ninth record as shown in Figure 6-12, click the Find Next button until the ninth record displays. Each time you click the **Find Next button,** Excel advances to the next record in the database. If necessary, you can use the **Find Prev button** to go back to a previous record. You also can use the vertical scroll bar in the middle of the data form to move between records.

To change data in a record, you first display it on a data form. Next, you select the fields to change. Finally, you use the DOWN ARROW key or the ENTER key to confirm or enter the field changes. If you change field values on a data form and then select the Find Next button to move to the next record without entering the field changes, these changes will not be made.

To add a new record, click the **New button** on the data form. Excel automatically adds the new record to the bottom of the database and increases the range assigned to the name Database. To delete a record, you first display it on a data form and then click the **Delete button**. Excel automatically moves all records below the deleted record up one row.

Table 6-2

DATABASE SIZE AND WORKBOOK LOCATION

1. Do not enter more than one database per worksheet.

2. Maintain at least one blank row between a database and other worksheet entries.

3. Do not store other worksheet entries in the same rows as your database.

4. Define the name Database as the database range.

5. A database can have a maximum of 256 fields and 65,536 records on a worksheet.

COLUMN TITLES (FIELD NAMES)

1. Place column titles (field names) in the first row of the database.

2. Do not use blank rows or rows with dashes to separate the column titles (field names) from the data.

3. Apply a different format to the column titles and the data. For example, bold the column titles and display the data below the column titles using a regular style. Varying the format between the column titles and data is only necessary if you do not assign the name Database to the database range.

4. Column titles (field names) can be up to 32,767 characters in length.

CONTENTS OF DATABASE

1. Each column should have similar data. For example, employee hire date should be in the same column for all employees.

2. Format the data to improve readability, but do not vary the format in a column.

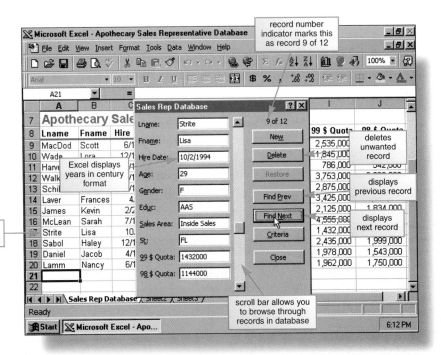

FIGURE 6-12

Printing a Database

To print the database, follow the same procedures you followed in earlier projects. If the worksheet includes data that is not part of the database you want to print, then follow these steps to print only the database.

TO PRINT A DATABASE

Step 1: Click Page Setup on the File menu.
Step 2: Click the Sheet tab in the Page Setup dialog box. Type Database in the Print Area box.
Step 3: Click the OK button.
Step 4: Ready the printer and click the Print button on the Standard toolbar.

Later, if you want to print the entire worksheet, delete the database range from the Print Area box on the Sheet tab in the Page Setup dialog box.

Sorting a Database

The data in a database is easier to work with and more meaningful if the records are arranged sequentially based on one or more fields. Arranging records in a specific sequence is called **sorting**. Data is in **ascending sequence** if it is in order from lowest to highest, earliest to most recent, or alphabetically from A to Z. For example, the records in the Apothecary Sales Representative Database were entered in order from the earliest hire date to the most recent hire date. Thus, the database in Figure 6-13 is sorted in ascending sequence by hire date. Data is in **descending sequence** if it is sorted from highest to lowest, most recent to earliest, or alphabetically from Z to A.

You can sort data by clicking the **Sort Ascending button** or **Sort Descending button** on the Standard toolbar or by clicking the **Sort command** on the Data menu. If you are sorting on a single field (column), use one of the Sort buttons on the Standard toolbar. If you are sorting on multiple fields, use the Sort command on the Data menu. Make sure you select a cell in the field on which to sort before you click the button. The field or fields you select to sort the records are called **sort keys**. The first sort example reorders the records by last name in ascending sequence.

Sorting the Database in Ascending Sequence by Last Name

Follow these steps to sort the records in ascending sequence by last name.

Steps To Sort a Database in Ascending Sequence by Last Name

1 **Click cell A9 and point to the Sort Ascending button on the Standard toolbar (Figure 6-13).**

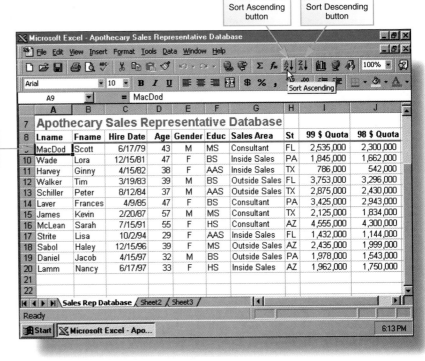

FIGURE 6-13

2 **Click the Sort Ascending button.**

Excel sorts the sales representative database in ascending sequence by last name (Figure 6-14).

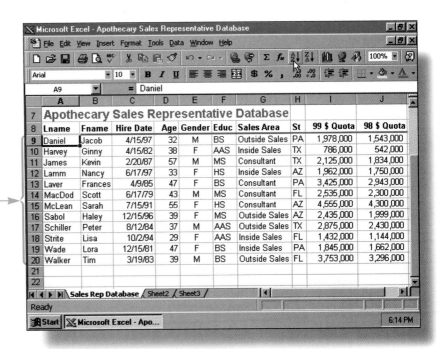

FIGURE 6-14

Other Ways

1. On Data menu click Sort, click field name in Sort By list, click OK button

Sorting a Database in Descending Sequence by Last Name

Follow these steps to sort the records in descending sequence by last name.

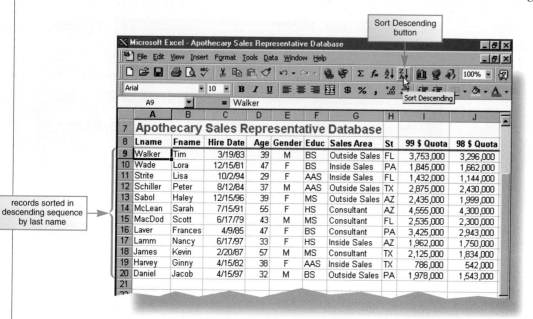

FIGURE 6-15

TO SORT A DATABASE IN DESCENDING SEQUENCE BY LAST NAME

Step 1: If necessary, click cell A9 to make it active.

Step 2: Click the Sort Descending button on the Standard toolbar.

Excel sorts the sales representative database in descending sequence by last name (Figure 6-15).

Returning a Database to its Original Order

Follow these steps to return the records back to their original order in ascending sequence by hire date.

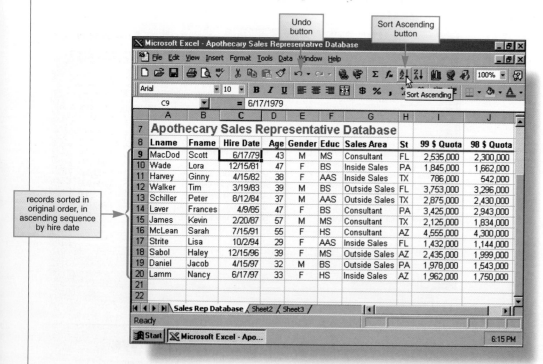

FIGURE 6-16

TO RETURN A DATABASE TO ITS ORIGINAL ORDER

Step 1: Click cell C9.

Step 2: Click the Sort Ascending button on the Standard toolbar.

Excel sorts the sales representative database in ascending sequence by hire date (Figure 6-16). The database displays in its original order.

You also can undo a sort operation by doing one of the following:

1. clicking the Undo button on the Standard toolbar; or
2. clicking the Undo Sort command on the Edit menu.

If you have sorted the database more than once, you can click the Undo button multiple times to undo the previous sorts, or you can click the Undo arrow and select the specific sort you want to undo in the Undo list.

Sorting a Database on Multiple Fields

Excel allows you to sort on a maximum of three fields in a single sort operation. For instance, in the sort example that follows, you will use the Sort command on the Data menu to sort the Apothecary Sales Representative Database by 1999 dollar quotas (column I) within education (column F) within gender (column E). The Gender and Education fields will be sorted in ascending sequence; the 99 $ Quota field will be sorted in descending sequence.

The phrase *sort by 1999 dollar quota within education within gender* means that the records first are arranged in ascending sequence by gender code. Within gender, the records are arranged in ascending sequence by education code. Within education, the records are arranged in descending sequence by the 99 $ Quota field.

In this case, gender is the **major sort key** (Sort By field), education is the **intermediate sort key** (first Then By field), and 99 $ Quota is the **minor sort key** (second Then By field).

More *About* the Database Range

After naming the database range Database, you still can select a subset of the database, such as the last ten records, before completing an activity, such a sort operation, and Excel only will manipulate the data in the selected range.

More *About* Sorting

Some Excel users use the fill handle to create a series in an additional field in the database that is used only to reorder the records into their original sequence.

 Steps To Sort a Database on Multiple Fields

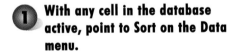

1 **With any cell in the database active, point to Sort on the Data menu.**

The Data menu displays as shown in Figure 6-17.

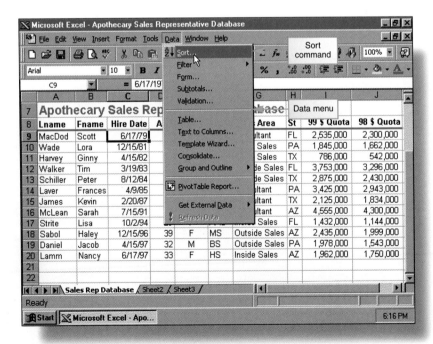

FIGURE 6-17

2 **Click Sort. When the Sort dialog box displays, click the Sort by arrow. Point to Gender in the Sort by list.**

The Sort by list includes the field names in the database (Figure 6-18).

FIGURE 6-18

3 **Click Gender. Click the first Then by arrow and then click Educ. Click the second Then by arrow and then click 99 $ Quota. Click the Descending option button in the second Then by area. Point to the OK button.**

The Sort dialog box displays as shown in Figure 6-19. The database will be sorted by the 1999 dollar quota within education within gender.

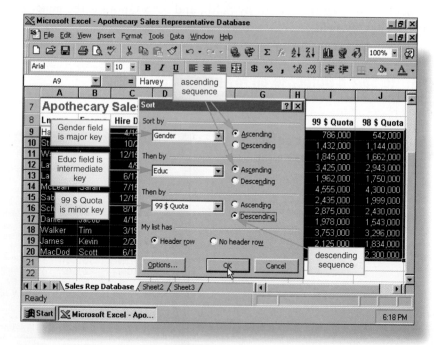

FIGURE 6-19

4 **Click the OK button.**

Excel sorts the sales representative database by the 1999 dollar quota within education within gender as shown in Figure 6-20.

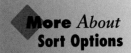

	A	B	C	D	E	F	G	H	I	J
7	**Apothecary Sales Representative Database**									
8	**Lname**	**Fname**	**Hire Date**	**Age**	**Gender**	**Educ**	**Sales Area**	**St**	**99 $ Quota**	**98 $ Quota**
9	Strite	Lisa	10/2/94	29	F	AAS	Inside Sales	FL	1,432,000	1,144,000
10	Harvey	Ginny	4/15/82	38	F	AAS	Inside Sales	TX	786,000	542,000
11	Laver	Frances	4/9/85	47	F	BS	Consultant	PA	3,425,000	2,943,000
12	Wade	Lora	12/15/81	47	F	BS	Inside Sales	PA	1,845,000	1,662,000
13	McLean	Sarah	7/15/91	55	F	HS	Consultant	AZ	4,555,000	4,300,000
14	Lamm	Nancy	6/17/97	33	F	HS	Inside Sales	AZ	1,962,000	1,750,000
15	Sabol	Haley	12/15/96	39	F	MS	Outside Sales	AZ	2,435,000	1,999,000
16	Schiller	Peter	8/12/84	37	M	AAS	Outside Sales	TX	2,875,000	2,430,000
17	Walker	Tim	3/19/83	39	M	BS	Outside Sales	FL	3,753,000	3,296,000
18	Daniel	Jacob	4/15/97	32	M	BS	Outside Sales	PA	1,978,000	1,543,000
19	MacDod	Scott	6/17/79	43	M	MS	Consultant	FL	2,535,000	2,300,000
20	James	Kevin	2/20/87	57	M	MS	Consultant	TX	2,125,000	1,834,000
21										

Callouts: *records are in ascending sequence by gender* — *within each gender, records in ascending sequence by education* — *within each education level, records in descending sequence by 1999 dollar quota*

FIGURE 6-20

As shown in Figure 6-20, Excel sorts the records in ascending sequence by the gender codes (F or M) in column E. Within each gender code, the records are in ascending sequence by the education codes (AAS, BS, HS, MS) in column F. Finally, within the education codes, the records are in descending sequence by the 1999 dollar quotas in column I. Remember, if you make a mistake in a sort operation, you can return the records to their original order by clicking the Undo button on the Standard toolbar.

Because Excel sorts the database using the current order of the records, the previous example could have been completed by sorting on one field at a time using the Sort buttons on the Standard toolbar, beginning with the minor sort key.

Sorting a Database on More than Three Fields

To sort on more than three fields, you must sort the database two or more times. The most recent sort takes precedence. Hence, if you plan to sort on four fields, you sort on the three least important keys first and then sort on the major key. For example, if you want to sort on the fields Lname within Title within St within Gender, you first sort on Lname (second Then By column) within Title (first Then By column) within St (Sort By column). After the first sort operation is complete, you sort on the Gender field by clicking one of the cells in the Gender column and then clicking the Sort Ascending or Sort Descending button on the Standard toolbar.

Displaying Automatic Subtotals in a Database

Displaying **automatic subtotals** is a powerful tool for summarizing data in a database. Excel only requires that you sort the database on the field for which you want subtotals to be based, and then use the **Subtotals command** on the Data menu. When the Subtotal dialog box displays, you select the subtotal function you want to use. The more often used subtotal functions are listed in Table 6-3.

Other Ways

1. Click cell in 99 $ Quota column, click Sort Descending button, click cell in Educ column, click Sort Ascending button, click cell in Gender column, click Sort Ascending button

---

◆ **More *About* Sort Options**

You can sort left to right across rows by clicking the Options button (Figure 6-19 on page E 6.18) and then clicking Sort left to right in the Orientation area. You also can click the Case sensitive check box, which would sort lower case letters ahead of the same capital letters for an ascending sort.

Table 6-3

SUBTOTAL FUNCTIONS	DESCRIPTION
Sum	Sums a column
Count	Counts the number of entries in a column
Average	Determines the average of numbers in a column
Max	Determines the maximum value in a column
Min	Determines the minimum value in a column

The field on which you sort prior to invoking the Subtotals command is called the **control field**. When the control field changes, Excel displays a subtotal for the numeric fields you select in the Subtotal dialog box. For example, if you sort on the St field and request subtotals for the 99 $ Quota and 98 $ Quota fields, then Excel recalculates the subtotal and grand total 99 $ quotas and 98 $ quotas each time the St field changes.

In addition to displaying subtotals, Excel also creates an outline for the database. The following example shows you how to display quota subtotals by state. Because the insertion of subtotals increases the number of rows, the Zoom box on the Standard toolbar is used to display the entire database.

Steps

To Display Subtotals in a Database

① **Select cell H9. Click the Sort Ascending button on the Standard toolbar.**

The Apothecary Sales Representative Database displays in ascending sequence by state as shown in Figure 6-21.

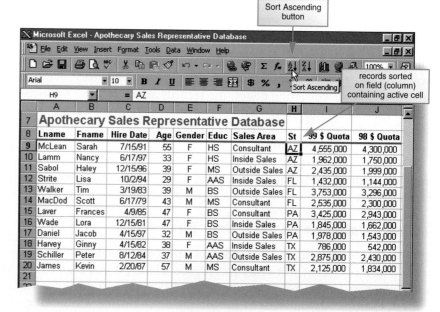

FIGURE 6-21

② **Point to Subtotals on the Data menu.**

The Data menu displays as shown in Figure 6-22.

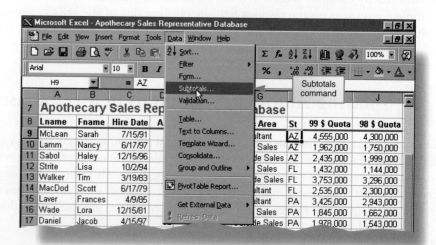

FIGURE 6-22

3 Click Subtotals. When the Subtotal dialog box displays, click the At each change in arrow and click St. If necessary, click Sum in the Use function list. Click the 99 $ Quota and 98 $ Quota check boxes in the Add subtotal to box. Point to the OK button.

The Subtotal dialog box displays as shown in Figure 6-23. The At each change in box contains the St field. The Use function box contains Sum. In the Add subtotal to box, both 99 $ Quota and 98 $ Quota are selected.

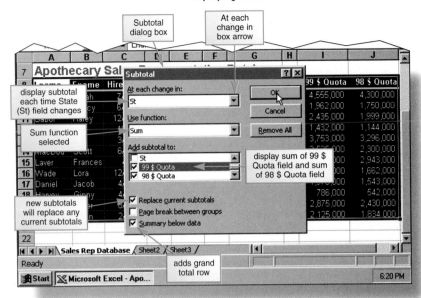

FIGURE 6-23

4 Click the OK button. Double-click the right boundary of column heading H to change the column width to best fit.

Excel inserts five new rows in the Apothecary Sales Representative Database. Four of the new rows contain quota subtotals for each state (Figure 6-24). The fifth row displays a grand total quota. The database also is outlined and thus extends beyond the window.

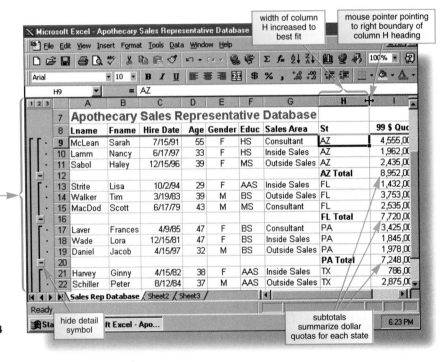

FIGURE 6-24

As shown in Figure 6-24, Excel has added four subtotal rows and one grand total row to the database. The names for each subtotal row are derived from the state names. Thus, in cell H12 of row 12, the text *AZ Total* precedes the actual quota totals for Arizona.

Zooming Out on a Worksheet and Hiding and Showing Detail Data in a Subtotaled Database

The steps on the next page show how to use the Zoom box on the Standard toolbar to reduce the magnification of the worksheet so that all records and fields display. The steps also illustrate how to use the outline features of Excel to display only the total rows.

Steps To Zoom Out on a Worksheet and Hide and Show Detail Data in a Subtotaled Database

1 **Click the Zoom box arrow on the Standard toolbar. Click 75%. If necessary, change widths of columns I and J to best fit.**

Excel reduces the magnification of the worksheet so that all rows and columns in the database, including the subtotals and grand total, display (Figure 6-25).

FIGURE 6-25

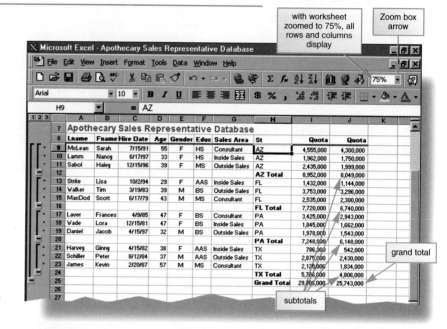

2 **Click the row level 2 symbol next to the Select All button on the left side of the screen.**

Excel hides all detail rows and displays only the subtotal and grand total rows (Figure 6-26).

3 **Click the row level 3 symbol next to the Select All button on the left side of the screen to display hidden detail rows. Click the Zoom box arrow and then click 100% in the list.**

Excel displays the worksheet in normal size (Figure 6-24 on page E 6.21).

FIGURE 6-26

4 **Change the width of column H to 2.71. If necessary, change the widths of columns I and J to 11.00.**

Other Ways

1. On View menu click Zoom
2. Click hide detail symbol or show detail symbol

By utilizing the outlining features of Excel, you quickly can hide and show detail data.

Removing Subtotals From the Database

You can remove subtotals and the accompanying outline from a database in two ways: you can click the Undo button on the Standard toolbar, or you can click the Remove All button in the Subtotal dialog box. The following steps show how to use the Remove All button to remove subtotals from a database.

 Steps **To Remove Subtotals From a Database**

1 Click Subtotals on the Data menu.

Excel selects the database and displays the Subtotal dialog box (Figure 6-27).

2 When the Subtotal dialog box displays, click the Remove All button.

Excel removes all subtotal and total rows and the outline from the database.

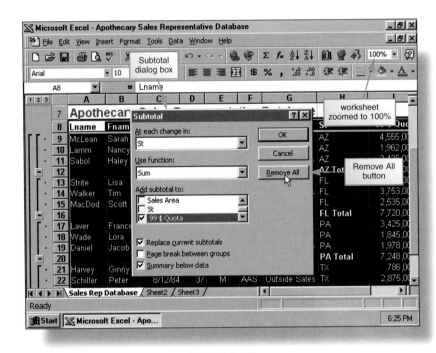

FIGURE 6-27

As shown in the previous sections, Excel makes it easy to add and remove subtotals from a database. You thus can quickly generate the type of information that database users need to help them make decisions about products or company direction.

Before moving on to the next section, complete the following steps to sort the Apothecary Sales Representative Database into its original order in ascending sequence by hire date.

TO SORT THE DATABASE BY HIRE DATE

Step 1: Click cell C9.
Step 2: Click the Sort Ascending button on the Standard toolbar.

The records in the Apothecary Sales Representative Database are sorted in ascending sequence by hire date (Figure 6-16 on page E 6.16).

More *About* **Outlining**

When you hide data using the outline features, you can chart the resulting rows and columns as if they were adjacent to one another. Thus, in Figure 6-26 you can chart the quotas by state as an adjacent range even though they are not in adjacent rows when the worksheet displays in normal form.

More *About*
Finding Records

Excel is not case sensitive. That is, Excel considers uppercase and lowercase characters in the comparison criteria to be the same. For example, =m is the same as =M.

Finding Records Using a Data Form

Once you have created the database, you might want to view only records that meet certain conditions, or comparison criteria. **Comparison criteria** are one or more conditions that include the field names and entries in the corresponding boxes on a data form. For example, you can instruct Excel to find and display only those records that pass the test:

Age >= 38 **AND** Gender = F **AND** Education <> BS **AND** 99 $ Quota < 3,000,000

You use the same relational operators (=, <, >, >=, <=, and <>) to enter comparison criteria on a data form that you used to formulate conditions in IF functions. For a record to display on the data form, it has to pass **ALL** four parts of the test. Finding records that pass a test is useful for viewing specific records, as well as maintaining the database. When a record that passes the test displays on the data form, you can change the field values or delete it from the database.

To find records in the database that pass a test made up of comparison criteria, you can use the Find Prev and Find Next buttons together with the Criteria button on the data form. The following steps illustrate how to use a data form to find records that pass the test described above.

 To Find Records Using a Data Form

1 **Click Form on the Data menu.**

The first record in the Apothecary Sales Representative Database displays on the data form (Figure 6-28).

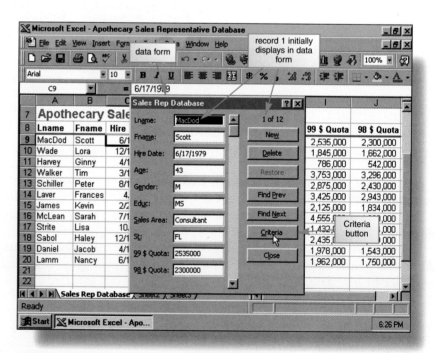

FIGURE 6-28

2 **Click the Criteria button on the data form.**

Excel clears the field values from the data form and displays a data form with blank text boxes.

3 **Enter** >=38 **in the Age box,** =F **in the Gender box,** <>BS **in the Educ box, and** <3,000,000 **in the 99 $ Quota box. Point to the Find Next button.**

The data form displays with the comparison criteria entered as shown in Figure 6-29.

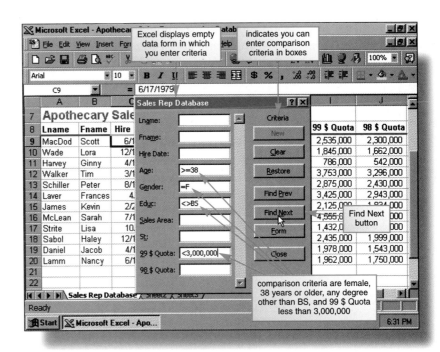

FIGURE 6-29

4 **Click the Find Next button.**

Excel immediately displays the third record in the database because it is the first record that meets the comparison criteria (Figure 6-30). Ms. Ginny Harvey is a 38-year old female with an AAS degree whose 99 $ Quota is $786,000. The first two records in the sales representative database did not meet the comparison criteria.

5 **Use the Find Next and Find Prev buttons to display the other record in the database that passes the test (Ms. Haley Sabol). When you are finished displaying the record, click the Close button on the data form.**

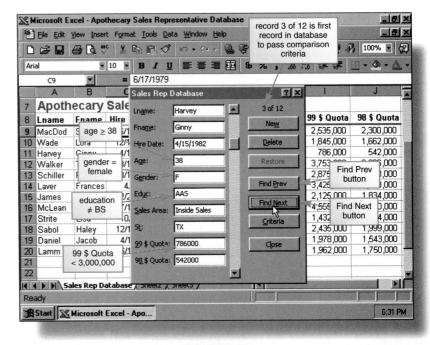

FIGURE 6-30

Two records in the database pass the test: record 3 (Ms. Ginny Harvey) and record 10 (Ms. Haley Sabol). Each time you click the Find Next button, Excel displays the next record that passes the test. You also can use the Find Prev button to display the previous record that passed the test.

In Figure 6-29, no blank characters appear between the relational operators and the values. As you enter comparison criteria, remember that leading or trailing blank characters have a significant impact on text comparisons. For example, there is a big difference between =M and = M.

You also should note that Excel is not **case sensitive**. That is, Excel considers uppercase and lowercase characters in a comparison criterion to be the same. For example, =m is the same as =M.

Using Wildcard Characters in Comparison Criteria

If you are searching on text fields, you can use **wildcard characters** to find records that have certain characters in a field. Excel has two wildcard characters, the question mark (?) and the asterisk (*). The **question mark** represents any single character in the same position as the question mark. For example, if the comparison criteria for Lname (last name) is =Wa?e, then any last name must have the following to pass the test: Wa as the first two characters, any third character, and the letter e as the fourth character. In this database, only Wade (record 2 in row 10) passes the test.

An **asterisk** (*) can be used in a comparison criteria to represent any number of characters in the same position as the asterisk. Ja*, *e, La*m, are examples of valid text entries with the asterisk wildcard character. Ja* means all text that begins with the letters Ja. James (record 7 in row 15) passes the test. The second example, *e, means all text that ends with the letter e. Wade (record 2 in row 10) and Strite (record 10 in row 17) pass the test. The third example, La*m, means all text that begins with the letters La and ends with the letter m. Only Lamm (record 12 in row 20) passes the test.

Using Computed Criteria

Using **computed criteria** involves using a formula in comparison criteria. For example, using the computed criterion > 99 $ Quota / 1000 in the Age field on a data form finds all records whose Age field is greater than the corresponding 99 $ Quota field divided by 1000.

Filtering a Database Using AutoFilter

An alternative to using a data form to find records that meet comparison criteria is to use AutoFilter. Whereas the data form displays only one record at a time, **AutoFilter** displays all records that meet certain criteria as a subset of the database. AutoFilter hides records that do not pass the test, thus displaying only those that pass the test.

To apply AutoFilter to a database, point to Filter on the Data menu and then click AutoFilter on the Filter submenu. Excel responds by adding drop-down arrows directly to the cells containing the field names at the top of the database (row 8). Clicking an arrow displays a list of all the items in the field (column). If you select an item from the list, Excel immediately hides records that do not contain the item. The item you select from the list is called the **filter criterion**. If you then select a filter criterion from a second field, Excel displays a subset of the first subset.

The following steps show how to use AutoFilter to display those records in the Apothecary Sales Representative Database that pass the following test:

Gender = M **AND** Sales Area = Consultant

Steps **To Apply AutoFilter to a Database**

1 Select any cell in the database. Point to Filter on the Data menu and then point to AutoFilter on the Filter submenu (Figure 6-31).

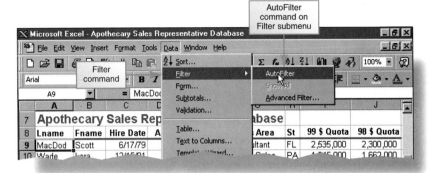

FIGURE 6-31

2 Click AutoFilter.

Drop-down arrows display to the right of each field name in row 8 (Figure 6-32).

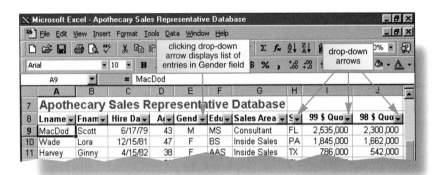

FIGURE 6-32

3 Click the Gender arrow and point to M in the Gender list.

A list of the entries in the Gender field displays (Figure 6-33). The entries (All), (Top 10…), and (Custom…) are found in every AutoFilter list. When you first click AutoFilter on the Filter submenu, the filter criteria for each field in the database is set to All. Thus, all records display.

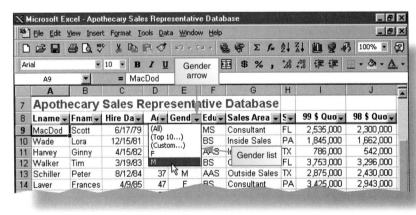

FIGURE 6-33

4 Click M. Click the Sales Area arrow and point to Consultant in the list.

Excel hides all records representing females, so that only records representing males display (Figure 6-34). The Sales Area list displays.

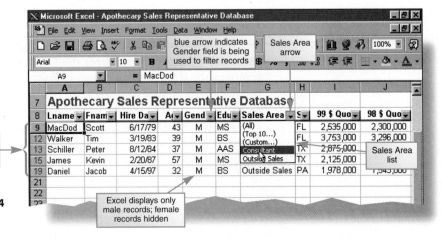

FIGURE 6-34

5 Click Consultant in the Sales Area list.

*Excel hides all records representing males that are not consultants. As shown in Figure 6-35, only two records pass the filter criteria Gender = M **AND** Sales Area = Consultant.*

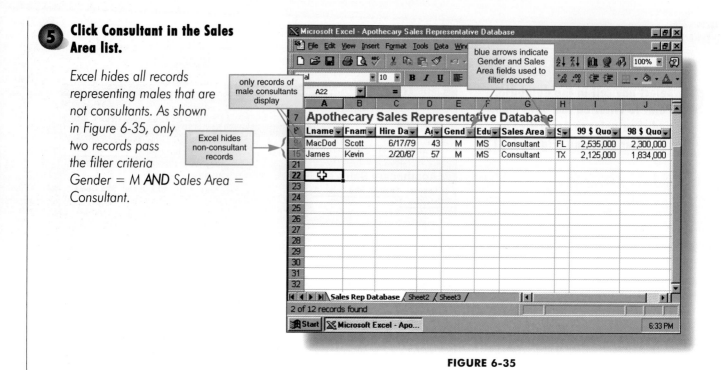

FIGURE 6-35

When you select a second filter criterion, Excel adds it to the first. Hence, in the case of the previous steps, each record must pass two tests to display as part of the final subset of the database. Other important points regarding AutoFilter include the following:

1. When AutoFilter is active, Excel displays the drop-down arrows used to establish the filter and the row headings of the selected records in blue.
2. If you have multiple lists (other columns of data) on the worksheet, be sure to select a cell within the database prior to invoking AutoFilter.
3. If a single cell is selected prior to applying AutoFilter, Excel assigns arrows to all field names in the database. If you select certain field names, Excel assigns arrows only to the selected field names.
4. To remove a filter criteria for a single field, select the All option from the list for that field.
5. If you plan to have Excel determine automatic subtotals for a filtered database, apply AutoFilter first and then apply Subtotals because Excel does not recalculate after selecting the filter criteria.

Removing AutoFilter

AutoFilter is like a toggle switch. That is, if you click it once, Excel adds drop-down arrows to the field names in the database. If you click it again, Excel removes the drop-down arrows from the field names and displays all records in the database. If you want to keep the drop-down arrows but display all the records, click the Show All command on the Filter submenu.

The following steps show how to display all records and remove the drop-down arrows from the field names by clicking AutoFilter on the Filter submenu.

Steps **To Remove AutoFilter**

1 **Select a cell in the database below one of the field names. Point to Filter on the Data menu and then point to AutoFilter on the Filter submenu.**

The Data menu and Filter submenu display as shown in Figure 6-36.

2 **Click AutoFilter.**

All the records in the Apothecary Sales Representative Database display.

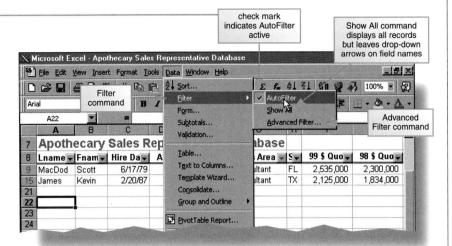

FIGURE 6-36

Entering Custom Criteria with AutoFilter

One of the options available in all of the AutoFilter lists is (Custom...). **(Custom...)** allows you to select custom criteria, such as multiple options or ranges of numbers. The following steps show how to enter custom criteria to display records in the Apothecary Sales Representative Database that represent employees whose ages are in the range 40 to 50 inclusive ($40 \le Age \le 50$).

 To Enter Custom Criteria

1 **Point to Filter on the Data menu and then click AutoFilter on the Filter submenu. Click the Age arrow and then point to (Custom...) in the Age list.**

The Age list displays (Figure 6-37).

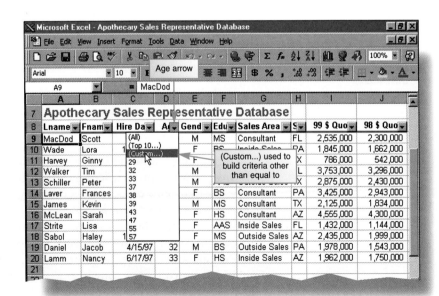

FIGURE 6-37

2 Click (Custom...). When the Custom AutoFilter dialog box displays, click the drop-down arrow in the top left box and then click **is greater than or equal to** in the list. Type 40 in the top right box. Click **is less than or equal to** in the bottom left list. Type 50 in the bottom right box. Point to the OK button.

The Custom AutoFilter dialog box displays as shown in Figure 6-38.

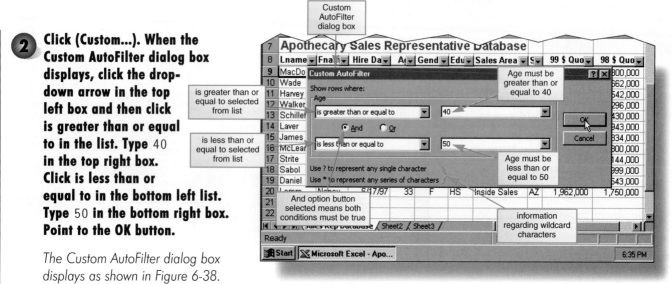

FIGURE 6-38

3 Click the OK button.

The records in the database that represent sales representatives whose ages are between 40 and 50 inclusive display (Figure 6-39). Records that represent employees whose ages are not between 40 and 50 inclusive are hidden.

4 When you are finished viewing the records that meet the custom criteria, point to Filter on the Data menu and then click AutoFilter on the Filter submenu to display all the records in the database.

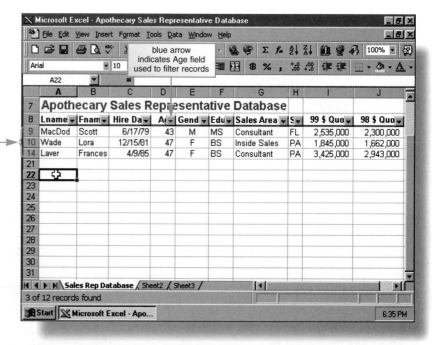

FIGURE 6-39

In Figure 6-38 in the Custom AutoFilter dialog box, you can click the And or Or option button to select the AND or OR operator. The AND operator indicates that both parts of the criteria must be true; the OR operator indicates that only one of the two must be true. Use the AND operator when the custom criteria is continuous over a range of values, such as Age between 40 **AND** 50 inclusive ($40 \leq Age \leq 50$). Use the OR operator when the custom criteria is not continuous, such as Age less than or equal to 40 **OR** greater than or equal to 50 ($40 \geq Age \geq 50$).

As indicated at the bottom of the Custom AutoFilter dialog box in Figure 6-38, you can use wildcard characters to build custom criteria just as you do with data forms.

Using a Criteria Range on the Worksheet

Rather than using a data form or AutoFilter to establish criteria, you can set up a **criteria range** on the worksheet and use it to manipulate records that pass the comparison criteria. Using a criteria range on the worksheet involves two steps:

1. Create the criteria range and name it Criteria.
2. Use the Advanced AutoFilter command on the Filter submenu (Figure 6-36 on page E 6.29).

Creating a Criteria Range on the Worksheet

To set up a criteria range, you first copy the database field names to another area of the worksheet. If possible, copy the field names above the database, in case the database is expanded downward or to the right in the future. Next, you enter the comparison criteria in the row immediately below the field names you just copied to the criteria range. You then use the Name Box in the formula bar to name the criteria range Criteria. The following steps show how to set up a criteria range in the range A2:J3 to find records that pass the test:

Age > 36 **AND** Gender = M **AND** Educ = MS

> ◆ **More** *About*
> **Logical Operators**
>
> AND means each and every one of the comparison criteria must be true. OR means only one of the comparison criteria must be true.

Steps To Set Up a Criteria Range on the Worksheet

1 Select the range A7:J8. Click the Copy button on the Standard toolbar. Select cell A1. Press the ENTER key to copy the contents of the Clipboard to the paste area A1:J2. Change the title in cell A1 to Criteria Area. Enter >36 in cell D3. Enter M in cell E3. Enter MS in cell F3.

The worksheet displays as shown in Figure 6-40.

2 Select the range A2:J3. Click the Name Box in the formula bar and type Criteria as the range name. Press the ENTER key.

Excel assigns the name Criteria to the range A2:J3.

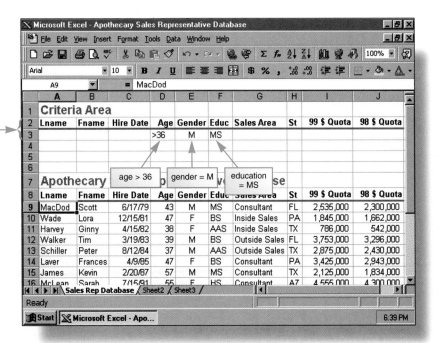

FIGURE 6-40

More *About* **Custom Criteria**

As with comparison criteria in data forms, you can use wildcard characters (?, *) to build the custom criteria as described at the bottom of the Custom AutoFilter dialog box in Figure 6-38 on page E 6.30. If the comparison criteria calls for searching for a question mark (?) or asterisk (*), precede either one with a tilde (~). For example, to search for the text What? enter What~? in the comparison criteria.

As you set up a criteria range, remember the following important points:

1. To ensure the field names in the criteria range are spelled exactly the same as in the database, use the Copy command to copy the database field names to the criteria range as shown in the previous set of steps.
2. The criteria range is independent of the criteria set up on a data form.
3. Unlike a data form, you do not begin a test for equality involving text with an equal sign (= M) because Excel will assume the text (M) is a range name rather than text. Instead, just type the text (M).
4. If you include a blank row in the criteria range (for example, rows 2 and 3 and the blank row 4) all records will pass the test.
5. You can print the criteria range by entering the name Criteria in the Print Area box on the Sheet tab in the Page Setup dialog box, just as you printed the database range (see page E 6.14).

Filtering a Database Using the Advanced Filter Command

The Advanced Filter command is similar to the AutoFilter command, except that it does not filter records based on comparison criteria you select from a list. The Advanced Filter command instead uses the comparison criteria set up in a criteria range (A2:J3) on the worksheet. Follow these steps to apply an Advanced Filter to display the records in the Apothecary Sales Representative Database that pass the test established in Figure 6-40 (Age > 36 **AND** Gender = M **AND** Educ = MS).

 Steps To Apply an Advanced Filter to a Database

① **Click cell A9. Point to Filter on the Data menu and then point to Advanced Filter on the Filter submenu.**

The Data menu and Filter submenu display as shown in Figure 6-41.

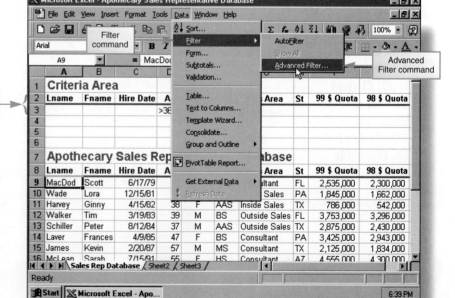

FIGURE 6-41

2 **Click Advanced Filter.**

The Advanced Filter dialog box displays (Figure 6-42). In the Action area, the Filter the list, in-place option button is selected automatically. Excel also automatically selects the database (A8:J20) in the List range box, because the active cell (cell A9) is within the database range. Excel also selects the criteria range (A2:J3) in the Criteria range box, because you assigned the name Criteria to the range A2:J3.

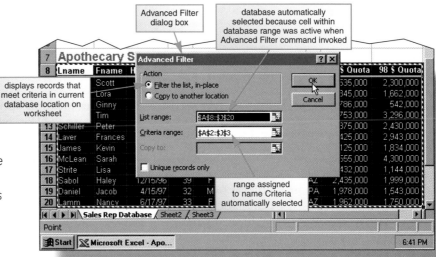

FIGURE 6-42

3 **Click the OK button.**

Excel hides all records that do not meet the comparison criteria, leaving only two records on the worksheet (Figure 6-43). Scott MacDod and Kevin James are the only two sales representatives listed in the sales representative database that are older than 36, male, and have an MS degree.

FIGURE 6-43

Like the AutoFilter command, the Advanced Filter command displays a subset of the database. The primary difference between the two is that the Advanced Filter command allows you to create more complex comparison criteria, because the criteria range can be as many rows long as necessary, allowing for many sets of comparison criteria.

To display all the records in the Apothecary Sales Representative Database, complete the following steps:

TO DISPLAY ALL RECORDS IN THE DATABASE

Step 1: Point to Filter on the Data menu.
Step 2: Click Show All on the Filter submenu.

All the records in the database display.

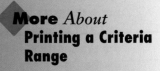

More *About*
Printing a Criteria Range

You can print the criteria range by entering the name Criteria in the Print Area box on the Sheet tab in the Page Setup dialog box.

Extracting Records

If you select the Copy to another location option button in the Action area of the Advanced Filter dialog box (Figure 6-42 on page E 6.33), Excel copies the records that meet the comparison criteria to another part of the worksheet, rather than displaying them as a subset of the database. The location where the records are copied to is called the **extract range**. The extract range is set up much like the criteria range was set up earlier. Once the records that meet the comparison criteria in the criteria range are **extracted** (copied to the extract range), you can manipulate and print them as a group.

Creating an Extract Range

To create an extract range, copy the field names of the database to an area on the worksheet, preferably well below the database range. Next, name this range Extract by using the Name Box in the formula bar. Finally, use the Advanced Filter command to extract the records. The following steps show how to set up an extract range below the Apothecary Sales Representative Database and extract records that meet the following criteria, as entered in the Criteria area (Figure 6-43 on page E 6.33):

Age > 36 **AND** Gender = M **AND** Educ = MS

Steps To Create an Extract Range on the Worksheet and Extract Records

① Select the database title and field names in the range A7:J8. Click the Copy button on the Standard toolbar. Select cell A24. Press the ENTER key to copy the contents of the Clipboard to the paste area A24:J25. Change the title in cell A24 from Apothecary Sales Representative Database to Extract Area. Select the range A25:J25. Type the name Extract in the Name Box in the formula bar and then press the ENTER key. Click cell A20 to make a cell in the database active. Point to Filter on the Data menu and then point to Advanced Filter on the Filter submenu.

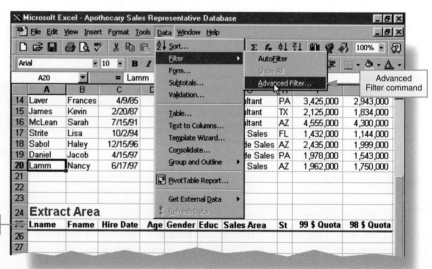

FIGURE 6-44

The worksheet displays as shown in Figure 6-44. The name Extract is assigned only to the field names in row 25. When the records are extracted, Excel automatically will copy the records to the rows below the range named Extract.

2 **Click Advanced Filter on the Filter submenu. When the Advanced Filter dialog box displays, select the Copy to another location option button in the Action area. Point to the OK button.**

The Advanced Filter dialog box displays (Figure 6-45). Excel automatically assigns the range A8:J20 to the List range box because the active cell (A20) is within the range of the database. Excel also automatically assigns the range named Criteria (A2:J3) to the Criteria range box and the range named Extract (A25:J25) to the Copy to box.

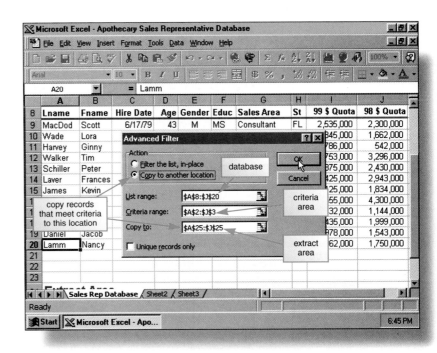

FIGURE 6-45

3 **Click the OK button.**

Excel copies any records that meet the comparison criteria in the criteria range (see Figure 6-43) from the Apothecary Sales Representative Database to the extract range (Figure 6-46).

FIGURE 6-46

When you set up the extract range, you do not have to copy all of the field names in the database to the proposed extract range. Instead, you can copy only those field names you want and they can be in any order. You also can type the field names rather than copy them, although this method is not recommended.

When you invoke the Advanced Filter command and select the Copy to another location option button, Excel clears all the cells below the field names in the extract range. Hence, if you change the comparison criteria in the criteria range and invoke the Extract command a second time, Excel clears the previously extracted records before it copies a new set of records that pass the new test.

In the previous example, the extract range was defined as a single row containing the field names (A25:J25). When you define the extract range as just one row, any number of records can be extracted from the database; Excel will expand the extract range to include all rows below the first row (row 25) to the bottom of the worksheet, if needed. The alternative is to define an extract range with a fixed number of rows. If you define a fixed-size extract range, however, and if more records are extracted than there are rows available, Excel displays a dialog box with a diagnostic message indicating the extract range is full.

More About Comparison Criteria

The way you set up the comparison criteria in the criteria range determines the records that will pass the test when you use the Filter command. The following describes examples of different comparison criteria.

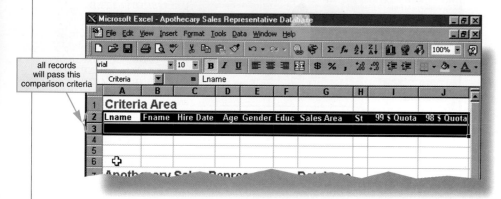

FIGURE 6-47

FIGURE 6-48

A Blank Row in the Criteria Range

If the criteria range contains a blank row, it means that no comparison criteria have been defined. All records in the database thus pass the test. For example, the blank row in the criteria range in Figure 6-47 means all records will pass the test.

Using Multiple Comparison Criteria with the Same Field

If the criteria range contains two or more entries under the same field name, then records that pass either comparison criterion pass the test. For example, based on the criteria range in Figure 6-48, all records that represent sales representatives that have an HS degree **OR** an MS degree will pass the test.

If an **AND** operator applies to the same field name (Age > 50 **AND** Age < 55) then you must duplicate the field name (Age) in the criteria range. That is, add the field name Age to the right of 98 $ Quota (cell K2), delete the name Criteria by using the Name command on the Insert menu, and then redefine the name Criteria to include the second Age field using the Name Box in the formula bar.

Comparison Criteria in Different Rows and Under Different Fields

When the comparison criteria under different field names are in the same row, then records pass the test only if they pass all the comparison criteria. If the comparison criteria for the field names are in different rows, then the records must pass only one of the tests. For example, in the criteria range in Figure 6-49, all records that represent sales representatives who are greater than 50 years old **OR** have a 99 $ Quota greater than $2,000,000 pass the test.

More *About* the Criteria Area

When you add items in multiple rows to a Criteria area, you must redefine the range of the name Criteria before you use it. To redefine the name Criteria, delete the name using the Create command on the Name submenu. The Name command is on the Insert menu. The Define Name dialog box allows you to delete names using the Delete button. Next, select the new Criteria area and name it Criteria using the Name Box.

Using Database Functions

Excel has 13 database functions that you can use to evaluate numeric data in a database. One of the functions is called the DAVERAGE function. As the name implies, you use the DAVERAGE function to find the average of numbers in a database field that pass a test. This function serves as an alternative to finding an average using the Subtotals command on the Data menu. The general form of the DAVERAGE function is:

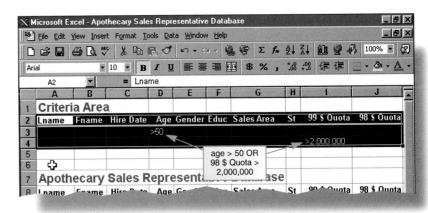

FIGURE 6-49

=DAVERAGE(database, "field name", criteria range)

where database is the name of the database, field name is the name of the field in the database, and criteria range is the comparison criteria or test to pass.

In the following steps the DAVERAGE function is used to find the average age of the female sales representatives and the average age of the male sales representatives in the database.

TO USE THE DAVERAGE DATABASE FUNCTION

Step 1: Click cell A40 and enter Gender as the field name. Enter the same field name in cell B40. Enter F in cell A41 as the code for females. Enter M in cell B41 as the code for males.

Step 2: Enter Average Female Age =====> in cell A43. Enter Average Male Age =======> in cell A44.

Step 3: Click cell D43. Enter the database function =daverage(database, "Age", A40:A41) in cell D43.

Step 4: Click cell D44. Enter the database function =daverage(database, "Age", B40:B41) in cell D44.

Excel computes and displays the average age of the females in the sales representative database (41.14) in cell D43 and the average age of the males in the sales representative database (41.6) in cell D44 (Figure 6-50).

In Figure 6-50, the first value in the function, database, references the sales representative database defined earlier in this project (A8:J20). The second value, "Age", identifies the field on which to compute the average. Excel requires that you surround the field name with quotation marks unless the field has been assigned a name through the Name Box in the formula bar. The third value, B40:B41, defines the criteria range for the male average.

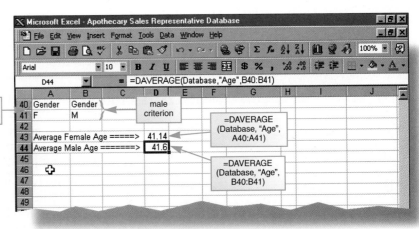

FIGURE 6-50

Other database functions that are similar to the functions described in previous projects include the DCOUNT, DMAX, DMIN, and DSUM functions. For a complete list of the database functions, click the Paste Function button on the Standard toolbar. When the Paste Function dialog box displays, select Database in the Function category list. The database functions display in the Function name box.

Using Excel's Lookup Functions

The HLOOKUP and VLOOKUP functions are useful for looking up values in tables, such as tax tables, discount tables, parts tables, and grade scale tables. Both functions look up a value in a table and return a corresponding value from the table to the cell assigned the function. The HLOOKUP function is used when the table direction is horizontal or across the worksheet. The VLOOKUP function is used when a table direction is vertical or down the worksheet. The VLOOKUP function is by far the most often used, because most tables are vertical. Therefore, the VLOOKUP function will be illustrated in this section.

Assume Kelsy Young, national sales manager for Apothecary, wants to grade the sales representatives on the percent of the 1999 dollar quota met thus far by state. The percent of the 1999 dollar quota met thus far by state is shown in Table 6-4. Kelsy uses the grading scale shown in Table 6-5. Using the information from these two tables, the states would grade out as follows: AZ = F; FL = A; PA = C; and TX = B.

The VLOOKUP function searches the leftmost column of a table (called the **table arguments**) for a particular value (called the **search argument**) and then returns the value from the specified column (called the **table values**). In this example, the table values are the grades. The general form of the VLOOKUP function is:

=VLOOKUP(search argument, table range, column number)

In this example, the VLOOKUP function will use the total state percent of 1999 dollar quota met (the search argument) in Table 6-4 and look up the grade in Table 6-5. For the VLOOKUP function to work correctly, the table arguments must be in ascending sequence, because the VLOOKUP function will return a table value based on the search argument being less than or equal to the table arguments. Thus, if the percent of sales quota met is 77%, then the VLOOKUP function returns a grade of C because 77% is greater than or equal to 75% and less than 85%, which is the minimum percent for a grade of B.

The following steps show how to enter the two tables of information shown in Tables 6-4 and 6-5 and use the VLOOKUP function to determine the letter grades for the states.

Table 6-4

STATE	% OF 99 $ QUOTA MET
AZ	62
FL	95
PA	76
TX	85

Table 6-5

QUOTA SCORE	GRADE
Below 65	F
65 and below 75	D
75 and below 85	C
85 and below 93	B
93 and above	A

TO CREATE A LOOKUP TABLE AND USE THE VLOOKUP FUNCTION

Step 1: Click cell A50 and enter State as the column title. Enter % of 99 $ Quota in cell B50, and Grade in cell C50. Press ALT+ENTER after 99 in cell B50.

Step 2: Enter AZ in cell A51, 62 in cell B51, FL in cell A52, 95 in cell B52, PA in cell A53, 76 in cell B53, TX in cell A54, and 85 in cell B54.

Step 3: Enter Quota Score in cell E50 and Grade in cell F50. Press ALT+ENTER after Quota in the cell E50.

Step 4: Enter 0 in cell E51, F in cell F51, 65 in cell E52, D in cell F52, 75 in cell E53, C in cell F53, 85 in cell E54, B in cell F54, 93 in cell E55, and A in cell F55.

Step 5: Enter =VLOOKUP(B51, $E$51:$F$55,2) in cell C51. Use the fill handle to copy the function to the range C52:C54.

The VLOOKUP function returns the grades shown in column C from the table of grades in columns E and F for the corresponding scores in column B (Figure 6-51).

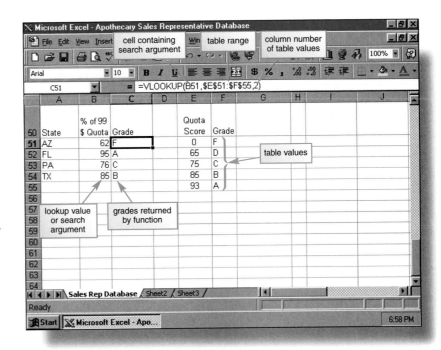

FIGURE 6-51

As shown in Figure 6-51, any percent met below 65 returns a grade of F. Thus, AZ receives a grade of F because its percent of the 1999 dollar quota met is 62%. A percent of 65 is required to move up to the next letter grade. FL receives a grade of A because its percent of the 99 dollar quota met is 95%. Any percent of 93 or greater returns a letter grade of A.

From the example in Figure 6-51, you can see that the VLOOKUP function is not searching for a table argument that matches the search argument exactly. The VLOOKUP function begins the search at the top of the table and works downward. As soon as it finds the first table argument greater than the search argument, it returns the previous table value. For example, when it searches the table with the AZ score of 62%, it determines the score is less than 65% in the first column in the table and returns the grade of F from the second column in the table, which actually corresponds to 0 in the table. Thus, the letter grade of F is returned for any value greater than or equal to 0 (zero) and less than 65. A score less than 0 (zero) would return an error message (#N/A) to the cell assigned the VLOOKUP function.

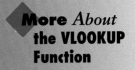

More *About* **the VLOOKUP Function**

A score less than the least table argument (zero in Figure 6-51) will return an error message (#N/A) to the cell assigned the VLOOKUP function.

Creating a Data Map

Microsoft Excel includes a mapping feature, called **Microsoft Map,** which you can use to see the relationships between numbers and geographic regions. With a few clicks of the mouse, you can embed a **data map** of any location in the world in the worksheet and then format it. For example, you can add labels, text, and pins to a data map to display and analyze the sales representative quotas by state. Figure 6-52 on the next page shows the data map required for this project. It is a data map of the 48 contiguous United States. The four states where Apothecary has offices are highlighted in gray. The Column chart on top of each of the four states compares the 1999 $ Quota to the 1998 $ Quota.

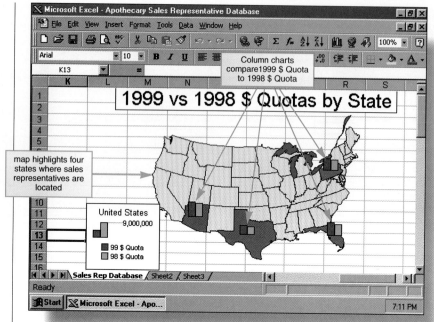

FIGURE 6-52

To use the mapping feature of Excel, you select a range of cells on your worksheet that includes geographic data, such as countries or states, and then click the **Map button** on the Standard toolbar. When the mouse pointer changes to a cross hair, drag it to an open area on your worksheet to define the data map location and size.

The data you plan to use to create a data map must be in columnar form with the names or abbreviations of the states (or countries) in the leftmost column. For example, the data shown in Table 6-6 could be used to create a data map. Before clicking the Map button, you would select the entire range of data, including the column titles Country and Employees.

Excel determines which countries to include on the map based on the data in the first column in Table 6-6. The data in the second column then can be used to format the map to emphasize the numbers and their corresponding countries.

Table 6-6	
COUNTRY	EMPLOYEES
Albania	100
Greece	600
Italy	1,200
Poland	2,700

Creating the Data Map

Follow the steps below to create a data map in the range L1:S17 using the three rightmost columns (H8:J20) of the Apothecary Sales Representative Database.

 Steps To Create a Data Map

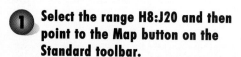

Select the range H8:J20 and then point to the Map button on the Standard toolbar.

Excel highlights the selected range (Figure 6-53).

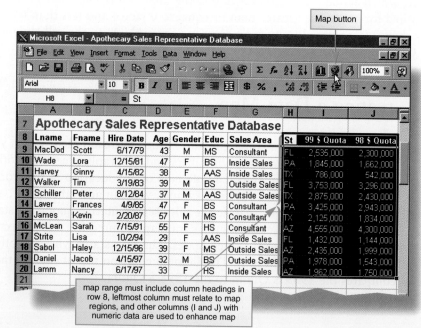

FIGURE 6-53

2 Click the Map button. Use the scroll bars to display cell L1. Point to the upper-left corner of cell L1. Drag to the lower-right corner of cell S17 and hold.

The map location L1:S17 is surrounded by a thin border (Figure 6-54).

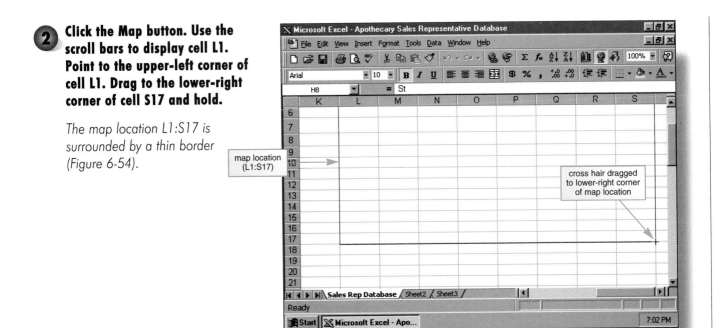

FIGURE 6-54

3 Release the left mouse button.

Microsoft Map's menu and toolbar display at the top of the screen in place of Excel's menu and toolbars. A thick gray border surrounds the map location indicating it is active, and the **Multiple Maps Available** *dialog box displays (Figure 6-55).*

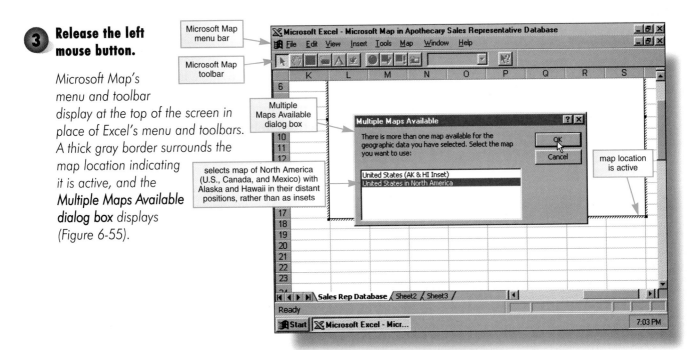

FIGURE 6-55

4 **Select United States in North America and then click the OK button.**

*Microsoft Map draws a map of North America and displays the **Microsoft Map Control dialog box** (Figure 6-56). The four states with sales representatives (Arizona, Texas, Pennsylvania, and Florida) display in varying shades.*

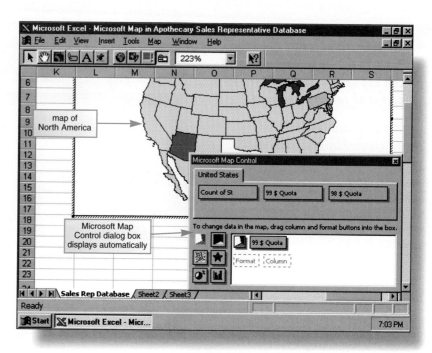

FIGURE 6-56

OtherWays

1. On Insert menu click Map

The basic data map is complete. The data map soon will be formatted so that it appears as shown in Figure 6-52 on page E 6.40. When the data map is active (the gray border indicates it is active) the menu and toolbar at the top of the screen can be used to manipulate the data map. The functions of the buttons on the **Microsoft Map toolbar** are described in Figure 6-57. When you first create a data map, two of the buttons on the toolbar are recessed (active) — Select Objects and Show/Hide Microsoft Map Control.

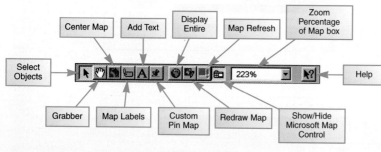

FIGURE 6-57

When the **Select Objects button** is recessed, you can select items within the data map location, such as legends and the data map title, and move and format them. When the **Show/Hide Microsoft Map Control button** is recessed, the Microsoft Map Control dialog box displays, which allows you to format the data map. The **Grabber button** allows you to grab the data map and move it. This button is especially useful when the data map is zoomed out and you want to see hidden parts.

Changing, Deleting, and Formatting a Data Map

When the data map is **selected** (click data map), a set of handles surrounds the data map and you can resize it, move it, or delete it. When the data map is **active** (double-click data map), a heavy gray border surrounds the data map and you can change its features and format it.

More *About* **Drawing the Data Map Location**

Holding down the ALT key while you drag to define the data map location instructs Excel to snap the data map location to the nearest gridline on the worksheet.

Changing the Map's Features

The Features command on the shortcut menu allows you to add or delete countries from the active data map. For example, Canada or Mexico can be removed from the data map, because Apothecary's sales are limited to the United States. The following steps show you how to change the features of a data map.

Steps **To Change the Features of a Data Map**

1 **Right-click the data map and then point to Features.**

The shortcut menu displays as shown in Figure 6-58.

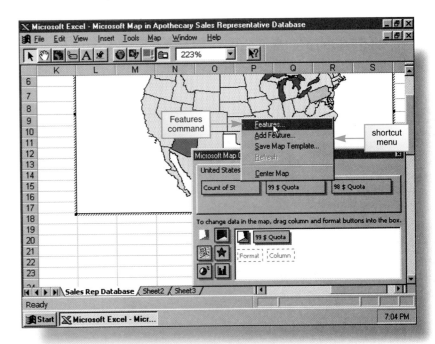

FIGURE 6-58

2 **Click Features. When the Map Features dialog box displays, click Canada, Canada Lakes, and Mexico to remove the corresponding check marks from the Visible box.**

The Map Features dialog box displays as shown in Figure 6-59.

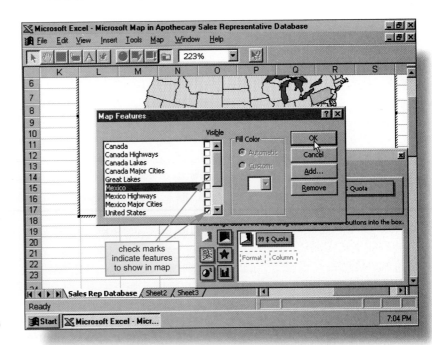

FIGURE 6-59

3 **Click the OK button.**

The data map displays without Mexico, Canada, and Canada Lakes (Figure 6-60). Only the continental United States and the Great Lakes display.

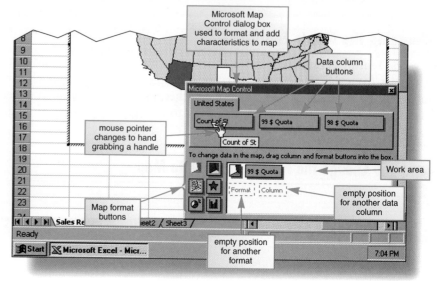

FIGURE 6-60

OtherWays

1. On Map menu click Features, click categories to remove, click OK button

2. Right-click data map, click Features, click map feature in Visible box on Map Features dialog box, click Remove button, click OK button

Formatting a Data Map and Adding Column charts

The Microsoft Map Control dialog box that displays when the data map first is created is used to format the map and add charts. The Microsoft Map Control dialog box is divided into three areas: the Data column buttons area, the Map format buttons area, and the Work area. The **Data column buttons area** includes a button for each column heading at the top of the range (H8:J20) used to create the data map. The **Map format buttons area** includes six format buttons as described in Table 6-7. The **Work area** in the Microsoft Map Control dialog box is where you drag buttons from the other two areas to format the data map.

Table 6-7		
MAP FORMAT BUTTON	*BUTTON NAME*	*FUNCTION*
	Value Shading	Shades each category (state) on the data map according to the value in the corresponding data column. This button is the default. Figure 6-60 shows this button in the Work area; the result is the four states in different shades.
	Category Shading	Shades each category (state) on the data map a different color than an adjacent category (state).
	Dot Density	Displays dots within the boundaries of each category (state) on the data map. The dot density is based on the values in one column of data in the data map range.
	Graduated Symbols	Displays graduated symbols, such as varying size circles at the center of each category (state) on the data map. The size of each symbol is based on the values in one of the columns of data in the data map range.
	Pie Chart	Displays a Pie chart for each category (state) on the data map. The slices in the Pie chart are dependent on the values of the selected column of data.
	Column Chart	Displays a Column chart for each category (state) on the data map. The number of columns in the chart is dependent on the number of columns selected. The heights of the columns are dependent on the magnitude of the data for each different category (state).

As shown in Figure 6-52 on page E 6.40, the data map for this project calls for the same shading for each of the four states with sales representatives (AZ, TX, PA, and FL). By default, Microsoft Map activates the **Value Shading button** in the Work area and shades the states based on the first numeric column in the data map range, column I (99 $ Quota). To shade the four states the same, drag the Count of St button on top of the 99 $ Quota button in the Work area of the Microsoft Map Control dialog box. When you drag one button on top of another in the Work area, the dragged button replaces the current button. To add the Column charts, drag the **Column Chart button** and then the 99 $ Quota button and the 98 $ Quota button onto the Work area. The following steps describe how to format the data map.

Steps **To Format the Data Map**

More *About*
Data Map Features

There are additional characteristics you can add to a data map, such as major highways, cities, airports, lakes, or a combination of these. Right-click the data map, then click Add Feature on the shortcut menu.

1 **Point to the Count of St button in the Data column buttons area of the Microsoft Map Control dialog box.**

The mouse pointer changes to a hand grabbing a handle.

2 **Drag the Count of St button on top of the 99 $ Quota button in the Work area. Point to the Column Chart button in the Map format buttons area.**

Microsoft Map shades the four states the same (Figure 6-61).

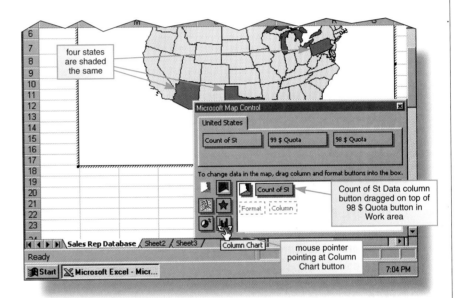

FIGURE 6-61

3 **Drag the Column Chart button onto the word Format in the Work area. One by one, drag the 99 $ Quota button and the 98 $ Quota button from the Data column buttons area onto the word Column in the Work area.**

The Work area on the Microsoft Map Control dialog box displays as shown in Figure 6-62. Each of the four states with sales representatives are assigned a Column chart on the data map. The leftmost column represents the total 99 $ Quota for a given state. The rightmost column represents the total 98 $ Quota.

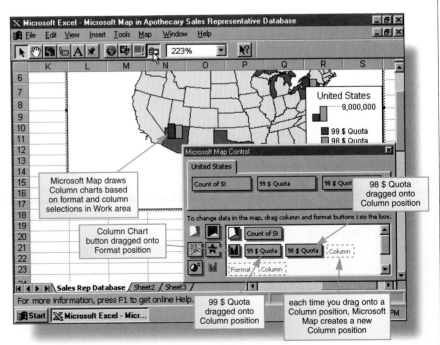

FIGURE 6-62

4 Click the Show/Hide Microsoft Map Control button on the toolbar. Click the Shade legend in the lower-right corner of the data map location.

The Microsoft Map Control dialog box closes. The data map displays with two legends in the lower-right corner of the data map location. The **Shade legend** *defines the shading; the* **Column chart legend** *defines the Column charts. The Shade legend is selected (Figure 6-63).*

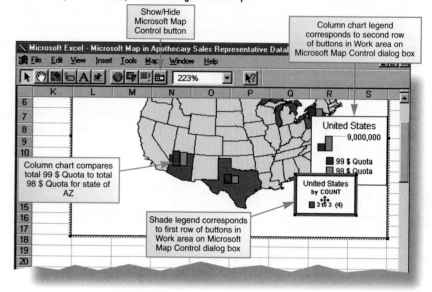

FIGURE 6-63

5 Press the DELETE key to delete the Shade legend. Drag the Column chart legend to the lower-left corner of the data map location and then resize it as shown in Figure 6-64. Scroll up so cell L1 displays. Point to the immediate left of the letter N in the map title North America and double-click. Enter the title shown in Figure 6-64. Resize and center the new data map title. Click cell K13 to deactivate the data map. Click the Save button on the Standard toolbar.

The data map is complete.

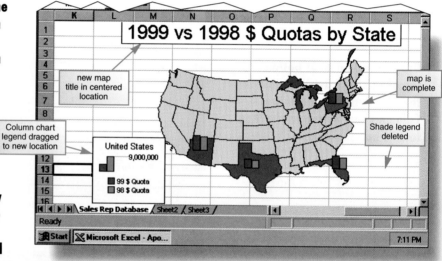

FIGURE 6-64

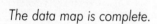
As you can see from Figure 6-64, you can create sophisticated data maps with just a few clicks of the mouse button.

Creating a Pivot Table to Analyze Data

A **pivot table** gives you the ability to summarize data in the database and then rotate the table's row and column titles to obtain different views of the summarized data. While you usually create a pivot table on a separate worksheet in the workbook containing the database you are analyzing, you can create a pivot table on the same worksheet as the data.

The **PivotTable command** on the Data menu starts the **PivotTable Wizard**, which guides you through creating a pivot table. The PivotTable Wizard does not modify the database in any way; it simply uses the data in the database to generate information on a new worksheet, similar to the way the Scenarios command worked in Project 5.

The pivot table to be created in this project is shown in Figure 6-65. The table summarizes 1998 and 1999 dollar quota information by sales area and state for the Apothecary Sales Representative Database. To create the pivot table in Figure 6-65, you only need to select four fields from the database when prompted by the PivotTable Wizard: row field; column field; and two data fields. As shown in Figure 6-65, the row field is Sales Area. The column field is St. The two data fields are 99 $ Quota and 98 $ Quota.

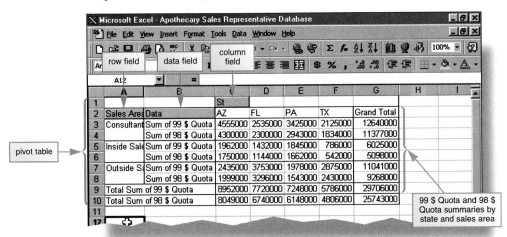

FIGURE 6-65

Grand total quotas for the row and column fields automatically display in rows 9 and 10 and in column G. For example, in the pivot table in Figure 6-65, column G displays the 99 $ Quota and 98 $ Quota totals for Consultants — $12,640,000 and $11,377,000, respectively. Cells G9 and G10 show the grand totals for each year's dollar quota.

Pivot tables are powerful data analysis tools because they allow you to view the data in various ways by interchanging or pairing up the row and column fields by dragging the buttons located over cells A2, B2, and C1 in Figure 6-65. The process of rotating the field values around the data fields will be discussed later in this project.

To create the pivot table shown in Figure 6-65, perform the following steps.

Steps **To Create a Pivot Table**

1 **Click cell A9. Point to PivotTable Report on the Data menu (Figure 6-66).**

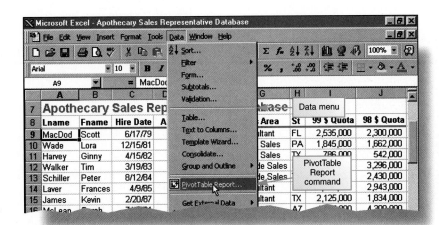

FIGURE 6-66

2 Click PivotTable Report.

The PivotTable Wizard – Step 1 of 4 dialog box displays (Figure 6-67). The option Microsoft Excel list or database is selected automatically.

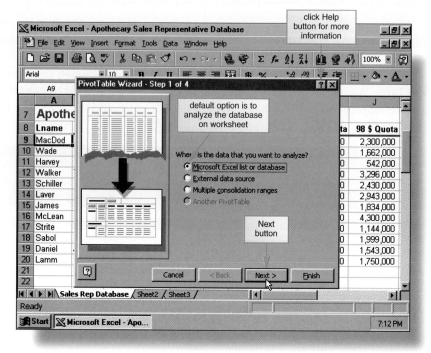

FIGURE 6-67

3 Click the Next button.

Excel displays the PivotTable Wizard – Step 2 of 4 dialog box with the named range Database (A8:J20) automatically selected in the Range box (Figure 6-68). The database on the worksheet is surrounded by a marquee.

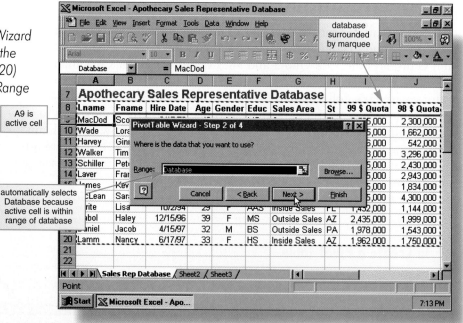

FIGURE 6-68

4 **Click the Next button.**

Excel displays the PivotTable Wizard – Step 3 of 4 dialog box (Figure 6-69). At the top of the dialog box are instructions and a diagram that help you create the pivot table. On the right side of the dialog box are field buttons, one for each field in the Apothecary Sales Representative Database. You construct the pivot table by dragging the field buttons to locations (PAGE, ROW, COLUMN, and DATA) on the diagram on the left of the dialog box.

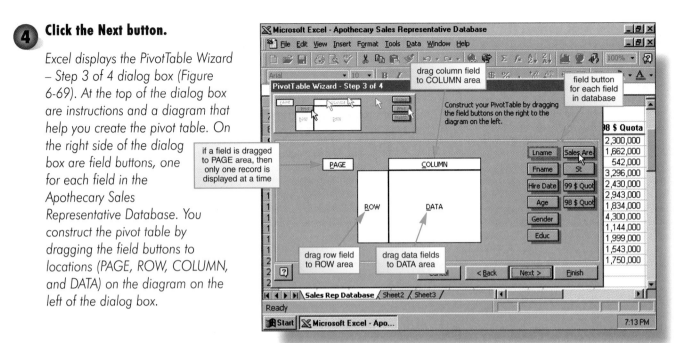

FIGURE 6-69

5 **Drag the Sales Area button to the ROW area. Drag the St button to the COLUMN area. Drag the 99 $ Quota and 98 $ Quota buttons to the DATA area.**

The PivotTable Wizard – Step 3 of 4 dialog box displays as shown in Figure 6-70.

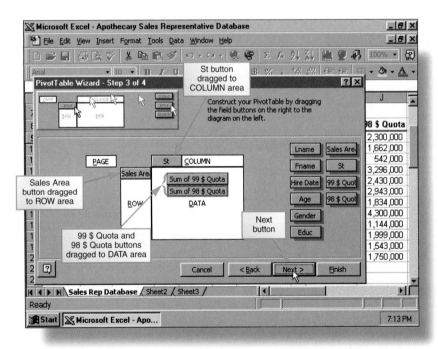

FIGURE 6-70

6 **Click the Next button. If necessary, click the New worksheet option button.**

The PivotTable Wizard – Step 4 of 4 dialog box displays as shown in (Figure 6-71).

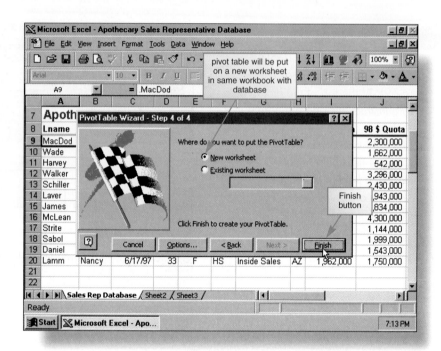

FIGURE 6-71

7 **Click the Finish button. Double-click the sheet tab and rename the sheet Pivot Table. Drag the Pivot Table sheet to the immediate right of the Sales Rep Database sheet.**

Excel creates and displays the pivot table on a new sheet as shown in Figure 6-72. The pivot table summarizes the 1998 and 1999 dollar quotas by sales area and state.

8 **Click the Save button on the Standard toolbar to save the workbook using the file name Apothecary Sales Representative Database.**

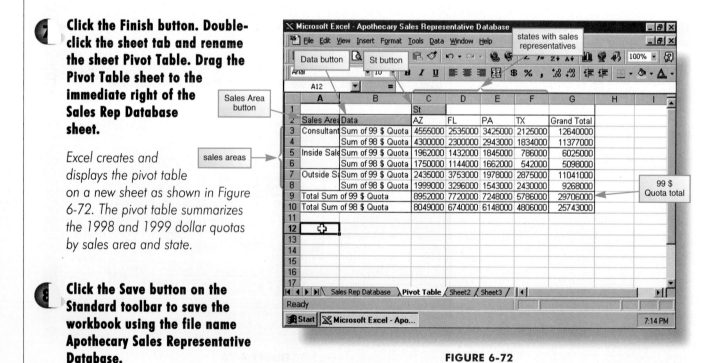

FIGURE 6-72

Once the pivot table is created, you can treat it like any other worksheet. Thus, you can print or chart a pivot table. If you update the data in the sales representative database, click Refresh Data on the Data menu or click the Refresh button on the PivotTable toolbar to update the corresponding pivot table.

Changing the View of a Pivot Table

You can rotate the row and column fields around the data field by dragging the buttons on the pivot table from one side of the data to another. For example, if you drag the St button to the lower-right corner of the Data button so that the mouse displays as a vertical table, the pivot table changes to provide a different view of the data. If you then drag the Sales Area button to the top of the total row so that the mouse pointer displays as a horizontal table, you change the view of the pivot table to the one in Figure 6-73.

If you drag the Sales Area button to the left of the Data button, and then drag the St button to the top of the column A heading so that the mouse pointer changes to three bars, you get the view shown in Figure 6-74. Each time you change the view of the pivot table, Excel gives you a new look at the same data. Notice that the St button in Figure 6-74 has a box and drop-down arrow to the right. Click the arrow to display the State list box and select another state whose totals you wish to view.

PivotTable Toolbar

When you create a pivot table, Excel may display the **PivotTable toolbar** shown in Figure 6-75. If the PivotTable toolbar does not display, you can display it by right-clicking any toolbar and then clicking Pivot-Table. The buttons on the toolbar allow you to modify quickly the appearance of the pivot table. You also can use the buttons to restart the PivotTable Wizard and refresh the data after updating the database with which the pivot table is associated.

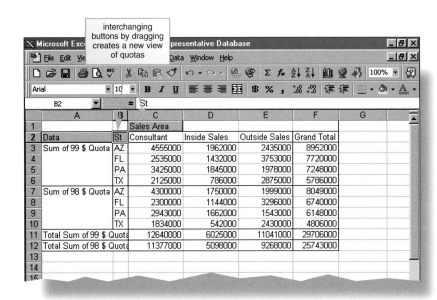

FIGURE 6-73

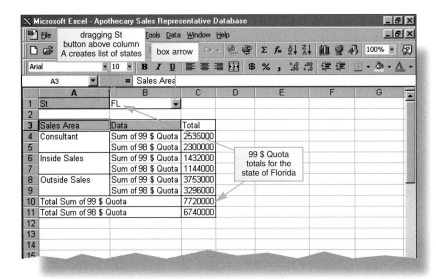

FIGURE 6-74

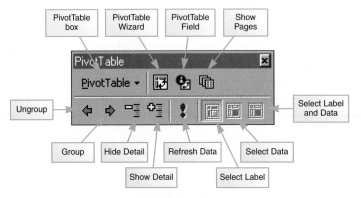

FIGURE 6-75

Quitting Excel

The project is complete. To exit Excel, follow the steps below.

TO QUIT EXCEL

Step 1: Click the Close button on the right side of the title bar.
Step 2: If the Microsoft Excel dialog box displays, click the No button.

Project Summary

The Apothecary Sales Representative Database and pivot table created in this project will allow Kelsy Young, the national sales manager, to generate information that will help her make decisions regarding the sales force. She also can use the data map for presentations to the company's management teams and to potential customers interested in knowing more about the company.

In this project you learned how to create, sort, and filter a database. Creating a database involves naming a range in the worksheet Database. You then can add, change, and delete records in the database through a data form. Sorting a database can be done using the Sort Ascending and Sort Descending buttons on the Standard toolbar or by using the Sort command on the Data menu.

Once a database is sorted, you can use the Subtotals command on the Data menu to generate subtotals that display within the database range. Filtering a database involves displaying a subset of the database or copying (extracting) records that pass a test. This project also showed you how to use database functions and lookup functions. Finally, you learned how to create and format data maps and how to use pivot tables to analyze data in a database.

What You Should Know

Having completed this project, you should be able to perform the following tasks:

- Apply an Advanced Filter to a Database *(E 6.32)*
- Apply AutoFilter to a Database *(E 6.27)*
- Change the Features of a Data Map *(E 6.43)*
- Create a Data Map *(E 6.40)*
- Create a Lookup Table and Use the VLOOKUP Function *(E 6.38)*
- Create a Pivot Table *(E 6.47)*
- Create an Extract Range on the Worksheet and Extract Records *(E 6.34)*
- Display all Records in the Database *(E 6.33)*
- Display Subtotals in a Database *(E 6.20)*
- Enter Custom Criteria *(E 6.29)*
- Enter Records into a Database Using a Data Form *(E 6.10)*
- Find Records Using a Data Form *(E 6.24)*
- Format the Data Map *(E 6.45)*
- Name the Database *(E 6.9)*
- Print a Database *(E 6.14)*
- Quit Excel *(E 6.52)*
- Remove AutoFilter *(E 6.29)*
- Remove Subtotals From a Database *(E 6.23)*
- Return a Database to its Original Order *(E 6.16)*
- Set Up a Criteria Range on the Worksheet *(E 6.31)*
- Set Up a Database *(E 6.8)*
- Sort the Database by Hire Date *(E 6.23)*
- Sort a Database in Ascending Sequence by Last Name *(E 6.15)*
- Sort a Database in Descending Sequence by Last Name *(E 6.16)*
- Sort a Database on Multiple Fields *(E 6.17)*
- Start Excel *(E 6.7)*
- Use the DAVERAGE Database Function *(E 6.37)*
- Zoom Out on a Worksheet and Hide and Show Detail Data in a Subtotaled Database *(E 6.22)*

Test Your Knowledge

1 True/False

Instructions: Circle T if the statement is true or F if the statement is false.

T F   1. When the AutoFilter is active, Excel displays the row headings and drop-down arrows used to establish the filter in red.

T F   2. Saving your database before creating a pivot table is important because the PivotTable Wizard modifies the database.

T F   3. Records can be added to the database using the Data Form function.

T F   4. In one sort operation, you can sort on up to three fields in a database.

T F   5. To use the Name Box in the formula bar to name a database, first select the column headings (field names) and the cells in the row immediately below the field names.

T F   6. The Features command on the shortcut menu allows you to add or delete countries on a data map.

T F   7. To add a new record in the data form, press the TAB key.

T F   8. After sorting the database, you can return it to its original order by clicking the Undo button.

T F   9. To display subtotals in a database, point to the Filter command on the Data menu and click Totals.

T F 10. You can use the Criteria button and comparison criteria to find records in the database using the data form.

2 Multiple Choice

Instructions: Circle the correct response.

1. Column titles need to be placed in the _____ of the database.
   a. second row
   b. first column
   c. second column
   d. first row

2. A blank row in the criteria range causes _____.
   a. all the records in the database to pass the test
   b. an error
   c. no records to pass the test
   d. none of the above

3. For the VLOOKUP function to work correctly, the search arguments in the table must be in _____ sequence.
   a. no particular
   b. ascending
   c. descending
   d. none of the above

(continued)

A+ Test Your Knowledge

Multiple Choice *(continued)*

4. Which of the following is an example of a computed criteria?
   a. Sales * 0.05
   b. >= 500
   c. = M
   d. both a and c

5. The question mark (?) wildcard character represents any _____ the question mark.
   a. single character positioned before or after
   b. single character in the same position as
   c. number of characters in the same position as
   d. all of the above

6. The _____ command enables you to display all records that meet a criteria as a subset of the database.
   a. AutoFilter
   b. Data Form
   c. Extract
   d. PivotTable

7. A _____ is a powerful tool that allows you to summarize data in the database and rotate rows and columns to get different views.
   a. pivot table
   b. data map
   c. VLOOKUP function
   d. criteria range

8. Which one of the following commands adds drop-down arrows to all field names at the top of the database?
   a. Subtotals
   b. AutoFilter
   c. Form
   d. Validation

9. To select a field in a database on which to sort when the Sort dialog box displays, enter the _____ in the Sort by box.
   a. cell reference of any cell in the field (column)
   b. cell reference of the field (column) in the first record
   c. cell reference of the field (column) in the last record
   d. all of the above

10. The _____ function will find the average of numbers in a database field that pass a test.
    a. =DAVERAGE(database, field name, comparison range)
    b. =DAVERAGE(database, "field name", criteria range)
    c. =DAVERAGE(database, 'field name', extract range)
    d. =DAVERAGE(database, field name, criteria range)

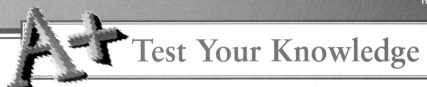

3 Understanding Sorting

Instructions: Name the fields in Figure 6-76 that have been sorted. In the blanks below indicate the sort order (minor field *within* intermediate field *within* major field). Also indicate the sort sequence (ascending or descending) for each field.

Order: _____ in _____ sequence within _____ in _____ sequence within _____ in _____ sequence

4 Understanding Comparison Criteria

Instructions: Assume that the figures that accompany each of the six problems on the next page make up the criteria range. Fill in the comparison criteria to select records from the database in Figure 6-76 according to these problems. So that you better understand what is required for this assignment, the answer is given for the first problem.

	A	B	C	D	E	F	G	H	I	J
7	**Apothecary Sales Representative Database**									
8	**Lname**	**Fname**	**Hire Date**	**Age**	**Gender**	**Educ**	**Sales Area**	**St**	**99 $ Quota**	**98 $ Quota**
9	McLean	Sarah	7/15/91	55	F	HS	Consultant	AZ	4,555,000	4,300,000
10	Sabol	Haley	12/15/96	39	F	MS	Outside Sales	AZ	2,435,000	1,999,000
11	Lamm	Nancy	6/17/97	33	F	HS	Inside Sales	AZ	1,962,000	1,750,000
12	Strite	Lisa	10/2/94	29	F	AAS	Inside Sales	FL	1,432,000	1,144,000
13	MacDod	Scott	6/17/79	43	M	MS	Consultant	FL	2,535,000	2,300,000
14	Walker	Tim	3/19/83	39	M	BS	Outside Sales	FL	3,753,000	3,296,000
15	Laver	Frances	4/9/85	47	F	BS	Consultant	PA	3,425,000	2,943,000
16	Wade	Lora	12/15/81	47	F	BS	Inside Sales	PA	1,845,000	1,662,000
17	Daniel	Jacob	4/15/97	32	M	BS	Outside Sales	PA	1,978,000	1,543,000
18	Harvey	Ginny	4/15/82	38	F	AAS	Inside Sales	TX	786,000	542,000
19	James	Kevin	2/20/87	57	M	MS	Consultant	TX	2,125,000	1,834,000
20	Schiller	Peter	8/12/84	37	M	AAS	Outside Sales	TX	2,875,000	2,430,000
21										
22										

FIGURE 6-76

(continued)

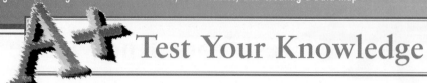

Test Your Knowledge

Understanding Comparison Criteria *(continued)*

1. Select records that represent females under 40.

LNAME	FNAME	HIRE DATE	AGE	GENDER	EDUC	SALES AREA	ST	99 $ QUOTA	98 $ QUOTA
			<40	F					

2. Select records that represent sales representatives who are assigned to offices in Pennsylvania (PA) or Texas (TX).

LNAME	FNAME	HIRE DATE	AGE	GENDER	EDUC	SALES AREA	ST	99 $ QUOTA	98 $ QUOTA

3. Select records that represent sales representatives with a BS degree or higher, whose last names begin with the letter S, and who are assigned to the Texas (TX) office.

LNAME	FNAME	HIRE DATE	AGE	GENDER	EDUC	SALES AREA	ST	99 $ QUOTA	98 $ QUOTA

4. Select records that represent female sales representatives who are at least 39 years old and were hired before 1/1/90.

LNAME	FNAME	HIRE DATE	AGE	GENDER	EDUC	SALES AREA	ST	99 $ QUOTA	98 $ QUOTA

5. Select records that represent female sales representatives or sales representatives who are at most 40 years old.

LNAME	FNAME	HIRE DATE	AGE	GENDER	EDUC	SALES AREA	ST	99 $ QUOTA	98 $ QUOTA

6. Select records that represent male consultants who are at least 29 years old and whose last names begin with the letter J.

LNAME	FNAME	HIRE DATE	AGE	GENDER	EDUC	SALES AREA	ST	99 $ QUOTA	98 $ QUOTA

Use Help

1 Reviewing Project Activities

Instructions: Perform the following tasks using a computer.

1. Start Excel. Click the Contents and Index command on the Help menu to display the Help Topics: Microsoft Excel dialog box. Click the Contents tab. Double-click the Displaying Data in a Map book. Double-click the link About displaying data in a map. Click, read, and print all links. To print a link topic, right-click it, and then click Print Topic. Next, click the Help Topics button and then double-click the link Add data to a map. Read and print the information. Click all link buttons labeled How?, reading and printing each link topic. Hand the printouts in to your instructor.

2. If the Help Topics: Microsoft Excel dialog box is not on the screen, click the Contents and Index command on the Help menu to display it. Click the Find tab. Type sorting in the top text box labeled 1. In the lower list box labeled 3, double-click the What's new with data analysis in PivotTable? topic. Read and print the information. Hand the printout in to your instructor.

3. If the Help Topics: Microsoft Excel dialog box is not on the screen, click the Contents and Index command on the Help menu to display it. Click the Index tab. Type filter in the top text box labeled 1. Under the topic filters in the middle list box labeled 2, double-click the topic overview. One at a time double-click the topics Display a subset of rows in a list by using filters and Ways to find values in a list by using filters. For the first topic, click the links and read the information. For the second topic, click the links and read and print the information. Hand the printouts in to your instructor. Close all Help windows.

4. Click the Office Assistant button on the Standard toolbar. Type vlookup in the balloon text box and then click the Search button. Click the VLOOKUP button and then read and print the information. Click the See Also link immediately below the title VLOOKUP. Read and print the information about HLOOKUP. Hand the printouts in to your instructor.

2 Expanding on the Basics

Instructions: Perform the following tasks using a computer.

1. Start Excel. Click the Contents and Index command on the Help menu to display the Help Topics: Microsoft Excel dialog box. Click the Index tab. Type database in the top text box labeled 1. In the middle list box labeled 2, double-click the topic database functions. Read and print the information. At the bottom of the page, choose three buttons and read and print the information about each topic. Hand the printouts in to your instructor. Close all Help windows.

2. Click the Contents and Index command on the Help menu. Click the Find tab. Type subtotal in the top text box labeled 1. Scroll down in the lower list box labeled 3 and double-click the topic Insert subtotal values into a list. Click each link. Read and print the information. Hand the printouts in to your instructor. Close all Help windows.

3. Click the Office Assistant button on the Standard toolbar. Type outline a worksheet in the balloon text box and then click the Search button. Click the Summarize data by using subtotals and outlines button. One at a time, click the buttons under the What do you want to do? question. Read and print the information for each link. Hand the printouts in to your instructor.

Apply Your Knowledge

1 Filtering a Database

Instructions: Start Excel. Open the workbook World of Flowers from the Excel folder on the Data Disk that accompanies this book. The worksheet displays with drop-down arrows as shown in Figure 6-77. Step through each filter exercise in Table 6-8 and print the results for each.

To complete a filter exercise, select the appropriate drop-down arrow(s) and option(s) in the lists. Use the (Custom...) option for field names that do not contain appropriate selections. After printing each filtered solution, point to Filter on the Data menu and click Show All on the Filter submenu. After the last filter exercise, remove the drop-down arrows by clicking the AutoFilter on the Filter submenu. You should end up with the following number of records for Filters 1 through 10: 1 = 2; 2 = 8; 3 = 4; 4 = 2; 5 = 3; 6 = 2; 7 = 3; 8 = 0; 9 = 2; and 10 = 12.

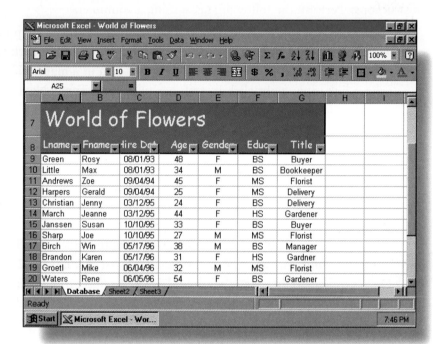

FIGURE 6-77

Table 6-8							
FILTER	LNAME	FNAME	HIRE DATE	AGE	GENDER	EDUC	TITLE
1	Begins with B						
2					F		
3				>27 and < 45		BS or MS	
4			After 1/1/95				Florists
5		Begins with J					
6							Delivery
7				>30	M		
8		Ends with E		>50	F	HS	
9				<35	F		Delivery
10	All	All	All	All	All	All	All

In the Lab

1 Building and Sorting a Database and Determining Subtotals

Problem: The company you consult for, NetWeb Computers, Inc., manufactures network computers. They have asked you to create a sales report database (Figure 6-78) and then generate subtotal information as shown in Figure 6-79 on the next page.

Part 1 Instructions: Create the database shown in Figure 6-78 using the techniques learned in this project. In particular, enter and format the database title and field names in rows 1 and 2. Name the range A2:E3 Database. Use a data form to enter the data in rows 3 through 15. Enter your name, course number, laboratory assignment (Lab 6-1), date, and instructor name in the range A20:A24. Save the workbook using the file name NetWeb Computers.

Part 2 Instructions: Sort the database according to the six sort problems below. Print the database for each sort problem. After completing each sort problem, save the workbook using the file name NetWeb Computers x, where x is the sort problem number. Open the original workbook NetWeb Computers to begin each sort problem.

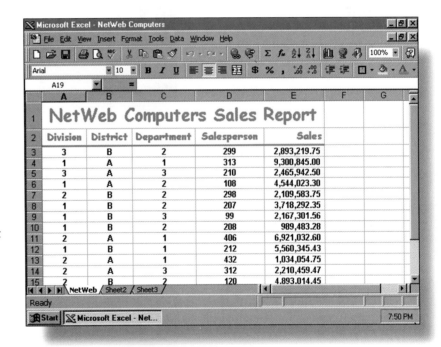

FIGURE 6-78

1. Sort the database in ascending sequence by division.
2. Sort the database by department within district within division. All three sort keys are to be in ascending sequence.
3. Sort the database by district within division. Both sort keys are to be in descending sequence.
4. Sort the database by salesperson within department within district within division. All four sort keys are to be in ascending sequence.
5. Sort the database in descending sequence by sales.
6. Sort the database by department within district within division. All three sort keys are to be in descending sequence.

Part 3 Instructions: Close all the workbooks created in Part 2 by holding down the SHIFT key and clicking Close All on the File menu. Next, open the workbook NetWeb Computers (Figure 6-78) created in Part 1. Sort the database by department within district within division. Select ascending sequence for all three sort keys. Use the Subtotals command on the Data menu to generate subtotals for sales by

(continued)

In the Lab

Building and Sorting a Database and Determining Subtotals *(continued)*

division. Click 75% in the Zoom list on the Standard toolbar so the worksheet appears as shown in Figure 6-79. Change column E to best fit. Print the database with the subtotals. Use the Subtotals command to remove the subtotals. Click 100% in the Zoom list on the Standard toolbar. Close the workbook without saving it.

FIGURE 6-79

	Division	District	Department	Salesperson	Sales
			NetWeb Computers Sales Report		
3	1	A	1	313	9,300,845.00
4	1	A	2	108	4,544,023.30
5	1	B	1	212	5,560,345.43
6	1	B	2	207	3,718,292.35
7	1	B	2	208	989,483.28
8	1	B	3	99	2,167,301.56
9	1 Total				26,280,290.92
10	2	A	1	406	6,921,032.60
11	2	A	1	432	1,034,054.75
12	2	A	3	312	2,210,459.47
13	2	B	2	298	2,109,583.75
14	2	B	2	120	4,893,014.45
15	2 Total				17,168,145.02
16	3	A	3	210	2,465,942.50
17	3	B	2	299	2,893,219.75
18	3 Total				5,359,162.25
19	Grand Total				48,807,598.19

2 Building, Sorting, and Filtering a Database of River Kayakers

Problem: Waters Odyssey Kayakers specializes in guiding kayak and canoe trips in the Inland Northwest. The owner and his clients are interested in the range of experience and years of experience of the company's river guides. Create the database shown in Figure 6-80 using the field information listed in Table 6-9.

Part 1 Instructions: Perform the following tasks.

1. Enter the database title and column titles (field names) beginning in row 6. Use the Name Box in the formula bar to define the name Database as the range A7:J8. Use the Form command in the Data menu to enter the records shown in the Figure 6-80.

2. Enter your name, course, computer laboratory exercise (Lab 6-2), date, and instructor's name in the range A30:A34. Print the worksheet. Save the workbook using the file name Waters Odyssey Kayakers.

Waters Odyssey Kayakers

Guide Names	Age	Gender	St	Yrs Exp	Rating	Sea Kayak	River Kayak	Canoe	Rapid Class
Anderson, Rene	31	F	MT	5	Standard	Yes	Yes	No	4
Chase, Ryan	34	F	WA	3	Standard	Yes	No	Yes	3
Green, Jason	32	M	ID	20	Expert	Yes	Yes	Yes	5
Mason, Marsh	36	M	OR	15	Expert	Yes	Yes	Yes	5
Priest, Morgan	26	M	WA	4	Standard	Yes	Yes	No	3
Rivers, Joan	29	F	OR	7	Standard	Yes	Yes	Yes	4
Rouen, Andy	38	M	MT	6	Standard	Yes	Yes	Yes	4
Rush, Josie	22	F	CA	1	Grunt	No	Yes	No	2
Sanders, Kevin	41	M	ID	9	Expert	Yes	Yes	Yes	5
Trent, Troy	44	M	ID	11	Expert	Yes	Yes	Yes	5
Webb, George	30	M	CO	1	Grunt	Yes	Yes	No	2
Jackson, Trace	44	M	ID	9	Expert	Yes	Yes	Yes	5

FIGURE 6-80

In the Lab

3. Sort the records in the database by years experience (descending), within rapid class (descending), within gender (ascending). Print the sorted version.

4. Sort the records in the database by age within rating. Select ascending sequence for both. Print the sorted version. Close the workbook without saving it.

Table 6-9

COLUMN HEADINGS (FIELD NAMES)	COLUMN	TYPE OF DATA	COLUMN WIDTH
Guide Names	A	Text	15.43
Age	B	Numeric	4.57
Gender	C	Text	7.71
St	D	Text	3.57
Yrs Exp	E	Numeric	4.71
Rating	F	Text	8.00
Sea Kayak	G	Text	9.29
River Kayak	H	Text	9.29
Canoe	I	Text	7.14
Rapid Class	J	Numeric	7.43

Part 2 Instructions: Open the workbook Waters Odyssey Kayakers (Figure 6-80). Use the Criteria button on a data form to enter the comparison criteria for the following tasks. Use the Find Next button on the data form to find the records that pass the comparison criteria. Write down and submit the names of the kayakers who pass the comparison criteria for Items 1 through 4. Close the data form after each query and then reopen it by clicking the Data Form command on the Data menu. You should end up with the following number of records for Items 1 through 4: 1 = 8; 2 = 9; 3 = 8; 4 = 7.

1. Find all kayak guides who can guide a sea kayak with at least five years of experience.
2. Find all kayak guides who can guide a river kayak in rapid class 3 or better.
3. Find all kayak guides who can guide a canoe in rapid class 3 or better.
4. Find all kayak guides who can guide all three crafts with at least five years of experience.

All standard kayak guides who were not familiar with a canoe were sent on expeditions to receive this experience. Use the Find Next button on the Data Form menu to update the appropriate records, changing the No in the Canoe field to a Yes for each appropriate record. Make sure you press the ENTER key or press the DOWN ARROW after changing a record. Save the database using the file name Waters Odyssey Kayakers Experience.

Part 3 Instructions: Open the workbook Waters Odyssey Kayakers (Figure 6-80). Use the AutoFilter command on the Filter submenu and redo Part 2 Items 1, 2, 3, and 4. Use the Show All command on the Filter submenu after each filter. Print the worksheet for each problem. Change the exercise number in the range A30:A34 to Lab 6-23x, where x is the problem letter. Click the AutoFilter command on the Filter submenu to remove the box arrows. Close the workbook without saving it.

Part 4 Instructions: Open the workbook Waters Odyssey Kayakers (Figure 6-80). Add a criteria range by copying the database title and field names (A6:J7) to A1:J2. Change cell A1 to Criteria Area. Use the Name Box in the formula bar to name the criteria range (A2:J3) Criteria. Add an extract range by copying the database title and field names (A6:J7) to A21:J22. Change cell A21 to Extract Area. Use the Name Box in the formula bar to name the extract range (A22:J22) Extract. The top of your worksheet should look similar to the top screen in Figure 6-81 on the next page.

(continued)

In the Lab

Building, Sorting, and Filtering a Database of River Kayakers *(continued)*

Select a cell within the database range and use the Advanced Filter command on the Filter submenu to extract records that pass the tests in Items 1 through 5 below. Change the laboratory exercise number in the range A30:A34 to Lab 6-24x, where x is the problem letter. Print the entire worksheet after each extraction.

1. Extract the records that represent river guides who are female (Figure 6-82).

2. Extract the records that represent river guides who can navigate a river kayak but not a canoe.

3. Extract the records that represent female river guides who can navigate rapid class 3 or better.

4. Extract the records that represent male river guides who can navigate river and sea kayaks.

5. Extract the records that represent river guides with a grunt rating.

After you complete the extraction in Item 5, save the workbook using the file name Waters Odyssey Kayakers Criteria.

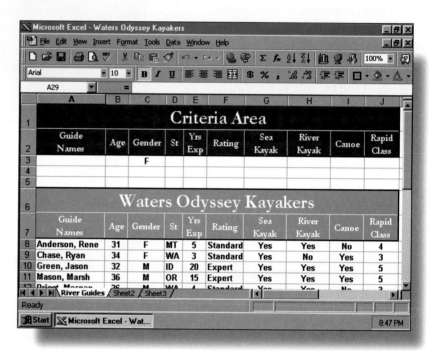

FIGURE 6-81

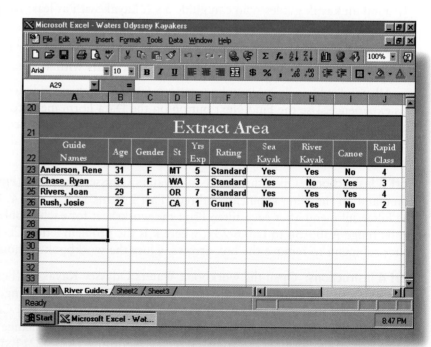

FIGURE 6-82

Part 5 Instructions: Open the workbook Waters Odyssey Kayakers (Figure 6-80 on page E 6.60). Draw a data map of the United States (Figure 6-83) that highlights the states where the company's river kayakers originated. Select the range D7:D19 as the basis for the data map. Use the data map location M1:S20. Save the workbook using the file name Waters Odyssey Kayakers Data Map.

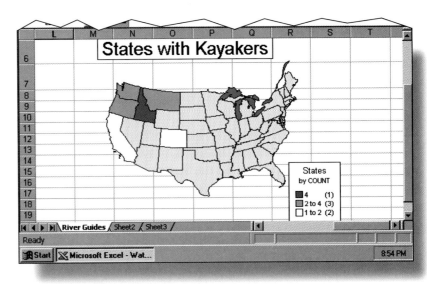

FIGURE 6-83

3 Finding Subtotals and Creating a Pivot Table for an Order Entry Database

Problem: You are employed as a spreadsheet specialist in the order entry department of Luke's Restaurant Supplies. You have been assigned to do the following:

1. Develop an order entry database that keeps track of the orders (Figure 6-84).
2. Display subtotals of the number ordered and amount (Figure 6-85 on the next page).
3. Create a pivot table to summarize the amount (Figure 6-86 on the next page).

FIGURE 6-84

Part 1 Instructions: Complete the following to create the database shown in the range A5:G17 in Figure 6-84.

1. Change the font of the worksheet to bold. Change the column widths to the following: A = 11.29, B = 11.00, C = 7.86, D = 21.00, E = 5.71, F = 9.29, and G = 12.00. Enter and format the database heading and field names in the range A5:G6. Center entries in columns A and B. Left-align the field names in columns A through D and right-align columns E through G, as shown in Figure 6-84.

(continued)

In the Lab

Finding Subtotals and Creating a Pivot Table for an Order Entry Database *(continued)*

2. Enter the first record without using a data form. Enter the formula =E7 * F7 in cell G7. Define the name Database as the range A6:G7. Use a data form to enter the remaining order records.
3. Enter your name, course, computer laboratory exercise (Lab 6-3a), date, and instructor name in the range A20:A24.
4. Save the workbook using the file name Luke's Restaurant Supplies. Use the Page Setup command on the File menu or shortcut menu to change the left and right margins to 0.5. Print the worksheet. Click the Save button on the Standard toolbar to save the workbook.

Part 2 Instructions: Do the following to develop the subtotals shown in Figure 6-85.

1. Select a cell within the range of Database. Click the Subtotals command on the Data menu and determine totals for the Amount field by the Order No field.
2. Change the magnification of the worksheet to 75% (Figure 6-85).
3. Print the worksheet.
4. Hide detail records so that only total rows display. Print the worksheet.
5. Change the magnification back to 100%. Use the Subtotals command on the Data menu to remove subtotals.

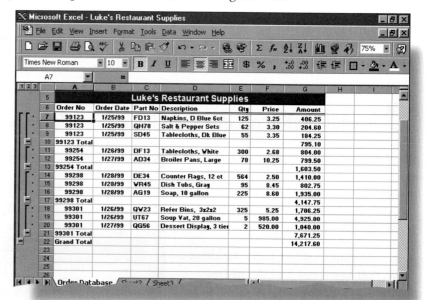

FIGURE 6-85

Part 3 Instructions: Using the database created in Part 1, create the pivot table shown in Figure 6-86 on a separate worksheet. The table summarizes dollar amount information by order number and order date. Use the Pivot Table command to create the pivot table. Print the pivot table. Drag the Order No and Order Date buttons around on the pivot table to obtain different views of the information. Save the workbook using the file name Luke's Restaurant Supplies.

FIGURE 6-86

Cases and Places

The difficulty of these case studies varies: ❿ are the least difficult, ❿❿ are more difficult, and ❿❿❿ are most difficult.

1 ❿ Your coaches have asked you to develop a database of information about last season's games so that they can better understand which teams pose the biggest challenge to this year's team. Create a database with records for 15 games, using the following fields: Team, City, Their Score, Our Score, and Home/Away. Sort the database by team name in ascending order. Use the advanced filter to find out how many games were won by your team away from home. Use the DAVERAGE to find your team's average score for the season.

2 ❿ As part of a class project, you have decided to create a database that compares the favorite hobby or sport of your closest ten friends and family members and the length of time they have enjoyed their hobby or sport. Create the database with the following field names: Lname, Fname, Age, Gender, Friend or Relative, Hobby or Sport, and Years. Sort the entire database in ascending order by last name. Sort it again by gender within age within hobby or sport. Sort the database by years. Use the data form to find all your male friends who have enjoyed their hobby or sport for more than two years.

3 ❿❿ Develop a database made up of the professional basketball (or any other major sport) sports teams you and your friends enjoy watching on television. Include fields for the team names, sport, home state, and ranking this season. Sort the database by sport within team name within home state, all in ascending sequence. Create and format a data map to show each team's home state. Create a criteria and extract range to discover if any teams come from the same home state.

4 ❿❿ A multitude of software is available to help users manage a variety of tasks. Go to a software retailer or visit a software retailer's Web site and create a software database that includes the following information: name of the software, the software company, the type of application, the version number, and the cost. Sort the database by software company. Sort it again by software name within application within cost. Display subtotals for the software cost by application. Use the data form and find all versions greater than 2.0.

Cases and Places

5 ▶▶ You also can use a software database to generate information about the software that helps you choose a software package. Create the software database as described in Cases and Places 4. Use the AutoFilter to find all software products developed by Microsoft that retail for under $200.00. Set up a criteria and extract range to locate all software that has word processing capabilities and costs between $150.00 and $225.00.

6 ▶▶▶ Print shops offer a variety of services such as printing, stapling, cutting, and they usually offer a price break for higher quantities. Visit a local print shop and find out the prices for printing, collating, cutting, folding, and stapling. Obtain the quantity needed for three price breaks and the corresponding prices. Create a database with the information and then create a worksheet below it to enter print jobs. Use the VLOOKUP to obtain the prices for four different jobs, combining a variety of services and price breaks. *Hint:* You can copy the formula using the fill handle if you use the absolute cell references for the first and second arguments.

7 ▶▶▶ Major electronics stores do not have the luxury of being able to depend on their profits by the quantity of sales. They need to keep track of the items that sell versus those that do not. Visit a local major electronics store and gather information to create a database. Include the brand, item name, cost, place of manufacture, item type, and whether the item has increased or decreased in sales from last year. Sort the database a variety of ways, explaining the purpose of each sort. Display subtotals of costs, and use the data form, AutoFilter, and criteria range to find specific information. Use the DAVERAGE function to find the average cost between brands.

Embedding an Excel Worksheet into a Word Document Using Drag and Drop

INTEGRATION FEATURE

Case Perspective

Alex Hansen serves as treasurer of the High-Tech Stock Club. Each month he sends the members an investment report that summarizes the club's end-of-month financial status. Alex wants to use Word to create the monthly report and Excel to create the end-of-month financial summary worksheet. Alex even has been using object linking and embedding to paste the worksheet at the end of the report. Thus far, for instance, he has used the Paste Special command on the Edit menu to try both linking and embedding.

Alex recently learned that you can tile open application windows on the desktop and then embed an object by dragging it from one window and dropping it into another. Alex has asked you to show him how to tile application windows and then drag and drop an Excel worksheet and chart onto a Word document.

Introduction

In the earlier Excel Integration feature, you were introduced to using the Copy button and Paste Special command on the Edit menu to link a worksheet, also called the **source document**, to a Word document, also called the **destination document**. This Integration feature shows you how to use the OLE features of Microsoft Office to **embed**, rather than link, an Excel worksheet into a Word document using **drag and drop** techniques (Figure 1 on the next page). Table 1 summarizes the difference between linking and embedding.

| Table 1 | |
METHOD	CHARACTERISTICS
Embed	The source document becomes part of the destination document. An object can be edited in the destination application using the editing features of the source application. If you modify the worksheet in Excel, changes will not display in the Word document the next time you open it.
Link	The source document does not become part of the destination document even though it appears to be part of it. This method establishes a link between the two documents so that, when you open the Word document, the worksheet displays as part of it. When you attempt to edit a linked worksheet in Word, the system activates Excel. If you modify the worksheet in Excel, the changes will show in Word document the next time you open it.

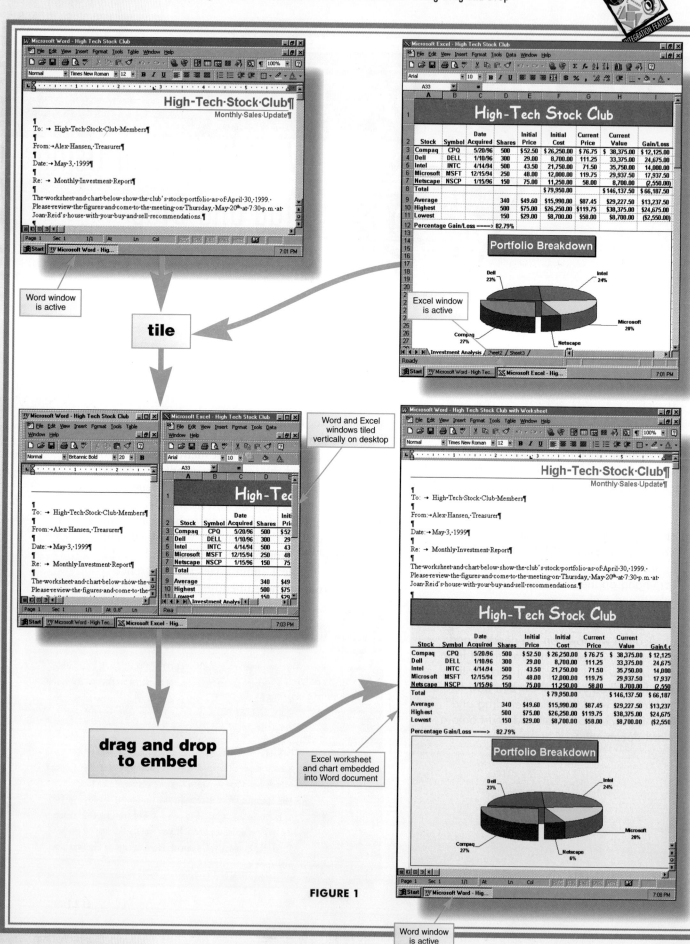

FIGURE 1

Starting Word and Excel

Both the Word document (High Tech Stock Club) and the Excel workbook (High Tech Stock Club) are in the Excel folder on the Data Disk that accompanies this book. The first step in embedding the Excel worksheet into the Word document is to open both the Word document and the Excel workbook as shown in the following steps.

TO OPEN A WORD DOCUMENT AND EXCEL WORKBOOK

Step 1: Insert the Data Disk that accompanies this book in drive A. Click the Start button. Click Open Office document on the Start menu. Click 3½ Floppy (A:) in the Look in box and then select the Excel folder. Double-click the Word document named High Tech Stock Club.

Word becomes active and the High Tech Stock Club document displays as shown in the upper-left screen in Figure 1.

Step 2: Click the Start button. Click Open Office document on the Start menu. Click 3½ Floppy (A:) in the Look in box and then select the Excel folder. Double-click the Excel workbook named High Tech Stock Club.

Excel becomes active and the High Tech Stock Club workbook displays as shown in the upper-right screen of Figure 1. At this point, Word is inactive but still in memory. The Excel window is active.

Step 3: Click the Word button on the taskbar to activate Word.

Word becomes the active application.

When you open an application, Windows automatically activates it and deactivates any applications that were active previously. As described in Step 3, with both Word and Excel in memory, you can click the application button on the taskbar to activate the corresponding application.

More *About*
Starting Applications

You can start an application through Explorer by double-clicking the file name. For example, if you display the contents of the Excel folder on the Data Disk in Explorer, then you can double-click the Word document High Tech Stock Club to start Word and open the document. Likewise, you can start Excel by double-clicking the workbook High Tech Stock Club.

Tiling Applications on the Desktop

To use the mouse to drag and drop an object from one application to another, both applications must be running and visible on your screen (lower-left screen in Figure 1). To make both applications visible at the same time, you tile the applications on your screen. **Tiling** is the process of arranging open applications in smaller windows that fit next to each other on the desktop. When tiled, each application displays in its own window. Follow the steps on the next page to tile the two application windows on the desktop in preparation for dragging and dropping the Excel worksheet onto the Word document.

Steps | **To Tile the Application Windows on the Desktop**

1 **Right-click an open area on the taskbar between the Excel button and the tray.**

The taskbar shortcut menu displays (Figure 2). Although the Word document displays on the screen, the Word button on the taskbar is no longer recessed because the displayed shortcut menu is associated with Windows, not Word.

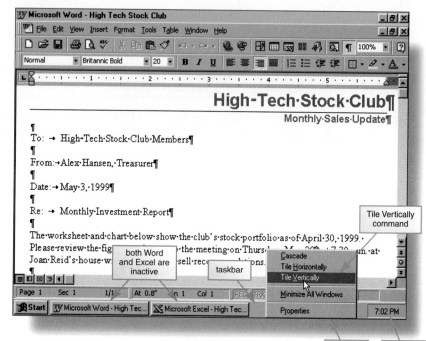

FIGURE 2

2 **Click Tile Vertically. Click the Excel button on the taskbar to activate Excel.**

Windows displays each open application in a separate window on the desktop. In this case, the Word document and Excel workbook display side-by-side in two vertical windows (Figure 3). Each tiled window has its own title bar, status bar, Minimize button, Maximize button, Close button, and scroll bars.

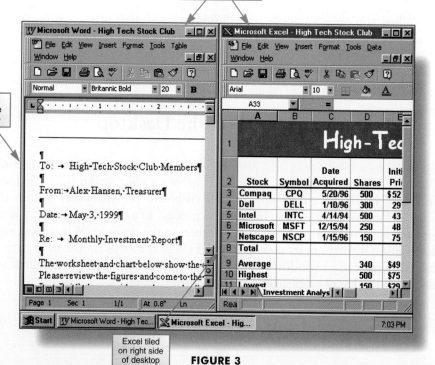

FIGURE 3

▶ *Other***Ways**

1. Right-click taskbar, type V

In addition to tiling vertically, Windows can tile horizontally or cascade the open application windows. To tile horizontally, click **Tile Horizontally** on the shortcut menu (Figure 2). The windows will display horizontally across the desktop, one above the other. To cascade the open application windows, click **Cascade** on the shortcut menu. The cascaded windows will overlap so each title bar is visible. When the windows are cascaded, you can make an application active by clicking on any part of its window.

You can switch back and forth between vertically tiled, horizontally tiled, and cascaded windows by right-clicking the taskbar and then clicking the appropriate command on the shortcut menu.

Embedding Using Drag and Drop

With each open application in a separate window on the desktop, the next step is to embed the Excel worksheet into the Word document. As shown in the following steps, you will use the mouse to drag and drop the worksheet onto the document.

Steps To Embed Using Drag and Drop

1 **With the Excel window active, select the range A1:I29. Point to the right or bottom border of the selected range so the mouse pointer displays as a block arrow. Press and hold down the CTRL key.**

The worksheet and pie chart are selected. When you hold down the CTRL key, the mouse pointer displays as a block arrow with a plus sign above and to the right (Figure 4).

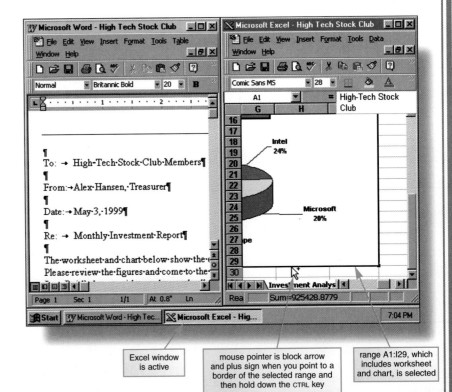

Excel window is active

mouse pointer is block arrow and plus sign when you point to a border of the selected range and then hold down the CTRL key

range A1:I29, which includes worksheet and chart, is selected

FIGURE 4

② **While holding down the CTRL key, drag the mouse to the last paragraph mark in the Word document and hold.**

The mouse pointer changes to a block arrow with a shadow and a plus sign in a square. The insertion point indicates where the object will be placed in the Word document (Figure 5).

shaded insertion point indicates where object will be placed

status bar indicates worksheet will be copied, not moved

mouse pointer changes to this symbol when the Excel range is dragged onto the Word window with the CTRL key pressed

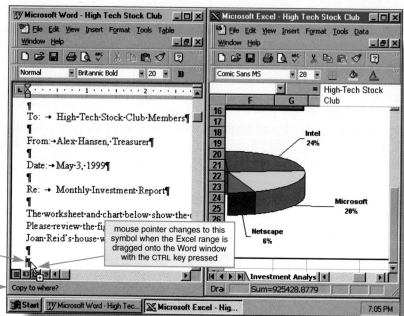

FIGURE 5

③ **Release the left mouse button.**

The system embeds the worksheet range A1:I29 in the Word document, beginning at the location of the insertion point. The embedded worksheet range displays in the Word window (Figure 6). The worksheet also remains intact in the Excel window.

worksheet and chart embedded into Word document

worksheet and chart in Excel is copied, rather than moved, and thus displays in both windows

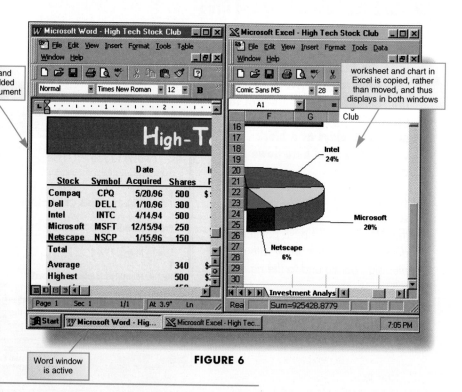

Word window is active

FIGURE 6

▶ **Other Ways**

1. Select range to embed in source document, click Copy button, click point of insertion in destination document, on Edit menu click Paste Special, click Paste option button, click Float over text check box, click OK button

The Excel worksheet now is embedded into the Word document. Because you held down the CTRL key while dragging, the worksheet is copied to the Word document. If you drag the Excel worksheet onto the Word document without holding down the CTRL key, then the worksheet is moved to the Word document, rather than copied. The next section shows how to undo the tile so the Word document with the embedded worksheet displays in a maximized window.

Undoing the Tiling of Application Windows on the Desktop

Once you are finished with the Excel window, you can undo the tile so that the Word document displays in a maximized window.

Steps To Undo the Tiling of Application Windows on the Desktop

1 **Click the Word button on the taskbar to ensure it is the active application.**

2 **Right-click an open area on the taskbar between the Excel button and the tray.**

The taskbar shortcut menu displays (Figure 7).

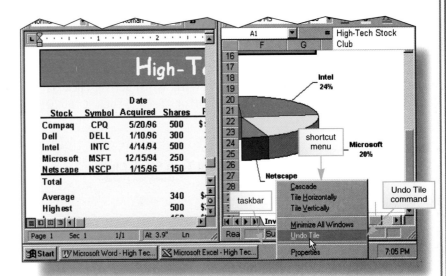

FIGURE 7

3 **Click Undo Tile. When the Word document displays in a maximized window, scroll to the top of the document.**

The embedded worksheet displays at the bottom of the Word document (Figure 8).

because Word was active when Undo Tile was clicked, Word document displays in a maximized window

4 **Click the Excel button on the taskbar. If necessary, click the Maximize button on the title bar. Click the Close button on the title bar. Do not save your changes.**

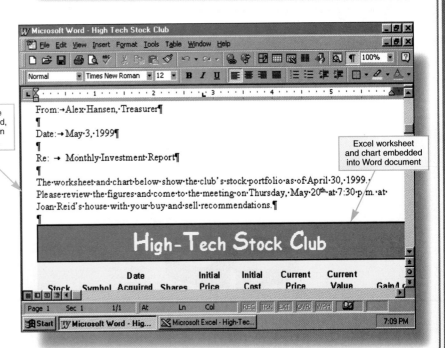

FIGURE 8

*Other***Ways**

1. In Excel window click Maximize button, click Close button, in Word window click Maximize button

If you embed an object such as the Excel worksheet, and the results are not what you expected, click the Undo button on the Standard toolbar or click the Undo command on the Edit menu. You can remove the embedded object at any time by clicking the embedded object to select it and then pressing the DELETE key.

Saving and Printing the Word Document with the Embedded Excel Worksheet

With the Word window maximized, the next step is to save and print the Word document with the embedded Excel worksheet.

TO SAVE AND PRINT THE WORD DOCUMENT WITH THE EMBEDDED EXCEL WORKSHEET

Step 1: With Word active, click Save As on the File menu. Type the file name `High Tech Stock Club with Worksheet` in the File name box. If necessary, click the Save in box arrow and then click the 3½ Floppy (A:) icon. Click the Save button.

The document with the embedded worksheet is saved on your floppy disk using the file name High Tech Stock Club with Worksheet.

Step 2: Click Page Setup on the File menu. Click the Margins tab. Type `.8` in the Top box. Type `.3` in the Bottom box. Click the OK button. Click the Print button on the Standard toolbar. Click the Save button on the Standard toolbar.

The memorandum prints as shown in Figure 9.

If you quit and then start Word and re-open the file High Tech Stock Club with Worksheet, the worksheet will display in the Word document. The worksheet displays even though Excel is not running, because it is part of the Word document. The next section describes what happens when you attempt to edit the embedded worksheet while Word is active.

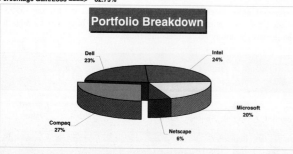

High-Tech Stock Club
Monthly Sales Update

To: High-Tech Stock Club Members

From: Alex Hansen, Treasurer

Date: May 3, 1999

Re: Monthly Investment Report

The worksheet and chart below show the club's stock portfolio as of April 30, 1999. Please review the figures and come to the meeting on Thursday, May 20th at 7:30 p.m. at Joan Reid's house with your buy and sell recommendations.

High-Tech Stock Club

Stock	Symbol	Date Acquired	Shares	Initial Price	Initial Cost	Current Price	Current Value	Gain/Loss
Compaq	CPQ	5/20/96	500	$52.50	$26,250.00	$76.75	$ 38,375.00	$ 12,125.00
Dell	DELL	1/10/96	300	29.00	8,700.00	111.25	33,375.00	24,675.00
Intel	INTC	4/14/94	500	43.50	21,750.00	71.50	35,750.00	14,000.00
Microsoft	MSFT	12/15/94	250	48.00	12,000.00	119.75	29,937.50	17,937.50
Netscape	NSCP	1/15/96	150	75.00	11,250.00	58.00	8,700.00	(2,550.00)
Total					$ 79,950.00		$ 146,137.50	$ 66,187.50
Average			340	$49.60	$15,990.00	$87.45	$29,227.50	$13,237.50
Highest			500	$75.00	$26,250.00	$119.75	$38,375.00	$24,675.00
Lowest			150	$29.00	$8,700.00	$58.00	$8,700.00	($2,550.00)
Percentage Gain/Loss ====>		82.79%						

Portfolio Breakdown

Dell 23%
Intel 24%
Microsoft 20%
Netscape 6%
Compaq 27%

FIGURE 9

Editing the Embedded Worksheet in the Word Document

To change information in the worksheet portion of the report, you do not have to make the changes in Excel, delete the worksheet from the letter, and then drag and drop to embed it again. Instead, you simply double-click the embedded worksheet while in Word.

When you double-click the embedded worksheet, the Word menu and tool-bars immediately change to the Excel menu and toolbars. The title bar, however, continues to identify the application as Word. When you make changes, you are using the editing capabilities of Excel while Word is the active application. This is called **in-place activation**. The following steps show how to change the value in cell G6 in the worksheet from 119.75 to 199.25 while Word is active. The change to cell G6 affects the totals, which in turn changes the size of the slices in the pie chart. The pie chart thus is redrawn immediately when you change the value in cell G6.

> **More** *About*
> ## Editing an Embedded Object
>
> In most cases, double-clicking an embedded object causes in-place activation of the source application. Some embedded objects such as video and sound clips, however, play when you double-click them.

 Steps To Edit an Embedded Worksheet in a Word Document

1 **With Word active, double-click the worksheet to activate it. When the heavy border displays around the worksheet, scroll down and click cell G6.**

Excel surrounds the worksheet with a heavy border as shown in Figure 10. The Excel menu bar, toolbars, column and row headings, and scroll bar display on the screen, even though the title bar and status bar indicate that Word is active.

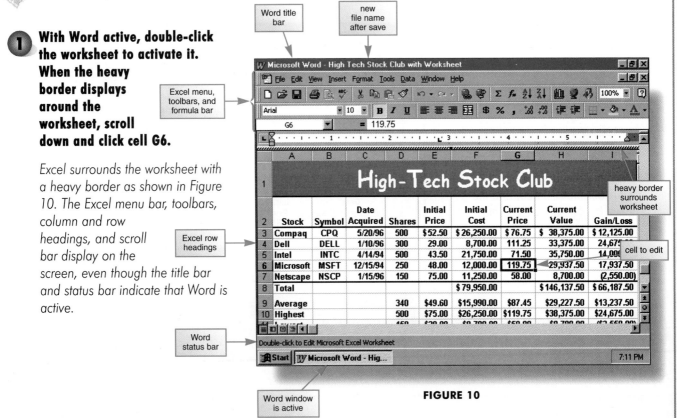

FIGURE 10

2 Type 199.25 **and click the Enter box or press the ENTER key.**

The value 119.75 in cell G6 changes to 199.25. The formulas in the worksheet are recalculated. New values display in cells H6, I6, H8, I8, and the range H9:I10 (Figure 11). Excel automatically redraws the pie chart based on the new values. The slice representing Microsoft increases in size and the remaining slices decrease in size.

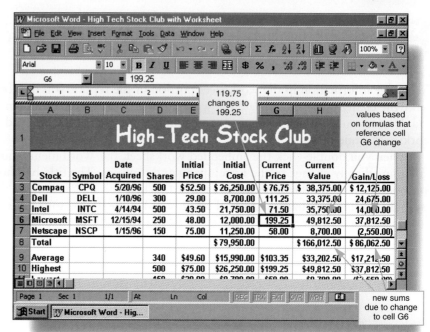

FIGURE 11

3 **Scroll up so that both the original document and embedded worksheet display. Click outside the heavy border surrounding the worksheet to activate Word.**

The Word menu, toolbar, ruler, and status bar are restored, and the heavy border surrounding the worksheet disappears. The mouse pointer changes to an I-beam and an insertion point displays in the Word document (Figure 12).

4 **Click the Close button on the title bar. Do not save the changes.**

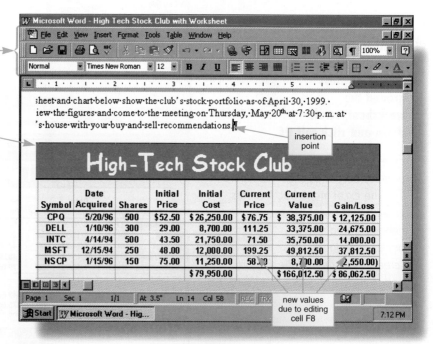

FIGURE 12

As shown in the previous steps, when an object is embedded into a document, you can activate the source application within the destination application by double-clicking the embedded object. You then can use the editing capabilities of the source application. The embedded object, however, has no connection to the original file from which it came; that is, it is not linked. Thus, any changes made to the worksheet while Word is active will not show up in the worksheet if you later open it in Excel.

Summary

Once the Excel worksheet is embedded into the Word document, Alex Hansen easily can open the report with the embedded worksheet each month, make the appropriate modifications, and e-mail the report to the High-Tech Stock Club members.

This Integration Feature introduced you to using tiling and drag and drop to embed an object into a document. When you embed an object into a document and save it, the object becomes part of the document. When you save the document with the embedded object, the destination document increases by the size of the object. For example, embedding a 10KB worksheet into a 20KB document increases the file size to 30KB. You can edit an embedded object by double-clicking it.

What You Should Know

Having completed this Integration Feature, you now should be able to perform the following tasks:

▶ Edit an Embedded Worksheet in a Word Document *(EI 2.9)*

▶ Embed Using Drag and Drop *(EI 2.5)*

▶ Open a Word Document and Excel Workbook *(EI 2.3)*

▶ Save and Print the Word Document with the Embedded Excel Worksheet *(EI 2.8)*

▶ Tile the Application Windows on the Desktop *(EI 2.4)*

▶ Undo the Tiling of Application Windows on the Desktop *(EI 2.7)*

1 Using Help

Instructions: Perform the following tasks using a computer.

Start Excel. Click Contents and Index on the Help menu to display the Help Topics: Microsoft Excel dialog box. Click the Index tab. Type embed in the top text box labeled 1. Under the topic, embedded objects, in the lower list box labeled 2, double-click the subtopic, creating and inserting. When the Topics Found dialog box displays, read and print the information for the following topics: (a) About linked and embedded objects; and (b) Copy information from an existing file as a linked or embedded object. Hand the printouts in to your instructor.

In the Lab

2 Embedding Using Drag and Drop

Problem: You have been assigned the task of embedding a monthly expense worksheet into a memo using drag and drop techniques.

Instructions: Perform the following tasks.

1. One at a time, open the document Monthly Expense Memo and the workbook Monthly Expense Summary from the Excel folder on the Data Disk that accompanies this book. Tile the two applications on the desktop.
2. Use the mouse to drag and drop the range A1:E17 to the bottom of the Monthly Expense Memo document.
3. Print and then save the document using the file name Monthly Expense with Worksheet.
4. Double-click the worksheet and increase each of the nine expense amounts by $200. Print the document with the new values. Close the document and workbook without saving your changes.

3 Embedding a Word Document into an Excel Workbook as an Icon

Problem: You have been asked to embed a Word document as an icon into an Excel workbook.

Instructions: Complete the following tasks.

1. One at a time, open the document Monthly Expense Memo and the workbook Monthly Expense Summary from the Excel folder on the Data Disk that accompanies this book. Tile the two applications on the desktop.
2. Click within the Word window and then select the entire document. Click the Copy button on the Standard toolbar in Word. Activate the Excel window. Click Paste Special on the Edit menu in Excel to embed the Word document as an icon. When the Paste Special dialog box displays, click the Display as icon check box. Position the icon beginning in cell G1.
3. Print the worksheet and then save the workbook as Monthly Expense with Icon.
4. With the Excel window active, double-click the icon representing the embedded document and then delete the second sentence. Print the revised memo. Close the workbook and document without saving your changes.

NOTE TO READER: This index contains references for Projects 1 through 6 and the Integration Features of the book, *Microsoft Excel 97: Complete Concepts and Techniques*. The same references can be used for Excel Projects 1 through 3 and Integration Feature 1 in the book, *Microsoft Office 97: Introductory Concepts and Techniques*, and Excel Projects 4 through 6 and Integration Feature 2 in the book, *Microsoft Office 97: Advanced Concepts and Techniques*.

Microsoft **Excel 97**

Index

Microsoft

Access 97

Microsoft Access 97

Reports, Forms, and Publishing Reports to the Web

Objectives

You will have mastered the material in this project when you can:

◗ Create a query for a report
◗ Use the Report Wizard to create a report
◗ Use the Report window to modify a report design
◗ Move between Design view and Print Preview
◗ Recognize sections in a report
◗ Save a report
◗ Close a report
◗ Print a report
◗ Create a report with grouping and subtotals
◗ Change headings in a report
◗ Move and resize controls on a report
◗ Use the Form Wizard to create an initial form
◗ Use the Form window to modify a form design
◗ Move fields on a form
◗ Place a calculated field on a form
◗ Change the format of a field on a form
◗ Place a combo box on a form
◗ Place a title on a form
◗ Change colors on a form
◗ View data using a form
◗ Publish database data to the Web

Outrageous Oddities

and
Meaningful
Data

Pelicans on the moon? In 1834, the *New York Sun* had its readers believing exactly that. Later, Edgar Allen Poe displayed a similar zest for practical jokes when he published a "news" dispatch detailing a bogus trans-Atlantic hot air balloon crossing. These were blatant hoaxes, but people loved them. Into this climate of practical jokes and humbug strode a man who was arguably the all-time giant of American entertainment. For sixty years, Phineas Taylor Barnum reigned as "The Showman to the World."

Best remembered today for his monumental circuses, he promoted some of the more outrageous oddities America and the world have ever seen, most of them legitimate, others born of Barnum's fertile imagination and love for a prank.

After it became known that the Feejee Mermaid was the head and torso of an orangutan sewn onto the body of a fish, crowds still flocked to see it. The public not only expected the outrageous from Barnum, but required it.

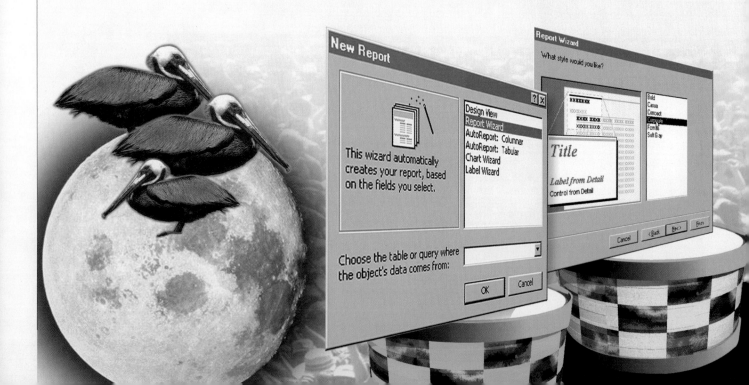

Far outweighing his hoaxes was the unending stream of genuine rarities he produced: Jenny Lind, the Swedish Nightingale; General Tom Thumb, measuring 25 inches tall and weighing 15 pounds, who became the toast of Europe and Commodore Nutt, who was even tinier; Anna Swan, the Nova Scotia giantess; Chang and Eng, Siamese Twins who fathered 22 children between them; Mrs. Myers, the bearded lady; *industrious* fleas trained to pull tiny wagons; a knitting machine operated by a dog; the armless man who loaded and fired a pistol and played musical instruments — with his feet; and Jumbo the Elephant, the mainstay of Barnum circuses.

What made Barnum's name a household word around the world? A consummate master of the art of presentation, he preceded each new attraction with a concentrated public relations campaign. Editors then were just as desperate as now for news and advertising and Barnum fed them a steady diet of both, always well-written and humorous. Above all, he loved people.

Although you may never have the opportunity to manage an event of such magnitude as a grand-scale Barnum circus, you are likely to require in your profession the Microsoft Access tools illustrated in this project to present data. If relational database power had existed in the days of P.T. Barnum, he might have used an Access Event Management database. Access eases the tasks of report and form creation with improved Report and Form Wizards that create tables and reports from database information with little user intervention.

Today, almost 100 years since Barnum first introduced "The Greatest Show on Earth," you can access information about it on the World Wide Web. The new Access Internet tool, Publish to the Web Wizard, shown in this project, automates the publishing of your database information dynamically. Now, you can share timely data on the World Wide Web.

With Microsoft Access 97, you get organized, get connected, and get results, quickly.

Project 4

Microsoft
Access 97

Reports, Forms, and Publishing Reports to the Web

Case Perspective

Pilotech Services has realized several benefits from its database of clients and technicians. The management and staff of Pilotech Services greatly appreciate, for example, the ease with which they can query the database. They hope to realize additional benefits using two custom reports that meet their exact needs. The first report includes the number, name, address, city, state, zip code, and outstanding amount (billed amount minus paid amount) of all clients. The second report groups the records by technician number. Subtotals of the billed and paid amounts appear after each group, and grand totals appear at the end of the report. They also want to improve the data entry process by using a custom form. In addition to a title, the form will contain the fields arranged in two columns and display the outstanding amount, which will be calculated automatically by subtracting the paid amount from the billed amount. To assist users in entering the correct technician number, users should be able to select from a list of existing technician numbers. Finally, Pilotech would like to make copies of the reports available on the Web.

Introduction

This project creates two reports and a form. The two reports will be printed and made available on the Web. The first report is shown in Figure 4-1. This report includes the number, name, address, city, state, zip code, and outstanding amount (Billed minus Paid) of all clients. It is similar to the one produced by clicking the Print button on the toolbar. It has two significant differences, however.

First, not all fields are included. The Client table includes a Client Type field (added in Project 3), a Billed field, a Paid field, and a Tech Number field, none of which appears on this report. Second, this report contains an Outstanding Amount field, which does not appear in the Client table.

The second report is shown in Figure 4-2 on page A 4.8. It is similar to the report in Figure 4-1, but contains an additional feature, grouping. **Grouping** means creating separate collections of records sharing some common characteristic. In the report in Figure 4-2, for example, the records have been grouped by Technician Number. Three separate groups exist: one for Technician 11, one for Technician 12, and one for Technician 17. The appropriate Technician Number appears before each group, and the total of the billed and paid amounts for the clients in the group (called a **subtotal**) appears after the group. At the end of the report is a grand total of the billed and paid amounts.

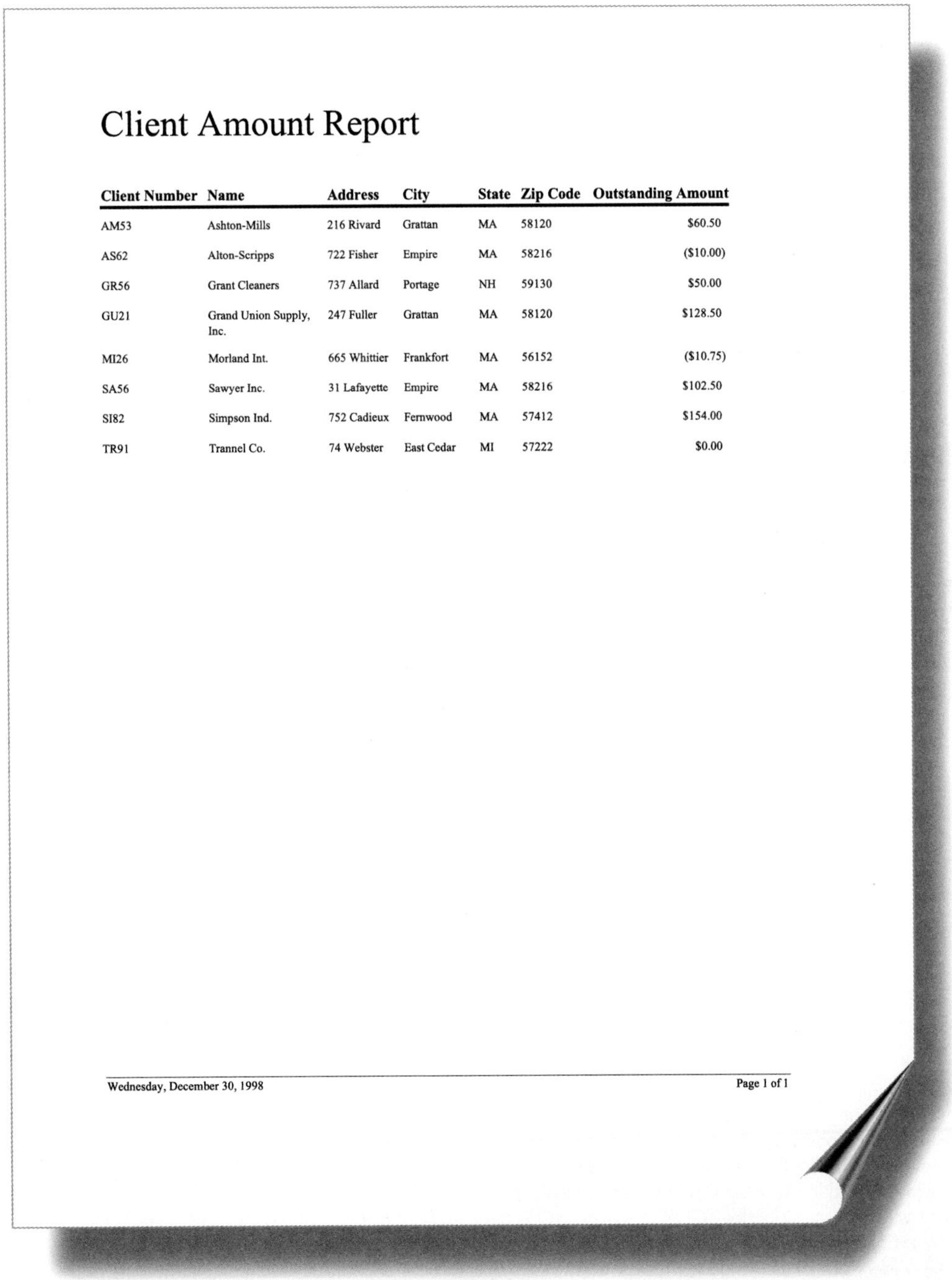

Client Amount Report

Client Number	Name	Address	City	State	Zip Code	Outstanding Amount
AM53	Ashton-Mills	216 Rivard	Grattan	MA	58120	$60.50
AS62	Alton-Scripps	722 Fisher	Empire	MA	58216	($10.00)
GR56	Grant Cleaners	737 Allard	Portage	NH	59130	$50.00
GU21	Grand Union Supply, Inc.	247 Fuller	Grattan	MA	58120	$128.50
MI26	Morland Int.	665 Whittier	Frankfort	MA	56152	($10.75)
SA56	Sawyer Inc.	31 Lafayette	Empire	MA	58216	$102.50
SI82	Simpson Ind.	752 Cadieux	Fernwood	MA	57412	$154.00
TR91	Trannel Co.	74 Webster	East Cedar	MI	57222	$0.00

Wednesday, December 30, 1998 — Page 1 of 1

FIGURE 4-1

Clients by Technician

Technician Number	First Name	Last Name	Client Number	Name	Billed	Paid
11	Joanna	Levin				
			AM53	Ashton-Mills	$215.50	$155.00
			GR56	Grant Cleaners	$215.00	$165.00
			MI26	Morland Int.	$212.50	$223.25
			TR91	Trannel Co.	$0.00	$0.00
					$643.00	$543.25
12	Brad	Rogers				
			AS62	Alton-Scripps	$425.00	$435.00
			GU21	Grand Union Supply, Inc.	$128.50	$0.00
			SI82	Simpson Ind.	$154.00	$0.00
					$707.50	$435.00
17	Maria	Rodriguez				
			SA56	Sawyer Inc.	$352.50	$250.00
					$352.50	$250.00
					$1,703.00	1,228.25

FIGURE 4-2

The **custom form** to be created is shown in Figure 4-3. Although similar to the form created in Project 1, it offers some distinct advantages. Some of the differences are merely aesthetic. The form has a title and the fields have been rearranged in two columns. In addition, two other major differences are present. This form displays the outstanding amount and will calculate it automatically by subtracting the amount paid from the amount billed. Second, to assist users in entering the correct technician, the form contains a **combo box**, which is a box that allows you to select entries from a list. An arrow displays in the Technician Number field. Clicking the arrow causes a list of the technicians in the Technician table to display as shown in the figure. You then can type either the desired technician number or simply click the desired technician.

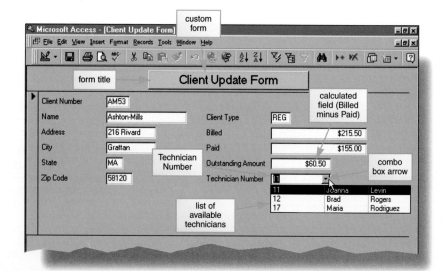

FIGURE 4-3

Note: The Data Disk that accompanies this book contains an Access folder containing compressed versions of five databases: Pilotech Services, Green Thumb, Museum Mercantile, City Telephone System, and City Scene. Pilotech Services is required if you plan to step through the project on a PC. The other files are required for the exercises at the end of the project. It is recommended that you create a copy of the Data Disk for each database you will be using.

To create a copy for an individual database, do the following: [1] Insert the Data Disk in drive A; [2] start Explorer; [3] right-click the 3½ Floppy (A:) folder in the All Folders side of the window; [4] click Copy Disk; [5] click Start and OK as required; [6] insert the blank floppy disk when requested; [7] delete any folder other then the Access folder from the newly-created floppy disk; [8] double-click the Access folder in the All Folders side of the window and then double-click the name of the database on the Contents of 'Access' side of the window; and [9] clearly label this floppy disk with the name of the database. The database will be contained in the Access folder.

If possible, you should place your data on your hard disk or on a network drive, because the databases can become rather large, especially after adding the pictures in Project 5. If this is not possible, you should not insert the pictures in Project 5. (There is a note in Project 5, showing you precisely which steps you should skip.)

Project Four – Creating Custom Reports and a Form for Pilotech Services

You are to create the reports requested by the management of Pilotech Services. You also must create the form that the management deems to be important to the data-entry process.

Overview of Project Steps

The database preparation steps give you an overview of how the reports and form shown in Figures 4-1 through 4-3 will be created in this project.

1. Start Access and open the Pilotech Services database.
2. Create a query for the first report.
3. Use the Report Wizard to create an initial version of the first report.
4. Use the Report window to complete the creation of the first report by changing one of the properties.
5. Create a query for the second report.
6. Use the Report Wizard to create an initial version of the second report.
7. Use the Report window to complete the creation of the second report.
8. Remove unwanted controls from the second report.
9. Enlarge the Page Header section on the second report.
10. Change the column headings on the second report.
11. Use the Form Wizard to create an initial version of the form.
12. Use the Form window to complete the creation of the form.
13. Move fields on the form.
14. Add a new field to the form.
15. Change the format of a field on the form.
16. Add a combo box to the form.
17. Add a title to the form.
18. Enhance the title on the form by changing some of its properties.
19. Publish the reports created in this project to the Web.

The following pages contain a detailed explanation of these steps.

Opening the Database

Before creating reports or forms, first you must open the database. Perform the following steps to complete this task.

TO OPEN A DATABASE

Step 1: Click the Start button.
Step 2: Click Open Office Document on the Start menu and then click 3½ Floppy (A:) in the Look in list box. If necessary, double-click the Access folder. Make sure the database called Pilotech Services is selected.
Step 3: Click the Open button.

The database is open and the Pilotech Services : Database window displays.

Report Creation

The simplest way to create a report design is to use the **Report Wizard**. For some reports, the Report Wizard can produce exactly the desired report. For others, however, first use the Report Wizard to produce a report that is as close as possible to the desired report. Then use the **Report window** to modify the report, transforming it into exactly the correct report. In either case, once the report is created and saved, you can print it at any time. Access will use the current data in the database for the report, formatting and arranging it in exactly the way you specified when the report was created.

If a report uses only the fields in a single table, use the table as a basis for the report. If the report uses extra fields (such as Outstanding Amount) or uses multiple tables, however, the simplest way to create the report is first to create a query using the steps you learned in Project 2. The query should contain exactly the fields and tables required for the report. This query forms the basis for the report.

Creating a Query

The process of creating a query for a report is identical to the process of creating queries for any other purpose. Perform the following steps to create the query for the first report.

Steps **To Create a Query**

1 In the Database window, click the Tables tab, if necessary, and then click the Client table. Click the New Object: AutoForm button arrow on the toolbar. Click Query. Be sure Design View is selected, and then click the OK button. Maximize the Select Query window. Resize the upper and lower panes and the Client field list so all the fields in the Client table display.

2 Double-click Client Number. Select Ascending as the sort order for the field. Include the Name, Address, City, State, and Zip Code fields in the design grid. Click the right scroll arrow to shift the fields to the left so the space for an extra field is visible. Right-click in the Field row of the space for the extra field. Point to Zoom on the shortcut menu.

The shortcut menu for the extra field displays (Figure 4-4).

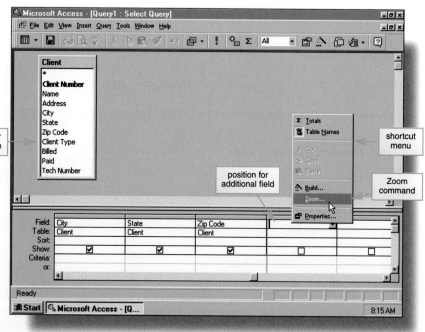

FIGURE 4-4

3 Click Zoom on the shortcut menu. Type `Outstanding Amount:[Billed]-[Paid]` in the Zoom dialog box and point to the OK button (Figure 4-5).

4 Click the OK button. Click the Close button for the Select Query window and then click the Yes button.

5 Type `Client Amount Query` as the name of the query and then click the OK button.

The query is saved.

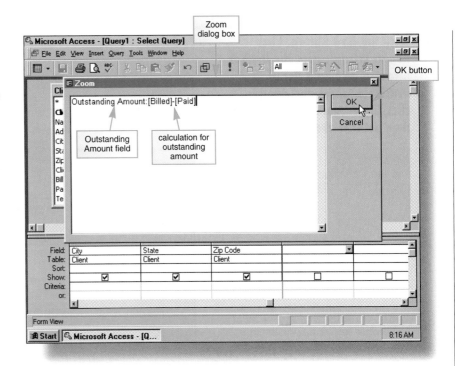

FIGURE 4-5

Creating a Report

Next, you will create a report using the Report Wizard. Access leads you through a series of choices and questions, and then creates the report automatically. Perform the following steps to create the report shown in Figure 4-1 on page A 4.7.

Steps To Create a Report

1 Click the Reports tab in the Database window and then point to the New button (Figure 4-6).

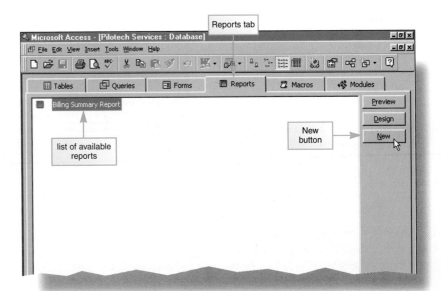

FIGURE 4-6

2 Click the New button. Click Report Wizard, click the list box arrow to display a list of available tables and queries, click Client Amount Query, and then point to the OK button.

The New Report dialog box displays and the Client Amount Query is selected (Figure 4-7).

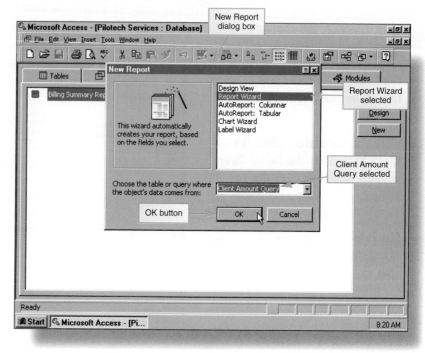

FIGURE 4-7

3 Click the OK button and then point to the Add All Fields button.

The Report Wizard dialog box displays, requesting the fields for the report (Figure 4-8). To add the selected field to the list of fields on the report, use the Add Field button. To add all fields, use the Add All Fields button.

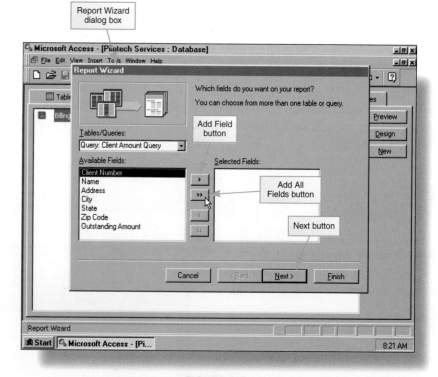

FIGURE 4-8

4 Click the Add All Fields button to add all the fields, and then click the Next button.

The next Report Wizard dialog box displays, requesting the field or fields for grouping levels (Figure 4-9). No grouping takes place in this report being created.

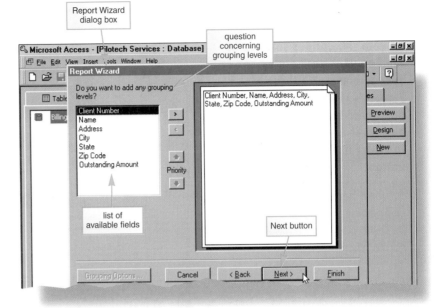

FIGURE 4-9

5 Click the Next button. No grouping levels are required.

The next Report Wizard dialog box displays, requesting the sort order for the report (Figure 4-10).

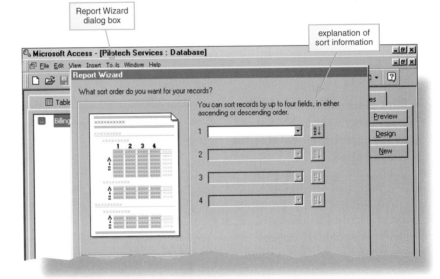

FIGURE 4-10

6 Click the Next button. The query already is sorted in the appropriate order, so you need not specify a sort order.

The next Report Wizard dialog box displays, requesting your report lay-out preference (Figure 4-11).

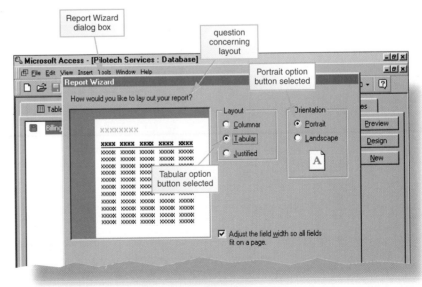

FIGURE 4-11

7 Be sure the options selected in the Report Wizard dialog box on your screen match those in Figure 4-11 on the previous page, and then click the Next button. If necessary, click Formal to select it. Point to the Next button.

The next Report Wizard dialog box displays, requesting a style for the report (Figure 4-12). The Formal style is selected.

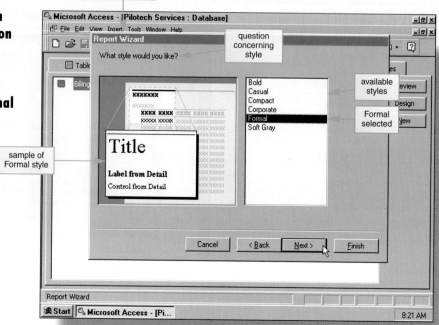

FIGURE 4-12

8 Click the Next button and then type Client Amount Report as the report title. Point to the Finish button.

The next Report Wizard dialog box displays, requesting a title for the report (Figure 4-13). Client Amount Report is entered as the title.

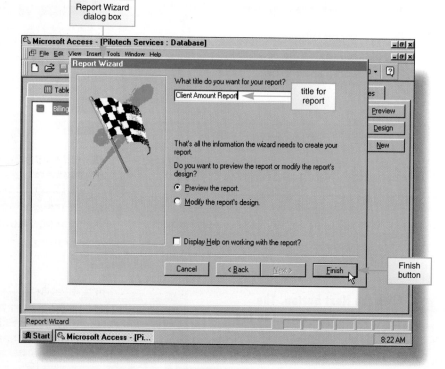

FIGURE 4-13

9 Click the Finish button.

The report design is complete and displays in Print Preview (Figure 4-14). (If your computer displays an entire page of the report, click the portion of the report where the mouse pointer displays in the figure.)

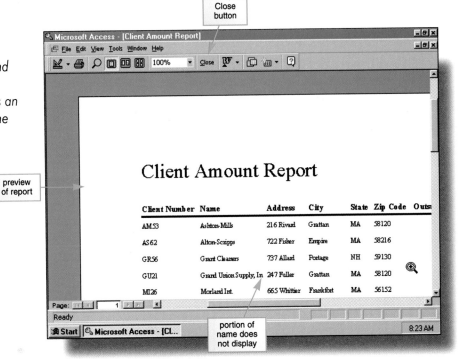

FIGURE 4-14

Because of insufficient space allowed in the report shown in Figure 4-14, some of the data does not display completely. The final portion of the name of Grand Union Supply, Inc. does not display, for example. You will need to correct this problem.

Using Design View

Within the Report window, the different possible views are Design view and Print Preview. Use **Design view** to modify the design (layout) of the report. Use **Print Preview** to see the report with sample data. To move from Design view to Print Preview, click the Print Preview button on the toolbar. To move from Print Preview to Design view, click the button labeled Close on the toolbar.

Within Print Preview, you can switch between viewing an entire page or a portion of a page. To do so, click somewhere within the report (the mouse pointer will change shape to a magnifying glass).

In Design view, you can modify the design of the report. A **toolbox** is available in Design view that allows you to create special objects for the report. The toolbox obscures a portion of the report, so it is common practice to remove the toolbox when you are not using it by clicking the Toolbox button on the toolbar. You can return the toolbox to the screen whenever you need it by clicking the Toolbox button again.

Perform the steps on the next page to move from Print Preview to Design view and remove the toolbox from the screen.

OtherWays

1. With table selected, click New Object button arrow on toolbar, click Report, click Report Wizard to create report
2. On Insert menu click Report, click Report Wizard to create report

More About Previewing a Report

You can view two pages at the same time when previewing a report by clicking the Two Page button on the toolbar. You can view multiple pages by clicking View on the menu bar, clicking Pages, and then clicking the number of pages to view.

Steps To Move to Design View and Remove the Toolbox

1 **Click the Close button on the Print Preview toolbar (see Figure 4-14). If Access returns to the Database window, right-click the report, and then click Design on the shortcut menu. If the toolbox displays, point to the Toolbox button on the Report Design toolbar. In the list, click Design View. Then click the Close button on the Print Preview toolbar.**

Print Preview is replaced by Design view (Figure 4-15). In the figure, the toolbox displays, obscuring some of the left edge of the report design.

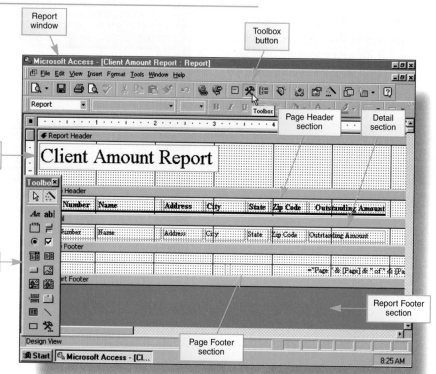

FIGURE 4-15

2 **If the toolbox displays, click the Toolbox button on the toolbar.**

The toolbox no longer displays.

Other Ways

1. Click View button arrow on toolbar, click Design View
2. On View menu click Design View

Report Sections

Each of the different portions of the report is described in what is termed a **section**. The sections are labeled on the screen (see Figure 4-15). Notice the following sections: the Report Header section, Page Header section, Detail section, Page Footer section, and Report Footer section.

The contents of the **Report Header section** print once at the beginning of the report. The contents of the **Report Footer section** print once at the end of the report. The contents of the **Page Header section** print once at the top of each page, and the contents of the **Page Footer section** print once at the bottom of each page. The contents of the **Detail section** print once for each record in the table.

The various rectangles appearing in Figure 4-15 (Client Amount Report, Client Number, Name, and so on) are called **controls**. The control containing Client Amount Report displays the report title; that is, it displays the words, Client Amount Report. The control in the Page Header section containing Name displays the word, Name.

The controls in the Detail section display the contents of the corresponding fields. The control containing Name, for example, will display the client's name. The controls in the Page Header section serve as **captions** for the data. The Client Number control in this section, for example, will display the words, Client Number, immediately above the column of client numbers, thus making it clear to anyone reading the report that the items in the column are, in fact, client numbers.

More *About*
Report Sections

Another common term for the sections in a report is "band." The term "band-oriented" applied to a report tool means that the tool is very similar to the report tool in Access; that is, you design a report by simply modifying the contents of the various sections (bands).

To move, resize, delete, or modify a control, click it. Small squares called **sizing handles** appear around the border of the control. Drag the control to move it, drag one of the sizing handles to resize it, or press the DELETE key to delete it. Clicking a second time produces an insertion point in the control in order to modify its contents.

Changing Properties

Some of the changes you may make will involve using the property sheet for the control to be changed. The **property sheet** is a list of properties for the control that can be modified. By using the property sheet, you can change one or more of the control's properties. To produce the property sheet, right-click the desired control and then click Properties on the shortcut menu.

The problem of missing data in the report in Figure 4-14 on page A 4.15 can be corrected in several ways.

1. Move the controls to allow more space in between them. Then, drag the appropriate handles on the controls that need to be expanded to enlarge them.
2. Use the Font Size property to select a smaller font size. This would enable more data to print in the same space.
3. Use the Can Grow property. By changing the value of this property from No to Yes, the data can be spread over two lines, thus enabling all the data to print. The name of customer GU21, for example, will have Grand Union Supply, on one line and Inc. on the next. Access will split data at natural break points, such as commas, spaces, and hyphens.

The first approach will work, but it can be cumbersome. The second approach would work, but makes the report difficult to read. The third approach, changing the Can Grow property, is the simplest and produces a very readable report. Perform the following steps to change the Can Grow property for the Detail section.

▶ **More** *About*
**Changing
Properties**

There are a large number of properties that can be changed using the property sheet. The properties determine the structure and appearance of a control. They also determine the characteristics of the data the control contains. For details on a particular property, click the Help button, then click the property.

 Steps **To Change the Can Grow Property**

① **Point below the section selector for the Detail section (Figure 4-16).**

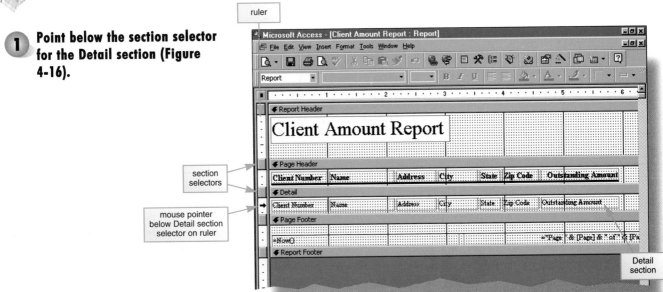

FIGURE 4-16

2 Right-click and then point to Properties on the shortcut menu.

The shortcut menu displays (Figure 4-17).

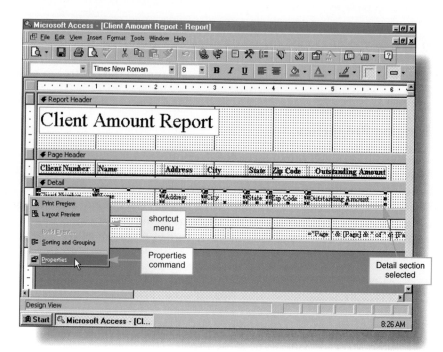

FIGURE 4-17

3 Click Properties and then click the All tab, if necessary, to ensure that all available properties display. Click the Can Grow property, click the Can Grow box arrow, and then click Yes in the list that displays.

The Multiple selection property sheet displays (Figure 4-18). All the properties display on the All sheet. The value for the Can Grow property has been changed to Yes.

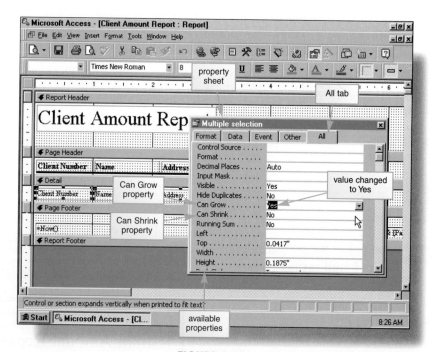

FIGURE 4-18

④ Close the property sheet by clicking its Close button, and then point to the Print Preview button on the toolbar (Figure 4-19).

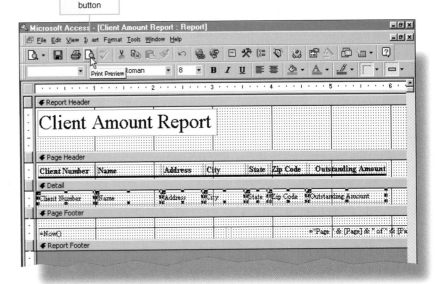

FIGURE 4-19

⑤ Click the Print Preview button.

A portion of the report displays (Figure 4-20). The names now display completely by extending to a second line. (If your computer displays an entire page, click the portion of the report where the mouse pointer displays in the figure.)

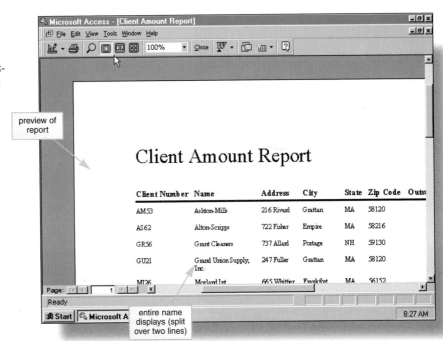

FIGURE 4-20

Closing and Saving a Report

To close a report, close the window using the window's Close button in the upper-right corner of the window. Then indicate whether or not you want to save your changes. Perform the following step to close the report.

TO CLOSE AND SAVE A REPORT

Step 1: Close the Report window and then click the Yes button to save the report.

OtherWays

1. On File menu click Close

Printing a Report

To print a report, right-click the report in the Database window, and then click Print on the shortcut menu. Perform the following steps to print the Client Amount Report.

 Steps To Print a Report

1 In the Database window, if necessary, click the Reports tab. Right-click the Client Amount Report. Point to Print on the shortcut menu.

The shortcut menu for the Client Amount Report displays (Figure 4-21).

2 Click Print.

The report prints. It should look like the report shown in Figure 4-1 on page A 4.7.

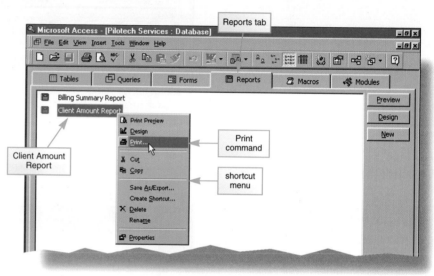

FIGURE 4-21

OtherWays

1. Click Reports tab, select report, click Print button on toolbar
2. Click Reports tab, select report, on File menu click Print
3. Click Reports tab, select report, press CTRL+P

Grouping in a Report

Grouping arranges the records in your report. When records are grouped in a report, separate collections of records are created that share some common characteristic. In the report in Figure 4-2 on page A 4.8, for example, the records are grouped by Technician Number. Three separate groups exist, one for each technician.

In grouping, reports typically include two other types of sections: a group header and a group footer. A **group header** is printed before the records in a particular group and a **group footer** is printed after the group. In Figure 4-2, the group header indicates the technician number and name. The group footer includes the total of the billed and paid amounts for the clients of that technician. Such a total is called a **subtotal**, because it is just a subset of the overall total.

Again, you should create an appropriate query before creating the report. Perform the following steps to create the query for the report shown in Figure 4-2.

Creating a Query

Because the report involves data from two tables, the query needs to draw data from two tables. To create such a query, you will need to create a multi-table query. Perform the following steps to create a query for the report.

More *About*
Grouping in a Report

To force each group to begin on a new page of the report, change the value of the ForceNewPage property for the group header section from None to Before Section. You can change the ForceNewPage property for any section except the page header and page footer.

TO CREATE A QUERY

Step 1: In the Database window, click the Tables tab and then, if necessary, click the Client table. Click the New Object: AutoForm button arrow on the toolbar. Click Query. Be sure Design View is selected, and then click the OK button.

Step 2: If necessary, maximize the Select Query window. Resize the upper and lower panes and the Client field list so that all fields in the Client table display. Add the Technician table by right-clicking any open area in the upper pane of the Select Query window, clicking Show Table on the shortcut menu, clicking the Technician table, clicking the Add button, and clicking the Close button. Expand the size of the field list so all the fields display.

Step 3: Include the Tech Number field from the Technician table and then select Ascending as the sort order. Include the First Name and Last Name fields from the Technician table. Include the Client Number, Name, Billed, and Paid fields from the Client table.

All the necessary fields are included (Figure 4-22), although currently some are off the right edge of the design grid.

Step 4: Click the Close button for the Select Query window, click the Yes button, type `Clients by Technician` as the name, and click the OK button.

The query is created and saved.

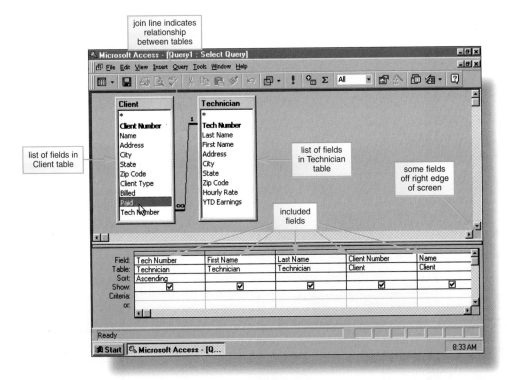

FIGURE 4-22

Creating a Second Report

As you did when creating the first report, you will use the Report Wizard to create the second report. Perform the steps on the next page to create the report shown in Figure 4-2 on page A 4.8.

Steps To Create a Second Report

1 In the Database window, click the Reports tab and then click the New button. Click Report Wizard, select the Clients by Technician query, and then point to the OK button.

The New Report dialog box displays and the Clients by Technician query is selected (Figure 4-23).

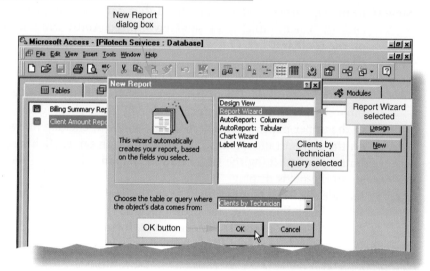

FIGURE 4-23

2 Click the OK button and then point to the Add All Fields button.

The Report Wizard dialog box displays, requesting the fields for the report (Figure 4-24).

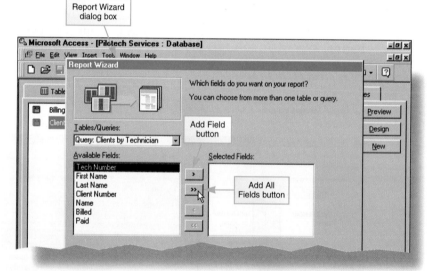

FIGURE 4-24

3 Click the Add All Fields button to add all the fields, and then click the Next button.

The next Report Wizard dialog box displays (Figure 4-25). Because two tables are in the query, the wizard is asking you to indicate how the data is to be viewed; that is, the way the report is to be organized. The report may be organized by Technician or by Client.

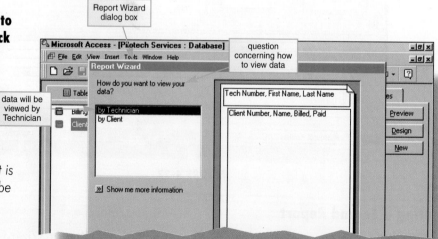

FIGURE 4-25

4 **Because the report is to be viewed by technician and by Technician already is selected, click the Next button.**

Access groups the report automatically by Tech Number, which is the key to the Technician table. The next Report Wizard dialog box displays, asking for additional grouping levels other than the Tech Number.

5 **Because no additional grouping levels are required, click the Next button. Click the box 1 arrow and then click the Client Number field. Point to the Summary Options button.**

The next Report Wizard dialog box displays, requesting the sort order for detail records in the report; that is, the way in which records will be sorted within each of the groups (Figure 4-26). The Client Number field is selected for the sort order, indicating that within the group of clients of any technician, the clients will be sorted by client number.

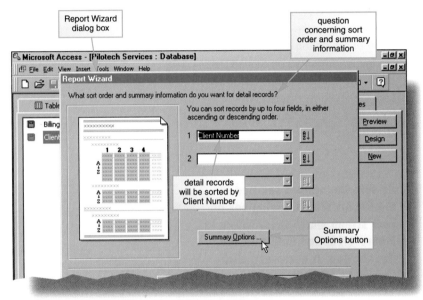

FIGURE 4-26

6 **Click the Summary Options button. Point to the Sum check box in the row labeled Billed.**

The Summary Options dialog box displays (Figure 4-27). This dialog box allows you to indicate any statistics you want calculated in the report by clicking the appropriate check box.

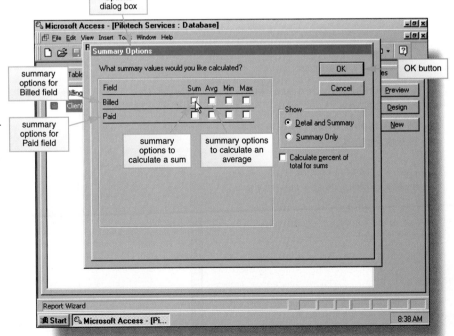

FIGURE 4-27

7 Click the Sum check box in the Billed row and the Sum check box in the Paid row. Click the OK button in the Summary Options dialog box, and then click the Next button.

The next Report Wizard dialog box displays, requesting your report layout preference (Figure 4-28). The Stepped layout, which is the correct one, already is selected. To see the effect of any of the others, click the appropriate option button. The sample layout displayed on the left side of this screen will change to represent the layout you select. The Stepped option button should be selected before you proceed.

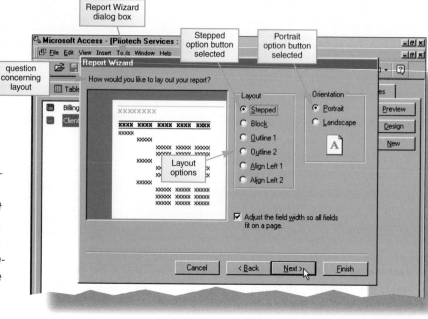

FIGURE 4-28

8 Be sure the options selected in the Report Wizard dialog box on your screen match those shown in Figure 4-28, and then click the Next button. If necessary, click Formal to select it.

The next Report Wizard dialog box displays, requesting a style for the report. The Formal style is selected (Figure 4-29).

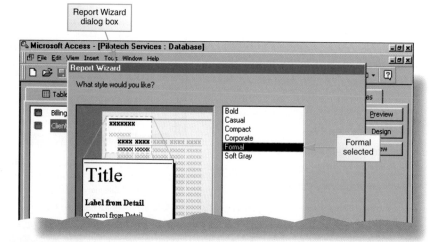

FIGURE 4-29

9 Click the Next button and then type Clients by Technician as the report title. Point to the Finish button.

The next Report Wizard dialog box displays, requesting a title for the report (Figure 4-30). Clients by Technician is typed as the title.

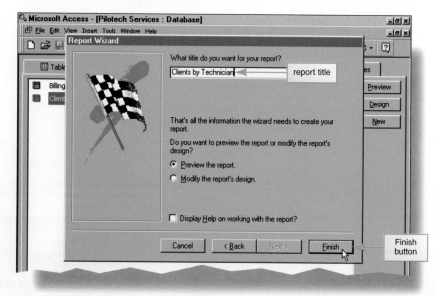

FIGURE 4-30

10 **Click the Finish button.**

The report design is complete and displays in the Print Preview window (Figure 4-31).

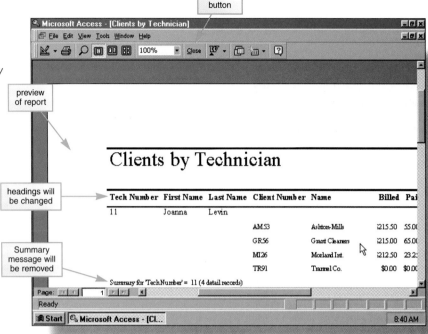

FIGURE 4-31

Reviewing the Report Design

Three major differences exist between the report in Figure 4-31 and the one in Figure 4-2 on page A 4.8. The first is that all the column headings in Figure 4-31 are on a single line, whereas they extend over two lines in the report in Figure 4-2. The first column heading in Figure 4-2 is Technician Number, rather than Tech Number. The second difference is that the report in Figure 4-2 does not contain the message that begins, Summary for Tech Number. Other messages are on the report in Figure 4-31 that are not on the report in Figure 4-2, but they are included on a portion of the report that currently does not display. The final difference is that the Billed and Paid fields do not display completely.

To complete the report design, you must change the column headings and remove these extra messages. In addition, you will move and resize the Billed and Paid fields so the values display completely. (Changing the Can Grow property would not work here because it places part of the number on one line and the rest on the next line. While this is appropriate for names, it is not appropriate for numbers.)

Removing Unwanted Controls

To remove the extra messages, or any other control, first click the control to select it. Then press the DELETE key to remove the unwanted control. Perform the steps on the next page to remove the unwanted controls from the report.

Steps **To Remove Unwanted Controls**

1 Click the Close button on the toolbar to return to the Report window. Point to the control that begins, ="Summary for " (Figure 4-32).

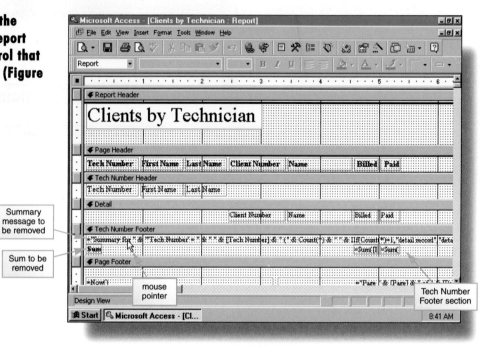

FIGURE 4-32

2 Click the control to select it, and then press the DELETE key to delete it. In a similar fashion, delete the control below that reads, Sum. Click the down scroll arrow so the Report Footer displays and then delete the control that begins, Grand.

The controls have been removed (Figure 4-33).

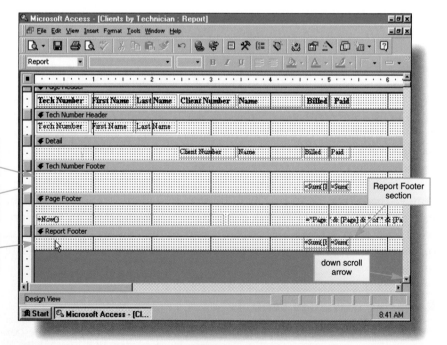

FIGURE 4-33

Enlarging the Page Header Section

The current Page Header section is not large enough to encompass the desired column headings because several of them extend over two lines. Thus, before changing the column headings, you must **enlarge** the Page Header. To do so, drag the bottom border of the Page Header section down. A bold line in the Page Header section immediately below the column headings also must be dragged down.

Perform the following steps to enlarge the Page Header section and move the bold line.

 Steps To Enlarge the Page Header Section

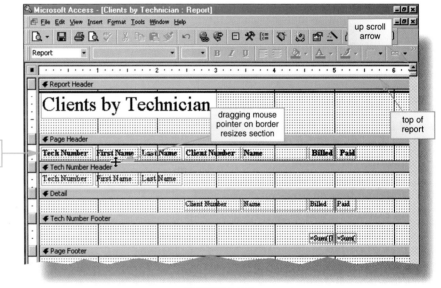

1 Click the up scroll arrow to move to the top of the report. Point to the bottom border of the Page Header section (Figure 4-34). The mouse pointer shape changes to a two-headed vertical arrow.

FIGURE 4-34

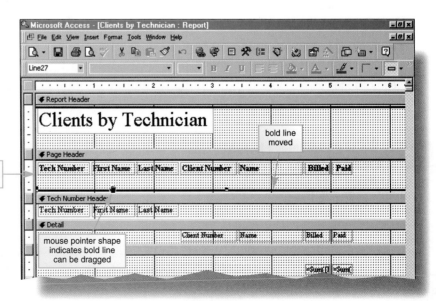

2 Drag the mouse pointer down to enlarge the size of the Page Header section to that shown in Figure 4-35 and then drag the bold line in the Page Header section down to the position shown in the figure. The mouse pointer will display as a hand as you drag the line.

FIGURE 4-35

Changing Column Headings

To change a column heading, point to the position at which you would like to produce an insertion point. Click once to select the heading. Handles will appear around the border of the heading after clicking. Then, click a second time to produce the insertion point. Once you have produced the insertion point, you can make the desired changes. To delete a character, press the DELETE key to delete the character following the insertion point, or the BACKSPACE key to delete the character preceding the insertion point. To insert a new character, simply type the character. To move the portion following the insertion point to a second line, press the SHIFT+ENTER keys.

If you click the second time too rapidly, Access will assume that you have double-clicked the heading. Double-clicking a control is another way to produce the control's property sheet. If this happens, simply close the property sheet and begin the process again.

Perform the following steps to change the column headings.

Steps **To Change the Column Headings**

1 **Point immediately in front of the N in Number in the heading for the first field. Click the column heading for the first field to select it. Click it a second time to produce an insertion point in front of the N, and then press the SHIFT + ENTER keys. Click immediately after the h in Tech and then type** nician **to complete the word, Technician, on the first line.**

The heading is split over two lines (Figure 4-36). The heading has been changed to Technician Number.

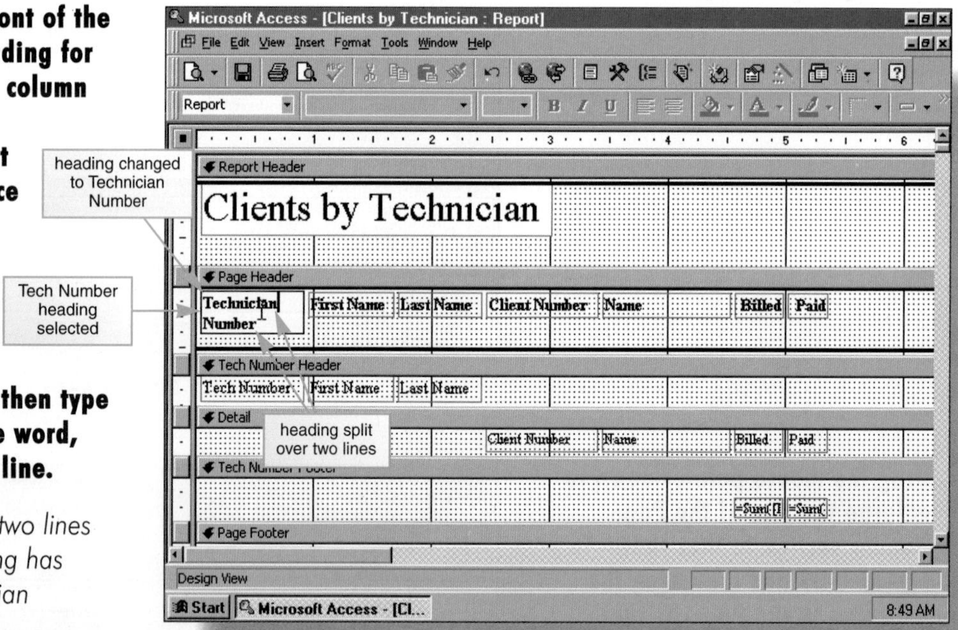

2 **Use the same technique to split the headings for the First Name, Last Name, and Client Number fields over two lines.**

FIGURE 4-36

The changes to the header now are complete.

Moving and Resizing Controls

To move, resize, delete, or modify a single control, click it. **Sizing handles** display around the border of the control. To move the control, point to the boundary of the control, but away from any sizing handle. The mouse pointer changes shape to a hand. You then can drag the control to move it. To resize the control, drag one of the sizing handles.

You can move or resize several controls at the same time by selecting them all before dragging. This is especially useful when controls must line up in a column. For example, the Paid control in the Page Header should line up above the Paid control in the Detail section. These controls also should line up with the controls in the Tech Number Footer and Report Footer sections that will display the sum of the paid amounts.

To select multiple controls, click the first control you wish to select. Then hold down the SHIFT key while you click each of the others. The following steps first will select the controls in the Page Header, Detail, Tech Number Footer, and Report Footer sections that relate to the Paid amount. You then will move and resize all these controls at once. Next, you will use the same technique to move and resize the controls that relate to the Billed amount. Finally, to ensure enough room for complete names, you will enlarge the Name controls in the Page Header and Detail sections.

 Steps To Move and Resize Controls

1 **Click the down scroll arrow so the Report Footer displays. Click the Paid control in the Page Header section to select it. Hold down the SHIFT key and click the Paid control in the Detail section, the control for the sum of the Paid amounts in the Tech Number Footer section, and the control for the sum of the Paid amounts in the Report Footer section. Release the SHIFT key. Point to the border of the Paid control in the Page Header section but away from any handle.**

Multiple controls are selected (Figure 4-37).

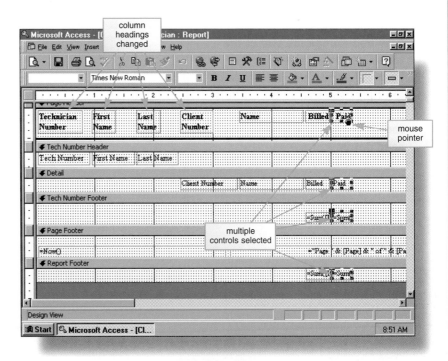

FIGURE 4-37

2 Drag the Paid control in the Page Header section to the position shown in Figure 4-38. Drag the right sizing handle of the Paid control in the Page Header section to change the size of the control to the one shown in the figure. (You need not be exact.)

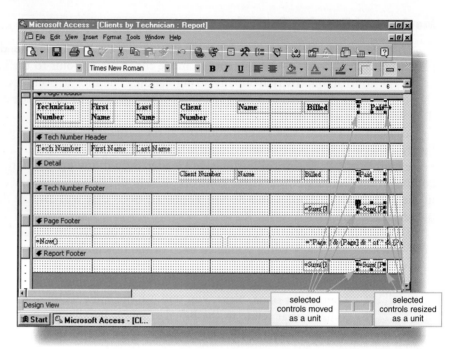

FIGURE 4-38

3 Use the same technique to move the controls for the Billed field to the position shown in Figure 4-39 and change the size of the controls to those shown in the figure. Use the same technique to change the size of the controls for the Name field to those shown in the figure. (Again, you need not be exact.)

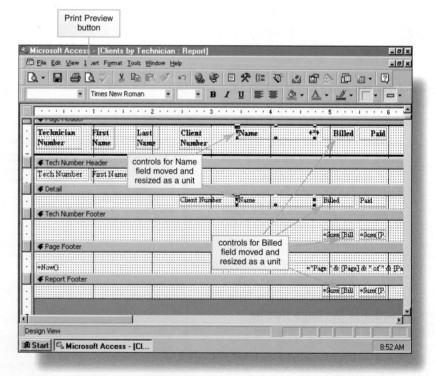

FIGURE 4-39

Previewing a Report

To see what the report looks like with sample data, preview the report by clicking the Print Preview button on the toolbar as illustrated in the following step.

TO PREVIEW A REPORT

Step 1: Click the Print Preview button on the toolbar. If the entire width of the report does not display, click anywhere within the report.

A preview of the report displays (Figure 4-40). The extra messages have been removed. The column headings have been changed and now extend over two lines.

Closing and Saving a Report

To close a report, close the window using the window's Close button. Then, indicate whether you want to save your changes. Perform the following step to close and save the report.

TO CLOSE AND SAVE A REPORT

Step 1: Click the window's Close button to close the window. Click the Yes button to save the design of the report.

Printing a Report

To print the report, right-click the report name in the Database window, and then click Print on the shortcut menu as shown in the following step.

TO PRINT A REPORT

Step 1: Make sure that the reports display in the Database window. Right-click the Clients by Technician report and then click Print on the shortcut menu.

The report prints. It should look like the report shown in Figure 4-2 on page A 4.8.

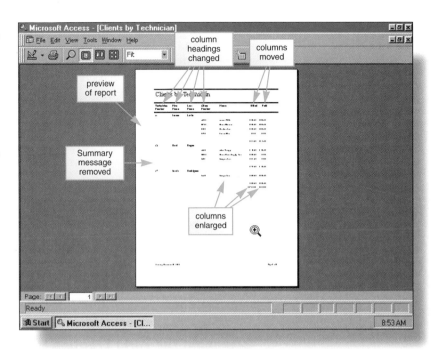

FIGURE 4-40

Report Design Considerations

When designing and creating reports, keep in mind the following guidelines.

1. The purpose of any report is to provide specific information. Ask yourself if the report conveys this information effectively. Are the meanings of the rows and columns in the report clear? Are the column captions easily understood? Are any abbreviations contained on the report that may not be clear to those looking at the report?

2. Be sure to allow sufficient white space between groups. If you feel the amount is insufficient, add more by enlarging the group footer.

3. You can use different fonts and sizes, but do not overuse them. Using more than two or three different fonts and/or sizes often gives a cluttered and amateurish look to the report.
4. Be consistent when creating reports. Once you have decided on a general style, stick with it.

Creating and Using Custom Forms

More *About*
Creating Forms

There are two alternatives to using the Form Wizard to create forms. You can use AutoForm to create a very simple form that includes all fields in the table or query. You also can use Design View to create a form totally from scratch.

Thus far, you have used a form to add new records to a table and change existing records. When you did, you created a basic form using the New Object: AutoForm button. Although the form did provide some assistance in the task, the form was not particularly pleasing. The standard form stacked fields on top of each other at the left side of the screen. This section covers custom forms that you can use in place of the basic form created by the Report Wizard. To create such a form, first use the Form Wizard to create a basic form. Then, you can modify the design of this form, transforming it into the one you want.

Beginning the Form Creation

To create a form, first click the Forms tab and then click the New button. Next, use the Form Wizard to create the form. The Form Wizard leads you through a series of choices and questions. Access then will create the form automatically.

Perform the following steps to create an initial form. This form later will be modified to produce the form shown in Figure 4-3 on page A 4.8.

Steps To Begin Creating a Form

1 **Click the Forms tab, click the New button, click Form Wizard, click the list box arrow, and then click the Client table.**

The New Form dialog box displays. Form Wizard and the Client table are both selected.

2 **Click the OK button and then point to the Add Field button.**

The Form Wizard dialog box displays (Figure 4-41). The Client Number field is selected.

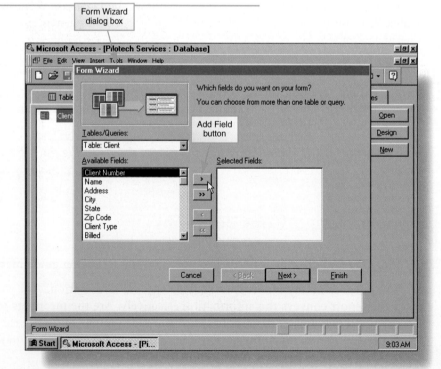

FIGURE 4-41

3 Use the Add Field button to add all the fields except the Tech Number field, and then click the Next button. When asked for a layout, be sure Columnar is selected, and then click the Next button again.

The Form Wizard dialog box displays, requesting a form style (Figure 4-42).

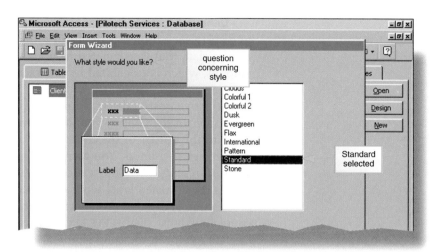

FIGURE 4-42

4 Be sure Standard is selected, click the Next button, type `Client Update Form` as the title for the form. Click the Finish button to complete and display the form.

The form displays (Figure 4-43).

5 Click the Close button for the Client Update Form window to close the form.

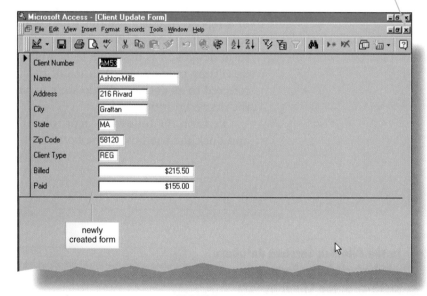

FIGURE 4-43

Modifying the Form Design

To modify the design of an existing form, right-click the form in the Database window, and then click Design on the shortcut menu. Then, modify the design. The modifications can include moving fields, adding new fields, and changing field characteristics. In addition, they can include adding special features, such as combo boxes and titles. The modifications also can involve changes to colors.

Just as with reports, the various items on a form are called **controls**. The three types are **bound controls**, which are used to display data that comes from the database, such as the client number and name. Bound controls have attached labels that typically display the name of the field that furnishes the data for the control. The **attached label** for the Client Number field, for example, is the portion of the screen immediately to the left of the field. It contains the words, Client Number.

OtherWays

1. With table selected, click New Object button arrow on toolbar, click Form, click Form Wizard to create form
2. On Insert menu click Form, click Form Wizard to create form

More *About*
Attached Labels

You can remove an attached label by clicking the label and then pressing the DELETE key. The label will be removed, but the control will remain. To attach a label to a control, create the label, click the Cut button, click the Control, and then click the Paste button.

Unbound controls are not associated with data from the database and are used to display such things as the form's title. Finally, **calculated controls** are used to display data that is calculated from data in the database, such as the outstanding amount, which is calculated by subtracting the paid amount from the billed amount.

To move, resize, delete, or modify a control, click it. Handles display around the border of the control and, if appropriate, around the attached label. If you point to the border of the control, but away from any handle, the pointer shape will change to a hand. You then can drag the control to move it. If an attached label is present, it will move along with the control. If you wish to move the control or the attached label separately, drag the large handle in the upper-left corner of the control or label. You also can drag one of the sizing handles to resize the control, or press the DELETE key to delete it. Clicking a second time produces an insertion point in the control in order to modify its contents.

Just as with reports, some of the changes involve using the property sheet for the control to be changed. You will use the property sheet of the Outstanding Amount control, for example, to change the format that Access uses to display the contents of the control.

The toolbox also can obscure a portion of the form as it obscured a portion of a report. You can use the Toolbox button to remove it and return it to the screen when needed. Because you use the toolbox frequently when modifying form designs, it is desirable to be able to leave it on the screen, however. You can do this by moving it to a different position on the screen, which is a process referred to as **docking**. To do so, you simply drag the title bar of the toolbox to the desired position.

Perform the following steps to modify the design of the Client Update Form and dock the toolbox at the bottom of the screen.

Steps To Modify the Form Design

1 In the Pilotech Services database window, click the Forms tab. Right-click the Client Update Form to display its shortcut menu.

The shortcut menu for the Client Update Form displays.

2 Click Design on the shortcut menu. Maximize the window, if necessary. Be sure the toolbox displays. (If it does not, click the Toolbox button on the toolbar). Point to the title bar of the toolbox (Figure 4-44).

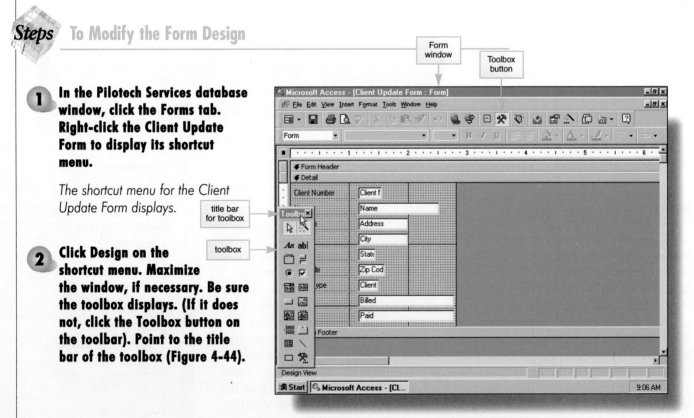

FIGURE 4-44

3 If the toolbox is not already docked at the bottom of the screen, drag the title bar of the toolbox below the scroll bar at the bottom of the screen and release the left mouse button.

The toolbox is docked at the bottom of the screen (Figure 4-45).

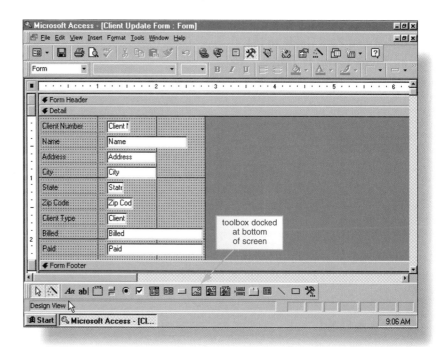

FIGURE 4-45

4 Click the control for the Client Type field, and then move the mouse pointer until the shape changes to a hand. (You will need to point to the border of the control but away from any handle.)

Move handles display, indicating the field is selected (Figure 4-46). The shape of the mouse pointer has changed to a hand.

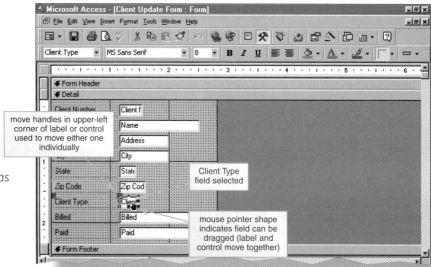

FIGURE 4-46

5 Drag the Client Type field to the approximate position shown in Figure 4-47. The form will expand automatically in size to accommodate the new position for the field.

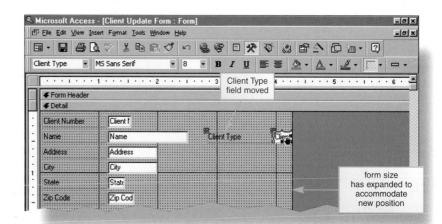

FIGURE 4-47

6 Use the same steps to move the Billed and Paid fields to the positions shown in Figure 4-48.

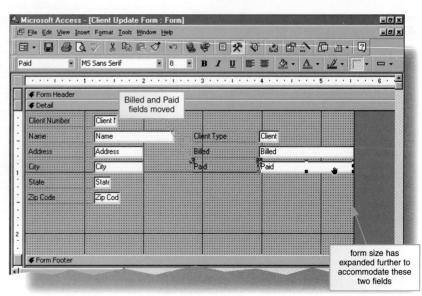

FIGURE 4-48

Adding a New Field

To add a new field, use the **Text Box button** in the toolbox to add a field. After clicking the Text Box button, click the position for the field on the form, and then indicate the contents of the field. Perform the following steps to add the Outstanding Amount field to the form.

 Steps To Add a New Field

1 Point to the Text Box button in the toolbox (Figure 4-49).

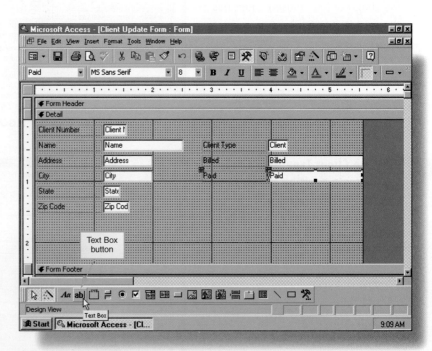

FIGURE 4-49

2 Click the Text Box button in the toolbox, and then move the mouse pointer, which has changed shape to a small plus sign accompanied by a text box, to the position shown in Figure 4-50.

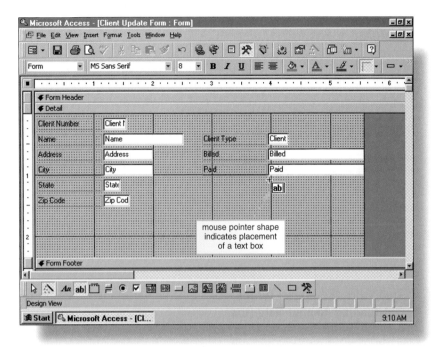

FIGURE 4-50

3 Click the position shown in Figure 4-50 to place a text box. **Type** =[Billed]-[Paid] **as the expression in the text box. Click the field label (the box that contains the word Text) twice, once to select it and a second time to produce an insertion point. Use the DELETE key or the BACKSPACE key to delete the current entry. Type** Outstanding Amount **as the new entry.**

The expression for the field has been entered and the label has been changed to Outstanding Amount (Figure 4-51).

4 Click outside the Outstanding Amount control to deselect it. Then, click the control to select it once more. Handles will display around the control. Move the label portion so its left edge lines up with the labels for the Client Type, Billed, and Paid fields by dragging the move handle in its upper-left corner.

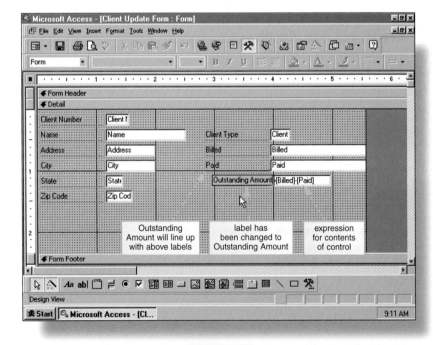

FIGURE 4-51

More *About*
Changing a Format

Access assigns formats to database fields, but these formats can be changed by changing the Format property. The specific formats that are available depend on the data type of the field. The Format list also contains samples of the way the data would display with the various formats.

Changing the Format of a Field

Access automatically formats fields from the database appropriately, because it knows their data types. Usually, you will find the formats assigned by Access to be acceptable. For calculated fields, such as Outstanding Amount, however, Access just assigns a general format. The value will not display automatically with two decimal places and a dollar sign.

A special format, such as Currency, which displays the number with a dollar sign and two decimal places, requires using the field's property sheet to change the Format property. Perform the following steps to change the format for the Outstanding Amount field to Currency.

Steps **To Change the Format of a Field**

1 **Right-click the control for the Outstanding Amount field (the box containing the expression) to produce its shortcut menu and then click Properties on the shortcut menu. Click the All tab, if necessary, so all the properties display, and then click the Format property. Point to the Format box arrow.**

The property sheet for the field displays in the Text Box window (Figure 4-52).

2 **Click the Format box arrow to produce a list of available formats. Scroll down so Currency displays and then click Currency. Close the property sheet by clicking its Close button.**

The values in the Outstanding Amount field now display in Currency format, which includes a dollar sign and two decimal places.

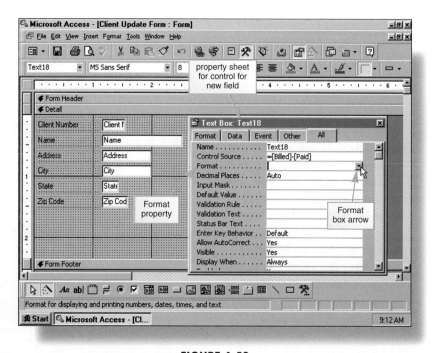

FIGURE 4-52

Placing a Combo Box

To place a combo box, use the Combo Box button in the toolbox. If the **Control Wizards button** in the toolbox is recessed, you can use a wizard to guide you through the process of creating the combo box. Perform the following steps to place a combo box for the Tech Number on the form.

Steps To Place a Combo Box

1 Make sure the Control Wizards button in the toolbox is recessed. Point to the Combo Box button in the toolbox (Figure 4-53).

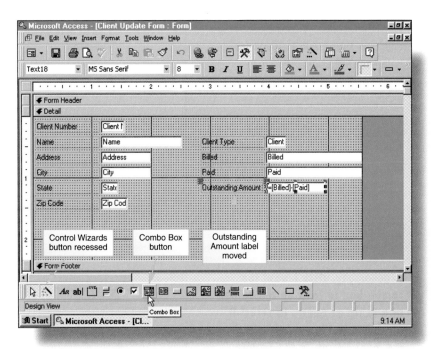

FIGURE 4-53

2 Click the Combo Box button in the toolbox, and then move the mouse pointer, whose shape has changed to a small plus sign accompanied by a combo box, to the position shown in Figure 4-54.

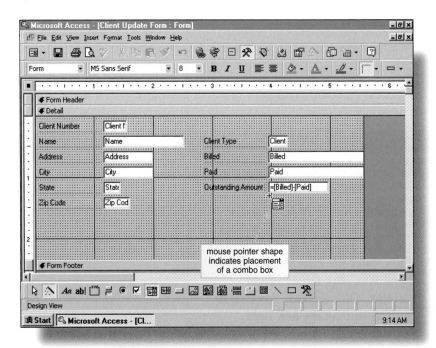

FIGURE 4-54

3 **Click the position shown in Figure 4-54 on the previous page to place a combo box.**

The Combo Box Wizard dialog box displays, requesting that you indicate how the combo box is to receive values for the list (Figure 4-55).

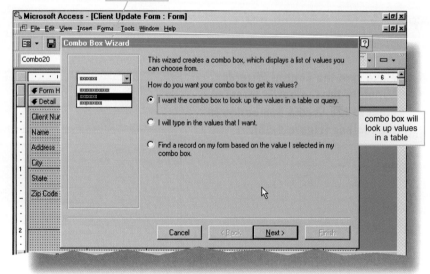

FIGURE 4-55

4 **If necessary, click I want the combo box to look up the values in a table or query. to select it as shown in Figure 4-55. Click the Next button in the Combo Box Wizard dialog box, click the Technician table, and then point to the Next button.**

The Technician table is selected as the table to provide values for the combo box (Figure 4-56).

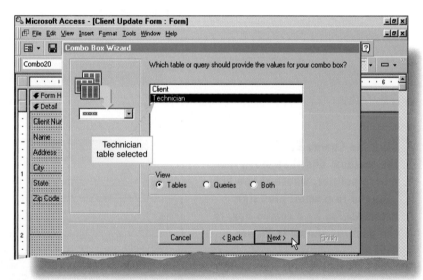

FIGURE 4-56

5 **Click the Next button. Click the Add Field button to add the Tech Number as a field in the combo box. Click the First Name field and then click the Add Field button. Click the Last Name field and then click the Add Field button. Point to the Next button.**

The Tech Number, First Name, and Last Name fields are selected for the combo box (Figure 4-57).

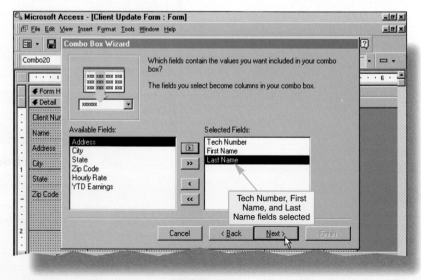

FIGURE 4-57

6 **Click the Next button. Point to the Hide key column (recommended) check box.**

The next Combo Box Wizard dialog box displays (Figure 4-58). You can use this dialog box to change the sizes of the fields. You also can use it to indicate whether the key field, in this case the Tech Number field, should be hidden.

7 **Click Hide key column (recommended) to remove the check mark to ensure the Tech Number field displays along with the First Name and Last Name fields. Resize each column to best fit the data by double-clicking the right-hand border of the column heading. Click the Next button.**

The Combo Box Wizard dialog box displays, asking you to choose a field that uniquely identifies a row in the combo box. The Tech Number field, which is the correct field, already is selected.

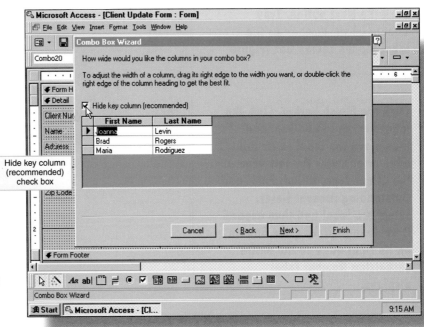

FIGURE 4-58

8 **Click the Next button. Click Store that value in this field. Click the Store that value in this field box arrow, scroll down and then click Tech Number.**

The Store that value in this field option button is selected and the Tech Number field is selected (Figure 4-59).

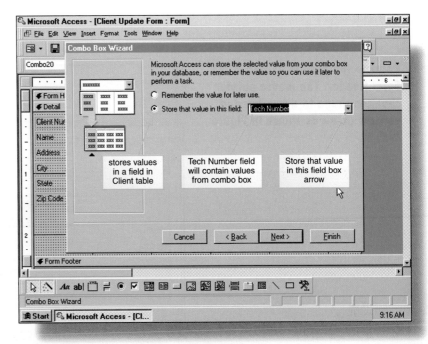

FIGURE 4-59

9 Click the Next button. Type Technician Number as the label for the combo box (Figure 4-60).

10 Click the Finish button. Click the label for the combo box, and then move the label so its left edge aligns with the left edge of the Client Type, Billed, Paid, and Outstanding Amount fields. Select the label and then expand it by double-clicking the handle on its right edge so the entire Technician Number label displays.

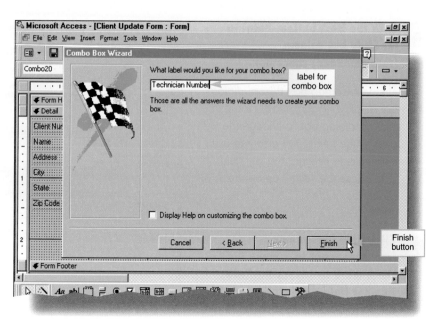

FIGURE 4-60

Adding a Title

The form in Figure 4-3 on page A 4.8 contains a title, Client Update Form that displays in a large, light blue label at the top of the form. To add a title, first expand the Form Header to allow room for the title. Next, use the Label button in the toolbox to place the label in the Form Header. Finally, type the title in the label. Perform the following steps to add a title to the form.

Steps To Add a Title

1 Point to the bottom border of the Form Header. The mouse pointer changes shape to a two-headed vertical arrow as shown in Figure 4-61.

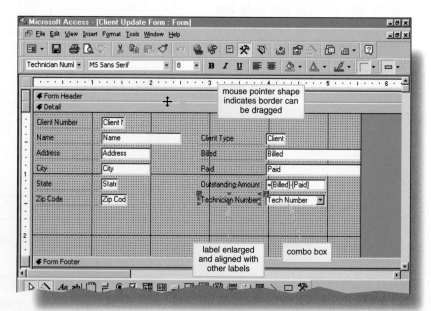

FIGURE 4-61

2 Drag the bottom border of the Form Header to the approximate position shown in Figure 4-62, and then point to the Label button in the toolbox.

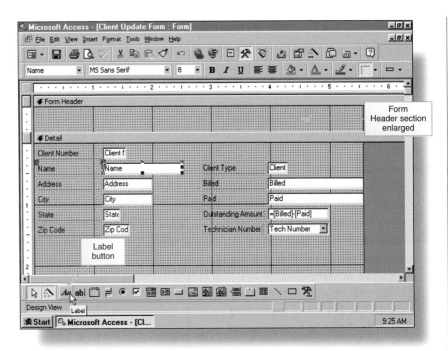

FIGURE 4-62

3 Click the Label button in the toolbox and move the mouse pointer, whose shape has changed to a small plus sign accompanied by a label, into the position shown in Figure 4-63.

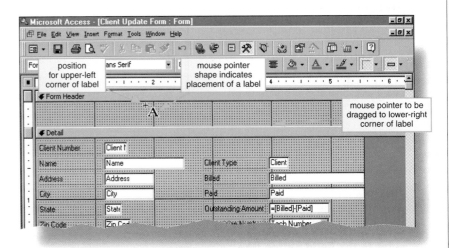

FIGURE 4-63

4 Press the left mouse button and drag the pointer to the opposite corner of the Form Header to form the label shown in Figure 4-64.

5 Type Client Update Form as the form title.

The title is entered.

FIGURE 4-64

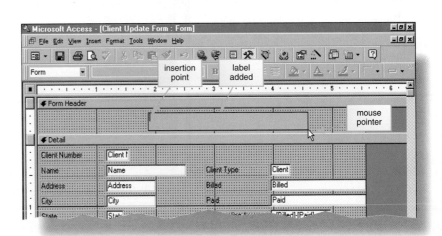

Enhancing a Title

The form now contains a title. You can enhance the appearance of the title by changing various properties of the label containing the title. The following steps change the color of the label, make the label appear to be raised from the screen, change the font size of the title, and change the alignment of the title within the label.

Steps To Enhance a Title

① **Click somewhere outside the label containing the title to deselect the label. Deselecting is required or right-clicking the label will have no effect. Next, right-click the label containing the title. Point to Properties on the shortcut menu.**

The shortcut menu for the label displays (Figure 4-65).

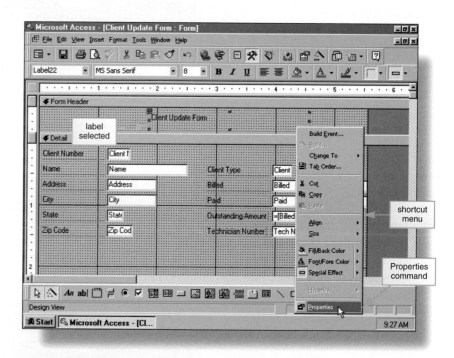

FIGURE 4-65

② **Click Properties. If necessary, click the All tab on the property sheet. Click Back Color and then point to the Build button (the button with the three dots).**

The property sheet for the label displays. The insertion point displays in the Back Color property (Figure 4-66).

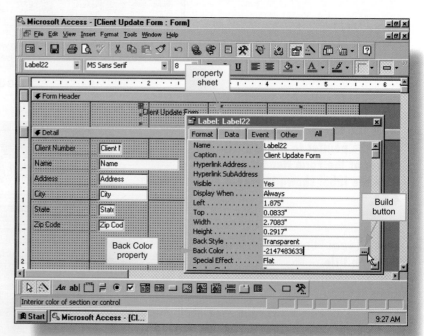

FIGURE 4-66

3 Click the Build button and then point to the color light blue in the Color dialog box that displays (Figure 4-67).

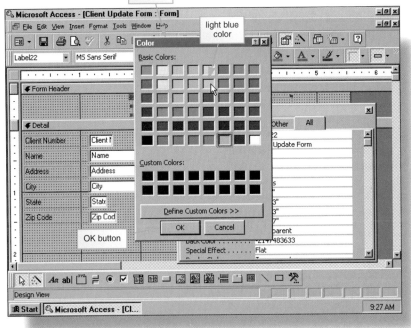

FIGURE 4-67

4 Click the color light blue, and then click the OK button. Click the Special Effect property, and then click the Special Effect box arrow.

The list of available values for the Special Effect property displays (Figure 4-68).

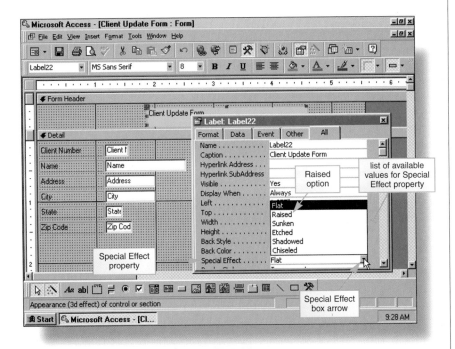

FIGURE 4-68

5 Click Raised. Scroll down the property sheet and then click the Font Size property. Click the Font Size box arrow. Click 14 in the list of font sizes that displays.

6 Scroll down and then click the Text Align property. Click the Text Align box arrow.

The list of available values for the Text Align property displays (Figure 4-69).

7 Click Center. Close the property sheet by clicking its Close button.

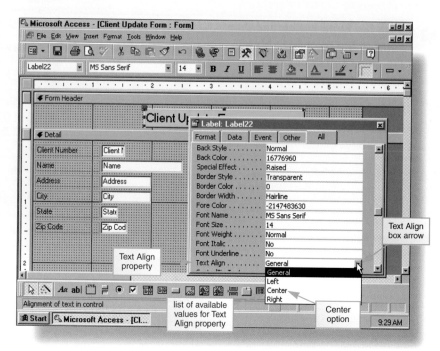

FIGURE 4-69

The enhancements to the title now are complete.

Closing and Saving a Form

To close a form, close the window using the window's Close button. Then indicate whether you want to save your changes. Perform the following step to close and save the form.

Other Ways
1. On File menu click Close

TO CLOSE AND SAVE A FORM

Step 1: Click the window's Close button to close the window, and then click the Yes button to save the design of the form.

Opening a Form

To open a form, right-click a form in the Database window, and then click Open on the shortcut menu. The form will display and can be used to examine and update data. Perform the following steps to open the Client Update Form.

Steps To Open a Form

1 Right-click the Client Update Form to display the shortcut menu. Point to Open on the shortcut menu.

The shortcut menu for the Client Update Form displays (Figure 4-70).

2 Click Open on the shortcut menu.

The form displays. It should look like the form shown in Figure 4-3 on page A 4.8.

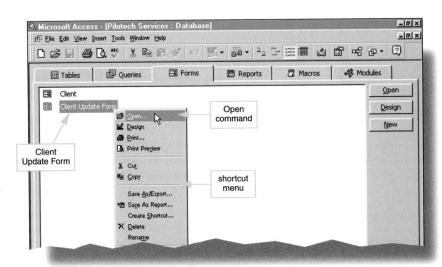

FIGURE 4-70

*Other***Ways**
1. Select form, click Open button on toolbar
2. Double-click form

Using a Form

You use this form as you used the form in Project 3, with two differences. Access will not allow changes to the outstanding amount, because Access calculates this amount automatically by subtracting the paid amount from the billed amount. The other difference is that this form contains a combo box, which you can use to select a Technician Number (Figure 4-3 on page A 4.8).

To use the combo box, click the arrow. The numbers and names of available technicians display as shown in Figure 4-3. Either you can type the appropriate technician number from the list you see on the screen or you can click the appropriate technician. In either case, the combo box helps you make sure you enter the correct number.

Closing a Form

To close a form, simply close the window containing the form. Perform the following step to close the form.

TO CLOSE A FORM

Step 1: Click the Close button for the Form window.

Form Design Considerations

As you design and create custom forms, keep in mind the following guidelines.

1. Remember that someone using your form may be looking at the form for several hours at a time. Forms that are cluttered excessively or that contain too many different effects (colors, fonts, frame styles, and so on) can become very hard on the eyes.

2. Place the fields in logical groupings. Fields that relate to each other should be close to each other on the form.
3. If the data that a user will enter comes from a paper form, make the screen form resemble the paper form as closely as possible.

Publishing to the Web

Access provides the capability of creating a version of a datasheet, form, or report in a format that can be viewed on the **Internet**, specifically on a portion of the Internet called the **World Wide Web**, or simply the **Web**. (It also could be viewed on an organization's **intranet**.) To do so, the version of the object to be viewed must be stored as a **Web page**. Web pages are stored in a language called **HTML** (**hypertext markup language**). Fortunately, you do not need to know the details of this language, because Access will create this version for you automatically. The process of creating such a version is referred to as **publishing to the Web**. The tool in Access that assists you in the process is the Publish to the Web Wizard.

Publishing an Object to the Web

To publish an object to the Web, you first must save the object as HTML. The Publish to the Web Wizard then will lead you through the necessary steps to create the HTML version of the object. Perform the following steps to publish the Client Amount Report to the Web.

Steps To Publish a Report to the Web

1 **With the Database window on the screen, click File on the menu bar and then click Save as HTML. Point to the Next button.**

The Publish to the Web Wizard dialog box displays (Figure 4-71).

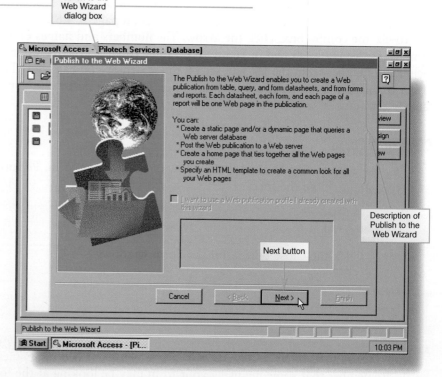

FIGURE 4-71

2 Click the Next button. Click the Reports tab in the next Publish to the Web Wizard dialog box that displays, and then click the check box for the Client Amount Report.

The Publish to the Web Wizard dialog box displays, requesting you to select the objects you wish to publish (Figure 4-72). The Client Amount Report is selected.

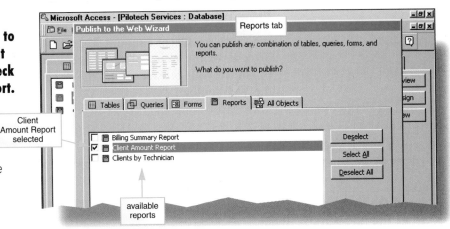

FIGURE 4-72

3 Click the Next button. No HTML document is to be used as a template in this project. Click the Next button. Be sure Static HTML is selected as the default format type, and then click the Next button. Point to the Browse button.

The Publish to the Web Wizard dialog box displays, asking where you want to place the Web publication (Figure 4-73).

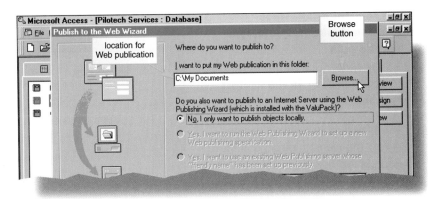

FIGURE 4-73

4 Click the Browse button. Click the Look in box arrow, click 3½ Floppy (A:), click the Access folder, and then click the Select button. Click the Next button.

The Publish to the Web Wizard dialog box displays, asking if you want to create a home page (Figure 4-74). If you were publishing several objects at once, a home page would be a convenient way to tie them together.

5 Be sure the Yes, I want to create a home page. check box is not checked and then click the Next button. Click the Finish button to complete the process.

The Publish to the Web Wizard creates a Web page for the Client Amount Report.

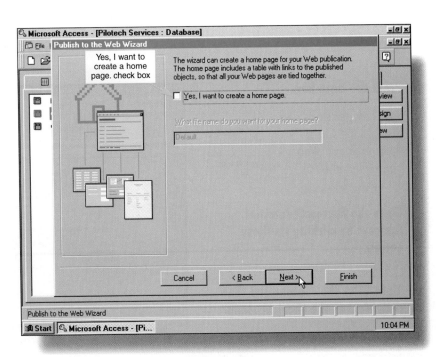

FIGURE 4-74

Viewing a Web Page

Once the Client Amount Report is saved as a Web page, you can use your browser or the **Web toolbar** in Access to display it. The following steps show how to launch your browser using the Access Web toolbar and Address text box on the Web toolbar.

Steps To View a Web Page

1 Insert the floppy disk with the HTML file into drive A. Right-click the toolbar and then click Web on the shortcut menu. When the Web toolbar displays, type the file path a:\access\Client Amount Report_1.html in the Address text box.

The Web toolbar displays (Figure 4-75). The file path displays in the Address text box.

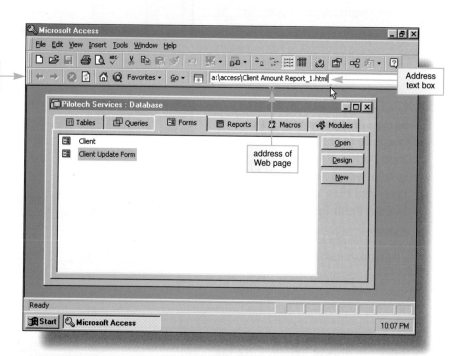

FIGURE 4-75

2 Press the ENTER key.

Your browser starts and displays the Client Amount Report Web page (Figure 4-76).

3 Close the Microsoft Internet Explorer by clicking its Close button.

4 Right-Click the toolbar and then click Web on the shortcut menu.

The Web toolbar no longer displays.

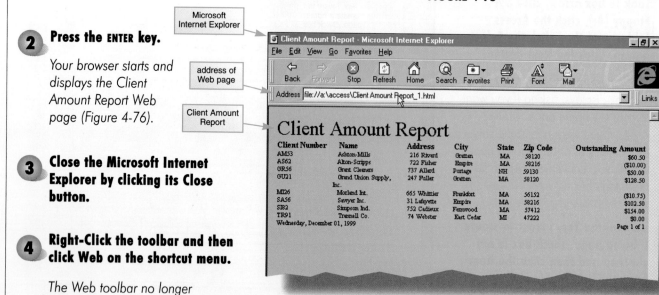

FIGURE 4-76

Closing a Database

The following step closes the database by closing its Database window.

TO CLOSE A DATABASE

Step 1: Click the Close button for the Pilotech Services : Database window.

Project Summary

Project 4 covered the creation of reports and forms. To create the reports for Pilotech Services, you learned the purpose of the various sections and how to modify their contents. You used grouping in a report. You created and used a custom form. Steps and techniques were presented showing you how to move controls, create new controls, add combo boxes, and add a title. You changed the characteristics of various objects in a form. General principles to help you design effective reports and forms were explained. Finally, you learned how to publish an object to the Web (or an intranet connection) using the Publish to the Web Wizard.

What You Should Know

Having completed this project, you now should be able to perform the following tasks:

▶ Add a New Field (A 4.36)

▶ Add a Title (A 4.42)

▶ Begin Creating a Form (A 4.32)

▶ Change the Can Grow Property (A 4.17)

▶ Change the Column Headings (A 4.28)

▶ Change the Format of a Field (A 4.38)

▶ Close a Database (A 4.51)

▶ Close a Form (A 4.47)

▶ Close and Save a Form (A 4.46)

▶ Close and Save a Report (A 4.19, A 4.31)

▶ Create a Report (A 4.11)

▶ Create a Second Report (A 4.22)

▶ Create a Query (A 4.10, A 4.21)

▶ Enhance a Title (A 4.44)

▶ Enlarge the Page Header Section (A 4.27)

▶ Modify the Form Design (A 4.34)

▶ Move and Resize Controls (A 4.29)

▶ Move to Design View and Remove the Toolbox (A 4.16)

▶ Open a Database (A 4.9)

▶ Open a Form (A 4.47)

▶ Place a Combo Box (A 4.39)

▶ Preview a Report (A 4.31)

▶ Print a Report (A 4.20, A 4.31)

▶ Publish a Report to the Web (A 4.48)

▶ Remove Unwanted Controls (A 4.26)

▶ View a Web Page (A 4.50)

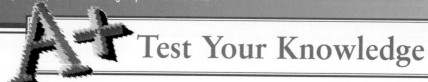

Test Your Knowledge

1 True/False

Instructions: Circle T if the statement is true or F if the statement is false.

T F 1. Only a report that does not need to be modified in any way can be created with the Report Wizard.

T F 2. The contents of the Page Footer section will display only once on a report.

T F 3. The Report window uses small squares called sizing handles to indicate which portion of a report currently is selected.

T F 4. The various entries appearing in a report, such as the report title and a column heading, are called containers.

T F 5. To remove a control from a report, select the control and press the CTRL+D keys.

T F 6. To split a column heading over two lines, place the insertion point at the position where you would like to split the heading, and then press the TAB+ENTER keys.

T F 7. The three types of controls on a form are bound controls, unbound controls, and calculated controls.

T F 8. On a form, unbound controls are used to display the title.

T F 9. To add a new field to a form, use the Label button in the toolbox.

T F 10. A combo box is a box that allows you to select entries from a list.

2 Multiple Choice

Instructions: Circle the correct response.

1. The process of creating separate collections of records sharing some common characteristic is known as _____.
   a. collecting
   b. matching
   c. categorizing
   d. grouping

2. By changing the value of the _____ property, data can be split over two lines on a report.
   a. Enlarge
   b. Can Grow
   c. Magnify
   d. Expand

3. To remove a control from a report, select the control and then _____.
   a. press the DELETE key
   b. press the CTRL+DELETE keys
   c. press the CTRL+D keys
   d. right-click

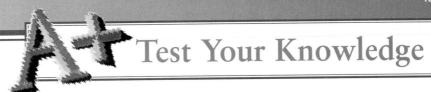 Test Your Knowledge

4. Portions of the Report window such as Report Header or Page Header are called _____.
   a. segments
   b. sections
   c. areas
   d. bands

5. The Report window uses small squares called _____ to indicate which portion of the report currently is selected.
   a. handholds
   b. braces
   c. handles
   d. grippers

6. To split a column heading over two lines, place the insertion point at the position where you would like to split the heading, and then press the _____ keys.
   a. SHIFT+ENTER
   b. ENTER
   c. ALT+ENTER
   d. TAB+ENTER

7. On a custom form, controls that are used to display data in a database are called _____ controls.
   a. bound
   b. field
   c. unbound
   d. data

8. On a form, _____ controls are used to display data that is calculated from data in the database.
   a. tabulated
   b. calculated
   c. defined
   d. extended

9. Controls that are not associated with data in a database are called _____ controls.
   a. text
   b. bound
   c. unbound
   d. outside

10. To add a new field to a form, use the _____ button in the toolbox.
    a. Object Box
    b. Control Box
    c. Field Box
    d. Text Box

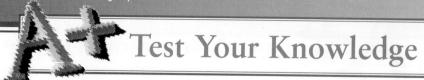

3 Understanding the Report Window

Instructions: In Figure 4-77, arrows point to the major components of the Report window. Identify the various parts of the Report window in the spaces provided. Answer the following questions about the window on your own paper.

1. How many times will the control with the label =Sum([Balance]) print?

   1. _____

2. How can you delete the control that begins ="Summary for"?

   2. _____

   3. _____

   4. _____

3. What values will print once at the top of every page?

FIGURE 4-77

4 Understanding the Form Design Window

Instructions: In Figure 4-78, arrows point to various items in the Form Design window. Identify these items in the spaces provided. Answer the following questions about the window on your own paper.

1. Which control currently is selected?

2. Identify the unbound control(s) on the form.

3. Identify the bound control(s) on the form.

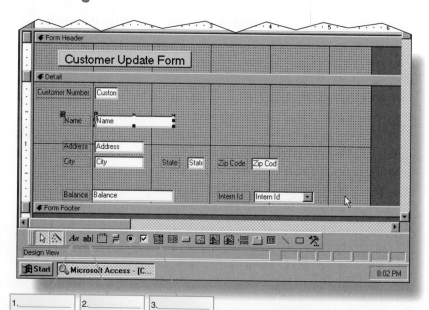

1. _____

2. _____

3. _____

FIGURE 4-78

? Use Help

1 Reviewing Project Activities

Instructions: Perform the following tasks using a computer.

1. Start Access.
2. If the Office Assistant is on your screen, then click it to display its balloon. If the Office Assistant is not on your screen, click the Office Assistant button on the toolbar.
3. Type `property sheet` in the What would you like to do? text box. Click the Search button. Click What is a property sheet?.
4. Read the Help information in the Microsoft Access 97 Help window. Next, right-click within the box, and then click Print Topic. Hand the printout in to your instructor. Click the Help Topics button to the return to the Help Topics: Microsoft Access 97 dialog box.
5. Click the Index tab. Type `grouping` in the top text box labeled 1, and then double-click grouping records in reports in the middle list box labeled 2. Double-click Example of grouped records in a report in the Topics Found dialog box. Read the Help information. Use the page number buttons in the upper-left corner of the screen to move to the next Help windows. Three Help windows will display. When you are finished, click the Close button.
6. Click the Office Assistant. Type `controls` in the What would you like to do? text box. Click the Search button. Click Move a control and its label. Read and print the Help information. Hand the printout in to your instructor.

2 Expanding the Basics

Instructions: Use Access Help to better understand the topics listed below. If you cannot print the Help information, then answer the question on your own paper.

1. Using the Office Assistant, answer the following questions:
   a. How can you change the page orientation for a report?
   b. Do you need to reset special page setup options each time you print a report?
   c. How can you preview just the layout of a report?
2. Use the Index tab in the Help Topics: Microsoft Access 97 dialog box to answer the following questions about fonts on forms and reports:
   a. How do you italicize text using the property sheet?
   b. What is the Formatting toolbar?
   c. Where is the Formatting toolbar located?
   d. How else can you italicize text?
3. Use the Find tab in the Help Topics: Microsoft Access 97 dialog box to display and print information on adding the current date and time to a form.
4. Use the Office Assistant to display and print information on exporting a table, query, form, or report to HTML format. Then, answer the following questions:
   a. What is an HTML template file?
   b. When do you use dynamic HTML format?

Apply Your Knowledge

1 Presenting Data in the Green Thumb Database

Instructions: Start Access and open the Green Thumb database from the Access folder on the Data Disk that accompanies this book. Perform the following tasks.

1. Create a query that includes both the Customer and Intern tables. Include the Intern Id, First Name, and Last Name from the Intern table. Include the Customer Number, Name, and Balance from the Customer table.
2. Using the query, create the report shown in Figure 4-79.

Customers by Intern

Intern Id	First Name	Last Name	Customer Number	Name	Balance
102	Chou	Dang			
			AS36	Asterman Ind.	$85.00
			CJ16	CJ's Music and Videos	$105.00
					$190.00
105	Lois	Eckels			
			KL55	Klingon Toys	$115.00
					$115.00
109	Michelle	Hyde			
			AU54	Author Books	$50.00
			BI92	Bike Shop	$40.00
			JO62	Jordan Diner	$74.00
			RO32	Royal Mfg Co.	$93.00
					$257.00
113	Javier	Lopez			
			CI76	Cinderton Co.	$0.00
			MO13	Moore Foods	$0.00
					$0.00
					$562.00

Wednesday, December 30, 1998

Page 1 of 1

FIGURE 4-79

Apply Your Knowledge

3. Print the report.
4. Using the Form Wizard, create a form for the Customer table. Include all fields except Intern Id on the form. Use Customer Update Form as the title for the form.
5. Modify the form in the Design window to create the form shown in Figure 4-80. The form includes a combo box for the Intern Id field.

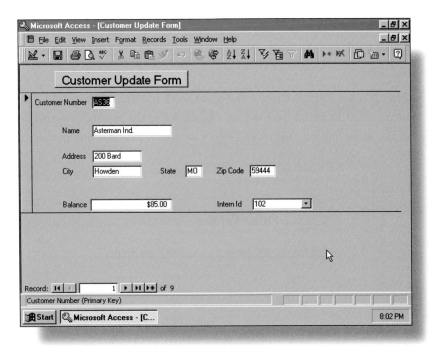

FIGURE 4-80

6. Print the form. To print the form, open the form, click File on the menu bar and then click Print. Click Selected Record(s) as the Print Range. Click the OK button.

In the Lab

1 Presenting Data in the Museum Mercantile Database

Problem: Museum Mercantile already has realized the benefits from the database of products and vendors that you created. The Museum director must now prepare reports for auditors as well as the executive board of the Museum. The director and volunteer staff greatly appreciate the validation rules that were added to ensure that data is entered correctly. They now feel they can improve the data entry process even further by creating custom forms.

Instructions: Open the Museum Mercantile database in the Access folder (see the note on page A 4.8). Perform the following tasks.

1. Create the On Hand Value Report shown in Figure 4-81 for the Product table. On Hand Value is the result of multiplying On Hand by Cost. In Figure 4-81, the report title and column headings are italicized. (*Hint*: Use information from Use Help Exercise 2 to solve this problem.)

On Hand Value Report

Product Id	Description	On Hand	Cost	On Hand Value
CH04	Chess Set	11	$26.75	$294.25
DI24	Dinosaurs	14	$3.75	$52.50
GL18	Globe	2	$27.50	$55.00
JG01	Jigsaw Puzzle	3	$5.40	$16.20
MN04	Mancala	4	$17.50	$70.00
PC03	Pick Up Sticks	5	$8.50	$42.50
ST23	Stationery	8	$3.95	$31.60
WI10	Wizard Cards	10	$7.50	$75.00
WL34	Wildlife Posters	15	$2.50	$37.50
YO12	Wooden YoYo	9	$1.60	$14.40

FIGURE 4-81

2. Print the report.
3. Create the Products by Vendor report shown in Figure 4-82. Profit is the difference between Selling Price and Cost.

In the Lab

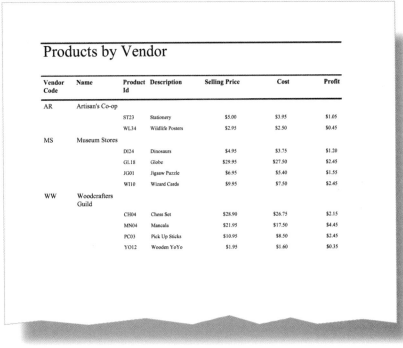

Products by Vendor

Vendor Code	Name	Product Id	Description	Selling Price	Cost	Profit
AR	Artisan's Co-op					
		ST23	Stationery	$5.00	$3.95	$1.05
		WL34	Wildlife Posters	$2.95	$2.50	$0.45
MS	Museum Stores					
		DI24	Dinosaurs	$4.95	$3.75	$1.20
		GL18	Globe	$29.95	$27.50	$2.45
		JG01	Jigsaw Puzzle	$6.95	$5.40	$1.55
		WI10	Wizard Cards	$9.95	$7.50	$2.45
WW	Woodcrafters Guild					
		CH04	Chess Set	$28.90	$26.75	$2.15
		MN04	Mancala	$21.95	$17.50	$4.45
		PC03	Pick Up Sticks	$10.95	$8.50	$2.45
		YO12	Wooden YoYo	$1.95	$1.60	$0.35

FIGURE 4-82

4. Print the report.
5. Create the form shown in Figure 4-83. On Hand Value is a calculated control and is the result of multiplying On Hand by Cost. Include a combo box for Vendor Code.
6. Print the form. To print the form, open the form, click File on the menu bar and then click Print. Click Selected Record(s) as the Print Range. Click the OK button.

FIGURE 4-83

In the Lab

2 Presenting Data in the City Telephone System Database

Problem: The Telephone manager already has realized several benefits from the database of users and departments that you created. The manager now would like to prepare reports from the database that can be used for hourly rate purposes. She greatly appreciates the validation rules that were added to ensure that data is entered correctly. She now feels that the data entry process can be improved even further by creating custom forms.

Instructions: Open the City Telephone System database in the Access folder (see the note on page A 4.8). Perform the following tasks.

1. Create the Total Charges Report shown in Figure 4-84. Total Charges is the sum of Basic Charge and Extra Charges. The report is sorted by last name. (*Hint*: Sort the query by last name rather than using the Report Wizard to sort the records.)

2. Print the report.

3. Create the Users by Department report shown in Figure 4-85. Notice that the date appears at the top of the report. (*Hint*: Use information from Use Help Exercise 1 to solve this problem.)

Total Charges Report

User Id	Last Name	First Name	Phone Ext	Office	Total Charges
T087	Anders	Jane	3923	531	$10.00
T129	Bishop	Fred	3383	212	$32.00
T238	Chan	Rose	3495	220	$42.95
T347	Febo	Javier	4267	323	$17.75
T451	Ginras	Mary Catherin	3156	444	$69.85
T536	Hanneman	William	3578	317	$31.75
T645	Johnsen	Paul	4445	234	$28.75
T780	Mentor	Melissa	3418	525	$90.95
T851	Sanchez	Alfredo	3134	438	$17.25
T890	Tartar	Joan	4655	240	$10.00
T888	TenClink	Brian	3414	521	$47.45

Wednesday, December 30, 1998   Page 1 of 1

FIGURE 4-84

Users by Department

Wednesday, December 30, 1998

Dept Code	Dept Name	User Id	Last Name	First Name	Basic Charge	Extra Charges	Total Charges
APV	Assessment						
		T451	Ginras	Mary Catherin	$17.00	$52.85	$69.85
		T851	Sanchez	Alfredo	$11.00	$6.25	$17.25
					$28.00	$59.10	$87.10
HRS	Housing						
		T347	Febo	Javier	$10.00	$7.75	$17.75
		T536	Hanneman	William	$13.00	$18.75	$31.75
		T890	Tartar	Joan	$10.00	$0.00	$10.00
					$33.00	$26.50	$59.50
ITD	Income Tax						
		T129	Bishop	Fred	$10.00	$22.00	$32.00
		T238	Chan	Rose	$13.00	$29.95	$42.95
		T645	Johnsen	Paul	$21.00	$7.75	$28.75
					$44.00	$59.70	$103.70
PLN	Planning						
		T087	Anders	Jane	$10.00	$0.00	$10.00
		T780	Mentor	Melissa	$17.00	$73.95	$90.95
		T888	TenClink	Brian	$10.00	$37.45	$47.45
					$37.00	$111.40	$148.40
					$142.00	$256.70	$398.70

Page 1 of 1

FIGURE 4-85

4. Print the report.
5. Create the form shown in Figure 4-86 on the next page. Total Charges is a calculated control and is the sum of Basic Charge and Extra Charges. Dept Code is a combo box.
6. Print the form. To print the form, open the form, click File on the menu bar and then click Print. Click Selected Record(s) as the Print Range. Click the OK button.
7. Publish the Total Charges Report to the Web.

(continued)

In the Lab

Presenting Data in the City Telephone System Database *(continued)*

FIGURE 4-86

3 Presenting Data in the City Scene Database

Problem: *City Scene* magazine already has realized several benefits from the database of accounts and account reps that you created. The managing editor now would like to prepare reports from the database that can be used for financial analysis and future planning. He greatly appreciates the validation rules that were added to ensure that data is entered correctly. He now feels that the data entry process can be improved even further by creating custom forms.

Instructions: Open the City Scene database in the Access folder (see the note on page A 4.8). Perform the following tasks.

1. Create the Advertising Income Report shown in Figure 4-87. Advertising Income is the sum of Balance and Amount Paid.

In the Lab

Advertising Income Report

Advertiser Number	Name	City	Balance	Amount Paid	Advertising Income
A226	Alden Books	Fernwood	$60.00	$535.00	$595.00
B101	Bud's Diner	Crestview	$155.00	$795.00	$950.00
C134	Baker & Clover Clothes	New Castle	$100.00	$835.00	$935.00
D216	Dogs 'n Draft	Crestview	$260.00	$485.00	$745.00
G080	Green Thumb	New Castle	$185.00	$825.00	$1,010.00
L189	Lighthouse Inc.	Crestview	$35.00	$150.00	$185.00
M121	Shoe Salon	Fernwood	$50.00	$0.00	$50.00
N034	New Releases	Fernwood	$435.00	$500.00	$935.00
S010	Skates R You	New Castle	$85.00	$235.00	$320.00

Wednesday, December 30, 1998

Page 1 of 1

FIGURE 4-87

2. Print the report.
3. Create the Advertisers by Ad Rep report shown in Figure 4-88 on the next page.

(continued)

In the Lab

Presenting Data in the City Scene Database *(continued)*

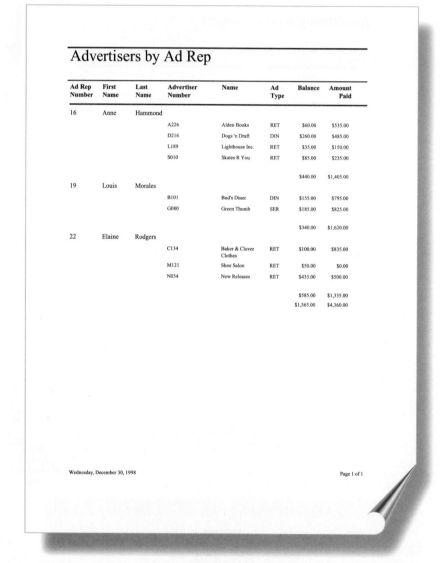

Advertisers by Ad Rep

Ad Rep Number	First Name	Last Name	Advertiser Number	Name	Ad Type	Balance	Amount Paid
16	Anne	Hammond					
			A226	Alden Books	RET	$60.00	$535.00
			D216	Dogs 'n Draft	DIN	$260.00	$485.00
			L189	Lighthouse Inc.	RET	$35.00	$150.00
			S010	Skates R You	RET	$85.00	$235.00
						$440.00	$1,405.00
19	Louis	Morales					
			B101	Bud's Diner	DIN	$155.00	$795.00
			G080	Green Thumb	SER	$185.00	$825.00
						$340.00	$1,620.00
22	Elaine	Rodgers					
			C134	Baker & Clover Clothes	RET	$100.00	$835.00
			M121	Shoe Salon	RET	$50.00	$0.00
			N034	New Releases	RET	$435.00	$500.00
						$585.00	$1,335.00
						$1,365.00	$4,360.00

Wednesday, December 30, 1998   Page 1 of 1

FIGURE 4-88

4. Print the report.
5. Create the form shown in Figure 4-89. Advertising Income is a calculated control and is the sum of Balance and Amount Paid. Ad Rep Number is a combo box.

In the Lab

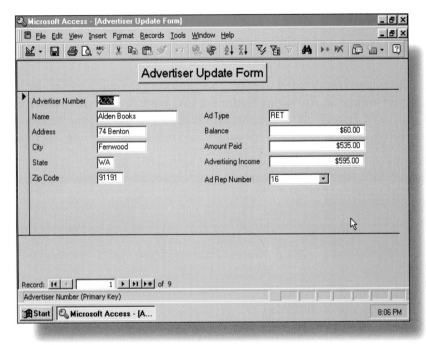

FIGURE 4-89

6. Add the current date to the form. (*Hint*: Use information from Use Help Exercise 2 to solve this problem.)
7. Print the form. To print the form, open the form, click File on the menu bar and then click Print. Click Selected Record(s) as the Print Range. Click the OK button.
8. Publish the Advertisers by Ad Rep report to the Web.

Cases and Places

The difficulty of these case studies varies: ❿ are the least difficult, ❿❿ are more difficult; and ❿❿❿ are the most difficult.

1 ❿ The Athletic department has decided to offer golf clinics emphasizing particular skills. Create a Lesson Revenue Report similar in format to Figure 4-81 on page A 4.58 that shows the maximum revenue that can be generated in each class. Use the data in Figure 4-90. Use the heading, Maximum Revenue, for the last column, and calculate the maximum revenue by multiplying Maximum Students by Fee. Print the report.

Lesson Revenue Table

CLASS ID	DESCRIPTION	MAXIMUM STUDENTS	FEE	PRO'S SALARY	PRO'S INITIALS
101	Grip	25	$15	$135	GC
102	Setup	15	$22	$168	CW
103	Alignment	20	$18	$180	VM
104	Posture	25	$20	$180	VM
105	Pitching	20	$25	$168	VM
106	Bunker Play	10	$30	$210	CW
107	Chipping	15	$28	$388	GC
108	Putting	10	$30	$388	SP
109	Finishing and Balance	15	$24	$158	GC
110	Distance	10	$20	$175	SP

FIGURE 4-90

2 ❿ Using the database from Case Study 1 above, create a Classes By Pro report similar in format to Figure 4-82 on page A 4.59 that shows each pro's name, classes taught, maximum revenue in the classes, pro's salary, and profit. Profit is calculated by subtracting the pro's salary from the maximum revenue. Use the data in Figure 4-91. Print the report.

FIGURE 4-91

Pro Table

PRO'S INITIALS	PRO'S NAME
GC	Greg Cotter
CW	Christy Walton
VM	Vishnu Mahraj
SP	Sue Pendleton

Cases and Places

3 ▶▶ Using the database from Case Studies 1 and 2, create a Class Update Form similar to the one in Figure 4-83 on page A 4.59. Use a calculated control called Revenue that is the result of multiplying Maximum Students by Fee. Include a combo box for Pro's Initials. Print the form.

4 ▶▶ The textbook exchange system you created in Case Study 1 of the Cases and Places section of Project 1 has become extremely successful. Student government has had a tremendous response and has decided to charge a 10 percent commission on each book exchanged. The money collected will be used to fund various student activities. Create and print a Textbook Exchange Report that shows book title, author, seller's name, seller's telephone number, price, and commission. Commission is calculated by multiplying the price by 10 percent (0.10). In addition, create and print a form that helps you input and delete books in the textbook database.

5 ▶▶▶ Finding restaurants that match an individual's food preferences and schedule often is a time-consuming process. Restaurants seem to open and close overnight, or the hours and cuisine of the established restaurants change frequently depending on seasons and trends. You have found the database you created in Case Study 2 of the Cases and Places section of Project 1 to be valuable, so you need a form to help you make frequent updates easily. Create and print this form. In addition, create and print a report organized by food type.

6 ▶▶▶ You have a part-time job on campus working at the Information Desk. Visitors often approach you to ask the room number of particular instructors and offices, and callers ask for telephone extensions and office hours. Currently, you must consult several directories and guides to answer their questions, so you decide to create a database resembling the one in Case Study 6 of the Cases and Places section of Project 1. Create and print a report showing pertinent campus information in the categories of faculty, administration, and services. In addition, create and print a form to help you update the database easily.

Cases and Places

7 ▶▶▶ Few people have addressed adequately the goal of financial security in retirement. The rule of thumb is a retiree needs 80 percent of annual, after-tax pre-retirement income to live comfortably. To estimate how much you will need to have saved on your last day on the job, compute 80 percent of your current annual, after-tax income and divide that number by four percent, which is the annual rate of return you can expect from investments adjusted for inflation. With that investing goal in mind, your accounting instructor wants you to add $20,000 you have inherited from your favorite aunt to the $1,000 he had you invest in an Individual Retirement Account in Case Study 7 of the Cases and Places section of Project 1. Create and print an IRA Future Value Report that shows the names, addresses, and telephone numbers of financial institutions, current interest rates, and total values of the IRAs by age 65. Include a column comparing these IRA values to how much you will need to have invested when you retire.

Microsoft *Access* 97

Enhancing Forms with OLE Fields, Hyperlinks, and Subforms

Objectives

You will have mastered the material in this project when you can:

▶ Use date, memo, and OLE fields
▶ Enter data in date fields
▶ Enter data in memo fields
▶ Enter pictures into OLE fields
▶ Change row and column spacing in tables
▶ Save table properties
▶ Create a form with a subform
▶ Move and resize fields on a form
▶ Use a form that contains a subform
▶ Change styles and colors of labels
▶ Use date and memo fields in a query

Illuminate Your Work

In futuristic 32 A.D., carefully avoiding the Valley of the Misborn, feckless Brother Francis rode a scrawny burro along a narrow trail, carrying a most sacred manuscript concealed beneath his robe. For fifteen years he had toiled, first copying the wondrous drawing created by the *Beatus*, Irving E. Leibowitz, onto bleached sheepskin, then illuminating the copy with brilliantly hued letters, embellished with leaves and vines, and inlaid with scrollwork of gold and silver. Now, he was en route to New Rome, where he would deliver the holy document to Pope Leo XXII, who soon would canonize Leibowitz as a saint. Just when Brother Francis thought he had passed out of harm's way, however, three humanoid creatures — one of them sporting two heads — sprang from hiding. Not satisfied with seizing his poor burro as the main course for their dinner, they plucked the precious manuscript — a copy of a blueprint entitled *Transistorized Control System for Unit Six-B*.

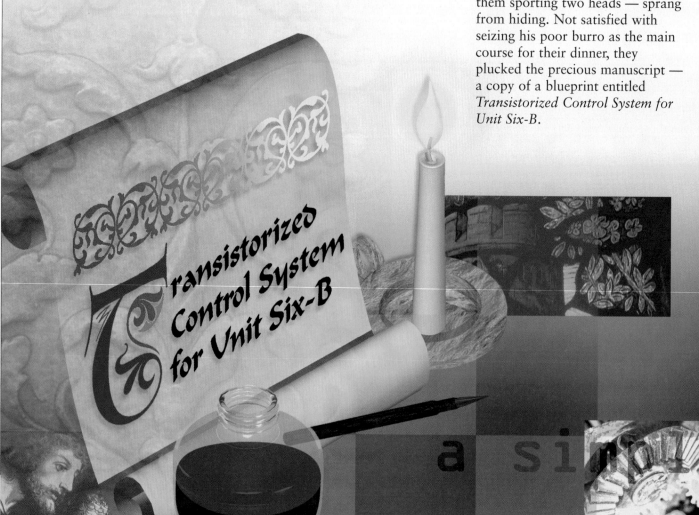

In *A Canticle for Leibowitz*, written during the height of 50s concern over the danger of nuclear war, *Canticle* was the most literarily successful science fiction novel written on the subject. Walter Michael Miller, Jr. paints a world where knowledge has been lost after the great Flame Deluge of the twentieth century. The setting is post-holocaust America where scraps of pre-war knowledge are gathered and preserved by monks who no longer understand that knowledge. After the fall of the Roman Empire, knowledge was preserved in Western Europe almost exclusively in small, isolated communities of priests and monks during a centuries-long dark age, recopied by men who often understood little of the ancient manuscripts of which they were the custodians.

An unexpected by-product of that activity was the enhanced works of art that these copies became; priceless pieces often bound in covers of gold or carved ivory. More importantly, they preserved knowledge that might otherwise have been lost and passed it on.

In today's world, knowledge flourishes. It is preserved, recalled, manipulated, enhanced, and stored. The process of enhancing documents is simplified by the capabilities of integration such as object linking an embedding (OLE). In Microsoft Access, along with other Microsoft products offering the OLE feature, it now is a simple matter to enhance a form in a database by inserting objects such as scanned-in photographs, clip art from the Microsoft Clip Gallery, and text from other applications.

In the topics presented in this project, you will experience the ease with which you can enter data and pictures into OLE fields, change styles and colors, and move and redesign objects on your forms. Data is everywhere on your PC, on local networks, and on the Internet. With such power at your fingertips, perhaps a form you create will become a model for the future.

Microsoft

Access 97

Enhancing Forms with OLE Fields, Hyperlinks, and Subforms

Case Perspective

The management of Pilotech Services has found it needs to maintain additional data on its technicians. Managers need to keep the start date of each technician in the database. They also would like the database to contain a description of the specialties of each technician as well as the technician's picture. In addition, each technician now has a page on the Web and the managers want to access this page easily from the database.

Once these fields have been added to the database, they would like to have a form created that incorporates the four new fields along with several existing fields. In addition, they would like the form to contain the client number, name, billed, and paid amounts for the clients of the technician. They would like to have two or three clients display on the screen at the same time, and the ability to scroll through all the clients of the technician. Finally, they would like to be able to access the technician's Web page directly from the form.

Introduction

This project creates the form shown in Figure 5-1. The form incorporates the following features not covered in previous projects:

▶ Four new fields are added to the Technician table. The Start Date field gives the date the technician began working for Pilotech Services. A Specialties field allows the organization to store a paragraph describing the specialties of the technician. The Specialties entry can be as long or short as the organization desires. The Picture field holds a picture of the technician. Finally, the Web Page field gives the ability to access the Technician's Web page directly from the database.

▶ The form not only shows data concerning the technician, but also the technician's clients. The clients are displayed as a table on the form. The form also contains the Web Page field. Clicking this field will access the technician's Web page automatically.

Project Five – Enhancing the Pilotech Services Forms

Before creating the form required by the management of Pilotech Services, first you must change the structure of the Technician table to incorporate the four new fields:

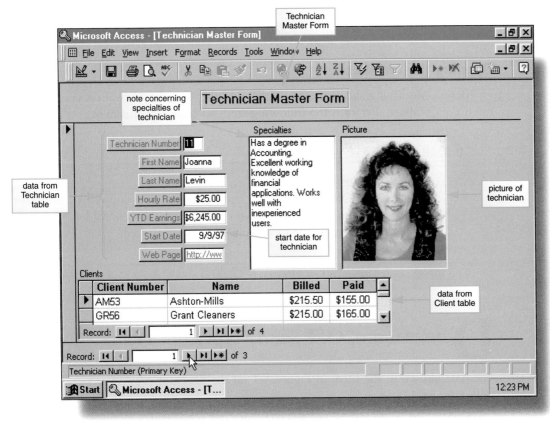

FIGURE 5-1

Start Date, Specialties, Picture, and Web Page. Each of the new fields uses a field type you have not encountered before. Then, you must fill in these new fields with appropriate data. The way this is achieved depends on the field type. After filling in the fields, you are to create the form including the table of client data. Finally, you will create queries to obtain the answer to two important questions that reference the new fields.

Overview of Project Steps

The database preparation steps give you an overview of how the new fields will be added and the form shown in Figure 5-1 will be created. The following tasks will be completed in this project.

1. Start Access.
2. Open the Pilotech Services database.
3. Add the Start Date, Specialties, Picture, and Web Page fields to the Technician table.
4. Update the Start Date, Specialties, Picture, and Web Page fields for the three technicians currently in the table.
5. Create a form that includes both technician and client data.

6. Move and resize objects on the form.
7. Change the size mode of the picture on the form so the entire picture displays.
8. Change special effects and colors of objects on the form.
9. Add a title to the form.
10. Use the form to view data.
11. Use the form to access the technicians' Web pages.
12. Create a query that uses the Start Date and Specialties fields.

The following pages contain a detailed explanation of these steps.

Opening the Database

Before modifying the Technician table and creating the form, first you must open the database. Perform the following steps to complete this task.

TO OPEN A DATABASE

Step 1: Click the Start button.
Step 2: Click Open Office Document, and then click 3½ Floppy (A:) in the Look in list box. If necessary, double-click the Access folder. Make sure the database called Pilotech Services is selected.
Step 3: Click the Open button.

The database is open and the Pilotech Services : Database window displays.

Date, Memo, OLE, and Hyperlink Fields

The data shown in the form in Figure 5-1 on the previous page incorporates the following field types:

1. **Date (D)** — The field can contain only valid dates.
2. **Memo (M)** — The field can contain text that is variable in length. The length of the text stored in memo fields virtually is unlimited.
3. **OLE (O)** — The field can contain objects created by other applications that support **OLE (Object Linking and Embedding)** as a server. Object Linking and Embedding is a special feature of Microsoft Windows that creates a special relationship between Microsoft Access and the application that created the object. When you edit the object, Microsoft Access returns automatically to the application that created the object.
4. **Hyperlink (H)** — This field can contain links to other office documents or to Web pages. If the link is to a Web page, the field will contain the **URL (Uniform Resource Locator)** of the Web page.

Adding Fields to a Table

You add the new fields to the Technician table by modifying the design of the table and inserting the fields at the appropriate position in the table structure. Perform the following steps to add the Start Date, Specialties, Picture, and Web Page fields to the Technician table.

Steps To Add Fields to a Table

1 If necessary, click the Tables tab. Right-click the Technician table, and then point to Design on the shortcut menu.

The shortcut menu for the Technician table displays (Figure 5-2).

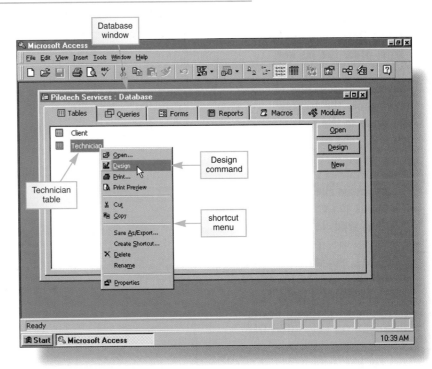

FIGURE 5-2

2 Click Design on the shortcut menu and then maximize the Technician : Table window. Point to the position for the new field (the Field Name column in the row following the YTD Earnings field).

The Technician : Table window displays (Figure 5-3).

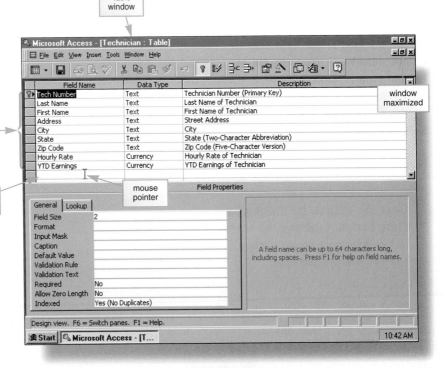

FIGURE 5-3

3 Click the position for the new field. Type Start Date as the field name, press the TAB key, select Date/Time as the data type, press the TAB key, type Start Date as the description, and then press the TAB key to move to the next field.

4 Type Specialties as the field name, press the TAB key, select Memo as the data type, press the TAB key, type Note Containing Details of Technician's Specialties as the description, and then press the TAB key to move to the next field. Type Picture as the field name, press the TAB key, select OLE Object as the data type, press the TAB key, type Picture of Technician as the description, and then press the TAB key to move to the next field. Type Web Page as the field name, press the TAB key, select Hyperlink as the data type, press the TAB key, and type Address of Technician's Web Page as the description. Point to the Close button.

The new fields are entered (Figure 5-4).

5 Close the window by clicking its Close button. Click the Yes button in the Microsoft Access dialog box to save the changes.

The new fields have been added to the structure.

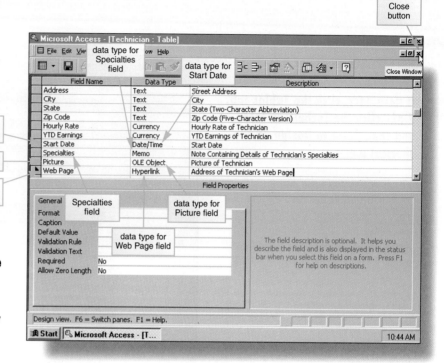

FIGURE 5-4

Updating the New Fields

After adding the new fields to the table, the next task is to enter data into the fields. The manner in which this is accomplished depends on the field type. The following sections cover the methods for updating date fields, memo fields, OLE fields, and Hyperlink fields.

Updating Date Fields

To enter **date fields**, simply type the dates including slashes (/). Perform the following steps to add the Start Dates for all three technicians using Datasheet view.

 Steps To Enter Data in Date Fields

1 **With the Database window on the screen, right-click the Technician table. Point to Open on the shortcut menu.**

The shortcut menu displays (Figure 5-5).

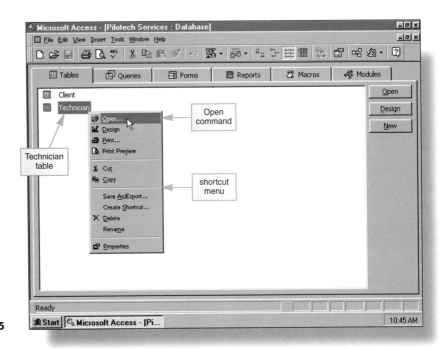

FIGURE 5-5

2 **Click Open on the shortcut menu and then, if necessary, maximize the window. Point to the right scroll arrow.**

The Technician table displays in Datasheet view in a maximized window (Figure 5-6).

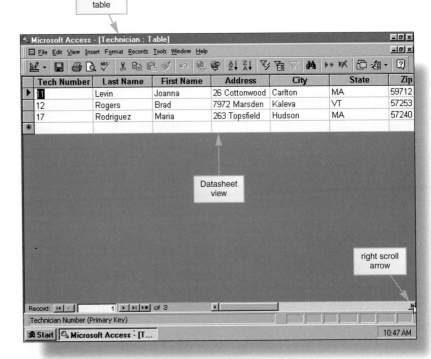

FIGURE 5-6

3 Repeatedly click the right scroll arrow until the new fields display (Figure 5-7). Point to the Start Date field on the first record.

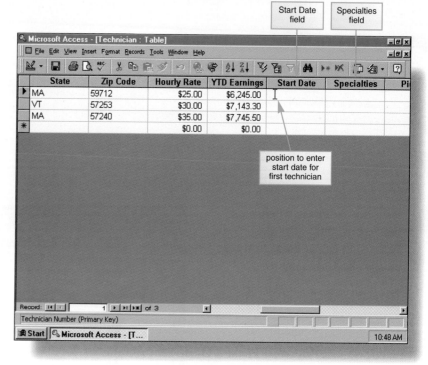

FIGURE 5-7

4 Click the Start Date field on the first record and then type 9/9/97 as the date. Press the DOWN ARROW key. Type 10/6/98 as the Start Date on the second record and then press the DOWN ARROW key. Type 11/12/98 as the date on the third record.

The dates are entered (Figure 5-8).

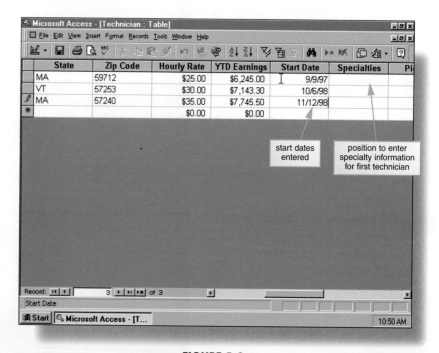

FIGURE 5-8

Updating Memo Fields

To **update a memo field**, simply type the data in the field. With the current spacing on the screen, only a small portion of the memo will display. To correct this problem, you later will change the spacing to allow more room for the memo. Perform the following steps to enter each technician's specialties.

Steps To Enter Data in Memo Fields

1 If necessary, click the right scroll arrow so that the Specialties field displays. Click the Specialties field on the first record. Type Has a degree in Accounting. Excellent working knowledge of financial applications. Works well with inexperienced users. **as the entry.**

The last portion of the memo displays (Figure 5-9).

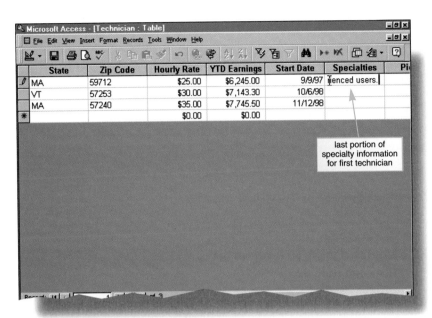

FIGURE 5-9

2 Click the Specialties field on the second record. Type Specializes in network design and maintenance. Is a certified network administrator. Teaches networking courses at local community college. **as the entry.**

3 Click the Specialties field on the third record. Type Excellent diagnostic skills. Enjoys challenging hardware problems. Works well with inexperienced users. **as the entry.**

The Specialties are all entered (Figure 5-10). The first portion of the specialty information for the first two Technicians displays. Because the insertion point is still in the field for the third Technician, only the last portion displays.

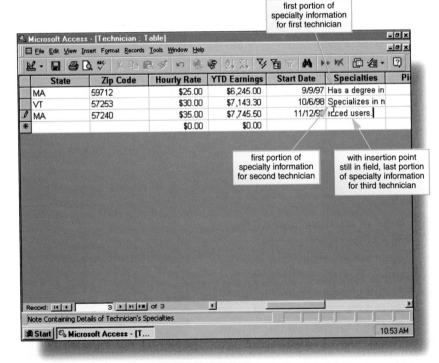

FIGURE 5-10

More *About*
Changing the Row and Column Size

The Undo command cannot be used to reverse (undo) changes to the row and/or column size. To undo the changes to the sizes, close the datasheet without saving the changes. Once you have saved the changes, there is no automatic way to restore the original sizes.

Changing the Row and Column Size

Only a small portion of the specialties display in the datasheet. To allow more of the specialties to display, you can expand the size of the rows and the columns. You can change the size of a column using the field selector. The **field selector** is the bar containing the field name. To select an entire column, you click the field selector. You then drag to change the size of the column. To change the size of a row, you use a record's **row selector**, which is the small box at the beginning of each record. You then click to select the record and drag to resize the row.

The following steps resize the column containing the Specialties field and resize the rows of the table so a larger portion of the Specialties field text will display.

Steps To Change the Row and Column Size

1 Click the right scroll arrow so the Web Page field displays. Point between the two column headings for the Specialties and Picture columns.

The mouse pointer shape changes to a two-headed vertical arrow, indicating you can drag the line to resize the column (Figure 5-11).

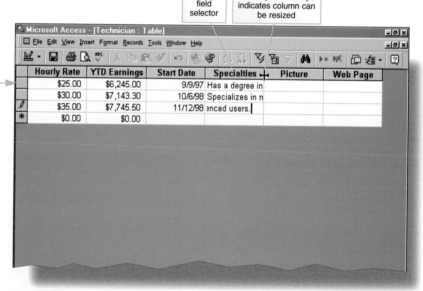

FIGURE 5-11

2 Drag to the right to resize the Specialties column to the approximate size shown in Figure 5-12 and then point between the first and second row selectors as shown in the figure.

The mouse pointer shape changes to a double-headed arrow with a horizontal bar, indicating you can drag the line to resize the row.

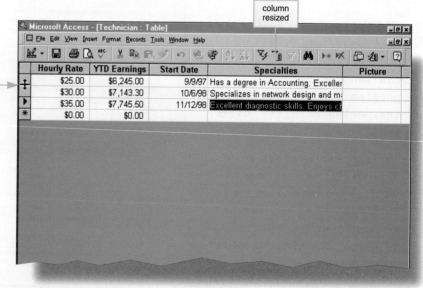

FIGURE 5-12

3 Drag the edge of the row to approximately the position shown in Figure 5-13.

All the rows are resized at the same time (Figure 5-13). The specialties now display in their entirety. The last row has a different appearance from the other two because it still is selected.

Hourly Rate	YTD Earnings	Start Date	Specialties	Picture
$25.00	$6,245.00	9/9/97	Has a degree in Accounting. Excellent working knowledge of financial applications. Works well with inexperienced users.	
$30.00	$7,143.30	10/6/98	Specializes in network design and maintenance. Is a certified network administrator. Teaches networking courses at local community college.	
$35.00	$7,745.50	11/12/98	Excellent diagnostic skills. Enjoys	

row resized

FIGURE 5-13

Updating OLE Fields

To insert data into an OLE field, you will use the **Insert Object command** on the OLE field's shortcut menu. The Insert Object command presents a list of the various types of objects that can be inserted. Access then opens the corresponding application that is used to create the object, for example, Microsoft Drawing. If the object already is created and stored in a file, as is the case in this project, you simply can insert it directly from the file.

Perform the following steps to insert pictures into the Picture field. The pictures are located in the Access folder on the Data Disk that accompanies this book. If you are not using this floppy disk for your database, you will need to copy the files pict1.pcx, pict2.pcx, and pict3.pcx from the Data Disk to your floppy disk.

The quality of the pictures you see on your screen depends on the particular video driver your system is using. If your pictures do not appear to be as sharp as the ones shown in the text, it simply means your system is using a different video driver.

Note: If you are working on a floppy disk, skip these steps so that your database will not become too large for your disk.

Steps To Enter Data in OLE Fields and Convert the Data to Pictures

1 Click the right scroll arrow so the Picture field displays. Right-click the Picture field on the first record. Point to Insert Object on the shortcut menu.

The shortcut menu for the Picture field displays (Figure 5-14).

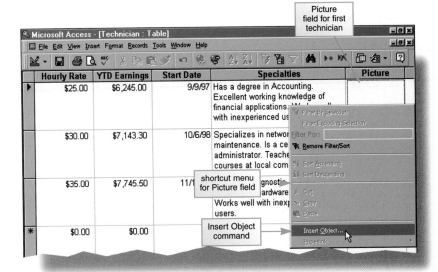

FIGURE 5-14

2 Click the Insert Object command on the shortcut menu. Point to Create from File in the Insert Object dialog box.

The Insert Object dialog box displays (Figure 5-15).

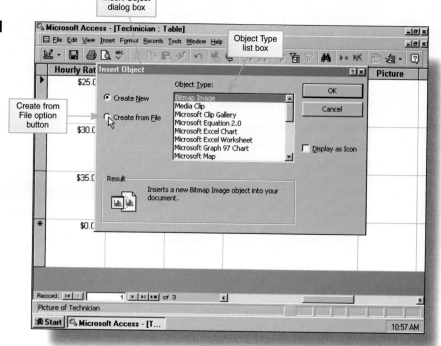

FIGURE 5-15

3 Click Create from File. If necessary, type a:\ in the File text box and then point to the Browse button.

The Create from File option button is selected (Figure 5-16).

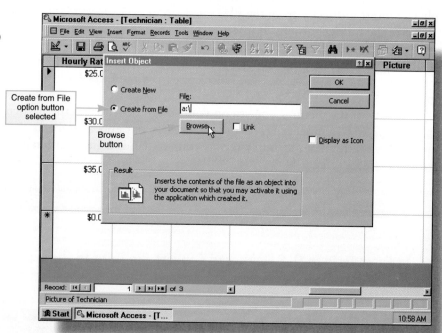

FIGURE 5-16

4 Click the Browse button. If necessary, select a:\, double-click the Access folder in the Directories list to select it, and then point to pict1.pcx.

The Browse dialog box displays (Figure 5-17). If you do not have the pcx files, you will need to locate the folder in which yours are stored.

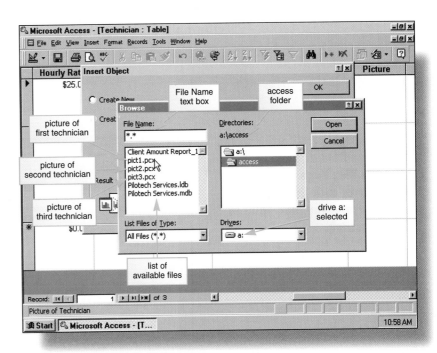

FIGURE 5-17

5 Double-click pict1.pcx and then point to the OK button.

The Browse dialog box closes and the Insert Object dialog box displays (Figure 5-18). The name of the selected picture displays in the File text box.

6 Click the OK button.

7 Insert the pictures in the second and third records using the techniques illustrated in Steps 1 through 6. For the second record, select the picture named pict2.pcx. For the third record, select the picture named pict3.pcx.

The pictures are inserted.

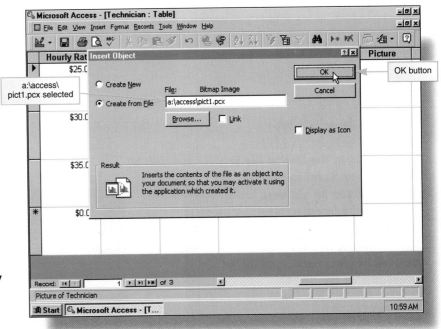

FIGURE 5-18

OtherWays

1. On Insert menu click Object

Updating Hyperlink Fields

To insert data into a Hyperlink field, you will use the **Hyperlink command** on the Hyperlink field's shortcut menu. You then edit the hyperlink. You either can enter the URL for the appropriate Web page or specify a file that contains the document to which you wish to link.

Perform the following steps to insert data into the Web Page field.

Steps To Enter Data in Hyperlink Fields

1 Click the right scroll arrow so the Web Page field displays. Right-click the Web Page field on the first record, click Hyperlink on the shortcut menu, and point to Edit Hyperlink.

The shortcut menu for the Web Page field displays (Figure 5-19).

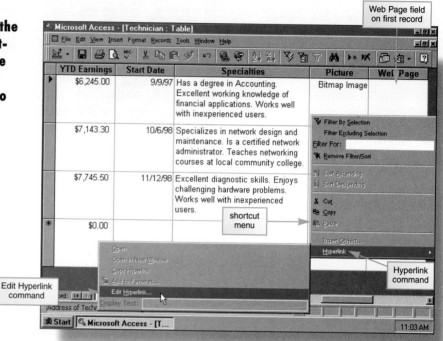

FIGURE 5-19

2 Click Edit Hyperlink. Type www.scsite.com/ac97/tech1.htm **in the Link to file or URL text box. Point to the OK button. (If you do not have access to the Internet, type** a:\access\tech1.html **in the Link to file or URL text box instead of www.scsite.com/ac97/tech1.htm as the URL.)**

The Insert Hyperlink dialog box displays (Figure 5-20).

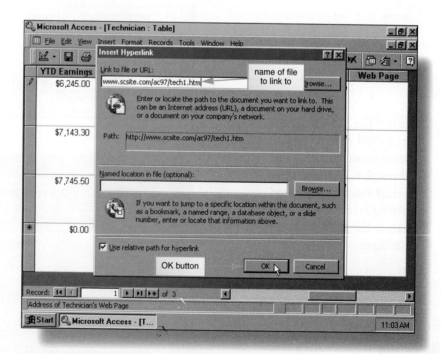

FIGURE 5-20

3 Click the OK button. Use the techniques in Steps 1 and 2 to enter Web page data for the second and third technicians. For the second technician, type `www.scsite.com/ac97/ tech2.htm` **as the URL and for the third, type** `www.scsite.com/ac97/ tech3.htm` **as the URL. (If you do not have access to the Internet, type** `a:\access\tech2.html` **for the second technician, and** `a:\access\tech3.html` **for the third technician.)**

The Web page data is entered (Figure 5-21).

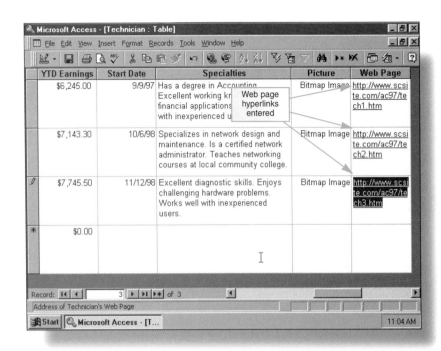

FIGURE 5-21

Other Ways
1. On Insert menu click Hyperlink

Saving the Table Properties

The row and column spacing are **table properties**. When changing any table properties, the changes apply only as long as the table is active *unless they are saved*. If saved, they will apply every time the table is open. To save them, simply close the table. If any properties have changed, a Microsoft Access dialog box will ask if you want to save the changes. By answering Yes, the changes will be saved.

Perform the following steps to close the table and save the properties that have been changed.

 Steps To Close the Table and Save the Properties

1 Close the table by clicking its Close button. Point to the Yes button.

The Microsoft Access dialog box displays (Figure 5-22).

2 Click the Yes button to save the table properties.

The properties now are saved.

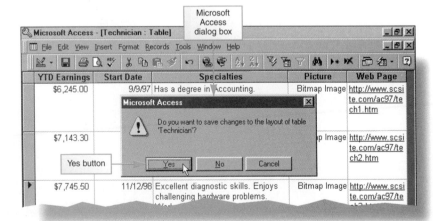

FIGURE 5-22

More *About* Updating OLE Fields

OLE fields can occupy a great deal of space. To save space in your database, you can convert a picture from "Bitmap Image" to "Picture (Device Independent Bitmap)." To do so, right-click the field, click Bitmap Image Object, click Convert, and then double-click Picture.

More *About* Subforms

When creating forms with sub-forms, the tables for the main form and the subform must be related. The relationship must have been set previously in the Relationships window. To see if your tables are related, click the Relationships button. Previously created relationships display as a line connecting the tables.

Although the pictures do not display on the screen, you can view them at any time. To view the picture of a particular *Technician*, point to the Picture field for the *Technician*, and then right-click to produce the shortcut menu. Click Bitmap Image Object on the shortcut menu, and then click Open. The picture then will display. Once you have finished viewing the picture, close the window containing the picture by clicking its Close button. You also can view the Web page for a technician, by clicking the technician's Web Page field.

Advanced Form Techniques

The form in this project includes data from both the Technician and Client tables. The form will display data concerning one technician. It also will display data concerning the technician's many clients. Formally, the relationship between technicians and clients is called a **one-to-many relationship** (*one* technician has *many* clients).

To include the data for the many clients of a technician on the form, the client data must appear in a **subform**, which is a form that is contained in another form. The form in which the subform is contained is called the main form. Thus, the **main form** will contain technician data and the subform will contain client data.

Creating a Form with a Subform

No special action is required to create a form with a subform if you use the Form Wizard. The **Form Wizard** will create both the form and subform automatically once you have selected the tables and indicated the general organization of your data. Perform the following steps to create the form and subform.

Steps To Create a Form with a Subform Using the Form Wizard

1 **With the Database window on the screen, click the Forms tab and then point to the New button.**

The Database window and the Forms sheet display (Figure 5-23).

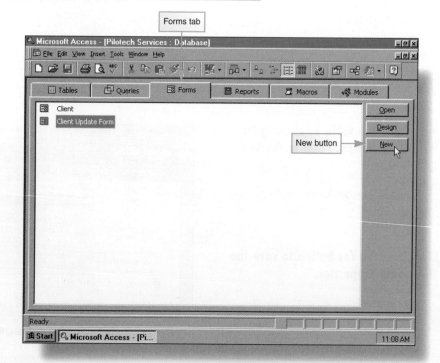

FIGURE 5-23

2 Click the New button, click Form Wizard, click the list box arrow, and then click Technician. Point to the OK button.

The New Form dialog box displays (Figure 5-24). Form Wizard and the Technician table both are selected.

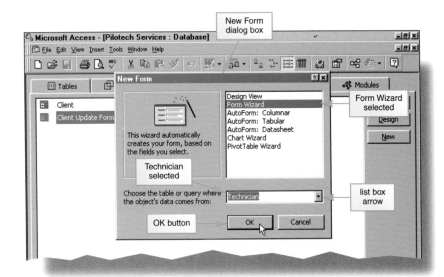

FIGURE 5-24

3 Click the OK button. With the Tech Number field selected in the Available Fields list box, click the Add Field button. Select the First Name, Last Name, Hourly Rate, YTD Earnings, Start Date, Specialties, Picture, and Web Page fields by clicking the field and then clicking the Add Field button. Point to the Table/Queries box arrow.

The fields from the Technician table are selected for the form (Figure 5-25).

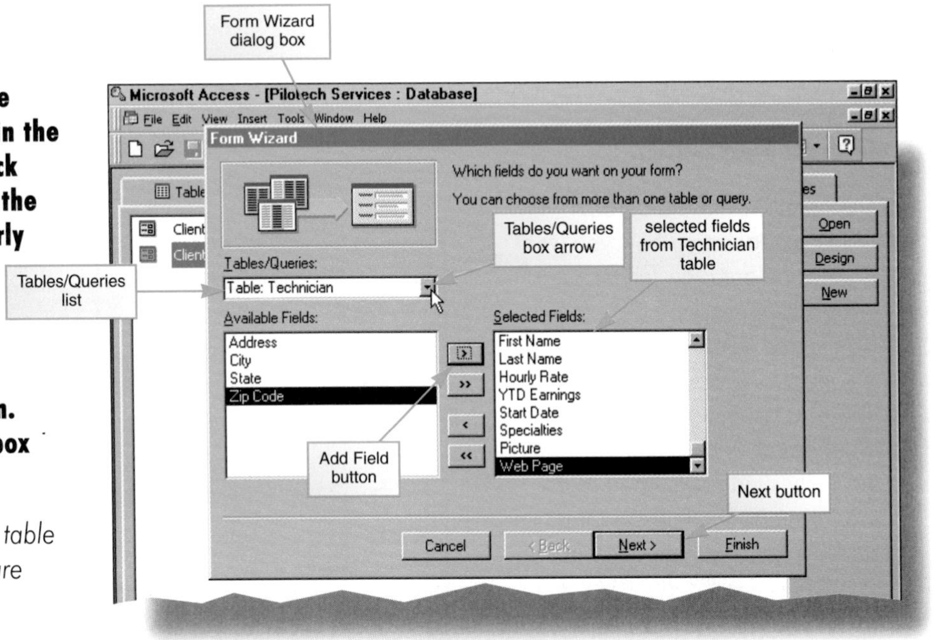

FIGURE 5-25

4 Click the Tables/Queries box arrow. Point to Table: Client in the list that displays (Figure 5-26).

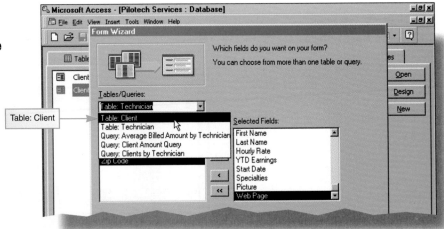

FIGURE 5-26

5 Click Table: Client. Select the Client Number, Name, Billed, and Paid fields. Point to the Next button.

All the fields are selected (Figure 5-27).

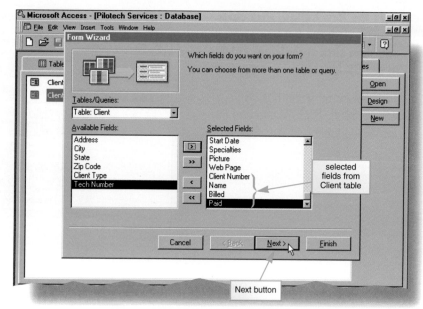

FIGURE 5-27

6 Click the Next button.

The Form Wizard dialog box displays, requesting how you want to view the data: by Technician or by Client (Figure 5-28). The highlighted selection, by Technician, is correct. The box on the right indicates visually that the main organization is by Technician, with the Technician fields listed at the top. Contained within the form is a subform that contains Client data.

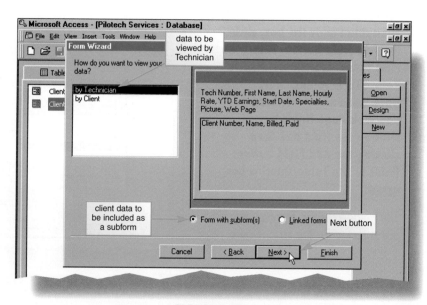

FIGURE 5-28

7 Click the Next button.

The Form Wizard dialog box displays, requesting the layout for the subform (Figure 5-29). This subform is to display in Datasheet view.

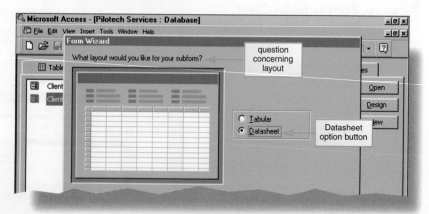

FIGURE 5-29

8 If necessary, click Datasheet and then click the Next button. Make sure the Standard style is selected.

The Form Wizard dialog box displays, requesting a style for the report (Figure 5-30).

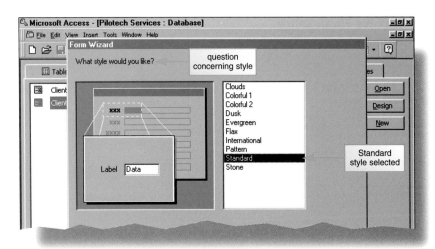

FIGURE 5-30

9 Click the Next button.

The Form Wizard dialog box displays (Figure 5-31). You use this dialog box to change the titles of the form and subform.

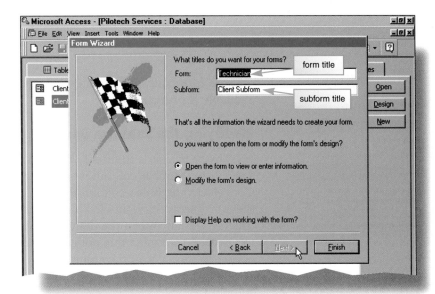

FIGURE 5-31

10 Type Technician Master Form as the title of the form. Click the Subform text box, use the DELETE or BACKSPACE key to erase the current entry, and then type Clients as the name of the subform. Point to the Finish button.

The titles are changed (Figure 5-32).

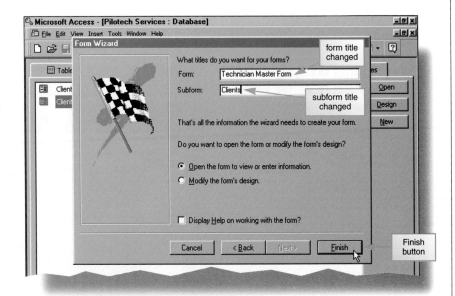

FIGURE 5-32

11 Click the Finish button.

The form displays (Figure 5-33).

12 Close the form by clicking its Close button.

FIGURE 5-33

More *About*
Subform Design

To change the appearance of the subform, make sure the subform control is not selected, double-click inside the subform, right-click the form selector for the subform, click Properties, and then change the Default-View property.

The form and subform now have been saved as part of the database and are available for future use.

Modifying the Subform Design

The next task is to modify the spacing of the columns in the subform. The Client Number column is so narrow that only the letters, Clien, display. Conversely, the Billed column is much wider than is needed. You can correct these problems, by right-clicking the subform in the Database window and then clicking Design. When the design of the subform displays, you then can convert it to Datasheet view. At this point, you resize each column by double-clicking the border to the right of the column name.

Perform the following steps to modify the subform design to improve the column spacing.

Steps **To Modify the Subform Design**

1 On the Forms sheet, right-click Clients. Point to Design on the shortcut menu.

The shortcut menu for the subform displays (Figure 5-34).

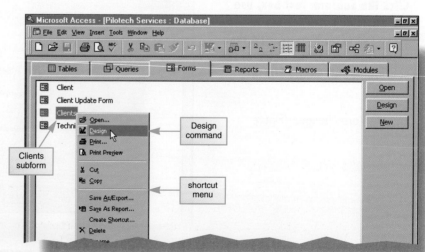

FIGURE 5-34

2 Click Design on the shortcut menu. If necessary, maximize the window. Point to the View button on the toolbar.

The form design displays in a maximized window (Figure 5-35).

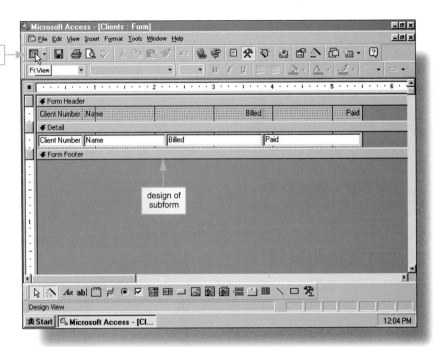

FIGURE 5-35

3 Click the View button to display the subform in Datasheet view. Resize each of the columns by pointing to the right edge of the field selector (the right of the column name) and double-clicking. Point to the Close button.

The subform displays in Datasheet view (Figure 5-36). The columns have been resized. You also can resize each column by dragging the right edge of the field selector.

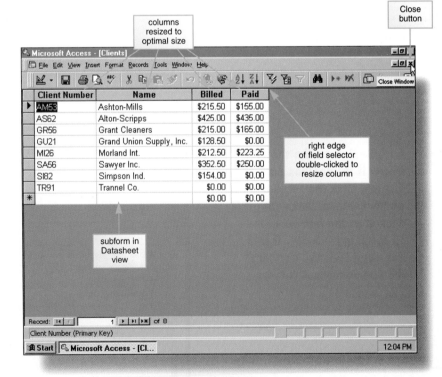

4 Close the subform by clicking its Close button.

The changes are made and saved.

FIGURE 5-36

Modifying the Form Design

The next step is to make several changes to the form. Various objects, including the subform, need to be moved and/or resized. The properties of the picture need to be adjusted so the entire picture displays. The appearance of the labels needs to be changed, and a title needs to be added to the form.

You can make these or other changes to the design of the form by right-clicking the form in the Database window and then clicking Design. If the toolbox is on the screen, make sure it is docked at the bottom of the screen. Perform the following steps to begin the modification of the form design.

 Steps To Modify the Form Design

1 **Right-click Technician Master Form. Point to Design on the shortcut menu.**

The shortcut menu for the form displays (Figure 5-37).

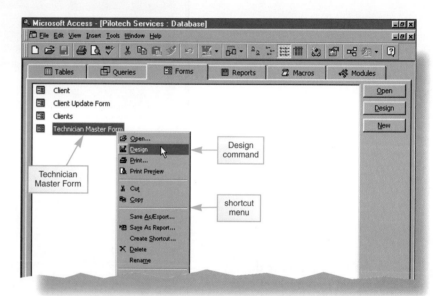

FIGURE 5-37

2 **Click Design on the shortcut menu. If the toolbox does not display, click the Toolbox button on the toolbar. Make sure it is docked at the bottom of the screen (Figure 5-38). If it is not, drag it to the bottom of the screen to dock it there.**

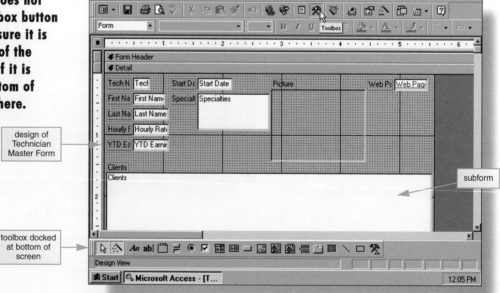

FIGURE 5-38

Resizing and Moving the Subform

To resize or move the subform, click it. **Sizing handles** display around the border of the subform. Drag the control to move it or drag one of the sizing handles to resize it. Perform the following steps first, to reduce the size of the subform, and then to move it to the bottom of the form.

 Steps To Resize and Move the Subform

1. **Click the down scroll arrow so the bottom portion of the form design displays (Figure 5-39).**

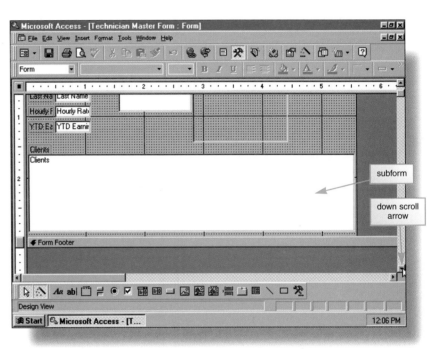

FIGURE 5-39

2. **Click the subform. Point to the sizing handle in the middle of the lower border of the subform.**

The subform is selected (Figure 5-40). Sizing handles display on the border of the subform. The shape of the mouse pointer has changed, indicating that you can drag the sizing handle to resize the subform.

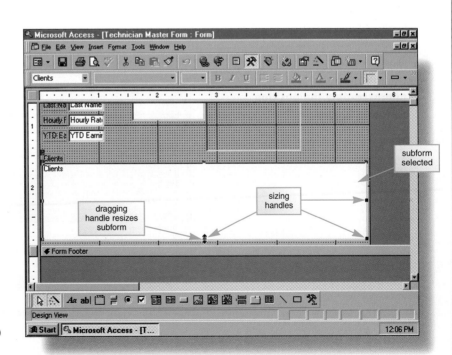

FIGURE 5-40

3 Drag the handle to approximately the position shown in Figure 5-41.

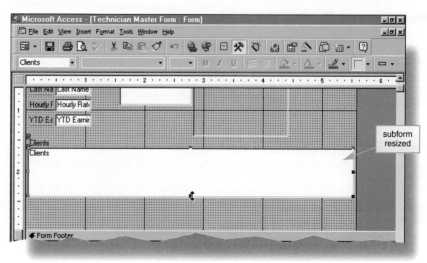

FIGURE 5-41

4 Point to the lower border of the subform, but not to a sizing handle. The shape of the mouse pointer will change to a hand (Figure 5-42).

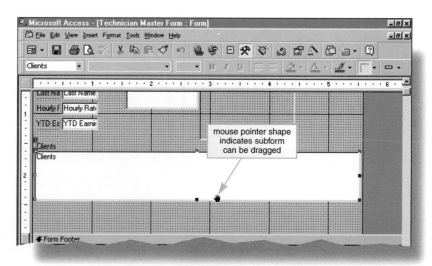

FIGURE 5-42

5 Move the subform by dragging the lower border to approximately the position shown in Figure 5-43.

The subform now has been resized and moved.

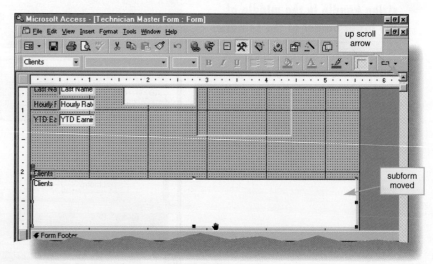

FIGURE 5-43

Moving and Resizing Fields

Fields on this form can be moved or resized just as they were in the form created in the previous project. First, click the field. To move it, move the mouse pointer to the boundary of the field so it becomes a hand, and then drag the field. To resize a field, drag the appropriate sizing handle. The following steps move certain fields on the form. They also resize the fields appropriately.

Steps To Move and Resize Fields

1 Click the up scroll arrow to scroll up to the top of the form. Click the Start Date control, and then move the mouse pointer until the shape changes to a hand.

Sizing handles display, indicating the control is selected (Figure 5-44).

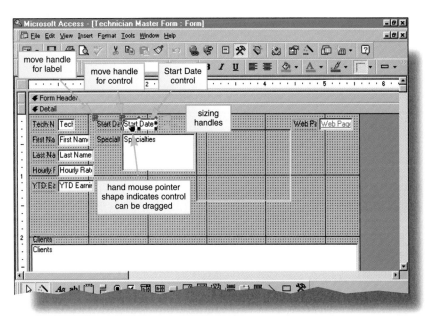

FIGURE 5-44

2 Drag the Start Date control to the position shown in Figure 5-45.

The control now has been moved.

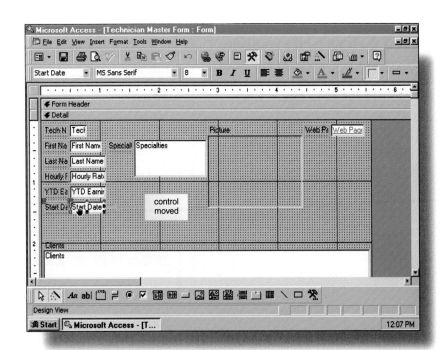

FIGURE 5-45

3 Move the Web Page control to the position shown in Figure 5-46. Move and resize the Picture control to the approximate position and size shown in the figure, and then move and resize the Specialties control to the approximate position and size shown in the figure.

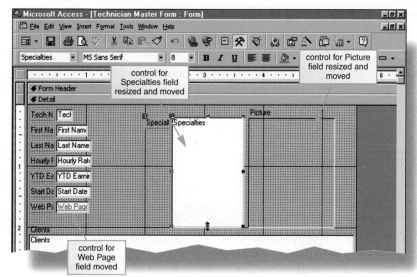

FIGURE 5-46

Moving Labels

To move a label independently from the field with which the label is associated, point to the large, **move handle** in the upper-left corner of the label. The shape of the mouse pointer changes to a hand with a pointing finger. By dragging this move handle, you will move the label without moving the associated field. Perform the following steps to move the label of the Specialties field without moving the field itself.

 Steps To Move Labels

1 Click the label for the Specialties field and then drag the handle in the upper-left corner to the position shown in Figure 5-47.

The shape of the mouse pointer changes to a hand with a pointing finger.

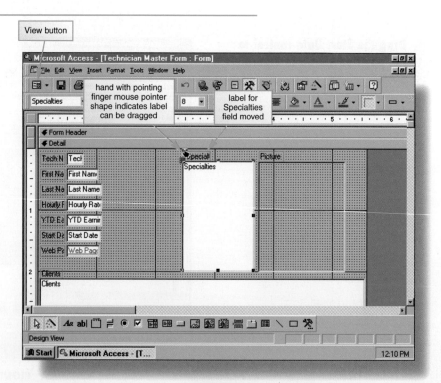

FIGURE 5-47

2 Click the View button to view the form with the changes.

The form displays (Figure 5-48).

FIGURE 5-48

Changes to the Form

Several changes need to be made to this form to produce the form shown in Figure 5-1 on page A 5.5. The Tech Number, First Name, Last Name, Hourly Rate, YTD Earnings, Start Date, and Web Page fields are not in the correct positions. In addition, the labels for these fields need to be changed in a variety of ways. The label for the Specialties field has the last few letters cut off and only a portion of the picture displays.

Resizing a Label

To resize a label, select the label by clicking it, and then drag an appropriate sizing handle. To resize a label to optimum size, select the label and then double-click an appropriate sizing handle. Perform the steps on the next page to resize the label for the Specialties field by double-clicking the sizing handle on the right.

Steps To Resize a Label

1 **Click the View button to return to the design grid. Make sure the label for the Specialties field is selected, and then point to the middle sizing handle on the right edge of the label.**

The shape of the mouse pointer changes to a two-headed arrow (Figure 5-49).

2 **Double-click the sizing handle to expand the label to the appropriate size.**

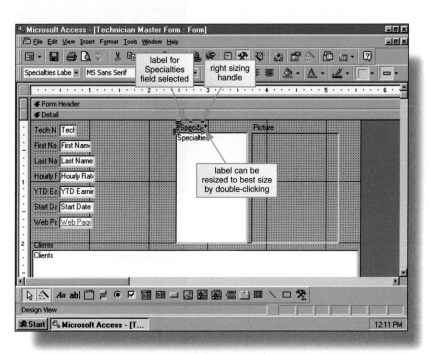

FIGURE 5-49

Changing the Size Mode of a Picture

The portion of a picture that displays as well as the way it displays is determined by the **size mode**. The possible size modes are as follows:

1. **Clip** — Displays only the portion of the picture that will fit in the space allocated to it.
2. **Stretch** — Expands or contracts the picture to fit the precise space allocated on the screen. For photographs, usually this is not a good choice, because fitting a photograph to the allocated space can distort the image, giving it a stretched appearance.
3. **Zoom** — Do the best job of fitting the picture to the allocated space without changing the look of the picture. The entire picture will display and will be proportioned correctly. Some white space may be visible either above or to the right of the picture, however.

Currently, the size mode is Clip and that is why only a portion of the picture displayed. To see the whole picture, use the shortcut menu for the picture to change the size mode to Zoom as in the following steps.

More *About* Size Mode

The Clip size mode is the most rapid to display, but may only show a portion of a picture. If your pictures have been created with a size such that the entire picture will display on the form with Clip as the size mode, Clip is the best choice.

Steps To Change the Size Mode of a Picture

1 **Right-click the Picture control to produce its shortcut menu, and then point to Properties.**

The shortcut menu displays (Figure 5-50).

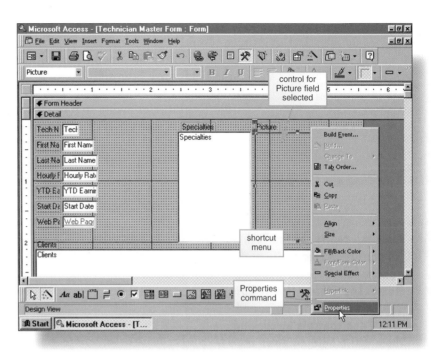

FIGURE 5-50

2 **Click Properties on the shortcut menu. Click the Size Mode property and then click the Size Mode box arrow. Point to Zoom.**

The Bound Object Frame: Picture property sheet displays (Figure 5-51). The list of Size Mode options displays.

3 **Click Zoom and then close the property sheet by clicking its Close button.**

The Size Mode is changed. The entire picture now will display.

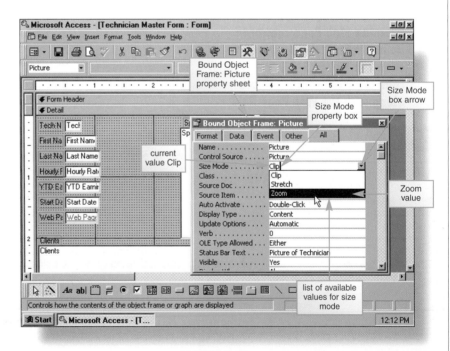

FIGURE 5-51

Other Ways

1. Click Properties button on toolbar
2. On View menu click Properties

More *About*
Selecting Multiple Controls

To select all the controls in a given column or row, you can use the rulers. To select all the controls in a column, click the horizontal ruler above the column. To select all the controls in a row, click the vertical ruler to the left of the row.

Moving a Group of Fields

Fields may be moved individually just as you have done previously. If you need to move a group of fields as a single block, however, a shortcut is available. You can move the group of fields in a single operation by selecting all the fields at once. To do so, click the first field to select it. To select more than one object at a time, press and hold down the SHIFT key as you click the additional objects. Once all the fields have been selected, drag any field to its new position. All the other selected fields will move along with it.

Perform the following step to move the Tech Number, First Name, Last Name, Hourly Rate, YTD Earnings, Start Date, and Web Page fields.

Steps **To Move a Group of Fields**

1 Click the control of the Tech Number field (the white portion, not the label). Select the First Name, Last Name, Hourly Rate, YTD Earnings, Start Date, and Web Page controls by clicking them while holding down the SHIFT key. Release the SHIFT key. Move the mouse pointer until its shape changes to a hand. Drag the Web Page control to approximately the position shown in Figure 5-52. The other controls will move as a block along with the Web Page field.

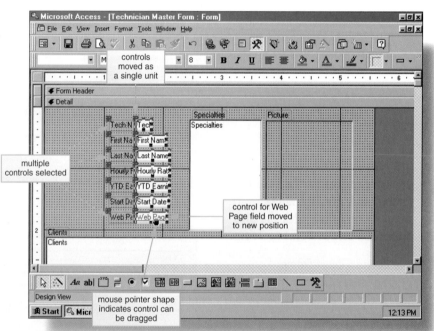

FIGURE 5-52

Changing the Contents of a Label

To change the contents of a label, right-click the label, and then click Properties on the shortcut menu. Select the Caption property and type the new **caption**; that is, the new entry that will display within the label. Perform the following steps to change the contents of the label for the Tech Number field from Tech Number to Technician Number.

To Change the Contents of a Label

1 Right-click the label for the Tech Number field. Click Properties on the shortcut menu. Click the Caption property, and then change the caption from Tech Number to Technician Number.

The Label: Tech Number Label property sheet displays (Figure 5-53). The caption has been changed to Technician Number.

2 Close the Label: Tech Number Label property sheet by clicking its Close button.

The label is changed.

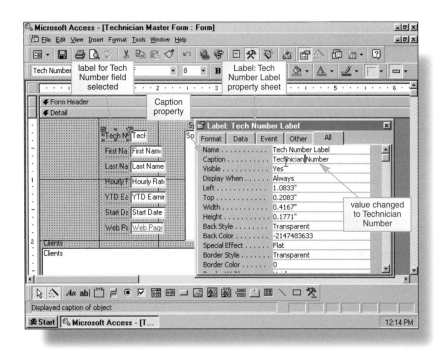

FIGURE 5-53

Changing Label Alignment

The labels for the Technician Number, First Name, Last Name, Hourly Rate, YTD Earnings, Start Date, and Web Page fields in Figure 5-1 on page A 5.5 are **right-aligned**, that is, aligned with the right margin. Because the labels currently are left-aligned, the alignment needs to be changed. To change the **alignment**, you must click the label, right-click to produce the shortcut menu, click Properties, and then click the Text Align property. In the property sheet, you then can select the appropriate alignment.

In some cases, you will want to make the same change to several objects, perhaps to several labels at once. Rather than making the changes individually, you can select all the objects at once, and then make a single change. Perform the steps on the next page to change the alignment of the labels.

Steps To Change Label Alignment

1 If necessary, click the label for the Technician Number field to select it. Select the labels for the First Name, Last Name, Hourly Rate, YTD Earnings, Start Date, and Web Page fields by clicking them while holding down the SHIFT key. Release the SHIFT key. Right-click the Web Page field. Click Properties on the shortcut menu and then click the down scroll arrow until the Text Align property displays. Click the Text Align property, and then click the Text Align box arrow. Point to Right.

The labels are selected (Figure 5-54). The Multiple selection property sheet displays. The Text Align property is selected and the list of available values for the Text Align property displays.

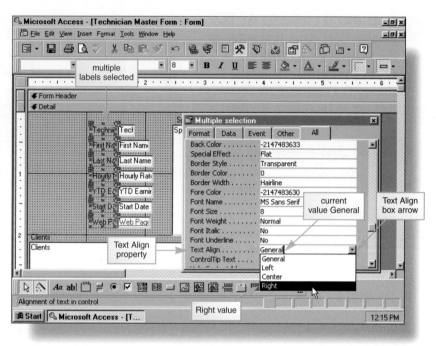

FIGURE 5-54

2 Click Right to select right alignment for the labels. Close the Multiple selection property sheet by clicking its Close button.

The alignment is changed.

Resizing the Labels

To resize a label to optimum size, select the label by clicking it, and then double-click an appropriate sizing handle. Perform the following steps to resize the label for the Technician Number, First Name, Last Name, Hourly Rate, YTD Earnings, Start Date, and Web Page fields just as you resized the label for the Specialties field earlier. The only difference is that you will double-click the sizing handles at the left edge of the labels instead of the right edge. You could resize them individually. It is easier, however, to make sure they are all selected and then resize one of the labels. Access will resize all the others automatically as demonstrated in the following step.

Steps To Resize a Label

1 With all the labels selected, double-click the middle sizing handle on the left edge of the Technician Number label to resize all the labels to the optimal size.

The labels are resized (Figure 5-55).

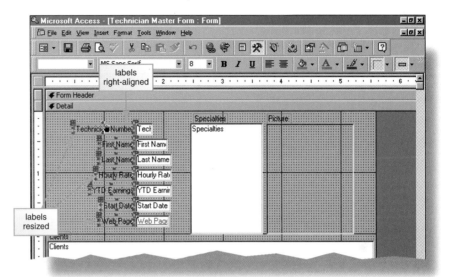

FIGURE 5-55

Changing Special Effects and Colors of Labels

Access allows you to change a variety of **characteristics of the labels** in the form. You can change the border style and color, the background color, the font, and the font size. You also can give the label **special effects**, such as raised or sunken. To change characteristics of a label, such as special effects and colors, perform the following steps.

 Steps To Change Special Effects and Colors of Labels

◆**More** *About*
Colors of Labels

There are two different colors you can change for many objects, including labels. Changing Fore Color (foreground) changes the color of the letters that appear in the label. Changing Back Color (background) changes the color of the label itself.

1 Be sure the labels for the Technician Number, First Name, Last Name, Hourly Rate, YTD Earnings, Start Date, and Web Page fields are selected. Right-click one of the selected labels, and then click Properties on the shortcut menu that displays. Click the Special Effect property and then click the Special Effect box arrow. Point to Raised.

The Multiple selection property sheet displays (Figure 5-56). The Special Effect property is selected and the list of values for the Special Effect property displays.

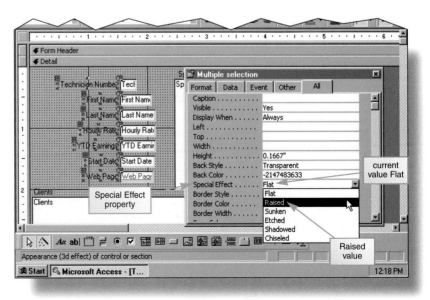

FIGURE 5-56

2 Click Raised. If necessary, click the down scroll arrow until the Fore Color property displays, and then click the Fore Color property. Point to the Build button (the button containing the three dots).

The Fore Color property is selected (Figure 5-57).

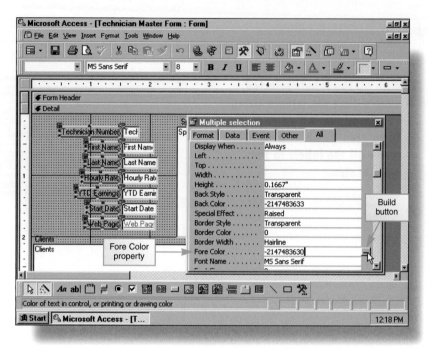

FIGURE 5-57

3 Click the Build button to produce the Color dialog box, and then point to the color blue in row 4, column 5, as shown in Figure 5-58.

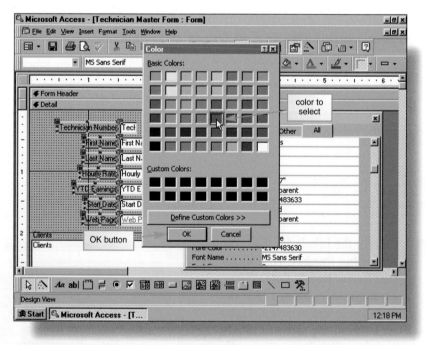

FIGURE 5-58

4 Click the color blue, and then click the OK button. Close the Multiple selection property sheet by clicking its Close button.

The changes to the labels are complete.

5 Click the View button to view the form.

The form displays (Figure 5-59). The fields have been moved and the appearance of the labels has been changed.

6 Click the View button a second time to return to the design grid.

The form design displays.

FIGURE 5-59

Adding a Form Title

Notice in Figure 5-1 on page A 5.5 that the form includes a title. To add a title to a form, add the title as a label in the Form Header section. To accomplish this task, first you will need to expand the size of the Form Header to accommodate the title by dragging the bottom border of the Form Header. Then, you can use the **Label button** in the toolbox to place the label. After placing the label, you can type the title in the label. Using the Properties command on the label's shortcut menu you can change various properties to improve the title's appearance, as well.

Perform the following steps to place a title on the form.

> ◆ **More** *About*
> **Form Headers**
>
> You might wish to add more than just a title to a form header. For example, you may wish to add a picture such as a company logo. To do so, click the Image button in the toolbox, click the position where you want to place the picture, and then select the picture to insert.

 Steps To Add a Form Title

1 Point to the line separating the Form Header section from the Detail section.

The shape of the mouse pointer changes to a two-headed horizontal arrow, indicating you can drag the line to resize the Form Header section (Figure 5-60).

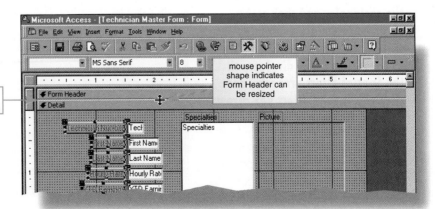

FIGURE 5-60

2 Drag the line to expand the size of the Form Header section to approximately the size shown in Figure 5-61. Point to the Label button in the toolbox as shown in the figure.

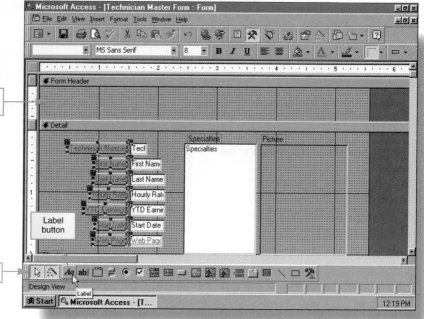

FIGURE 5-61

3 Click the Label button and then position the mouse pointer as shown in Figure 5-62. The shape of the mouse pointer has changed, indicating you are placing a label.

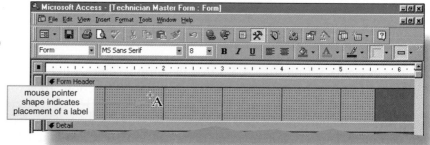

FIGURE 5-62

4 Click the position shown in the figure to place the label on the form. Type Technician Master Form as the title. Click somewhere outside the rectangle containing the title to deselect the rectangle, and then right-click the rectangle containing the title. Click Properties on the shortcut menu that displays, click the Special Effect property, and click the Special Effect box arrow. Point to Etched.

The Label: Label21 property sheet displays (Figure 5-63). The Special Effect property is selected. (Your Label property sheet may contain a different number.)

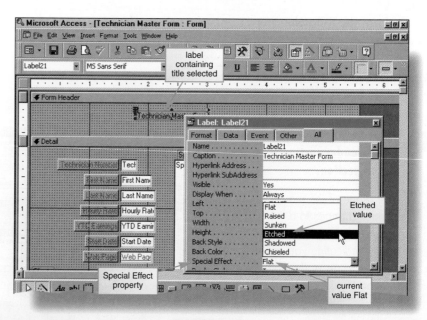

FIGURE 5-63

5 Click Etched. Click the down scroll arrow so the Font Size property displays. Click the Font Size property, click the Font Size box arrow, and then click 12. If necessary, click the down scroll arrow to display the Font Weight property. Click the Font Weight property, click the Font Weight box arrow, and then click Bold. Close the property sheet by clicking its Close button. Resize the label to display the title completely in the larger font size.

The Form Header is complete (Figure 5-64).

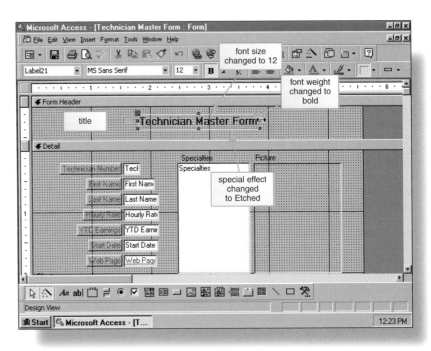

FIGURE 5-64

Adjusting the Subform

After viewing the form in Figure 5-59 on page A 5.37, you can see a problem with the subform. It is wider than it needs to be. The following steps change the size of the subform to remove the extra space.

 Steps To Adjust the Subform

1 Scroll down to the bottom of the form. Click the subform and then point to the right middle sizing handle (Figure 5-65).

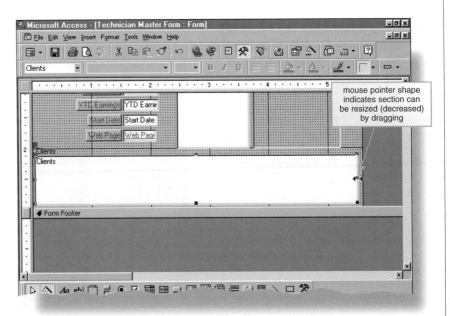

FIGURE 5-65

2 Drag the right edge to approximately the position shown in Figure 5-66.

3 Close the window containing the form. When asked if you want to save the changes to the design of the form, click Yes.

The form is complete.

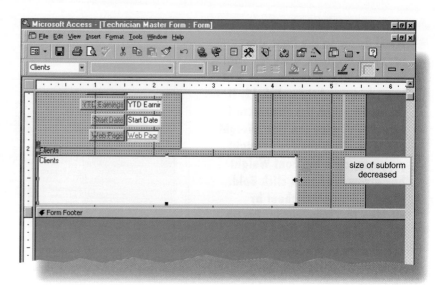

FIGURE 5-66

Viewing Data and Web Pages Using the Form

To use a form to view data, right-click the form in the Database window, and then click Open on the shortcut menu that displays. You then can use the navigation buttons to move among technicians or to move among the clients of the technician who currently is displayed on the screen. By clicking the technician's Web Page field, you can display the technician's Web page. As soon as you close the window containing the Web page, Access returns to the form.

Perform the following steps to display data using the form.

 Steps To Use the Form to View Data and Web Pages

1 If necessary, click the Forms tab and then right-click Technician Master Form. Point to Open on the shortcut menu.

The shortcut menu displays (Figure 5-67).

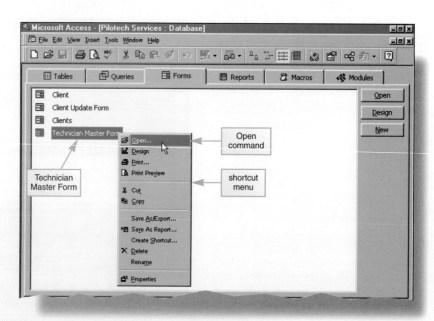

FIGURE 5-67

2 Click Open on the shortcut menu. Be sure the window containing the form is maximized. Point to the Next Record button for the Technician table.

The data from the first record displays in the form (Figure 5-68).

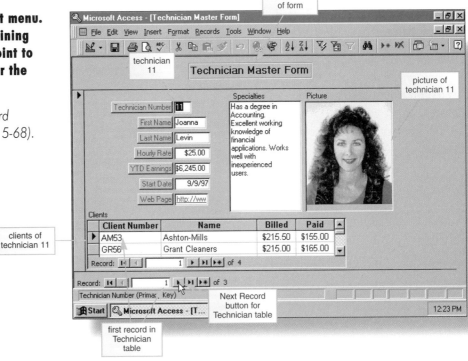

FIGURE 5-68

3 Click the Next Record button to move to the second technician. Point to the Next Record button for the Clients subform (the Next Record button in the set of navigation buttons immediately below the subform).

The data from the second record displays (Figure 5-69). (The records in your form may display in a different order.) Because more clients are included than will fit in the subform at a single time, Access automatically adds a **vertical scroll bar**. You can use the scroll bar or the navigation buttons to move among clients.

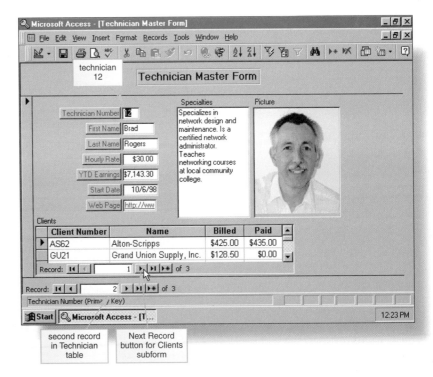

FIGURE 5-69

4 Click the subform's Next Record button twice.

The data from the third client of technician 12 displays in the subform (Figure 5-70).

FIGURE 5-70

5 Point to the control for the technician's Web page (Figure 5-71).

FIGURE 5-71

6 Click the control for the technician's Web page. If a dialog box displays in either this step or the next, follow the directions given in the dialog box.

The technician's Web page displays (Figure 5-72).

7 When you have finished viewing the technician's Web page, click the Close button to return to the form. Close the form by clicking its Close button.

The form no longer displays.

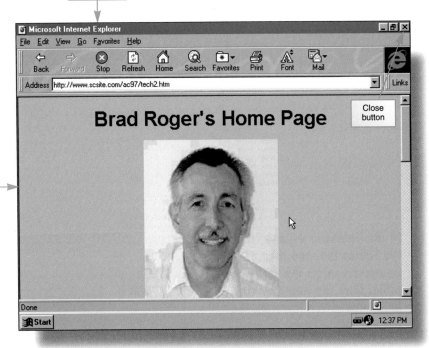

FIGURE 5-72

The previous steps have illustrated the way you work with a main form and subform, as well as how to use a hyperlink (the Web Page control in this form). Clicking the navigation buttons for the main form moves to a different technician. Clicking the navigation buttons for the subform moves to a different client of the technician who displays in the main form. Clicking a hyperlink moves to the corresponding document or Web page. The following are other actions you can take within the form:

1. To move from the last field in the main form to the first field in the subform, press the TAB key. To move back to the last field in the main form, press the CTRL+SHIFT+TAB keys.
2. To move from the last field in the subform to the first field in the main form, press the CTRL+TAB keys. In the process, you also will move to the next record.
3. To switch from the main form to the subform using the mouse, click anywhere in the subform. To switch back to the main form, click any control in the main form. Clicking the background of the main form is not sufficient.

Using Date and Memo Fields in a Query

To use date fields in queries, you simply type the dates including the slashes. To search for records with a specific date, you must type the date. You also can use **comparison operators**. To find all the technicians whose start date is prior to January 1, 1998, for example, you would type the criterion <1/1/98.

**More *About*
Date Fields in Queries: Using Date( )**

In a query, to test for the current date, type Date( ) in the criteria row of the appropriate column. Placing <Date( ) in the criteria row for Renewal Date, for example, would find those therapists whose renewal date occurs anytime before the date on which you run the query.

**More *About*
Date Fields in Queries: Using Expressions**

Expressions have a special meaning in date fields in queries. Numbers that appear in expressions represent numbers of days. The expression <Date( )+30 for Renewal Date would find therapists whose renewal date occurs anytime prior to 30 days after the day on which you run the query.

You also can use memo fields in queries. Typically, you will want to find all the records on which the memo field contains a specific word or phrase. To do so, you use wildcards. For example, to find all the technicians who have the word, inexperienced, in the Specialties field, you would type the criterion like *inexperienced*.

Perform the following steps to create and run queries that use date and memo fields.

Steps To Use Date and Memo Fields in a Query

1 In the Database window, click the Tables tab, and then, if necessary, select the Technician table. Click the New Object: AutoForm button arrow on the toolbar. Click Query. Be sure Design View is highlighted, and then click the OK button.

2 Maximize the Select Query window that displays. Resize the upper and lower panes and the Technician field list to the sizes shown in Figure 5-73. Double-click the Tech Number, First Name, Last Name, Start Date, and Specialties fields to include them in the query (you may need to scroll down the field list before double-clicking the Specialties field). Click the Criteria row under the Specialties field and then type like *inexperienced* (Figure 5-73). Point to the Run button on the toolbar.

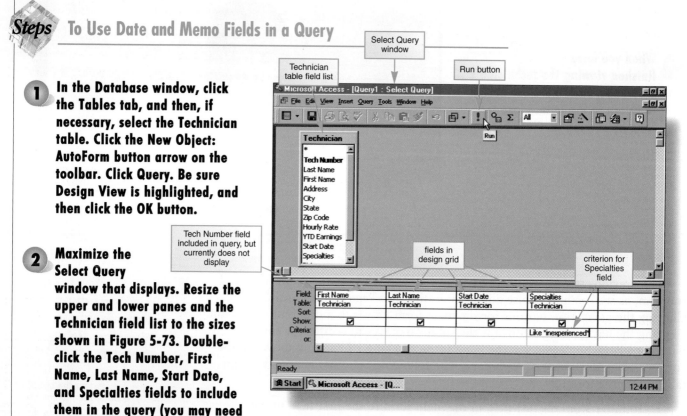

FIGURE 5-73

3 Click the Run button on the toolbar to run the query.

The results display in Datasheet view (Figure 5-74). Two records are included.

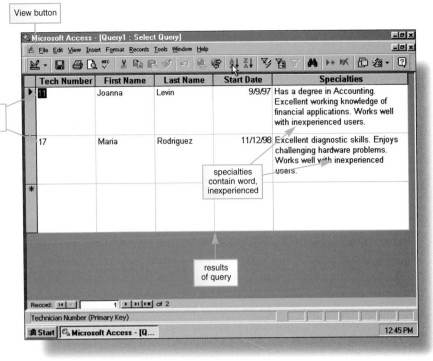

View button

two records included

specialties contain word, inexperienced

results of query

FIGURE 5-74

4 Click the View button to return to the Select Query window. Click the Criteria row under the Start Date field, and then type <1/1/98 **(Figure 5-75).**

5 Click the Run button on the toolbar to run the query.

The result contains only a single row, because only one technician was hired before January 1, 1998 and has a specialty entry that contains the word, inexperienced.

6 Close the Select Query window by clicking its Close button. When asked if you want to save the query, click the No button.

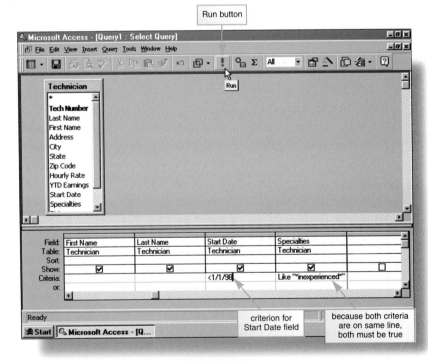

Run button

Run

criterion for Start Date field

because both criteria are on same line, both must be true

FIGURE 5-75

The results of the query are removed from the screen and the Database window again displays.

Closing the Database

The following step closes the database by closing its Database window.

TO CLOSE A DATABASE

Step 1: Click the Close button for the Pilotech Services : Database window.

Project Summary

Project 5 introduced you to some additional field types. To maintain the additional data required at Pilotech Services, you needed to learn how to create and work with date, memo, OLE, and Hyperlink fields. You also learned how to use such fields in a form. You then learned how to build a form on a one-to-many relationship in which you had several records from one of the tables displaying on the screen at the same time in order to create the form required for Pilotech Services. You learned how to use the form to view technician and client data as well as to view the technician's Web page. Finally, you learned how to use date and memo fields in queries to answer two important questions for the organization.

What You Should Know

Having completed this project, you now should be able to perform the following tasks:

- Add a Form Title *(A 5.37)*
- Add Fields to a Table *(A 5.7)*
- Adjust the Subform *(A 5.39)*
- Change Label Alignment *(A 5.34)*
- Change Special Effects and Colors of Labels *(A 5.35)*
- Change the Contents of a Label *(A 5.33)*
- Change the Row and Column Size *(A 5.12)*
- Change the Size Mode of a Picture *(A 5.31)*
- Close a Database *(A 5.46)*
- Close the Table and Save the Properties *(A 5.17)*
- Create a Form with a Subform Using the Form Wizard *(A 5.18)*
- Enter Data in Date Fields *(A 5.9)*
- Enter Data in Hyperlink Fields *(A 5.16)*
- Enter Data in Memo Fields *(A 5.11)*
- Enter Data in OLE Fields and Convert the Data to Pictures *(A 5.13)*
- Modify the Form Design *(A 5.24)*
- Modify the Subform Design *(A 5.22)*
- Move a Group of Fields *(A 5.32)*
- Move and Resize Fields *(A 5.27)*
- Move Labels *(A 5.28)*
- Open a Database *(A 5.6)*
- Resize a Label *(A 5.30, A 5.35)*
- Resize and Move the Subform *(A 5.25)*
- Use Date and Memo Fields in a Query *(A 5.44)*
- Use the Form to View Data and Web Pages *(A 5.40)*

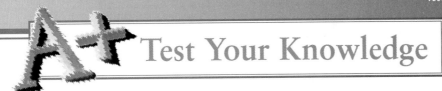 Test Your Knowledge

1 True/False

Instructions: Circle T if the statement is true or F if the statement is false.

T F   1. The term OLE means Object Linking and Embedding.

T F   2. To change the size of a row, position the mouse pointer on the lower border of any record's row selector and drag.

T F   3. To insert data into an OLE field, right-click the field to produce the shortcut menu, and then click Add Picture on the shortcut menu.

T F   4. You can import pictures from files on disk and place them in an OLE field.

T F   5. You cannot resize OLE fields on a form.

T F   6. To change the color of a field label, right-click the object, and then click Color on the shortcut menu.

T F   7. To select more than one object at a time, press and hold down the CTRL key as you select additional objects.

T F   8. You cannot use comparison operators with date fields.

T F   9. To find all records where the text, Java, is included in a memo field, enter Java in the criteria row of the design grid.

T F   10. When you enter date fields in a record, it is not necessary to enter the slashes.

2 Multiple Choice

Instructions: Circle the correct response.

1. The term OLE means _____.
   a. Object Linking and Encoding
   b. Object Locking and Encoding
   c. Object Linking and Embedding
   d. Object Locking and Embedding

2. To enter data in a Hyperlink field, right-click the field, and then click _____ on the shortcut menu.
   a. Hyperlink
   b. WWW
   c. URL
   d. Link

3. In a table, the row containing the list of field names is called the _____.
   a. column selector panel
   b. field label
   c. field selector
   d. column label panel

(continued)

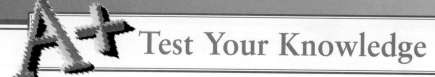

Test Your Knowledge

Multiple Choice *(continued)*

4. The box at the beginning of a record that you can click to select a record is called the _____.
   a. row selector   c. record highlighter
   b. row identifier   d. record identifier

5. To insert data in an OLE field, right-click the field, and then click _____ on the shortcut menu.
   a. Insert OLE   c. Object
   b. Insert Object   d. OLE

6. A technician may represent many clients but a client can be represented by only one technician. This is a _____ relationship.
   a. one-to-none   c. one-to-one
   b. one-to-many   d. many-to-many

7. To select all field objects on a form, click the first object and then press and hold down the _____ key as you click each of the others.
   a. left CTRL
   b. SHIFT
   c. right CTRL
   d. ALT

8. To change the color of a field label, right-click the field, click _____ on the shortcut menu, and then click the Fore Color property.
   a. Color
   b. Label
   c. Properties
   d. Image

9. The Technician table contains a Start Date field. To find all technicians who started after January 1, 1998, enter the criterion _____ in the Criteria row of the Start Date field in the design grid.
   a. >'1/1/98'
   b. >1/1/98
   c. >=1/1/98
   d. >='1/1/98'

10. The Technician table includes a Specialties field that contains notes describing important characteristics of the technicians. To find all technicians with the word, network, in the Specialties field, enter the criterion _____ in the Criteria row of the Specialties field in the design grid.
   a. like ?network
   b. like ?network?
   c. like *network
   d. like *network*

3 Understanding Forms

Instructions: Figure 5-76 shows a partially completed form for the Intern table. Answer the following questions about the form on your own paper.

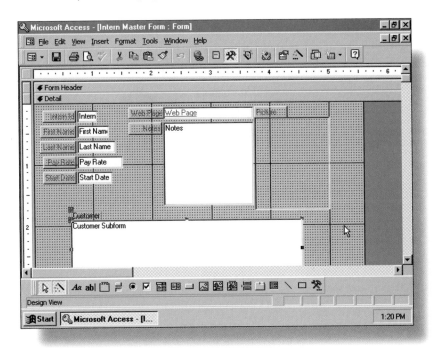

FIGURE 5-76

1. How can you select more than one field object at a time?
2. How would you change the color of the field labels on the form?
3. The form includes a Customer subform. What is a subform?
4. How would you add a title to the form?

4 Understanding the Green Thumb Database

Instructions: In Figure 5-77 on the next page, arrows point to various fields in the Intern table in the Green Thumb database. Identify the data types for these fields in the spaces provided. Answer the following questions about the Green Thumb database on your own paper.

(continued)

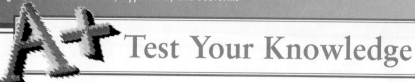

Test Your Knowledge

Understanding the Green Thumb Database *(continued)*

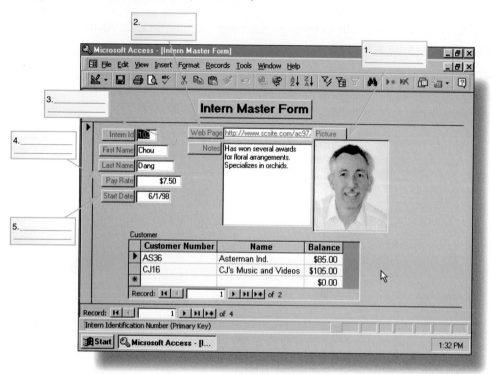

FIGURE 5-77

1. The Intern Master Form depicts a one-to-many relationship between the Intern table and the Customer table. What is a one-to-many relationship?
2. Using the keyboard, how can you move from the last field in the main form to the first field in the subform?
3. Using the mouse, how can you move from the subform to the main form?

Use Help

1 Reviewing Project Activities

Instructions: Perform the following tasks using a computer.

1. Start Access.
2. Click the Contents and Index command on the Help menu to display the Help Topics: Microsoft Access 97 dialog box.

Use Help

3. Click the Contents tab. Double-click the Working with Forms book. Double-click the Creating Multiple-Table or Linked Forms (Subforms) book and then double-click How Microsoft Access links main forms and subforms.

4. Read the Help information when it displays. Next, ready the printer, right-click within the Help window, and then click Print Topic. Hand the printout in to your instructor. Click the Help Topics button to return to the Help Topics: Microsoft Access 97 dialog box.

5. Click the Index tab. Type relationships in the top text box labeled 1 and then double-click forms and subforms under relationships in the middle list box labeled 2. Double-click Subforms - What they are and how they work in the Topics Found dialog box. When the Help information displays, read it, ready the printer, right-click, and click Print Topic. Hand the printout in to your instructor. Click the Help Topics button to return to the Help Topics: Microsoft Access 97 dialog box.

6. Click the Find tab. Type hyperlink in the top text box labeled 1. Double-click About hyperlink addresses in hyperlink fields and controls in the lower list box labeled 3. When the Help information displays, read it, ready the printer, right-click, and click Print Topic. Hand the printout in to your instructor. Click the Close button.

7. If the Office Assistant is on your screen, click it to display its balloon. If the Office Assistant is not on your screen, click the Office Assistant button on the toolbar.

8. Type special effects in the What would you like to do? text box. Click the Search button. Click Make a control appear raised, sunken, shadowed, chiseled, or etched. When the Help information displays, read it, ready the printer, right-click, and click Print Topic. Hand the printout in to your instructor. Click the Close button.

2 Expanding the Basics

Instructions: Use Access Help to better understand the topics listed below. If you cannot print the Help information, then answer the questions on your own paper.

1. Using the Office Assistant, answer the following questions:
   a. What is the maximum size of a text field?
   b. What is the maximum size of a memo field?
   c. Can you create an index for a memo field?
   d. What is the default size for a text field?

2. Using the keyword, sizemode, and the Index sheet in the Help Topics: Microsoft Access 97 dialog box, display and print information on adjusting the size and proportions of a picture. Then, answer the following question. Which setting may distort the image?

3. Use the Find sheet in the Help Topics: Microsoft Access 97 dialog box to display and then print information about changing the layout of a subform displayed in Datasheet view. Then, answer the following questions:
   a. How can you hide a column?
   b. How can you freeze a column?

4. Use the Office Assistant to display and print information on creating hyperlink data types.

Apply Your Knowledge

1 Enhancing the Green Thumb Database

Instructions: Start Access. Open the Green Thumb database from the Access folder on the Data Disk that accompanies this book. Perform the following tasks.

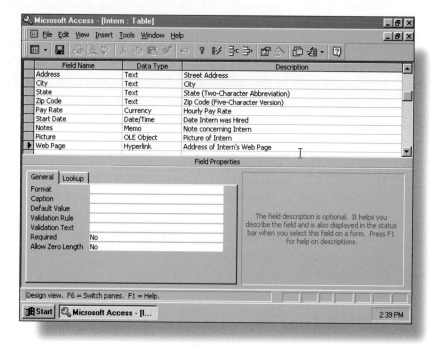

FIGURE 5-78

1. Add the fields, Start Date, Notes, Picture, and Web Page to the Intern table structure as shown in Figure 5-78.

2. Save the changes to the structure.

3. Add the data shown in Figure 5-79 to the Intern table. Add pictures and hyperlinks for all interns. Use the same pictures and hyperlinks that you used for the Technician table in this project. You can use the same file for more than one record. Pict1.pcx, and pict3.pcx are pictures of females; pict2.pcx is a male. Adjust the row and column spacing for the table, if necessary.

4. Print and then close the table.

INTERN ID	START DATE	NOTES
102	6/1/98	Has won several awards for floral arrangements. Specializes in orchids.
105	8/1/98	Has an environmental engineering background. Very knowledgeable on plant toxins and allergies.
109	1/9/99	Has a reputation for innovative floral arrangements. Bonsai enthusiast.
113	3/1/99	Prefers outdoor gardening chores. Has some experience with irrigation systems.

FIGURE 5-79

5. Query the Intern table to find all interns who do floral arrangements. Include the Intern's first name, last name, and pay rate in the query. Print the query results. Do not save the query.

6. Use the Form Wizard to create a form/subform for the Intern table. Include the Intern Id, Last Name, First Name, Pay Rate, Start Date, Notes, Picture, and Web Page from the Intern table. Include the Customer Number, Name, and Balance fields from the Customer table.

7. Modify the form design to create the form shown in Figure 5-77 on page A 5.50.

8. Print the form. To print the form, open the form, click File on the menu bar, click Print, and click Selected Record(s) as the Print Range. Click the OK button.

In the Lab

1 Enhancing the Museum Mercantile Database

Problem: The Museum director has found that Museum Mercantile needs to maintain additional data on vendors. They need to know the last date that they placed an order with a vendor. They also would like to store some notes about each vendor's return policy as well as the URL of each vendor's Web page. The committee requires a form that displays information about the vendor as well as the products that the vendor sells.

Instructions: Open the Museum Mercantile database from the Access folder on the Data Disk that accompanies this book. Perform the following tasks.

1. Add the fields Last Order Date, Notes, and Web Page to the Vendor table structure as shown in Figure 5-80 and then save the changes to the structure.

2. Add the data shown in Figure 5-81 to the Vendor table. Adjust the row and column spacing for the table, if necessary.

FIGURE 5-80

VENDOR CODE	LAST ORDER DATE	NOTES
AR	1/5/99	Can return all unsold merchandise. No extra charges.
MS	1/17/99	Can return all unsold merchandise. Charges a fee.
WW	2/14/99	Can return only those items ordered for the first time. Charges a fee.

FIGURE 5-81

3. Print the table.

4. Create the form shown in Figure 5-82 on the next page for the Vendor table. Use Vendor Master Form as the name of the form and Products of Vendor (Subform) as the name of the subform.

(continued)

In the Lab

Enhancing the Museum Mercantile Database (continued)

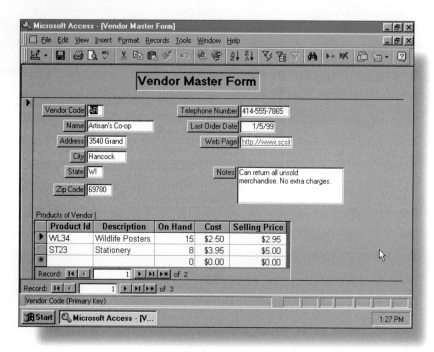

FIGURE 5-82

5. Print the form. To print the form, open the form, click File on the menu bar, click Print, and click Selected Record(s) as the Print Range. Click the OK button.

6. Query the Vendor table to find all vendors that allow all unsold merchandise to be returned. Include the Vendor Code and Name in the query. Print the results. Do not save the query.

2 Enhancing the City Telephone System Database

Problem: The Telephone manager has found that she needs to maintain additional data on the departments. For auditing purposes, she needs to know the start date for each manager. She also needs to store some notes on the billing rate procedures for each department. The manager would like you to create a form that displays information about the department as well as the users in the department.

Instructions: Open the City Telephone System database from the Access folder on the Data Disk that accompanies this book. Perform the following tasks.

1. Add the fields Start Date and Notes to the Department table structure as shown in Figure 5-83. Save the changes to the structure.

In the Lab

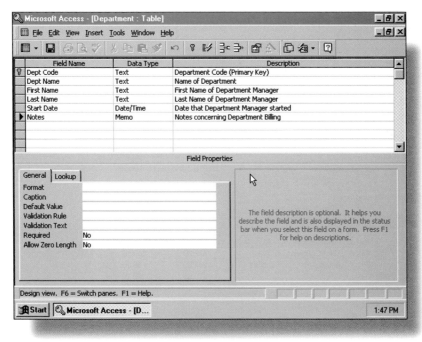

FIGURE 5-83

2. Add the data shown in Figure 5-84 to the Department table. Adjust the row and column spacing for the table, if necessary.

DEPT CODE	START DATE	NOTES
APV	9/1/97	Send all invoices to manager.
ENG	2/1/99	Send invoices to users with summary to manager.
HRS	7/1/98	Send all invoices to manager. Requires two copies.
ITD	3/1/98	Send invoices to users with summary to manager.
PLN	4/1/99	Send all invoices to manager. Also send invoices to users.

FIGURE 5-84

3. Print the table.
4. Create the form shown in Figure 5-85 on the next page. Use Department Master Form as the name of the form and Users as the name of the subform.

(continued)

In the Lab

Enhancing the City Telephone System Database *(continued)*

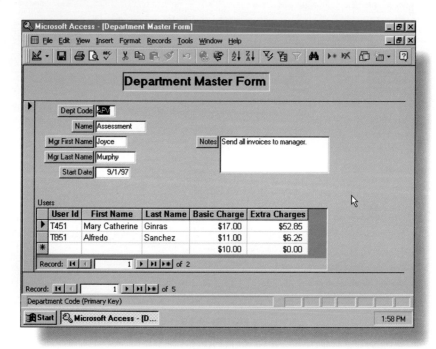

FIGURE 5-85

5. Print the form. To print the form, open the form, click File on the menu bar, click Print, and click Selected Record(s) as the Print Range. Click the OK button.

6. Query the Department table to find all departments whose manager started prior to July 1, 1998. Include the Dept Code, Name, First Name, and Last Name in the query. Print the results. Do not save the query.

3 Enhancing the City Scene Database

Problem: The managing editor has found that he needs to maintain additional data on the advertising representatives. He needs to maintain the date an ad rep started as well as some notes concerning a representative's abilities. He also would like to store a picture of the representative as well as a link to each representative's Web page. The manager wants you to create a form that displays advertising representative information and the advertisers for which they are responsible.

Instructions: Open the City Scene database from the Access folder on the Data Disk that accompanies this book. Perform the following tasks.

1. Add the Start Date, Notes, Picture, and Web Page fields to the Ad Rep table as shown in Figure 5-86. Save the changes to the structure.

In the Lab

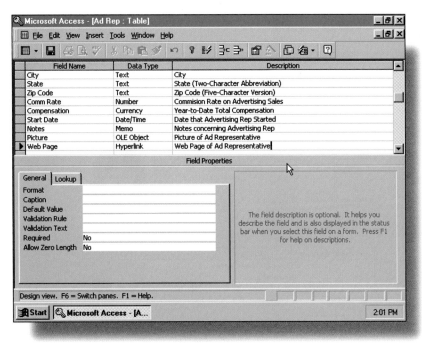

FIGURE 5-86

2. Add the data shown in Figure 5-87 to the Ad Rep table. Add pictures and hyperlinks for each representative. Use the same picture and hyperlink files that you used for the Technician table in this project. Pict1.pcx and pict3.pcx are pictures of females; pict2.pcx is a male.

AD REP NUMBER	START DATE	NOTES
16	4/1/98	Also works as freelance journalist.
19	9/7/98	Records radio advertisements for magazine.
22	3/4/99	Excellent proofreader.

FIGURE 5-87

3. Print the table.
4. Create the form shown in Figure 5-88 on the next page. Use Advertising Rep Master Form as the name of the form and Accounts as the name of the subform.

(continued)

In the Lab

Enhancing the City Scene Database *(continued)*

FIGURE 5-88

5. Add the current date to the form. (*Hint*: Use information from Use Help Exercise 2 of the previous project to solve this problem.)

6. Print the form. To print the form, open the form, click File on the menu bar, click Print, and click Selected Record(s) as the Print Range. Click the OK button.

7. Query the Ad Rep table to find all ad reps who also will work as freelance journalists. Include the Ad Rep Number, Last Name, and First Name in the query. Print the query results. Do not save the query.

8. Query the Ad Rep table to find all ad reps who started before 1999. Include the Ad Rep Number, Last Name, First Name, Compensation, and Comm Rate in the query. Print the query results. Do not save the query.

200 MHz

Cases and Places

The difficulty of these case studies varies: ❱ are the least difficult; ❱❱ are more difficult; and ❱❱❱ are the most difficult.

1 ❱ Use the database created in Case Study 1 of the Cases and Places section of Project 4 for this assignment. Athletic department personnel need additional data on the golf pros. Add the fields and data in Figure 5-89 to the Pro table. Print the Pro table. Create and print a Pro Master Form for the Pro table, which is similar in format to Figure 5-82 on page A 5.54. Query the Pro table to find the instructors who prefer teaching in the afternoons.

INSTRUCTOR	PREFERRED TIMES	PREFERRED STUDENTS
GC	Mornings	Children
CW	Weekends	Beginners
VM	Afternoons	Advanced
SP	Afternoons	Beginners

FIGURE 5-89

2 ❱ Enhance the database created in Case Study 1 above by adding pictures of the four golf pros. Use the same picture files used for the Technician table in Project 5. (Use the picture file of the male for both male golf pros.) In addition, change the special effects and colors of the labels.

3 ❱❱ Use the database created in Case Study 3 of the Cases and Places section of Project 1 for this assignment. Add a memo field to describe the plot of each movie and a date field to indicate when nursing home residents last watched the movie. Use the following data: *The Little Princess*, a sweet child is mistreated at a strict boarding school, 10/15/96; *North by Northwest*, mistaken identity entangles a New York man in murder and espionage, 2/19/98; *Of Mice and Men*, migrant life during the Depression on a California ranch, 4/2/97; *The Quiet Man*, an American ex-boxer returns to Ireland and falls in love, 5/4/98; *On the Waterfront*, corruption in New York tests morality 3/6/98; *Pardon My Sarong*, two Chicago bus drivers experience a Pacific island, 8/25/97; *Ride 'em Cowboy*, two New York peanut vendors experience a dude ranch 12/16/96; *You Can't Take It with You*, an unconventional grandfather and the parents of his granddaughter's fiancé meet, 4/29/98; *The Undefeated*, a Yankee colonel and a Confederate colonel join forces to sell wild horses to the French, 7/31/96; and *Operation Pacific*, a submarine commander tackles the Japanese, 2/7/98. Query the table to find all movies with a New York setting and all movies that have not been watched in the past two years.

Cases and Places

4 ▶▶ You have been using the restaurant form created in Case Study 5 of the Cases and Places section of Project 4 in your meal delivery service. Now, you want to add a memo field to record notes regarding these eating establishments. Add the following facts to the records in the table: Ole Tacos has outstanding taco salads; Little Venice, Red Rose, and House of China accept reservations; Noto's has extremely slow service; Pan Pacific and New Crete have entertainment on weekends; Napoli's Pizza has a romantic decor; Ye Old Cafe and Texas Diner have outdoor seating. Query the table to find all restaurants open past 10:00 p.m. that have outdoor seating and all restaurants open for lunch that accept reservations.

5 ▶▶▶ Although the textbook exchange system you enhanced in Case Study 4 of the Cases and Places section of Project 4 is quite profitable, you believe the system would be more successful by using additional marketing data in the advertisements you have been running on the student government's Web page. Add fields to the table for the current selling price in the bookstore, copyright date, and edition. Use the following data: *Sociology Today*, $35, 1998, 3rd ed.; *Creative Writing*, $27, 1997, 2nd ed.; *Reach for the Stars*, $42, 1996, 4th ed.; *Ethics for Today's Society*, $35, 1998, 3rd ed.; *Electronic Circuitry*, $52, 1997, 3rd ed.; *Nutrition for Our Souls*, $26, 1998, 2nd ed.; *Geriatric Nursing*, $54, 1997, 3rd ed. Query the table for books published after 1996 and for books selling for less than $30.

6 ▶▶▶ The campus directory database you created in Case Study 6 of the Cases and Places section of Project 4 has been very useful. Add fields and data for: (a) athletic coaches and dates of athletic events and (b) computer lab room numbers, open lab times, and telephone extensions. Query the table to find all computer labs that are open on the weekends, all faculty members with office hours on Fridays, and the coaches in charge of the next three athletic events.

7 ▶▶▶ Financial planners suggest saving 10 percent of income as a good start toward preparing for retirement. Your accounting instructor wants you to diversify your investments by putting 10 percent of last year's after-tax income in certificates of deposit. Visit five local banks, credit unions, or savings and loan associations to determine current rates, maturity dates, and the total values of the CDs by age 65. Add fields and this data to the table you created in Case Study 7 of the Cases and Places Section of Project 4, and then print a revised report with the new title of Investment Future Value Report. Query the table to find all the financial institutions with interest rates above 6 percent and all CDs maturing before January 2001.

Microsoft *Access 97*

Creating an Application System Using Macros, VBA, and the Switchboard Manager

Objectives

You will have mastered the material in this project when you can:

▶ Create a macro
▶ Add actions and comments to a macro
▶ Modify arguments in a macro
▶ Run a macro
▶ Add command buttons to forms
▶ Modify VBA code associated with a command button
▶ Add a combo box to a form
▶ Modify properties of a combo box
▶ Use a combo box
▶ Create a switchboard
▶ Modify switchboard pages
▶ Modify switchboard items
▶ Use a switchboard

CREATION
and
CULTURES
by
Design

Four days the dark cloud rested at the summit of the peak, until Talking God ascended the mountain to investigate. At the place where the cloud rested, he found rain softly falling and heard the cry of an infant. Beneath a rainbow, a baby girl lay on a bed of flowers. Born of Darkness, she was fathered by Dawn. Talking God named her Changing Woman, then gave her to First Man and First Woman to rear. When Changing Woman came of age, one day she awoke from a deep sleep, knowing that she would bear a child. Within four days, she gave birth to Monster Slayer, and four days after that, Child Born of Water entered the world. After seeking out their father — the Sun — these Hero Twins became the founders of the Navaho Nation.

This story about the origins of the Navaho people first became familiar to non-Navahos through the novel of

Tony Hillerman. It is but one of untold numbers of creation legends, since virtually every culture in the history of the world has conceived a story to explain its own existence.

In his landmark work, *The Historical Atlas of World Mythologies*, noted scholar Joseph Campbell illustrates the remarkable similarities between mythologies of cultures not only widely separated by distance and custom, but by centuries of time.

Genesis, the basis for Judeo-Christian beliefs, tells of Adam and Eve, who with Cain and Abel, founded the human race. A Pygmy tale from the Congo and a Bassari legend of Togo contain the story of a woman tempted to eat forbidden fruit. In Plato's *Protagoras Myth*, the gods of Greek legend gave to Epimetheus and Prometheus the task of distributing powers and characteristics to man and the beasts. In the Brahman *Upanishad*, the Universal Self divides into two — a man and a woman — then transforms into pairs of every type of animal in order to populate the earth. In the Icelandic *Prose Edda*, written by Snorre Sturlasons, a single god created heaven and earth and Adam and Eve, but two of the main heroes are named Thor and Odin. In the Japanese *Kojiki*, Izanagi and Izanami are the gods from whom the eight great islands of Japan and the Japanese people sprang.

A story of another beginning involves database creation and its associated application systems. In this project, you will use Microsoft Access to create a switchboard system, which includes adding command buttons and a combo box to carry out specific tasks with greatly enhanced performance. The improved design environment of Access provides developer-oriented features with powerful tools such as macros, Visual Basic for Applications, and the Switchboard Manager. These tools assist you in both the way you work and the speed at which you create database applications, allowing you to be productive and save valuable time.

With all that extra time, you may be able to produce a personal database to chronicle your own family origins.

Project 6

Microsoft
Access 97

Case Perspective

The management of Pilotech Services is pleased with the tables, forms, and reports that you have created thus far. They have two additional requests, however. First, they would like some improvements to the Client Update Form, which would include placing buttons on the form for moving to the next record, moving to the previous record, adding a record, deleting a record, and closing the form. Then, they want a simple way of searching for a client given the client's name. They also require an easier way to access the various tables, forms, and reports merely by clicking a button or two to open any form or table, preview any report, or print any report. They believe this will increase employee productivity at the organization if employees do not have to remember all the steps required to perform any of these tasks.

Creating an Application System Using Macros, VBA, and the Switchboard Manager

Introduction

In previous projects, you created tables, forms, and reports. Each time you want to use any of these, you must follow the correct series of steps. To open the Client Update Form in a maximized window, for example, first you must click the Forms tab in the Database window, and then right-click the correct form. Then, you will click Open on the shortcut menu and finally, click the Maximize button for the window containing the form.

All these steps are unnecessary if you create your own switchboard system, such as the one shown in Figures 6-1a and 6-1b. A **switchboard** is a form that includes buttons to perform a variety of actions. In this system, you just click a button — View Form, View Table, View Report, Print Report, or Exit Application — to indicate the action you wish to take. Other than Exit Application, clicking a button leads to another switchboard. For example, clicking the View Form button leads to the View Form switchboard as shown in Figures 6-1a and 6-1b. You then click the button that identifies the form you want to view. Similarly, clicking the View Table button would lead to a switchboard on which you would click a button to indicate the table you want to view. Thus, viewing any form, table, or report, or printing any report requires clicking only two buttons.

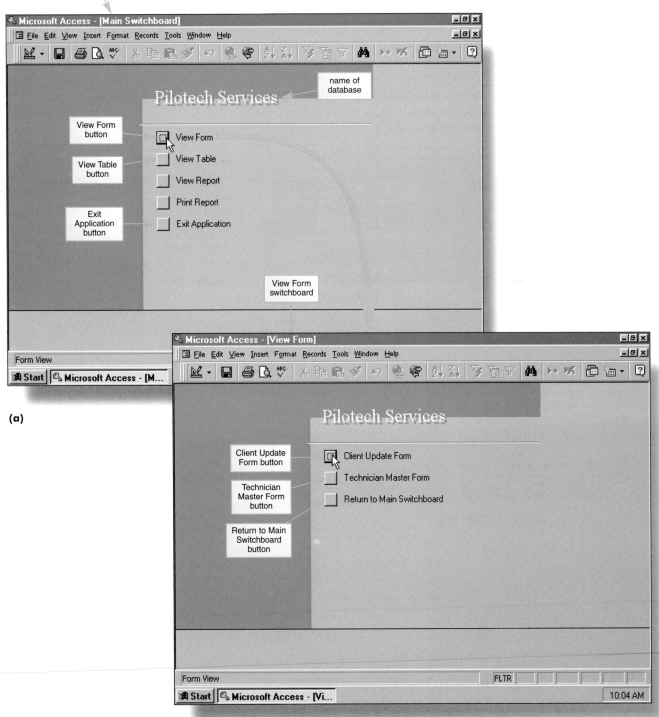

FIGURE 6-1

(a)

(b)

More *About*
Switchboards

An application system is simply an easy-to-use collection of forms, reports, and/or queries designed to satisfy the needs of some specific user or groups of users, like the users at Pilotech Services. A switchboard system is one type of application system that is very popular in the Windows environment.

In this project, you will create the switchboard system represented in Figures 6-1a and 6-1b. You will begin by creating **macros**, which are collections of actions designed to carry out specific tasks, such as opening a form and maximizing the window containing the form. You can run the macros directly from the Database window. When you do, Access will execute the various steps, called **actions**, in the macro. You also can use the macros in the switchboard system. Clicking certain buttons in the switchboard system you create will cause appropriate macros to be run.

By including both command buttons and a combo box that allows users to search for clients by name, you will enhance the Client Update Form you created earlier (Figure 6-2). When you add the command buttons and the combo box to the form, you will use appropriate Access wizards. The **wizards** create the button or the combo box to your specifications and place it on the form. They also create an event procedure for the button or the combo box. An **event procedure** is a series of steps that Access will carry out when an event, such as the clicking of a command button, occurs. For example, when you click the Delete Record button, the steps in the event procedure created for the Delete Record button will be executed. This procedure actually will cause the record to be deleted. Event procedures are written in a language called **Visual Basic for Applications**, or **VBA**. This language is a standard throughout Microsoft applications.

Generally, you do not even need to be aware that these event procedures exist. Access creates and uses them automatically. Occasionally, however, you may wish to make changes to an event procedure. Without making changes, for example, clicking the Add Record button blanks out the fields on the form so you can enter a new record. Yet, it would not produce an insertion point in the Client Number field. It would require you to take special action, such as clicking the Client Number field, before you could begin entering data. You can rectify this by making a change to the event procedure for the Add Record button.

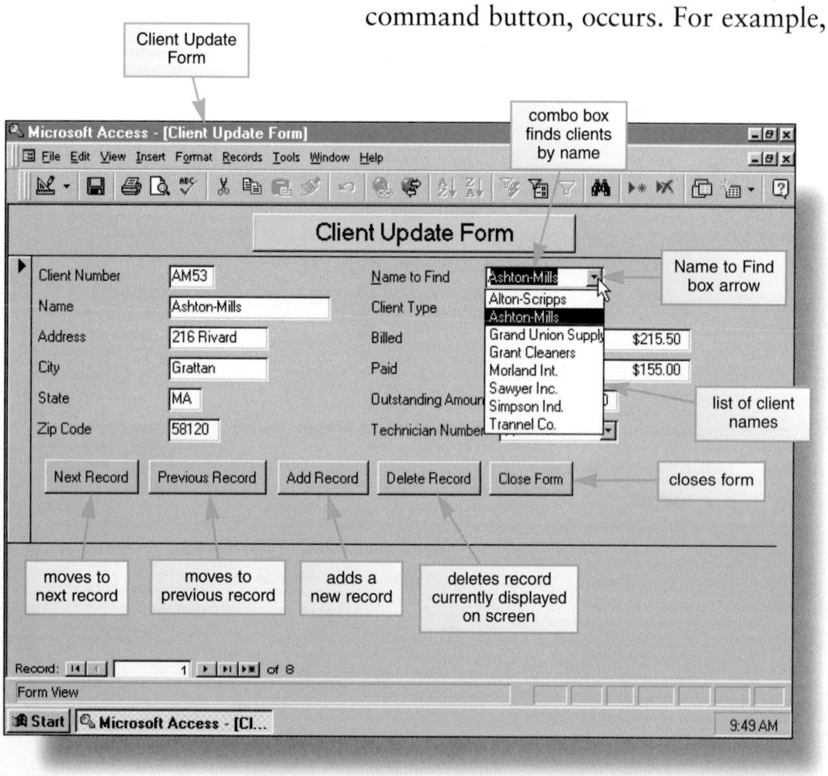

FIGURE 6-2

Project Six – Creating an Application System for Pilotech Services

Before creating the switchboard system required by the management of Pilotech Services, first you must create and test the macros that will be used in the system. In addition, you must add the necessary buttons to the Client Update Form. Then, you must add the combo box that allows users to find a client given the client's name. Finally, you must create the switchboard system that will allow users to access any form, table, or report simply by clicking the appropriate buttons.

Overview of Project Steps

The project steps create the macros necessary to implement the switchboard system in Figures 6-1a and 6-1b on page A 6.5. They add the command buttons and combo box to the Client Update Form in Figure 6-2. Finally, they create the switchboard system in Figures 6-1a and 6-1b. The following tasks will be completed in this project.

1. Start Access.
2. Create the macros needed for the switchboard system.
3. Place command buttons on the Client Update Form.
4. Modify the VBA code for the Add Record button.
5. Place a combo box on the Client Update Form.
6. Modify the properties of the combo box.
7. Create a switchboard.
8. Create the switchboard pages.
9. Create the switchboard items.

The following pages contain a detailed explanation of these steps.

Opening the Database

Before creating the macros, modifying the form, or creating the switchboard system, first you must open the database. Perform the following steps to complete this task.

TO OPEN A DATABASE

Step 1: Click the Start button on the taskbar.
Step 2: Click Open Office Document on the Start menu, and then click 3½ Floppy (A:) in the Look in list box. If necessary, double-click the Access folder. Make sure the Pilotech Services database is selected.
Step 3: Click the Open button.

The database opens and the Pilotech Services : Database window displays.

Creating and Using Macros

A **macro** consists of a series of actions that Access will perform when the macro is run; therefore, you will need to specify the actions when you create the macro. The actions are entered in a special window called a **Macro window**. Once a macro is created, you can run it from the Database window by right-clicking it and then clicking Run on the shortcut menu. Macros also can be associated with items on switchboards. When you click the corresponding button on the switchboard, Access will run the macro. Whether a macro is run from the Database window or from a switchboard, the effect is the same. Access will execute the actions in the macro in the order in which they are entered.

In this project, you will create macros to open forms and maximize the windows; open tables in Datasheet view; open reports in preview windows; and print reports. As you enter actions, you will select them from a list box. The names of the actions are self-explanatory. The action to open a form, for example, is OpenForm. Thus, it is not necessary to memorize the specific actions that are available.

More *About* **Macros**

The actions in a macro are executed when a particular *event* occurs. The event simply could be a user clicking Run on the macro's shortcut menu. It also could be the clicking of a button on a form or switchboard, provided the macro is associated with the button.

To create a macro, perform the following steps to begin the process.

To Create a Macro

1 **Click the Macros tab and point to the New button.**

The list of previously created macros displays (Figure 6-3). Currently, no macros exist.

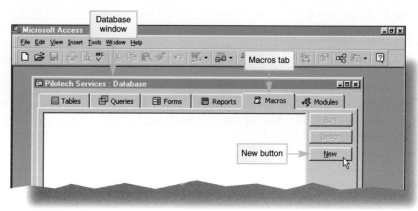

FIGURE 6-3

2 **Click the New button.**

The Macro1: Macro window displays (Figure 6-4).

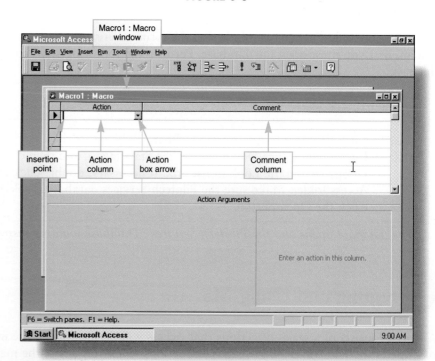

FIGURE 6-4

The Macro Window

The first column in the Macro window is the **Action column**. You enter the **actions** you want the macro to perform in this column (Figure 6-4). To enter an action, click the arrow in the Action column and select the action from the list that displays. Many actions require additional information, called the **arguments** of the action. If you select such an action, the arguments will display in the lower portion of the Macro window and you can make any necessary changes to them.

The second column in the Macro window is the **Comment column**. In this column, you enter **comments**, which are brief descriptions of the purpose of the corresponding action. The actions, the arguments requiring changes, and the comments for the first macro you will create are shown in Table 6-1.

Table 6-1

ACTION	ARGUMENT TO CHANGE	NEW VALUE FOR ARGUMENT	COMMENT
Echo	Echo On	No	Turn echo off to avoid screen flicker
Hourglass			Turn on hourglass
OpenForm	Form Name	Client Update Form	Open Client Update Form
Hourglass	Hourglass On	No	Turn off hourglass
Echo			Turn echo on

The macro begins by turning off the echo. This will eliminate the screen flicker that can be present when a form is being opened. The second action changes the shape of the mouse pointer to an hourglass to indicate that some process currently is taking place. The third action opens the form called Client Update Form. The fourth turns off the hourglass and the fifth turns the echo back on so the Client Update Form will display.

Adding Actions to a Macro

Turning on and off the echo and the hourglass are not absolutely necessary. On computers with faster processors, you might not notice a difference between running a macro that included these actions and one that did not. For slower processors, however, they can make a noticeable difference and that is why they are included here.

To create this macro, enter the actions. For each action, fill in the action and comment, and then make the necessary changes to any arguments. Once the actions have been entered, close the macro, click the Yes button to save the changes, and assign the macro a name. Perform the following steps to create, add actions to, and save the macro.

Steps To Add Actions to a Macro

1 **Click the box arrow in the first row of the Action column. Point to Echo.**

The list of available actions displays (Figure 6-5).

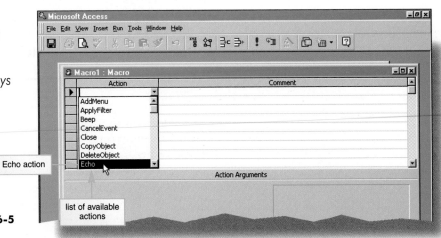

Echo action

list of available actions

FIGURE 6-5

2 Click Echo. Press the F6 key to move to the Action Arguments for the Echo action. Click the Echo On box arrow. Point to No.

The arguments for the Echo action display (Figure 6-6). The list of values for the Echo On argument displays. Pressing the F6 key switches panes.

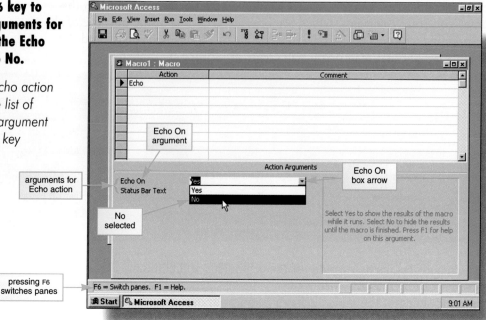

FIGURE 6-6

3 Click No. Press the F6 key to move back to Echo in the Action column. Press the TAB key. Type `Turn echo off to avoid screen flicker` **in the Comment column and then press the TAB key.**

The first action and comment are entered (Figure 6-7).

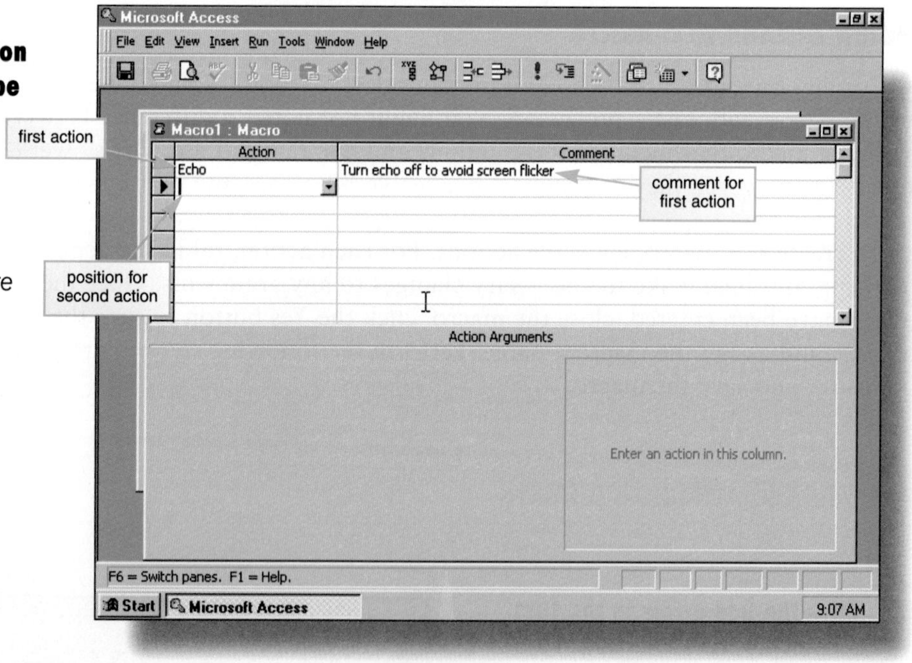

FIGURE 6-7

4 Select Hourglass as the action on the second row. Press the TAB key and then type Turn on hourglass as the comment on the second row. Press the TAB key and then select OpenForm as the third action. Press the F6 key to move to the Action Arguments and then click the Form Name box arrow. Point to Client Update Form.

A list of available forms displays (Figure 6-8).

5 Click Client Update Form, press the F6 key, press the TAB key, and type Open Client Update Form as the comment.

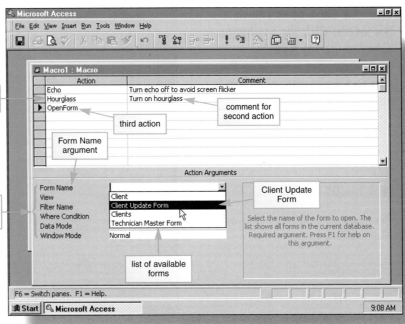

FIGURE 6-8

6 Select Hourglass as the fourth action. Change the Hourglass On argument to No and then type Turn off hourglass as the comment.

7 Select Echo as the fifth action. Type Turn echo on as the comment.

The actions and comments are entered (Figure 6-9).

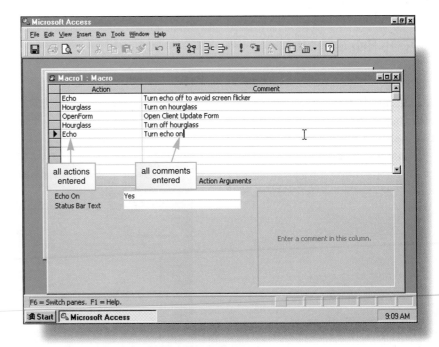

FIGURE 6-9

8 Click the Close button to close the macro, click the Yes button to save the macro, type `Open Client Update Form` as the name of the macro, and then point to the OK button.

The Save As dialog box displays (Figure 6-10).

9 Click the OK button.

The macro is created and saved.

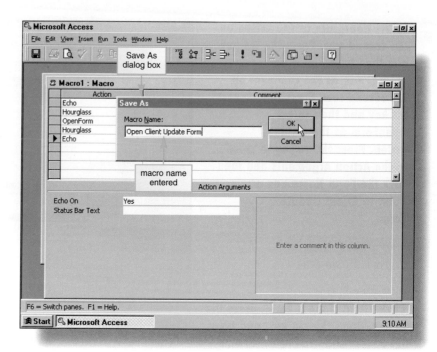

FIGURE 6-10

Running a Macro

To **run a macro**, click the Macros tab in the Database window, right-click the macro, and then click Run on the shortcut menu. The actions in the macro then will be executed. Perform the following steps to run the macro you just created.

 Steps To Run a Macro

1 Right-click the Open Client Update Form macro and then point to Run on the shortcut menu.

The shortcut menu displays (Figure 6-11).

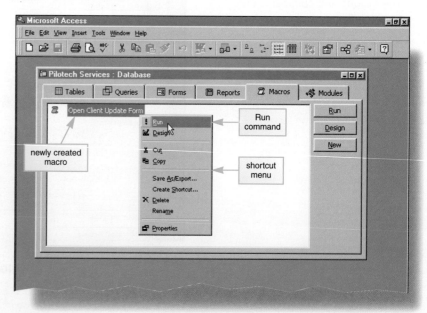

FIGURE 6-11

2 Click Run on the shortcut menu.

The macro runs and the Client Update Form displays (Figure 6-12). The window containing the form is not maximized.

3 Close the Client Update Form by clicking its Close button.

The form no longer displays.

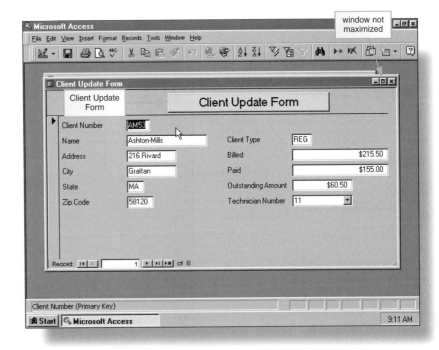

FIGURE 6-12

Modifying a Macro

To **modify a macro**, right-click the macro in the Database window, click Design on the shortcut menu, and then make the necessary changes. To insert a new action, click the position for the action. If the action is to be placed between two actions, press the INSERT key to insert a new blank row. Then enter the new action, change the values for any necessary arguments, and enter a comment.

The following steps modify the macro just created, adding a new step to maximize the form automatically.

Steps To Modify a Macro

1 Right-click the Open Client Update Form macro and then point to Design on the shortcut menu.

The shortcut menu displays (Figure 6-13).

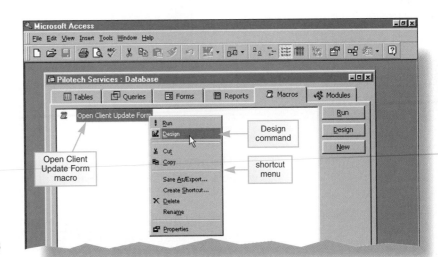

FIGURE 6-13

2 Click Design on the shortcut menu. Point to the row selector in the fourth row, which is directly to the left of the second Hourglass action.

The Open Client Update Form : Macro window displays (Figure 6-14).

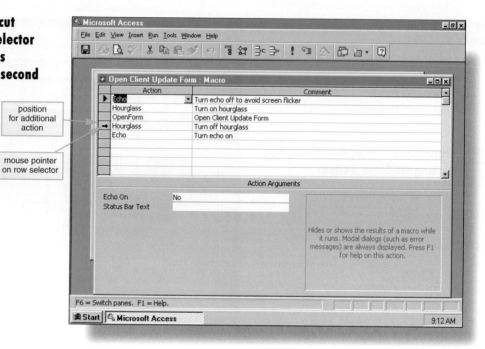

FIGURE 6-14

3 Click the row selector to select the row, and then press the INSERT key to insert a new row. Click the Action column on the new row, select Maximize as the action, and type Maximize the window as the comment.

The new action is entered (Figure 6-15).

4 Click the Close button, and then click the Yes button to save the changes.

The macro has been changed.

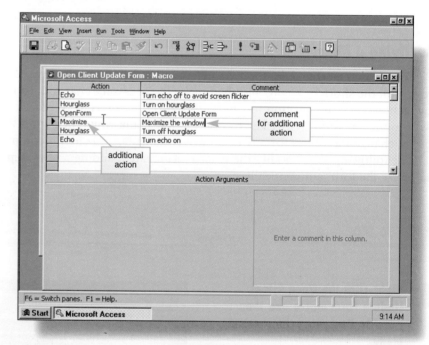

FIGURE 6-15

The next time the macro is run, the form not only will be opened, but the window containing the form also will be maximized.

Errors in Macros

Macros can contain **errors**. For example, if you typed the name of the form in the Form Name argument of the OpenForm action instead of selecting it from the list, you might type it incorrectly. Access then would be unable to execute the desired action. In that case, a Microsoft Access dialog box would display, indicating the error and solution (Figure 6-16).

More *About* **Inserting an Action**

If you inadvertently press the DELETE key rather than the INSERT key when you are inserting a new line in a macro, you will delete the selected action from the macro. To return the deleted action to the macro, click the Undo button on the toolbar.

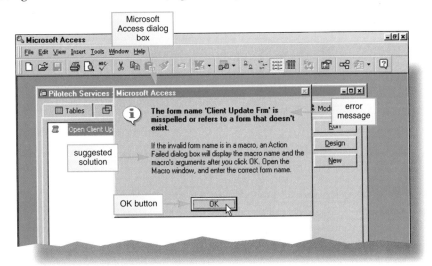

FIGURE 6-16

If such a dialog box displays, click the OK button. The Action Failed dialog box then displays (Figure 6-17). It indicates the macro that was being run, the action that Access was attempting to execute, and the arguments for the action. This information tells you which action needs to be corrected. To make the correction, click the Halt button, and then modify the design of the macro.

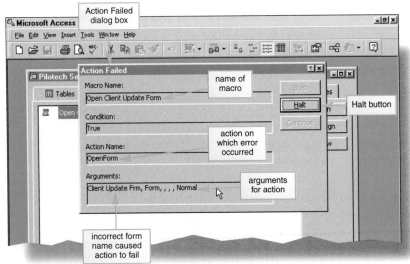

FIGURE 6-17

Creating Additional Macros

The additional macros to be created are shown in Table 6-2 on the next page. The first column gives the name of the macro and the second indicates the actions for the macro. The third contains the values of the arguments that need to be changed and the fourth contains the comments.

Table 6-2

MACRO NAME	ACTION	ARGUMENT(S)	COMMENT
Open Technician Master Form	Echo	Echo on: No	Turn echo off to avoid screen flicker
	Hourglass	Hourglass On: Yes	Turn on hourglass
	OpenForm	Form Name: Technician Master Form	Open Technician Master Form
	Maximize		Maximize the window
	Hourglass	Hourglass On: No	Turn off hourglass
	Echo	Echo on: Yes	Turn echo on
Open Client Table	OpenTable	Table Name: Client View: Datasheet	Open Client Table
	Maximize		Maximize the window
Open Technician Table	OpenTable	Table Name: Technician View: Datasheet	Open Technician Table
	Maximize		Maximize the window
Preview Billing Summary Report	OpenReport	Report Name: Billing Summary Report View: Print Preview	Preview Billing Summary Report
	Maximize		Maximize the window
Print Billing Summary Report	OpenReport	Report Name: Billing Summary Report View: Print	Print Billing Summary Report
Preview Client Amount Report	OpenReport	Report Name: Client Amount Report View: Print Preview	Preview Client Amount Report
	Maximize		Maximize the window
Print Client Amount Report	OpenReport	Report Name: Client Amount Report View: Print	Print Client Amount Report
Preview Clients by Technician	OpenReport	Report Name: Clients by Technician View: Print Preview	Preview Clients by Technician
	Maximize		Maximize the window
Print Clients by Technician	OpenReport	Report Name: Clients by Technician View: Print	Print Clients by Technician

Some macros require a change to more than one argument. For example, the action being entered in Figure 6-18 requires changes to both the Report Name argument and the View argument.

You can create additional macros using the same steps you used to create the first macro. Perform the following step to create the additional macros shown in Table 6-2.

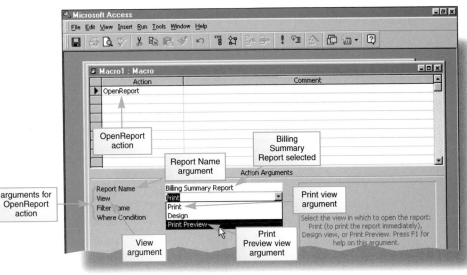

FIGURE 6-18

TO CREATE ADDITIONAL MACROS

Step 1: Using the same techniques you used to create the Open Client Update Form macro (page A 6.9), create each of the other macros in Table 6-2.

Running the Other Macros

To run any of the other macros, right-click the appropriate macro in the Database window and then click Run on the shortcut menu, just as you ran the first macro. The appropriate actions then are carried out. Running the Preview Billing Summary Report macro, for example, would display the Billing Summary Report in a maximized preview window.

Creating and Using Command Buttons

A **command button** executes a command when clicked. For example, after creating the Next Record command button, clicking it will move to the next record; clicking the Delete Record command button will delete the record currently on the screen; and clicking the Close Form command button will close the form.

Adding Command Buttons to a Form

To add command buttons, you will use the **Control Wizards button** and Command Button button in the toolbox. Using the series of **Command Button Wizard dialog boxes**, you must provide the action that should be taken when the button is clicked. Several categories of actions are available.

In the **Record Navigation category,** you will select the action Go to Next Record for one of the buttons. From the same category, you will select Go to Previous Record for another. Other buttons will use the Add New Record and the Delete Record actions from the **Record Operations category.** The Close Form button will use the Close Form action from the **Form Operations category.**

Perform the steps on the next page to add command buttons to move to the next record, move to the previous record, add a record, delete a record, and close the form.

▶ **More** *About*
Creating Additional Macros

To create a macro that is identical to an existing macro, highlight the existing macro in the database window, click the Copy button on the toolbar, click the Paste button on the toolbar, and type a name for the new macro. You then can edit the new macro.

▶ **More** *About*
Control Wizards

There are wizards associated with many of the controls. The wizards lead you through screens that assist you in creating the control. To use the wizards, the Control Wizards button must be recessed. If not, you will need to specify all the details of the control without any assistance.

Steps To Add Command Buttons to a Form

1 **Click the Forms tab, right-click Client Update Form, and point to Design on the shortcut menu.**

The shortcut menu displays (Figure 6-19).

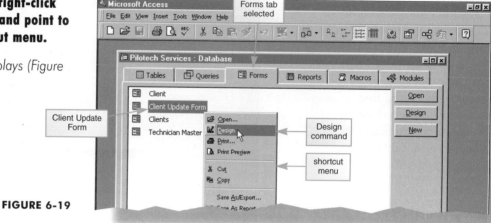

FIGURE 6-19

2 **Click Design on the shortcut menu, and then, if necessary, maximize the window. Be sure the toolbox displays and is docked at the bottom of the screen. (If it does not display, click the Toolbox button on the toolbar. If it is not docked at the bottom of the screen, drag it to the bottom of the screen to dock it there.) Make sure the Control Wizards button is recessed, and then point to the Command Button button in the toolbox.**

The design of the form displays in a maximized window (Figure 6-20).

FIGURE 6-20

3 **Click the Command Button button and move the mouse pointer, whose shape has changed to a plus sign with a picture of a button, to the position shown in Figure 6-21.**

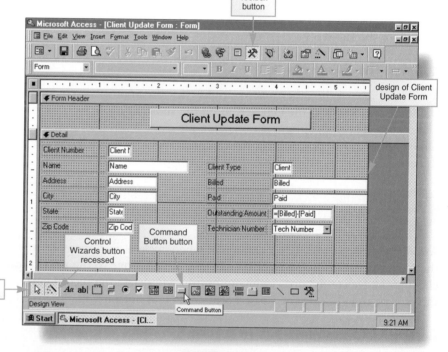

FIGURE 6-21

4 Click the position shown in Figure 6-21. With Record Navigation selected in the Categories list box, click Go to Next Record in the Actions list box. Point to the Next button.

The Command Button Wizard dialog box displays (Figure 6-22). Go to Next Record is selected as the action. A sample of the button displays in the Sample box.

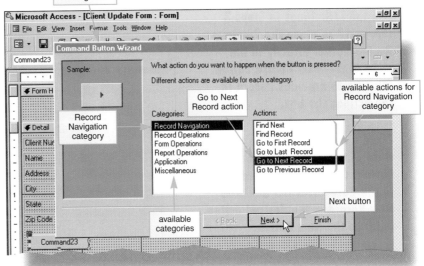

FIGURE 6-22

5 Click the Next button. Point to the Text option button.

The next Command Button Wizard dialog box displays, asking what to display on the button (Figure 6-23). The button can contain either text or a picture.

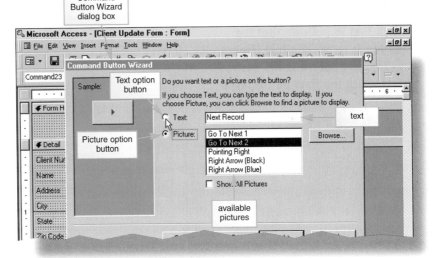

FIGURE 6-23

6 Click Text. Next Record is the desired text and does not need to be changed. Click the Next button, and then type Next Record as the name of the button. Point to the Finish button.

The name of the button displays in the text box (Figure 6-24).

7 Click the Finish button.

The button displays on the form.

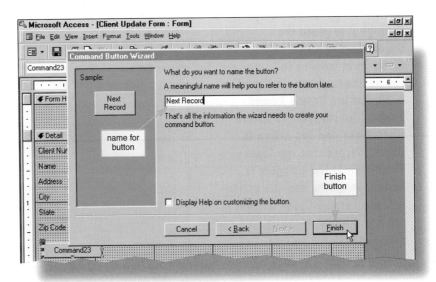

FIGURE 6-24

8 Use the techniques in Steps 3 through 7 to place the Previous Record button directly to the right of the Next Record button. Click Go to Previous Record in the Actions list box.

9 Place a button directly to the right of the Previous Record button. Click Record Operations in the Categories list box. Add New Record is the desired action. Point to the Next button.

The Command Button Wizard dialog box displays with the selections (Figure 6-25).

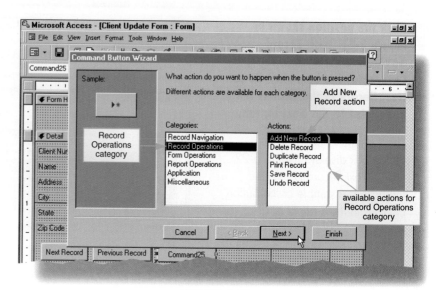

FIGURE 6-25

10 Click the Next button, and then click Text to indicate that the button is to contain text (Figure 6-26). Add Record is the desired text. Click the Next button, type Add Record as the name of the button, and then click the Finish button.

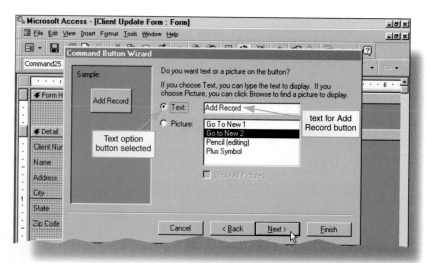

FIGURE 6-26

11 Use the techniques in Steps 3 through 7 to place the Delete Record and Close Form buttons in the positions shown in Figure 6-27. For the Delete Record button, the category is Record Operations and the action is Delete Record. For the Close Form button, the category is Form Operations and the action is Close Form. (If your buttons are not aligned properly, you can drag them to the correct positions.) Point to the View button on the toolbar.

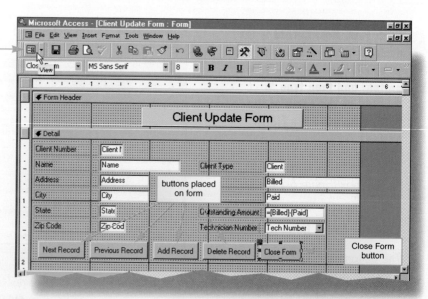

FIGURE 6-27

12 **Click the View button.**

The form displays with the added buttons (Figure 6-28).

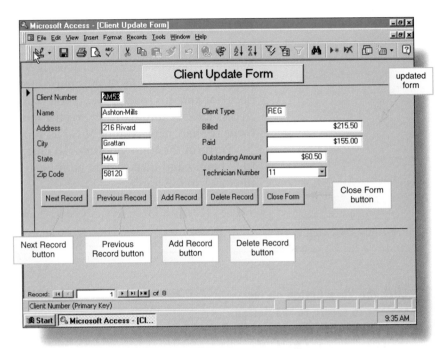

FIGURE 6-28

After creating the command buttons, you will use them. You also may need to modify them.

Using the Buttons

To move around on the form, you can **use the buttons** to perform the actions you specify. To move to the next record, click the Next Record button. Click the Previous Record button to move to the previous record. Clicking the Delete Record button will delete the record currently on the screen. You will get a message requesting you to verify the deletion before the record actually is deleted. Clicking the Close Form button will remove the form from the screen.

Clicking the Add Record button will clear the contents of the form so you can add a new record (Figure 6-29). Notice on the form in Figure 6-29, however, that an insertion point does not display. Therefore, to begin entering a record, you will have to click the Client Number field before you can start typing. To ensure that an insertion point displays in the field text box when you click the Add Record button, you must change the focus. **Focus** is the capability to receive user input through mouse or keyboard actions. The Add Record button needs to update the focus to the Client Number field.

More *About*
Focus

There is a visual way to determine which object on the screen has the focus. If a field has the focus, an insertion point will display in the field. If a button has the focus, a small rectangle will appear inside the button.

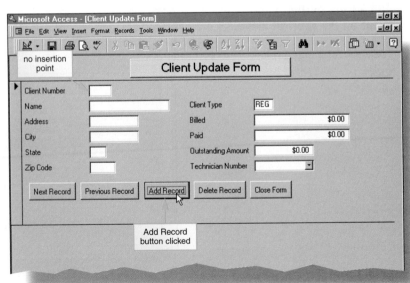

FIGURE 6-29

Modifying the Add Record Button

To display an insertion point automatically when you click the Add Record button, two steps are necessary using **Visual Basic for Applications (VBA)**. First, you must change the name of the control for the Client Number field to a name that does not contain spaces. Next, you must add a command to the VBA code that Access creates automatically for the button. The added command will move the focus to the Client Number field as soon as the button is clicked.

Perform the following steps to change the name of the Client Number control to ClNumb and then add an additional command to the VBA code that will set the focus to ClNumb.

Steps   To Modify the Add Record Button

Click the View button on the toolbar to return to the design grid. Right-click the control for the Client Number field (the white space, not the label), and then click Properties on the shortcut menu. Click the Name property, use the DELETE or BACKSPACE key to erase the current value, and then type ClNumb **as the new name.**

The name is changed (Figure 6-30).

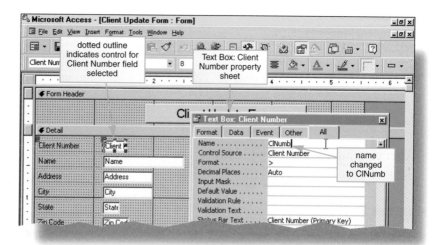

FIGURE 6-30

Click the Close button to close the Text Box: Client Number property sheet. Right-click the Add Record button. Point to Build Event on the shortcut menu.

The shortcut menu displays (Figure 6-31).

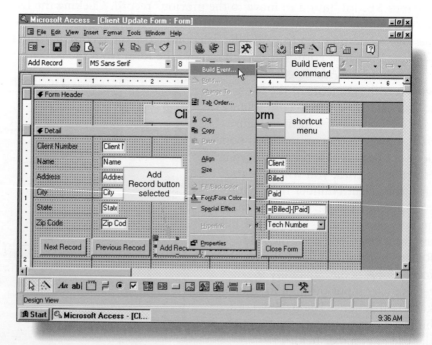

FIGURE 6-31

3 **Click Build Event on the shortcut menu.**

The VBA code for the Add Record button displays (Figure 6-32). The important line in this code is DoCmd, which stands for Do Command. Following DoCmd, is the command, formally called a method, that will be executed; in this case GoToRecord. Following GoToRecord are the arguments, which are items that provide information that will be used by the method. The only argument necessary in this case is acNewRec. This is a code that indicates that Access is to move to the new record at the end of the table; that is, the position where the new record will be added. This command will not set the focus to any particular field automatically, however, so an insertion point still will not be produced.

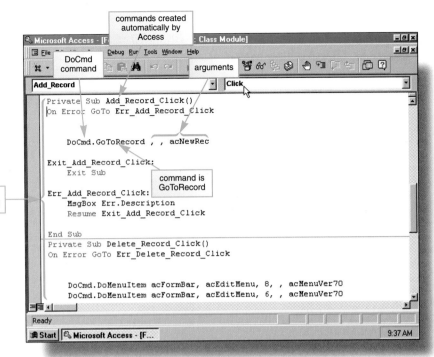

FIGURE 6-32

4 **Press the down arrow key four times, press the TAB key, and type** ClNumb.SetFocus **as the additional command. Press the ENTER key.**

The command is entered (Figure 6-33). While typing, a list box may display indicating selections for the command. You may ignore this list. This command will set the focus in the control named ClNumb as soon as the previous command (GoToRecord) is executed.

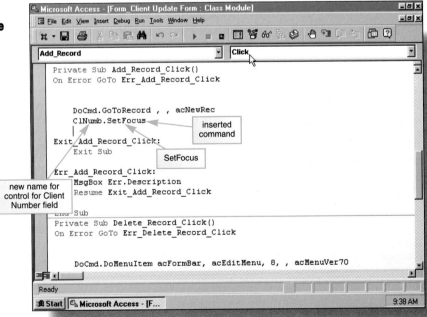

FIGURE 6-33

5 Close the window containing the VBA code. Click the View button on the toolbar and then click the Add Record button.

An insertion point displays in the Client Number field (Figure 6-34).

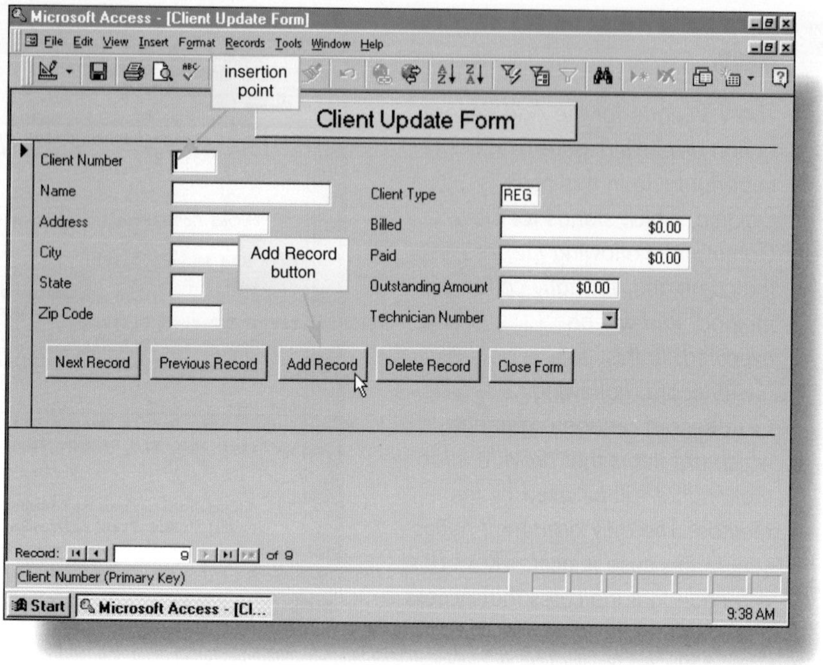

FIGURE 6-34

Creating and Using Combo Boxes

A **combo box**, such as the one shown in Figure 6-2 on page A 6.6, combines the properties of a **text box**, a box into which you can type an entry, and a **list box**, a box you can use to display a list. You could type the client's name directly into the box. Alternatively, you can click the Name to Find box arrow, and Access will display a list of client names. To select a name from the list, simply click the name.

Creating a Combo Box

To create a combo box, use the **Combo Box button** in the toolbox. The **Combo Box Wizard** then will guide you through the steps in adding the combo box. Perform the following steps to place a combo box for names on the form.

More *About*
the Add Record Button

If your spelling was not consistent, you will get an error message when you click the Add Record button. To correct the problem, return to the form design. Check to make sure the name you gave to the Client Number control and the name in the SetFocus command are both the same (ClNumb).

Steps To Create a Combo Box

1 Click the View button on the toolbar to return to the design grid. Make sure the Control Wizards button is recessed, and then point to the Combo Box button in the toolbox (Figure 6-35).

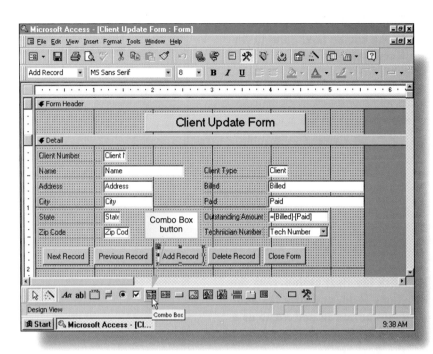

FIGURE 6-35

2 Click the Combo Box button and then move the mouse pointer, whose shape has changed to a small plus sign with a combo box, to the position shown in Figure 6-36.

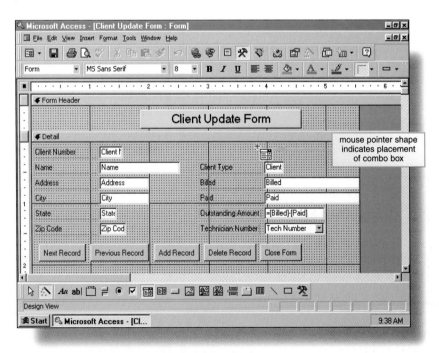

FIGURE 6-36

3 Click the position shown in Figure 6-36 to place a combo box. Click Find a record on my form based on the value selected in the combo box. Point to the Next button.

The Combo Box Wizard dialog box displays, instructing you to indicate how the combo box is to obtain values for the list (Figure 6-37).

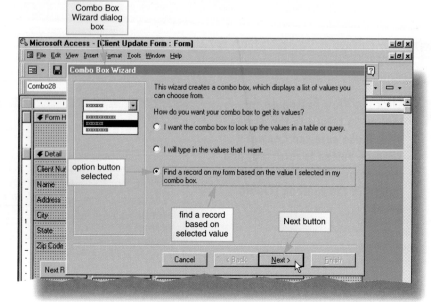

FIGURE 6-37

4 Click the Next button, click the Name field, and click the Add Field button to add Name as a field in the combo box. Point to the Next button.

The Name field is selected (Figure 6-38).

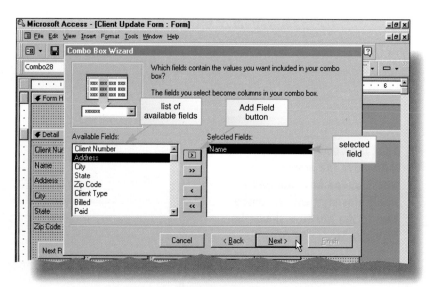

FIGURE 6-38

5 Click the Next button.

The Combo Box Wizard dialog box displays (Figure 6-39), giving you an opportunity to resize the columns in the combo box.

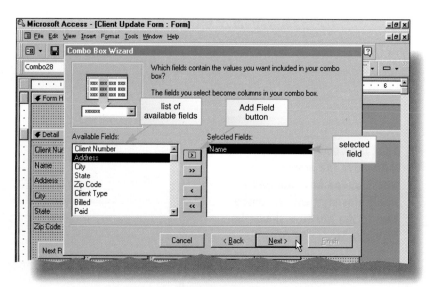

FIGURE 6-39

6 Click the Next button, and then type &Name to Find as the label for the combo box. Point to the Finish button.

The label is entered (Figure 6-40). The ampersand (&) in front of the letter N indicates that users can select the combo box by pressing the ALT+N keys.

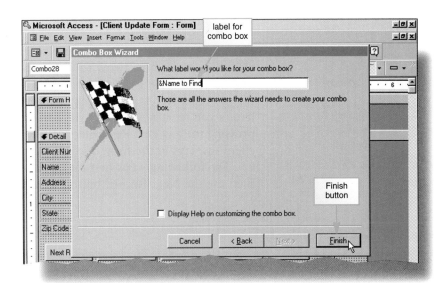

FIGURE 6-40

7 Click the Finish button. Click the label for the combo box. Point to the sizing handle on the right edge of the label.

The shape of the mouse pointer changes to a two-headed horizontal arrow, indicating that you can drag the right edge (Figure 6-41).

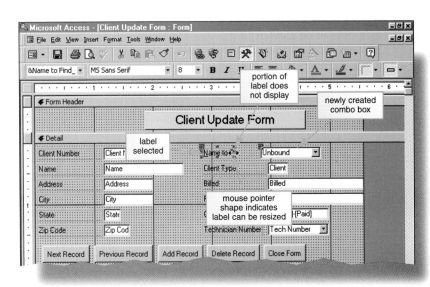

FIGURE 6-41

8 Double-click the handle so the entire label displays. Point to the View button on the toolbar.

The combo box is added and the label has been resized (Figure 6-42). The N in Name is underlined indicating that you can press the ALT+N keys to select the combo box.

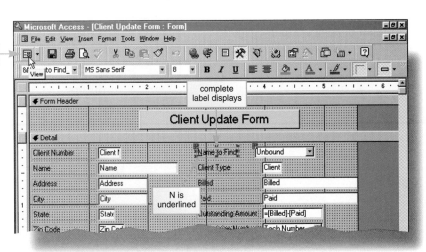

FIGURE 6-42

Using the Combo Box

Using the combo box, you can search for a client in two ways. First, you can click the combo box arrow to display a list of client names, and then select the name from the list by clicking it. Alternatively, you can begin typing the name. As you type, Access will display automatically the name that begins with the letters you have typed. Once the correct name is displayed, select the name by pressing the TAB key. Regardless of the method you use, the data for the selected client displays in the form once the selection is made.

The following steps first locate the client whose name is Morland Int., and then use the Next Record button to move to the next client.

Steps To Use the Combo Box

1 **Click the View button on the toolbar to display the form.**

The form displays (Figure 6-43).

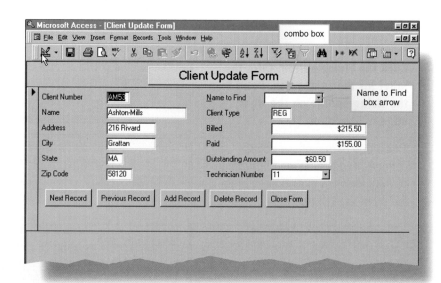

FIGURE 6-43

2 **Click the Name to Find box arrow and then point to Morland Int.**

The list of names displays (Figure 6-44).

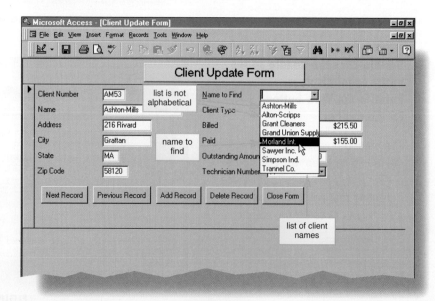

FIGURE 6-44

3 **Click Morland Int.**

The data for the client whose name is Morland Int. displays in the form (Figure 6-45).

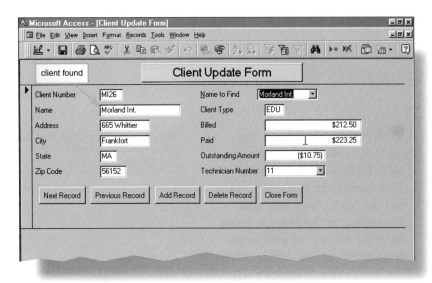

FIGURE 6-45

4 **Click the Next Record button.**

The data for the client whose name is Sawyer Inc. displays in the form (Figure 6-46). The combo box still contains Morland Int.

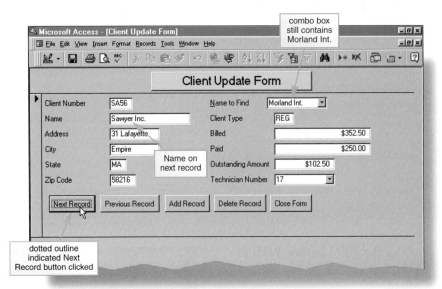

FIGURE 6-46

Issues with the Combo Box

Consider the following **issues with the combo box**. First, if you examine the list of names in Figure 6-44, you will see that they are not in alphabetical order. Second, when you move to a record without using the combo box, the name in the combo box does not change to reflect the name of the client currently on the screen. Third, pressing the TAB key should not move to the combo box.

Modifying the Combo Box

The steps on the next page modify the query that Access has created for the combo box so that first the data is sorted by name and then by the **On Current property** of the entire form. The modification to the On Current property will ensure that the combo box is kept current with the rest of the form; that is, it contains the name of the client whose number currently displays in the Client Number field. The final step changes the Tab Stop property for the combo box from Yes to No.

Perform the following steps to modify the combo box.

Steps To Modify the Combo Box

1 **Click the View button on the toolbar to return to the design grid. Right-click the Name to Find combo box (the white space, not the label), and then click Properties on the shortcut menu. Note the number of your combo box, which may be different from the one shown in Figure 6-47, because it will be important later. Click the Row Source property, and then point to the Build button for the Row Source property.**

The Combo Box: Combo28 property sheet displays (Figure 6-47). The combo box number is 28 (Combo28). The Row Source property is selected. Depending on where you clicked the Row Source property, the value may or may not be highlighted.

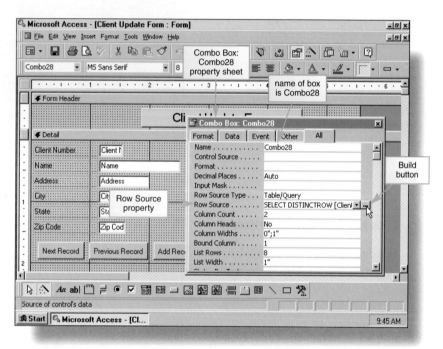

FIGURE 6-47

2 **Click the Build button. Point to the Sort row under the Name field.**

The SQL Statement : Query Builder window displays (Figure 6-48). This screen allows you to make changes just as you did when you created queries.

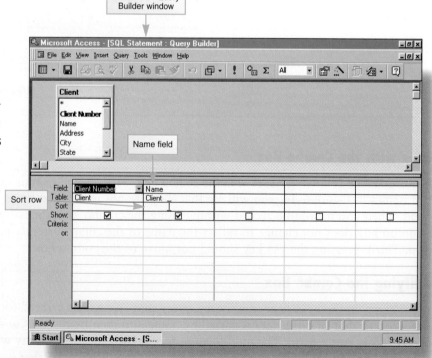

FIGURE 6-48

3 Click the Sort row in the Name field, click the box arrow that displays, and click Ascending. Point to the Close button for the SQL Statement : Query Builder window.

The sort order is changed to Ascending (Figure 6-49).

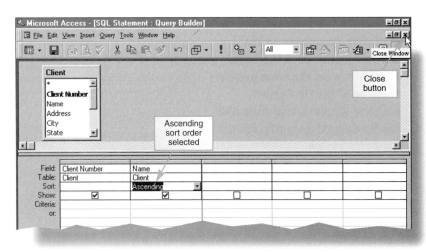

FIGURE 6-49

4 Close the SQL Statement : Query Builder window by clicking its Close button. Point to the Yes button.

The Microsoft Access dialog box displays (Figure 6-50).

5 Click the Yes button to change the property, and then close the Combo Box: Combo28 property sheet.

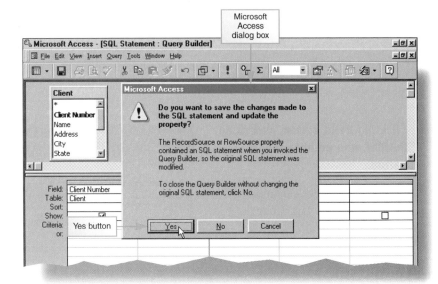

FIGURE 6-50

6 Point to the form selector, the box in the upper-left corner of the form (Figure 6-51).

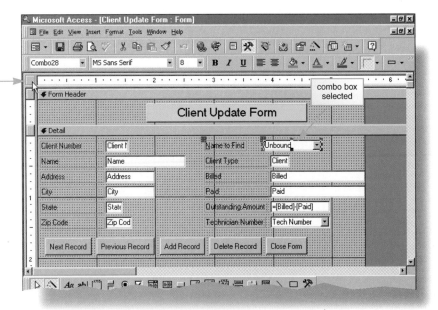

FIGURE 6-51

7 Right-click the form selector, and then click Properties on the shortcut menu. Click the down scroll arrow on the Form property sheet until the On Current property displays, and then click the On Current property. Point to the Build button.

The Form property sheet displays (Figure 6-52).

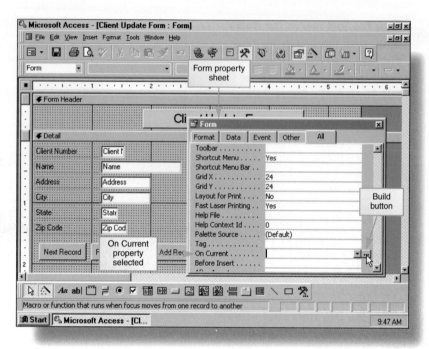

FIGURE 6-52

8 Click the Build button, click Code Builder, and point to the OK button.

The Choose Builder dialog box displays (Figure 6-53). Code Builder is selected.

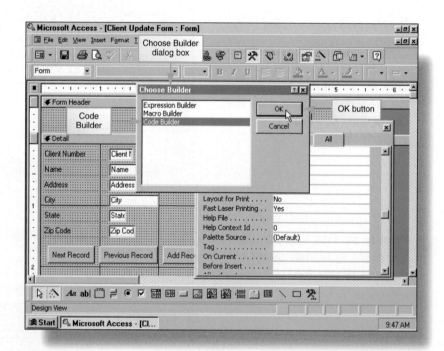

FIGURE 6-53

⑨ Click the OK button.

The code generated by Access for the form displays (Figure 6-54).

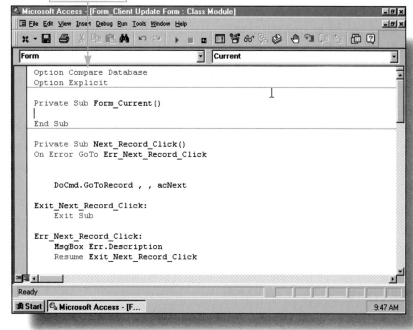

FIGURE 6-54

⑩ Type Combo28 = ClNumb ' Update the combo box **in the position shown in Figure 6-55, and then point to the Close button.**

This command assumes your combo box is Combo28. If yours has a different number, use your number in the command instead of 28. This command will update the contents of the combo box using the client number currently in the ClNumb control. The portion of the command following the apostrophe is called a **comment.** *It describes the purpose of the command.*

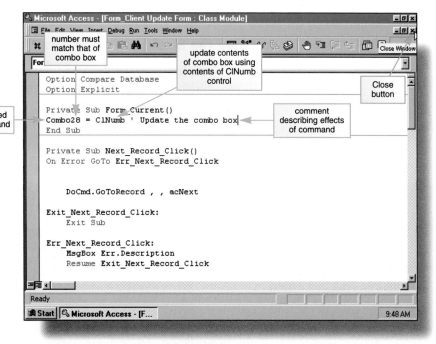

FIGURE 6-55

11 Click the Close button, and then close the Form property sheet. Right-click the combo box, and then click Properties on the shortcut menu. Click the down scroll arrow until the Tab Stop property displays, click the Tab Stop property, click the Tab Stop box arrow, and point to No (Figure 6-56).

12 Click No, and then close the Combo Box: Combo28 property sheet.

The modifications to the combo box are complete.

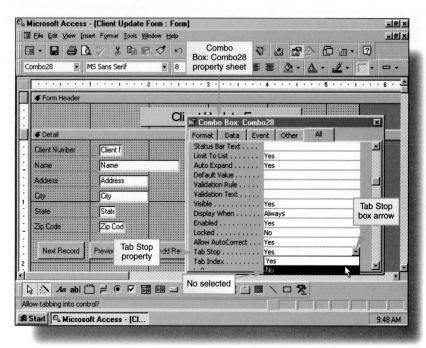

FIGURE 6-56

Using the Modified Combo Box

The problems with the combo box now are corrected. The search conducted in the following steps first search for the client whose name is Morland Int., and then move to the next record in the table to verify that the combo box also will be updated. Perform the following steps to search for a client.

 Steps To Use the Combo Box to Search for a Client

1 Click the View button on the toolbar to display the Client Update Form, and then click the Name to Find box arrow.

A list of names displays (Figure 6-57).

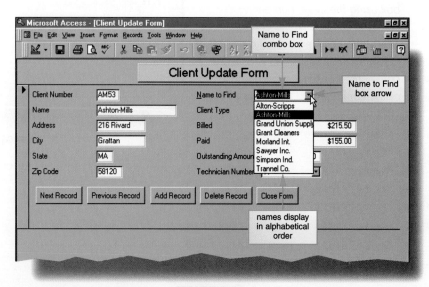

FIGURE 6-57

2 **Click Morland Int., and then point to the Next Record button.**

Client MI26 displays in the form (Figure 6-58).

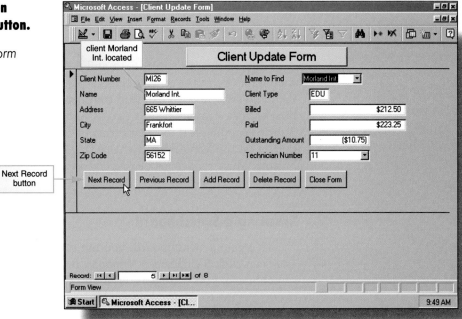

FIGURE 6-58

3 **Click the Next Record button.**

Client SA56 displays on the form (Figure 6-59). The client's name also displays in the combo box.

4 **Close the form by clicking its Close button, and then click the Yes button to save the changes.**

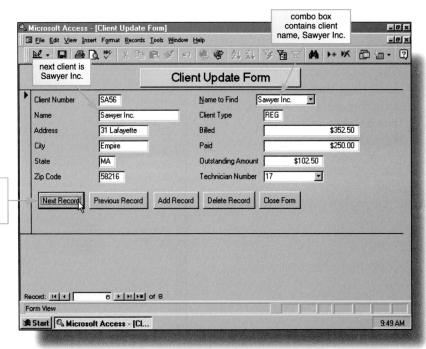

FIGURE 6-59

More *About*
Switchboards

A switchboard is considered a form and is run like any other form. There is a special tool to create it, however, called the Switchboard Manager. Although you could modify the design of the form by clicking Design on its shortcut menu, it is easier to use the Switchboard Manager for modifications.

Creating and Using a Switchboard

A **switchboard** (see Figures 6-1a and 6-1b on page A 6.5) is a special type of form. It contains buttons you can click to perform a variety of actions. Buttons on the main switchboard can lead to other switchboards. Clicking the View Form button, for example, causes Access to display the View Form switchboard. Buttons can be used to open forms or tables. Clicking the Client Update Form button on the View Form switchboard opens the Client Update Form. Still other buttons cause reports to be displayed in a preview window. Other buttons print reports.

Creating a Switchboard

To create a switchboard, you use the Add-Ins command on the Tools menu and then click **Switchboard Manager**. If you have not previously created a switchboard, you will be asked if you want to create one. Clicking the Yes button causes Access to create the switchboard. Perform the following steps to create a switchboard for the Pilotech Services database.

Steps To Create a Switchboard

1 **With the Database window displaying, click Tools on the menu bar, point to Add-Ins, and then point to Switchboard Manager.**

The Tools menu displays (Figure 6-60). The Add-Ins submenu displays. (The menu you see may be different.)

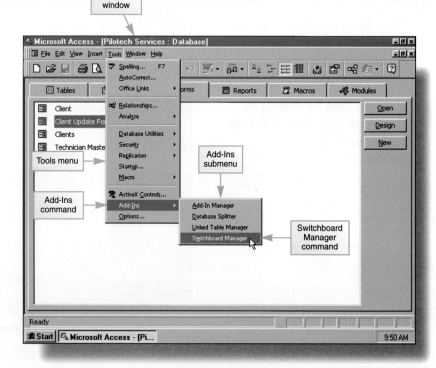

FIGURE 6-60

2 Click Switchboard Manager and then point to the Yes button.

The Switchboard Manager dialog box displays (Figure 6-61). The message indicates that no switchboard currently exists for this database.

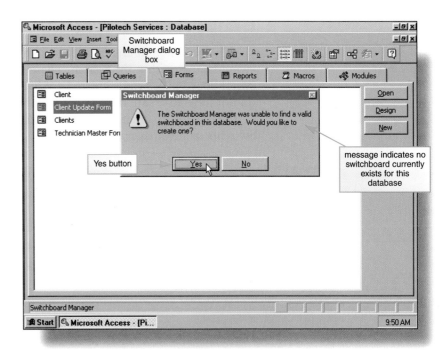

FIGURE 6-61

3 Click the Yes button to create a new switchboard. Point to the New button.

The Switchboard Manager dialog box displays (Figure 6-62).

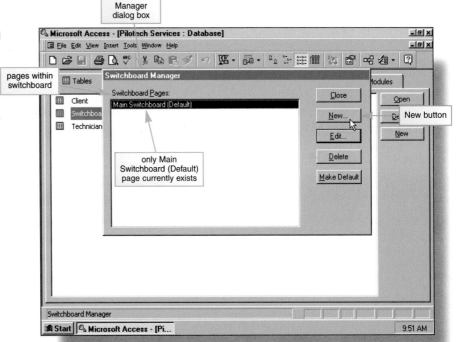

FIGURE 6-62

Creating Switchboard Pages

The next step in creating the switchboard system is to create the individual switchboards within the system. These are called the **switchboard pages**. The switchboard pages to be created are listed in the first column of Table 6-3. You do not have to create the Main Switchboard page, because Access has created it automatically. To create each of the other pages, click the New button in the Switchboard Manager dialog box, and then type the name of the page.

Table 6-3

SWITCHBOARD PAGE	SWITCHBOARD ITEM	COMMAND	ARGUMENT
Main Switchboard	View Form	Go to Switchboard	Switchboard: View Form
	View Table	Go to Switchboard	Switchboard: View Table
	View Report	Go to Switchboard	Switchboard: View Report
	Print Report	Go to Switchboard	Switchboard: Print Report
	Exit Application	Exit Application	none
View Form	Client Update Form	Run Macro	Macro: Open Client Update Form
	Technician Master Form	Run Macro	Macro: Open Technician Master Form
	Return to Main Switchboard	Go to Switchboard	Switchboard: Main Switchboard
View Table	Client Table	Run Macro	Macro: Open Client Table
	Technician Table	Run Macro	Macro: Open Technician Table
	Return to Main Switchboard	Go to Switchboard	Switchboard: Main Switchboard
View Report	View Billing Summary Report	Run Macro	Macro: Preview Billing Summary Report
	View Client Amount Report	Run Macro	Macro: Preview Client Amount Report
	View Clients by Technician	Run Macro	Macro: Preview Clients by Technician
	Return to Main Switchboard	Go to Switchboard	Switchboard: Main Switchboard
Print Report	Print Billing Summary Report	Run Macro	Macro: Print Billing Summary Report
	Print Client Amount Report	Run Macro	Macro: Print Client Amount Report
	Print Clients by Technician	Run Macro	Macro: Print Clients by Technician
	Return to Main Switchboard	Go to Switchboard	Switchboard: Main Switchboard

Perform the following steps to create the switchboard pages.

Steps To Create Switchboard Pages

1 **Click the New button in the Switchboard Manager dialog box. Type** View Form **as the name of the new switchboard page. Point to the OK button.**

The Create New dialog box displays (Figure 6-63). The name of the new page displays.

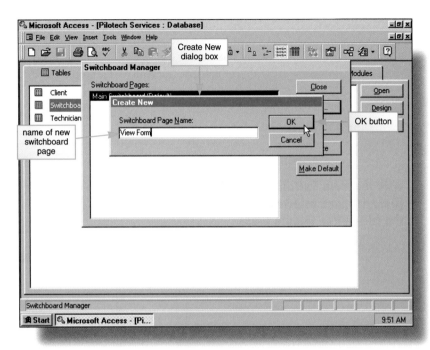

FIGURE 6-63

2 **Click the OK button to create the View Form switchboard page. Use the same technique to create the View Table, View Report, and Print Report switchboard pages.**

The newly created switchboard pages display in the Switchboard Manager dialog box in alphabetical order (Figure 6-64).

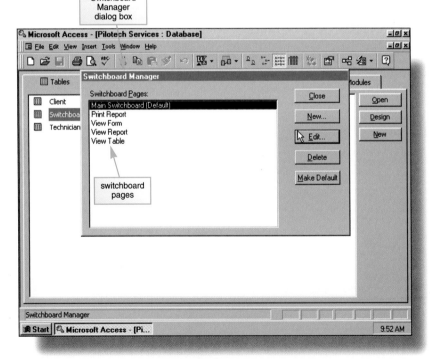

FIGURE 6-64

Modifying Switchboard Pages

To **modify a switchboard page,** after selecting the page in the Switchboard Manager dialog box, you click the **Edit button**. You can add new items to the page, move existing items to a different position in the list of items, or delete items. For each item, you can indicate the command to be executed when the item is selected.

Perform the following steps to modify the Main Switchboard page.

Steps To Modify the Main Switchboard Page

1. **With the Main Switchboard (Default) page selected, point to the Edit button (Figure 6-65).**

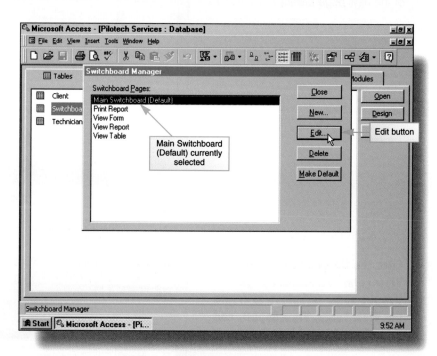

FIGURE 6-65

2 Click the Edit button, and then point to the New button in the Edit Switchboard Page dialog box.

The Edit Switchboard Page dialog box displays (Figure 6-66).

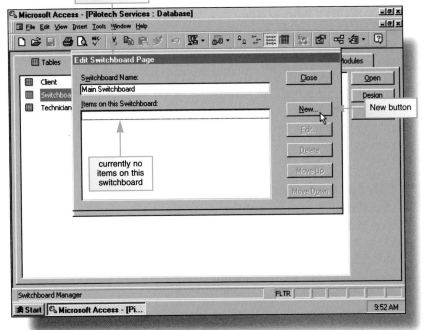

FIGURE 6-66

3 Click the New button, type View Form as the text, click the Switchboard box arrow, and then point to View Form.

The Edit Switchboard Item dialog box displays (Figure 6-67). The text is entered, the command is Go to Switchboard, and the list of available switchboards displays.

4 Click View Form, and then click the OK button to add the item to the switchboard.

5 Using the techniques in Steps 3 and 4, add the View Table, View Report, and Print Report items to the Main Switchboard page. In each case the command is Go to Switchboard. The names of the switchboards are the same as the name of the items. For example, the switchboard for the View Table item is called View Table.

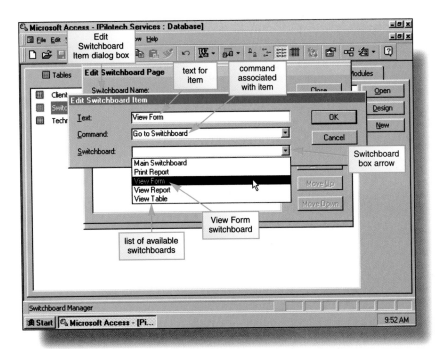

FIGURE 6-67

6 **Click the New button, type** Exit Application **as the text, click the Command box arrow, and then point to Exit Application.**

The Edit Switchboard Item dialog box displays (Figure 6-68). The text is entered, and the list of available commands displays.

7 **Click Exit Application, and then click the OK button to add the item to the switchboard. Click the Close button in the Edit Switchboard Page dialog box to indicate you are finished editing the Main Switchboard.**

The Main Switchboard page now is complete. The Edit Switchboard Page dialog box closes, and the Switchboard Manager dialog box displays.

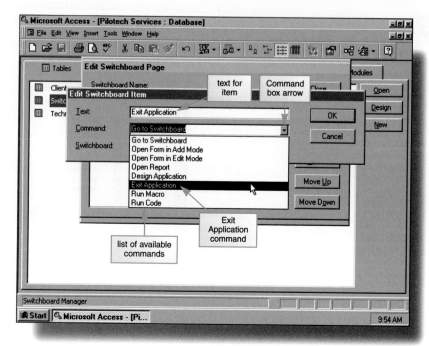

FIGURE 6-68

Modifying the Other Switchboard Pages

The other switchboard pages from Table 6-3 on page A 6.38 are modified in exactly the same manner you modified the Main Switchboard page. Perform the following steps to modify the other switchboard pages.

Steps To Modify the Other Switchboard Pages

1 **Click the View Form switchboard page, and then point to the Edit button.**

The View Form page is selected (Figure 6-69).

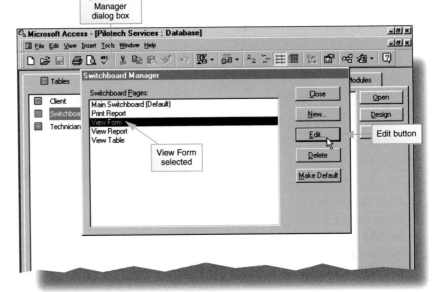

FIGURE 6-69

2 **Click the Edit button, click the New button to add a new item, type** Client Update Form **as the text, click the Command box arrow, and then click Run Macro. Click the Macro box arrow, and then point to Open Client Update Form.**

The Edit Switchboard Item dialog box displays (Figure 6-70). The text is entered, and the command has been selected. The list of available macros displays.

3 **Click Open Client Update Form, and then click the OK button.**

The Open Client Update Form item is added to the View Form switchboard.

4 **Click the New button, type** Technician Master Form **as the text, click the Command box arrow, and then click Run Macro. Click the Macro box arrow, click Open Technician Master Form, and then click the OK button.**

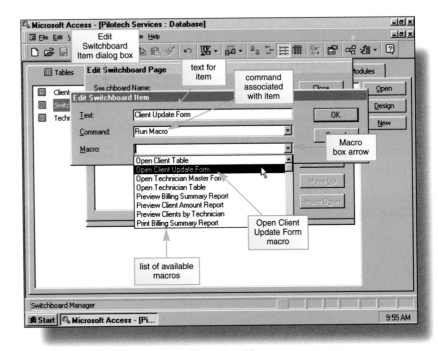

FIGURE 6-70

5 Click the New button, type Return to Main Switchboard as the text, click the Command box arrow, and then click Go to Switchboard. Click the Switchboard box arrow, and then click Main Switchboard. Point to the OK button.

The text is entered (Figure 6-71). The command and switchboard are selected.

6 Click the OK button. Click the Close button in the Edit Switchboard Page dialog box to indicate you are finished editing the View Form switchboard.

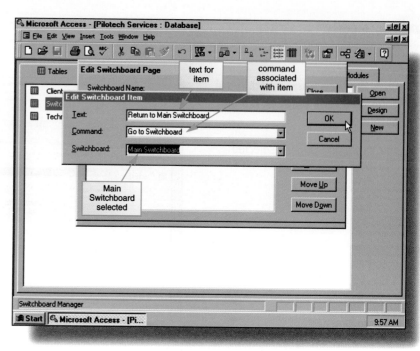

FIGURE 6-71

7 Use the techniques in Steps 1 through 6 to add the items indicated in Table 6-3 on page A 6.38 to the other switchboards. When you have finished, point to the Close button in the Switchboard Manager dialog box (Figure 6-72). •

8 Click the Close button.

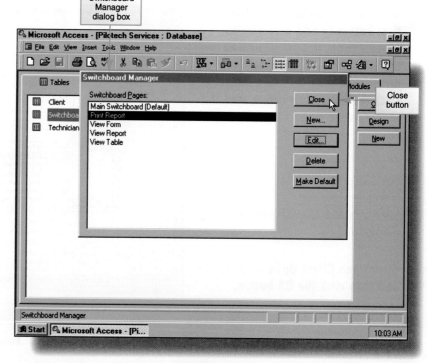

FIGURE 6-72

The switchboard is complete and ready for use. Access has created a form called Switchboard that you will run to use the switchboard. It also has created a table called Switchboard Items. *Do not modify this table.* It is used by the Switchboard Manager to keep track of the various switchboard pages and items.

Using a Switchboard

To use the switchboard, click the Forms tab, right-click the switchboard, and then click Run on the shortcut menu. The main switchboard then will display. To take any action, click the appropriate buttons. When you have finished, click the Exit Application button. The switchboard will be removed from the screen, and the database will be closed. The following steps illustrate the use of the switchboard system.

> **More** *About*
> **Displaying a**
> **Switchboard**
>
> It is possible to have the switchboard display automatically when the database is opened. To do so, click Tools on the menu bar and click Startup. Click the Display Form box arrow, select the Switchboard form, and click the OK button.

 Steps To Use a Switchboard

1 **Click the Forms tab, and then right-click Switchboard. Point to Open on the shortcut menu.**

The shortcut menu for Switchboard displays (Figure 6-73).

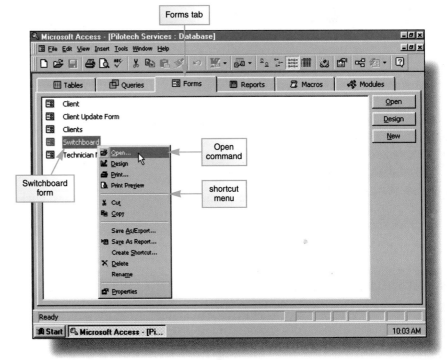

FIGURE 6-73

2 **Click Open.**

The Main Switchboard displays (Figure 6-74).

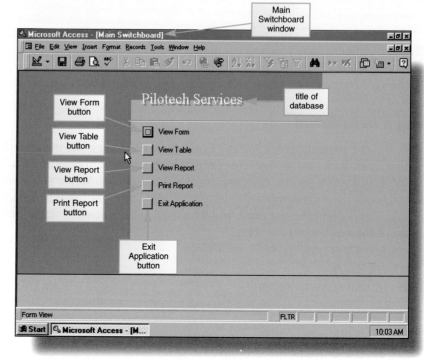

FIGURE 6-74

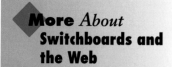
Click the View Form button to display the View Form switchboard page. Click the View Table button to display the View Table switchboard page. Click the View Report button to display the View Report switchboard page. Click the Print Report button to display the Print Report switchboard page. On each of the other switchboard pages, click the button for the form, table, or report you wish to view, or the report you wish to print. To return from one of the other switchboard pages to the Main Switchboard, click the Return to Main Switchboard button. To leave the switchboard system, click the Exit Application button.

If you discover a problem with the switchboard, click Tools on the menu bar, click Add-Ins, and click Switchboard Manager. You then can modify the switchboard system using the same techniques you used to create it.

Closing the Switchboard and Database

To close the switchboard and the database, click the Exit Application button. Perform the following step to close the switchboard.

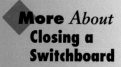
TO CLOSE THE SWITCHBOARD AND DATABASE

Step 1: Click the Exit Application button.

The switchboard is removed from the screen. The database also closes.

Project Summary

Project 6 introduced you to creating a complete switchboard system. To create the system required at Pilotech Services, you created and used several macros. In addition, you modified the Client Update Form to make it more functional for the users at Pilotech Services. You incorporated several command buttons to make it easier for the users to perform certain tasks. Then, you added a combo box to allow users to search for a client either by typing the client's name or selecting the name from a list. Using Switchboard Manager, you created the switchboard, the switchboard pages, and the switchboard items. You also used the Switchboard Manager to assign actions to the buttons on the switchboard pages.

What You Should Know

Having completed this project, you now should be able to perform the following tasks:

- Add Actions to a Macro *(A 6.9)*
- Add Command Buttons to a Form *(A 6.18)*
- Close the Switchboard and Database *(A 6.46)*
- Create a Combo Box *(A 6.25)*
- Create a Macro *(A 6.8)*
- Create Additional Macros *(A 6.17)*
- Create a Switchboard *(A 6.36)*
- Create Switchboard Pages *(A 6.39)*
- Modify a Macro *(A 6.13)*
- Modify the Add Record Button *(A 6.22)*
- Modify the Combo Box *(A 6.30)*
- Modify the Main Switchboard Page *(A 6.40)*
- Modify the Other Switchboard Pages *(A 6.43)*
- Open a Database *(A 6.7)*
- Run a Macro *(A 6.12)*
- Use the Combo Box *(A 6.28)*
- Use the Combo Box to Search for a Client *(A 6.34)*
- Use a Switchboard *(A 6.45)*

 Test Your Knowledge

1 True/False

Instructions: Circle T if the statement is true or F if the statement is false.

T F 1. Macros are collections of actions designed to carry out some specific task.

T F 2. To create a macro, click the Macros tab in the Database window, and then click the Create button.

T F 3. Many actions that you enter in the Macro window require additional information called the parameters of the action.

T F 4. Setting the Hourglass action to No eliminates screen flicker.

T F 5. To run a macro, click the Macros tab in the Database window, right-click the macro, and then click Run on the shortcut menu.

T F 6. When you create a command button, you can specify only the text that appears on the button.

T F 7. A combo box combines the properties of a text box and a list box.

T F 8. To sort entries in a combo box, right-click the combo box, click Properties on the shortcut menu, and then click the Row Arrange property.

T F 9. A switchboard is a special type of form.

T F 10. To create a switchboard, click Insert on the menu bar, click Add-Ins, and then click Switchboard Manager.

2 Multiple Choice

Instructions: Circle the correct response.

1. In Access, a(n) _____ is a collection of actions designed to carry out some specific task.
   a. script
   b. button
   c. option group
   d. macro

2. Many actions require additional information called the _____ of the action.
   a. parameters
   b. properties
   c. arguments
   d. options

3. To run a macro, click the Macros tab in the Database window, right-click the macro, and then click _____ on the shortcut menu.
   a. Execute
   b. Run
   c. Do
   d. Perform

 Test Your Knowledge

4. To insert a new macro action between two existing actions, select the row below where you want to insert the action, and press the _____ key(s).
    a. CTRL+N
    b. CTRL+I
    c. CTRL+INSERT
    d. INSERT

5. To sort entries in a combo box, right-click the combo box, click Properties on the shortcut menu, and click the _____ property.
    a. Row Arrange
    b. Row Source
    c. Row Sort
    d. Sort

6. A switchboard is a special type of _____.
    a. report
    b. table
    c. module
    d. form

7. To create a switchboard, click _____ on the menu bar, click Add-Ins, and then click Switchboard Manager.
    a. Edit
    b. View
    c. Insert
    d. Tools

8. Individual switchboards within a switchboard system are referred to as switchboard _____.
    a. pages
    b. frames
    c. boxes
    d. buttons

9. To move between the Action column and the Action Arguments in the Macro window, press the _____ key.
    a. F5
    b. F6
    c. F7
    d. F8

10. To keep a combo box current with the rest of a form, modify the _____ property of the entire form.
    a. On Target
    b. On Record
    c. On Current
    d. On Focus

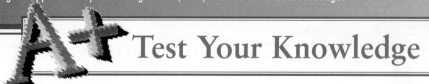

3 Understanding Macros

Instructions: In Figure 6-75, arrows point to various items in the Macro window. Identify these items in the spaces provided and use this figure to answer the following questions on your own paper.

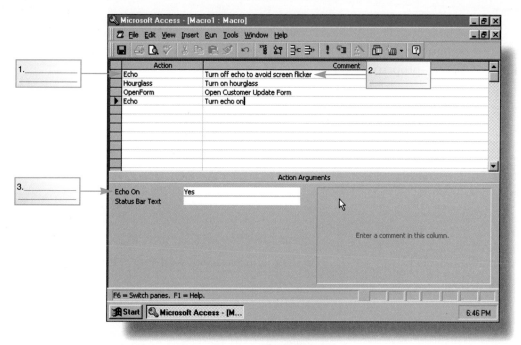

FIGURE 6-75

1. The Hourglass action to turn off the hourglass should be inserted between the OpenForm and Echo action. How can you insert a new action?
2. What value would you assign to the argument for this new action?
3. How can you maximize the form when it is opened?
4. How do you execute a macro?

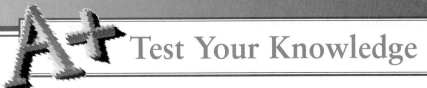

Test Your Knowledge

4 Understanding Combo Boxes

Instructions: Figure 6-76 shows the design grid for the Customer Update Form. The properties for the Name to Find combo box display in the window. Use this figure to answer the following questions on your own paper.

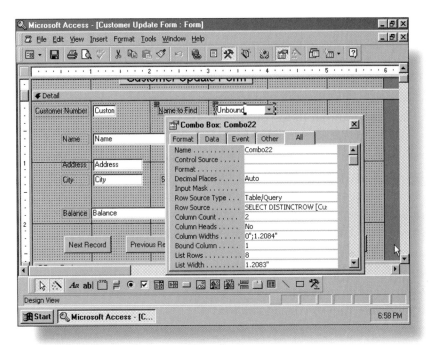

FIGURE 6-76

1. When do you place a combo box on a form?
2. What is the purpose of the Row Source property?
3. What is the purpose of the Tab Stop property?
4. What is the purpose of the On Current property?

Use Help

1 Reviewing Project Activities

Instructions: Perform the following tasks using a computer.

1. Start Access.
2. If the Office Assistant is on your screen, then click it to display its balloon. If the Office Assistant is not on your screen, click the Office Assistant button on the toolbar.
3. Type switchboard in the What would you like to do? text box. Click the Search button. Click Create and manage a switchboard form.
4. When the Help information displays, read it. Click the Create a switchboard form using the Switchboard Manager link. Read the information. Next, right-click within the box, and then click Print Topic. Hand the printout in to your instructor. Click the Help Topics button to return to the Help Topics: Microsoft Access 97 dialog box.
5. Click the Index tab. Type command bu in the top text box labeled 1 and then double-click Command Button Wizard in the middle list box labeled 2. Double-click Create a command button in the Topics Found dialog box. When the Help information displays, read it, ready the printer, right-click, and click Print Topic. Hand the printout in to your instructor. Click the Help Topics button to return to the Help Topics: Microsoft Access 97 dialog box.
6. Click the Find tab. Type combo in the top text box labeled 1. Click Combo in the middle list box labeled 2. Double-click Combo boxes: What they are and how they work in the lower list box labeled 3. When the Help information displays, read it, ready the printer, right-click, and click Print Topic. Hand the printout in to your instructor.

Use Help

2 Expanding the Basics

Instructions: Use Access Help to learn about the topics listed below. If you are unable to print the Help information, then answer the questions on your own paper.

1. Using the Office Assistant, answer the following questions:
   a. How can you save a copy of a macro under a different name?
   b. How can you delete a macro?
   c. How can you rename a macro?
2. Using the keywords, command bu, and the Index sheet in the Help Topics: Microsoft Access 97 dialog box, display and print information on adding a picture to a command button. Then, answer the following questions:
   a. How can you add a picture and a caption to a command button?
   b. How do you add a picture if you are not sure of the path and file name?
3. Use the Find sheet in the Help Topics: Microsoft Access 97 dialog box to display and then print information about deleting a switchboard.
4. Use the Office Assistant to display and print information on when you should use a macro versus when you should use Visual Basic. Then, answer the following questions:
   a. When must you use a macro instead of Visual Basic?
   b. Why does using Visual Basic instead of macros make your database easier to maintain?

Apply Your Knowledge

1 Creating and Using Macros in the Green Thumb Database

Instructions: Start Access. Open the Green Thumb database from the Access folder on the Data Disk that accompanies this book. Perform the following tasks.

1. Create a macro to open the Customer Update Form you created in Project 4. The macro should maximize the form automatically when it is opened.
2. Save the macro as Open Customer Update Form.
3. Create a macro to print the Customers by Intern report you created in Project 4.
4. Save the macro as Print Customers by Intern.
5. Run the Print Customers by Intern macro and print the report.
6. Modify the Customer Update Form you created in Project 4 to create the form shown in Figure 6-77. The form includes command buttons and a combo box to search for the customer's name.

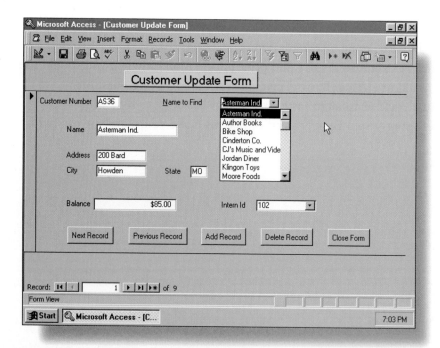

FIGURE 6-77

7. Print the form. To print the form, open the form, click File on the menu bar and then click Print. Click Selected Record(s) as the Print Range. Click the OK button.

In the Lab

1 Creating an Application System for the Museum Mercantile Database

Problem: The Museum Mercantile volunteers are pleased with the tables, forms, and reports you have created. They have two additional requests, however. First, they require some improvements to the Product Update Form. They would like to have buttons placed on the form for moving to the next record, moving to the previous record, adding a record, deleting a record, and closing the form. Then, they want a simple way of searching for a product given the product's description. They also would like an easy way to access the various tables, forms, and reports simply by clicking a button or two. This would make it much easier to train the volunteers that maintain and update the database.

Instructions: Open the Museum Mercantile database from the Access folder on the Data Disk that accompanies this book. Perform the following tasks.

1. Create macros that will perform the following tasks:
   a. Open the Product Update Form
   b. Open the Vendor Master Form
   c. Open the Product Table
   d. Open the Vendor Table
   e. Preview the Inventory Report
   f. Preview the Products by Vendor
   g. Preview the On Hand Value Report
   h. Print the Inventory Report
   i. Print the Products by Vendor
   j. Print the On Hand Value Report
2. Modify the Product Update Form to create the form shown in Figure 6-78. The form includes command buttons and a combo box to search for products by description.
3. Save and print the form. To print the form, open the form, click File on the menu bar and then click Print. Click Selected Record(s) as the Print Range. Click the OK button.

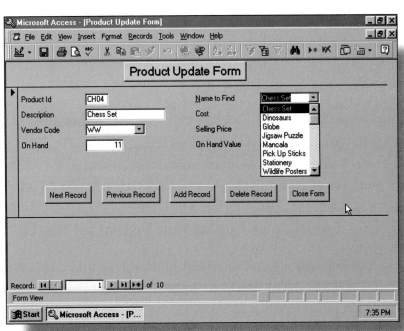

FIGURE 6-78

(continued)

In the Lab

Creating an Application System for the Museum Mercantile Database *(continued)*

4. Create the switchboard for the Museum Mercantile database shown in Figure 6-79. Use the same design for your switchboard pages as that shown in this project. For example, the View Form switchboard page should have three choices: Open Product Update Form, Open Vendor Master Form, and Return to Main Switchboard. Include all the forms, tables, and reports for which you created macros in Step 1 on the previous page.

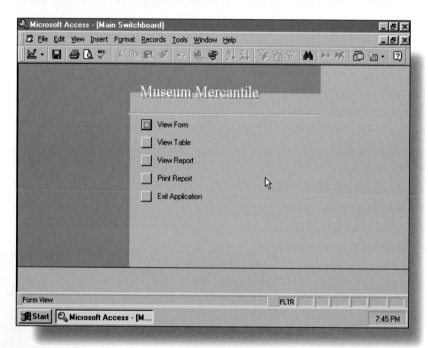

FIGURE 6-79

5. Run the switchboard and correct any errors.

2 Creating an Application System for the City Telephone System Database

Problem: The telephone manager is pleased with the tables, forms, and reports you have created. She has two additional requests, however. First, she requires some improvements to the User Update Form. She would like to have buttons placed on the form for moving to the next record, moving to the previous record, adding a record, deleting a record, and closing the form. Then, she wants a simple way of searching for a user given the user's last name. She also would like an easy way to access the various tables, forms, and reports simply by clicking a button or two. She feels that this would make the employees much more productive than if they have to remember all the steps required to perform any of these tasks.

Instructions: Open the City Telephone System database from the Access folder on the Data Disk that accompanies this book. Perform the following tasks.

1. Create macros that will perform the following tasks:
   a. Open the User Update Form
   b. Open the Department Master Form
   c. Open the User Table
   d. Open the Department Table
   e. Preview the Telephone List
   f. Preview the Users by Department
   g. Preview the Total Charges Report
   h. Print the Telephone List
   i. Print the Users by Department
   j. Print the Total Charges Report
2. Modify the User Update Form to create the form shown in Figure 6-80. The form includes command buttons and a combo box to search for users by the user's last name.

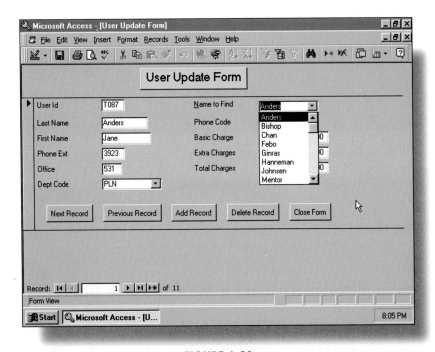

FIGURE 6-80

3. Save and print the form. To print the form, open the form, click File on the menu bar and then click Print. Click Selected Record(s) as the Print Range. Click the OK button.

(continued)

In the Lab

Creating an Application System for the City Telephone System Database *(continued)*

4. Create the switchboard for the City Telephone System database shown in Figure 6-81. Use the same design for your switchboard pages as that shown in this project. For example, the View Form switchboard page should have three choices: Open User Update Form, Open Department Master Form, and Return to Main Switchboard. Include all the forms, tables, and reports for which you created macros in Step 1 on the previous page.

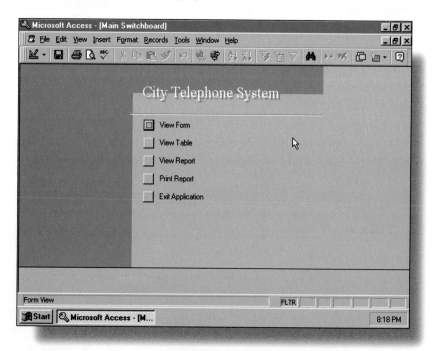

FIGURE 6-81

5. Run the switchboard and correct any errors.

3 Creating an Application System for the City Scene Database

Problem: The managing editor is pleased with the tables, forms, and reports that you have created. He has two additional requests, however. First, he requires some improvements to the Advertiser Update Form. He would like to have buttons placed on the form for moving to the next record, moving to the previous record, adding a record, deleting a record, and closing the form. He also would like a simple way of searching for an advertiser given the advertiser's name. Then, he wants an easy way to access the various tables, forms, and reports simply by clicking a button or two. He feels that this would make the employees much more productive than if they have to remember all the steps required to perform any of these tasks.

In the Lab

Instructions: Open the City Scene database from the Access folder on the Data Disk that accompanies this book. Perform the following tasks.

1. Create macros that will perform the following tasks:
   a. Open the Advertiser Update Form
   b. Open the Ad Rep Master Form
   c. Open the Advertiser Table
   d. Open the Ad Rep Table
   e. Preview the Status Report
   f. Preview the Advertisers by Ad Rep
   g. Preview the Advertising Income Report
   h. Print the Status Report
   i. Print the Advertisers by Ad Rep
   j. Print the Advertising Income Report

2. Modify the Advertiser Update Form to create the form shown in Figure 6-82. The form includes command buttons and a combo box to search for accounts by the account name.

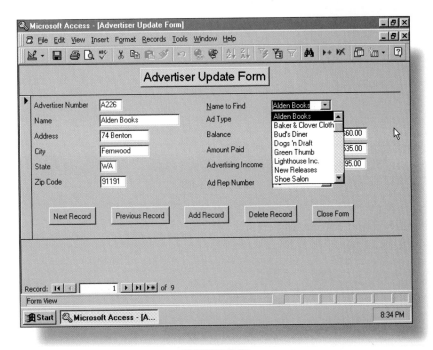

FIGURE 6-82

3. Save and print the form. To print the form, open the form, click File on the menu bar and then click Print. Click Selected Record(s) as the Print Range. Click the OK button.

(continued)

In the Lab

Creating an Application System for the City Scene Database *(continued)*

4. Create the switchboard for the City Scene database shown in Figure 6-83. Use the same design for your switchboard pages as that shown in this project. For example, the View Form switchboard page should have three choices: Open Advertiser Update Form, Open Ad Rep Master Form, and Return to Main Switchboard. Include all the forms, tables, and reports for which you created macros in Step 1 on the previous page.

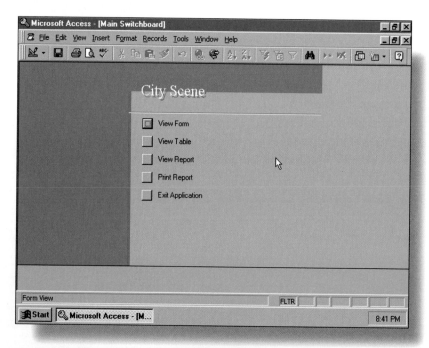

FIGURE 6-83

5. Run the switchboard and correct any errors.

Cases and Places

The difficulty of these case studies varies: ❱ are the least difficult; ❱❱ are more difficult; and ❱❱❱ are the most difficult.

1 ❱ Use the golf lesson database modified in Case Study 1 of the Cases and Places section of Project 5 for this assignment. Create macros to (a) open the Class Update and Pro Master Forms, (b) open the Lesson Revenue and Pro Tables, (c) preview the Lesson Revenue and Classes By Pro Reports, and (d) print the Lesson Revenue and Classes By Pro Reports. Also, create and run a switchboard for the golf lesson database.

2 ❱ Modify the Class Update Form created in Case Study 3 of the Cases and Places section of Project 4 to include command buttons and a combo box to search for classes by description. Save and print the form.

3 ❱❱ Use the textbook database modified in Case Study 5 of the Cases and Places section of Project 5 for this assignment. Create macros to (a) open the book form, (b) open the book table and maximize the window, (c) preview the Textbook Exchange Report, and (d) print the Textbook Exchange Report. Also, create and run a switchboard that includes these four macros.

4 ❱❱ Use the restaurant database modified in Case Study 4 of the Cases and Places section of Project 5 for this assignment. Modify the restaurant form to include command buttons. Also, create a combo box to search for restaurant names. Save and print the form.

5 ❱❱ Use the movie database modified in Case Study 3 of the Cases and Places section of Project 5 for this assignment. Create macros to (a) open the table and maximize the window, (b) open a movie report in a preview window, and (c) print the movie report. Also, create and run a switchboard that includes these three macros.

6 ❱❱❱ Use the campus directory database modified in Case Study 6 of the Cases and Places section of Project 5 for this assignment. Modify the information form to include command buttons. Also, create a combo box to serch for faculty, administration, coaches, and other key names. Save and print the form.

Cases and Places

7 ▶▶▶ Use the financial institutions database modified in Case Study 7 of the Cases and Places section of Project 5 for this assignment. Create macros to (a) open the investment table and maximize the window, (b) preview the Investment Future Value Report, and (c) print the Investment Future Value Report. Also, create and run a switchboard that includes these three macros.

Linking Excel Worksheets to an Access Database

INTEGRATION FEATURE

Case Perspective

Lamatec Industries has been using Excel to automate a variety of tasks for several years. Lamatec has maintained data on its departments and employees in an Excel worksheet, but recently, the management decided to convert this data to an Access database. After performing the conversion, they intended to discontinue using Excel for the employee data, relying instead on Access exclusively.

As the management at Lamatec reviewed its uses of the data, however, it appeared that some operations existed for which it might be better to maintain the data in an Excel workbook rather than convert the data to Access. The management at Lamatec is keenly interested in being able to use the Query, Form, and Report features of Access. Fortunately, they found that by linking the worksheets to an Access database, they could have the best of both. They can use Excel to store and manipulate the data and use Access for queries, forms, and reports.

They decided to try the approach using both Excel and Access first. They intended to analyze their usage of Excel over the next year. If later they found they were no longer realizing any benefit from it, then they would convert the data to Access and no longer rely on Excel.

Introduction

It is possible to **link** data stored in a variety of formats to Access databases. The available formats include several other database management systems (for example, dBASE, FoxPro, and Paradox). They also include a variety of non-database formats, including Excel worksheets.

When an external table or worksheet is imported, or converted, into an Access database, a copy of the data is placed as a table in the database. The original data still exists, just as it did before, but no further connection is maintained between it and the data in the database. Changes to the original data do not affect the data in the database. Likewise, changes in the database do not affect the original data.

With **linking**, the connection is retained. When an Excel worksheet is linked, for example, the worksheet is not stored in the database. Instead, Access simply establishes a connection to the worksheet so you can view or edit the data in either Access or Excel.

Figures 1a through 1d on the next page illustrate the linking process. The type of worksheet that can be linked is one where the data is stored as a **list**, which is a labeled series of rows, with each row containing the same type of data. For example, in the worksheets shown in Figures 1a and 1b, the first rows contain the labels, which are entries indicating

AI 2.1

the type of data found in the column. The entry in the first column of the Department worksheet, for example, is Dept Code, indicating that all the other values in the column are department codes. The entry in the second column is Name, indicating that all the other values in the column are department names. Other than the first row, which contains the labels, all the rows contain precisely the same type of data: a department code in the first column, a name in the second column, a location in the third column, and so on.

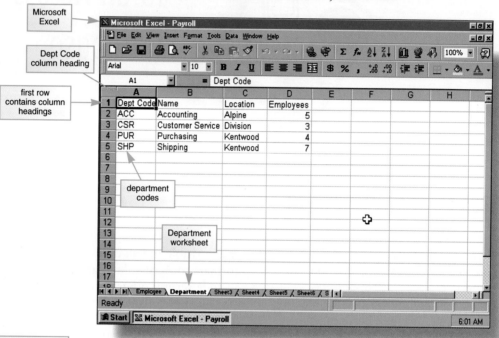

FIGURE 1a

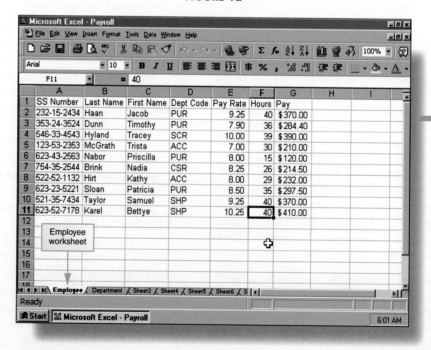

FIGURE 1b

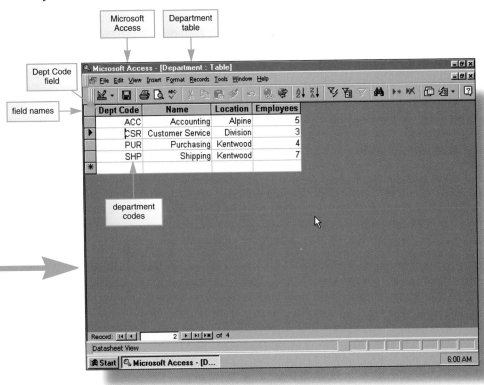

FIGURE 1c

FIGURE 1d

linked worksheets
appear to be
Access tables

As Figures 1a and 1b on page AI 2.2 illustrate, the worksheets are linked to the database and then can be displayed as typical database tables, as shown in Figures 1c and 1d on the previous page.
The columns in the worksheet become the *fields*. The column headings in the first row of the worksheets become the *field names*. The rows of the worksheets, other than the first rows, which contain the labels, become the *records* in the table. In the process, each field will be assigned the data type that seems the most reasonable, given the data currently in the worksheet.

Creating the Database

Before linking the data, you must start Access. If the database already exists, you must open it. If not, you must create it. Perform the following steps to start Access and create a new database called Payroll. The data will be linked to this database.

TO START ACCESS AND CREATE A DATABASE

Step 1: Click the Start button on the taskbar.
Step 2: Click New Office Document on the Start menu. If the General tab is not selected, click the General tab.
Step 3: Make sure the Blank Database icon is selected, and then click the OK button.
Step 4: Click 3½ Floppy (A:) in the Save in list box. Type Payroll in the File name text box.
Step 5: Click the Create button.

The Payroll database is created and the Database window displays.

Linking the Data

To **link the data,** you will use the **Get External Data command** on the File menu, and then click **Link Tables.** After selecting the desired type of linked file (Microsoft Excel, in this case), then you select the workbook containing the worksheets to be linked. Next, you will select the specific worksheet to be linked and also indicate that the first row contains the column headings. These column headings become the field names in the Access table. Perform the following steps to link the Employee and Department worksheets to the Access database.

More *About* Linking Data: Spreadsheets

By selecting the TransferSpreadsheet action, you can use a macro to link spreadsheet data. Select Link for the Transfer Type argument, select the spreadsheet type (for example, Microsoft Excel 5-7) for the Spreadsheet Type argument, enter the name of the Access table, and the file name of the spreadsheet.

More *About* Linking Data: Databases

By selecting the TransferDatabase action, you can use a macro to link data from an external database. Select Link for the Transfer Type argument, select the database type (for example, dBASE IV), enter the name of the source table, and the name of the destination table.

More *About* Linking Data: Text Data

By selecting the TransferText action, you can use a macro to link text data. Select the appropriate file type as the value for the Transfer Type argument, enter the name of the Access table and the name of the file containing the data.

Steps To Link Worksheets to an Access Database

1 **Click File on the menu bar, point to Get External Data, and then click Link Tables.**

*The **Link dialog box** displays. You can use this dialog box to select the file that is to be linked.*

2 **Click the Files of type box arrow and then point to Microsoft Excel.**

The list of available file types displays (Figure 2).

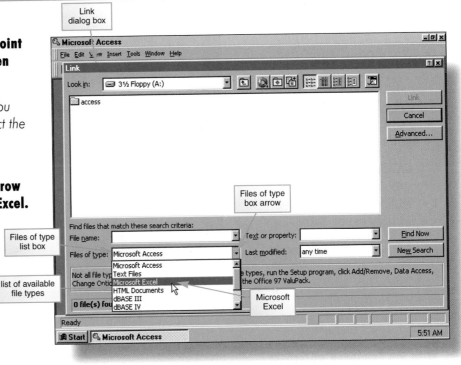

FIGURE 2

3 **Click Microsoft Excel. If the Access folder does not display in the Look in list box, point to the Access folder (Figure 3).**

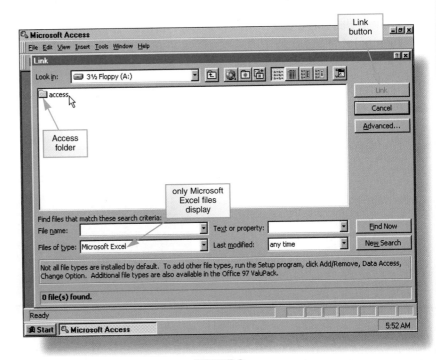

FIGURE 3

4 **If necessary, click the Access folder.**

The list of available Excel workbooks in the Access folder displays.

5 **Click the Payroll workbook, and then click the Link button. Point to the Next button.**

The Link Spreadsheet Wizard dialog box displays (Figure 4). You can use this dialog box to select the worksheet to be linked.

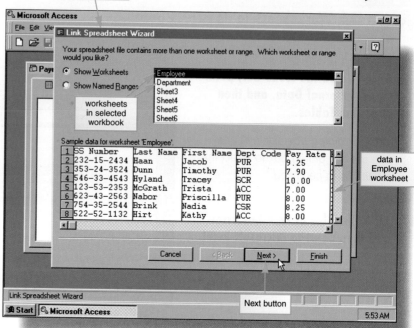

FIGURE 4

6 **With the Employee worksheet selected, click the Next button. Click First Row Contains Column Headings, and then point to the Next button.**

The Link Spreadsheet Wizard dialog box displays (Figure 5). You can use this dialog box to indicate that the first row contains the field names.

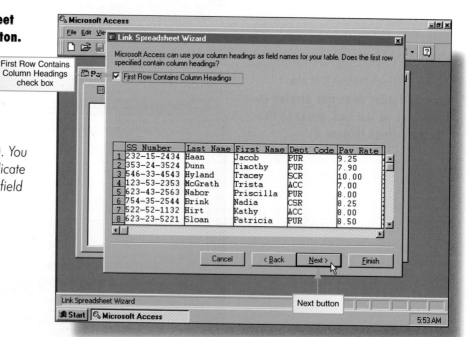

FIGURE 5

7 **Click the Next button. Make sure the Linked Table Name is Employee, and then point to the Finish button.**

The Link Spreadsheet Wizard dialog box displays (Figure 6). The name of the linked table will be Employee.

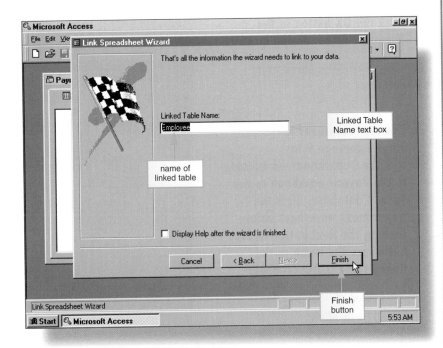

FIGURE 6

8 **Click the Finish button.**

The Microsoft Access dialog box displays when the process is complete (Figure 7). The name of the linked table displays in the Database window. The arrow in front of the name indicates that it is a linked object rather than a true Access table.

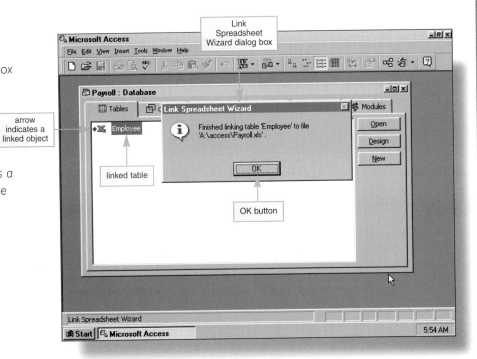

FIGURE 7

9 Click the OK button in the Microsoft Access dialog box.

The worksheet is linked to the database.

10 Use the techniques in Steps 1 through 9 to link the Department worksheet in the Payroll workbook to the Payroll database. Click the Department worksheet before clicking the Next button in Step 6. Be sure the name of the linked table is Department.

The Microsoft Access dialog box displays when the process is complete (Figure 8). The worksheets are linked to the database and display as tables in the Payroll database.

11 Click the OK button. Close the Database window by clicking its Close button, and then quit Access.

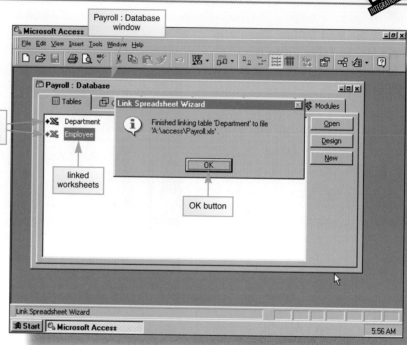

FIGURE 8

Using the Linked Worksheets

Generally, you can use the linked worksheets just as if they were regular Access tables. You can use Datasheet view or Form view to change the data. When you do, you actually are changing data within the Excel worksheets. You also can use Excel to change the data directly.

Using the linked worksheets, you can create queries such as the one shown in Figure 9. In addition, you can use the worksheets in forms and reports. The one operation you cannot perform with the linked worksheets that you can with tables is to alter their design.

When you run a query, the query will be executed using the current data in the linked worksheets. Running the query shown in Figure 9, for example, would produce the results shown in Figure 10.

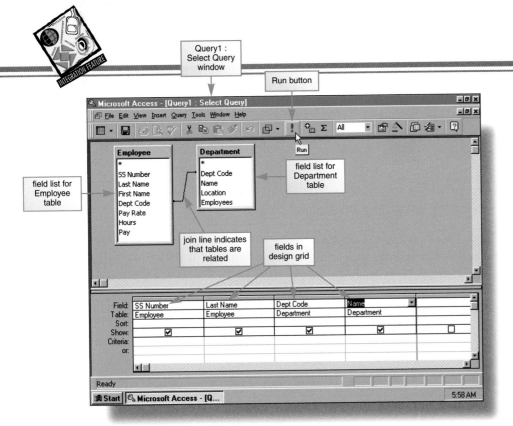

Query1 : Select Query window

Run button

field list for Employee table

field list for Department table

join line indicates that tables are related

fields in design grid

FIGURE 9

Summary

The Integration Feature covered the process of linking worksheets in an Excel workbook to an Access database. To link a worksheet to an Access database, you learned to use the Link Spreadsheet Wizard. Working with the wizard, you first identified the specific worksheet to be linked, identified that the first row of the worksheet contained the column headings, and then assigned a name to the linked worksheet. The wizard linked the worksheet to the database, enabling you to manipulate the worksheet from within Access just as you would a table.

data from Employee worksheet

data from Department worksheet

SS Number	Last Name	Dept Code	Name
522-52-1132	Hirt	ACC	Accounting
123-53-2353	McGrath	ACC	Accounting
754-35-2544	Brink	CSR	Customer Service
623-23-5221	Sloan	PUR	Purchasing
623-43-2563	Nabor	PUR	Purchasing
353-24-3524	Dunn	PUR	Purchasing
232-15-2434	Haan	PUR	Purchasing
623-52-7178	Karel	SHP	Shipping
521-35-7434	Taylor	SHP	Shipping

results of query

FIGURE 10

What You Should Know

Having completed this Integration Feature, you now should be able to perform the following tasks:

▶ Link Worksheets to an Access Database *(AI 2.5)*

▶ Start Access and Create a Database *(AI 2.4)*

In the Lab

1 Use Help

Instructions: Perform the following tasks using a computer.

1. Start Access.
2. If the Office Assistant is on your screen, click it to display its balloon. If the Office Assistant is not on your screen, click the Office Assistant button on the toolbar.
3. Type linking spreadsheets in the What would you like to do? text box. Click the Search button. Click Import or link data from a spreadsheet. When the Help information displays, read it. Next, right-click within the box and then click Print Topic. Hand the printout in to your instructor. When you are finished, close the Microsoft Access 97 Help window.
4. Start Excel.
5. Click the Office Assistant to display its balloon. Type naming cells in the What would you like to do? text box. Click the Search button. Click Name cells in a workbook. When the Help information displays, read it and then click the Name a cell or range of cells link. Read the Help information, right-click within the box and then click Print Topic. Hand the printout in to your instructor.

2 Linking Excel Worksheets to the Sales Database

Problem: Midwest Computer Supply has been using Excel to automate a variety of tasks and recently converted some of its data to an Access database. As Midwest reviewed its uses of the data, however, it decided that some financial operations are better performed in Excel. The management of Midwest would like to be able to use the Query, Form, and Report features of Access while maintaining the data in Excel worksheets.

Instructions: Perform the following tasks.

1. Create a new database in which to store all the objects related to the sales data. Use Sales as the name of the database.
2. Link the Customer and Sales Representative worksheets shown in Figures 11a and 11b to the Sales database. The worksheets are in the Sales workbook in the Access folder on the Data Disk that accompanies this book.
3. Open and print the tables in Access.

In the Lab

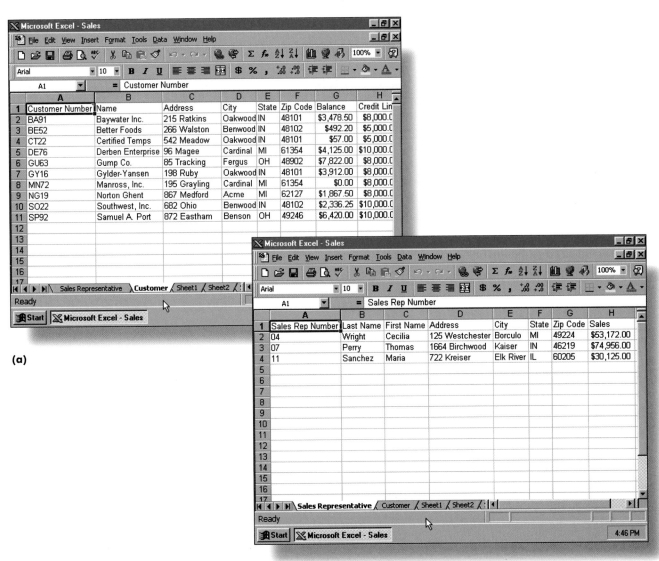

(a)

FIGURE 11

(b)

3 Linking Excel Worksheets to the Inventory Stock Database

Problem: Tennis Is Everything has been using Excel to automate a variety of tasks and recently converted some of its data to an Access database. As Tennis Is Everything reviewed its uses of the data, however, it decided that some financial operations are better performed in Excel. The management of Tennis Is Everything would like to be able to use the Query, Form, and Report features of Access while maintaining the data in Excel worksheets.

(continued)

In the Lab

Linking Excel Worksheets to the Inventory Stock Database *(continued)*

Instructions: Perform the following tasks.

1. Create a new database in which to store all the objects related to the inventory data. Use Inventory Stock as the name of the database.

2. The Product worksheet shown in Figure 12a in the Inventory Stock workbook includes formulas that do not need to be linked to the Inventory Stock database. Link only the named range, inv_data, in the Product worksheet to the Inventory Stock database. Use Product for the Linked Table Name. The worksheet is in the Inventory Stock workbook in the Access folder on the Data Disk that accompanies this book. (*Hint*: Use Help on page AI 2.10 to help you solve this problem.)

3. Link the Vendor worksheet shown in Figure 12b to the Inventory Stock database. The worksheet is in the Inventory Stock workbook in the Access folder on the Data Disk that accompanies this book.

4. Open and print the tables in Access.

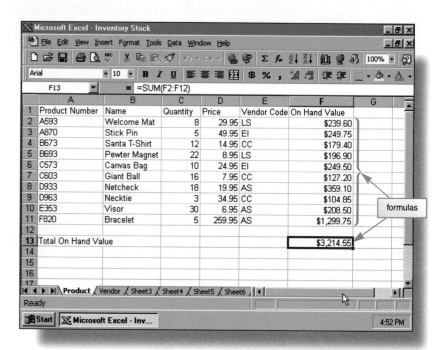

Figure 12a

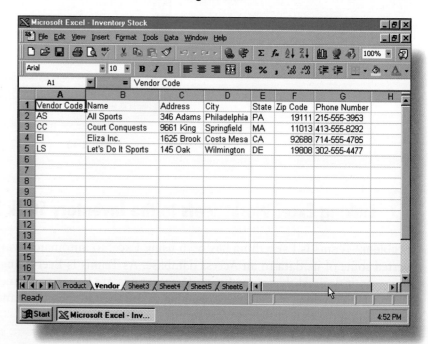

FIGURE 12b

NOTE TO READER: This index contains references for Projects 1 through 6 and the Integration Features of the book, *Microsoft Access 97: Complete Concepts and Techniques*. The same references can be used for Access Projects 1 through 3 and Integration Feature 1 in the book, *Microsoft Office 97: Introductory Concepts and Techniques*, and Access Projects 4 through 6 and Integration Feature 2 in the book, *Microsoft Office 97: Advanced Concepts and Techniques*.

Microsoft **Access 97**

Index

Microsoft PowerPoint 97

Microsoft PowerPoint 97

Using Embedded Visuals to Enhance a Slide Show

Objectives:

You will have mastered the material in this project when you can:

▶ Import an outline created in Microsoft Word
▶ Create a slide background using a picture
▶ Embed an Excel chart
▶ Create and embed an organization chart
▶ Move text
▶ Embed a picture
▶ Resize objects
▶ Create a PowerPoint clip art object
▶ Scale objects
▶ Ungroup clip art
▶ Apply slide transition and text preset animation effects
▶ Print handouts

Project 3

Presentations Provide Fuel for *Top Performance*

Amoco Corporation is one of the world's leading integrated petroleum and chemical companies, with revenues of approximately $30 billion a year and operations in 40 countries. Amoco's operating strategies are based on financial performance, core business leadership, environmental leadership, and improvement.

The Company's 17 business sectors: exploration and chemicals.

Exploration Amoco exploring focusing potent Egypt United

Gasoline. Sportswear. Carpeting. Cassette tapes. Paint. Tires. Home insulation. On first glance, these products seem unrelated. But they are all manufactured from petroleum and chemicals developed and marketed by the Amoco Corporation, one of the world's largest industrial organizations. More than 40,000 employees in 40 countries worldwide implement Amoco's cutting-edge technologies, and once a year the corporation's 350 top executives travel to one location from all corners of the globe to determine strategies that will help keep Amoco an international leader.

Central to this three-day Worldwide Senior Management event is a $100,000 multimedia presentation combining Microsoft PowerPoint slides with video, audio, and special effects. The slide show is produced by the Presentation Graphics team at Amoco's Graphic Resources department in Chicago. The department offers complete project management, including graphic design of publications and manuals, displays for exhibits, photography, printing, writing assistance, and new media, such as intranets and the Internet.

The department creates more than 60 new presentations annually. When Amoco employees contact Graphic Resources with a project idea, the Graphics team first determines the users' needs. Previously, users wanted 35mm slides, but now they request computer presentations incorporating multimedia and overhead transparencies. The team uses PowerPoint and other drawing and graphics programs to design and produce presentations, color overheads, and color prints. The presentations incorporate text, video, music, animation, and graphics that are saved on a CD-ROM distributed throughout the corporation.

The Graphic Resources department often imports Microsoft Word files, just as you will import the Internet Training Outline file in Project 3. These Word documents often are written by Amoco corporate writers or speech writers. Then the presentations can be enhanced by photos supplied by the employees and digitized by passing the pictures through a scanner. In addition, the department can select clip art and computer graphics from its digital library, which has files dating back to Amoco's first graphics computer system installed more than 15 years ago at a cost of one million dollars.

In addition to creating new slide shows, the Presentation Graphics team updates and enhances many files. If information on a previous slide show needs to be changed, employees can modify the information themselves or bring the data disk containing the presentation to the Graphic Resources department for revisions.

Occasionally, employees come to the department with original PowerPoint slide shows they have created themselves. If their layouts are not pleasing, Graphics team members suggest using different templates, slide masters, colors, type sizes, or fonts. You will make similar changes to the slide show in Project 3 when you create a slide background using a digitized photograph and apply the Contemporary Portrait design template. Graphics personnel also suggest style changes, such as using uppercase letters in the main title text, and they recommend dividing some slides into two different slides for a less-cluttered appearance.

Amoco sells more gasoline than any other company, and the presentations produced by the Graphic Resources department help steer top executives and employees down the road to a productive future.

Project

Microsoft
PowerPoint 97

Using Embedded Visuals to Enhance a Slide Show

Case Perspective

Computers are found in nearly 40 million households in the United States, and that number is expected to double by the end of the decade. About one-half of these computers have modems, which allow users to connect to the Internet — a collection of networks that allows you to do research, shop, send messages, and converse with other computer users throughout the world.

Thousands of new Internet users, or newbies, come online each month. Even though the Internet has become more user-friendly recently, these people need training to help them learn the various components of the Internet. The Net-Train Corporation specializes in Internet training, and company executives have asked you to produce a presentation to help them market their upcoming seminar scheduled for the Presidents' Day weekend in Park City, Utah, which is the site of the 2002 Winter Olympics.

Net-Train employees use an outline created in Microsoft Word for their advertisements and sales promotions, and they have modified it to reflect this seminar's content. You use this outline to develop the marketing presentation. Then you enhance the presentation by creating a custom background, embedding an Excel chart showing Internet use, creating and embedding an organization chart, and inserting pictures and clip art.

Create Exciting Presentations Using Embedded Visuals

Bulleted lists and simple graphics are the starting point for most presentations, but they can become boring. Advanced PowerPoint users want exciting presentations — something to impress their audiences. With PowerPoint, it is easy to develop impressive presentations by creating a custom background, embedding graphs and organization charts, inserting pictures, and creating new graphics.

One problem you may experience when developing a presentation is finding the proper graphic to convey your message. One way to overcome this obstacle is to modify clip art from the Microsoft Clip Gallery. Another solution is to import charts created in another application, such as Microsoft Excel. PowerPoint design templates offer a limited number of slide backgrounds and allow you to create your own background using a picture or clip art.

This project introduces several techniques to make your presentations more exciting.

Project Three – Internet Training Seminar

Project 3 expands on the basic PowerPoint presentation features by importing existing files and embedding objects. This project creates a presentation that is used to promote the Internet Training Seminar. The workshop provides intense training sessions for various Internet components, including electronic mail, the World Wide

Web, newsgroups, chat rooms, netiquette, search engines, creating Web pages, and privacy issues. The project begins by building the presentation from an outline created in Microsoft Word and saved as a Rich Text Format (RTF) file. Then, several objects are inserted to customize the presentation. These objects include an Excel chart, an organization chart, and pictures.

Slide Preparation Steps

The preparation steps summarize how the slide presentation shown in Figures 3-1a through 3-1e will be developed in Project 3. The following tasks will be completed in this project.

1. Start PowerPoint.
2. Import the Training Outline file from the PowerPoint folder on the Data Disk that accompanies this book.
3. Apply a design template.
4. Save the presentation as Internet Training.
5. Insert a picture to create a slide background (Figure 3-1a).
6. Embed an Excel chart on Slide 2 (Figure 3-1b).
7. Create and embed an organization chart on Slide 3 (Figure 3-1c).
8. Insert a picture in Slide 4 (Figure 3-1d).
9. Insert clip art and ungroup pieces of this art (Figure 3-1e).

FIGURE 3-1a

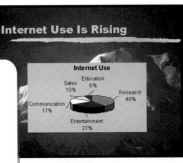

FIGURE 3-1b

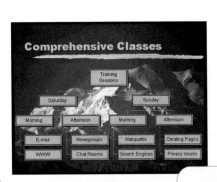

FIGURE 3-1c

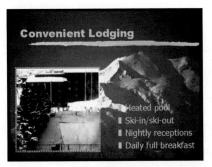

FIGURE 3-1d

FIGURE 3-1e

10. Apply slide transition and text preset animation effects.
11. Save the presentation again.
12. Print handouts.
13. Close PowerPoint.

Importing Outlines Created in Another Application

You may be asked to present the findings of a research paper. Instead of typing the presentation outline, you can import the outline from the research paper. If you did not create an outline for the research paper, you can create it by first saving the research paper document as an RTF file, removing all text except topic headings, and then saving the RTF file again. Once the research paper outline is saved as an RTF file, you can import the outline into PowerPoint.

You also can create a presentation by opening an outline created in Microsoft Word or another word processing program. The advantage of using an outline saved as a Microsoft Word document or as an RTF file is the text attributes and outline heading levels are maintained. Documents saved as plain text (.txt) files can be opened in PowerPoint but do not maintain text attributes and outline heading levels. Consequently, each paragraph becomes a slide title.

To create a presentation using an existing outline, select All Outlines from the Files of type box in the Open dialog box. When you select All Outlines, PowerPoint displays a list of outlines. Next, you select the file that contains the outline. PowerPoint then creates a presentation using your outline. Each major heading in your outline becomes a slide title, and subheadings become a bulleted list.

More About Presentation Design

Taking the time to design effective presentation graphics really pays off. Some research studies conclude that well-prepared electronic presentations can reduce meeting times by more than 25 percent.

Opening an Existing Outline Created in Another Application

After starting PowerPoint, the first step in this project is to open an outline created in Microsoft Word. PowerPoint can produce slides from an outline created in Microsoft Word or another word processing program if the outline was saved in a format that PowerPoint can recognize. The outline created by the workshop organizing team was saved as an RTF file.

Opening an outline into PowerPoint requires two steps. First, you must tell PowerPoint you are opening an existing presentation. Then, to open the outline, you need to select the proper file type from the Files of type box in the Open dialog box. The following steps explain how to start PowerPoint and to open an outline created in Microsoft Word.

Note: The Data Disk that accompanies this book contains a PowerPoint folder with three executable files that include compressed versions of the files for Projects 3 and 4 and the Integration Feature of PowerPoint. Some of these files are required if you plan to step through the PowerPoint projects on a PC. The other files are required for the exercises at the end of the projects. It is recommended that you copy the executable file for a project to a blank floppy disk and then expand it. The paragraph below explains how to expand the files for Project 3. To expand the files for Project 4 and the Integration Feature, replace Project3 with Project4 or Integrat.

To expand the executable file for Project 3, do the following: (1) insert the Data Disk in drive A; (2) start Windows Explorer and, if necessary, click the Restore button so that part of the desktop displays; (3) click the plus sign to the left of the 3½ Floppy (A:) icon in the All Folders side of the window and then click the PowerPoint icon; (4) right-drag Project3 on to the desktop and click Copy Here on the shortcut menu; (5) insert a blank floppy disk in drive A; (6) right-drag Project3 from the desktop on to the 3½ Floppy (A:) icon in the All Folders side of the window and then click Move Here on the shortcut menu; (7) double-click Project3 in the Contents of '3½ Floppy (A:)' side of the window and then click the Proceed button when the PowerPoint 97 Project3 Data Disk dialog box displays (do not change the folder location unless installing to a hard disk); (8) If necessary, click Yes to create the new folder; (9) right-click Project3 and click Delete on the shortcut menu, and then click the Yes button in the Confirm File Delete dialog box; (10) clearly label the newly created floppy disk as PowerPoint 97 Project3 Data Disk.

Steps To Start PowerPoint and Open an Outline

1 Insert your PowerPoint 97 Project 3 Data Disk into drive A. Click the Start button on the taskbar. Point to Programs on the Start menu. Click Microsoft PowerPoint on the Programs submenu.

2 When the PowerPoint startup dialog box displays, click Open an existing presentation. Click the OK button.

The Open dialog box displays (Figure 3-2). The current folder is My Documents. The current file type is Presentations and Shows as displayed in the Files of type box.

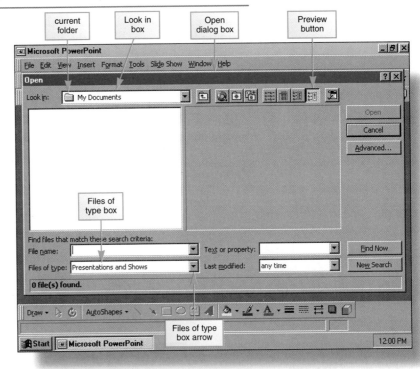

FIGURE 3-2

3 Click the Look in box arrow, and then click 3½ Floppy (A:). Double-click the PowerPoint folder in the list box. Click the Files of type box arrow, and then scroll down and click All Outlines.

A list displays the types of files that PowerPoint can open. Your list may be different depending on the software installed on your computer.

4 Double-click Training Outline in the list box.

PowerPoint opens Training Outline and displays it in Outline View (Figure 3-3). The title on Slide 1 is highlighted. The outline text displays bulleted, indicating the slide layout is Bulleted List. The position of the elevator on the scroll bar indicates more outline text exists than can display in the Outline View window. The current design template is Default Design as identified on the status bar.

FIGURE 3-3

More *About*
Font Color

If you want to change the text back to its original default color, highlight the text, click the Font Color button arrow on the Drawing toolbar and then click Automatic.

When opening a file created in another presentation graphics program, such as Harvard Graphics or Aldus Persuasion, PowerPoint picks up the outline structure from the styles used in the file (heading level one becomes a title, heading level two becomes the first level of text, and so on). If the file does not contain heading styles, PowerPoint uses paragraph indents to create the outline. For **plain text files**, which are files saved without formatting, PowerPoint uses the tabs at the beginning of paragraphs to define the outline structure.

Imported outlines can have up to nine outline levels, whereas PowerPoint outlines can have only six (one for titles and five for text). When you import an outline, all text in outline levels six through nine is treated as outline level six.

Changing the Font Color of the Existing Outline

Colored type can make your presentation visually interesting. Perform the following steps to change the font color of all the text in the outline from black to gold.

Steps To Change the Font Color of the Entire Outline

1 **Click Edit on the menu bar and then click Select All.**

The characters in the outline are selected (Figure 3-4).

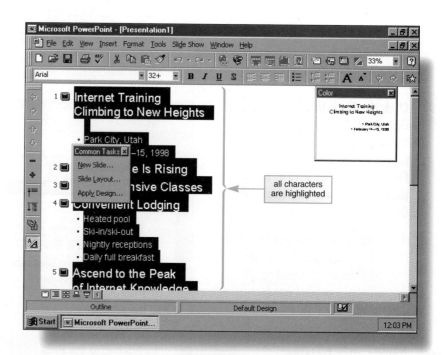

FIGURE 3-4

2 **Right-click the selection. Click Font on the shortcut menu. In the Font dialog box, click the Color box arrow and then point to More Colors.**

PowerPoint displays the Font dialog box (Figure 3-5). In the Font dialog box, you can set the font typeface, font style, font size, effects, and color of characters. More Colors is highlighted in the Color list.

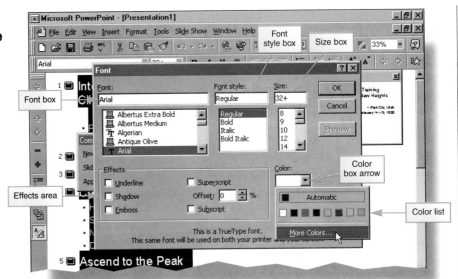

FIGURE 3-5

3 **Click More Colors. When the Colors dialog box displays, if necessary, click the Standard tab and then click the color gold as shown in Figure 3-6.**

The Colors dialog box displays the Standard sheet (Figure 3-6). The color gold is selected. Colors on the Standard sheet are arranged in varying shades of the color groups. White, black, and varying shades of gray display at the bottom of the Standard sheet. The preview box at the lower-right corner of the Standard sheet displays the new color and the current color. The object color on the slide does not change until you click the OK button.

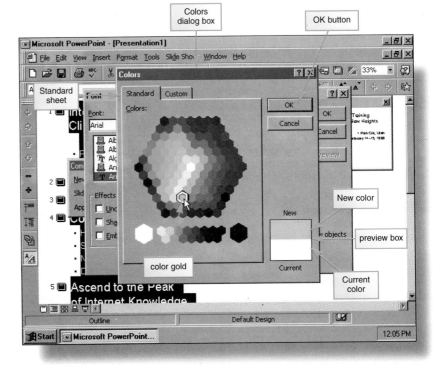

FIGURE 3-6

4 **Click the OK button in the Colors dialog box.**

The Font dialog box displays. The gold font color displays in the Color box.

5 **Click the OK button.**

The outline text displays in the gold font in the Color View window.

Changing Presentation Design Templates

Recall that **design templates** format the look of your presentation. You can change the design template any time you wish to change the appearance of your presentation, not just when you create a new presentation. The current design template is Default Design. Applying the Contemporary Portrait design template complements the custom slide background you will create later in this project. Perform these steps to change design templates.

Steps **To Change Design Templates**

1 **Point to the Apply Design button on the Common Tasks toolbar (Figure 3-7).**

2 **Click the Apply Design button. Click the Preview button if it is not already recessed. Click Contemporary Portrait in the list box.**

The Apply Design dialog box displays. The Preview button is recessed (refer to the location of the Preview button as shown in Figure 3-2 on page PP 3.9). Contemporary Portrait is highlighted in the list box and a preview of the Contemporary Portrait design template displays in the preview area.

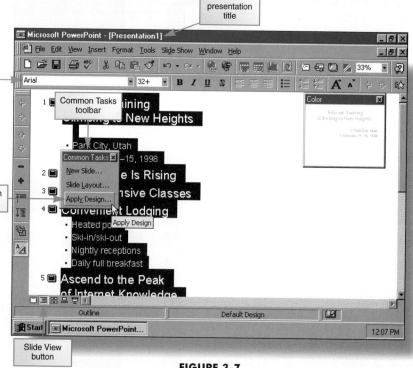

FIGURE 3-7

3 **Click the Apply button.**

PowerPoint applies the Contemporary Portrait design template as indicated by the change to the font and bullets.

> ▶**Other**Ways
>
> 1. Click Apply Design button on Standard toolbar, click Contemporary Portrait, click Apply button

Recall that slide attributes change when you select a different design template. The Contemporary Portrait design template format determines the slide attributes of the slide master and the title master. For example, when you compare Figure 3-3 on page PP 3.9 to your screen, you see the font changed from Arial to Arial Black and Tahoma and the bullets changed from small squares to large rectangles.

Saving the Presentation

You now should save your presentation because you created a presentation from an RTF file and changed the design template. The following steps summarize how to save a presentation.

◢ **More** *About*
Design Templates

Each design template has been professionally designed to give your presentation a consistent look. You can select any Auto-Layout and be assured that the color scheme, slide and title masters, and fonts will all harmonize with each other.

TO SAVE A PRESENTATION

1. Click the Save button on the Standard toolbar.
2. Type Internet Training in the File name text box.
3. Click the Save button.

The presentation is saved with the file name, Internet Training. The presentation title, Internet Training, displays on the title bar, instead of the default, Presentation.

Creating a Custom Background

PowerPoint has 17 design templates in the Presentation Designs folder. Sometimes you want a background, however, that is not found in one of the design templates, such as the picture of the mountains in Figures 3-1a through 3-1e on page PP 3.7. PowerPoint allows you to create that background by inserting a picture. PowerPoint also allows you to customize the background color, shading, pattern, and texture.

You perform two tasks to create the customized background for this presentation. First, you change the layout of Slide 1 to the Title Slide AutoLayout. Then, you create the slide background by inserting a picture of mountains.

The next two sections explain how to create a slide background using a picture.

Changing the Slide Layout to Title Slide

When you import an outline to create a presentation, PowerPoint assumes the text is bulleted text. Because Slide 1 is the title slide for this presentation, you want to change the AutoLayout to the Title Slide layout. You cannot change the slide layout in Outline View, however. Therefore, you want to change to Slide View and then change the AutoLayout.

The following steps summarize how to change to Slide View and change the layout of Slide 1 to the Title Slide layout.

TO CHANGE SLIDE LAYOUT TO TITLE SLIDE

1. Click the Slide View button.
2. Click the Slide Layout button on the Common Tasks toolbar.
3. Double-click Title Slide, the first layout in the Slide Layout dialog box.

Slide 1 displays in Slide View with the Contemporary Portrait design template (Figure 3-8).

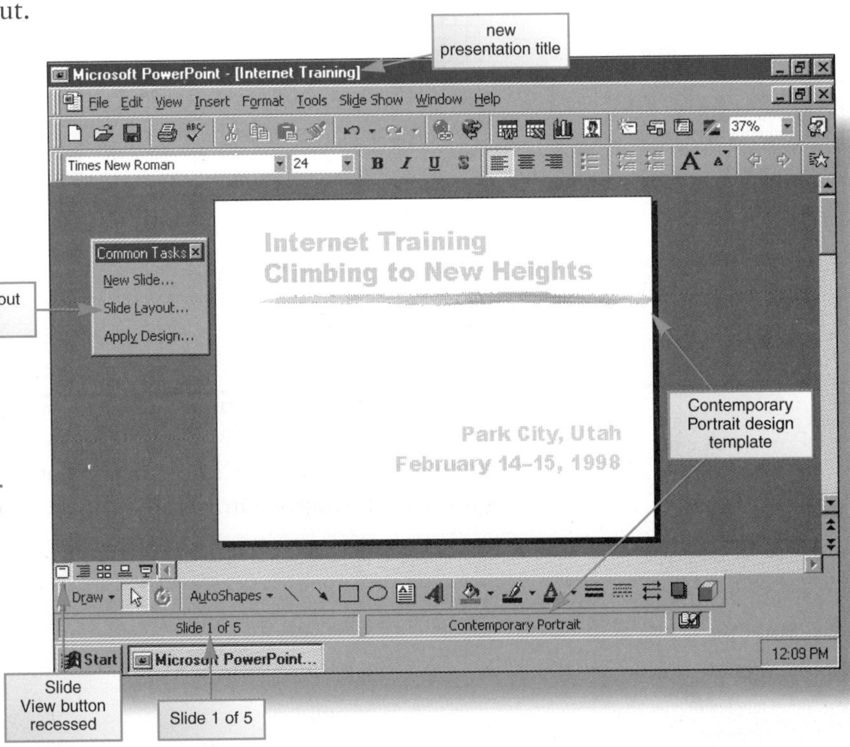

FIGURE 3-8

PowerPoint provides two alternative methods to double-clicking the Auto-Layout in Step 3 on the previous page. The first alternative is to type the layout number of one of the 24 AutoLayouts and press the ENTER key. A layout number corresponds to each AutoLayout, with the four slides in the first row numbered one through four from left to right, the next row of AutoLayouts numbered five through eight, and so on. The second alternative is to type the layout number and click the Apply button. PowerPoint interprets the number you type as the corresponding AutoLayout and applies it when you press the ENTER key (alternative one) or click the Apply button (alternative two). For example, the Title Slide AutoLayout is layout number one. When the Slide Layout dialog box displays, you would type 1 and press the ENTER key instead of double-clicking the Title Slide layout.

Inserting a Picture to Create a Custom Background

The next step in creating the Internet Training presentation is to insert a picture to create a custom background. In PowerPoint, a **picture** is any graphic created in another application. Pictures usually are saved in one of two **graphic formats**: bitmap or vector.

A **bitmap graphic** is a piece of art that has been stored as a pattern of dots called pixels. A **pixel**, short for **picture element**, is one dot in a grid. A picture that is produced on the computer screen or on paper by a printer is composed of thousands of these dots. Just as a bit is the smallest unit of information a computer can process, a pixel is the smallest element that can display or that print hardware and software can manipulate in creating letters, numbers, or graphics. For example, the letter A shown in Figure 3-9 actually is made up of a pattern of pixels in a grid.

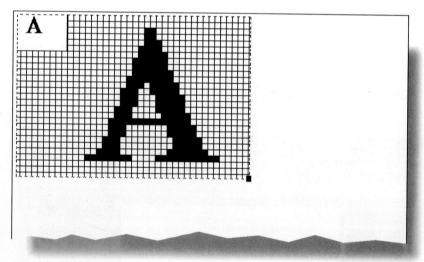

FIGURE 3-9

Bitmap graphics are created in paint programs such as Microsoft Paint. Bitmap graphics also can be produced from **digitizing** art, pictures, or photographs by passing the artwork through a scanner. A **scanner** is a hardware device that converts lines and shading into combinations of the binary digits 0 and 1 by sensing different intensities of light and dark. The scanner shines a beam of light on the picture being scanned. The beam passes back and forth across the picture, sending a digitized signal to the computer's memory. A **digitized signal** is the conversion of input, such as the lines in a drawing, into a series of discrete units represented by the binary digits 0 and 1. **Scanned pictures** are bitmap pictures and have jagged edges. The jagged edges are caused by the individual pixels that create the picture. Bitmap graphics also are known as **raster images**. Additionally, bitmap files cannot be ungrouped into smaller object groups.

The other graphic format in which pictures are stored is vector graphics. A **vector graphic** is a piece of art that has been created by a drawing program such as CorelDRAW! or AutoCAD. Vector graphic objects are created as a collection of lines instead of patterns of individual dots (pixels), as are bitmap graphics. Vector graphic files store data either as picture descriptions or as calculations. These files describe a picture mathematically as a set of instructions for creating the objects in the picture. These mathematical descriptions determine the position, length, and direction in which the lines are to be drawn. These calculations allow the drawing program to re-create the picture on the screen as necessary. Because vector graphic objects are described mathematically, they also can be layered, rotated, and magnified with relative ease. Vector graphics also are known as **object-oriented pictures**. Clip art pictures in the Microsoft Clip Gallery that have the file extension of **.wmf** are examples of vector files. Vector files can be ungrouped and manipulated by their component objects.

PowerPoint allows you to insert vector files because it uses **graphic filters** to convert the various graphic formats into a format PowerPoint can use. These filters are installed with the initial PowerPoint installation or can be added later by running the Setup program.

The Internet Training presentation will be used to help Net-Train market its seminar in Park City, Utah, so you want to emphasize the beautiful mountain scenery. To create the desired effect, you insert a picture of mountains to cover the Contemporary Portrait design template.

Perform the following steps to create a custom background.

More *About* **Graphic Filters**

PowerPoint allows you to directly insert many graphic file formats in your presentation. No separate filter is needed for these graphics types: Enhanced Metafile (.emf), Joint Photographic Experts Group (.jpg), Portable Network Graphics (.png), Windows Bitmap (.bmp, .rle, .dib), and Windows Metafile (.wmf). A separate filter is needed for all other file formats.

More *About* **Adding Colors**

A maximum of eight additional colors you have added will display on the Line Color list. If you select additional colors, the more recent ones display and the oldest ones drop off.

 Steps **To Insert a Picture to Create a Custom Background**

1 **Right-click anywhere on Slide 1 except the title object or subtitle object. Click Background on the shortcut menu. When the Background dialog box displays, point to the down arrow in the Background fill area.**

The Background dialog box displays (Figure 3-10).

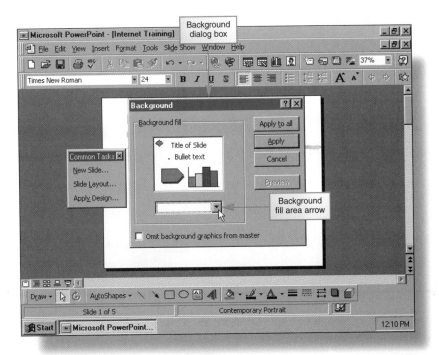

FIGURE 3-10

2 **Click the down arrow. When the list displays, point to Fill Effects.**

The list contains options for filling the slide background (Figure 3-11). The current background fill is Automatic, which is the Contemporary Portrait design template default. Fill Effects is highlighted.

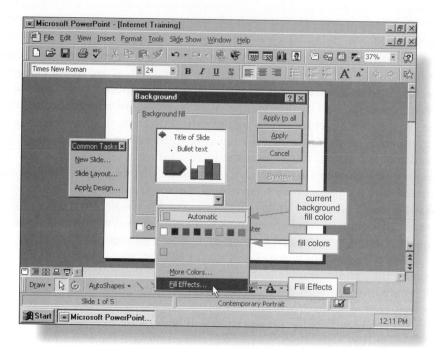

FIGURE 3-11

3 **Click Fill Effects. Click the Picture tab and then click the Select Picture button. Click the Preview button if it is not recessed. Click Mountains in the list box.**

The Select Picture dialog box displays (Figure 3-12). The Preview button is recessed. The selected file, Mountains, displays in the preview box.

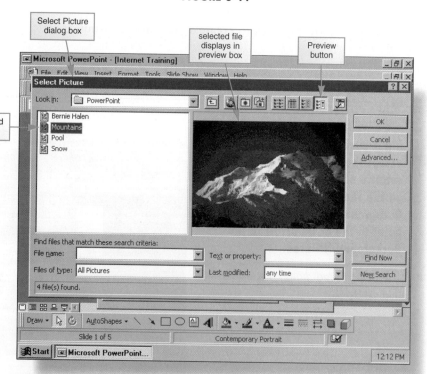

FIGURE 3-12

4 Click the OK button. When the Fill Effects dialog box displays, click the OK button. When the Background dialog box displays, point to the Apply to all button.

The Background dialog box displays the Mountains picture in the Background fill area (Figure 3-13a).

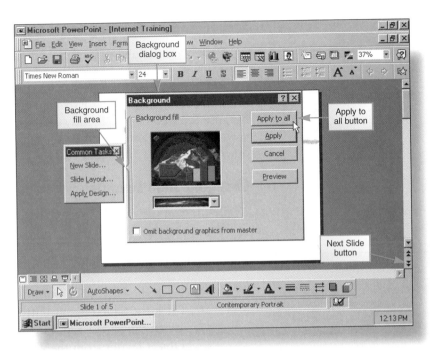

FIGURE 3-13a

5 Click the Apply to all button.

Slide 1 displays the Mountains picture as the slide background (Figure 3-13b). Although not shown in this figure, the Mountains picture is the background for all slides in the presentation. The Contemporary Portrait design template text attributes display on the slide.

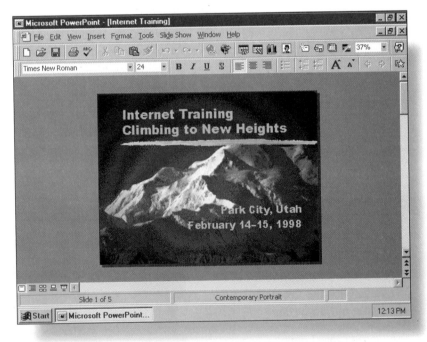

FIGURE 3-13b

When you customize the background, the design template text attributes remain the same, but the slide background changes. For example, inserting the Mountains picture for the slide background changes the appearance of the slide background but maintains the text attributes of the Contemporary Portrait design template.

The next section explains how to embed an Excel chart into the presentation.

Embedding an Existing Excel Chart

PowerPoint allows you to embed many types of objects into a presentation. In this project, you embed an existing Excel chart into the slide. The Excel chart is located in the PowerPoint folder on the Data Disk that accompanies this book.

Embedding an existing Excel chart is similar to embedding other objects. Because the Excel chart already exists, you must retrieve it from the file in which it was saved instead of opening the supplementary application and creating the object. Then you embed and edit the Excel chart.

Changing Slide Layouts

Before you embed the Excel chart, you need to display Slide 2 and change the slide layout to the Object layout.

OtherWays

1. Move scroll bar elevator downward to display Object layout, double-click Object layout

TO DISPLAY THE NEXT SLIDE AND CHANGE THE SLIDE LAYOUT

1. Click the Next Slide button to display Slide 2.
2. Click the Slide Layout button on the Common Tasks toolbar.
3. When the Slide Layout dialog box displays, type 16 to select the Object layout from the 24 available AutoLayouts. Click the Apply button.

Slide 2 displays the slide title and subtitle object.

Slide 2 now displays the title of the slide and a subtitle object. The next section explains how to embed an Excel chart.

Embedding an Excel Chart

The next step in modifying the PowerPoint object for Slide 2 is to embed an Excel chart. The Excel chart already is created and saved on the Data Disk. The following steps explain how to embed an existing Excel chart.

Steps To Embed an Excel Chart

1. **Double-click the object placeholder in the middle of Slide 2. Click the Create from file option button.**

The Insert Object dialog box displays (Figure 3-14). Drive A is the current drive and PowerPoint is the current folder.

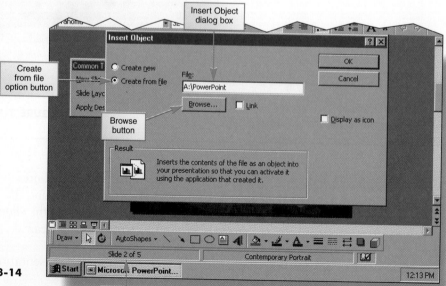

FIGURE 3-14

Slide 2 of 5

2 Click the Browse button. When the Browse dialog box displays, click Internet Use.

The Browse dialog box displays the files in the PowerPoint folder on the Data Disk (Figure 3-15). Internet Use is the Excel file you will embed into Slide 2, and it displays in the preview box.

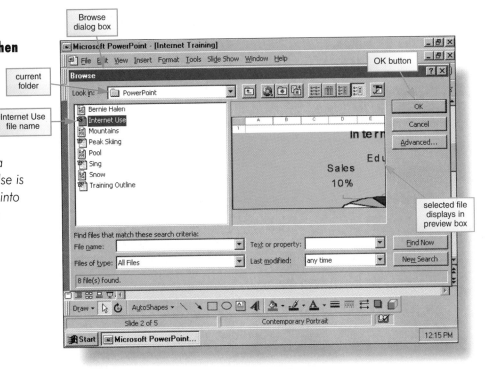

FIGURE 3-15

3 Click the OK button. When the Insert Object dialog box displays, point to the OK button.

The Insert Object dialog box now displays A:\PowerPoint\Internet Use.xls in the File text box (Figure 3-16).

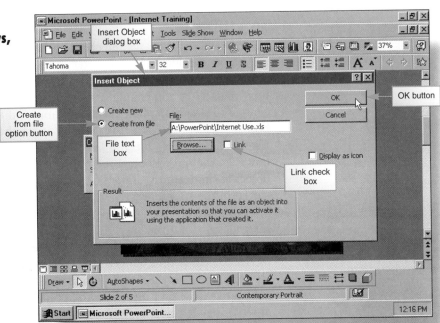

FIGURE 3-16

4 **Click the OK button.**

After a short time, Slide 2 displays a blue rectangle, which is part of the background of the Internet Use Pie chart (Figure 3-17).

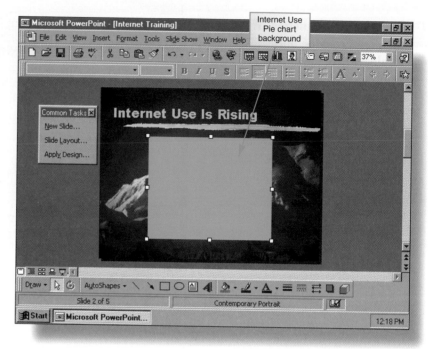

FIGURE 3-17

More *About*
Embedding Visuals

If you embed a chart or photograph obtained from another source, you should acknowledge this source either on the slide or when you verbally give the presentation. The same plagiarism rules apply to slide shows and written documents.

PowerPoint displays the chart in the middle of Slide 2 because you did not have a placeholder selected. Later in this project, you will edit the chart.

When you click the Create from file option button in the Insert Object dialog box, the dialog box changes. The File box replaces the Object type box. Another change to the dialog box is the addition of the **Link check box**. If the Link check box is selected, the object is inserted as a linked, instead of an embedded, object. Like an embedded object, a **linked object** also is created in another application; however, the linked object maintains a connection to its source. If the original object is changed, the linked object on the slide also changes. The linked object is stored in the source file where it was created.

For example, the Excel chart you inserted into the slide is stored in the Internet Use file from the PowerPoint folder on the Data Disk that accompanies this book. If you were to link the Internet Use file to your presentation, every time the Internet Use file changed in Excel, the changes would display on the chart in Slide 2. Your PowerPoint presentation stores a representation of the original Internet Use file and information about its location. Therefore, if later you move or delete the source file, the link will be broken, and the object will not be available. Hence, if you make a presentation on a computer other than the one on which the presentation was created and the presentation contains linked objects, be certain to include a copy of the source files. The source files must be stored in the exact location as originally specified when you linked them to your presentation.

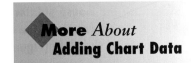

When you select a source file from the Browse dialog box, PowerPoint associates the file with a specific application, which is based on the file extension. For example, if you select a source file with the file extension .DOC, PowerPoint recognizes the file as a Microsoft Word file. Additionally, if you select a source file with the file extension **.xls**, PowerPoint recognizes the file as a Microsoft Excel file.

Slide 2 now displays the title of the slide and the upper-left corner of the embedded Internet Use Pie chart object. The next section explains how to edit the Excel chart so the entire chart object displays.

Editing an Excel Chart

The next step in creating Slide 2 is to edit the embedded Excel Pie chart. The following steps explain how to edit the embedded Excel chart object.

 Steps To Edit an Embedded Excel Chart

1 **Double-click the blue rectangle in the center of the slide, which is the upper-left corner of the Internet Use Pie chart object. Point to the right center sizing handle on the right side of the object.**

PowerPoint starts Excel and opens the Internet Use Pie chart object for editing (Figure 3-18). The mouse pointer displays as a two-headed arrow.

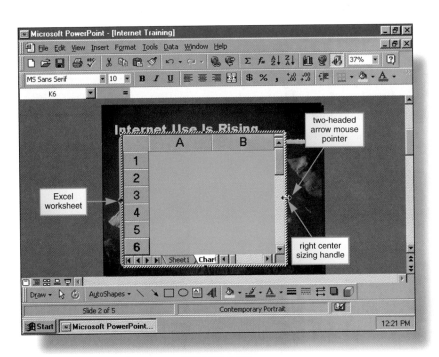

FIGURE 3-18

2 Drag the mouse pointer to the black border along the right edge of the slide (Figure 3-19).

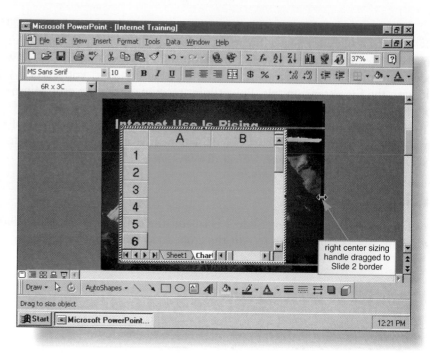

FIGURE 3-19

3 Click anywhere along the right edge of the Excel object border, which looks like rope (Figure 3-20a).

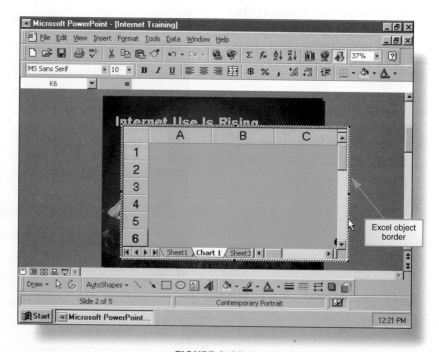

FIGURE 3-20a

4 **Click anywhere on the slide other than the Excel chart.**

The Excel Pie chart displays in Slide 2 (Figure 3-20b).

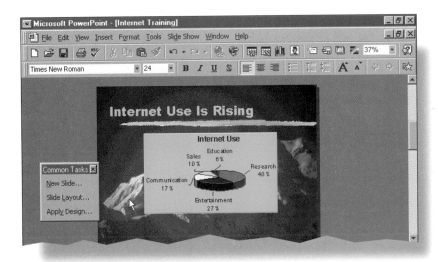

FIGURE 3-20b

You now will position the Excel chart object in a more desirable area of the slide.

Positioning an Embedded Object

Now that the Excel Pie chart object displays in its entirety, you need to move it downward to a more central area of the slide. The steps on the next page explain how to position the embedded Excel chart object.

 To Position an Embedded Excel Chart Object

1 **Right-click the Internet Use Pie chart object. Click Format Object on the shortcut menu.**

2 **Click the Position tab in the Format Object dialog box. Triple-click the Horizontal text box in the Position on slide area. Type 1.9 and then triple-click the Vertical text box in the Position on slide area. Type 2.8 as the entry.**

The Format Object dialog box displays (Figure 3-21a). The upper-left corner of the Internet Use Pie chart object will be positioned at 1.9 inches to the right of the top left corner and 2.8 inches down from the top of the slide.

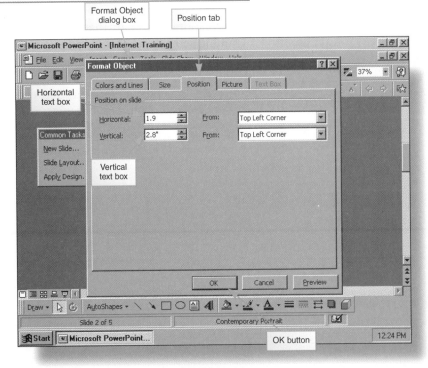

FIGURE 3-21a

3 **Click the OK button. Click above or to the left of the Pie chart.**

The Excel Pie chart object displays in the center of Slide 2 (Figure 3-21b).

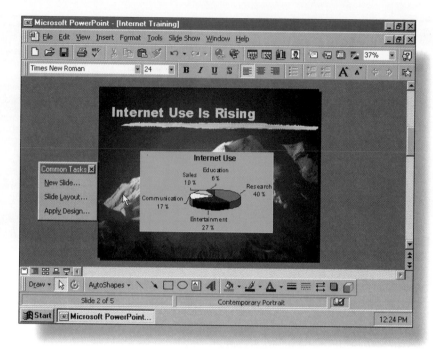

FIGURE 3-21b

PowerPoint displays the embedded chart in the center of Slide 2. This slide is now complete. The next section describes how to embed an organization chart in a slide.

Creating and Embedding an Organization Chart

Slide 3 contains a chart that elaborates on the daily schedule for the Internet Training seminar as shown in Figure 3-22. This type of chart is called an **organization chart**, which is a hierarchical collection of elements depicting various functions or responsibilities that contribute to an organization or to a collective function. Typically, an organization chart is used to show the structure of people or departments within an organization, hence the name, organization chart.

Figure 3-23 illustrates how a company uses an organization chart to describe the relationships between the company's departments. In the information sciences, organization charts often are used to show the decomposition of a process or program. When used in this manner, the chart is called a **hierarchy chart**.

PowerPoint contains a supplementary application called **Microsoft Organization Chart 2.0** that allows you to create an organization chart. When you open Microsoft Organization Chart, its menus, buttons, and tools are available to you directly in the PowerPoint window. Microsoft Organization Chart is an object linking and embedding (OLE) application. The organization chart you create for Slide 3 (Figure 3-22) is an embedded object because it is created in an application other than PowerPoint.

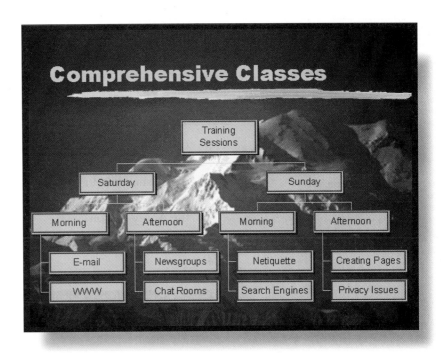

FIGURE 3-22

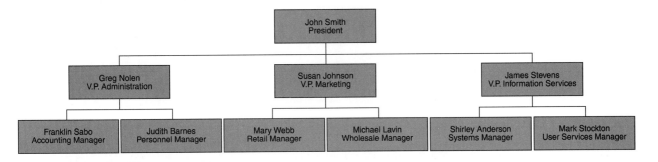

FIGURE 3-23

Creating an organization chart requires several steps. First, you display the slide that will contain the organization chart in Slide View and change the AutoLayout to the Organization Chart layout. Then, you open the Microsoft Organization Chart application. Finally, you enter and format the contents of the boxes in the organization chart window.

Perform the steps on the following pages to create the organization chart for this project.

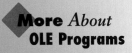

More *About*
OLE Programs

When you install PowerPoint, you install four OLE programs to help you create embedded objects. Microsoft Organization Chart 2.0, Microsoft Photo Editor 3.0 Photo, Microsoft Graph 97 Chart, and Microsoft Equation 3.0 (Equation Editor) all allow you to share information between programs. To verify these programs exist on your system, click Object on the Insert menu, and then scroll down through the Object type list.

Changing Slide Layouts

Before you open Microsoft Organization Chart 2.0, you need to display Slide 3 and change the AutoLayout to the Organization Chart layout.

TO DISPLAY THE NEXT SLIDE AND CHANGE THE SLIDE LAYOUT

1️⃣ Click the Next Slide button.

2️⃣ Click the Slide Layout button on the Common Tasks toolbar.

3️⃣ When the Slide Layout dialog box displays, type 7 to select the Organization Chart layout from the 24 available AutoLayouts. Click the Apply button.

Slide 3 displays the organization chart placeholder and the slide title (Figure 3-24).

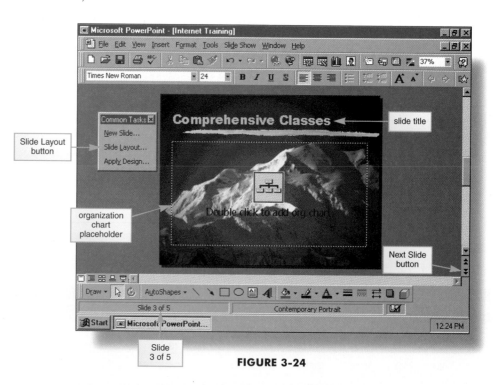

FIGURE 3-24

Slide 3 now displays the placeholder for the organization chart. The next section explains how to open the Microsoft Organization Chart application.

Opening the Microsoft Organization Chart Application

To create the organization chart on Slide 3, you first must open the organization chart application, Microsoft Organization Chart 2.0, which is included within PowerPoint. Recall that when this supplementary application is active, the menus, buttons, and tools in the organization chart application are made available in the PowerPoint window. Once active, Microsoft Organization Chart displays a sample four-box organization chart in a work area in the middle of the PowerPoint window, as explained in the following step.

Steps To Open Microsoft Organization Chart

1 **Double-click the Organization Chart placeholder in the middle of Slide 3.**

Organization Chart displays the Microsoft Organization Chart - [Object in Internet Training] window in a work area in the PowerPoint window (Figure 3-25). Notice the sample organization chart is composed of four boxes connected by lines. When Microsoft Organization Chart is active, the first line of the top box automatically is selected. Depending on the version of Microsoft Organization Chart installed on your computer, the display on the screen may vary slightly.

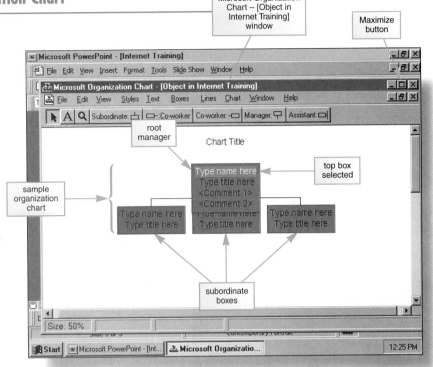

FIGURE 3-25

Microsoft Organization Chart displays a sample organization chart to help you create your chart. The sample is composed of one **manager box**, located at the top of the chart, and three **subordinate boxes**. A manager box has one or more subordinates. The topmost manager is called the **root manager**. A subordinate box is located at a level lower than its manager. A subordinate box has only one manager. When a lower-level subordinate box is added to a higher-level subordinate box, the higher-level subordinate box becomes the manager of the lower-level subordinate box.

Maximizing the Microsoft Organization Chart Window

When Microsoft Organization Chart is active, the Microsoft Organization Chart window is not maximized. Maximizing the Microsoft Organization Chart window makes it easier to create your organization chart because it displays a larger area in which to view the chart.

TO MAXIMIZE THE MICROSOFT ORGANIZATION CHART WINDOW

1 Click the Maximize button in the upper-right corner of the Microsoft Organization Chart window.

The Microsoft Organization Chart window fills the desktop. Clicking the Restore button returns the Microsoft Organization Chart window to its original size.

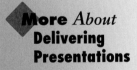

More *About*
Delivering Presentations

If you are delivering your PowerPoint presentation in front of a group, consider using a laser pointer to direct the audience's attention to objects projected on the screen. Some laser pointer models have dot, underline, and arrow images. Other features are clocks and countdown timers that beep at set intervals, such as five minutes prior to the scheduled slide show ending time.

Creating the Title for the Root Manager Box

In this presentation, the organization chart is used to communicate the daily training schedule. The topmost box, the root manager, identifies the purpose of this organization chart: Comprehensive Classes. Recall that when Microsoft Organization Chart became active, the first line in the root manager box was selected. The following step explains how to create the title for the root manager box.

Steps **To Create the Title for the Root Manager Box**

1 **Type** Training **in the root manager box on level one and then press the ENTER key. Type** Sessions **on the second line.**

Training Sessions displays in the root manager box (Figure 3-26). <Comment 1> and <Comment 2> prompts display in brackets under the root manager box title.

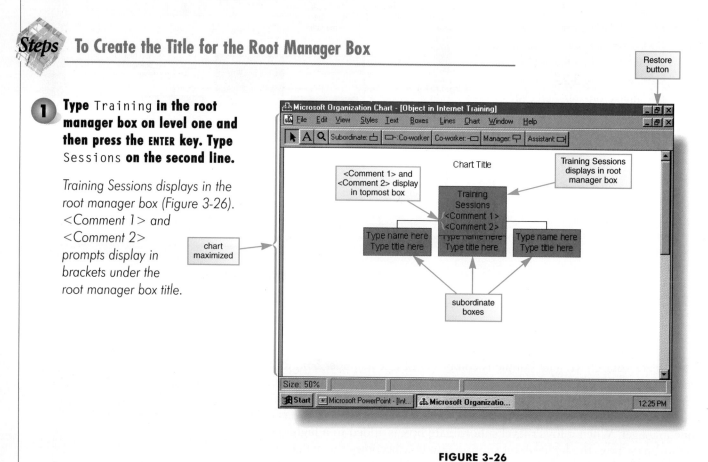

FIGURE 3-26

Deleting Subordinate Boxes

The organization chart in this presentation has two boxes on level 2 immediately below the root manager. The schedules for both days of the training are similar, so you create the schedule for Saturday, copy it, and make editing changes. Before proceeding with the remaining boxes for Saturday, you want to delete the level 2 unnecessary boxes as shown in the following steps.

Steps To Delete Subordinate Boxes

1 Click the level 2 middle subordinate box located directly under the root manager box.

2 Press and hold the SHIFT key. Then click the rightmost subordinate box in level 2. Release the SHIFT key.

The middle and right subordinate boxes are selected (Figure 3-27). <Comment 1> and <Comment 2> do not display in the root manager box because text was not entered at their prompts. Name and title prompts, however, display in the subordinate boxes without entering text at their prompts. The technique of selecting more than one object by pressing and holding the SHIFT key while clicking the objects is called SHIFT+click.

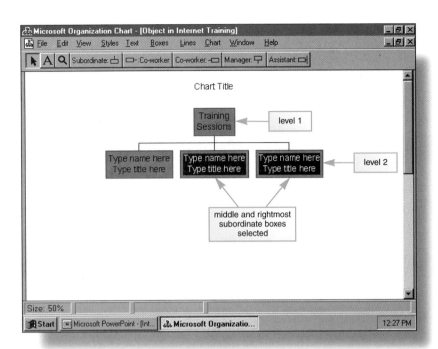

FIGURE 3-27

3 Press the DELETE key.

Microsoft Organization Chart displays two boxes: the root manager and one subordinate (Figure 3-28).

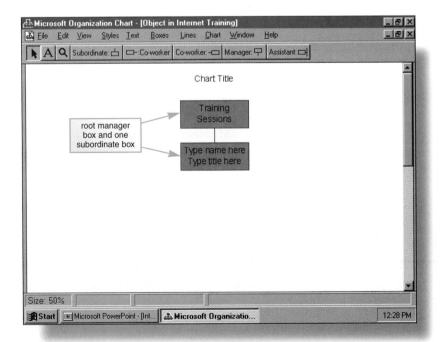

FIGURE 3-28

Titling the Subordinate Box

The process of adding a title to a subordinate box is the same as adding the title to the root manager box except that you first must select the subordinate box. The following step explains how to title a subordinate box.

 Steps   To Title a Subordinate Box

1 **Click the subordinate box. Type** Saturday **and then press the** ENTER **key. Press the** DELETE **key.**

Saturday displays as the title for the subordinate box (Figure 3-29). You pressed the DELETE *key because only one line of text is needed.*

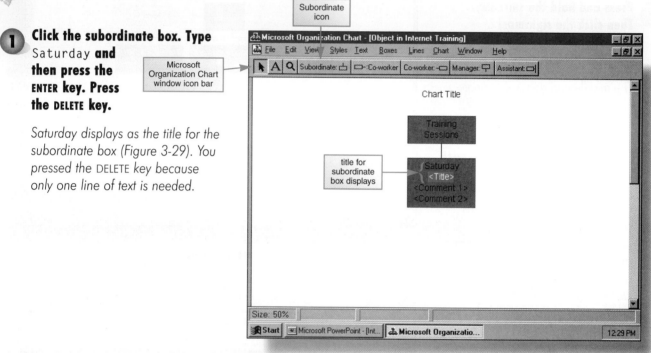

FIGURE 3-29

Adding Subordinate Boxes

Microsoft Organization Chart has five **types of boxes** you can add to a chart. Each box type has a corresponding **box tool** on the Microsoft Organization Chart window **icon bar**. Because the daily activities for the workshop in this project are divided into morning and afternoon sessions, you need to add two subordinate boxes to Saturday's schedule.

To add a single subordinate box, click the **Subordinate icon** and then click the box on the organization chart to which the subordinate reports. When you want to add several subordinate boxes, you can click the Subordinate icon once for each box you want to add to the organization chart. For example, if you want to add two subordinate boxes, click the Subordinate icon two times. If the Subordinate icon is recessed and you decide not to add subordinate boxes, you can deselect the Subordinate icon by clicking the Selection Arrow icon on the Microsoft Organization Chart window icon bar or pressing the ESC key.

The following steps explain how to use the Subordinate box tool to add two subordinate boxes to the Saturday box.

Steps **To Add Multiple Subordinate Boxes**

1 **Click the Subordinate icon on the Microsoft Organization Chart window icon bar two times. Point to the Saturday box.**

The Subordinate icon is recessed (Figure 3-30). The status bar displays the number of subordinate boxes Microsoft Organization Chart is creating, which is two. The mouse pointer shape changes to a subordinate box.

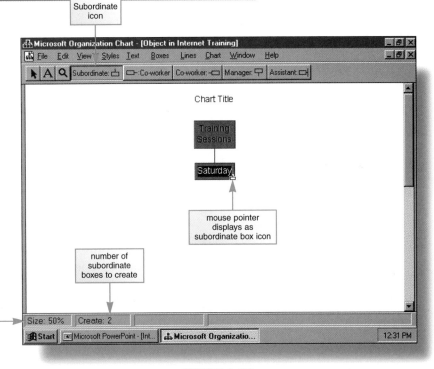

FIGURE 3-30

2 **Click the Saturday box.**

Two subordinate boxes display below the Saturday box (Figure 3-31). The new subordinate boxes display one level lower than the box to which they are attached. Saturday is now the manager to the new subordinate boxes. The left subordinate box on level 3 is selected.

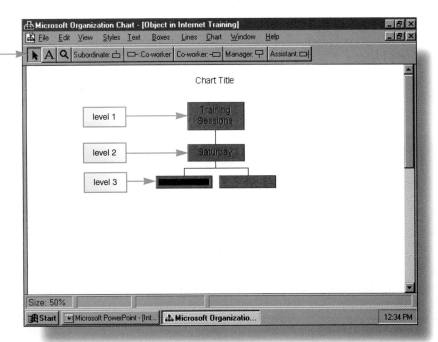

FIGURE 3-31

Adding Another Level of Subordinate Boxes

To further develop the organization chart in this project, you need to add a fourth level of subordinate boxes for the workshop sessions. This workshop presents two classes during the morning session and two classes during the afternoon session. Workshop participants must decide which four-hour class they want to attend. For example, a participant can attend the E-mail session on Saturday morning and then attend the Netiquette session on Sunday morning. The same decision will need to be made for the afternoon sessions.

The following steps summarize adding multiple subordinate boxes to a higher-level box.

TO ADD ANOTHER LEVEL OF SUBORDINATE BOXES

1. Click the Subordinate icon on the icon bar two times, and then click the left subordinate box on level 3.
2. Click the Subordinate icon two times, and then click the right subordinate box on level 3.

Two subordinate boxes display under each level 3 subordinate box (Figure 3-32).

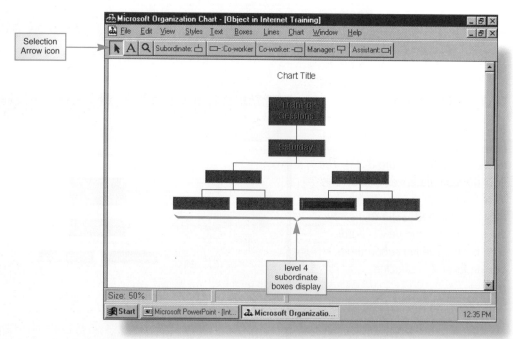

FIGURE 3-32

The structure of the organization chart is complete. The next step is to add titles to the boxes in the chart.

Adding Names to the Subordinate Boxes

To complete the organization chart, you must add names to all boxes subordinate to the Saturday box. Before you can add the names, however, you must deactivate the Subordinate box tool and activate the Selection Arrow tool. When the **Selection Arrow tool** is active, the mouse pointer displays as a left-pointing block arrow. Because the subordinate boxes in this project have names but do not have titles, the Title, Comment 1, and Comment 2 prompts display in brackets under the box name when the box is selected. The brackets indicate the label is optional, and it displays only when replaced by text. The following steps summarize adding a title to each level 4 subordinate box.

TO ADD NAMES TO SUBORDINATE BOXES

① Click the left subordinate box on level 3. Type Morning in the subordinate box.

② Click the right subordinate box on level 3. Type Afternoon in the subordinate box.

③ Click the left subordinate box under the Morning box. Type E-mail in the subordinate box.

④ Click the right subordinate box under the Morning box. Type WWW in the subordinate box.

⑤ Click the left subordinate box under the Afternoon box. Type Newsgroups in the subordinate box.

⑥ Click the right subordinate box under the Afternoon box. Type Chat Rooms in the subordinate box.

All level 4 subordinate boxes under the Saturday box display session names (Figure 3-33).

> ◆**M**ore *About*
> **Text**
>
> Avoid using all capital letters in your slides. If you use more than seven consecutive words in uppercase letters, most audience members will need to read the slide a second time.

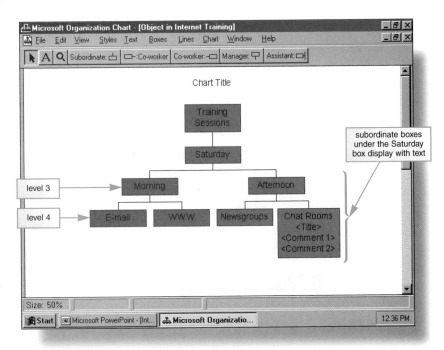

FIGURE 3-33

Changing Organization Chart Styles

Now that the boxes for the Saturday branch are labeled, you want to change the way the organization chart looks. With the addition of each new box, the chart expanded horizontally. Before you add Sunday's schedule, you must change the style of selected boxes from horizontal to vertical.

Steps To Change the Organization Chart Style

1 **Click anywhere outside the Organization Chart boxes. Press and hold the SHIFT key. Click the four lowest-level boxes: E-mail, WWW, Newsgroups, and Chat Rooms. Release the SHIFT key.**

The four lowest-level boxes are selected (Figure 3-34).

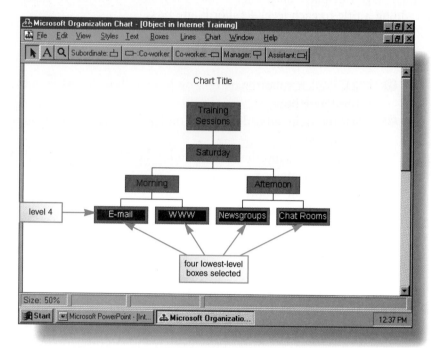

FIGURE 3-34

2 **Click Styles on the menu bar and then point to the vertical style icon (row 1, column 2) in the top set of Groups styles.**

The default group style is selected, which is indicated by the recessed icon (Figure 3-35). The verticle style icon is highlighted. The Styles menu icons allow you to change the arrangement of boxes in your chart. The top set of styles changes the arrangement of boxes in a group. The middle style creates assistant boxes. The bottom style is used to show co-managers.

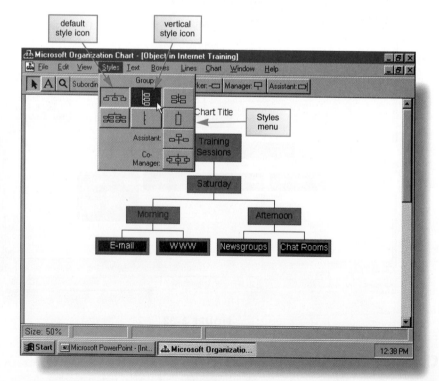

FIGURE 3-35

3 **Click the vertical style icon.**

The organization chart displays the two morning sessions and the two afternoon sessions vertically (Figure 3-36). The Morning box and the Afternoon box still display horizontally under the Saturday box because only the selected boxes change styles.

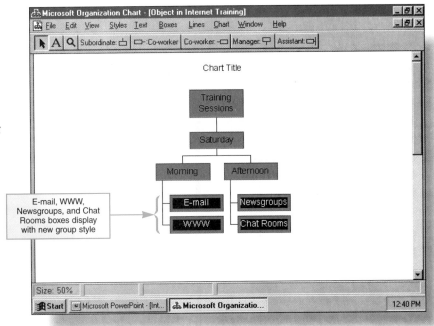

FIGURE 3-36

If you select the wrong group style or decide to retain the previous style, immediately click Undo Chart Style on the Edit menu.

Copying a Branch of an Organization Chart

Saturday's schedule is complete, and Sunday's schedule is similar. Instead of creating Sunday's schedule by adding and labeling boxes, you can copy Saturday's schedule and add it under the Training Sessions box. When you work with a whole section of an organization chart, it is referred to as working with a branch, or an appendage, of the chart. The following steps explain how to copy a branch of the chart.

More *About*
**Delivering
Presentations**

Use the "one-person-per-two-inch-rule" when deciding the maximum number of audience members who should view your slide show on a monitor. One person can comfortably view the screen for every two diagonal inches on the monitor. For example, 16 people can be seated comfortably around a 32-inch monitor.

Steps To Copy a Branch of an Organization Chart

1 Press and hold the SHIFT key. Click the Saturday box, the Morning box, and the Afternoon box. If not already selected, click the E-mail box, the WWW box, the Newsgroups box, and the Chat Rooms box. Release the SHIFT key (Figure 3-37).

2 Right-click one of the selected boxes and then click Copy on the shortcut menu.

*Microsoft Organization Chart copies the Saturday branch of the organization chart to the Clipboard. Recall that the **Clipboard** is a temporary Windows storage area.*

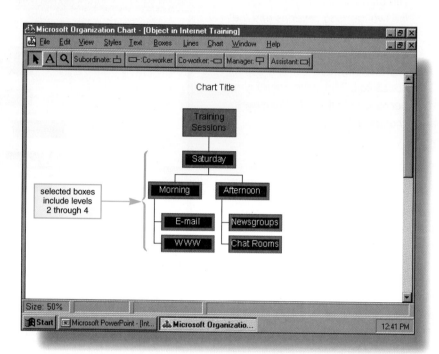

FIGURE 3-37

The next section explains how to paste the Saturday branch of the organization chart to another location on the chart.

Pasting a Branch of an Organization Chart

Now that a copy of the Saturday branch of the organization chart is on the Clipboard, the next step is to paste it from the Clipboard to the Comprehensive Classes slide.

Steps To Paste a Branch of an Organization Chart

1 Right-click the root manager box labeled Training Sessions and then point to Paste Boxes on the shortcut menu.

Paste Boxes is highlighted on the shortcut menu (Figure 3-38). The Training Sessions box is selected.

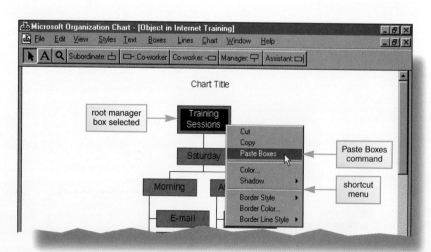

FIGURE 3-38

2 Click Paste Boxes on the shortcut menu.

The organization chart displays two Saturday branches (Figure 3-39).

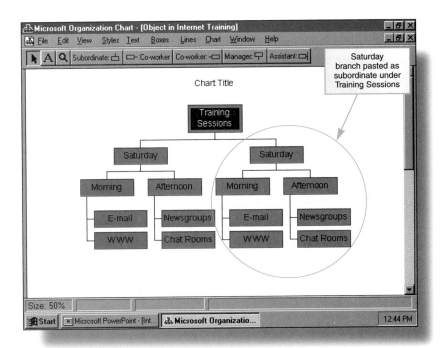

FIGURE 3-39

Editing an Organization Chart

After you have copied and pasted a branch of the organization chart, you need to **edit** the title of the first subordinate level so it displays as Sunday. You also need to edit the four sessions scheduled for Sunday. Editing a box requires you first to select the box and then make your edits.

 Steps To Edit Text in an Organization Chart

1 Click the Saturday box at the top of the right branch of the organization chart. Type Sunday in the subordinate box.

The word Sunday replaces the word Saturday (Figure 3-40).

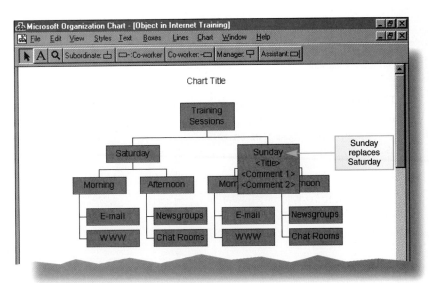

FIGURE 3-40

2 Click the E-mail box under the Sunday morning branch of the organization chart. Type Netiquette **in the subordinate box. For the other Sunday classes, type** Creating Pages **to replace Newsgroups, type** Search Engines **to replace WWW, and type** Privacy Issues **to replace Chat Rooms. Click anywhere outside the organization chart boxes.**

The Sunday training sessions schedule is revised (Figure 3-41).

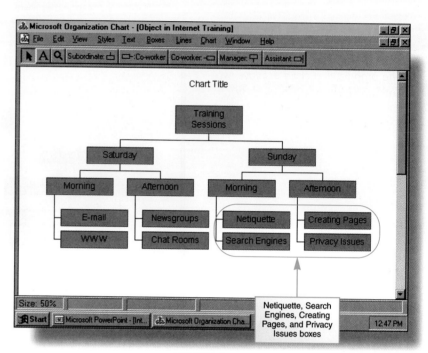

FIGURE 3-41

The text on the organization chart is complete. The next section explains how to format an organization chart.

Formatting an Organization Chart

Microsoft Organization Chart allows you to format a box simply by selecting it. To make your organization chart look like the chart shown in Figure 3-22 on page PP 3.25, you must add shadow effects and a border to every box. Then, you change the color of the boxes and the lines connecting the boxes. The following sections explain how to select all the boxes in the chart, change the box attributes to shadow and border, and then change the color of the organization chart boxes and lines.

More About
Color Choices

Black and white visuals usually are the least effective color choices for holding an audience's attention. Black absorbs light and pulls the eye into the visual, whereas white reflects light and causes the audience to look away. If you need to use black and white visuals, use as few words as possible and display the slide for a brief time.

Steps **To Select All Boxes in an Organization Chart**

1 **Click Edit on the menu bar, point to Select, and then point to All (Figure 3-42).**

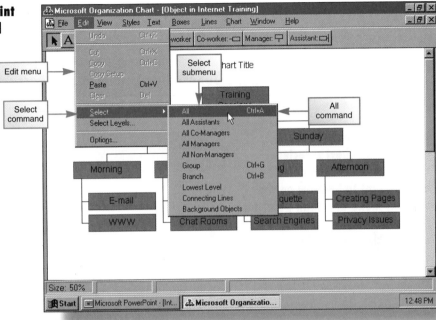

FIGURE 3-42

2 **Click All on the submenu.**

Microsoft Organization Chart selects all the boxes in the chart (Figure 3-43).

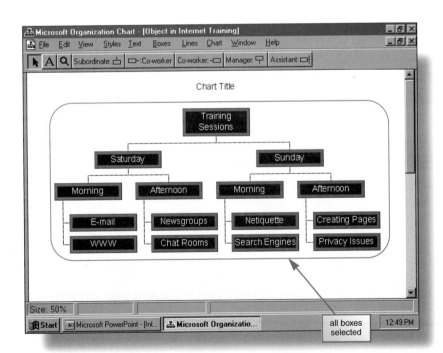

FIGURE 3-43

OtherWays

1. Press CTRL+A

Adding Shadow Effects to the Boxes in an Organization Chart

Now that all the boxes are selected, you can add shadow effects. Microsoft Organization Chart has eight shadow effects from which to choose. One style is None, which has no shadow. The following steps explain how to add shadow effects to all the boxes in an organization chart.

Steps **To Add Shadow Effects to the Boxes in an Organization Chart**

① **With all the boxes in the organization chart selected, right-click one of the selected boxes. Point to Shadow on the shortcut menu and then point to the shadow style in row 2, column 2 on the Shadow submenu.**

Microsoft Organization Chart displays the Shadow submenu (Figure 3-44). The default shadow style for Microsoft Organization Chart is None. The desired shadow style is highlighted.

② **Click the highlighted shadow style on the Shadow submenu.**

Microsoft Organization Chart adds the shadow effect to all the boxes in the organization chart.

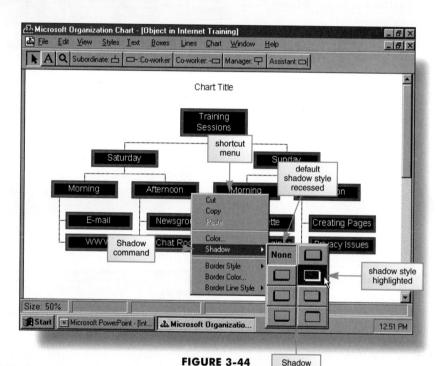

FIGURE 3-44

Changing Border Styles in an Organization Chart

To enhance the boxes in the organization chart, you must change the border style. Microsoft Organization Chart has 12 border styles from which to choose. One style is None, which has no border. The default border style is a thin line. The steps on the next page explain how to change border styles.

Steps **To Change the Border Style**

1 With all the boxes in the organization chart selected, right-click one of the selected boxes. Point to Border Style on the shortcut menu and then point to the border style in row 4, column 1 on the Border Style submenu.

Microsoft Organization Chart displays the Border Style submenu (Figure 3-45). The default border style for Microsoft Organization Chart is recessed in row 2, column 1. The desired border style is highlighted.

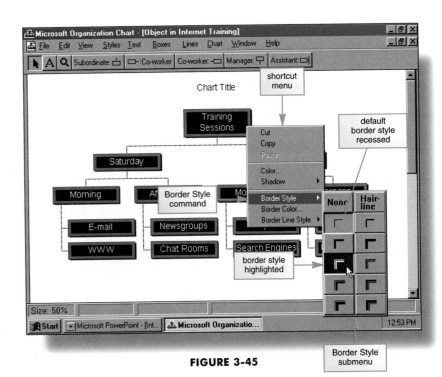

FIGURE 3-45

2 Click the highlighted border style on the Border Style submenu.

Microsoft Organization Chart applies the new border style to all the boxes in the organization chart.

Changing Box Color in an Organization Chart

To enhance the boxes in the organization chart, you need to change their color. Microsoft Organization Chart uses orange as the default box color, but you can choose 31 other colors. The following steps explain how to change box colors.

Steps To Change the Box Color

1 **With all the boxes in the organization chart still selected, right-click one of the selected boxes. Click Color on the shortcut menu.**

Microsoft Organization Chart displays the Color dialog box with a palette of 32 colors for the boxes (Figure 3-46). Orange is selected as the default box color.

2 **Point to the color gold in row 1, column 4.**

3 **Click the gold box and then click the OK button.**

Microsoft Organization Chart applies the new color to all boxes in the organization chart.

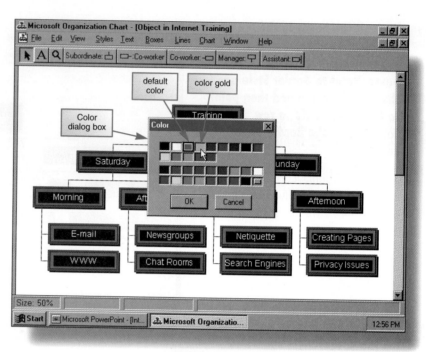

FIGURE 3-46

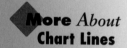 **More** *About* **Chart Lines**

Solid lines on an organization chart represent a formal chain of command between the boxes, as when one person is a direct supervisor of another person. On the other hand, dotted or dashed lines represent an open line of communication for reporting out of the chain of authority.

Changing Line Color in an Organization Chart

To enhance the lines connecting the boxes in the organization chart, you need to change their color. Microsoft Organization Chart uses black as the default line color, but you can choose 30 other colors. The steps on the next page explain how to change line colors.

Steps To Change the Line Color

1 With all the boxes in the organization chart still selected, click Lines on the menu bar and then click Color.

2 Click the color gold in row 1, column 4, which is the same color you selected for the box color. Click the OK button.

Microsoft Organization Chart applies the new color gold to all lines in the organization chart (Figure 3-47).

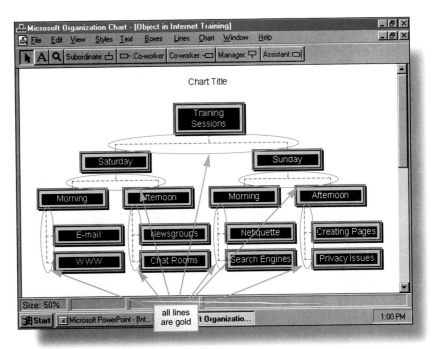

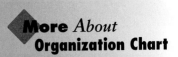

FIGURE 3-47

The organization chart now is complete. The next step is to return to the PowerPoint window.

Quitting Microsoft Organization Chart and Returning to the PowerPoint Window

After you create and format an organization chart, you quit Microsoft Organization Chart and return to the PowerPoint window. The steps on the next page explain how to return to the PowerPoint window.

More *About*
Organization Chart

If you want to modify your organization chart object after you have inserted it in your PowerPoint slide, just double-click it. PowerPoint will open Microsoft Organization Chart and allow you to make your changes. When you click the Close button, you will return to the PowerPoint window.

Steps To Quit Microsoft Organization Chart and Return to the PowerPoint Window

1 **Click the Close button on the Microsoft Organization Chart - [Object in Internet Training] title bar. When the Microsoft Organization Chart dialog box displays, point to the Yes button.**

The Microsoft Organization Chart dialog box warns you that the organization chart object has changed and asks you if you want to update the object in the PowerPoint presentation, Internet Training, before proceeding (Figure 3-48).

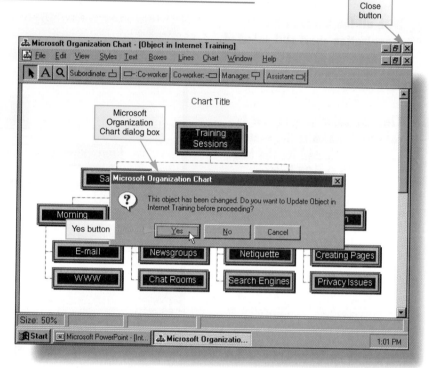

FIGURE 3-48

2 **Click the Yes button.**

Microsoft Organization Chart updates the organization chart object and closes, and then PowerPoint displays the organization chart on Slide 3 (Figure 3-49).

FIGURE 3-49

Scaling an Organization Chart Object

The organization chart on Slide 3 is sized to fit the Organization Chart placeholder. The organization chart would be easier to read if it were enlarged. The **Scale command** allows you to enlarge or reduce an object by very precise amounts while retaining the object's original proportions.

Perform the following steps to scale an organization chart object.

TO SCALE AN ORGANIZATION CHART OBJECT

1 Right-click the selected organization chart object and then click Format Object on the shortcut menu.

2 Click the Size tab. In the Scale area, triple-click the Height text box. Type 110 as the entry.

3 Click the OK button.

The organization chart is scaled to 110 percent of its original size (Figure 3-50).

D *Other* **Ways**

1. On Format menu click Object, click Size tab, type 110 in Scale Height text box, click OK button

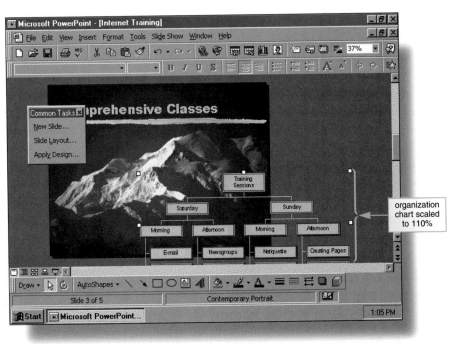

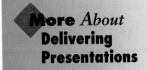

FIGURE 3-50

Moving the Organization Chart

Now that the organization chart is scaled to a readable size, you need to move it onto the slide. The following step explains how to move the organization chart.

▶ More *About* **Delivering Presentations**

Electronic presentations enhance our ability to remember information. Some studies estimate that when we communicate verbally without any visual cues, we misinterpret or forget as much as 75 percent of the information.

Steps **To Move the Organization Chart**

1 Drag the organization chart onto the middle of the blank area of Slide 3 (Figure 3-51).

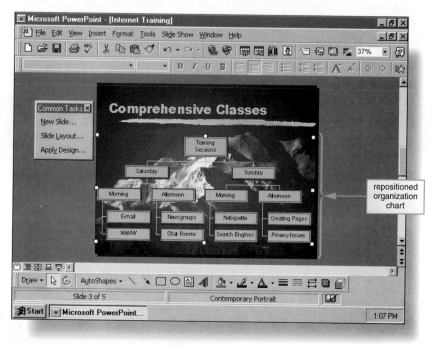

FIGURE 3-51

Slide 3 now is complete. The next section introduces you to moving text and embedding a picture into a slide.

FIGURE 3-52

Moving Text and Embedding a Picture into a Slide

Slide 4 is included in this presentation to inform prospective attendees that convenient lodging and social activities are included in their work-shop package. You list features of the weekend seminar package and insert a picture of the hotel and heated outdoor pool to reinforce that message. Another graphic object often inserted into a slide is a picture. Slide 4 contains a bulleted list and an embedded picture as shown in Figure 3-52. Recall that a **picture** is any graphic image from another application.

Moving Text in a Slide

The first step is to display the next slide and to move the bulleted list to the right side of the slide.

Perform these steps to move the text.

Steps **To Move Text in a Slide**

1 **Click the Next Slide button to display Slide 4.**

Slide 4 displays the Bulleted List layout (Figure 3-53).

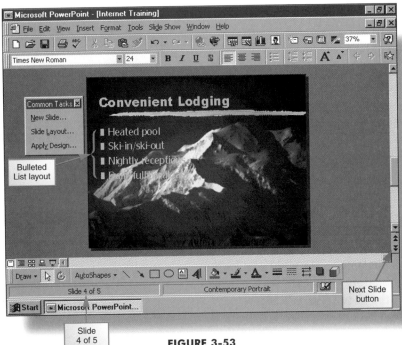

FIGURE 3-53

2 **Click any of the bulleted list text.**

All the text becomes highlighted and a border displays around the subtitle object (Figure 3-54).

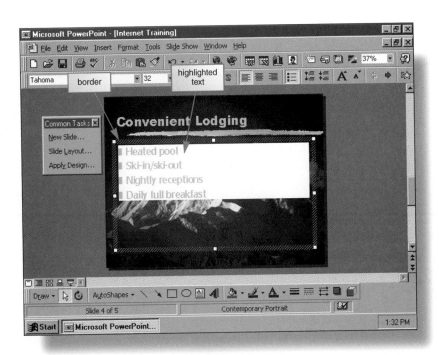

FIGURE 3-54

3 Click the bottom right fill handle and drag it diagonally so the border frames the text (Figure 3-55).

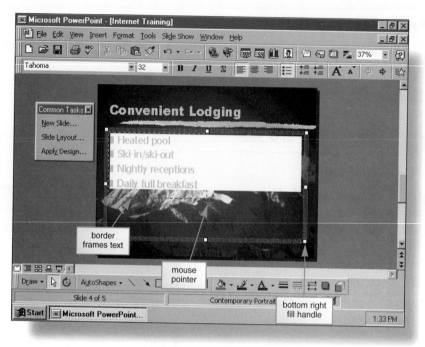

FIGURE 3-55

4 Point to the border around the subtitle object. Drag the border to the lower-right quadrant of the slide so the right and bottom borders align with the edges of the slide (Figure 3-56).

5 Click anywhere outside the box.

The border disappears.

FIGURE 3-56

Inserting a Picture

The picture you insert on Slide 4 is a scanned picture that has been stored as a bitmap graphic and saved as a TIF file. The Pool file is from the PowerPoint folder on the Data Disk that accompanies this book.

Perform the following steps to insert this picture.

To Insert a Picture

1 Click Insert on the menu bar, point to Picture, and then point to From File (Figure 3-57).

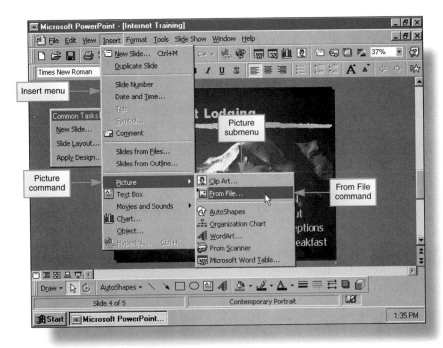

FIGURE 3-57

2 Click From File. When the Insert Picture dialog box displays, if necessary, click 3½ Floppy (A:) in the Look in box. Double-click Pool in the list box.

The Pool.tif file displays on Slide 4 (Figure 3-58).

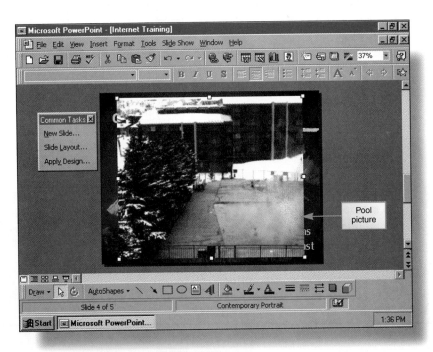

FIGURE 3-58

When the Insert Picture dialog box displays, PowerPoint does not require that you specify which format your picture is in. The default includes all the formats installed on your system that PowerPoint recognizes.

Resizing a Picture

PowerPoint automatically placed the picture in the middle of Slide 4 because a placeholder was not selected. To balance the text object and the picture, you must drag the picture to the left of the bulleted list. **Balance** means that the slide possesses a harmonious, or satisfying, arrangement of proportions of its objects. The height of the picture is not in balance with the bulleted text. To correct this, you need to change the proportions of the picture.

PowerPoint allows you to **constrain**, or control, resizing an object from its center by holding down the CTRL key while dragging a sizing handle. This method of constraining is called **resizing about center**.

Perform the following steps to resize a picture about its center.

Steps To Resize a Picture

1 **Point to the right center sizing handle on the right side of the picture.**

The mouse pointer shape changes to a two-headed arrow when it is positioned on a sizing handle (Figure 3-59).

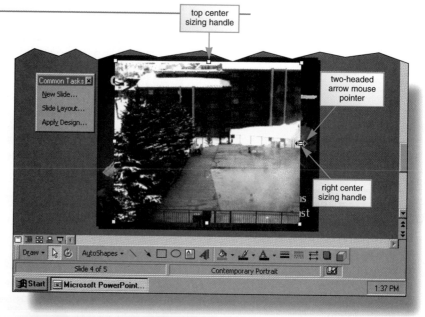

FIGURE 3-59

2 **Press and hold the CTRL key. Drag the mouse pointer inward toward the middle of the picture until the right edge of the picture aligns with the swimmer in the pool. Release the mouse button. Then, release the CTRL key (Figure 3-60).**

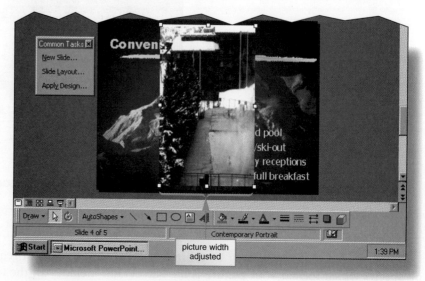

FIGURE 3-60

3 Point to the top center sizing handle. Press and hold the CTRL key. Drag the mouse pointer inward toward the middle of the picture until the top edge of the picture aligns with the bottom of the gold line at the top of the slide. Release the mouse button. Then, release the CTRL key.

The picture is resized about its center (Figure 3-61). Resize about center means changing the size of an object proportionally from its center.

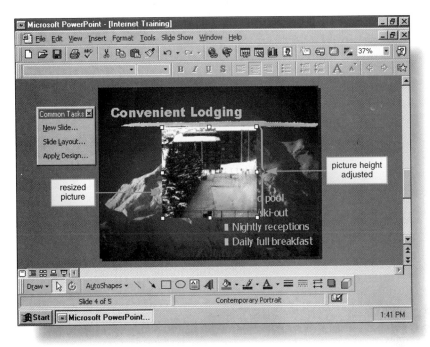

FIGURE 3-61

4 Drag the picture to the bottom-left corner of the slide (Figure 3-62).

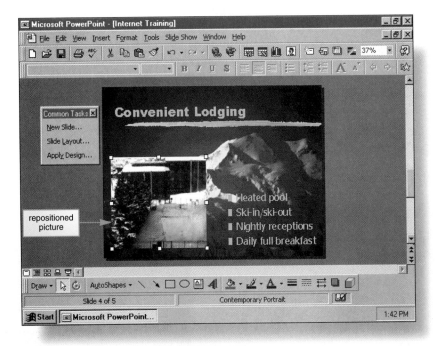

FIGURE 3-62

Caution should be exercised when resizing an object about its center. In Step 3, releasing the CTRL key before releasing the left mouse button does not resize about center; it resizes only the bottom of the picture. To correct this error, click the Undo button on the Standard toolbar and perform Steps 2 and 3 again, making certain first to release the mouse button and then release the CTRL key.

Table 3-1	
METHOD	*CONSTRAINING WITH RESIZING AN OBJECT*
SHIFT+drag a corner sizing handle	Resizes a selected object proportionally from a corner
CTRL+drag a sizing handle	Resizes a selected object vertically, horizontally, or diagonally from the center outward
CTRL+SHIFT+drag a corner sizing handle	Resizes a selected object proportionally from the center
ALT+drag a sizing handle	Resizes a selected object while temporarily overriding the settings for the grid and guides

PowerPoint has other methods of constraining objects when resizing. Table 3-1 explains the various constraining methods.

You can **restore** a resized object to its original proportions by selecting and then right-clicking the object to produce a shortcut menu. Click Format Picture on the shortcut menu, click the Size tab, click Reset in the Original size area, and then click the OK button.

Changing the size of the object can be achieved simply by dragging a sizing handle. This action resizes the picture in the direction toward which you drag. Dragging a sizing handle, however, changes the proportions of the picture. Recall that evenly resizing the object from a center point in the object is called resizing about center. This method of resizing the picture maintains the object's proportions.

Adding a Border to the Picture

The next step is to add a border to the picture. A **border** is the visible line around the edge of an object. The border draws attention to the object by defining its edges. A border has line style and line color attributes. The **line style** determines the line thickness and line appearance of the border. For example, you could choose a thick, solid line for your border. **Line color** determines the color of the line that forms the border. The picture illustrated in Figure 3-52 on page PP 3.46 has a three-line white border.

Perform these steps to format the picture by adding a three-line border.

Steps **To Add a Border to a Picture**

1 **Verify the picture is selected. Click the Line Style button on the Drawing toolbar.**

The Line Style list displays (Figure 3-63).

2 **Click the last line style in the list, which is the 6 pt thin-thick-thin three-line style.**

A three-line style displays around the picture.

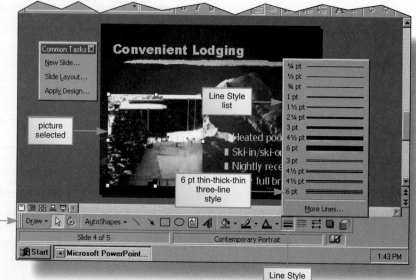

FIGURE 3-63

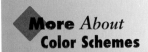

Changing the Border Line Color

To draw the attention of the audience to the picture, you can add color to the lines of the border. Recall that the design template establishes the attributes of the title master and the slide master. When you click the Line Color button arrow on the Drawing toolbar, a list displays line colors. A portion of the list contains the eight colors used to create the design template. One of the colors is identified as the line color and is labeled Automatic.

Perform the following steps to add the Contemporary Portrait design template default line color to the border around the picture on Slide 4.

 Steps **To Change the Border Line Color**

1 **Click the Line Color button arrow on the Drawing toolbar.**

The Line Color list displays (Figure 3-64a). The current line color is black.

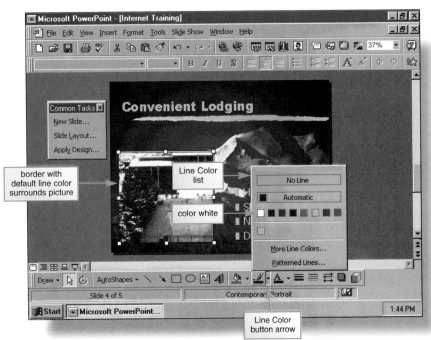

FIGURE 3-64a

2 **Click the color white, which is the first box in the row of available colors.**

A white border displays around the pool picture (Figure 3-64b).

3 **Click the Save button on the Standard toolbar to save the presentation again.**

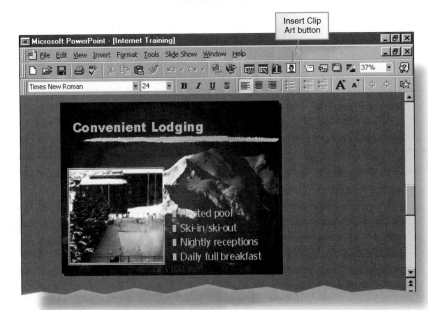

FIGURE 3-64b

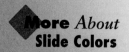

More *About*
Delivering
Presentations

A presentation is most effective when all audience members can see your slides easily. The maximum viewing distance is eight times the width of the slide. For example, if your slide is five feet wide when it projects on a screen, the farthest distance anyone should sit is 40 feet.

Slide 4 now is complete. The next section describes how to ungroup clip art and insert pieces of it in your closing slide in the onscreen slide show.

Creating a PowerPoint Clip Art Object

A **clip art picture** is composed of many objects grouped together to form one object. PowerPoint allows you to alter clip art by disassembling the objects. **Disassembling** a clip art object, also called **ungrouping**, separates one object into multiple objects. Once ungrouped, you can manipulate the individual objects as needed to form a new object. When you ungroup a clip art picture in PowerPoint, it becomes a **PowerPoint object** and loses its link to the Microsoft Clip Gallery. Therefore, you cannot double-click the new picture to open the Microsoft Clip Gallery.

Slide 5 contains a modified version of the Opportunity Challenge Difficult Objective picture from the Microsoft Clip Gallery. You may want to modify clip art for various reasons. Many times you cannot find clip art that precisely illustrates your topic. For example, you might want a picture of a man and woman shaking hands, but the only available clip art picture has two men and a woman shaking hands.

Occasionally, you may want to remove or change a portion of a clip art picture or you may want to combine two or more clip art pictures. For example, you can use one clip art picture for the background and another picture as the foreground. Still other times, you may want to combine clip art with another type of object. The types of objects you can combine with clip art depend on the software installed on your computer. The Object type list box in the Insert Object dialog box identifies the types of objects you can combine with clip art.

Modifying the clip art picture on Slide 5 requires several steps. First, you display Slide 5. Then, you change the AutoLayout to Object. Next, you insert the Opportunity Challenge Difficult Objective clip art into the object placeholder. Then, you scale the clip art to increase its size. Then, you ungroup the clip art and delete unwanted pieces. The steps on the following pages explain in detail how to insert, scale, and ungroup clip art.

Inserting Clip Art

The first step in modifying a clip art picture is to insert the picture on a slide. You insert the Opportunity Challenge Difficult Objective clip art from the Microsoft Clip Gallery. In later steps, you modify the clip art.

The following steps explain how to insert the Opportunity Challenge Difficult Objective clip art onto Slide 5 of this presentation.

More *About*
Slide Colors

If you are using at least three colors on your slide, use the darker colors at the bottom and the lighter colors at the top. The viewers' eyes will scan the slide naturally and quickly, leaving more time for them to focus on you.

TO INSERT CLIP ART

1. Click the Next Slide button to display Slide 5.
2. Click the Slide Layout button on the Common Tasks toolbar. Type 16 to select the Object AutoLayout. Press the ENTER key.
3. Click the object placeholder to select it.
4. Click the Insert Clip Art button on the Standard toolbar. Then, click the Find button in the Microsoft Clip Gallery 3.0 dialog box.
5. When the Find Clip dialog box displays, type Opportunity Challenge Difficult Objective in the Keywords text box.

6 Click the Find Now button.

7 Click the Insert button in the Microsoft Clip Gallery 3.0 dialog box.

Slide 5 displays the Opportunity Challenge Difficult Objective clip art picture (Figure 3-65).

Scaling Clip Art

Now that the clip art picture is inserted onto Slide 5, you must increase its size by **scaling**. Perform the following steps to scale the clip art picture.

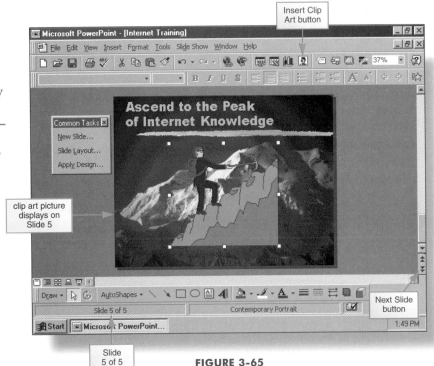

FIGURE 3-65

TO SCALE CLIP ART

1 Making sure the Opportunity Challenge Difficult Objective clip art picture still is selected, right-click the clip art picture.

2 Click Format Picture on the shortcut menu.

3 If necessary, click the Size tab.

4 In the Scale area, triple-click in the Height text box. Type 175 and then click the OK button.

The Opportunity Challenge Difficult Objective clip art picture is scaled to 175 percent of its original size (Figure 3-66).

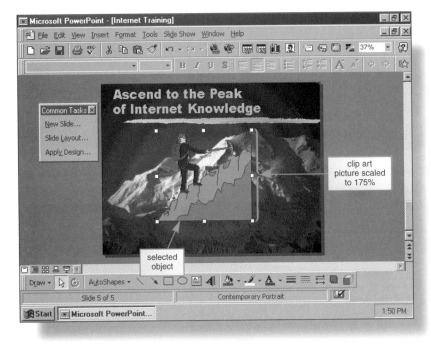

FIGURE 3-66

Ungrouping Clip Art

The next step is to ungroup the Opportunity Challenge Difficult Objective clip art picture in Slide 5. When you **ungroup** a clip art picture, PowerPoint breaks it into its component objects. These new groups can be ungrouped repeatedly until they decompose into individual objects. A clip art picture may be composed of a few individual objects or several complex groups of objects.

The steps on the next page explain how to ungroup clip art.

Steps **To Ungroup Clip Art**

1 **With the Opportunity Challenge Difficult Objective clip art picture selected, right-click the clip art. Point to Grouping on the shortcut menu. Click Ungroup on the Grouping submenu.**

A Microsoft PowerPoint dialog box displays explaining that this clip art object is an imported object and that converting it to a Microsoft Office drawing permanently discards any embedded data or linking information it contains. Finally, you are asked if you want to convert the object to a Microsoft Office drawing.

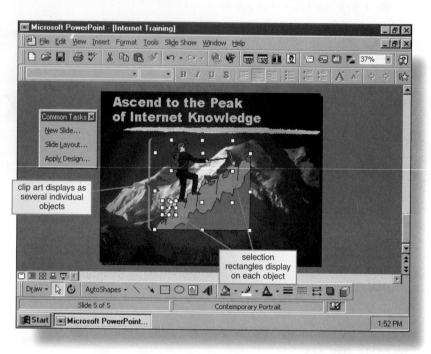

FIGURE 3-67

2 **Click the Yes button.**

*The clip art picture now displays as several PowerPoint objects (Figure 3-67). Selection rectangles display around the ungrouped objects. Recall that a **selection rectangle** is the box framed by the sizing handles when a graphic is selected.*

*Other***Ways**

1. On Draw menu click Ungroup

When you ungroup a clip art object and click the Yes button in the Microsoft PowerPoint information box (Step 2 above), PowerPoint converts the clip art object to a PowerPoint object. Recall that a PowerPoint object is an object *not* associated with a supplementary application. As a result, you lose the capability to double-click the clip art picture to open the Microsoft Clip Gallery. To replace a PowerPoint object with a clip art object, click the Insert Clip Art button on the Standard toolbar or click Insert on the menu bar. Click Object and then click Microsoft Clip Gallery. If for some reason, you decide not to ungroup the clip art picture, click the No button in the Microsoft PowerPoint dialog box. Clicking the No button terminates the Ungroup command, and the clip art picture displays on the slide as a clip art object.

Because clip art is a collection of complex groups of objects, you may need to ungroup a complex object into less complex objects before being able to modify a specific object.

If you accidentally ungroup an object, you immediately can **regroup** it by clicking Group on the Grouping submenu. If only one composite object is selected or you made changes to the composite objects, you can regroup the composite objects using the **Regroup command** on the Grouping submenu.

Recall that clip art is an object imported from the Microsoft Clip Gallery. Disassembling imported, embedded, or linked objects eliminates the embedding data or linking information the object contains that ties it back to its original source.

Use caution when objects are not completely regrouped. Dragging or scaling affects only the selected object, not the entire collection of objects.

Deselecting Clip Art Objects

All of the ungrouped objects in Figure 3-67 are selected. Before you can manipulate an individual object, you must **deselect** all selected objects to remove the selection rectangles, and then you must select the object you want to manipulate. For example, in this slide you will remove the clip art mountains under the man. The following step explains how to deselect objects.

TO DESELECT A CLIP ART OBJECT

(1) Click outside the clip art area.

Slide 5 displays without selection rectangles around the objects.

The Opportunity Challenge Difficult Objective clip art picture now is ungrouped into many objects. The next two sections explain how to drag a PowerPoint object and delete unwanted objects.

Moving a PowerPoint Object

To make deleting the unwanted clip art mountains easier, you must move the mountain climber away from the other clip art objects. Perform the following steps to move a PowerPoint object.

 Steps To Move a PowerPoint Object

1 **Click the torso of the mountain climber object.**

A selection rectangle displays around the mountain climber object (Figure 3-68). If you inadvertently select a different object, click the center of the mountain climber object.

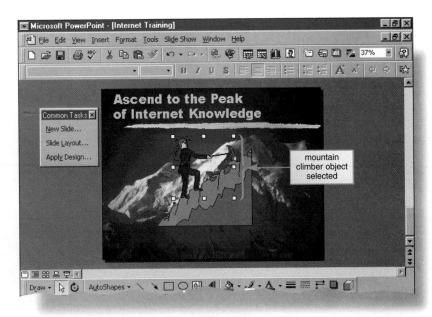

FIGURE 3-68

2 Drag the mountain climber object downward and away from the clip art mountain so his pick is reaching into a mountain peak in the mountain photograph (Figure 3-69).

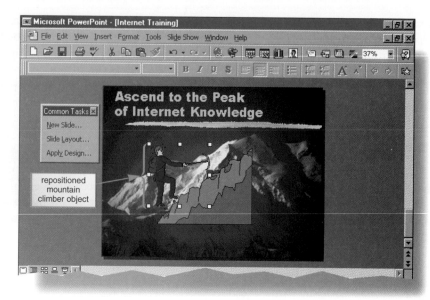

FIGURE 3-69

You moved the mountain climber object away from the other objects to make it easier to delete the unwanted objects.

Deleting PowerPoint Objects

Now that the mountain climber object is separated from the other objects in the Opportunity Challenge Difficult Objective clip art picture, you can delete the mountain objects that are part of this clip art. Perform the following steps to delete unwanted PowerPoint objects.

 Steps **To Delete PowerPoint Objects**

1 Select the gray clip art mountain object under the mountain climber's feet.

A selection rectangle displays around the mountain object (Figure 3-70). If you inadvertently select a different object, click the center of the mountain object.

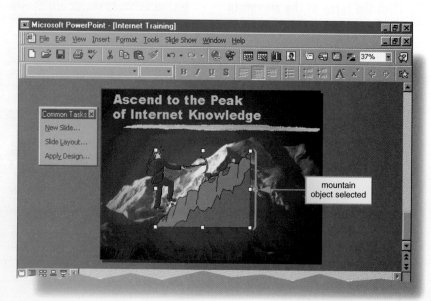

FIGURE 3-70

2 **Press the DELETE key.**

The mountain object is deleted (Figure 3-71).

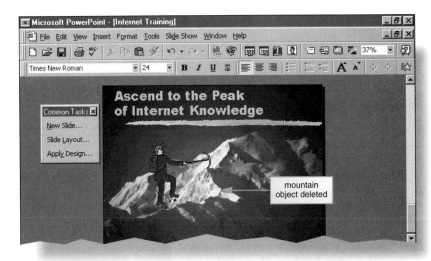

Other Ways
1. On Edit menu click Clear

FIGURE 3-71

Other Ways
1. In Slide View or Slide Sorter View, select slide to add transitions, right-click selected slide, click Slide Transition, click Effect area box arrow, choose desired transition, click Apply button
2. Select slide to add transitions, on Slide Show menu click Slide Transition, click Effect area box arrow, choose desired transition, click Apply button

Slide 5 now is complete. The next section shows you how to add effects for switching from one slide to the next when you give your presentation.

Adding Slide Transition and Text Preset Animation Effects

The final step in preparing the Internet Training presentation is to add slide transition and text preset animation effects. Perform the following steps to add the slide transition and text preset animation effects.

TO ADD SLIDE TRANSITION AND TEXT PRESET ANIMATION EFFECTS

1 Click the Slide Sorter View button.

2 Press and hold the SHIFT key. Click Slide 2, Slide 3, and Slide 4. Release the SHIFT key.

3 Click the Slide Transition Effects box arrow. Click Box In.

4 Click Slide 1. Press and hold the SHIFT key and then click Slide 4. Release the SHIFT key.

5 Click the Text Preset Animation box arrow. Scroll down and click Spiral.

The presentation displays in Slide Sorter View (Figure 3-72). Slides 1 and 4 are selected. Text preset animation effects are applied to Slides 1 and 4. Slide transition effects are applied to Slides 2, 3, 4, and 5.

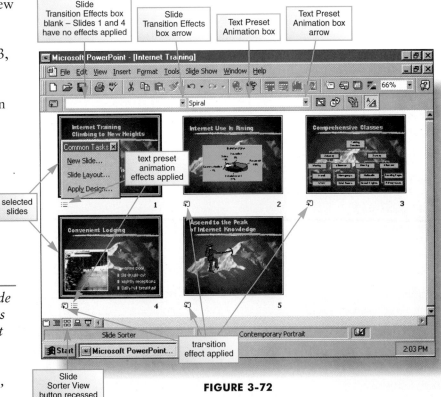

FIGURE 3-72

Printing Slides as Handouts

Perform the following steps to print the presentation slides as handouts, six slides per page.

Steps To Print Slides as Handouts

1 **Click File on the menu bar and then click Print. When the Print dialog box displays, click the Print what box arrow and click Handouts (6 slides per page) in the Print what list box. Then click Scale to fit paper (Figure 3-73).**

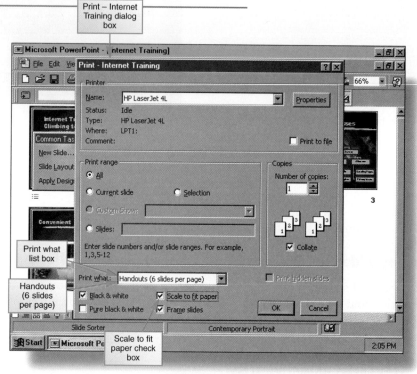

FIGURE 3-73

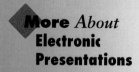

More *About*
Electronic Presentations

PowerPoint allows you to change slides quickly and effortlessly. As a result, presenters often need to develop three times as many slides for their speeches than they would have needed had they been using overhead transparencies or 35mm slides.

2 **Click the OK button to begin printing.**

The handout prints as shown in Figure 3-74.

FIGURE 3-74

Project Summary

Project 3 introduced you to several methods of enhancing a presentation with embedded visuals. You began the project by creating the presentation from an outline that was created in Word. Then, you learned how to create a special slide background using a picture. When you created Slide 2, you learned how to embed an existing Excel chart. Slide 3 introduced you to creating and embedding an organization chart using the supplementary application Microsoft Organization Chart 2.0. You then learned how to embed a picture on Slide 4. Then, you learned how to ungroup objects for Slide 5. Finally, you learned how to print your presentation slides as handouts.

What You Should Know

Having completed this project, you now should be able to perform the following tasks:

▶ Add a Border to a Picture *(PP 3.52)*

▶ Add Another Level of Subordinate Boxes
(PP 3.32)

▶ Add Multiple Subordinate Boxes *(PP 3.31)*

▶ Add Names to Subordinate Boxes *(PP 3.33)*

▶ Add Shadow Effects to Boxes in an Organization
Chart *(PP 3.40)*

▶ Add Slide Transition and Text Preset Animation
Effects *(PP 3.59)*

▶ Change the Box Color *(PP 3.42)*

▶ Change the Border Line Color *(PP 3.53)*

▶ Change the Border Style *(PP 3.41)*

▶ Change Design Templates *(PP 3.12)*

▶ Change the Font Color of the Entire Outline
(PP 3.10)

▶ Change the Line Color *(PP 3.43)*

▶ Change the Organization Chart Style *(PP 3.34)*

▶ Change Slide Layout to Title Slide *(PP 3.13)*

▶ Copy a Branch of an Organization Chart
(PP 3.36)

▶ Create the Title for the Root Manager Box
(PP 3.28)

▶ Delete PowerPoint Objects *(PP 3.58)*

▶ Delete Subordinate Boxes *(PP 3.29)*

▶ Deselect a Clip Art Object *(PP 3.57)*

▶ Display the Next Slide and Change the Slide
Layout *(PP 3.18, 3.26)*

▶ Edit an Embedded Excel Chart *(PP 3.21)*

▶ Edit Text in an Organization Chart *(PP 3.37)*

▶ Embed an Excel Chart *(PP 3.18)*

▶ Insert a Picture *(PP 3.49)*

▶ Insert a Picture to Create a Custom Background
(PP 3.15)

▶ Insert Clip Art (PP 3.54)

▶ Maximize the Microsoft Organization Chart
Window *(PP 3.27)*

▶ Move a PowerPoint Object *(PP 3.57)*

▶ Move Text in a Slide *(PP 3.47)*

▶ Move the Organization Chart *(PP 3.46)*

▶ Open Microsoft Organization Chart *(PP 3.27)*

▶ Paste a Branch of an Organization Chart
(PP 3.36)

▶ Position an Embedded Excel Chart Object
(PP 3.23)

▶ Print Slides as Handouts *(PP 3.60)*

▶ Quit Microsoft Organization Chart and Return
to the PowerPoint Window *(PP 3.44)*

▶ Resize a Picture *(PP 3.50)*

▶ Save a Presentation *(PP 3.13)*

▶ Scale an Organization Chart Object *(PP 3.45)*

▶ Scale Clip Art *(PP 3.55)*

▶ Select All Boxes in an Organization Chart
(PP 3.39)

▶ Start PowerPoint and Open an Outline *(PP 3.9)*

▶ Title a Subordinate Box *(PP 3.30)*

▶ Ungroup Clip Art *(PP 3.56)*

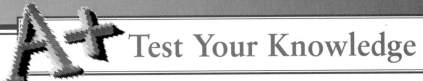

Test Your Knowledge

1 True/False

Instructions: Circle T if the statement is true or F if the statement is false.

T F 1. RTF is an abbreviation for Real Text Font.

T F 2. The default design template is named Auto Design.

T F 3. You can change presentation design templates when you are creating a presentation and also any time you wish to change the look of your presentation.

T F 4. Bitmap and vector are the two types of graphic formats used to save pictures.

T F 5. The smallest element that can display or that print hardware and software can manipulate is called a pixel.

T F 6. A linked object on a slide does not change if the original object changes.

T F 7. An organization chart shows various functions or responsibilities that contribute to an organization or to a collective function.

T F 8. In Microsoft Organization Chart, the top box is called the root manager.

T F 9. To resize an object about its center, press and hold the CTRL key and double-click the object.

T F 10. When a PowerPoint object is disassembled, it becomes a clip art picture.

2 Multiple Choice

Instructions: Circle the correct response.

1. When PowerPoint opens an outline created in Microsoft Word and saved as a(n) _____ file, the text attributes and outline heading levels are maintained.
   a. Microsoft Word
   b. PowerPoint
   c. Rich Text Format (RTF)
   d. plain text (.txt)

2. Which slide attributes can change when a different design template is selected?
   a. font
   b. bullets
   c. color
   d. all of the above

3. A(n) _____ is a piece of art that has been stored as a pattern of dots called pixels.
   a. graphic filter
   b. vector graphic
   c. digitized signal
   d. bitmap graphic

(continued)

Test Your Knowledge

Multiple Choice *(continued)*

4. A(n) _____ object is created in another application but maintains a connection to its source.
   a. inserted
   b. linked
   c. extended
   d. related

5. To select more than one object, such as two subordinate boxes, press and hold the _____ key while clicking the objects.
   a. ALT
   b. CTRL
   c. SHIFT
   d. TAB

6. To resize a picture about its center, press and hold the _____ key while dragging a sizing handle.
   a. ALT
   b. CTRL
   c. ESC
   d. TAB

7. A(n) _____ object can be embedded in a PowerPoint slide.
   a. Excel chart
   b. clip art
   c. picture
   d. all of the above

8. The _____ attribute(s) of an organization chart can be formatted.
   a. box color
   b. border style
   c. shadow effects
   d. all of the above

9. The OLE application used to create an organization chart is called _____.
   a. Microsoft Organization Chart
   b. Microsoft Hierarchy Chart
   c. Microsoft Embedded Chart
   d. Microsoft Department Chart

10. A PowerPoint sample organization chart has _____ boxes.
    a. two
    b. three
    c. four
    d. five

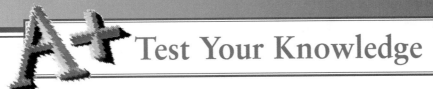

Test Your Knowledge

3 Understanding PowerPoint Menus and Commands

Instructions: Identify the menus and commands that carry out the operation or cause the dialog box to display and allow you to make the indicated changes.

	MENU	COMMAND
1. Add slide transition effects	_____	_____
2. Change design templates	_____	_____
3. Change AutoLayout to Title Slide	_____	_____
4. Delete subordinate boxes	_____	_____
5. Insert a picture	_____	_____
6. Insert clip art	_____	_____
7. Open an outline	_____	_____
8. Open Microsoft Organization Chart	_____	_____
9. Print slides as handouts	_____	_____
10. Scale an Organization Chart object to 110 percent	_____	_____

4 Working with an Organization Chart

Instructions: Write the step numbers below to indicate the sequence necessary to create the organization chart shown in Figure 3-75. Assume Microsoft Organization Chart is active, the design template and Organization Chart layout are selected, and the title text already is created. Label levels 1 and 2 before adding the level 3 subordinate boxes. Label new level 3 subordinate boxes before changing the chart style. Then add the level 4 subordinate boxes. Finally, format all the box border styles.

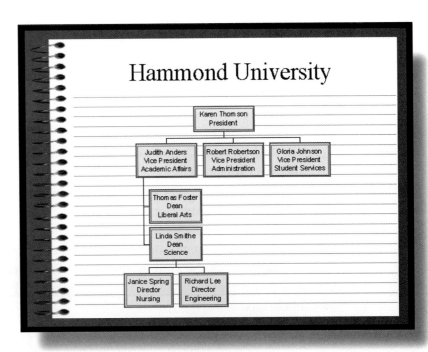

FIGURE 3-75

(continued)

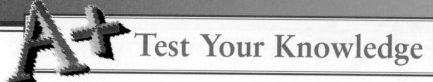

Test Your Knowledge

Working with an Organization Chart (*continued*)

Step _____: Click the box to the right of the Thomas Foster subordinate box. Type `Linda Smithe` and then press the ENTER key. Type `Dean` and then press the ENTER key. Type `Science` in the box.

Step _____: Click Styles on the menu bar and then click the vertical style icon in the Groups styles.

Step _____: On the Boxes menu, click Border Color. Click brown (row 3, column 2 in the Color dialog box). Click the OK button.

Step _____: Click the Subordinate icon on the Microsoft Organization Chart window icon bar two times. Click the left subordinate box labeled Judith Anders. Type `Thomas Foster` and then press the ENTER key. Type `Dean` and then press the ENTER key. Type `Liberal Arts` in the box.

Step _____: Click the Close button. Click the Yes button in the Microsoft Organization Chart dialog box.

Step _____: On level 2, click the left subordinate box. Type `Judith Anders` and then press the ENTER key. Type `Vice President` and then press the ENTER key. Type `Academic Affairs` in the box. Next, click the middle subordinate box. Type `Robert Robertson` and then press the ENTER key. Type `Vice President` and then press the ENTER key. Then, type `Administration` in the box. Click the right subordinate box. Type `Gloria Johnson` and then press the ENTER key. Type `Vice President` and then press the ENTER key. Type `Student Services` in the box.

Step _____: Click the box to the right of the Nursing subordinate box. Type `Richard Lee` and then press the ENTER key. Type `Director` and then press the ENTER key. Type `Engineering` in the box.

Step _____: Type `Karen Thomson` in the root manager box and then press the ENTER key. Type `President` in the root manager box.

Step _____: On the Microsoft Organization Chart Edit menu, point to Select and then click All on the Select submenu.

Step _____: Press and hold the SHIFT key. Click the two lowest-level boxes — Liberal Arts and Science. Release the SHIFT key.

Step _____: Double-click the organization chart placeholder.

Step _____: Click the Subordinate icon on the Microsoft Organization Chart window icon bar two times. Click the bottom subordinate box labeled Linda Smithe. Type `Janice Spring` and then press the ENTER key. Type `Director` and then press the ENTER key. Type `Nursing` in the box.

Use Help

1 Learning More about the Microsoft Clip Gallery

Instructions: Perform the following tasks using a computer.

1. Start PowerPoint. When the PowerPoint startup dialog box displays, double-click Blank presentation. Type 10 to select the Clip Art & Text AutoLayout. Click the OK button.
2. Double-click the Clip Art placeholder. When the Microsoft Clip Gallery 3.0 window displays, click the Help button and then click the Index tab.
3. In the Help Topics: Microsoft Clip Gallery 3.0 window, click Adding Clips from the Clip Gallery to a document. Click Display. When the Topics Found window displays, click What's the difference between clip art and pictures? Click the Display button and then read the information. Right-click in the dialog box, and click Print Topic on the shortcut menu. Click the OK button.
4. Click the Help Topics button. Scroll down and then click Pictures. Click Display. Scroll down and then click What if I can't find the clip I'm looking for? Click the Display button. Read and then print the information. Click How and read the information. Print the Import clips from Clip Gallery Live into the Clip Gallery information.
5. Click the Help Topics button. Double-click Properties of clips. In the Topics Found window, double-click What is a keyword? When the Help menu displays, read and then print the information.
6. Click the Help Topics button. Double-click Searching for clips. Display the Find a specific clip in the Clip Gallery information. Read and then print the information.
7. Click the Microsoft Clip Gallery 3.0 Help window Close button. Click the Microsoft Clip Gallery 3.0 window Close button. When the Microsoft PowerPoint – [Presentation1] window displays, click the Close button.
8. When the Microsoft PowerPoint window displays, quit PowerPoint without saving the presentation.
9. Hand in the printouts to your instructor.

2 Expanding on the Basics

Instructions: Use PowerPoint Help to better understand the topics listed below. Begin each of the following by clicking the Office Assistant button on the Standard toolbar. If you cannot print the Help information, answer the question on a separate piece of paper.

1. How do you recolor an organization chart?
2. How do you remove a border?
3. In what ways can you modify a picture in your presentation?
4. How do you edit an organization chart?
5. What is the default font for organization charts?
6. How can you rotate or flip a clip art object?
7. How do you change a slide background picture?
8. How can you crop or trim a picture?

Apply Your Knowledge

1 Creating a Presentation from an Outline, Inserting Clip Art, and Changing the Slide Background

Instructions: Start PowerPoint. Open the outline, Peak Skiing, from the PowerPoint folder on the Data Disk that accompanies this book.

1. Apply the Whirlpool design template.
2. Change the AutoLayout for Slide 1 to Title Slide (Figure 3-76a).
3. Create the custom background shown in Figure 3-76a using the Snow picture file from the Data Disk.
4. Change the AutoLayout for Slide 2 to Text & Clip Art. Move the bulleted text to look like Figure 3-76b. Insert the Screen Beans People Happy Joy clip art. Scale the height of the clip art picture to 110 percent.
5. Apply the Dissolve slide transition effect. Apply the Peek From Left text preset animation effect.
6. Save the presentation with the file name, Ski School.
7. Print the presentation.
8. Quit PowerPoint.

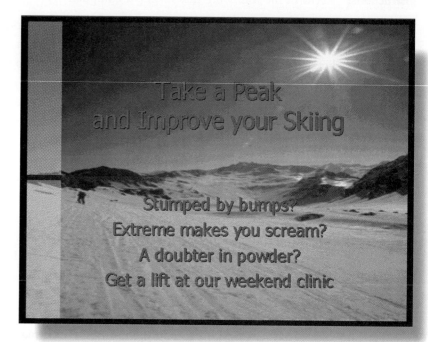

FIGURE 3-76a

FIGURE 3-76b

In the Lab

1 Creating a Custom Slide

Problem: You are the marketing manager for a new office building. One of the benefits of working in that building is the convenient parking lot next door. You are creating a sales presentation to persuade the business community to lease space from your company. You want a title slide with a rendering of office buildings and the parking lot. You modify various clip art objects to create this presentation.

Instructions: Perform the following tasks to create the slide shown in Figure 3-77.

1. Start PowerPoint, choose the Object AutoLayout, and apply the high voltage design template.
2. Type Park Close to the Office for the slide title. Change the font size to 48 and the text color to black.
3. Change the slide background color to light green.
4. Insert the clip art picture from the Microsoft Clip Gallery with a description Skyscraper Large Tall. Resize the clip art about center to increase the width of the buildings as shown in Figure 3-77.
5. Ungroup the Skyscraper Large Tall picture. Delete the purple building in the front row of buildings.
6. Insert the clip art picture with the description Success Victory Accomplishment Result. Ungroup the Success picture and delete everything in the clip art except the flag, flagpole, and hand. Scale the flag, flagpole, and hand height to 65 percent. Move the flag, flagpole, and hand to the right side of the orange building. Ungroup the flag, flagpole, and hand. Delete the hand from the flagpole. Color the flag red.
7. Change the fill effect of the pink building to Green marble in the Texture sheet in the Fill Effects dialog box.
8. Insert the clip art picture with the description Performance Fast Sports Car. Scale the car to a height of 25 percent. Then move the car into the vacant lot where the purple building originally stood.
9. Group the PowerPoint objects.
10. Save the presentation with the file name Park Close.
11. Print the slide using the Black & white option.
12. Quit PowerPoint.

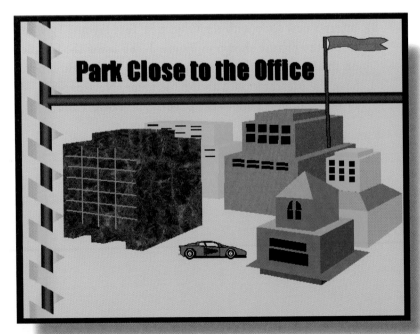

FIGURE 3-77

In the Lab

2 Embedding an Organization Chart and Inserting a Picture

Problem: You are the news editor of the *Observer*, the student newspaper at Hammond University. You want to print an organization chart in the *Observer* that will familiarize the campus with the student editors. You decide to use PowerPoint to create the organization chart shown in Figure 3-78a and the fact sheet about the editor shown in Figure 3-78b.

Instructions: Perform the following tasks.

1. Start PowerPoint. Click Blank presentation to create a new presentation. Apply the Organization Chart layout. Apply the Professional design template.
2. Type Hammond University in the slide title and then press the ENTER key. Type Observer Staff on the second line.
3. Create the organization chart shown in Figure 3-78a. Type your name in the News Editor text box.
4. Change the box color for the editor to red (row 1, column 9). Change the box color for the assistant editor to purple (row 2, column 5). Change the box color for the four news staff members to yellow (row 2, column 1). Change the box color for the two sports staff members to lime green (row 2, column 2). Change the box color for the three business staff members to light blue (row 2, column 3).
5. Add borders to all boxes. Use the border style in column 1, row 6 on the Border Style submenu. Change the border color for all boxes to royal blue (column 4, row 2).
6. Change the line color to red (column 9, row 1).
7. Quit Microsoft Organization Chart and return to Slide 1. Scale the organization chart to 115 percent. Then drag the organization chart onto the center of the blank area under the title object.
8. Insert a new slide with the Object & Text layout. Type the text shown in Figure 3-78b.
9. Insert the picture shown in Figure 3-78b using the file, Bernie Halen, from the PowerPoint folder on the Data Disk that accompanies this book. Add a border to the picture using the 3 pt single line.
10. Save the presentation with the file name, Newspaper.
11. Print handouts (2 slides per page). Quit PowerPoint.

In the Lab

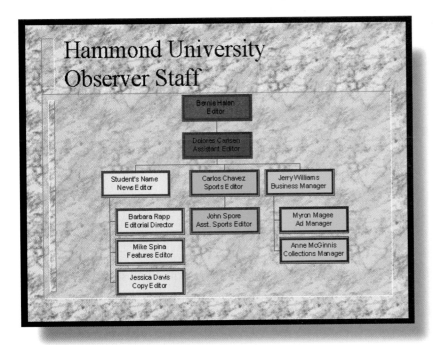

FIGURE 3-78a

FIGURE 3-78b

In the Lab

3 Opening an Existing Outline and Creating a New Clip Art Picture

Problem: You are in charge of recruiting new choir members for an informal choral group at school. The choir director has asked you to create a presentation to show to students enrolled in music and drama classes. Create the opening slide of the presentation from the outline developed for your program. Because you cannot find clip art of a choir, you create the object shown in Figure 3-79.

Instructions: Perform the following tasks.

1. Start PowerPoint. Open the Sing outline from the PowerPoint folder on the Data Disk that accompanies this book.
2. Apply the Blush design template. Change the AutoLayout to Text & Clip Art.
3. Select the title text and change the font size to 54.
4. Insert the clip art picture with the description of Leadership Information Test Communication Listen Dictate. Ungroup the clip art picture.
5. Delete the table and screen from the clip art. Move the people so they form a half-circle around the choir director.
6. Change the color of the choir director to the same color as the title text. Change the color of the baton to limegreen.
7. Change the color of the two end singers to yellow. Change the color of the middle two people to light blue. Change the color of the two remaining people to lime green, which is the same color as the baton.
8. Add a lime green border around the bulleted text using a ¼ pt line.
9. Group all the individual objects in the clip art picture into one object.
10. Scale the object to 110 percent.
11. Place the date, your name, and the slide number in the slide footer.
12. Save the presentation with the file name, Choir Practice. Print the presentation. Quit PowerPoint.

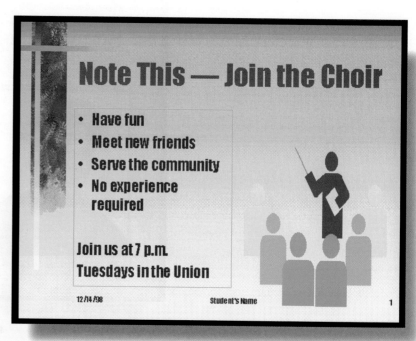

FIGURE 3-79

Cases and Places

The difficulty of these case studies varies: ❱ are the least difficult; ❱❱ are more difficult; and ❱❱❱ are the most difficult.

1 ❱ "I'll have a caffe latte macchiato extra-tall non." What's that? A coffee connoisseur would know it is an extra-large cup of nonfat steamed milk with a small amount of full-bodied coffee. Cappuccino, espresso, mocha, and latte are standard lingo for many coffee drinkers. Visit a coffeehouse or gourmet food store to learn the definitions and recipes for these drinks. Prepare a presentation that describes the various types of coffee beverages, the amounts of caffeine and calories in an eight-ounce serving, and price. Create a custom background. Include a title slide and clip art.

2 ❱ Skis, tennis rackets, and golf clubs have changed shape dramatically in recent years to help the infrequent or average user enjoy the sport. For instance, the parabolic shape of the new super-sidecut skis helps average skiers carve turns with ease. Visit a sporting goods store, read sports magazines, or use the Internet to learn about one of these new pieces of equipment. Find out why this new style makes using this equipment much easier than the traditional shape. What materials comprise this item? What are some of the leading brands? How much does this equipment cost? Use a word processing program to outline your research findings. Create a presentation from this outline. Design a custom background and add pictures or clip art. Use a title slide and apply slide transition and text preset animation effects.

3 ❱❱ When one thinks of leaders, President Bill Clinton, Gen. George Patton, and Lee Iacocca might come to mind. Leadership is defined as the process of exerting social influence on others in an attempt to obtain voluntary participation in efforts to reach a goal. Consider the student leaders at your school, such as the student government president, football team captain, or newspaper editor. Interview one of these individuals and create a presentation profiling major accomplishments and strategies on leading others successfully. Create a title slide with a bordered picture of this person, if possible.

4 ❱❱ Athletic organizations have a hierarchy of coaches and managers that often is highly specialized. In softball and baseball, for instance, hitting, pitching, catching and first base coaches and assistants may report to an infield coach who, in turn, reports to a manager. Visit the athletic department of your school and obtain the names and titles of coaches and managers associated with one sport. Then create a presentation that includes a hierarchy chart explaining this chain of command. Format the hierarchy chart to highlight the team's divisions. Include a slide showing the team's record for the past three years, a short biography of the team captain, and appropriate clip art or pictures.

200 MHz

Cases and Places

5 ▶▶ Treadmills are one of the more quickly selling products in the home-exercise market today. They provide an efficient means of burning calories and giving an aerobic workout. These machines vary widely in price, features, and guarantees. Visit a sporting goods store, read a fitness magazine, or use the Internet to examine the diverse treadmill market. Group the treadmills in three categories according to price: low-, middle-, and high-end. Compare features, such as walking surface size, speed, incline, motor horsepower, guarantee, and programming. Create a presentation comparing various treadmills on the basis of price and features. Use a title slide and apply slide transition and text preset animation effects.

6 ▶▶▶ Whether it is a high-rise condominium overlooking New York City's Central Park, a beach house in Tahiti, or an isolated cabin in the Colorado Rockies, we all dream of the ideal place to live. Use the Internet, magazines, or a travel agent to gather information about this dream house and then create a presentation. Include geographical information and a map. Scan a picture of this place and use it for the background of your title slide. Include another picture to depict one of the features of this location, such as a carriage ride through Central Park. Apply slide transition and text preset animation effects.

7 ▶▶▶ We eat, on average, one-third of our meals away from home. Often restaurants and fast-food places serve portions that are large enough to satisfy two or three people. For example, the U.S. Department of Agriculture classifies a serving of pancakes as two or three medium-sized pancakes, but many restaurants serve up to four large pancakes in an order. Obtain the standard serving size of three breakfast, lunch, dinner, and snack food items you normally consume away from home, such as bagels, french fries, pizza, and ice cream. You can find these serving sizes by looking at nutrition books or at the labels of these items in supermarkets. Then visit the restaurants where you typically eat these products and determine the serving sizes. Create a presentation that compares the official serving sizes to the restaurant serving sizes. Insert clip art and apply slide transition and text preset animation effects where appropriate.

Creating a Presentation Containing Interactive OLE Documents

Objectives:

You will have mastered the material in this project when you can:

▶ Open an existing presentation and save it with a new file name

▶ Create a custom background

▶ Modify a color scheme

▶ Draw an object

▶ Add a special text effect

▶ Embed an object into the slide master

▶ Change the organization chart formatting

▶ Create a slide using action buttons and hyperlinks

▶ Add text to a slide

▶ Use guides to position and size an object

▶ Modify PowerPoint options to end a presentation with a black slide

▶ Hide a slide

▶ Animate an object

▶ Run a slide show to display a hidden slide and activate an interactive document

Order in the High-Tech Court

Lawyers in today's courtrooms are using different types of cases that do not involve plaintiffs and defendants. Instead, these cases are the ones used to carry their notebook computers. They are installing presentation software on these notebooks to develop and project carefully prepared slide shows to juries.

Perry Mason, Clarence Darrow, and F. Lee Bailey are known for the art of effective lawyering, with jurors regularly influenced by their compelling and persuasive opening and closing arguments. Not every lawyer or every case, however, has the flair and drama to rest on mere words alone.

With a generation of jurors raised on MTV and VCRs, attorneys realize they need to turn to technology to enhance their messages.

One of their technological tools is a notebook computer equipped with electronic presentation software, such as Microsoft PowerPoint. They realize that convincing a jury means more than merely creating a presentation and running it on the computer. Their slide show must be

impressive, which means having effective design, color, graphics, photographs, animation effects, and transitions. The PowerPoint projects in this textbook have illustrated the techniques for creating powerful presentations. The More About features provide insight on delivering these slide shows. Lawyers follow these same principles to make their presentations effective and ensure that the jurors feel comfortable with the new courtroom technology.

Using this hardware in court presents special challenges. First, the attorneys usually need to seek permission and make arrangements with the appropriate personnel. Once approval is granted, they then have to examine the courtroom to determine where the electrical outlets are located, what type of lighting exists, and where to place a projection screen or monitor. Some courtrooms are equipped with televisions and videotape recorders to play taped depositions for the jury, so lawyers can plug their notebook computers into the jacks in this equipment. Many courtrooms also have overhead projectors, so attorneys can connect their computers into an LCD presentation panel that rests on top of the overhead projector.

Lawyers know they must expect the unexpected, so they come to court with extra extension cords, batteries, disks, and bulbs. If time permits, they rehearse in the courtroom to adjust the lighting and determine electrical loads. In addition, they prepare a set of overhead transparencies that duplicate the PowerPoint slides, just in case their notebook computers fail. They can make these overheads by placing transparency film sheets in color printers or copiers.

Lawyers are using the power of PowerPoint beyond the courtroom. They frequently prepare PowerPoint presentations to educate general community groups and such specialized audiences as insurance agents on the intricacies of estate planning, charitable giving, and life insurance products. Some firms then convert their presentations to HTML documents and post them on the World Wide Web or the firm's intranet.

As the computers gain acceptance in the courtroom, juries soon may be hearing, "Your Honor, my digital co-counsel and I rest our case."

Microsoft
PowerPoint 97

Creating a Presentation Containing Interactive OLE Documents

Case Perspective

The next Net-Train Corporation Internet Training seminar will be held in San Francisco, California. Company executives have asked you to modify the Internet presentation created for the Park City, Utah, seminar. You want to change design templates, but you cannot find one that exemplifies the California spirit and has a light, colorful background. You find a design template, however, on the Microsoft site on the Internet and decide to change the color scheme. You draw the company logo and insert it onto the title slide. You decide to animate the logo to fly across the title slide. You replace the convenient-housing picture with a picture of the Golden Gate Bridge. Finally, you add a slide to demonstrate two components of the Internet Training workshop: e-mail and the World Wide Web. Then you decide to display that slide only if time permits.

Introduction

Because every presentation is created for a specific audience, subsequent deliveries of the same presentation may require changes. These changes are necessary to accommodate the knowledge base or interest level of the audience. Sometimes, when running a slide show, you want to open another application to show the audience the effect of a change. For example, when presenting next year's projected sales, you may want to perform a what-if analysis during the slide show without leaving PowerPoint. PowerPoint allows you to do so using interactive documents. An **interactive document** is a file created in another application, such as Microsoft Word, and then opened during the running of a slide show. Other times you may want to refrain from showing one or more slides because you are short on time or the slides are not applicable to a particular audience.

PowerPoint has the capability of hiding slides. As the presenter, you decide whether to display them. Occasionally, you need to change the look of your presentation by adding special graphics, such as a company logo, adding borders to objects and text, adding shadow effects to objects, or changing the overall color scheme. Project 4 customizes the Internet Training seminar presentation created in Project 3 (see Figures 3-1a through 3-1e on page PP 3.7).

Slide Preparation Steps

The preparation steps are an overview of how the slide presentation shown in Figures 4-1a through 4-1h (shown on this and the next page) will be developed in Project 4. The following tasks will be completed in this project.

1. Start PowerPoint.
2. Open an existing presentation, save it with a new file name, and apply a new design template.
3. Select a new color scheme and then modify it.
4. Create a logo using drawing tools.
5. Embed the logo into the slide master.
6. Link Word and PowerPoint documents to create a slide containing interactive documents.
7. Replace the text and picture on the slide titled, Convenient Activities.
8. Change the PowerPoint options to end the presentation with a blank slide.
9. Hide a slide.
10. Animate two slides.
11. Save the presentation.
12. Run the slide show to display the hidden slide and activate the interactive documents.
13. Quit PowerPoint.

FIGURE 4-1a

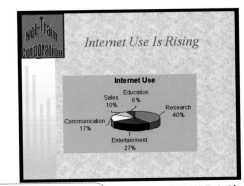

FIGURE 4-1b

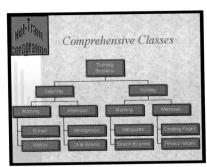

FIGURE 4-1c

hyperlinked file

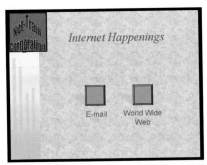

FIGURE 4-1d

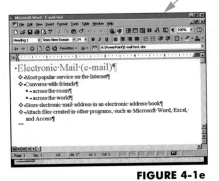

FIGURE 4-1e

(slide show continued on next page)

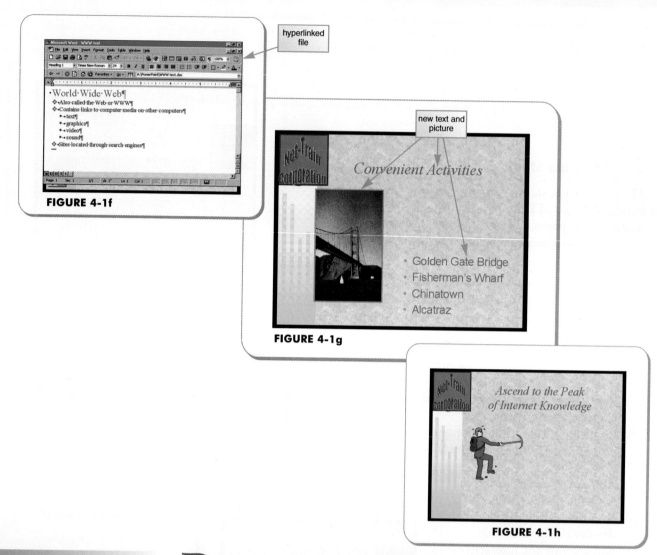

FIGURE 4-1f

FIGURE 4-1g

FIGURE 4-1h

Project Four – Customizing an Existing Presentation

Because you are customizing the Internet Training seminar presentation created in Project 3, the first step in this project is to open the Internet Training file. To ensure that the original presentation remains intact, you must save it with a new file name, Internet Training San Fran. Later in this project, you will modify the new presentation's slides by changing the design template, selecting a new color scheme, replacing a picture and bulleted text, and adding one new slide. The following steps illustrate these procedures.

Opening a Presentation and Saving It with a New File Name

After starting PowerPoint, the first step in this project is to open the Internet Training presentation saved in Project 3 and save it with the file name, Internet Training San Fran. This procedure should be done immediately to prevent inadvertently saving the presentation with the original file name. Perform the following steps to open an existing presentation and save it with a new file name. If you did not complete Project 3, see your instructor for a copy of the presentation.

TO OPEN A PRESENTATION AND SAVE IT WITH A NEW FILE NAME

1️⃣ Insert your PowerPoint 97 Project3 Data Disk into drive A.

2️⃣ Start Windows Explorer and, if necessary, click the Restore button so that part of the desktop displays.

3️⃣ Click the plus sign to the left of the 3½ Floppy (A:) icon in the All Folders side of the window, and then click the PowerPoint icon.

4️⃣ Right-drag Internet Training onto the desktop and click Copy Here on the shortcut menu.

5️⃣ Insert your PowerPoint 97 Project4 Data Disk into drive A.

6️⃣ Right-drag Internet Training from the desktop onto the 3½ Floppy (A:) icon on the All Folders side of the window, and then click Move Here on the shortcut menu.

7️⃣ Click the Close button on the Windows Explorer title bar.

8️⃣ Click the Start button on the taskbar, and then click Open Office Document.

9️⃣ When the Open Office Document dialog box displays, click the Look in box arrow, and then click 3½ Floppy (A:). Double-click Internet Training.

🔟 Click File on the menu bar, and then click Save As. If necessary, click the Look in box arrow, and then click 3½ Floppy (A:). Double-click the PowerPoint folder in the list.

⑪ Type Internet Training San Fran in the File name text box.

⑫ Click the Save button.

The presentation is saved on the PowerPoint 97 Project4 Data Disk in drive A with the file name, Internet Training San Fran (Figure 4-2).

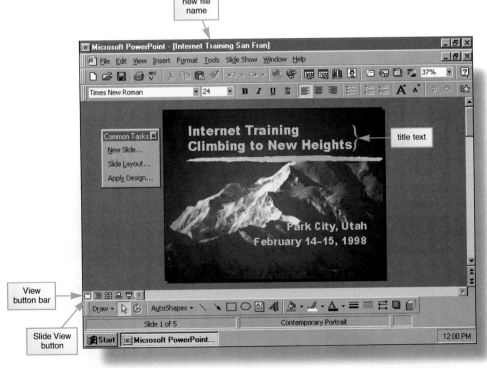

FIGURE 4-2

Editing Text

Because the location of the Internet Training seminar is changing, you must change the title and subtitle text on the title slide. Recall that text objects that display on a slide can be edited in slide view or outline view. Perform the following steps to display the title slide in slide view, and then revise the title and subtitle text.

TO CHANGE TEXT

1 If necessary, click the Slide View button on the View button bar.

2 Double-click the title text and then drag through the text, Climbing to New Heights, to select it.

3 Type `Bridging to the 21st Century` in place of the highlighted text.

4 Triple-click Park City, Utah.

5 Type `San Francisco, CA` in place of the highlighted text.

6 Double-click February.

7 Type `March` in place of the highlighted text.

8 Click anywhere on the slide other than the title or subtitle objects.

Slide 1 displays the updated title and subtitle text (Figure 4-3).

Changing Design Templates

The Internet Training seminar organizing team has requested that you change the Contemporary Portrait design template used in Project 3. You examine the design templates included in Office 97, but none has a colorful, lively feeling to correlate with a California setting. You search the Microsoft site on the Internet and find the design template, speed. The speed design template is located in the PowerPoint folder on the Data Disk that accompanies this book. Perform the following steps to change the design template.

More *About* Meeting Feedback

Meeting Minder is a handy feature to use while giving a PowerPoint presentation. By right-clicking a slide and clicking Meeting Minder, you can add items to the Meeting Minutes and Action Items dialog boxes and transfer them to Microsoft Word. The action items display on a separate slide at the end of the slide show and can be posted to the task list in Microsoft Outlook. You can leave the Meeting Minder open throughout the slide show.

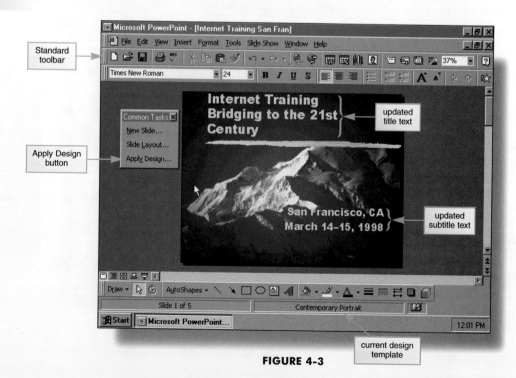

FIGURE 4-3

TO CHANGE THE DESIGN TEMPLATE

1 Click the Apply Design button on the Common Tasks toolbar.

2 When the Apply Design dialog box displays, click the Look in box arrow, click 3½ Floppy (A:), and double-click the PowerPoint folder in the list.

3 Double-click speed in the list.

Several messages will display before Slide 1 displays the new design template, speed, with the title master background graphics (Figure 4-4).

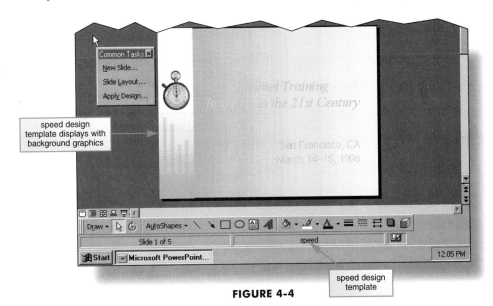

speed design template displays with background graphics

speed design template

FIGURE 4-4

More *About* **Color Schemes**

If you want to emphasize one aspect of your slide show, then you may want to apply a different color scheme to one slide. To do so, change to slide sorter view, on the Format menu, click Slide Color Scheme, select a different color scheme on the Standard sheet, and then click the Apply button.

Creating a Custom Background

Sometimes it is difficult to find a design template that has all the attributes your presentation requires. For example, you may find a design template with a pleasing design and attractive fonts, but you do not like the background objects or texture. Recall in Project 3, you modified the background by adding a picture of mountains. In this project, you want to modify the background by changing the texture. Perform the following steps to create a custom background.

TO CREATE A CUSTOM BACKGROUND

1 Right-click Slide 1 anywhere except the title or subtitle object. Click Background on the shortcut menu.

2 Click the Background fill area box arrow. Click Fill Effects in the list.

3 Click the Texture tab in the Fill Effects dialog box. Click the Bouquet texture (row 3, column 4).

4 Click the OK button and then click the Apply to all button in the Background dialog box.

When you customize the background, the design template text attributes remain the same, but the slide background changes (Figure 4-5 on the next page). Inserting the Bouquet texture for the slide background changes the appearance of the slide background but maintains the text attributes of the speed design template.

Clicking the Apply to all button applies the new background texture to every slide in the presentation. Clicking the Apply button in the Background dialog box, however, applies the new background texture only to the current slide or to any selected slides. If you click the Apply button by mistake, you can correct the error immediately by clicking the Undo button on the Standard toolbar and then reapplying the background texture to all slides.

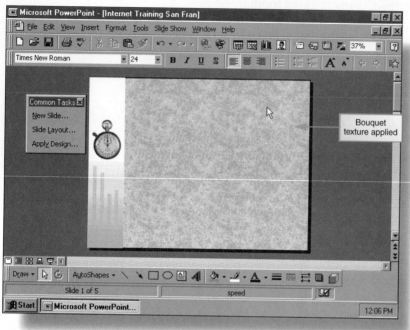

FIGURE 4-5

Modifying the Font Color

The gold text is difficult to read against the new Bouquet texture background, so you want to change the font color of the text. Recall in Project 3, you changed the text to the color gold. Now you want to change it to dark blue to complement the Bouquet texture background. Perform the following steps to change the font color of all text in the PowerPoint presentation from gold to dark blue.

TO CHANGE THE FONT COLOR

① Click the Outline View button on the View button bar.
② Click Edit on the menu bar, and then click Select All.
③ Right-click the selection. Click Font on the shortcut menu. Click the Color box arrow in the Font dialog box.
④ Click the Follow Title Text Scheme Color dark blue box (row 1, column 4).
⑤ Click the OK button.
⑥ Click the Slide View button on the View button bar.

Slide 1 displays the font color changes to the title and subtitle text (Figure 4-6).

FIGURE 4-6

The eight color samples in row 1 in the Color list in the Font dialog box represent the color scheme associated with the speed design template. A **color scheme** is a set of eight balanced colors you can apply to all slides, an individual slide, notes pages, or audience handouts. A color scheme consists of colors for a background, text and lines, shadows, title text, fills, accent, accent and hyperlink, and accent and followed hyperlink. Table 4-1 explains the components of a color scheme.

Table 4-1

COMPONENT	DESCRIPTION
Background color	The background color is the fundamental color of a PowerPoint slide. For example, if your background color is white, you can place any other color on top of it, but the fundamental color remains white. The white background shows everywhere you do not add color or other objects. The background color on a slide works the same way.
Text and lines color	The text and lines color contrasts with the background color of the slide. Together with the background color, the text and lines color sets the tone for a presentation. For example, a gray background with a black text and lines color sets a dreary tone. In contrast, a red background with a yellow text and lines color sets a vibrant tone.
Title text color	The title text color contrasts with the background color in a manner similar to the text and lines color. Title text displays in the title placeholder on a slide.
Shadow color	The shadow color is applied when you color an object. This color is usually a darker shade of the background color.
Fill color	The fill color contrasts with both the background color and the text and lines color. The fill color is used for graphs and charts.
Accent colors	Accent colors are designed as colors for secondary features on a slide. Additionally, accent colors are used as colors on graphs.

Creating a Logo

Many companies establish presentation standards to which every presentation must adhere. Very often, a company logo is part of those standards. Net-Train managers have asked you to create a new logo for the corporation (Figure 4-8 on the next page) and to display it on the title slide.

Creating and displaying the Net-Train Corporation logo requires several steps. First, you must open a new presentation and draw the square object. Next, you apply a border. Then, you use the company name to create a graphic text object using WordArt. The drawing and graphic text objects then are combined into one logo object. Finally, after copying the logo object onto the Clipboard, you paste it on the Internet Training San Fran title slide. The next several sections explain how to create the Net-Train Corporation logo.

Opening a New Presentation

Because you may want to reuse the Net-Train Corporation logo in other presentations, you should create it in a new presentation. Perform the steps on the next page to open a new presentation.

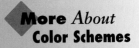

More *About*
Color Schemes

If you change color schemes, the colors you have added previously will remain displayed on the list. This feature is useful if you have mixed custom colors and need to display them on several slides.

TO OPEN A NEW PRESENTATION

① Click the New button on the Standard toolbar.
② Type 12 to select the Blank AutoLayout.
③ Click the OK button.
④ If necessary, click the Maximize button to maximize the PowerPoint window.

Slide 1 displays the Blank AutoLayout in a new presentation titled, Presentation1 (Figure 4-7).

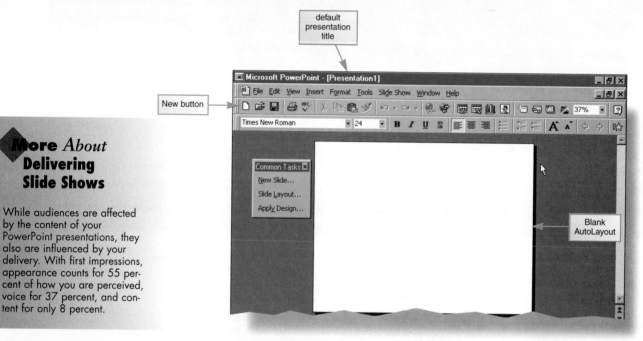

FIGURE 4-7

Drawing a Logo

The Net-Train Corporation logo is a square enclosing the company name. The logo is actually two objects, a square object and a text object. You create the square object using PowerPoint's drawing tools. Drawing the square object requires several steps. To help you draw the square object, display the horizontal and vertical rulers and guides to assist in aligning the objects. Next, increase the zoom percentage to see the detail of small objects better. Then, draw the outline of the square object using the Rectangle button on the Drawing toolbar. Finally, you add a border and change its line style. You will create the text object later in this project. The next several sections explain how to draw the square object shown in Figure 4-8.

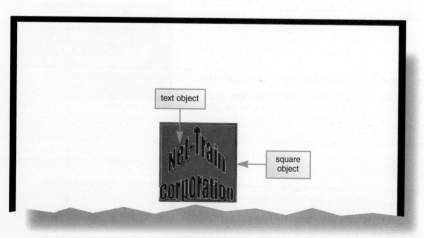

FIGURE 4-8

Displaying the Rulers

To help you align objects, PowerPoint provides two **rulers**: a horizontal ruler and a vertical ruler. The **horizontal ruler** displays at the top of the slide window. The **vertical ruler** displays at the left side of the slide window. When the zoom percentage is 25 or 33 percent, **tick marks** display in one-half-inch segments. When the zoom percentage is 50 percent or greater, tick marks display in one-eighth-inch segments. When you move the mouse pointer, a **pointer indicator** traces the position of the mouse pointer and displays its exact location on both rulers. You will use the rulers and pointer indicator later in this project when you draw the square object. In preparation for creating the logo, you display the rulers now. Perform the following steps to display the horizontal and vertical rulers.

 To Display the Rulers

① **Right-click anywhere on the blank slide, and then point to Ruler on the shortcut menu (Figure 4-9).**

② **Click Ruler.**

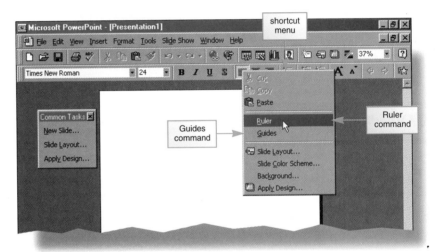

FIGURE 4-9

When the **Ruler command** is active, a check mark displays in front of the Ruler command on both the shortcut menu and the View menu. When you want to prohibit the rulers from displaying in the PowerPoint window, you hide them. To hide the rulers, right-click anywhere in the PowerPoint window except on an object, and then click Ruler.

Displaying the Guides

PowerPoint guides are used to align objects. The **guides** are two straight dotted lines, one horizontal and one vertical. When an object is close to a guide, its corner or its center (whichever is closer) *snaps*, or attaches itself, to the guide. You can move the guides to meet your alignment requirements. Because you are preparing the slide window to create the logo, perform this step to display the guides on the next page.

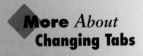

Steps To Display the Guides

1 Right-click anywhere on the blank slide, and then click Guides on the shortcut menu.

The horizontal and vertical guides intersect in the middle of the slide window and align with the 0-inch tick marks on the horizontal and vertical rulers (Figure 4-10).

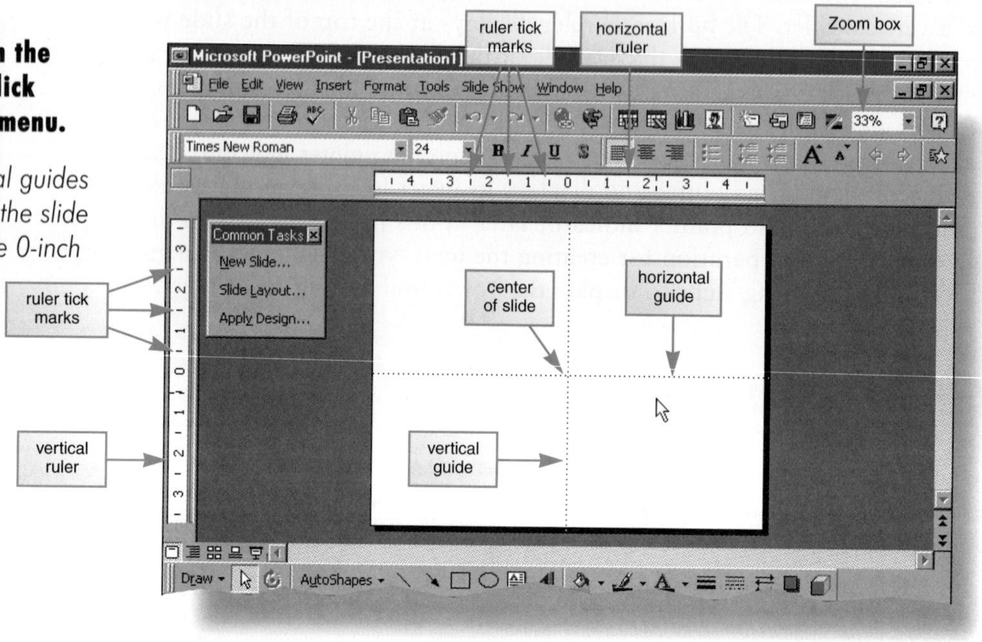

FIGURE 4-10

OtherWays

1. On View menu click Guides
2. Press ALT+V, press G

On the shortcut menu illustrated in Step 1, a check mark displays in front of the Ruler command because you activated it in the previous section. Recall that a check mark displays when a command is active, or turned on. In the same manner, when the Guides command is active, a check mark displays in front of the Guides command on both the shortcut menu and the View menu.

When you no longer want the guides to display on the screen or want to control the exact placement of objects, you can hide the guides. To hide the guides, right-click anywhere in the PowerPoint window except on an object, and click Guides.

More About Guides

You can display multiple vertical and horizontal guides on a screen. To display an additional guide, press and hold the CTRL key, and then drag one of the guides. When the new guide displays, drag it to the position where you want to place an object.

Increasing the Zoom Percentage

Increasing the zoom percentage reduces the editing view of a slide in slide view, but it increases the editing view of individual objects. You increase the zoom percentage to make working with detailed objects or small objects easier. In this project, you increase the zoom percentage to 100 percent because it allows you to work more easily with the two objects. The following steps summarize how to increase the zoom percentage.

TO INCREASE THE ZOOM PERCENTAGE

1. Click the Zoom box arrow on the Standard toolbar.
2. Click 100%.

The zoom percentage changes to 100% (Figure 4-11). When you compare Figure 4-10 to Figure 4-11, you see that the ruler tick marks display 1/8-inch increments. You may need to drag the vertical or horizontal scroll boxes so the 0-inch tick marks on the horizontal and vertical rulers display in the center of the screen.

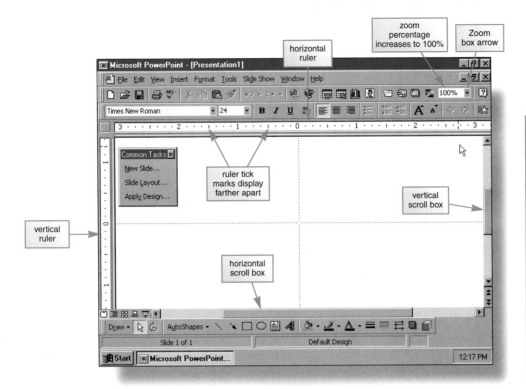

FIGURE 4-11

Drawing a Square

The next step in creating the Net-Train Corporation logo is drawing a square. A **square** is a plane with all sides at an equal distance from a given fixed point — the center. You draw a square using the **Rectangle button** on the Drawing toolbar. Because a Square button is not available, you constrain the shape of the object drawn using the Rectangle button. To draw a square, press and hold the CTRL+SHIFT keys, and then drag the mouse pointer as shown in the following steps.

Steps To Draw a Square

1 **Click the Rectangle button on the Drawing toolbar. Press and hold the CTRL+SHIFT keys. Position the crosshair mouse pointer at the intersection of the horizontal and vertical guides.**

The Rectangle button displays recessed, which indicates it is selected (Figure 4-12).

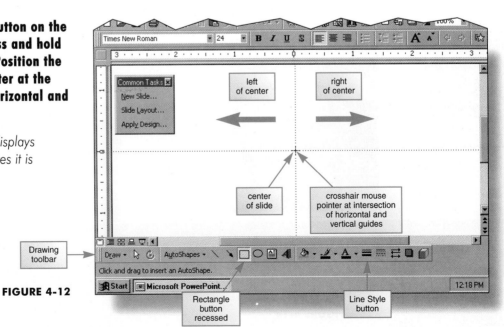

FIGURE 4-12

2 While holding the CTRL+SHIFT keys, drag the crosshair mouse pointer to the right of center until the pointer indicator on the horizontal ruler is on the 1¼ inch mark. Release the mouse button. Then release the CTRL+SHIFT keys.

A square displays the default attributes of the Default Design template: green fill color and black lines (Figure 4-13). Sizing handles around the square indicate it is selected. If necessary, drag the vertical or horizontal scroll boxes so the square displays in the center of the screen. The SHIFT key constrains the shape of the rectangle to draw a square. The CTRL key constrains the size of the square about center. When you release the CTRL+SHIFT keys, the Rectangle button is no longer recessed.

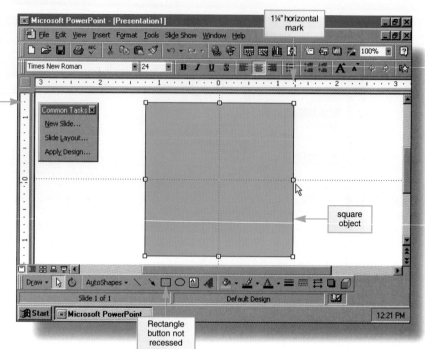

FIGURE 4-13

Changing the Logo Object Color

The next step in drawing the Net-Train Corporation logo is to change the logo object color from the default color green to the color pink. Perform the following steps to change the logo object color.

TO CHANGE THE LOGO OBJECT COLOR

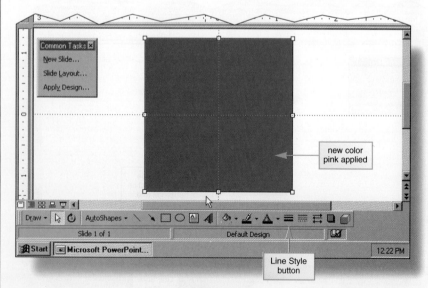

1 Right-click the square object. Click Format AutoShape on the shortcut menu.

2 If necessary, click the Colors and Lines tab.

3 Click the Color box arrow in the Fill area.

4 Click the Pink box (row 5, column 1 under Automatic).

5 Click the OK button.

The new color pink displays in the square object (Figure 4-14).

FIGURE 4-14

Changing a Logo Border

The next step in drawing the Net-Train Corporation logo is to add a border to the square object. Recall that a border is the visible line around the edge of an object and is composed of three attributes: line style, line color, and fill color. A border automatically displays around all objects you draw. The square shown in Figure 4-14 has a single-line border. Perform the following steps to add a two-line border.

TO CHANGE THE LOGO BORDER

1 If necessary, select the square object. Click the Line Style button on the Drawing toolbar.

2 Click the 3 pt two-line style from the Line Style list.

The new border displays around the square object (Figure 4-15).

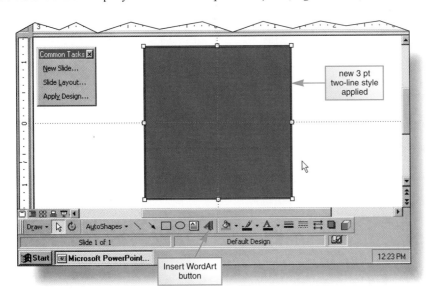

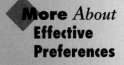

FIGURE 4-15

Adding Special Text Effects

The Net-Train Corporation logo contains letters that have been altered with special text effects. Using WordArt, you first will select a letter style for this text. Then, you will type the name of the corporation and shape these letters into a triangle, although many other predefined shapes could be used. Buttons on the WordArt toolbar also allow you to rotate, slant, curve, and alter the shape of letters. WordArt also can be used in the other Microsoft Office applications. The next several sections explain how to create the text object shown inside the square in Figure 4-8 on page PP 4.12.

Selecting a WordArt Style

PowerPoint supplies 30 predefined WordArt styles that vary in shape and color. Perform the steps on the next page to select a style for the Net-Train text.

Steps To Select a WordArt Style

1 **Click the Insert WordArt button on the Drawing toolbar. When the WordArt Gallery dialog box displays, click the WordArt style in row 2, column 5.**

The WordArt Gallery dialog box displays (Figure 4-16).

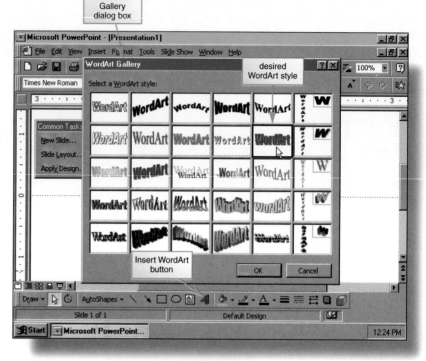

FIGURE 4-16

2 **Click the OK button.**

The Edit WordArt Text dialog box displays (Figure 4-17). The default text inside the dialog box is highlighted.

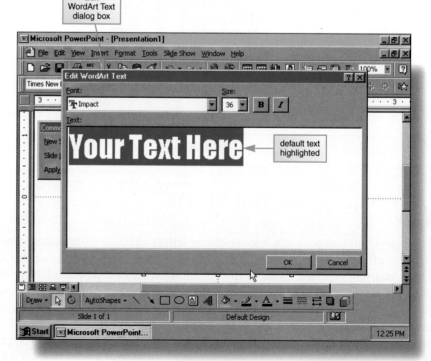

FIGURE 4-17

Entering the WordArt Text

To create a text object, you must enter text in the Edit WordArt Text dialog box. By default, the words, Your Text Here, in the Edit WordArt Text dialog box are highlighted. When you type the text for your logo, it replaces the selected text. When you want to start a new line, press the ENTER key. Perform the following steps to enter the text for the Net-Train Corporation logo.

 Steps **To Enter the WordArt Text**

1 **If necessary, select the text in the Edit WordArt Text dialog box. Type** Net-Train **and then press the ENTER key. Type** Corporation **but do not press the ENTER key.**

The two text lines display in the Text text box in the Edit WordArt Text dialog box (Figure 4-18). The default font is Impact, and the font size is 36.

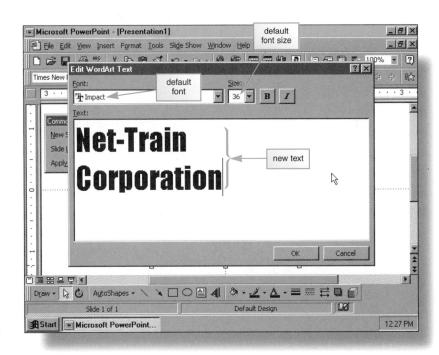

FIGURE 4-18

2 **Click the OK button. If necessary, display the WordArt toolbar by right-clicking a toolbar and clicking WordArt.**

The Net-Train Corporation text displays in front of the square object (Figure 4-19). The WordArt toolbar displays in the same location and with the same shape as it displayed the last time it was used.

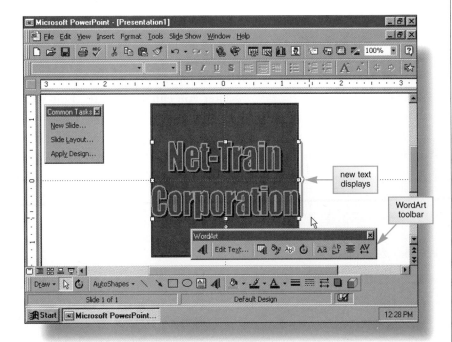

FIGURE 4-19

The WordArt toolbar contains the buttons that allow you to change an object's appearance. For example, you can rotate the letters, change the character spacing and alignment, scale the size, and add different fill and line colors. Table 4-2 explains the purpose of each button on the WordArt toolbar.

Table 4-2

BUTTON	BUTTON NAME	DESCRIPTION
◀	Insert WordArt	Creates a WordArt object
Edit Text...	WordArt Edit Text	Changes the text characters, font, and font size
▦	WordArt Gallery	Chooses a different WordArt style for the selected WordArt object
◈	Format WordArt	Formats the line, color, fill and pattern, size, position, and other properties of the selected object
Abc	WordArt Shape	Modifies the text shape
↺	Free Rotate	Turns an object around its axis
Aa	WordArt Same Letter Heights	Makes all letters the same height, regardless of case
Ab b↵	WordArt Vertical Text	Stacks the text in the selected WordArt object vertically — one letter on top of the other — for reading from top to bottom
≡	WordArt Alignment	Left-aligns, centers, right-aligns, word-aligns, letter-aligns, or stretch-aligns text
AV ↔	WordArt Character Spacing	Displays options (Very Tight, Tight, Normal, Loose, Very Loose, Custom, Kern Character Pairs) for adjusting spacing between text

The next section explains how to shape the WordArt text.

Shaping the WordArt Text

After you enter text in the Edit WordArt Text dialog box, you want to choose the basic shape of the letters. The text in the Net-Train Corporation logo in Figure 4-8 on PP 4.12 displays pointed at the top and wide at the bottom. Perform the following steps to choose a shape for the logo text object.

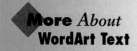

More *About*
WordArt Text

To create a graphic object in WordArt using text created in another application, highlight the text in that application, copy the text by using the CTRL+C keys, and then paste it inside PowerPoint's Edit WordArt Text dialog box by pressing the CTRL+V keys.

Steps **To Shape the WordArt Text**

1 **Click the WordArt Shape button on the WordArt toolbar. When the list displays, point to the Triangle Up shape (row 1, column 3).**

The WordArt shape list displays (Figure 4-20). By default, Plain Text is the selected shape.

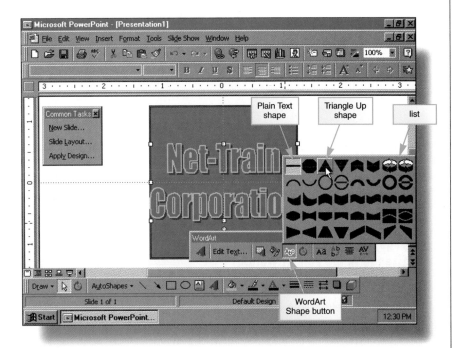

FIGURE 4-20

2 **Click Triangle Up.**

WordArt applies the Triangle Up shape to the text (Figure 4-21).

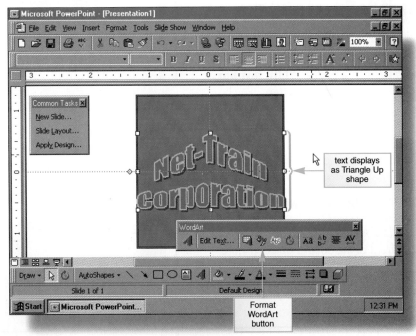

FIGURE 4-21

Changing the WordArt Height and Width

WordArt objects actually are drawing objects, not text. Consequently, they can be modified in various ways, including changing their height, width, line style, fill color, and shadows. Unlike text, however, they can neither display in outline view nor be spell checked. In this project, you will increase the height and decrease the width of the WordArt object. The Size tab in the Format WordArt dialog box contains two areas used to change an object's size. The first, the **Size and rotate area**, allows you to enlarge or reduce an object, and the rotate area allows you to turn an object around its axis. The second, the **Scale area**, allows you to change an object's size while maintaining its height-to-width ratio, or **aspect ratio**. If you want to retain the object's original settings, you click the Reset button in the **Original size area**. Perform the following steps to change the height of the WordArt object.

Steps **To Change the WordArt Height and Width**

① Click the Format WordArt button on the WordArt toolbar (see Figure 4-21 on the previous page). If necessary, click the Size tab in the Format WordArt dialog box.

The Size sheet displays in the Format WordArt dialog box.

② In the Size and rotate area, triple-click the Height text box. Type 2.4 in the Height text box. Triple-click the Width text box. Type 2.4 in the Width text box. Point to the OK button.

The Height and Width boxes display the new entries (Figure 4-22).

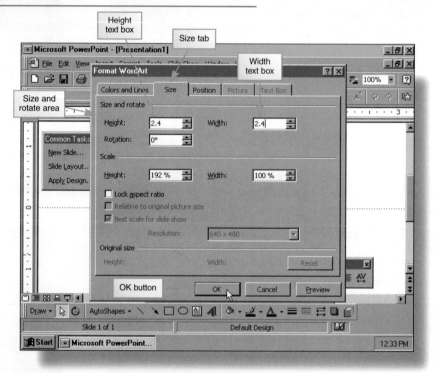

FIGURE 4-22

③ Click the OK button.

The WordArt text object displays in front of the square object (Figure 4-23).

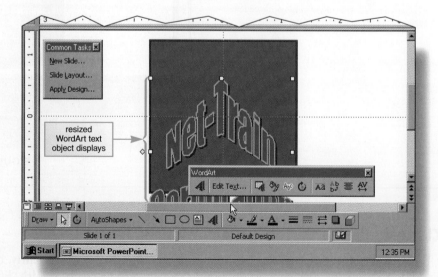

FIGURE 4-23

4 Drag the text object to the center of the square object. If necessary, you can make small adjustments in the position of the object by pressing the ARROW keys on the keyboard that correspond to the direction in which you want to move. Also, you can move the WordArt toolbar by dragging its title bar away from the text object.

The WordArt text object is centered in the square object (Figure 4-24).

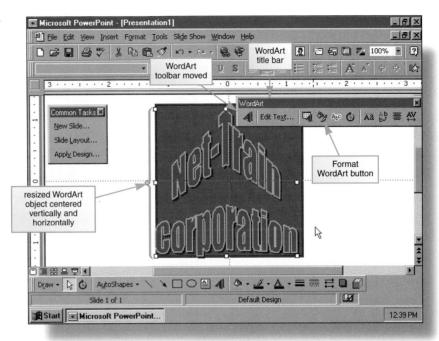

FIGURE 4-24

Changing the WordArt Fill Color

Now that the logo object is created, you want to change the font color to a dark blue. The Colors and Lines sheet in the Format WordArt dialog box contains an area to change the fill color. Perform the following steps to change the fill color.

 Steps **To Change the WordArt Fill Color**

1 Click the Format WordArt button on the WordArt toolbar. If necessary, click the Colors and Lines tab in the Format WordArt dialog box.

The Colors and Lines sheet displays in the Format WordArt dialog box (Figure 4-25).

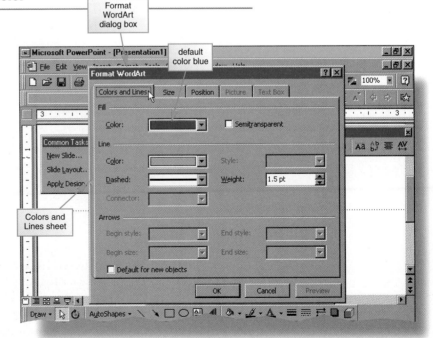

FIGURE 4-25

2 Click the Color box arrow in the Fill area. Click the color dark teal (row 2, column 5 under Automatic).

The color dark teal displays in the Fill area Color list box (Figure 4-26).

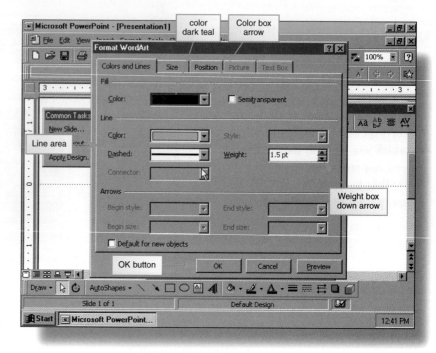

FIGURE 4-26

3 Click the Weight box down arrow in the Line area until 0.5 pt displays. Click the OK button.

The WordArt text object displays in front of the square object (Figure 4-27).

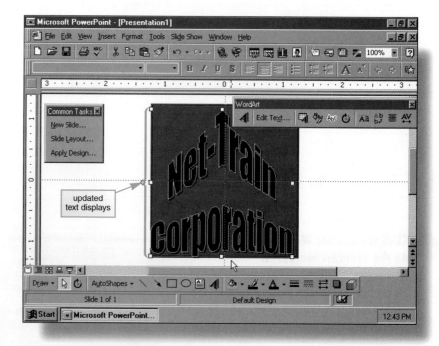

FIGURE 4-27

Grouping Objects

The final step in creating the Net-Train Corporation logo is to group the square object and the text object together to form one object. This action prevents one of the objects from being out of position when the logo is moved. Recall from Project 3 that you group objects together with the Group command on the short-cut menu. Perform the following steps to group the two objects.

TO GROUP OBJECTS

1. Click Edit on the menu bar, and then click Select All.
2. Right-click the selected objects, point to Grouping on the shortcut menu, and then click Group on the Grouping submenu.
3. Click the Save button on the Standard toolbar. If necessary, click the Look in box arrow, click 3½ Floppy (A:), and double-click the PowerPoint folder in the list. Type `Net-Train Logo` in the File name box. Press the ENTER key.

The two objects are grouped into one object (Figure 4-28). Sizing handles display around the grouped object. The logo is saved in the PowerPoint folder on the PowerPoint Project4 Data Disk in drive A.

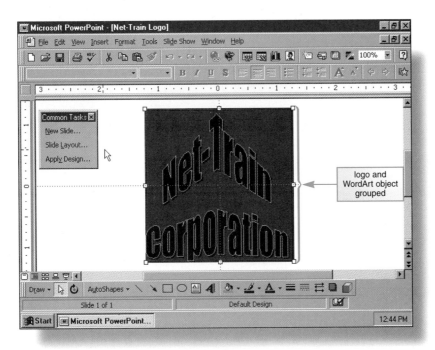

FIGURE 4-28

Grouping the text object with the square object converts the WordArt object into a PowerPoint object. If you need to modify the object, you must ungroup the logo, double-click the WordArt object, and then make the modifications.

Scaling an Object

The Net-Train logo object is too large to fit on the Internet Training San Fran seminar slides. To reduce the size of the object, you must scale it to 80 percent of its original size. Perform the steps on the next page to scale the logo object.

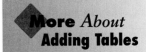

More *About*
Adding Tables

While PowerPoint does not have a Table feature, you can create a table on a slide in your presentation by using Microsoft Word's Table feature. To do so, click the Microsoft Word Table button on the Standard toolbar. Drag to indicate the number of rows and columns you want to insert. You can format the table by using Word tools and menus or by clicking Table on the menu bar and then clicking Table AutoFormat.

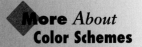

More *About*
Color Schemes

More than 15 percent of men have some form of red/green deficiency, which results in their seeing the color purple as blue and the color brown as green. This deficiency is more pronounced when they view these colors in small areas, such as the lines on charts. Thus, avoid using these colors in small areas of your slides, if possible.

Steps **To Scale the Logo Object**

1 If necessary, click the logo object to select it. Right-click the logo object and then click Format Object on the shortcut menu.

The Format Object dialog box displays.

2 Click the Size tab. Click Lock aspect ratio in the Scale area, and then click the Height text box down arrow until 80% displays. Point to the OK button.

The Height and Width text boxes both display 80% (Figure 4-29). When you change the percentage in the Height text box, the percentage in the Width text box also changes. In addition, the Height and Width text boxes in the Size and rotate area both change. The Lock aspect ratio check box is selected.

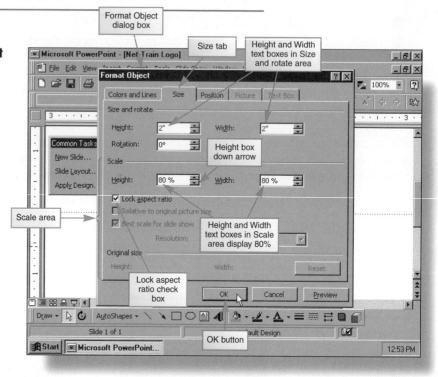

FIGURE 4-29

3 Click the OK button.

The logo object is reduced to 80 percent of its original size (Figure 4-30).

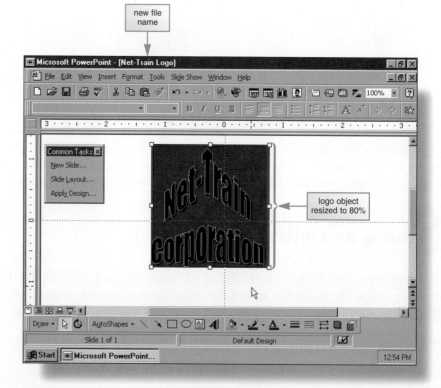

FIGURE 4-30

Adding an Object to the Slide Master

Your next step is to update the Internet Training San Fran presentation by adding your Net-Train logo object. You first must copy it from the Net-Train Logo presentation, and then paste it on the Internet Training San Fran presentation. If you want the logo to display on every slide, you must paste it on the slide master.

Perform the following steps to add the Net-Train Corporation logo to the slide master.

 Steps To Add an Object to the Slide Master

1 **Right-click the Net-Train Corporation logo, and then click Copy on the shortcut menu.**

A copy of the Net-Train Corporation logo is placed on the Clipboard.

2 **Click Window on the menu bar, and then point to 1 Internet Training San Fran (Figure 4-31).**

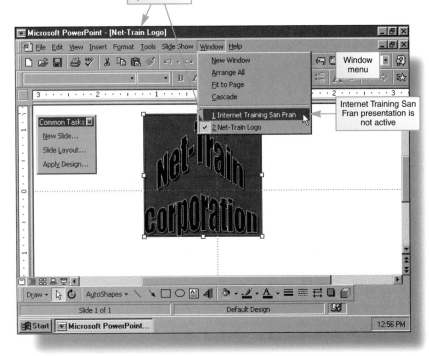

FIGURE 4-31

3 **Click 1 Internet Training San Fran.**

PowerPoint displays the Internet Training San Fran presentation (Figure 4-32). The Net-Train Logo presentation still is open but does not display.

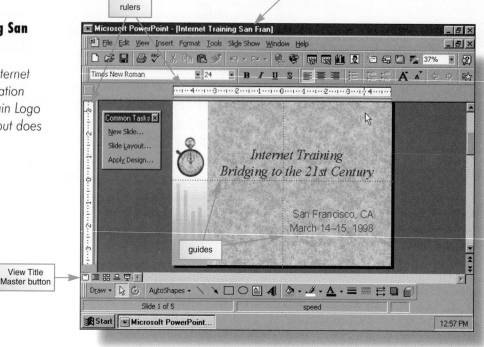

FIGURE 4-32

4 **Press and hold the SHIFT key, and then click the View Title Master button on the View button bar. Release the SHIFT key. Drag the vertical scroll box up to display the slide master.**

PowerPoint displays the slide master for the Internet Training San Fran presentation (Figure 4-33).

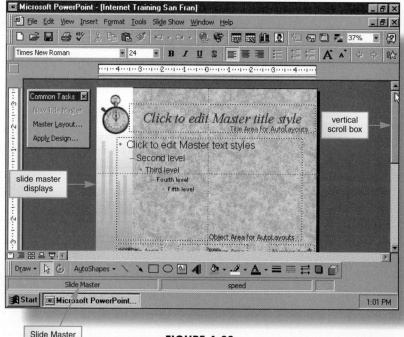

FIGURE 4-33

5 Right-click anywhere on the slide master, and then click Paste on the shortcut menu.

The logo object displays in the center of the slide master.

6 Drag the logo object to the upper left corner of the slide master so it covers the stopwatch object on the left side of the speed design template background.

The logo displays in the upper left corner of the slide master (Figure 4-34). If you want to make small adjustments in the position of the object, press the ARROW keys on the keyboard that correspond to the direction in which you want to move.

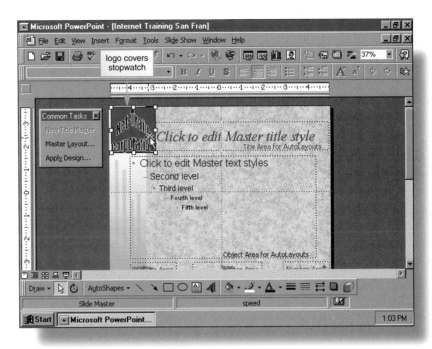

FIGURE 4-34

The rulers and guides stayed active when you changed presentation windows in Step 3. The Ruler command and the Guides command are PowerPoint settings, not slide attributes. Therefore, the rulers and guides display in the PowerPoint window whenever they are active, regardless of the presentation.

To inspect the logo and color scheme, click the Slide Show button. Notice the logo does not display on the title slide because the logo was pasted on the slide master, not the title master. Also notice the logo uses the color scheme of the slide. The next section explains how to paste the logo on the title slide.

Pasting an Object on a Title Slide

Because the San Francisco organizing team wants the Net-Train Corporation logo to display on every slide, you also must paste it on the title slide. Later in this project, you will animate the logo so it flies across the title slide from the right. Perform the steps on the next page to paste the logo on the title slide.

More *About*
Objects

Use an arrow to direct the viewers' eyes to an important area on the slide. Their eyes will move along the arrow's shape and then focus on the object or text at the arrowhead. By using the arrow to point to this content, you will not need to touch or point to the screen during the presentation.

Steps: To Paste an Object on a Title Slide

1 **Click the Slide View button on the View button bar. Right-click the slide and then click Paste on the shortcut menu.**

The logo displays in the center of Slide 1, the title slide (Figure 4-35).

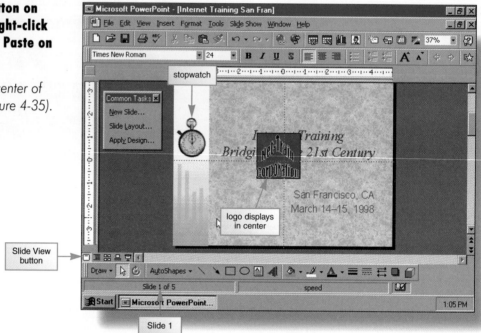

FIGURE 4-35

2 **Drag the logo to cover the stopwatch on the background graphic of the title slide (Figure 4-36).**

3 **Click the Save button on the Standard toolbar.**

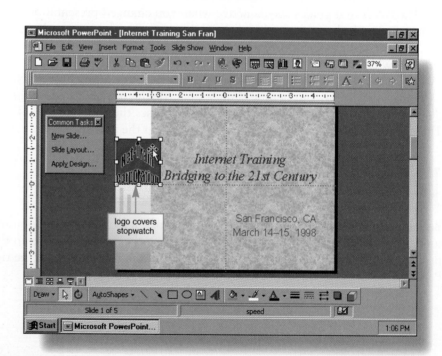

FIGURE 4-36

Because you do not need the rulers or guides when you modify the next slide, you want to hide them. Recall that a check mark displays in front of the Ruler and Guides commands on the shortcut menu and View menu when the commands are active. Perform the following steps to remove the check mark and deactivate, or hide, the rulers and guides.

TO HIDE THE RULERS AND GUIDES

① Right-click Slide 1 anywhere except the slide title or object placeholders.

② Click Ruler on the shortcut menu.

③ Right-click Slide 1 anywhere except the slide title or object placeholders.

④ Click Guides on the shortcut menu.

The rulers and guides no longer display.

Changing the Formatting of an Organization Chart

The black text and gold boxes and lines in the Microsoft Organization Chart on Slide 3 do not complement the new Bouquet texture. You therefore want to format the organization chart to change font color to white, the boxes color to pink, and the lines color to black. The shadow effects and border style selected in Project 3 can remain. Perform the following steps to change the organization chart formatting.

TO CHANGE THE ORGANIZATION CHART FORMATTING

① Click the Next Slide button twice to display Slide 3.

② Double-click an organization chart box to open the Microsoft Organization Chart application.

③ Click the Maximize button in the upper right corner of the Microsoft Organization Chart window.

④ Click Edit on the menu bar, point to Select, and then click All on the submenu.

⑤ Click Text on the menu bar, and then click Color.

⑥ Click the color White (row 1, column 2). Click the OK button.

⑦ With all the boxes in the organization chart still selected, click Lines on the menu bar, and then click Color.

⑧ Click the color Black (row 1, column 1). Click the OK button.

⑨ With all the boxes in the organization chart still selected, right-click one of the selected boxes. Click Color on the shortcut menu.

⑩ Click the color Pink (row 2, column 5). Click the OK button.

More *About*
Handouts

Handouts distributed to audience members should include more material than you cover verbally during the presentation. Do not merely reproduce all the slides in your slide show. If you use a slide that is detailed and complex, such as an organization chart, include that visual in your handouts and leave room for viewers to take notes.

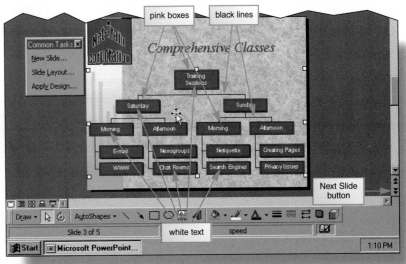

FIGURE 4-37

⑪ Click the Close button on the Microsoft Organization Chart – [Object in Internet Training San Fran] title bar. Click the Yes button in the Microsoft Organization Chart dialog box.

The Microsoft Organization Chart applies the new color white to the text, the color black to the lines, and the color pink to the boxes (Figure 4-37 on the previous page).

Creating an Interactive Document

The next step in customizing the Internet Training San Fran presentation is to add a slide to demonstrate two Internet Training sessions featured in the seminar. You add the new slide after Slide 3. Figure 4-38 illustrates the new Slide 4, which contains two action buttons to reference two sessions presented at the Internet Training San Fran seminar. An **action button** is a built-in 3-D button that can perform specific tasks such as display the next slide, provide help, give information, and play a sound. In addition, the action button can activate a **hyperlink**, which is a shortcut that allows you to jump to another program, in this case Microsoft Word, and load a specific document. A hyperlink also allows you to move to specific slides in a PowerPoint presentation or to an Internet address. In this slide, you will associate the hyperlink with an action button, but you also can use text or any object, including shapes, tables, or pictures. You specify which action you want PowerPoint to perform by using the **Action Settings** command on the Slide Show menu.

When you run the Internet Training San Fran presentation and click one of the action buttons on Slide 4, PowerPoint starts Microsoft Word and loads the designated file. For example, if you click the E-mail action button, PowerPoint opens the Microsoft Word application and loads the Word document, E-mail text.

Once you have finished viewing the E-mail text document, you want to return to Slide 4. To do so, you will create another hyperlink in the E-mail text file and specify that you want to jump to Slide 4 in the Internet Training San Fran slide show.

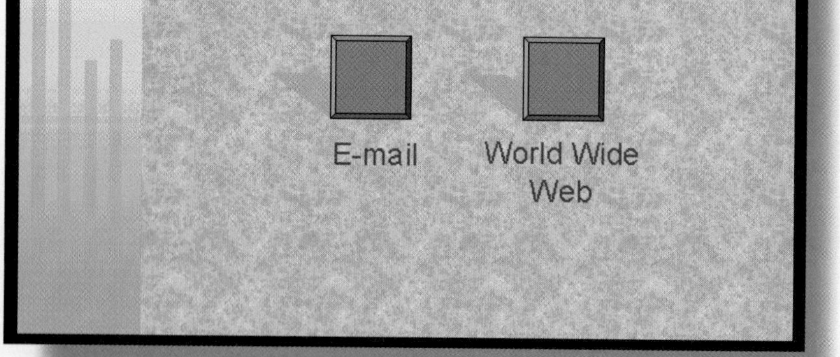

Creating the slide shown in Figure 4-38 requires several steps. First, you add a new slide to your presentation. Next, you display the guides. Then you add two action buttons, scale them, and add color and shadows. Then you create hyperlinks to the two Microsoft Word files and back to Slide 4. The next several sections explain how to create Slide 4.

Adding a New Slide

The first step in creating Slide 4 in this project is to add a new slide. Perform the following steps to add a new slide.

FIGURE 4-38

TO ADD A NEW SLIDE

① Click the New Slide button on the Common Tasks toolbar.

② When the New Slide dialog box displays, type 11 to select the Title Only AutoLayout.

③ Click the OK button.

The new Slide 4 displays the Title Only AutoLayout with the speed design template background graphics (Figure 4-39). PowerPoint automatically renumbers the original Slide 4 and Slide 5 as Slide 5 and Slide 6, respectively.

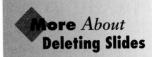

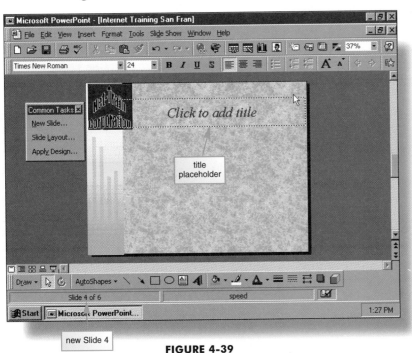

FIGURE 4-39

The title for Slide 4 is Internet Happenings. Perform the following step to add a slide title to Slide 4.

TO ADD A SLIDE TITLE

① Click the slide title placeholder and type Internet Happenings in that placeholder.

② Click anywhere on the slide except the slide title placeholder.

Internet Happenings displays in the title placeholder on Slide 4 (Figure 4-40).

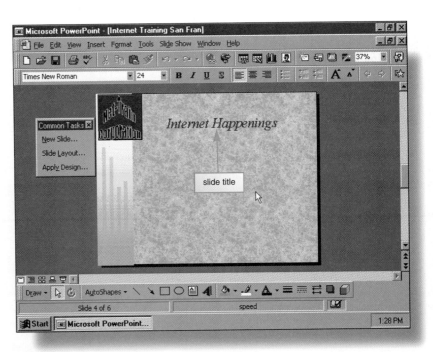

FIGURE 4-40

Adding Action Buttons and Action Settings

You want to feature two sessions that will be presented at the Internet Training seminar: E-mail and the World Wide Web. To obtain details on the E-mail session, you will click the left action button, and to obtain details on the World Wide Web session, you will click the right action button. When you click a button, a chime sound will play. The next section describes how to create the action buttons and place them on Slide 4.

Steps To Add an Action Button and Action Settings

① **Click Slide Show on the menu bar, and then point to Action Buttons.**

The Action Buttons submenu displays 12 built-in 3-D buttons (Figure 4-41).

FIGURE 4-41

② **Click the Action Button: Custom action button (row 1, column 1) in the list. Click anywhere on Slide 4 except the slide title placeholder.**

The action button is placed on Slide 4, and the Action Settings dialog box displays (Figure 4-42). None is the default Action on click.

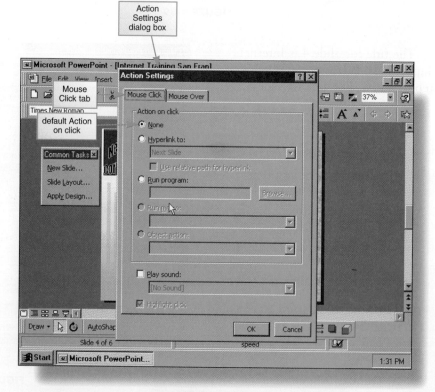

FIGURE 4-42

3 If necessary, click the Mouse Click tab. Click Hyperlink to in the Action on click area. Click the Hyperlink to box arrow. Point to Other File.

The list box displays the possible locations in the slide show or elsewhere where a hyperlink can be established (Figure 4-43).

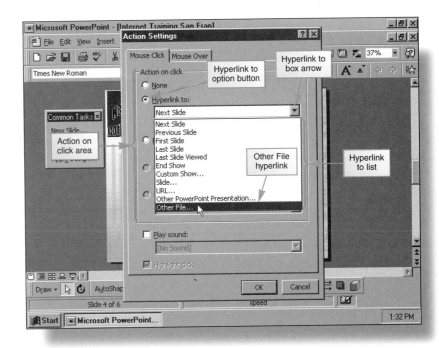

FIGURE 4-43

4 Click Other File. If necessary, click the Look in box arrow, click 3½ Floppy (A:), and then double-click the PowerPoint folder in the list. Click E-mail text in the list.

E-mail text is the Microsoft Word file you will link to the left action button (Figure 4-44).

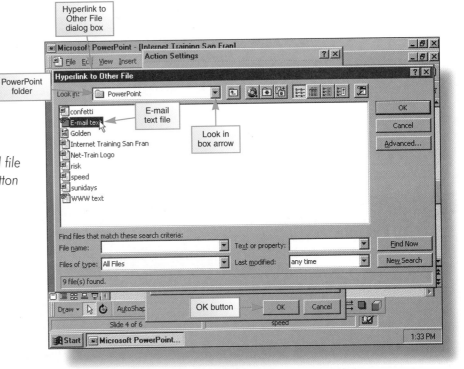

FIGURE 4-44

5 Click the OK button in the Hyperlink to Other File dialog box. Click Use relative path for hyperlink. Point to Play sound.

The Hyperlink to box displays E-mail text.doc (Figure 4-45).

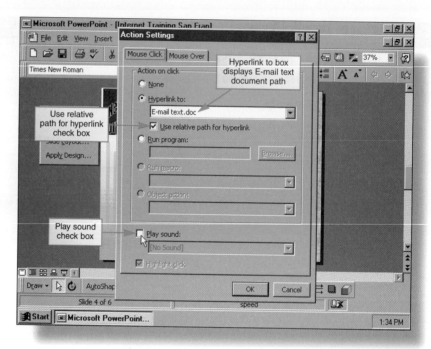

FIGURE 4-45

6 Click Play sound. Click the Play sound box arrow. Point to Chime.

The Play sound list displays sounds that can play when you click the action button (Figure 4-46).

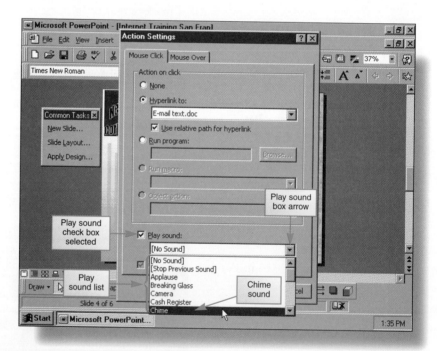

FIGURE 4-46

7 **Click Chime. Click the OK button.**

The action button is highlighted on Slide 4 (Figure 4-47).

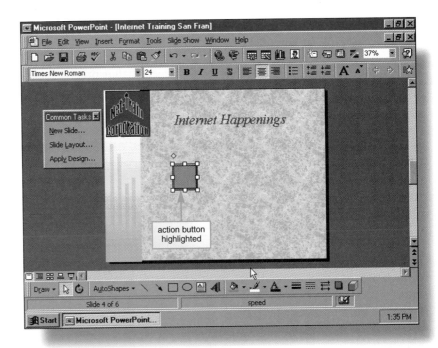

FIGURE 4-47

Now that you have created an action button and linked the E-mail text document, you need to repeat the procedure for the WWW text document. Perform the following steps to create another action button and to hyperlink the second Microsoft Word document to your PowerPoint presentation.

TO CREATE A SECOND ACTION BUTTON AND HYPERLINK

1 Click Slide Show on the menu bar, point to Action Buttons, and click the Action Button: Custom action button (row 1, column 1) in the list.

2 Click anywhere on Slide 4 except the slide title placeholder or the first action button.

3 Click Hyperlink to in the Action on click area on the Mouse Click sheet.

4 Click the Hyperlink to box arrow. Click Other File.

5 Double-click WWW text in the list. Click Use relative path for hyperlink.

6 Click Play sound. Click the Play sound box arrow and click Chime.

7 Click the OK button.

Slide 4 displays with the second action button for the World Wide Web hyperlink (Figure 4-48 on the next page).

More *About*
Microsoft Graph

You can create or modify a graph by using Microsoft Graph, which is a program installed when PowerPoint was installed on your system. To build a graph, click the Insert Chart button on the Standard toolbar. Then, replace the sample data by clicking a cell on the datasheet and typing your data. You also can replace the sample row and column labels on the datasheet. To return to PowerPoint, click anywhere on the PowerPoint slide other than the chart.

When creating a presentation with interactive documents, you can set the path to the hyperlinks as absolute or relative links. When you use an **absolute link**, you assume you will keep your files in the same location, such as on a floppy disk, and you specify that precise location in the Hyperlink to text area. In this project, however, you use a **relative link** because you may need to move or copy these files to a different location, such as a hard drive.

Displaying Guides and Positioning Action Buttons

Recall that the guides assist you in placing objects at specific locations on the slide. When an object is close to a guide, it jumps to the guide. In this project, you use the vertical and horizontal guides to help position the action buttons and captions on Slide 4. The center of a slide is 0.00 on both the vertical and the horizontal guides. You position a guide by dragging it to a new location. When you point to a guide and then press and hold the mouse button, PowerPoint displays a box containing the exact position of the guide on the slide in inches. An arrow displays under the guide position to indicate the vertical guide is either left or right of center. An arrow displays to the right of the guide position to indicate the horizontal guide is either above or below center. Perform the following steps to display and position the guides.

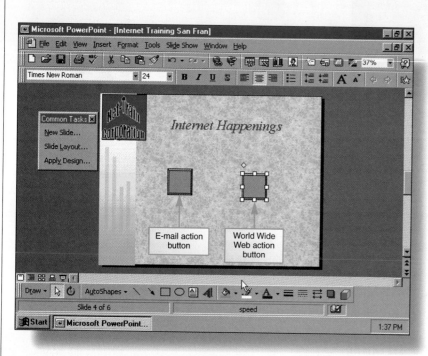

FIGURE 4-48

 Steps To Display and Position the Guides

① **Right-click Slide 4 anywhere except on the title placeholder or the action buttons. Click Guides on the shortcut menu.**

The horizontal and vertical guides display at the center of Slide 4.

② **Drag the vertical guide to 1.00 inch left of center (Figure 4-49).**

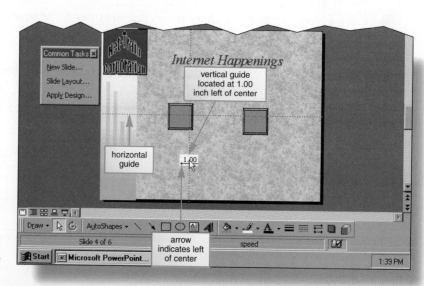

FIGURE 4-49

3 Click the horizontal guide to ensure it is displaying at the center (0.00) (Figure 4-50).

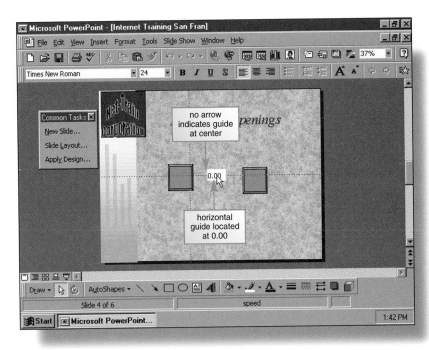

FIGURE 4-50

4 Drag the left action button for the E-mail text hyperlink until the top edge snaps to the horizontal guide and the left edge snaps to the vertical guide.

The top of the E-mail text action button aligns with the horizontal guide, and the left side of the button aligns with the vertical guide (Figure 4-51).

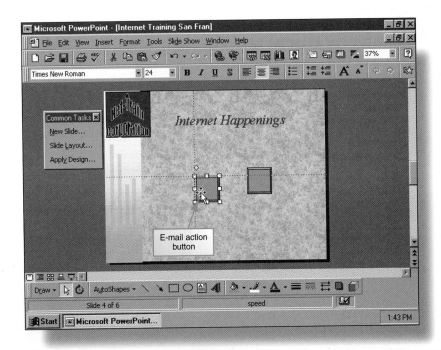

FIGURE 4-51

5 Drag the vertical guide to 1.50 inches right of center (Figure 4-52).

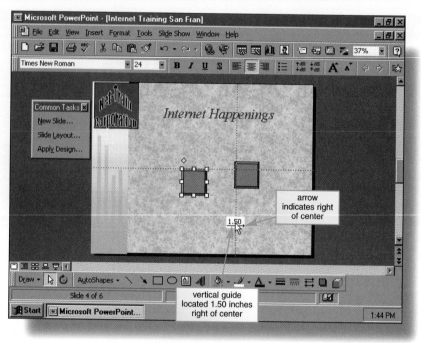

FIGURE 4-52

6 Drag the right action button for the WWW text hyperlink until the top edge snaps to the horizontal guide and the left edge snaps to the vertical guide.

The top of the World Wide Web action button aligns with the horizontal guide, and the left side of the button aligns with the vertical guide (Figure 4-53).

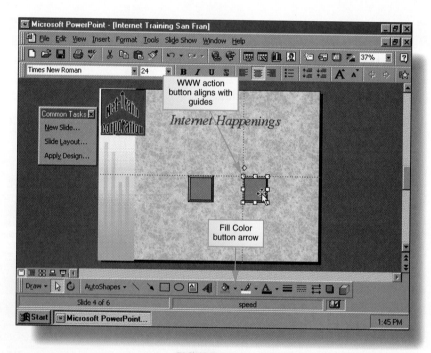

FIGURE 4-53

Scaling Objects

The action buttons on Slide 4 are too large in proportion to the screen. Perform the following steps to scale the two action buttons simultaneously.

TO SCALE ACTION BUTTONS

1 With the World Wide Web action button still selected, press and hold the SHIFT key. Click the E-mail action button. Release the SHIFT key.

2 Right-click either action button and then click Format AutoShape on the shortcut menu.

3 If necessary, click the Size tab. In the Scale area, click Lock aspect ratio, and then triple-click the Height text box. Type 90 in the Height text box.

4 Click the OK button.

Both action buttons are resized to 90 percent of their original size (Figure 4-54).

FIGURE 4-54

Adding Fill Color to the Action Buttons

To better identify the action buttons from the slide background, you must add fill color. Recall that fill color is the interior color of a selected object. Perform the following steps to add fill color to the action buttons on Slide 4.

 To Add Fill Color to the Action Buttons

1 **With the two action buttons still selected, click the Fill Color button arrow on the Drawing toolbar.**

The Fill Color list displays (Figure 4-55). Automatic is highlighted, indicating that gray is the current default fill color.

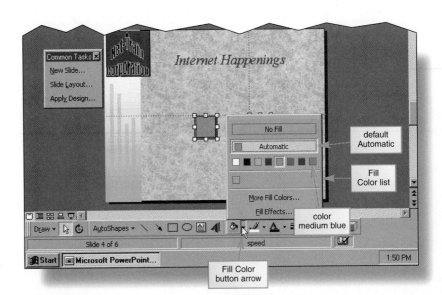

FIGURE 4-55

2 **Click the color medium blue (row 1, column 8 under Automatic).**

Both action buttons display filled with the color medium blue (Figure 4-56). Medium blue is the Follow Accent and Followed Hyperlink Scheme Color in the speed design template color scheme.

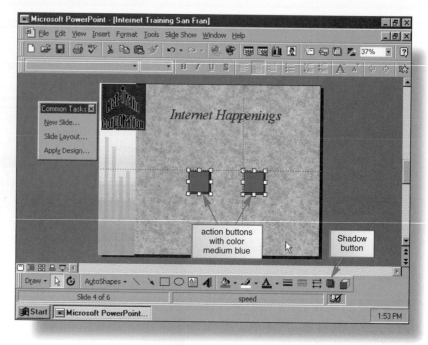

FIGURE 4-56

Adding Shadow Effects to the Action Buttons

To add depth to an object, you can **shadow** it by clicking the Shadow button on the Drawing toolbar. Perform the following steps to add shadows to the two action buttons on Slide 4.

TO ADD SHADOWS TO THE ACTION BUTTONS

1 Click the Shadow button on the Drawing toolbar.
2 Click Shadow Style 11 (row 3, column 3) in the style list.

PowerPoint adds the shadow to the two action buttons (Figure 4-57).

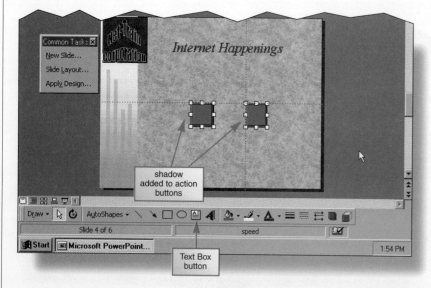

Adding Captions to the Action Buttons

The final components of Slide 4 that you need to add are the captions under the two action buttons. Perform the following steps to add captions to the action buttons on Slide 4.

FIGURE 4-57

TO ADD CAPTIONS TO THE ACTION BUTTONS

① Click the Text Box button on the Drawing toolbar.

② Click below the left action button. Type E-mail as the caption.

③ Click the Text Box button on the Drawing toolbar.

④ Click below the right action button, click the Center Alignment button on the Formatting tool- bar, type World Wide as the first caption line, and then press the ENTER key. Type Web as the second caption line.

The captions for the two action buttons display (Figure 4-58).

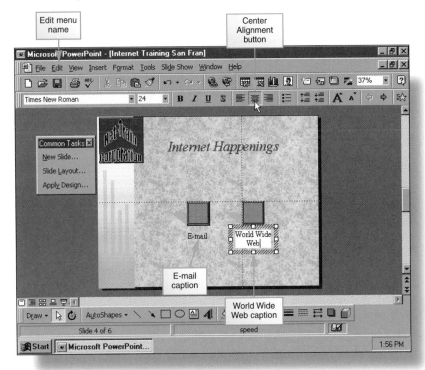

FIGURE 4-58

Formatting Text

To add visual appeal to the captions, you want to change the font to Arial, increase the font size to 28, and change the color to the same color as the title text. Perform the following steps to format the captions for the action buttons on Slide 4.

 Steps To Format Text

① With the World Wide Web caption text highlighted, click Edit on the menu bar, and then click Select All.

② Right-click the text and then click Font on the shortcut menu. When the Font list dialog box displays, click the Font box up arrow, and then scroll up and click Arial. Click the Size list box down arrow, and then click 28.

Arial displays in the Font list box, and the font size 28 displays in the Size list box (Figure 4-59).

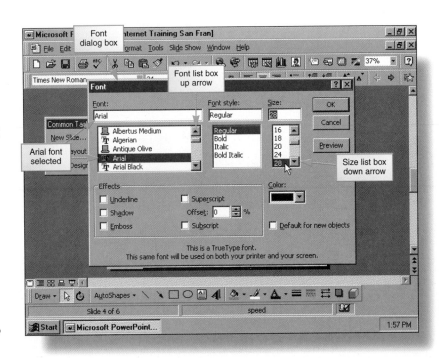

FIGURE 4-59

3 Click the Color box arrow and then point to the color dark blue (row 1, column 4 under Automatic).

The color dark blue is the Follow Title Text Scheme Color in the speed design template color scheme (Figure 4-60).

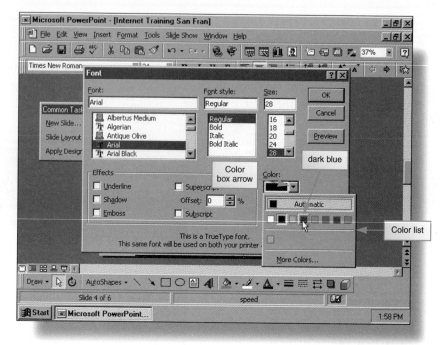

FIGURE 4-60

4 Click the color dark blue.

The color dark blue displays in the Color list box (Figure 4-61).

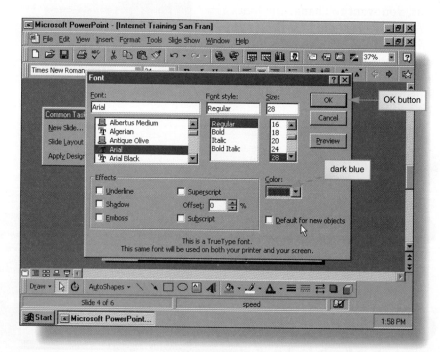

FIGURE 4-61

5 Click the OK button and then click anywhere on a blank area of the slide.

PowerPoint displays the World Wide Web caption with the 28-point Arial font and the color dark blue (Figure 4-62).

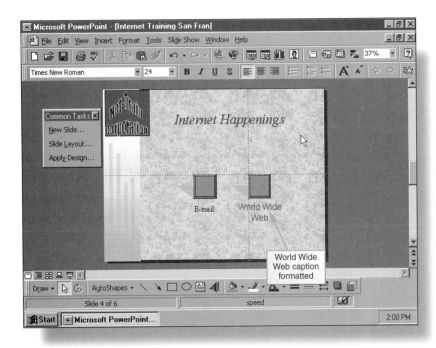

FIGURE 4-62

Now that you have formatted the World Wide Web caption text, you need to repeat the procedure to format the E-mail caption text. Perform the following steps to format the E-mail caption text.

TO FORMAT A SECOND CAPTION TEXT

1 Click the E-mail caption, click Edit on the menu bar, and then click Select All.

2 Right-click the text and click Font on the shortcut menu. When the Font dialog box displays, click the Font list box up arrow, and then scroll up and click Arial.

3 Click the Size list box down arrow, and then click 28.

4 Click the Color box arrow and then click the color dark blue (row 1, column 4 under Automatic).

5 Click the OK button and then click anywhere on a blank area of the slide.

Slide 4 is complete (Figure 4-63).

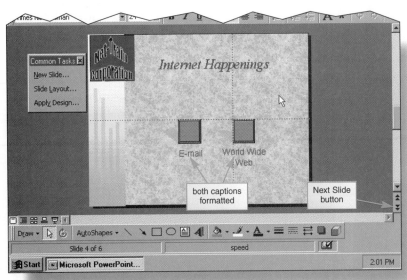

FIGURE 4-63

Now that the captions are added and formatted, you may need to make slight adjustments to their placement under the action buttons. If so, click the caption, click the border, and use the ARROW keys to position the text as shown in Figure 4-63.

Editing the Slide Title and Replacing a Picture

The Convenient Lodging slide, Slide 5, touts the features associated with staying at the housing in Park City, Utah. You want to change that slide to encourage prospective San Francisco workshop attendees to integrate educational activities with recreational activities in that city. Because this presentation is being customized for the San Francisco seminar, you will change the slide title and replace the picture of the lodge with the picture of the Golden Gate Bridge (Figure 4-72 on page PP 4.51). To replace a picture, first delete the existing picture and then insert the new picture, scale the picture, position and resize the picture to fit the slide, and then reapply the border. The next several sections explain how to replace the picture on Slide 5.

Editing the Slide Title

Because you want to emphasize the tourist activities available in San Francisco, you must change the title text on Slide 5. Recall that text objects that display on a slide can be edited in slide view or outline view and that you select text before editing it. Perform the following steps to display the title slide in slide view and then revise the title text.

TO EDIT TEXT

1 Click the Next Slide button to display Slide 5.
2 Double-click the word, Lodging, in the slide title.
3 Type Activities in place of the highlighted text.

Slide 5 displays the updated title text (Figure 4-64).

Editing a Bulleted List

You need to edit the bulleted list to change the text from housing features to tourist activities. Select the bulleted list on Slide 5 by dragging through all the text. Then type the replacement text. Perform the following steps to edit the bulleted list on Slide 5.

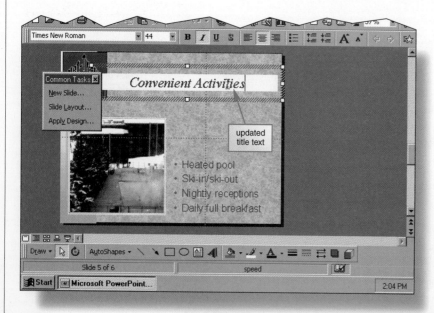

FIGURE 4-64

TO EDIT A BULLETED LIST

① Drag through the text in the bulleted list to select it.

② Type Golden Gate
Bridge and then press
the ENTER key. Type
Fisherman's Wharf and
then press the ENTER key.
Type Chinatown and
then press the ENTER key.
Type Alcatraz but do
not press the ENTER key.

Slide 5 displays the edited bulleted list (Figure 4-65).

Deleting an Object

A picture is an object. To delete any object in PowerPoint, you must select the object and then press the DELETE key. Perform the following steps to delete the Convenient Lodging picture on Slide 5.

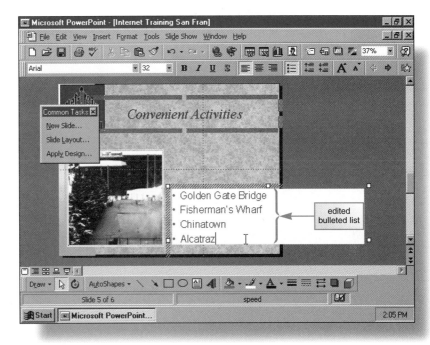

FIGURE 4-65

TO DELETE AN OBJECT

① Click the picture of the lodge.

② Press the DELETE key.

The picture is deleted (Figure 4-66).

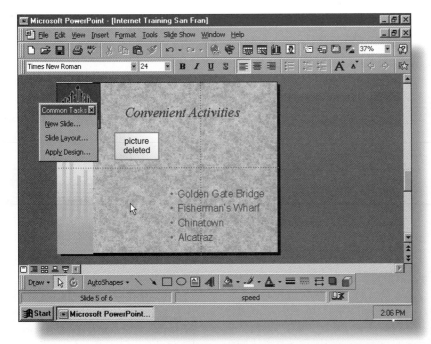

FIGURE 4-66

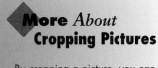

More *About* **Cropping Pictures**

By cropping a picture, you can focus on a specific portion of the picture and trim the parts you do not want to see. To crop a picture, click the picture, click the Crop button on the Picture toolbar, place the cropping tool over a sizing handle, and drag to frame the portion of the picture you want to include on your slide.

Inserting a Picture

The Internet Training San Fran presentation displays a picture of the Golden Gate Bridge to enhance the Convenient Activities slide. Perform the following steps to insert a picture on Slide 5.

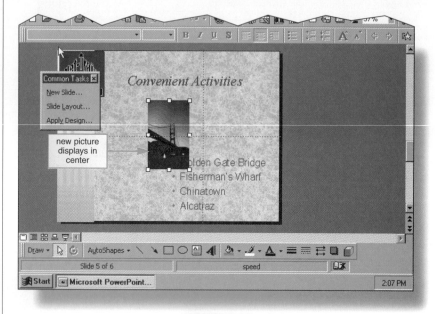

FIGURE 4-67

TO INSERT A PICTURE

① Click Insert on the menu bar, point to Picture, and then click From File on the Picture submenu.

② When the Insert Picture dialog box displays, if necessary, click the Look in box arrow, click 3½ Floppy (A:), and double-click the PowerPoint folder in the list. Double-click Golden.

The Golden Gate Bridge picture displays in the center of the slide (Figure 4-67).

Scaling an Object

To change the size of an object, you must scale it to retain the object's original proportions. Perform the following steps to scale the Golden Gate Bridge picture to 150 percent.

TO SCALE AN OBJECT

① With the Golden picture selected, right-click the picture, and then click Format Picture on the shortcut menu.

② Click the Size tab.

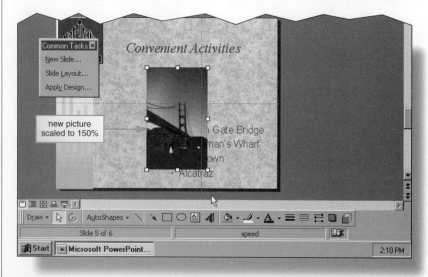

FIGURE 4-68

③ Triple-click the Height text box in the Scale area. Type 150 in the Height text box, and then click the OK button.

PowerPoint scales the picture to 150 percent of its original size (Figure 4-68).

Positioning and Resizing an Object

Recall that when an object is close to a guide, it jumps to the guide. Perform the following steps to position the Golden Gate Bridge picture using the vertical and horizontal guides.

Steps To Position and Resize an Object

1 Drag the vertical guide to 0.75 inch left of center (Figure 4-69).

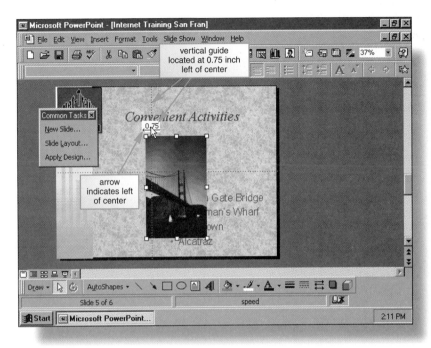

FIGURE 4-69

2 Drag the horizontal guide to 1.58 inches above center (Figure 4-70).

FIGURE 4-70

3 Drag the picture to the left until the top snaps to the horizontal guide and the right side snaps to the vertical guide.

The top of the picture aligns with the horizontal guide, and the right side of the picture aligns with the vertical guide (Figure 4-71).

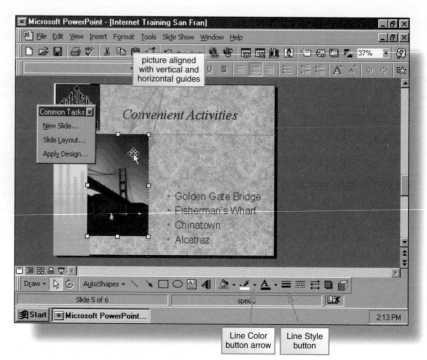

FIGURE 4-71

Now that the new picture is positioned correctly on Slide 5, the vertical and horizontal guides are not needed. Perform the following steps to hide the guides.

TO HIDE GUIDES

1 Right-click Slide 5 anywhere except on an object placeholder.
2 Click Guides on the shortcut menu.

The guides no longer display.

Adding a Border

The final step in replacing the picture on Slide 5, is to apply a two-line thin border. The Text and lines color in the speed design template color scheme is black. When you apply a line style, PowerPoint applies the text and lines color automatically. Perform the following steps to apply the 3 pt two-line border to the Golden Gate Bridge picture on Slide 5, and change the border color to dark blue.

TO ADD A BORDER

1 Click the picture.
2 Click the Line Style button on the Drawing toolbar.
3 Click the 3 pt two-line style on the list.
4 Click the Line Color button arrow on the Drawing toolbar. Click the color dark blue (row 1, column 4 under Automatic).

A dark blue, two-line border displays around the picture of the Golden Gate Bridge (Figure 4-72). The color dark blue is the Follow Title Text Scheme Color in the speed design template color scheme.

OtherWays

1. On View menu click Guides
2. Press ALT+V, press G

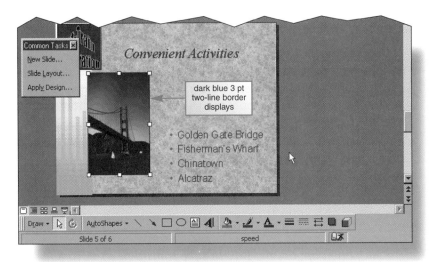

FIGURE 4-72

Ending a Presentation with a Black Slide

When you end a slide show, PowerPoint returns to the PowerPoint window. Recall that a closing slide allows you to end a slide show gracefully so the audience never sees the PowerPoint window. The Internet Training San Fran presentation currently uses Slide 6 for a closing slide.

The PowerPoint **End with black slide** option ends your presentation with a black slide. A black slide displays only when the slide show is running. A black slide ends all slide shows until the option setting is deactivated.

Ending with a Black Slide

To end with a black slide, complete the following steps.

 Steps To End a Slide Show with a Black Slide

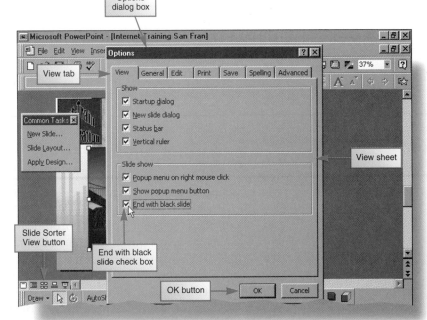

1 **Click Tools on the menu bar, and then click Options. If necessary, click the View tab. Click End with black slide.**

The Options dialog box displays (Figure 4-73). A check mark displays in the End with black slide check box.

2 **Click the OK button.**

The End with black slide option is activated.

FIGURE 4-73

Applying Slide Transition Effects

Slide 4 was added to the presentation and therefore does not have slide transition effects applied. Recall from Project 3 that the Box In slide transition effect was applied to all slides except Slide 1. To keep Slide 4 consistent with the other slides in the presentation, apply the Dissolve slide transition effect as described in the following steps.

TO APPLY SLIDE TRANSITION EFFECTS

1. Click the Slide Sorter View button on the View button bar.
2. Click Slide 4.
3. Click the Slide Transition Effects box arrow. Click Box In.

PowerPoint applies the Box In slide transition effect to Slide 4. An icon displays below Slide 4 indicating a slide transition effect is applied (Figure 4-74).

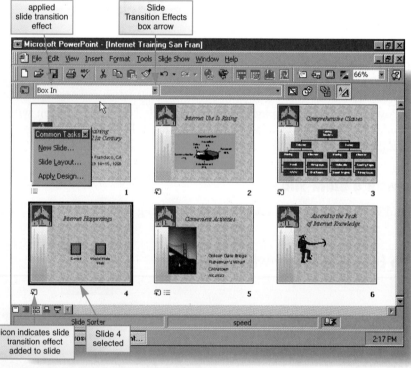

FIGURE 4-74

Hiding Slides

A **supporting slide** provides detailed information to supplement another slide in the presentation. For example, in a presentation to department chairpersons about the increase in student enrollment, one slide displays a graph representing the current year's enrollment and the previous three years' enrollment figures. The supporting slide for the slide with the graph displays a departmental student enrollment table for each year in the graph.

When running a slide show, you may not always want to display the supporting slide. You would display it when time permits and when you want to show the audience more detail about a topic. You should insert the supporting slide

More *About*
Black Slides

Black slides can be useful within the presentation when you want to pause for discussion and have the audience focus on the speaker. To create a black slide, click New Slide on the Common Tasks toolbar, select the Blank slide layout, click Format on the menu bar, click Background, click the Background fill box arrow, and click the color black fill color.

after the slide you anticipate may warrant more detail. Then, you use the Hide Slide command to hide the supporting slide. The **Hide Slide command** hides the supporting slide from the audience during the normal running of a slide show. When you want to display the supporting hidden slide, press the H key. No visible indicator displays to show that a hidden slide exists. You must be aware of the content of the presentation to know where the supporting slide is located.

Hiding a Slide

Slide 4 is a slide that supports the session information displayed in Slide 3. If time permits, or if the audience requires more information, you can display Slide 4. As the presenter, you decide whether to show Slide 4. You hide a slide in slide sorter view so you can see the slashed square surrounding the slide number, which indicates the slide is hidden. Perform the following step to hide Slide 4.

 Steps To Hide a Slide

1 **Right-click Slide 4 and then click Hide Slide on the shortcut menu.**

A square with a slash surrounds the slide number to indicate Slide 4 is a hidden slide (Figure 4-75). The Hide Slide button is recessed on the Slide Sorter toolbar and on the shortcut menu.

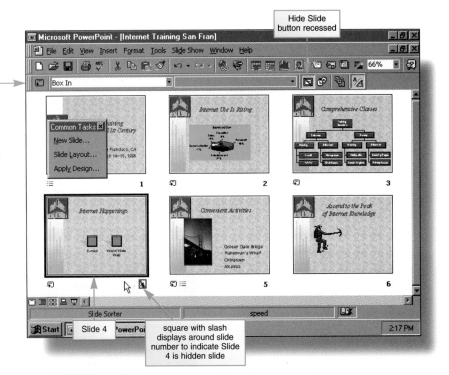

FIGURE 4-75

Other Ways

1. Click Hide Slide button on Slide Sorter toolbar
2. On Slide Show menu click Hide Slide
3. Press ALT+D, press H

The Hide Slide button is a toggle — it either hides or displays a slide. It also applies or removes a square with a slash surrounding the slide number. When you no longer want to hide a slide, change views to slide sorter view, right-click the slide, and then click Hide Slide on the shortcut menu. This action removes the square with a slash surrounding the slide number.

An alternative to hiding a slide in slide sorter view is to hide a slide in slide view, outline view, or notes page view. In these views, however, no visible indication is given that a slide is hidden. To hide a slide in slide view or notes page view, display the slide you want to hide, click Slide Show on the menu bar, and

More *About* Presentation Conferencing

PowerPoint's Conference Wizard helps you prepare your PowerPoint slide show to display over a Windows NT server and a Novell network, an intranet, and the Internet. You and your viewers all use the wizard to participate in the conference. You, as the presenter, can use Stage Manager tools such as the Slide Meter to time the presentation. All participants can write on the slides using the annotation pen. They will not be able to view embedded objects, however, such as the Excel chart on Slide 2 in this project.

then click Hide Slide. To hide a slide in outline view, select the slide icon of the slide you want to hide, click Slide Show on the menu bar, and then click Hide Slide. An icon displays in front of the Hide Slide command on the Slide Show menu, and it is recessed when the slide is hidden. You also can choose not to hide a slide in slide view, notes page view, and outline view by clicking Hide Slide on the Slide Show menu. The icon in front of the Hide Slide command no longer is recessed, and the slide then displays like all the other slides in the presentation.

When you run your presentation, the hidden slide does not display unless you press the H key when the slide preceding the hidden slide is displaying. For example, Slide 4 does not display unless you press the H key when Slide 3 displays in slide show view. You continue your presentation by clicking the mouse or pressing any of the keys associated with running a slide show. You skip the hidden slide by clicking the mouse and advancing to the next slide.

Animating Text and an Object

To seize the attention of the audience, the San Francisco Internet Training organizing committee wants the Net-Train Corporation logo to fly across the slide after the animated subtitle text automatically spirals onto the screen. The committee also wants you to make the mountain climber on Slide 6 move upward from the bottom of the slide. PowerPoint allows you to animate individual objects on a slide. The animation settings for objects are the same as those used for the text preset animation effects. Perform the following steps to animate the Net-Train Corporation logo object on Slide 1 and the mountain climber object on Slide 6.

To Animate the Logo Object

1 **Double-click Slide 1 and then right-click the Net-Train logo object.**

Slide 1 displays in slide view. The logo object is selected and the shortcut menu displays (Figure 4-76).

FIGURE 4-76

2 **Click Custom Animation on the shortcut menu. If necessary, click the Effects tab when the Custom Animation dialog box displays.**

The Custom Animation dialog box displays (Figure 4-77). No Effect is the default animation effect, as shown in the animation box. Text 2, the two lines of subtitle text, displays in the Animation order box because you applied the Spiral animation effect to it in Project 3.

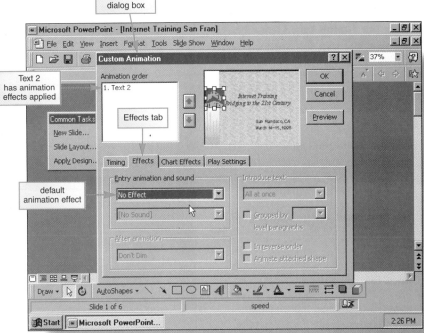

FIGURE 4-77

3 **Click the animation box arrow in the Entry animation and sound area. Click Fly From Right.**

Group 3, the Net-Train logo object, is added to the Animation order list box under Text 2 (Figure 4-78). When you run the presentation, each line of subtitle text will spiral onto the screen, and then the logo object will move across the screen from the right side.

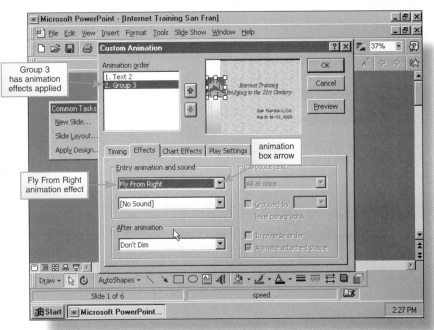

FIGURE 4-78

5 **Click the Timing tab. Click Automatically in the Start animation area.**

The logo object will move from the right edge of the screen automatically as soon as the subtitle text displays (Figure 4-79).

6 **Click the Preview button.**

The animation effects display in the preview area.

7 **Click the OK button.**

PowerPoint applies the animation settings and closes the dialog box.

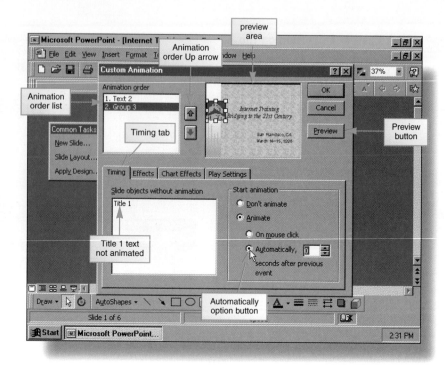

FIGURE 4-79

TO ANIMATE THE SUBTITLE TEXT AUTOMATICALLY

1 Right-click the subtitle text.
2 Click Custom Animation on the shortcut menu. If necessary, click the Timing tab when the Custom Animation dialog box displays.
3 Click Automatically in the Start animation area.
4 Click the Animation order Up arrow to move Text 2 as the first item in the Animation order list.
5 Click the Preview button.
6 Click the OK button.

PowerPoint applies the automatic animation settings and closes the custom animation dialog box.

Now that you have animated the logo object on Slide 1 and have set the subtitle text to display automatically, you want to animate the mountain climber on Slide 6 to have him move upward automatically from the bottom of the slide after the slide title displays. Perform the following steps to animate the mountain climber object on Slide 6.

To Animate the Mountain Climber Object

1 **Click the Next Slide button five times to display Slide 6. Right-click the mountain climber object. Point to Custom Animation on the shortcut menu.**

The mountain climber object in Slide 6 is selected. The shortcut menu displays (Figure 4-80).

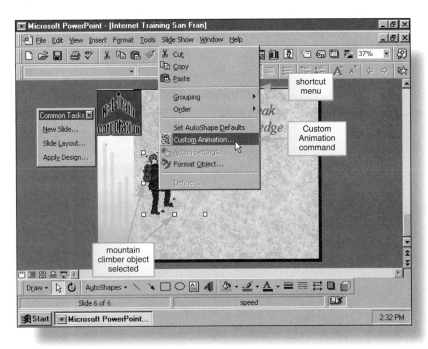

FIGURE 4-80

2 **Click Custom Animation. When the Custom Animation dialog box displays, click the animation box arrow. Scroll down through the list to select Crawl From Bottom. Click Crawl From Bottom.**

The Crawl From Bottom animation effect is selected (Figure 4-81). No Effects is the default animation effect.

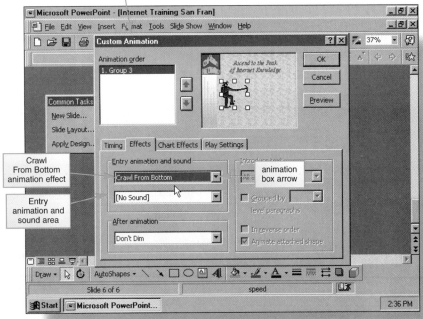

FIGURE 4-81

3 **Click the sound box arrow in the Entry animation and sound area. Point to Applause.**

The Applause sound effect is high-lighted (Figure 4-82). No Sound is the default sound effect. The Applause sound effect will play when the mountain climber object moves upward from the bottom of the screen.

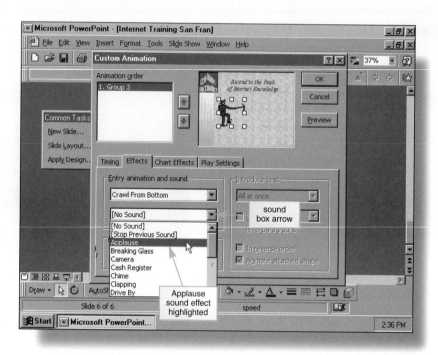

FIGURE 4-82

4 **Click Applause. Click the Timing tab. Click Automatically in the Start animation area.**

The mountain climber object will move upward from the bottom of the screen automatically as soon as the slide title displays (Figure 4-83). The slide title (Title 1) and small rocks object (Group 2) are not animated, as shown in the Slide objects without animation list box.

5 **Click the Preview button.**

The animation effect displays in the preview area, and the sound effect is applied.

6 **Click the OK button.**

PowerPoint applies the animation and sound effects and closes the custom animation dialog box.

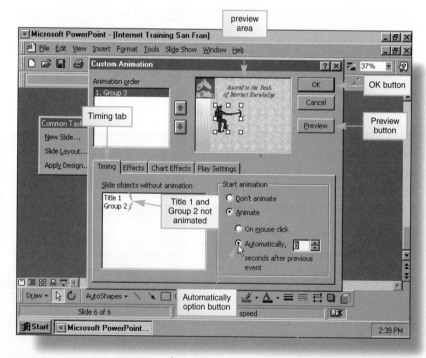

FIGURE 4-83

OtherWays

1. Click mountain climber object, press ALT+D, press M, press E, press C key three times, press TAB, press DOWN ARROW three times, press CTRL+SHIFT+TAB, press U, press ALT+P, press ENTER

Spell Checking and Saving the Presentation

The presentation is complete. You now should spell check the presentation and save it again.

Running a Slide Show with a Hidden Slide and Interactive Documents

Running a slide show that contains hidden slides or interactive documents basically is the same as running any other slide show. You must, however, know where slides are hidden. When a slide contains interactive documents, you can activate them by clicking the action button that represents the document. In Figure 4-84, the E-mail text document displays in Microsoft Word. When you are finished displaying or editing the interactive document and want to return to the presentation, click the Back button on the Web toolbar of the interactive document. Perform the following steps to run the Internet Training San Fran presentation.

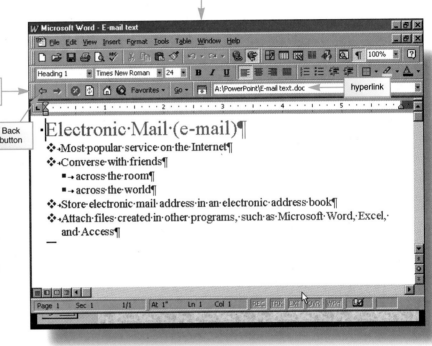

FIGURE 4-84

TO RUN A SLIDE SHOW WITH A HIDDEN SLIDE AND INTERACTIVE DOCUMENTS

1. Go to Slide 1. Click the Slide Show button on the View button bar.
2. After the subtitle text and logo display, click Slide 1 to display Slide 2. Click Slide 2 to display Slide 3.
3. Press the H key to display the hidden slide, Slide 4.
4. When Slide 4 displays, click the E-mail action button. If necessary, maximize the Microsoft Word window when the E-mail text document displays. Click the Back button on the Web toolbar.
5. Click the Word World Wide Web action button. If necessary, maximize the Microsoft Word window when the WWW text document displays. Click the Back button on the Web toolbar.
6. Click the background of Slide 4 to display Slide 5.
7. Click Slide 5 four times to display the bulleted list.
8. Click Slide 5 to display Slide 6.
9. Click Slide 6 to display the black slide that ends the slide show. Click the black slide to return to the PowerPoint window.
10. Click the Save button on the Standard toolbar.
11. Click the Close button on the title bar.

Slide 1 displays in slide view, PowerPoint quits, and then control returns to the desktop.

More *About* Meeting Notes

If you want to take notes during your presentation, PowerPoint includes a feature that allows you to record the comments and print them later using Microsoft Word. While running the presentation, right-click the slide and click Speaker Notes, type the notes, and then click the Close button. Click Black and White View on the Standard toolbar, click File on the menu bar, point to Send To, and then click Microsoft Word. You can choose how you want the notes to display, such as below an image of the slide or only as an outline.

Project Summary

Project 4 customized the Internet Training seminar presentation created in Project 3. The first step was to save the presentation with a new file name to preserve the Project 3 presentation. You then changed design templates and selected and modified a new color scheme. Next, you used the drawing tools and added special text effects to create a company logo and pasted it on the slide master and on the title slide. Next, you created a slide containing hyperlinks to two Microsoft Word documents. Then, you replaced a picture and activated the option to end every presentation with a black slide. You added slide transition effects to the slide added to this project. Next, you hid the new slide because you will display it during the slide show only if time permits. Then, you added animation effects to objects on the slides. You ran the slide show to display the hidden slide and hyperlinked documents. Finally, you closed both presentations and quit PowerPoint.

What You Should Know

Having completed this project, you now should be able to perform the following tasks:

- Add a Border *(PP 4.50)*
- Add a New Slide *(PP 4.33)*
- Add a Slide Title *(PP 4.33)*
- Add an Action Button and Action Settings *(PP 4.34)*
- Add an Object to the Slide Master *(PP 4.27)*
- Add Captions to the Action Buttons *(PP 4.43)*
- Add Fill Color to the Action Buttons *(PP 4.41)*
- Add Shadows to the Action Buttons *(PP 4.42)*
- Animate the Logo Object *(PP 4.54)*
- Animate the Mountain Climber Object *(PP 4.57)*
- Animate the Subtitle Text Automatically *(PP 4.56)*
- Apply Slide Transition Effects *(PP 4.52)*
- Change Text *(PP 4.8)*
- Change the Design Template *(PP 4.9)*
- Change the Font Color *(PP 4.10)*
- Change the Logo Border *(PP 4.17)*
- Change the Logo Object Color *(PP 4.16)*
- Change the Organization Chart Formatting *(PP 4.31)*
- Change the WordArt Fill Color *(PP 4.23)*
- Change the WordArt Height and Width *(PP 4.22)*
- Create a Custom Background *(PP 4.9)*
- Create a Second Action Button and Hyperlink *(PP 4.37)*
- Delete an Object *(PP 4.47)*

- Display and Position the Guides *(PP 4.38)*
- Display the Guides *(PP 4.14)*
- Display the Rulers *(PP 4.13)*
- Draw a Square *(PP 4.15)*
- Edit a Bulleted List *(PP 4.47)*
- Edit Text *(PP 4.46)*
- End a Slide Show with a Black Slide *(PP 4.51)*
- Enter the WordArt Text *(PP 4.19)*
- Format a Second Caption Text *(PP 4.45)*
- Format Text *(PP 4.43)*
- Group Objects *(PP 4.25)*
- Hide a Slide *(PP 4.53)*
- Hide Guides *(PP 4.50)*
- Hide the Rulers and Guides *(PP 4.31)*
- Increase the Zoom Percentage *(PP 4.14)*
- Insert a Picture *(PP 4.48)*
- Open a New Presentation *(PP 4.12)*
- Open a Presentation and Save It with a New File Name *(PP 4.7)*
- Paste an Object on a Title Slide *(PP 4.30)*
- Position and Resize an Object *(PP 4.49)*
- Run a Slide Show with a Hidden Slide and Interactive Documents *(PP 4.59)*
- Scale Action Buttons *(PP 4.41)*
- Scale an Object *(PP 4.48)*
- Scale the Logo Object *(PP 4.26)*
- Select a WordArt Style *(PP 4.18)*
- Shape the WordArt Text *(PP 4.21)*

 Test Your Knowledge

1 True/False

Instructions: Circle T if the statement is true or F if the statement is false.

T F 1. When you create a custom slide background, the new background is displayed on all screens in the presentation if you click the Apply button in the Background dialog box.

T F 2. Buttons on the WordArt toolbar allow you to modify letters by rotating, slanting, and curving their shapes.

T F 3. Tick marks on the rulers display in one-quarter-inch segments.

T F 4. A slide can be hidden in any PowerPoint view except slide show view.

T F 5. Either the corner or the center of an object snaps to a guide.

T F 6. If you want a hidden slide to display, you should press the ENTER key when you are displaying the slide preceding the hidden slide.

T F 7. Increasing the zoom percentage reduces the editing view of a slide in slide view.

T F 8. A hyperlink is a shortcut that allows you to jump to another program, to another slide in the PowerPoint presentation, or to an Internet address.

T F 9. The text and lines color is the fundamental color of a PowerPoint slide.

T F 10. To make small adjustments to the placement of a selected object, press the ARROW keys on the keyboard that correspond to the direction in which you want to move.

2 Multiple Choice

Instructions: Circle the correct response.

1. A color scheme is a set of _____ colors assigned to a slide.
   a. five   b. eight   c. ten   d. twelve

2. A built-in 3-D button that can perform specific tasks, such as display the next slide in a presentation, display the first slide, or play a sound, is called a(n) _____ button.
   a. settings   b. jump   c. hyperlink   d. action

3. You can add a special effect to letters by using tools on the _____ toolbar.
   a. WordArt   c. Common Tasks
   b. Microsoft Organization Chart   d. Web

4. An action button can activate a hyperlink to a(n) _____ document.
   a. Microsoft Word   c. Microsoft PowerPoint
   b. Microsoft Excel   d. all of the above

5. To double the size of an action button, you _____ the object 200 percent.
   a. zoom   b. link   c. scale   d. embed

6. You can activate a hyperlink by clicking a(n) _____.
   a. action button   c. picture
   b. text object   d. all of the above

7. PowerPoint displays the exact position of a guide when you point to the guide and press the _____.
   a. left mouse button   c. SHIFT key
   b. right mouse button   d. CTRL key

(continued)

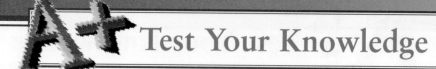

Test Your Knowledge

Multiple Choice *(continued)*

8. The two straight dotted lines, one horizontal and one vertical, used for aligning objects are
   _____.
   a. interactive objects   b. icons   c. rulers   d. guides
9. You can alter the appearance of an action button by changing its _____.
   a. fill color   b. shadow   c. size   d. all of the above
10. To add text to a slide, click the _____ button.
    a. Promote   b. Line Style   c. Text Box   d. New Slide

3 Understanding Guides in a PowerPoint Window

Instructions: Arrows in Figure 4-85 point to the major components of a window displaying guides. Identify the various parts of the window in the spaces provided.

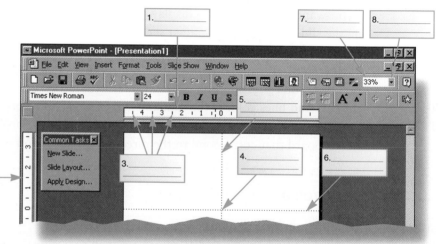

FIGURE 4-85

4 Understanding the WordArt Toolbar

Instructions: Answer the following questions using a separate piece of paper.

1. Which dialog box is used to enter text for an object?
2. How many predefined WordArt styles are available in the WordArt Gallery dialog box?
3. Which button on the WordArt toolbar allows you to display letters vertically?
4. How many shapes are available in the WordArt shape list?
5. Which WordArt shape resembles the shape of a stop sign?
6. Which button on the WordArt toolbar would you use to turn text 45 degrees?
7. How do you rotate text using the Format WordArt button?
8. What happens if you scale an object without selecting the Lock aspect ratio check box?
9. Which button on the WordArt toolbar allows you to make the spacing between letters very loose?
10. Which button on the WordArt toolbar makes all capital and lowercase letters the same height?

Use Help

1 Learning More about Running a Slide Show and Adding ActiveX Controls

You want to present your Internet Training San Fran slide show at an unattended booth at your school. In addition, you want interested people to enter their names, addresses, and telephone numbers so you can contact them with details on the seminar. Microsoft Help can provide assistance.

Instructions: Perform the following tasks using a computer.

1. Start PowerPoint. When the PowerPoint dialog box displays, double-click Blank presentation and then type 12 to select the Blank AutoLayout. Click the OK button in the New Slide dialog box.
2. Click the Office Assistant button on the Standard toolbar. Type How do I run a slide show in the What would you like to do? text box and then click the Search button. Click Ways to run a slide show, and read the information. Right-click in the window and then click Print Topic on the shortcut menu. Click the OK button in the Print dialog box.
3. Click the link at the end of the Browsed at a kiosk (full screen) paragraph to find more information on the About self-running presentations topic. When the About self-running presentations topic displays, read and print the material.
4. Click the link at the end of the first item in the bulleted list, Automatic or manual timings, to obtain information about the Set timings for a slide show topic.
5. When the Set timings for a slide show topic displays, read and print the information. Click Set slide show timings manually, and print the material. Click the Show me link in item 2. Click the Close button on the Slide Transition dialog box title bar. Click the Back button.
6. Click the Set slide show timings automatically while rehearsing link, and then read and print the information. Click the Back button twice.
7. The fourth bulleted item at the bottom of the About self-running presentations topic discusses ActiveX controls. Click the ActiveX controls link and read and print the information.
8. Click the See a list of ActiveX controls link at the bottom of the Use ActiveX controls in a presentation topic. Read and print the information.
9. Click the Microsoft PowerPoint Help window Close button. When the Microsoft PowerPoint window displays, quit PowerPoint without saving the presentation.
10. Hand in the printouts to your instructor.

2 Expanding on the Basics

Instructions: Use PowerPoint Help to better understand the topics listed below. Begin each of the following by clicking the Office Assistant button on the Standard toolbar. If you cannot print the Help information, answer the question on a separate piece of paper.

1. How do you automatically record the time each slide displays when you rehearse your slide shows?
2. How do you set each slide to advance automatically after 30 seconds?
3. How do you set different timings for each slide, such as having the first slide display for 10 seconds, the second slide for 2 minutes, and the third for 45 seconds?
4. What is an action button and how do you add one to your presentation?
5. How do you assign the mouse-over method to an object to start an interactive action?

Apply Your Knowledge

1 Editing a Logo Object and Changing a Color Scheme

Instructions: Start PowerPoint. Open the Net-Train Corporation logo you created in Project 4 and saved with the file name, Net-Train Logo. If you did not create the Net-Train Corporation logo in Project 4, ask your instructor for a copy. Perform the following tasks to modify the logo to look like Figure 4-86.

1. Click File on the menu bar, and then click Save As. Save the presentation with the file name, Student Logo.

2. Right-click the logo object, point to Grouping on the shortcut menu, and then click Ungroup on the Grouping submenu. Click outside the logo object to deselect the ungrouped objects.

3. Click the border around the square. Click the Line Style button on the Drawing toolbar. Click the 4½ pt thick-thin line style, which is the second line style from the bottom of the list.

4. With the border still selected, click the Fill Color button arrow on the Drawing toolbar. Change the fill color to light purple (row 1, column 7).

5. Press the TAB key to select the WordArt object. Click the WordArt Edit Text button on the WordArt toolbar. If necessary, select the text in the Edit WordArt Text dialog box. Type your first name, press the ENTER key, and then type your last name.

6. Click the Font box arrow. Scroll up the list and click Century Schoolbook. Click the OK button in the Edit WordArt Text dialog box.

7. Click the WordArt Shape button arrow on the WordArt toolbar. Click the Button (Curve) shape (row 2, column 4) in the shape list.

8. Click the Format WordArt button on the WordArt toolbar. If necessary, click the Colors and Lines tab. In the Fill area, click the Color box arrow. Then, click the color Violet (row 4, column 7 under Automatic). In the Line area, click the Color box arrow. Click the color Indigo (row 2, column 7 under Automatic). Click the OK button in the Format WordArt dialog box. Close the WordArt toolbar by clicking the Close button on the WordArt title bar.

9. Click the Shadow button on the Drawing toolbar. Click No Shadow in the list.

10. If necessary, scale the WordArt object about center so your name fits inside the square. Click Edit on the menu bar, and then click Select All. Right-click the selected objects and then point to Grouping and click Regroup on the Grouping submenu.

11. Save the logo object again.

12. Print the logo slide using the Black & white and Scale to fit paper options.

FIGURE 4-86

In the Lab

1 Creating a Title Slide Containing a Logo

Problem: Fun 4-U Tours has hired you to design a slide show promoting the company's annual Spring Break trip to Florida. Company representatives want to approve the title slide of your presentation before you work on the entire project. The title slide contains the Fun 4-U Tours maroon logo centered in a magnifying glass clip art object. You will create the title slide shown in Figure 4-87.

1. Open a blank presentation, apply the Title Slide AutoLayout, and then apply the sunidays design template from the PowerPoint folder on the Data Disk that accompanies this book. The sunidays design template was retrieved from the Microsoft site on the Internet. Type the text for the title slide as shown in Figure 4-87.
2. Save the presentation with the file name, Spring Break.
3. Open a new presentation and apply the Blank AutoLayout. Insert the magnifying glass clip art picture that has the description, Focus Investigation Identify Small.
4. Create the logo text by clicking the Insert WordArt button on the Drawing toolbar. In the WordArt Gallery dialog box, select the WordArt style in row 1, column 1. Type Fun 4-U Tours on three lines. Choose the Button (Pour) shape (row 2, column 8). Change the WordArt text color to Plum (row 5, column 7 under Automatic). Then, change the border line color to Olive Green (row 2, column 3 under Automatic) with a weight of 0.5 pt. Scale the height of the WordArt object to 82 percent, and then center it on the magnifying glass. Group the WordArt text and the magnifying glass clip art object. Save the Fun 4-U Tours WordArt logo with the file name, Fun 4-U Logo.
5. Paste a copy of the Fun 4-U Logo on the Spring Break title slide. Scale the logo to 95 percent. Drag the logo to the upper-right corner of the slide.
6. Save the Spring Break presentation. Print the title slide using the Black & white and Scale to fit paper options. Close both presentations and quit PowerPoint.

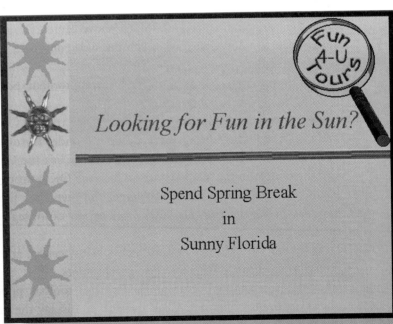

FIGURE 4-87

In the Lab

2 Designing a Title Slide Using AutoShapes

Problem: Members of the astronomy club, the Stargazers, have asked you to create a title slide promoting the organization. You examine the available design templates and determine that you will need to modify one to create the vibrant astronomy theme. You will create the title slide shown in Figure 4-88.

1. Open a blank presentation, apply the Title Slide AutoLayout, and then apply the confetti design template from the PowerPoint folder on the Data Disk that accompanies this book. The confetti design template was retrieved from the Microsoft site on the Internet.

2. Right-click the slide anywhere other than the title or subtitle objects. Click Slide Color Scheme on the shortcut menu. In the Color Scheme dialog box, click the middle color scheme on the Standard sheet. Click the Apply button.

3. Type the text for the title slide as shown in Figure 4-88. Remove the shadow from the title text by selecting the text, clicking the Shadow button on the Drawing toolbar, and then clicking No Shadow. Format the subtitle text to a font size of 40 and the same font color blue as the title text, to follow the title text scheme color.

4. Display the guides and rulers. If necessary, align the guides and rulers with the 0-inch tick marks on the horizontal and vertical rulers.

5. Click the AutoShapes button on the Drawing toolbar, point to Basic Shapes, and click the Sun object in row 6, column 3. Click the slide to display the sun object. Right-click the sun object and then click Format AutoShape on the shortcut menu. If necessary, click the Size tab. Click Lock aspect ratio, scale the sun to 300 percent, and click the OK button.

6. Click the Fill Color button arrow on the Drawing toolbar, and then click More Fill Colors. Double-click the color Bright Yellow.

7. Drag the horizontal ruler to 0.75inch above center. Drag the sun to the upper right corner of the slide so the top and right rays touch the slide edges and the point of the bottom ray touches the horizontal ruler.

8. Click the AutoShapes button on the Drawing toolbar, point to Stars and Banners, and click the 5-Point Star (row 1, column 4).

9. Click the slide to display the star object. Click the Fill Colors button arrow on the Drawing toolbar, and click the Orange box (row 1, column 6 under Automatic). Click the Fill Colors button arrow again, and then click Fill Effects. If necessary, click the Gradient tab, and then click the upper-left variant sample in the Variants area. Click the OK button in the Fill Effects dialog box.

10. Right-click the 5-Point Star AutoShape, and then click Format AutoShape on the shortcut menu. If necessary, click the Size tab. Click Lock aspect ratio, scale the star to 200 percent, and then click the OK button.

11. Drag the horizontal ruler to 1.50 inches below center, and align the upper point of the star with the intersection of the horizontal and vertical rulers.

12. Click the AutoShapes button on the Drawing toolbar, point to Basic Shapes, and click the Moon object in row 6, column 4. Click the slide to display the moon. Right-click the moon object and then click Format AutoShape on the shortcut menu. If necessary, click the Size tab. Click Lock aspect ratio, scale the moon to 500 percent, and then click the OK button.

In the Lab

13. Drag the vertical ruler to 2.00 inches left of center and the horizontal ruler to 2.75 inches below center. Drag the moon so the bottom point aligns with the intersection of the guides.

14. Click the Insert WordArt button on the Drawing toolbar. Choose the WordArt style in row 1, column 1, and then click the OK button. Enter the club information shown in the lower-right corner of the slide, and substitute your name for the words, Student Name. Click the WordArt Shape button on the WordArt toolbar, apply the Cascade Up shape (row 5, column 7), and change the text to the color Blue (row 3, column 6 under Automatic). Apply a 0.25 pt color Dark Blue (row 2, column 6 under Automatic) border to the text. Scale the text to 60 percent.

FIGURE 4-88

15. Drag the vertical guide to 1.25 inches right of center and the horizontal guide to 1.00 inch below center. Align the WordArt object with these guides. You might need to make minor adjustments with the scaling to accommodate your name.

16. Save the presentation with the file name, Stars. Print the slide using the Black & white and Scale to fit paper options. Quit PowerPoint.

3 Linking PowerPoint Presentations

Problem: Las Vegas has become one of the top tourist destinations in the United States, so your school band and choir are planning a trip to that location at the end of the school year. You have offered to create a PowerPoint presentation promoting the city. You decide an interactive slide show would be the best vehicle to answer the students' questions. Develop the presentation shown in Figures 4-89 through 4-94 on pages PP 4.68 through 4.70.

Instructions Part 1: Perform the following tasks to create four presentations: one consisting of Figures 4-89 and 4-90, one of Figure 4-91, one of Figure 4-92, and one of Figure 4-93 on the next two pages.

1. Open a blank presentation and apply the Bulleted List AutoLayout. Display rulers and guides. If necessary, align them with the 0-inch tick marks on the horizontal and vertical rulers. Apply the risk design template from the PowerPoint folder on the Data Disk that accompanies this book.

(continued)

In the Lab

Linking PowerPoint Presentations (*continued*)

Type and center the slide title, and then type the bulleted list item shown in Figure 4-89. Insert the clip art picture with the description, Risk (as shown in Figure 4-89), and then scale it to 200 percent. Drag the vertical ruler to 2.17 inches left of center and the horizontal ruler to 3.33 inches below center. Align the top-left edge of the 10-of-diamonds card with the vertical ruler and the bottom-left edge of that card with the horizontal ruler.

2. Create the bulleted list slide shown in Figure 4-90. Apply the Checkerboard Across slide transition effect to both slides. Apply the Fly From Top entry animation effect to animate the cards automatically on Slide 1. Save the presentation with the file name, Vegas Shows. Print the presentation slides using the Black & white option. Close the presentation.

3. Open a new presentation, apply the Bulleted List AutoLayout, and then apply the risk design template. Create the slide shown in Figure 4-91. Increase line spacing to .5 lines after each paragraph. Apply the Blinds Horizontal slide transition effect. Save the presentation with the file name, Vegas Tours. Print the presentation slide using the Black & white option. Close the presentation.

FIGURE 4-89

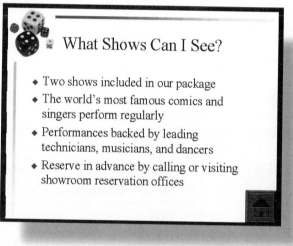

FIGURE 4-90

4. Open a new presentation, apply the 2 Column Text AutoLayout, and then apply the risk design template. Create the slide shown in Figure 4-92. Increase line spacing to .5 lines after each paragraph. Apply the Checkerboard Down slide transition effect. Save the presentation with the file name, Vegas Visit. Print the presentation slide using the Black & white option. Close the presentation.

5. Open a new presentation, apply the Bulleted List AutoLayout, and then apply the risk design template. Create the slide shown in Figure 4-93. Increase the line spacing for both paragraphs to .5 lines after each paragraph. Apply the Blinds Vertical slide transition effect. Save the presentation with the file name, Vegas Pack. Print the presentation slide using the Black & white option. Close the presentation.

In the Lab

What Tours Can I Take?

- ◆ Raft through scenic Black Canyon
- ◆ Visit the Grand Canyon
- ◆ Hike Red Rock Canyon
- ◆ Cruise Lake Mead

FIGURE 4-91

What Can I Visit?

- ◆ Museums
  - – Debbie Reynolds Hollywood Movie Museum
  - – King Tut Museum
  - – Liberace Museum
  - – Las Vegas Natural History Museum
- ◆ Attractions
  - – Imperial Palace Auto Collection
  - – Magic and Movie Hall of Fame
  - – Whiskey Pete's
  - – Hoover Dam/Hoover Dam Museum

FIGURE 4-92

What Should I Pack?

- ◆ Casual clothes, including shorts and sun dresses, for day attractions and tours
- ◆ Dresses and sports jackets for evening
- ◆ Forget the umbrella! Las Vegas has an average rainfall of 4.19 inches per year

FIGURE 4-93

(continued)

In the Lab

Linking PowerPoint Presentations *(continued)*

Instructions Part 2: Perform the following tasks to create the presentation shown in Figure 4-94.

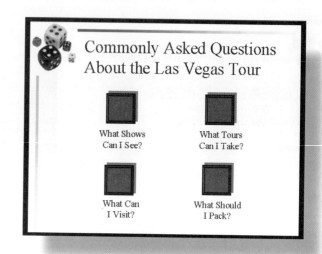

FIGURE 4-94

1. Open a new presentation, type 11 to apply the Title Only AutoLayout, and then apply the risk design template. Create the slide title shown in Figure 4-94.

2. Add the four action buttons, scale them to 90 percent, apply Shadow Style 2, change the border line style to 3 pt, and change the fill color to Red.

3. Type the caption What Shows Can I See? under the upper-left action button, What Can I Visit? under the lower-left action button, What Tours Can I Take? under the upper-right action button, and What Should I Pack? under the lower-right action button.

4. Create a hyperlink to the Vegas Shows presentation, created in Part 1, for the upper-left action button, the Vegas Visit presentation for the lower-left action button, the Vegas Tours presentation for the upper-right action button, and the Vegas Pack presentation for the lower-right action button.

5. Apply the Split Vertical Out slide transition effect. End the presentation with a black slide. Save the presentation with the file name, Vegas.

6. Add an action button to the lower-right corner of each of the four hyperlinked presentations, and hyperlink each button to the Vegas presentation. Change the buttons' fill color to Red. Save the four hyperlinked presentations.

7. Print the six presentation slides using the Black & white option.

8. Run the slide show. Click the What Shows Can I See? action button to display the hyperlinked presentation. Display both slides. Click the hyperlink at the bottom of the second slide to jump to the Vegas presentation. When the Commonly Asked Questions presentation returns, click the What Can I Visit? action button, read the new slide, and click the hyperlink at the bottom of the slide. Repeat this procedure for the What Tours Can I Take? and What Should I Pack? action buttons. Click to display the black closing slide. End the slide show and quit PowerPoint.

Cases and Places

The difficulty of these case studies varies: ❱ are the least difficult; ❱❱ are more difficult; and ❱❱❱ are the most difficult.

1 ❱ The latest dietary guidelines recommend eating two to four servings of fruit and three to five servings of vegetables daily. Although fruit and vegetables are less costly than snack foods, many adults and children buy junk food rather than the vitamin-laden fruit and vegetable alternatives. Vitamin A, found in oranges and dark green, leafy vegetables, helps repair and grow skin tissues and makes skin smooth and moist. Vitamin B is plentiful in bananas, sunflower seeds, lentils, and whole-grain cereals, and it helps prevent dry, cracking skin, especially at the corners of the mouth. The more active you are, the more you need vitamin B. Citrus juice and green and red peppers are rich in vitamin C. This vitamin helps your body manufacture the protein collagen, which keeps your skin firm. Your school cafeteria manager has asked you to prepare a PowerPoint presentation explaining the ABCs of fruits and vegetables to students. Using the techniques introduced in this chapter, create an interactive short slide show using three buttons that correspond to the three vitamins. Include your school logo, animated text, and slide transition effects. End with a black closing slide.

2 ❱ The marketing director of your local credit union has asked you to help with a membership campaign on campus. You decide to develop an interactive slide show to run in the bookstore during the start of the semester when students often stand in long lines to pay for their books and supplies. Prepare a short presentation aimed at encouraging students to join the credit union and begin a savings plan. One slide should show an Excel worksheet and 3-D Column chart explaining how saving even a small amount on a regular basis helps establish a nest egg. Other slides can feature additional credit union services, such as credit cards, vehicle loans, home equity loans, mortgages, and certificates of deposit. The final slide should give the address, telephone number, and hours of the office.

3 ❱❱ After completing the Internet Training San Fran presentation in Project 4, you are interested in attending the seminar. You inform your boss, who agrees that you and your company would benefit from the training. Funding is a problem, however, and the board of directors must approve the expenditure. Your boss believes you can persuade the board to release the money at the next board meeting if you develop a persuasive PowerPoint slide show. Prepare an Excel worksheet and Pie chart of your proposed expenses, and link them to the presentation as an interactive document. Include estimates of meals, housing, transportation, and incidental expenses, considering that two box lunches and one night's hotel room in central San Francisco are included in the $350 seminar fee. If you will be flying to the conference, visit a travel agent, search the Internet, or telephone several airlines to determine the least expensive airfare from your campus to San Francisco. Include other slides stating the components of the training sessions and how the company will benefit from your experience.

Cases and Places

4 ▶▶ Five of your friends have decided to form a jazz band, the Quintessential Quintet, and they want to perform at local events. They want you to help with their publicity, so you decide to create a slide show. You need to start by designing a logo that reflects the spirit of jazz music. Use PowerPoint and WordArt to create the logo. Then create a short slide show to present the logo to the Quintessential Quintet members. Explain your design and thoughts behind the logo component objects.

5 ▶▶ Many schools have an extracurricular or intramural athletic program to allow students to participate in a variety of sports in an informal, friendly atmosphere. Often the individual or team participants compete in tournaments at the end of the season. Research your school's athletic program by interviewing the athletic director or individual in charge of this student activity. Gather information about the sports, number of student participants, team standings, times and locations of games, and cost. Discuss how an interactive presentation might pique interest among students. Using this information, create the slide show. Enhance the presentation by including your school's logo, a modified design template background or color scheme, appropriate graphics, animated text, and slide transition effects. Deliver the presentation to the person with whom you spoke to collect your information.

6 ▶▶▶ Doctors and nutritionists recommend following a low-fat diet to help control body weight, prevent heart disease and diabetes, and reduce cholesterol. Many people, however, refuse to eliminate their favorite foods, such as potato chips and cookies. Fortunately, many food manufacturers have developed low- or no-fat alternatives to these high-fat foods, including salad dressings, ice cream, yogurt, desserts, candy bars, and pretzels. Visit a grocery store and compare labels of three dessert items, dairy products, and snack foods you normally eat that have both a regular and low- or no-fat version. Using this information and the techniques introduced in the project, prepare an interactive presentation that compares the serving sizes, calories, and fat grams of these foods. Enhance the presentation by adding graphics, using text preset animation effects, and applying slide transition effects. End the presentation with a black closing slide. Submit all files on a disk to your instructor.

7 ▶▶▶ Seventy-five percent of people older than 64 have an annual income of less than $10,000, including Social Security benefits. Fortunately, employees of public schools and certain not-for-profit organizations are eligible to participate in a 403(b) tax-deferred annuity (TDA) program. This special retirement benefit offers these employees the opportunity to reduce their tax liability while they are saving for retirement. Your school's business office has hired you to develop a PowerPoint presentation designed to encourage teachers to open a TDA. Call or visit life insurance companies to obtain information on this program. Research and then prepare an interactive slide show. Include an Excel worksheet demonstrating how much a teacher earning $30,000 annually would save on taxes after contributing $1,000 during the year. Prepare a second worksheet and a 3-D Column chart showing the power of tax-deferred growth during a 10- and 20-year period. Include slides answering questions of how the funds can be distributed and withdrawn and how much an employee can contribute during the year. Enhance the presentation by modifying a design template background or color scheme, adding appropriate graphics, animating text, and applying slide transition effects. Include a hidden slide. Run your presentation and perform a what-if scenario by increasing the contribution to $2,000 per year. Submit all files on a disk to your instructor.

Creating Web Pages from a PowerPoint Presentation

Case Perspective

The Park City, Utah, Net-Train Corporation Internet Training Seminar has generated much interest. Net-Train employees have received many telephone calls from prospective attendees asking for specific details. Among their questions are health-related topics regarding high elevations. Many prospective attendees have heard and read about the effects of reduced oxygen on the body, and they have concerns about adjusting to the mountain elevations.

You have decided the easiest way to provide this information to Net-Train employees and prospective attendees is to prepare a PowerPoint presentation and then transfer the file on World Wide Web pages posted to the Internet and to Net-Train's intranet. That way, you can disseminate important information easily and accurately to many people. The presentation is saved on your Data Disk that accompanies this book. To do the transfer, you will need to save the presentation again as an HTML file (Web page). Then you will view the Web page by launching your default Web browser and opening the HTML document.

Introduction

The graphic design power of PowerPoint allows you to create vibrant presentations that convey information in a clear, interesting manner. Some of these presentations are created for small, specific audiences, such as a subcommittee planning a department office picnic. In this case, the presentation may be shown in an office conference room. Other presentations are designed for large, general audiences, such as workers at a corporation's various offices across the country learning about a variety of health insurance options. These employees can view the presentation on their company's **intranet,** which is an internal network that uses Internet technologies. On a grand scale, you can inform the entire world about the contents of your presentation by posting your slide show to the World Wide Web. To publish to the World Wide Web, you need an **FTP (File Transfer Protocol)** program to copy your presentation and related files to an **Internet service provider (ISP)** computer.

PowerPoint allows you to create Web pages in two ways. First, you can start a new presentation, as you did in Project 3 when you produced the Net-Train Internet Training Seminar presentation for Park City, Utah. PowerPoint provides Internet or information kiosk presentation templates in the

AutoContent wizard option when you start PowerPoint. The wizard helps you design an effective slide show for an intranet or for the Internet.

Second, by using a **Save as HTML wizard**, you quickly can convert an existing presentation to a format compatible with popular Web browsers, such as Microsoft Internet Explorer. The wizard allows you to control the content and format options of the presentation. This Integration Feature illustrates saving the PowerPoint High Altitude Health Hints presentation on your Data Disk as an HTML file. Once the presentation is saved as an HTML file, you can view the presentation using your default browser (Figure 1).

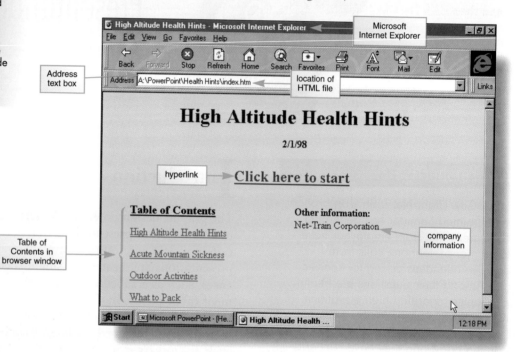

FIGURE 1

Saving the PowerPoint Presentation as Web Pages

Once your PowerPoint slide show is complete, you easily can save it as an HTML file by using the Save as HTML command on the file menu.

Because you are converting the High Altitude Health Hints presentation on your Data Disk to an HTML file, the first step in this project is to open the Health Hints file. Then you will start the Save as HTML wizard to turn the Health Hints presentation into a file for an intranet or for the Internet. Perform the following steps to convert the Health Hints presentation to Web pages.

Steps **To Save a PowerPoint Presentation as Web Pages**

1 **Start PowerPoint and then open the Health Hints file from the PowerPoint folder on your Data Disk that accompanies this book. Click File on the menu bar and then click Save as HTML.**

2 **Click the Next button. When the Layout selection panel displays, if necessary, click New layout and then point to the Next button.**

PowerPoint displays the Layout selection panel, requesting the type of layout (Figure 2). If you had designed and saved other HTML presentations previously, their file names would appear in the list box.

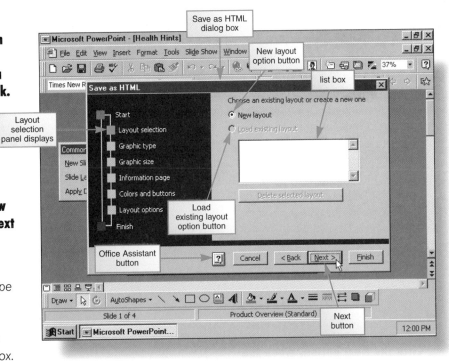

FIGURE 2

3 **Click the Next button. When the Select the page style area displays, if necessary, click Standard and then point to the Next button.**

PowerPoint displays the Select the page style area in the Save as HTML dialog box, asking for the layout style you want to use (Figure 3). A preview of each style displays beside its respective option button.

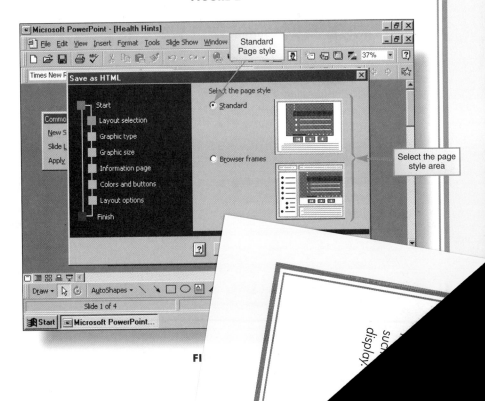

4 **Click the Next button. When the Graphic type panel displays, if necessary, click GIF – Graphics Interchange Format, and then point to the Next button.**

*PowerPoint displays the **Graphic type panel** in the Save as HTML dialog box (Figure 4). You would choose PowerPoint animation if you had graphics to animate. This animation option, however, requires a browser that supports the PowerPoint Animation Player, which is available on the Microsoft Web site.*

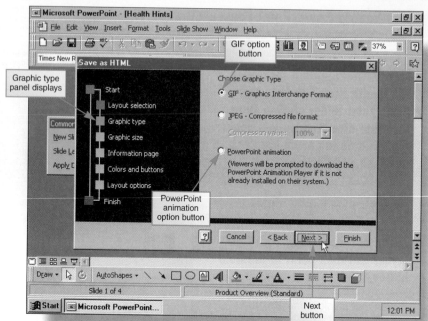

FIGURE 4

5 **Click the Next button. When the Graphic size panel displays, if necessary, click 640 by 480 and then point to the Next button.**

*PowerPoint displays the **Graphic size panel** in the Save as HTML dialog box, requesting the monitor resolution (Figure 5). All Web browsers can support the 640 by 480 monitor resolution; however, some graphics may look fuzzy on some monitors at this low resolution. If you are certain all users viewing the presentation have high-resolution monitors, you may choose one of the higher resolutions so sharper graphics display. Higher resolutions and width values create large bitmaps, which take a long time to load and may be too large to display on small monitors, such as on a notebook computer*

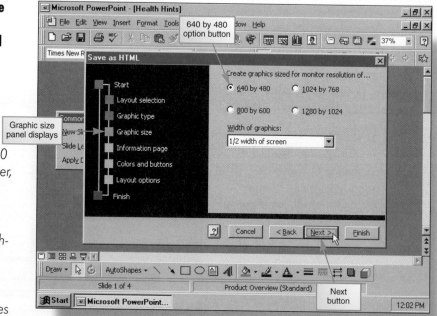

FIGURE 5

6 **Click the Next button. When the Information page panel displays, type** Net-Train Corporation **in the Other information text box. Point to the Next button.**

*PowerPoint displays the **Information page panel**, requesting information for the Table of Contents screen (Figure 6). The words, Net-Train Corporation, will display in the Other information area of the Table of Contents screen, which will be the first screen in your HTML presentation when you view it with a browser (see Figure 1 on page PPI 2.2). You also can add your e-mail and home page addresses to this title slide.*

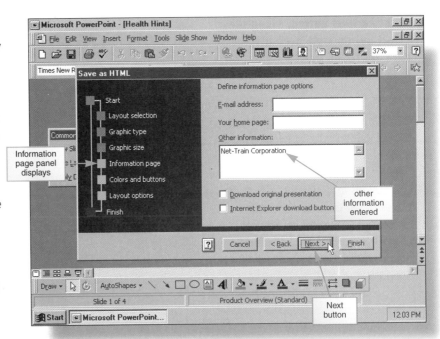

FIGURE 6

7 **Click the Next button. When the Colors and buttons panel displays, click Custom colors, and then click the Change Background button. Click the light blue basic color (row 1, column 5) in the Color dialog box, and then click the OK button in the Color dialog box. Click the Transparent buttons check box in the Save as HTML dialog box. Point to the Next button.**

*PowerPoint displays the **Colors and buttons panel**, asking for the colors you want to use on your Web page (Figure 7).*

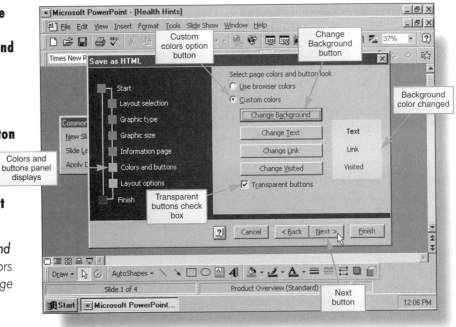

FIGURE 7

8 **Click the Next button. When the Select button style area displays, click the round button style, and then point to the Next button.**

PowerPoint displays the Select button style area, asking you to select the navigation button style you want to display on your Web page (Figure 8). You will click the navigation buttons to advance through the pages of the presentation or to review previous screens. You also can select text hyperlinks instead of buttons by clicking the Next slide option button.

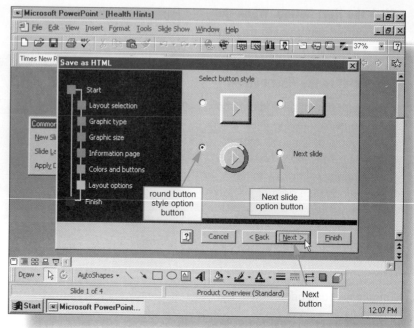

FIGURE 8

9 **Click the Next button. When the Layout options panel displays, click the lower right layout in the Place navigation buttons area. Point to the Next button.**

PowerPoint displays the Layout options panel, requesting you to select a layout option that sets the position and orientation of the navigation buttons (Figure 9). Each option button includes a graphic representation of the layout. The lower right layout places the navigation buttons to the right of the Web page slide. Clicking the Include slide notes in pages check box will include your presentation notes from the PowerPoint notes pages in your HTML document.

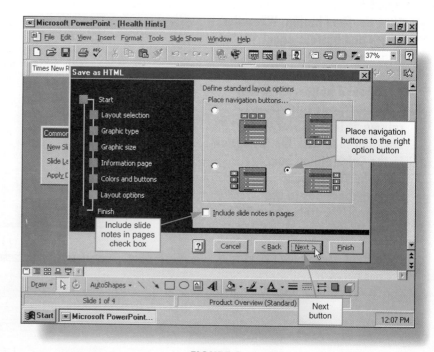

FIGURE 9

10 Click the Next button. Type
A:\PowerPoint\ in the Folder
text box. Point to the Next
button.

*PowerPoint will create an HTML
folder in the PowerPoint folder on
the Data Disk in drive A (Figure 10).*

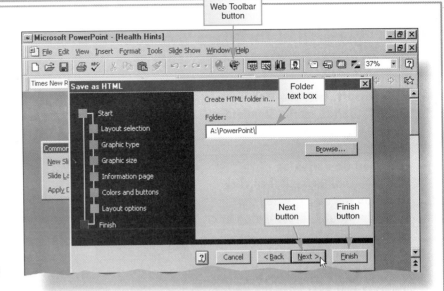

FIGURE 10

11 Click the Next button. When the
Finish panel displays, click the
Finish button. Click the Don't
Save button in the Save as HTML
dialog box (Figure 11). Click the
OK button in the Microsoft
PowerPoint dialog box.

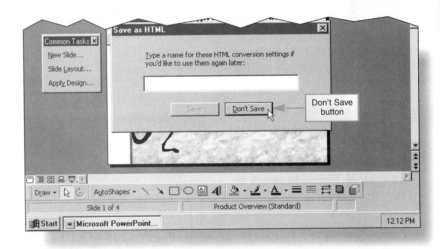

FIGURE 11

PowerPoint allows you to reuse HTML conversion settings, which is a
practical feature if you prepare many Web presentations with similar content and
format options, such as colors, button styles, and layout styles. Several HTML
export in progress messages display, indicating PowerPoint is creating Web pages
and exporting data as it is processing the four slides. PowerPoint creates a folder
with the file name Health Hints HTML, which contains the Web files needed for
the HTML pages.

Viewing a Web Page Document

Now that you have converted the PowerPoint presentation to HTML, you want
to view the Web pages in your default Web browser. These pages are located in
the Health Hints HTML folder created in the previous steps. You access these
pages by opening the index.htm file in this folder. Perform the following steps to
view your HTML pages.

More *About*
HTML

HTML may not support some
formatting in your PowerPoint
presentation. For example,
while you can bold, italicize,
and underline characters and
change their font size, you cannot apply shadows or set tabs.

Steps ## To View an HTML File Using a Web Browser

1 If necessary, click the Web Toolbar button on the Standard toolbar to display the Web toolbar (Figure 12). Click the Go button on the Web toolbar, and then click Open on the menu. When the Open Internet Address dialog box displays, type
`A:\PowerPoint\Health Hints\index.htm` in the Address text box. Click the OK button. When the browser window displays, click the Maximize button in the upper-right corner of the browser window.

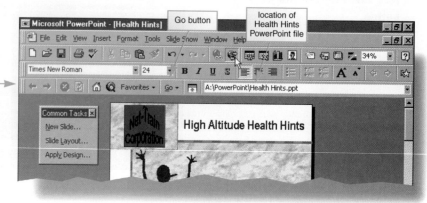

FIGURE 12

PowerPoint opens your Web browser in a separate window and displays the Table of Contents for the Health Hints HTML file in the browser window (see Figure 1 on page PPI 2.2).

2 Click the hyperlink, Click here to start. Click the Next navigation button three times to advance through the pages. Click the First navigation button to return to the first page.

The Next navigation button advances the presentation one slide forward, and the Previous navigation button reverses the presentation one slide (Figure 13). The First navigation button displays the first slide in the presentation, and the Last navigation button displays the final slide. The Index navigation button displays the Table of Contents slide (see Figure 1 on page PPI 2.2), and the Text navigation button launches a version of the Health Hints presentation with no graphics.

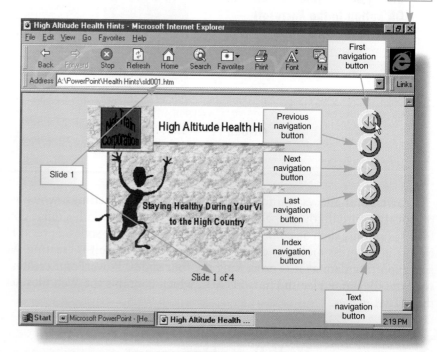

FIGURE 13

3 Click the Close button in the Web browser window.

PowerPoint closes the Health Hints HTML file, and the PowerPoint window redisplays.

The Web pages now are complete. The next step is to make your Web presentation available to others on your network, an intranet, or the World Wide Web. Ask your instructor how you can publish your presentation.

More *About*
Internet Explorer

You can place a button on your presentation that allows you to download the latest version of Microsoft Internet Explorer when connected to the World Wide Web.

Summary

This Integration Feature introduced you to creating Web pages by saving an existing PowerPoint presentation as an HTML file. You can customize the pages by selecting page styles, choosing graphic style types, selecting monitor resolution, picking custom colors and buttons for the Web page, and choosing a layout style. Now that the Health Hints presentation is converted to HTML format, you can post the file to an intranet or to the World Wide Web.

What You Should Know

Having completed this Integration Feature, you now should be able to perform the following tasks:

▶ Save a PowerPoint Presentation as Web Pages (PPI 2.3)

▶ View an HTML File Using a Web Browser (PPI 2.8)

In the Lab

1 Use Help

Instructions: Start PowerPoint. If the Office Assistant is on your screen, click it to display its balloon. If the Office Assistant is not on your screen, click the Office Assistant button on the Standard toolbar. Type Save as HTML in the What would you like to do? text box. Click the Search button. Click the Save a presentation in HTML format hyperlink. In the second bulleted item in the Tips section, click the button to display information about the animation player. Read and print the information. Click the Help Topics button to display the Help Topics: Microsoft PowerPoint window. If necessary, click the Contents tab. Double-click the Working with Presentations on Intranets and the Internet book icon. Double-click the Working with Hyperlinks book icon. Double-click the Add, edit, and remove hyperlinks in a presentation topic. Read and print the topic. Close any open Help windows. Close the Office Assistant.

2 Creating Web Pages from a PowerPoint Presentation

Problem: Net-Train employees want to expand the visibility of their Park City, Utah, Internet Training Seminar you created in Project 3. They believe the World Wide Web would be an excellent vehicle to promote the seminar, and they have asked you to help transfer the presentation to the Internet.

Instructions:

1. Open the Internet Training presentation shown in Figures 3-1a through 3-1e on page PP 3.7 that you created in Project 3. (If you did not complete Project 3, see your instructor for a copy of the presentation.)
2. Use the Save as HTML wizard to convert the presentation. Change the page color background to yellow (row 2, column 2) and the text to dark blue (row 4, column 5). Do not make the buttons transparent. Select the square navigation button style (row 1, column 1), and place the navigation buttons on the top of the Web page slide (row 1, column 1 option button).
3. View the HTML file in a browser.
4. Ask your instructor for instructions on how to post your Web pages so others may have access to them.

3 Creating a PowerPoint Presentation and Creating Web Pages

Problem: The band and choir students promoting the Las Vegas tour have asked you to post the presentation you created in Project 4 to the school's intranet. You need to combine the five slides in Figures 4-89 through 4-93 on pages PP 4.68 through 4.69 into one PowerPoint presentation and then convert that presentation to an HTML file.

Instructions:

1. Open the Vegas Shows presentation shown in Figures 4-89 and 4-90 on page PP 4.68. (If you did not create this presentation, see your instructor for a copy of the files.)
2. Click the Next Slide button to display Slide 2. Click Insert on the menu bar. Click Slides from Files.
3. If necessary, click the Find Presentation tab in the Slide Finder dialog box. In the File text box, type the location of the Vegas Tours file displayed in Figure 4-91 on page PP 4.69, click the Display button, and click the Insert All button. Then type the location of the Vegas Visit file displayed in Figure 4-92 on page PP 4.69, click the Display button, and click the Insert All button. Finally, type the location of the Vegas Pack file displayed in Figure 4-93 on page PP 4.69, click the Display button in the Slide Finder dialog box, and then click the Insert All button. Click the Close button.
4. Delete each action button in the lower-right corner of slides 2, 3, 4, and 5 by clicking it and pressing the DELETE key. Save the presentation with the file name, Vegas Package. Then use the Save as HTML wizard to convert the presentation. In the Information page panel, type Support Your Band and Choir in the Other information text box. Change the page color background to red (row 2, column 1), the text color to dark green (row 5, column 3), the link color to dark blue (row 5, column 5), and the Visited color to dark purple (row 6, column 7). Do not make the buttons transparent. Select the rectangle navigation button style (row 1, column 2), and place the navigation buttons on the left side of the Web page slide (row 2, column 1 option button).
5. View the HTML file in a browser.
6. Ask your instructor for instructions on how to post your Web pages so others may have access to them.

Index

NOTE TO READER: This index contains references for Projects 1 through 4 and the Integration Features of the book, *Microsoft PowerPoint 97: Complete Concepts and Techniques*. The same references can be used for PowerPoint Projects 1 and 2 and Integration Feature 1 in the book, *Microsoft Office 97: Introductory Concepts and Techniques*, and PowerPoint Projects 3 and 4 and Integration Feature 2 in the book, *Microsoft Office 97: Advanced Concepts and Techniques*.

Integration Case Studies

Introduction

In these case studies, you will use the concepts and techniques presented in the projects and integration features in this book to integrate all of the Office 97 applications. The first case study requires that you embed an existing Excel worksheet into a Word document, embed an Excel chart into a PowerPoint presentation, and then insert (attach) the Word document and PowerPoint presentation onto an e-mail message. The second case study requires you to use an existing Access database table as the data source for a Word form letter. It also requires you to use WordArt to create the letterhead for the form letter. In the third case study, you will create an Access database table and then convert the table twice, first to a Word document and then to an Excel worksheet. You then will convert the Word document to an Excel worksheet and vice versa. The files for the first and second case studies are provided on the Data Disk that accompanies this book.

Office 97 Integration Case Studies

1 Integrating Excel, Word, PowerPoint, and E-mail

Problem: In order to collect data on customer satisfaction, Northwest Local Cable enclosed a survey along with its February invoices. Lisa Travels, a marketing manager at Northwest, has received the completed surveys and summarized the results into an Excel worksheet. She also has charted the results using Excel. The worksheet and corresponding charts are saved in a workbook named Northwest Local Cable.

Lisa would like to schedule a meeting to discuss the survey's results with the steering committee of Northwest Local Cable. She plans to send an e-mail to the committee to schedule the meeting and ask for comments and suggestions. So that the committee can review the results prior to the meeting, Lisa will attach two documents to the e-mail message: (1) a memo that includes the Excel worksheet summarizing the survey results, and (2) a PowerPoint slide that includes the Excel chart depicting the survey results.

Lisa has asked you, her assistant, to create the memo in Word and the slide in PowerPoint, reminding you to embed the Excel worksheet into the Word document and the Excel chart into the PowerPoint slide. Finally, she asked you to create an e-mail message and insert the Word document and PowerPoint slide.

Part 1 Instructions:

Reviewing the Excel Workbook

Create the Northwest Local Cable workbook shown in Figures 1a and 1b or see your instructor for a copy of the Northwest Local Cable workbook. Before you begin creating the memo and slide, open the workbook and familiarize yourself with its contents. Print each sheet of the workbook.

Part 2 Instructions:

Creating a Memorandum in Word with a Link to an Excel Worksheet

Create a memorandum to schedule the meeting with the steering committee members, as shown in Figure 1d. After typing the text in the memo, embed the Customer Survey Results By Township table from the Excel workbook into the memo.

Leaving the Excel workbook open, start Word. Use the Contemporary Memo template to create the memo. Modify the template text so that the memo matches Figure 1d. Next, link the Customer Survey Results By Township table into the memo. (Do not type the table; rather embed it from Excel.) Save the document using the file name Northwest Local Cable. Print the memorandum with the embedded worksheet.

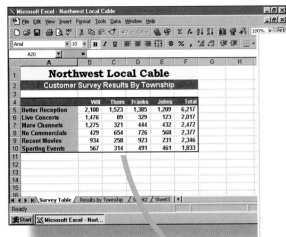

(a) Excel worksheet

(b) Excel chart

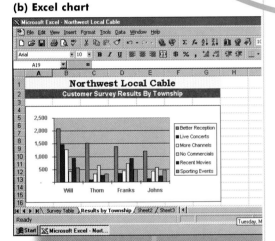

EMBED

EMBED

INSERT

(d) Word

Memorandum

To:	John Swain, Louis Jobbs, Kathleen Bates, Fred Swanson
CC:	Lora Friend
From:	Lisa Travels
Date:	May 30, 1999
Re:	Customer Satisfaction

Customer Survey Results
In our February invoices, we sent each customer a satisfaction survey. The goal of the survey was to determine why our customers chose to subscribe to our cable service. The table below summarizes the results of the survey, grouping customer responses by township.

Northwest Local Cable
Customer Survey Results By Township

	Will	Thom	Franks	Johns	Total
Better Reception	2,100	1,523	1,385	1,209	6,217
Live Concerts	1,476	89	329	123	2,017
More Channels	1,275	321	444	432	2,472
No Commercials	429	654	726	568	2,377
Recent Movies	934	258	923	231	2,346
Sporting Events	567	314	491	461	1,833

Sales Meeting
After reviewing these results, I feel it necessary to have a meeting to discuss our direction in the future. I have reserved Conference Room G102 for Thursday, April 8, for two hours beginning at 1:00 p.m.

CONFIDENTIAL

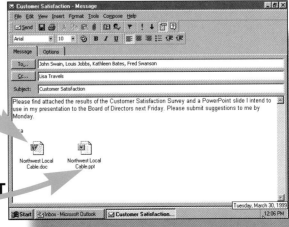

INSERT

(c) PowerPoint   **FIGURE 1**   **(e) e-mail message**

Part 3 Instructions:

Creating a Slide in PowerPoint with Links to Excel

You now are ready to create a slide (Figure 1c on the previous page) to be used in the presentation that Lisa will make to the Board of Directors.

Leaving the Excel workbook open, start PowerPoint. Select a blank slide for the slide's layout and color the background as shown in Figure 1c on the previous page. Use WordArt to create the title. Embed the Customer Survey Results By Township chart into the slide. Save the presentation using the file name Northwest Local Cable.

Part 4 Instructions:

Inserting the Files onto an E-mail Message

Using Word as your e-mail editor, create the e-mail message (Figure 1e on the previous page) and insert the Word document and PowerPoint slide onto the e-mail message. Print the e-mail message.

2 Integrating Word, WordArt, and Access

Problem: Every spring Sand Creek Country Club sends letters to its clients to verify the Club's internal records. In the past, the Club's Marketing Director, Marcell Webb, has used Word to type these letters to each client individually. This year, she wants to automate the process even further. She thus has entered the list of clients into an Access table (Figure 2a), which is saved in a database named Sand Creek Country Club. She has asked you to prepare a form letter to be sent to all clients using the Access database table as a data source. She also would like you to develop a creative letterhead for Sand Creek Country Club that can be used on all its business correspondence. The completed form letter, with letterhead, is shown in Figure 2b.

Part 1 Instructions:

Reviewing and Maintaining the Access Database Table

Create the Sand Creek Country Club database shown in Figure 2a or see your instructor for a copy. Open the database and then open the table named Client List. Familiarize yourself with the contents of the Client List table (Figure 2a). Add a record which contains information about yourself to the table — the table then should contain six records. Print the revised table and then close Access.

Mailing List ID	Prefix	First Name	Last Name	Address1	Address2	City	State	Postal Code	Home Phone	Work Phone	Fax Number	Email Address
1	Mr.	Edward	Hanks	4517 Tod Avenu	#316	Hamburg	NY	14075-	(716) 555-91	(315) 555-67	(315) 555-31	
2	Dr.	Joshua	Fields	1250 10th Street		Buffalo	NY	14201-	(716) 555-82	(607) 555-45	(716) 555-11	FieldsJ@jst.net
3	Ms.	Julie	Macon	32 Lincoln Street	Apt. 1A	Syracuse	NY	13201-	(315) 555-31	(716) 555-90	(315) 555-23	Shorty@xyz.com
4	Mr.	William	Lance	9946 Red Avenu		Binghamton	NY	13901-	(607) 555-52	(607) 555-15	(607) 555-66	
5	Mrs.	Helen	Banks	P.O. Box 341	Apt. 29	East Amher	NY	14051-	(716) 555-21	(315) 555-66	(716) 555-88	BanksH@nys.ed

(a) Access

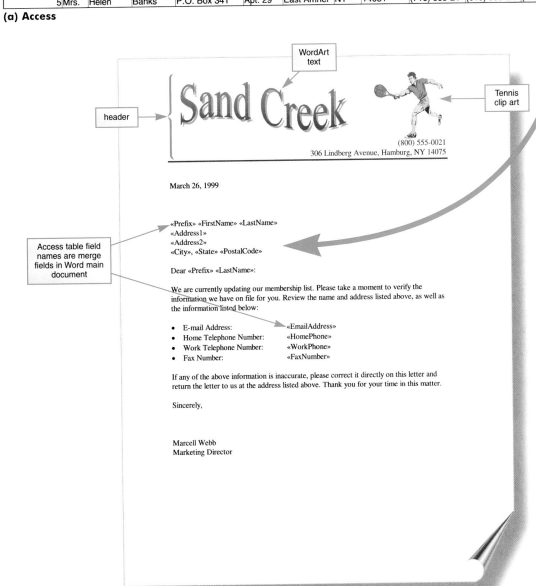

(b) Word   **FIGURE 2**

Part 2 Instructions:

Creating the Letterhead

Your first task is to develop the letterhead for the correspondence. Start Word and then display the header area. Insert and format a WordArt object, using the text Sand Creek as shown in Figure 2b on the previous page. Insert the Tennis clip art to the right of the WordArt object. Frame the picture, reposition and resize it, and then format it as shown in Figure 2b on the previous page. Finally, enter the telephone number and address of the club, add a bottom border, and color both dark magenta. When you are finished with the header, print it.

Part 3 Instructions:

Creating the Form Letter using an Access Database Table as the Data Source

You now are ready to create the form letter shown in Figure 2b on the previous page, which is to be sent to each client in the Client List table. The form letter is to verify the accuracy of the following information for each client: name, address, home and work telephone numbers, fax number, and e-mail address, if applicable.

Using the letterhead created in Part 2 above as the main document, create a form letter using the text shown in Figure 2b on the previous page and the Access database table as the data source. When specifying the data source, change the file type to MS Access Databases in the Open Data Source dialog box and then locate and click Sand Creek Country Club as the name of the data source. When prompted, click Client List as the table name. When you are finished with the main document, save the document using the file name Sand Creek Membership Update and then print it. Finally, merge and print the form letters for the six records.

Part 4 Instructions:

Setting Query Conditions

Marcell Webb has requested that you merge and print form letters for only those clients with a home area code of 716. On the resulting printed form letters, hand write the condition you specified. Next, she requests that you merge and print form letters for only those clients that have e-mail addresses. On the resulting printed form letters, hand write the condition you specified.

3 Integrating Access into Word and Excel

Problem: The owner of Growth Investors, Latanya Presley, would like to work with the daily stock records. The problem is that the records are stored in an Access database table (Figure 3a on the next page) and Latanya is unfamiliar with Access. Instead, she wants to work with the records in both Word and Excel. She thus has asked you to convert the Access table to both a Word document and an Excel worksheet. She also has asked you to show her how to convert in any direction between the three applications, Word, Excel, and Access.

Part 1 Instructions:

Creating the Access Table and Entering the Data

You are to design and create the Access database table that contains the stock information. The field names for the table are as follows: Stock Symbol, Today's High, Today's Low, Today's Close, 52 Week High, and 52 Week Low. Obtain a recent copy of the *Wall Street Journal* or use the Internet to obtain stock information for five different stocks. Enter the information as records in the table you create. The Access screen in Figure 3a on the next page shows a sample of the data entered into the Stock Portfolio table. The actual data you use will be different. When you finish creating the table, save the database using the file name Smart Investors. Print the Access table. Turn in the *Wall Street Journal* pages or printouts of the Web pages you used for stock quotes along with the Access table.

Part 2 Instructions:

Converting an Access Table to a Word Document

You now are ready to convert the Stock Portfolio table to a Word table so that Latanya can work with it. With the Access table highlighted in the Smart Investors: Database window, click the OfficeLinks button arrow on the Database toolbar and then click Publish It with MS Word. When the Word document window displays the stock information as a Word table, format it so that it is readable and professional, as shown in Figure 3b on the next page. Save the document using the file name Stock Portfolio. Print the resulting Word table.

Part 3 Instructions:

Converting an Access Table to an Excel Worksheet

You now are ready to convert the Stock Portfolio table to an Excel worksheet for Latanya. Return to the Access database table. With the Access table highlighted in the Smart Investors: Database window, click the OfficeLinks button arrow on the Database toolbar and then click Analyze It with MS Excel. When the Excel window displays the stock information as a worksheet, format it so that it is readable and professional, as shown in Figure 3c on the next page. Save the workbook using the file name Stock Portfolio. Below the table, add two rows that use Excel's statistical functions to determine the highest and lowest values for each of the numeric columns in the table. Print the resulting Excel worksheet.

Part 4 Instructions:

Converting Between Word, Excel, and Access

Use the techniques described earlier in this book to convert in any direction between Word, Excel, and Access. For example, open the Excel workbook Stock Portfolio and convert it to Word. Next, convert the workbook to Access. Do the same for the Word document Stock Portfolio. Print each of the four files created.

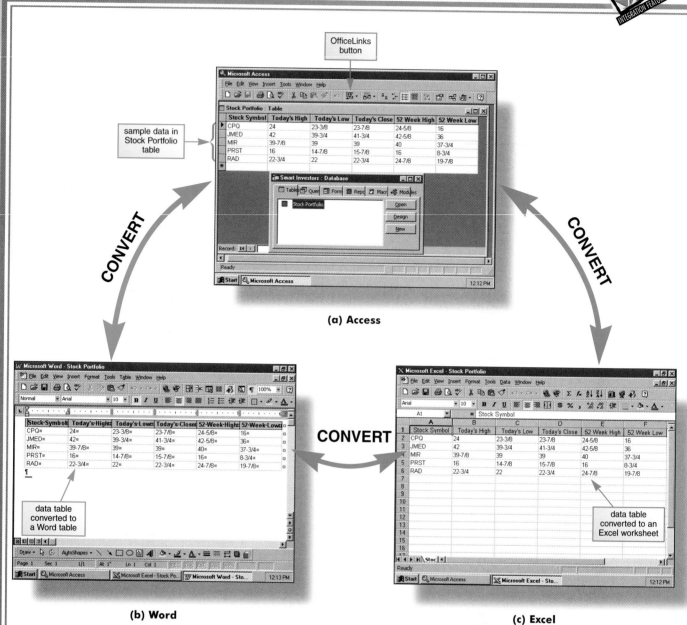

FIGURE 3

Index

I.4 • Index